THE ULTIMATE BOOK GUIDE

Over 600 great books for 8-12s

Editors: Daniel Hahn and Leonie Flynn
Associate editor: Susan Reuben

A & C Black • London

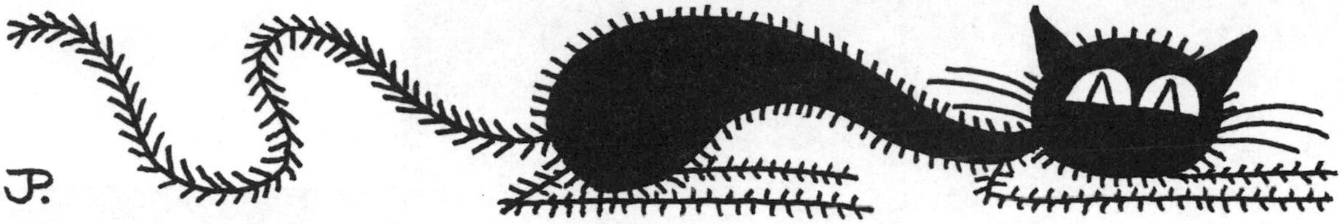

This book is dedicated to Rosemary Sutcliff (for Aquila)
and to L.M.H. (for everything) – L.F.

to Mr Reuben, with love from Mrs Reuben – S.R.

... and to Kalina, Lucas, Sebastian,
Aishwarya and Anjali, Sesha and Olivia. Eventually – D.H.

First published 2004 by
A & C Black Publishers Ltd
37 Soho Square, London, W1D 3QZ
www.acblack.com
www.ultimatebookguide.com

ISBN 0 7136 6718 4

A CIP catalogue for this book is available from the British Library.

A & C Black uses paper produced with elemental chlorine-free pulp,
harvested from managed, sustainable forests.

Printed in Great Britain by St Edmundsbury Press, Suffolk.

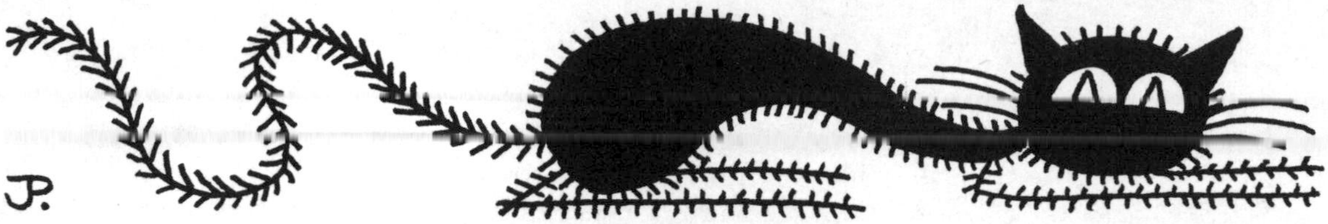

Contents

Before you begin …

Special features …

The Ultimate Readers' Poll results …

Other useful pages …

Introduction

by Anne Fine

It's every reader's worst nightmare: 'One day I shall run out of books I want to read.'

Trust me. It never happens. However young you are, however old you get, there are always more brilliant books waiting for you. That's partly because the more you read, the wider your tastes grow. But it's also because reading's something at which you get better and better. You soon find that even 'hard' books are a pleasure.

The right book brings enchantment. Books fill your mind, and there's nothing more tiresome to be around than unfurnished minds. Books make you think and make you feel. They teach you about the world, about others and even, sideways, about yourself. They show you you're never truly alone. There's always someone else who thinks, feels, worries or laughs the same way you do.

Yet what a shame it would be if you missed some of the books you might have enjoyed most, or if you didn't come across them at the perfect time. There's nothing sadder than the cry, 'Oh, I would have loved this when I was eleven!'

That's why Danny, Leonie and Susan have put together this amazing compendium of excellent suggestions. The range is astonishing – 'great classics' all the way to 'good laughs'. The only thing these books have in common is that some of your very favourite authors – and surely they should know! – liked them enormously, and want you to give them a try.

Once you've started, follow the pathways from one book to the next. 'If you've enjoyed this, try ...' Treat *The Ultimate Book Guide* as a really friendly and experienced librarian, flattened out into two hundred and eighty-eight pages. It's the *UBG*'s job always to have something else on offer, whether you want more of the same, or are ready to take some great leap in your reading. I've seen too many of you sticking with one author you're really a little bored with, and have just about grown out of, simply because you're not quite sure where to go next.

This book is your road map. So use it. If it does what it's supposed to do, and helps you find your way to more and more books you enjoy, it will become a favourite too.

Happy hunting!

love,

Anne

Anne Fine
Children's Laureate, 2001-2003

PS. A little note on tracking down books you want ...

One problem might be finding what you're looking for first time around. But be resourceful. (I can't see you failing to track down your favourite music.) If it's not on the library shelves, ask them to order it for you. If it doesn't arrive, go back and ask again.

If you can't get to the library, put the title on your birthday list and remind everyone books can be ordered in bookshops. (Little independent bookshops are sometimes the fastest at this.) Even long out-of-print books can be tracked down through the Internet or found in second-hand shops.

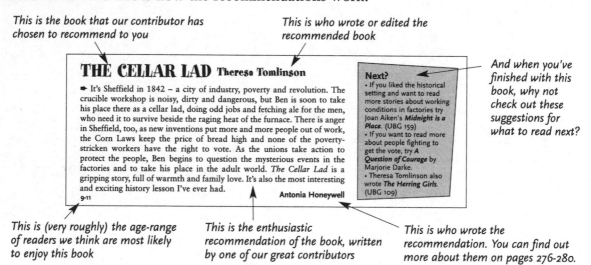

How to use this book

Most of this book is self-explanatory, and we hope you'll find it easy to use. But here is a bit of help in case you find any of it confusing.

Most of the *The Ultimate Book Guide* is made up of book recommendations. There are over six hundred books recommended for you by our team of contributors, and these titles are arranged in alphabetical order to make them easy to find. A useful tip: if you don't find what you're looking for first time, think about where else it might be listed. If you can't find **Narnia** under 'N', try looking under 'L' for *The Lion, the Witch and the Wardrobe* instead ... And this is how the recommendations work:

This is the book that our contributor has chosen to recommend to you

This is who wrote or edited the recommended book

THE CELLAR LAD **Theresa Tomlinson**

➨ It's Sheffield in 1842 – a city of industry, poverty and revolution. The crucible workshop is noisy, dirty and dangerous, but Ben is soon to take his place there as a cellar lad, doing odd jobs and fetching ale for the men, who need it to survive beside the raging heat of the furnace. There is anger in Sheffield, too, as new inventions put more and more people out of work, the Corn Laws keep the price of bread high and none of the poverty-stricken workers have the right to vote. As the unions take action to protect the people, Ben begins to question the mysterious events in the factories and to take his place in the adult world. *The Cellar Lad* is a gripping story, full of warmth and family love. It's also the most interesting and exciting history lesson I've ever had.

9-11

Antonia Honeywell

Next?
- If you liked the historical setting and want to read more stories about working conditions in factories try Joan Aiken's ***Midnight is a Place***. (UBG 159)
- If you want to read more about people fighting to get the vote, try ***A Question of Courage*** by Marjorie Darke.
- Theresa Tomlinson also wrote ***The Herring Girls***. (UBG 109)

And when you've finished with this book, why not check out these suggestions for what to read next?

This is (very roughly) the age-range of readers we think are most likely to enjoy this book

This is the enthusiastic recommendation of the book, written by one of our great contributors

This is who wrote the recommendation. You can find out more about them on pages 276-280.

The **Next?** box gives you ideas of what you might like to read once you've finished the recommended book. It might include other books by the same author, or books which are funny/exciting/scary in the same way as the book you've just finished, or which deal with a similar subject in a different way. The letters **UBG** means the book to read next has a recommendation in the *UBG* too, which you can find on the page indicated. For example, if you see ...

- Or for another book about a wizarding school, try ***Harry Potter and the Philosopher's Stone***. (UBG 106)

... then you can turn to page 106 to read about *Harry Potter*.

There are also eleven short features, not on particular books but on particular types of book – on fantasy books, historical books, school stories, etc. If you have a favourite genre of book, you'll find lots of good suggestions of what to read here. Or if you fancy trying something in a genre you don't know much about ('Hmm, I've never really read much fantasy ...') the features will give you a good idea of where to start. You'll find a list of these features on p. 3.

The features are all written by experts in the field – usually people who write that kind of book themselves (Susan Cooper on Fantasy, Dick King-Smith on Animals, Joan Aiken on Adventure, etc.). And next to them, you'll find lists of related titles too. If any of the titles in the lists sounds interesting, you can usually find out more about it by looking it up in this guide! Simple!

Finally, you'll come across reviews, illustrations and the results of our exclusive *UBG* top ten poll – voted by you, the readers! Check out our website at www.ultimatebookguide.com for more ways of becoming involved in the future.

About the editors

DANIEL HAHN is a writer, translator, editor and researcher (but he sometimes does other stuff too, like teaching or organising charity events). He has written a history of the first English zoo, translated an Angolan novel, edited a couple of reference books, researched an exhibition about Shakespeare's theatre, and now finds himself – rather to his own surprise – putting together a guide to children's books (which you're reading now). The children's books one is probably the most fun.

LEONIE FLYNN has worked with books for most of her life – from working at a small independent bookshop every Saturday when she was a teenager, to the heady delights of editing this book while also being librarian at a boys' prep school. The twin roles have shown that her true skills lie in being very strict, with both authors and boys, and in having serial nervous-breakdowns. She has also contributed essays on popular culture to various publications and reads voraciously, everything including the cornflakes packet.

SUSAN REUBEN never stopped reading children's books after she grew up, so decided she might as well produce them for a living. She spent five years editing picture books at Frances Lincoln, and is now Senior Publisher at Egmont Books, where she spends lots of time in the company of Thomas the Tank Engine and Winnie-the-Pooh. Susan enjoys cooking large meals for lots of people, and reading a good book while eating chocolate.

A.K. Peter Dickinson

➨ Paul Kagomi is a young boy, but the guns in his life are not a young boy's toys – they're real. His A.K.47 assault rifle is his most precious, almost his only, possession. So when the war he has been fighting in for most of his life is over, he doesn't want to give it up. Instead he buries it carefully in the soil out in the bush, and dutifully heads for school. But peace does not last long, and he knows he will need his A.K. again.

Though set in a mythical African country, *A.K.* is full of all-too-real experiences of modern African civil wars. More than just a war story, it also shows the emotional and moral struggles Paul faces to find another, more peaceful way of life.

10-12

Marcus Sedgwick

Next?

- Try some of Peter Dickinson's other books, such as the **Changes Trilogy** (UBG 44), or the strange ***Eva***. Another, set in a distant place torn apart by war, is ***Tulku***. (UBG 249)
- For a book about joining the resistance in a different war, read ***Match of Death*** by James Riordan. (UBG 157)

ABEL'S ISLAND William Steig

➨ Abelard Hassam de Chirico Flint is an Edwardian society mouse. He enjoys a comfortable and civilised life with his wife Amanda until one day, whilst enjoying a pleasant picnic of sandwiches, quail eggs, caviar and champagne, he is swept away and marooned on a river island. His new life as a castaway is very different from the one he is used to, but the proud and resourceful mouse struggles to overcome the many dangers and difficulties he faces, and never gives up hope of seeing his beloved wife again.

The text is mingled with Steig's own illustrations which perfectly complement and enhance his prose – a first-rate book by one of my favourite author/illustrators!

7-9

Neal Layton

Next?

- Why not try some other books by William Steig? ***Dominic*** is the philosophical tale of a piccolo-playing dog who decides to travel the road of adventure.
- For the story of a bear from dakest Peru in London, try ***A Bear Called Paddington*** by Michael Bond. (UBG 24)
- For more mice – or rather, a cat – but a cat who decides he's going to keep mice as pets! Read Dick King-Smith's ***Martin's Mice***.
- You might also enjoy W.J. Corbett's older read, ***The Song of Pentecost***. (UBG 223)

THE ADVENTURES OF ROBIN HOOD Roger Lancelyn Green

➨ My introduction to the tales of Robin Hood was by way of these books, and I've never read better versions. Roger Lancelyn Green went back to the earliest sources he could find – not all of them English – reinterpreted or refocused many of the tales, added his own spin here and there, and bound them together in continuous narratives where they were not always so bound previously. His language and style – dignified and rich, romantic yet business-like – stirred this young reader as much as the tales themselves.

There's chivalry, adventure, romance, skulduggery and cruelty in abundance here, and none of the watering-down and pussyfooting you find in some more recent interpretations. I'm glad I came upon R.L.G.'s versions at the age I did, in the age I did, before certain themes, attitudes, manners, customs and tastes were deemed inappropriate or offensive by lofty individuals keen to strip verve, sparkle and humour from stories too rich for their own impoverished sensibilities.

9-11

Michael Lawrence

Next?

- Compare this version to Michael Morpurgo's ***Robin Hood.***
- Oh, and do have a bash at ***Puck of Pook's Hill*** by Rudyard Kipling. (UBG 195)
- And more Roger Lancelyn Green? Read his great ***King Arthur and the Knights of the Round Table***. (UBG 134)

If you're looking for Adrian Mole's secret diaries, turn to p. 214

Next?

- Two other books by Mark Twain are ***The Adventures of Huckleberry Finn***, which is an older and darker story and ***The Prince and the Pauper*** (UBG 193).
- For characters with something of Tom about them, read ***Frindle*** (UBG 88) and ***A Week in the Woods*** by Andrew Clements.
- Looking for another high-spirited hero? Try Richmal Crompton's **Just William** stories – great for a laugh. (UBG 131)

THE ADVENTURES OF TOM SAWYER **Mark Twain**

➨ *Tom Sawyer* is a famous story. A classic. If you haven't read it, you've probably heard of it, and you might know a bit about the story. Tom lives with his aunt Polly in St. Petersburg on the banks of the Mississippi river, and is always getting into trouble. Oh, I didn't mention that besides being a very famous, classic story, it's also a pretty old story, written (and set) in the nineteenth century.

But here's the thing – it might surprise you to know that this old, famous, classic book is also really, really good! Tom is a great hero (and is bound to remind you of someone you know – or yourself, perhaps), and Mark Twain is a very funny, lively writer. Just read a page or two and you'll forget that this is one of those books people keep saying you *ought* to read – once you've met Tom you'll *want* to read it. You'll want to keep his company, to meet his friends (especially that other great troublemaker, Huck Finn), and follow their adventures up the Mississippi.

There's a good reason everyone remembers this book, and still talks about it more than a hundred years on. But don't take my word for it – just give it a try; you'll see why soon enough.

10+

Daniel Hahn

AESOP'S FUNKY FABLES

Vivian French, illustrated by Korky Paul

➨ Everyone knows some of these stories off by heart. Aesop wrote them two and a half thousand years ago. They must be good stories if they're still around after all that time!

Vivian French has taken old favourites like 'The Tortoise and the Hare' and 'The Boy who Cried Wolf', and made them funky! Yes ... funky! Can you hear the bass? Can you hear the drums? Get in the groove and me oh my, that Aesop was a funky guy. And the pictures? Man, they're off the wall. All of them drawn by Korky Paul!

6-8

Shoo Rayner

Next?

- If you enjoy these, you'll really like ***Groovy Greek Hero Raps*** by Tony Mitton – a load of stories that you know already, all done up in fancy rap rhyme.
- What about reading Marcia Williams's ***Greek Myths***? (UBG 166) Again, stories that you should know, but this time they are in a cartoon strip form ... good fun, too!
- If you like that, try ***Asterix the Gaul*** by René Goscinny and Albert Uderzo. (UBG 21)
- And what about the very funny ***Helping Hercules*** by Francesca Simon?

BY JOAN AIKEN

ADVENTURE STORIES

'X' marks the spot

When I was a child, my favourite room was my elder brother John's ground-floor bedroom. It had a brick floor, a bookcase full of his books, and an old purple sofa. John was away at college and I used to spend hours in there reading those books. And such books! *The Hound of the Baskervilles*, *King Solomon's Mines*, *Kidnapped*, *Treasure Island*, *Around the World in Eighty Days*, *Dracula*, *The Swiss Family Robinson*, *The Call of the Wild*, *The Man in the Iron Mask*, *The Prince and the Pauper*, *Tom Sawyer, Kim* … not only those but all the other books by Kipling, Mark Twain, Conan Doyle, Stevenson, Jules Verne, Dumas and the rest.

★ JOAN AIKEN'S TOP TEN ADVENTURE STORIES

- ***Captains Courageous*** by Rudyard Kipling
- ***Kim*** by Rudyard Kipling
- ***Emil and the Detectives*** by Erich Kästner
- ***The Hobbit*** by J.R.R. Tolkien
- ***The Midnight Folk*** by John Masefield
- ***The Bird of Dawning*** by John Masefield
- ***She*** by H. Rider Haggard
- ***The Sword in the Stone*** by T.H. White
- ***Tom Sawyer*** and ***Huckleberry Finn*** by Mark Twain

There were a lot of ghost stories, too. From age six to twelve I simply loved being terrified. I could gulp down books then that I'd hardly dare open now … Ballantyne's *Coral Island* had wonderful scenes in underwater coral caves but also TERRIFYING descriptions of South Sea savages and the things they did to their prisoners … *The Hound of the Baskervilles* was fairly hair-raising, too, and so were some of Kipling's short stories.

Kipling was just about my favourite author at around age seven or eight. I knew the poems in the *Jungle Books* by heart and spent whole afternoons being Mowgli on the thicketty South Downs, half a mile away. My favourite Mowgli story was the one in which he saves his friends the wolves from an invading pack of Dholes, wild red dogs … but there was another beauty about a wicked old white cobra guarding a hoard of long-forgotten royal treasure. And then there was *Kim*, which my mother and I read aloud to each other every evening. Meanwhile, I was made to drink a glass of milk every night; I cannot stand the taste of milk, still loathe it to this day, but the story of *Kim* was so marvellous that somehow I managed to get the milk down. I still link the taste of milk with the scene of Kim steering the old llama through the Himalayas and foiling the Russian spies.

A solitary child, I loved the company of those brave characters in my brother's adventure books. They seemed to come in fours: the Four Musketeers (including D'Artagnan), the Walker children in Arthur Ransome's *Swallows and Amazons* books, the Four Just Men, the four March girls in *Little Women* (that was my sister's); I collected a whole army of my own, using these warriors, and made up new exploits for them, led by me, riding on a white charger ... The Psammead's friends were my friends too.

Now I know that it was not the characters but the books – and their authors – who were my lifelong friends.

★ MORE FAVOURITES CHOSEN BY THE EDITORS

- **His Dark Materials** trilogy by Philip Pullman
- ***The Wolves of Willoughby Chase*** series by Joan Aiken
- ***Go Saddle the Sea*** by Joan Aiken
- ***The Hound of the Baskervilles*** by Arthur Conan Doyle
- ***Kidnapped!*** by R.L. Stevenson
- ***Treasure Island*** by R.L. Stevenson
- ***Stormbreaker*** and its sequels by Anthony Horowitz
- ***Around the World in Eighty Days*** by Jules Verne
- ***Journey to the River Sea*** by Eva Ibbotson
- ***Kensuke's Kingdom*** by Michael Morpurgo
- ***Hatchet*** by Gary Paulsen
- ***Amazon Adventure*** etc. by Willard Price
- ***Hornblower*** by C.S. Forester
- ***Biggles*** by Captain W.E. Johns
- ***Eagle of the Ninth*** by Rosemary Sutcliff
- ***Holes*** by Louis Sachar

EVERYBODY'S FAVOURITE...

ALICE'S ADVENTURES IN WONDERLAND **Lewis Carroll**

➨ Alice follows a white rabbit down through a rabbit hole into a strange world inhabited by playing cards. Babies turn into pigs, white roses are painted red, the Mad Hatter, the March Hare and the Dormouse are involved in an endless tea party. The book is alive with parodies of poems that were well known at the time. By now the original poems are forgotten: it is Lewis Carroll's parodies that we remember. Intelligent and puzzled, Alice moves through Wonderland, growing smaller then taller then smaller again until she finally grows so tall she pulls Wonderland into pieces around her.

Most Victorian stories had stern morals attached to them, but *Alice's Adventures in Wonderland* is told simply for the fun of Alice's adventures and for the fun of the language. Indeed, many of its situations and pronouncements have become part of the language and imagination of the English-speaking world.

Margaret Mahy

➨ This is the book that got me hooked on reading. I remember sitting on the stairs, transfixed by the dream-like quality of the story. It seemed, somehow, to be from my own dreams: a mixture of the strange, the funny, the absurd and the frightening. I was especially captured by the illustrations – the original ones by Tenniel, which portrayed Alice as stern and 'unpretty'. The book is a long journey during which she has a series of the most extraordinary encounters with bizarre characters, from the gently eccentric White Rabbit to the terrifying Queen of Hearts. This is a book that stretches your imagination and plays games with all that is logical and sensible, until nothing is what it seems and you start to see the world in a different way!

9+ **Jane Ray**

Next?

- Alice's next adventures, ***Through The Looking Glass***.
- Or Neil Gaiman's ***Coraline*** – also about a girl entering a different world uncannily like her own. (UBG 51)
- Charlotte Haptie's ***Otto and the Flying Twins*** has the same sense of oddness and wonder as Alice. (UBG 178)
- ***The Phantom Tollbooth*** by Norton Juster is another surreal story filled with strange events and verbal nonsense. (UBG 185)

If you're looking for the Alex Rider books by Anthony Horowitz, turn to p. 228

ALLY'S WORLD: THE PAST, THE PRESENT AND THE LOUD LOUD GIRL Karen McCombie

➡ The story of Ally (otherwise known as Alexandra, named after Alexandra Palace) is funny, cheerful and completely absorbing. Her family is mad. Her best friend, Sandie, is sane enough, but their friendship is tested by a new girl at school called Kyra. Kyra is pushy, arrogant and criticises everything. Life is complicated enough with two crazy dogs, one sister who's obsessed with fairy lights and sequins, another sister who's a control freak and a brother who can't understand why everyone doesn't love stick insects as much as he does. When Ally is set to complete a school project with Kyra, it seems things couldn't get worse.

Her dad, who's caring for the family on his own, is great, and he helps Ally to keep her sense of humour as she faces the challenge of Kyra – but what present will be good enough for his birthday?

9-12

Antonia Honeywell

Next?

- There are lots more great stories about Ally. Look out for ***A Guided Tour of Ally's World***, ***Daisy***, ***Dad and the Huge, Small Surprise*** and ***Pretty Weird Weirdness***.
- If you enjoyed the close relationship between Ally and her dad, try ***The Youngest Girl in the Fifth*** by Angela Brazil. (UBG 275)
- ***The Princess Diaries*** by Meg Cabot is a more fantastical young girl's life. (UBG 193)
- If you liked reading about the trials of school and family life, try the slightly harder ***Are You There, God? It's Me, Margaret*** by Judy Blume. (UBG 19)

COMPETITION WINNER ★ COMPETITION WINNER

ALLY'S WORLD: THE PAST, THE PRESENT AND THE LOUD LOUD GIRL
Karen McCombie

➡ I loved this book because it's exciting, down-to-earth, interesting and very, very funny. This book really grabbed me and was impossible to put down. People think I'm weird because when reading some books, I laugh out loud and this one practically had me falling off my chair. I think this book is a nice book to read after a dark horror novel, because it's relaxing. I've also read some of the other Ally's World books and they have also been super-duper so this gets a definite thumbs up!

Esther Burns, age 11, Deansfield Primary

THE AMAZING MAURICE AND HIS EDUCATED RODENTS Terry Pratchett

➡ Maurice is a cat who can think and talk, and his educated rodents are rats that can do the same. A change came over them when they ate some rubbish thrown over the wall of a wizard's castle. The rats have adopted names from the discarded tins they find on the dump: Sardines, Peaches, Hamnpork, Darktan and Dangerous Beans, to name but a few.

This hilarious book turns the story of the Pied Piper on its head. Maurice and the rats team up with a boy who looks stupid (but isn't) and can play a pipe. They travel round the country making money from townspeople who are afraid of rats. But then they reach Bad Blintz, and a terrifying battle begins.

I found this book impossible to put down, and so did my son (who is much younger than me). We just had to know what would become of Maurice and his wonderful rodents.

10+

Jenny Nimmo

Next?

- You'll want to read more of Terry Pratchett's amazing **Discworld** novels. My son recommends starting with ***The Colour of Magic***. (UBG 51)
- Or for longer books about rodents, try Brian Jacques's brilliant **Redwall** series. (UBG 199)
- Read about the original Pied Piper, in a poem by Robert Browning, 'The Pied Piper of Hamelin'.
- Or try ***Mouse Attack*** by Manjula Padma, about an educated mouse who is sent to be a pet, which, as you can imagine, he hates! (UBG 165)

Next?

- Other books in the series include ***Anastasia at Your Service, Anastasia Has the Answers*** and ***Anastasia on Her Own***.
- The **Betsy-Tacy** stories by Maud Hart Lovelace are also great fun. (UBG 27)
- Paula Danziger writes great books about families and friends. Try ***Everyone Else's Parents Said Yes!***
- You might enjoy ***Emily of New Moon*** by L.M. Montgomery, about an orphan who is sent to stay with her unwelcoming relations. (UBG 72)

ANASTASIA KRUPNIK Lois Lowry

➡ Ten-year-old Anastasia Krupnik is bright, precocious and funny. (A little like my heroine Flavia Gemina – see *The Thieves of Ostia*. [UBG 239])

Anastasia loves lists and keeps them in her green notebook. Her mother is an artist and her father a poet. Hers is a family so delightful that you long to be part of it. The first book charts Anastasia's amusing reactions to her mother's pregnancy and the birth of her brother, Sam, who becomes a delightful character in later books in the series.

Lowry never talks down to her readers which is why it's so much fun to read these books – even for adults!

9-11

Caroline Lawrence

AND THEN THERE WERE NONE

Agatha Christie

➡ This is the best murder-mystery story ever written. (For the record, I've just asked my fellow editors and they agree.) Agatha Christie was the grandmother of this sort of book, and her two regular sleuths, Hercule Poirot and Miss Marple, are among the world's favourites. But this story is different – for one thing, there's no detective. Just one murderer, and nine terrified victims ...

It's about the simplest plot you can imagine. Ten people stranded overnight in an isolated house. One is murdered. And then there were nine. Another murder. And then there were eight. And so on ...

You'd think that pretty quickly it'd become obvious who the killer is, wouldn't you? Especially as numbers start to dwindle. But try as you might, I'll bet you won't be able to work it out before Agatha Christie reveals her breathtaking ending. I've never yet met anyone who has. Awesome.

10+

Daniel Hahn

Next?

- Everything by Agatha Christie is worth reading. Personally, I tend to prefer the Poirot books, but any will do. ***The Pale Horse*** is recommended by Hugh Scott in the ***UBG*** on p. 182.
- Arthur Conan Doyle's Sherlock Holmes, of course: ***The Hound of the Baskervilles*** (UBG 117) and ***A Study in Scarlet*** (UBG 229).
- Dorothy L. Sayers wrote many stories about her detective, Lord Peter Wimsey – the first is ***Clouds of Witness***. They're all very good indeed.

Here

Next?

- Try ***The Transfer***, also by Terence Blacker, about football and a computer program that goes wrong. (UBG 246)
- Or ***Hacker*** by Malorie Blackman, about a girl who uses her hacking skills to save her father from prison. (UBG 102)
- What about being thrown into a parallel universe? Try ***Piggies*** by Nick Gifford, which is scary and a little older. (UBG 188)

THE ANGEL FACTORY Terence Blacker

➡ Thomas Wisdom lives a perfect life. Everything, including the dog, is exactly right. But one day, Tom and his friend Gip hack into Tom's father's computer. What they find blows Tom's so-called perfect life apart. Suddenly, he is plunged into a terrifying world where the future of mankind is at stake and treachery is all around him.

Tom learns to make some hard choices. And making hard choices when everyone around you seems so kind and caring is particularly difficult. Read this book and you will never look at people on the street in the same way again.

9-11

Karen Wallace

If you're looking for Anne Frank's diary, turn to p. 61

AN ANGEL FOR MAY Melvin Burgess

Next?
• Another great Melvin Burgess book is ***The Ghost Behind the Wall***. (UBG 90)
• For more ghosts and scary stuff, try Anthony Masters' ***Scary Tales to Tell in the Dark***.
• Justin Richards' **The Invisible Detective** series is full of mystery and adventure. (UBG 123)

➡ Tam hates his life. He hates his mum and he hates his dad for not wanting him. To get away from home he takes refuge in a burnt-out old farmhouse in the hills above his house. But the farmhouse is not quite what it seems, and there the hard line between past and present begins to blur, until suddenly Tam finds himself in the ruined house back when it was whole, and lived in by an old man and a strange young girl.

This is a very eerie story. Everything from the stray dog to the smelly old tramp Tam finds in the house have something weird about them. Spending more and more time back in the past, Tam begins to wonder if he wants to return home at all. But he has been taken back in time for a reason, and not all the answers lie in the past.

Leonie Flynn

9-11

THE ANGEL OF NITSHILL ROAD Anne Fine

➡ There's a bully at Nitshill Road School, and he makes life pretty miserable for the people around him. At least, he does until a new girl, Celeste, joins the class. Celeste is not frightened of Barry Hunter – she doesn't seem to be frightened of anything – and the way she deals with him and changes all the unhappiness he has caused makes for one of the cleverest books about bullying that you'll ever read.

None of the things Celeste does to the bully are what you'd expect. She doesn't fight him. She doesn't play tricks on him. She doesn't humiliate him. What she does is ...

No, I'm sorry ... You'll have to read it for yourself!

But I guarantee you won't regret it!

Andrew Norriss

7-10

Next?
• You'll probably enjoy many other books by Anne Fine. ***Flour Babies*** (UBG 86) and ***Goggle-eyes*** (UBG 95) will both make you laugh as well as think. They're slightly more challenging reads.
• If you like school stories, one where the bully is a teacher, not a pupil, is ***Matilda*** by Roald Dahl. (UBG 157)
• Teachers don't come any more fearsome than ***The Demon Headmaster*** by Gillian Cross! (UBG 59)
• ***See Andrew's SCHOOL STORIES recommendations on pp 212-213.***

ANGELS UNLIMITED Annie Dalton

Next?
• To read about some Earthbound girls' adventure, try **Ally's World** by Karen McCombie. (UBG 12)
• ***The Lottie Project*** by Jacqueline Wilson is another book about going back into the past – but in a different way. (UBG 149)
• For more fab sci-fi, try ***Aquila*** by Andrew Norriss. (UBG 18)

➡ What could be better than time-travelling with your best friends? That's why fast-talking and totally hip Mel Beeby just *loves* history – because she gets to live it! At the Angel Academy, the students often get pulled out of class to help solve a real-life crisis somewhere in the distant past. In *Flying High*, the Angels are off to mediaeval Jerusalem to help in the Children's Crusade. Intrigued already? But what *is* the Angel Academy? Well, that's where angels are trained, of course. Angels? Yep – Mel is formerly of this Earth and she has no idea why she was recruited. But her new life and her new friends are fantastic and there's never a dull moment (there are a few enemies to beware of, too – but aren't there always?) Mel and her friends travel back to sixteenth-century London (*Losing the Plot*) and forwards to Victorian times (*Fogging Over*) and way back to ancient Rome (*Fighting Fit*). And that's just for starters!

Jon Appleton

9-11

COMPETITION WINNER ★ COMPETITION WINNER

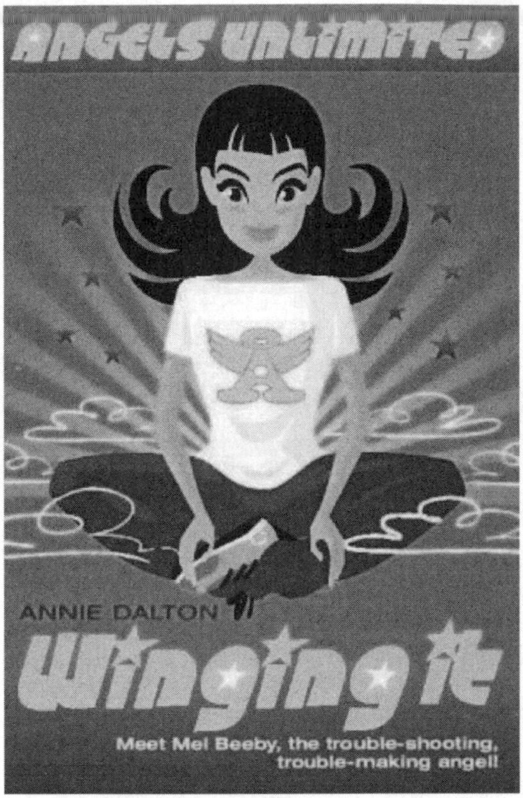

ANGELS UNLIMITED

Annie Dalton

➡ In *Winging It*, the first of the Angels Unlimited series, Annie Dalton tells the story of teenager, Mel Beeby, who finds herself in a posh angel academy after being involved in a major road accident. At first, Mel feels uncomfortable and out of place within the academy, but after her first term she finds something she might actually be good at …

Join Mel and her friends as she establishes her place in the academy, as she visits wartime London on her first angelic assignment with her major crush, Orlando, and her best mate, Lola. As she strives to impress Orlando, she goes to fight the opposition in one of her best dresses!

I really enjoyed reading this book because, personally, I enjoy reading fantasy/adventure genre stories. I would recommend this book to anyone seeking a funny, action-filled and stylish story of good and evil.

Priyanka Pal, age 10, Headington Junior School

ANIMAL ARK series

Lucy Daniels

➡ The first **Animal Ark** story, *Kittens in the Kitchen*, introduces us to thirteen-year-old Mandy Hope, who lives in the village of Welford with her parents, Adam and Emily Hope, who run Animal Ark, the local veterinary surgery. Mandy adores animals – and can't understand why anyone could possibly want to harm an innocent creature. The trouble is, sometimes people can't look after their pets properly – that's why Animal Ark is there to help. If there's a happy way to solve an animal problem, Mandy and her best friend, James, are determined to find it.

Throughout the series, we get to meet more of the locals in Welford, and even join the Hopes abroad for work or holidays – to Australia and Africa and the Arctic, where Mandy soon immerses herself in the world of the local wildlife.

8-10

Jon Appleton

Next?

- If you like spooky stories, try the **Animal Ark Hauntings** series, with spine-tingling scenarios and twisty plots.
- Look out in particular for Colin Dann's ***The Animals of Farthing Wood***. (UBG 17)
- Richard Adams wrote a much-loved, highly-acclaimed animal story in ***Watership Down***. (UBG 259)
- Or try the wonderful Dick King-Smith, who has written lots of books about animals, including ***Harry's Mad*** and ***Martin's Mice***.
- ***And see Dick's ANIMAL STORIES selections on pp. 16-17.***

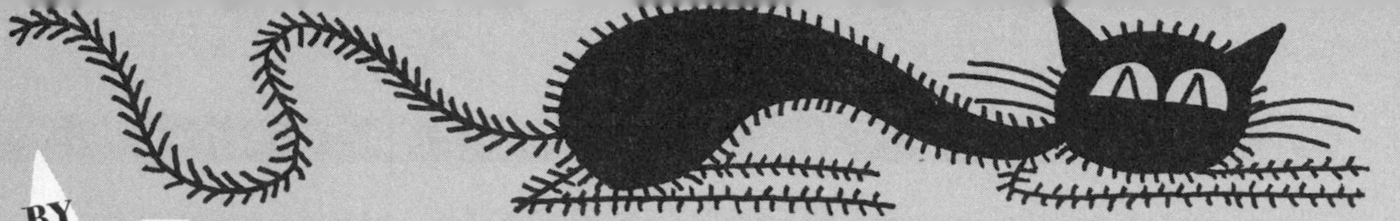

BY DICK KING-SMITH

ANIMAL STORIES

Two legs or four?

I like writing books about animals, mostly because I like animals. I'm interested in all the creatures that share this world with us, big or small, feathered or furry or finny. I'm interested in the look of an animal and in its habits. I'm not an expert, but with luck I don't make silly mistakes like one author (I won't tell you her name) who had partridges nesting up in the trees.

I've got favourite animals of course, like pigs, and in the kind of children's books I write, you're allowed to put words into their mouths. There's a posh word for this – anthropomorphism – which means giving human characteristics to what is not human, especially an animal.

So I can make my characters speak the Queen's English. That's all I do, really. I don't dress them up in human clothes (although that can be great fun – think of Beatrix Potter and her rabbits and mice and foxes), and I don't have billy-goats riding bicycles or pussycats playing the piano; I just let them talk. Apart from that, my pigs behave pretty much as all pigs do, and so do my hedgehogs or dogs or frogs or beetles or woodlice, or whatever other creatures I choose to put in my stories.

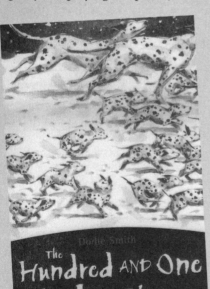

★ TEN BOOKS ABOUT ANIMALS AS REAL ANIMALS

(not talking, wearing clothes, driving cars etc.)

- ***Tarka the Otter*** by Henry Williamson
- ***The Call of the Wild*** by Jack London
- ***The Peppermint Pig*** by Nina Bawden
- ***National Velvet*** by Enid Bagnold
- ***White Fang*** by Jack London
- ***The Silver Brumby*** by Elyne Mitchell
- ***Blitzcat*** by Robert Westall
- ***The Midnight Fox*** by Betsy Byars

I think that most children enjoy reading books about animals because most children like animals, and of course there are so many different sorts of creatures, which means there's such a lot of choice, for both writer and reader.

'What shall I write about this time?' I say to myself when I sit down to start a new story.

Often I reply, 'A pig?'

But then I have to give myself a slap on the wrist (not too hard) and say, 'No, no, you've just done one about a pig; choose something else.'

So maybe I'll start thinking about the adventures of a mouse or a rabbit or a pigeon. Once I thought – how about an ostrich story? But then I found out I didn't know enough about ostriches and I didn't want to make silly mistakes (like those partridges nesting up in the trees). So the next time I was in London, I went to the Natural History Museum and made notes about the ostrich – how tall it is, how fast it can run, what noise it makes and so on. Out of all that came, eventually, a book called *The Cuckoo Child*.

There are all sorts of animal stories. They can be factual, about an animal that behaves completely naturally (no talking, let alone dressing up), like Henry Williamson's *Tarka the Otter*, or Jack London's *White Fang*. Or they can be about animals that behave in many ways exactly like humans (Beatrix Potter's creatures again, or Kenneth Grahame's *The Wind in the Willows*). Or they can be rather crazy stories, where animals do things they couldn't possibly do in real life. And of course there is always magic. Pigs might fly. There's so much to choose from.

★ TWENTY ANIMAL FANTASIES

(where they might talk, or wear clothes, or drive cars ...)

- ***The Sheep-Pig*** by Dick King-Smith
- ***The Hodgeheg*** by Dick King-Smith
- ***Charlotte's Web*** by E.B. White
- ***Watership Down*** by Richard Adams
- ***Silverwing*** by Kenneth Oppel
- ***The Jungle Book*** by Rudyard Kipling
- ***The Hundred and One Dalmatians*** by Dodie Smith
- ***I, Jack*** by Patricia Finney
- ***Winnie-the-Pooh*** – well, sort of ... by A. A. Milne
- ***Fire, Bed and Bone*** by Henrietta Branford
- ***Fantastic Mr Fox*** by Roald Dahl
- ***The Wind in the Willows*** by Kenneth Grahame
- **Paddington** series by Michael Bond
- **Mary Plain** series by Gwynedd Rae
- ***Mouse Attack*** by Manjula Padma
- **Redwall** series by Brian Jacques
- ***Varjak Paw*** by S.F. Said
- ***Doctor Dolittle*** by Hugh Lofting
- ***Abel's Island*** by William Steig
- ***Gobbolino the Witch's Cat*** by Ursula Moray Williams

THE ANIMALS OF FARTHING WOOD Colin Dann

➨ Disaster strikes Farthing Wood when the bulldozers crash in and a drought dries up all the water. How can the animals save themselves? They decide to leave their beloved home and take the long journey to White Deer Park, a faraway nature reserve. Under the leadership of Fox, with his trusted deputy Badger, they follow Toad who has told them stories of this wonderful place.

One of the best things about this book is that it is absolutely action-packed. Every single chapter has the animals facing a new danger: a forest fire, a motorway, angry farmers, flooding rivers and a fox hunt. So the story is not only very exciting but easy to read in short chunks. Each episode will keep you on the edge of your seat wondering how they will ever complete their journey.

8-10

Abigail Anderson

Next?

- The rest of the **Farthing Wood** books! They include ***The Fox Cub Bold*** and ***The Adventure Begins***.
- Try ***The Hodgeheg*** by Dick King-Smith. (UBG 112)
- ***The Wind in the Willows*** by Kenneth Grahame is about another group of animals' adventures, but animals who dress and act like humans. (UBG 265)

ANNE OF GREEN GABLES

L.M. Montgomery

➨ One day, Matthew Cuthbert, a shy and silent man, goes off to the station to pick up an orphan boy to help him on the farm; what he finds instead is a girl – Anne Shirley, an eleven-year-old orphan with bright red hair and freckles and a hot temper. Anne is desperate for a home, so Matthew quietly persuades his strict sister, Marilla, to let her stay at Green Gables. She is a tremendous talker and her imagination is quirky and interesting. It isn't long before she has won Matthew and Marilla's hearts and changed the way they look at the world.

Anne of Green Gables has always been my favourite children's book because of Anne herself – she could talk the hind leg off a donkey; she is spirited; she feels different to everyone else; she speaks her mind; and she's very self-conscious about her red hair. Such a brilliant character.

11+

Jackie Kay

Next?

- The story continues in ***Anne of Avonlea***, ***Anne of the Island***, ***Anne of Windy Willows***, ***Anne's House of Dreams***, ***Anne of Ingleside***, ***Rainbow Valley*** and ***Rilla of Ingleside***.
- You might also like ***Little Women*** by Louisa M. Alcott. (UBG 146)
- Or what about Jacqueline Wilson's ***The Story of Tracy Beaker***? (UBG 229)

THE APPRENTICES Leon Garfield

➨ These wonderful tales of London's apprentice children were first published separately, so you had to be patient and wait from one to the next. Now they're collected together and you can choose how to read them: you might read one a day, making friends gradually with trainee undertakers, printers' devils, silver thread spinners and hangmen, as they serve out their seven-year apprenticeships. But if I were you, I'd read them all in one go, and let the mysterious Link Boy whose flaming torch lights up every chapter guide you through Leon Garfield's brilliantly vivid world of eighteenth-century London. And my favourites? 'Mirror, Mirror', which is both terrifying and beautiful, and 'Filthy Beast'.

8-10

Gill Vickery

Next?
- Try more Leon Garfield. ***Smith*** (UBG 221) and ***Devil-in-the-Fog*** are historical adventures. ***The Strange Affair of Adelaide Harris*** is an hilarious comic romp about two boys who devise a crazy plan to kidnap a baby. (UBG 229)
- For a more light-hearted read, try Penelope Lively's witty and funny ***The Revenge of Samuel Stokes***, about a ghost who objects to a modern housing development being built on the site of his beautiful, old estate. (UBG 203)

AQUILA Andrew Norriss

➨ Geoff and Tom are on a school trip when they fall into an old quarry. Inside a cave at the bottom, they find a dead soldier and a weird-looking machine. Before they really think about what they're doing, they're climbing into the machine, pushing a few knobs and suddenly they're in the air.

Aquila is the sort of machine that dreams are made of. It runs on water, it answers questions. It can become invisible and it can immobilise people. Geoff and Tom, once the dunces of the class, suddenly become interested in power-technology, Latin, map-reading, maths and all the subjects that help them to understand Aquila. Their teachers are naturally suspicious, and it becomes increasingly difficult to keep Aquila a secret.

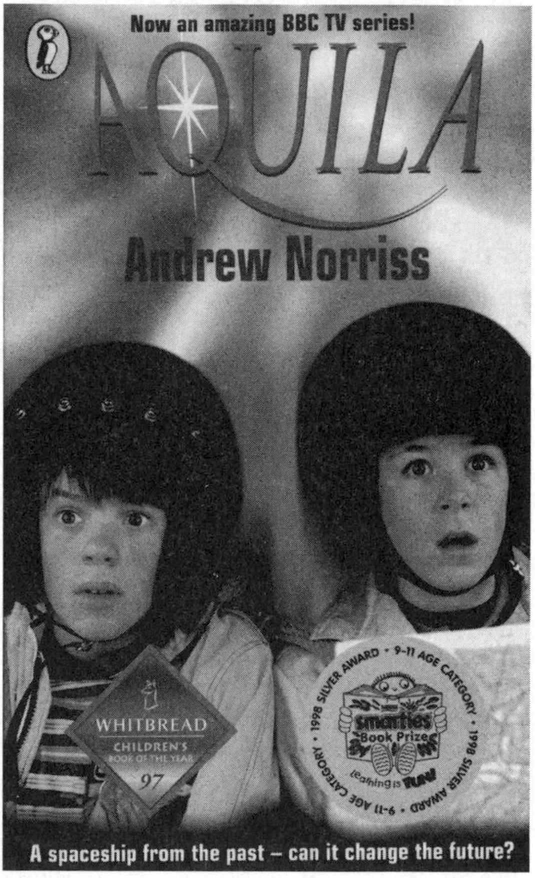

Now an amazing BBC TV series!
AQUILA
Andrew Norriss
WHITBREAD
CHILDREN'S BOOK OF THE YEAR
97
1998 SILVER AWARD • 9-11 AGE CATEGORY
smarties Book Prize
A spaceship from the past – can it change the future?

Next?
- In ***The House that Sailed Away*** by Pat Hutchins, a house moves, with a whole family inside.
- If you've a taste for ancient Rome, ***Nicobobinus*** by Terry Jones is a magical adventure.
- Andrew Clements's ***Frindle*** is about another boy for whom school suddenly becomes very interesting ... (UBG 88)
- ***The Big Bazoohley*** by Peter Carey is another wacky, eventful story – about a boy who gets locked out of his room, and then kidnapped! (UBG 27)

This story is tremendous fun. The reader is totally absorbed as the boys gradually discover Aquila's amazing powers. And the teachers' reactions are hilarious when you're in on the secret.

9-11

Jenny Nimmo

Next?
• Read some of the original translations by Richard Burton. Or a different modern translation by Husain Haddawy.
• Or ***The Land of Green Ginger*** by Noel Langley – a very funny book, all one story, set in a fictional land similar to that of the Arabian Nights. (UBG 139)
• Geraldine McCaughrean's magic retellings in ***The Orchard Book of Greek Myths*** are definitely worth reading too. (UBG 177)
• ***The Arthur Rackham Fairy Book*** is a great source of classic tales. (UBG 20)

THE ARABIAN NIGHTS

➡ Genies in lamps! Sparkling treasure! Splendid palaces! Magic carpets! Ferocious sword fights! Beautiful princesses! You might think you know all the stories, but think again. In addition to the favourites, such as 'Aladdin', 'Ali Baba and the Forty Thieves' and 'The Adventures of Sinbad', there are hundreds more to discover. There are lots of different collections – try Geraldine McCaughrean's *One Thousand and One Arabian Nights*.

The stories are supposed to be those told by the beautiful Princess Scheherazade to a powerful Emperor. The Emperor is planning to kill her but she manages to delay her execution by telling him stories of magic and wonder each night, and in the end he doesn't execute her – he marries her! Her stories certainly do cast a spell over you. They transport you to a hot, exotic world of sights, sounds and smells, far away from rainy old England.

9-12

Abigail Anderson

ARE YOU THERE, GOD? IT'S ME, MARGARET Judy Blume

➡ Margaret is eleven and just starting at a new school, far away from her beloved grandma in New York. Three girls invite her to join their gang, which meets in secret to discuss 'boys' and 'growing up'. We follow Margaret through Sixth Grade as she worries about her first bra and observes the boys in her class. Her most intimate concerns she addresses directly to God. Nothing much happens but she learns useful lessons, such as that even the most seemingly confident kids can exaggerate or even lie.

This isn't a book you'll want to re-read endlessly, but perfect if you're a ten- to eleven-year-old girl wondering what becoming a teenager is like.

10-12

Jane Darcy

Next?
• You might like other books by Judy Blume – try ***Iggie's House***.
• My niece recommends ***The Princess Diaries*** by Meg Cabot. (UBG 193) Also, anything by Jacqueline Wilson (turn to p. 288 for a list of titles in the *UBG*).
• ***Stargirl*** by Jerry Spinelli is about what it feels like not to fit in – and what happens when you suddenly do. (UBG 225) Or, on the same theme, ***The Wish*** by Gail Carson Levine.

Next?
• Other Jules Verne books, particularly ***Twenty Thousand Leagues Under the Sea*** (UBG 250) and ***Journey to the Centre of the Earth***.
• ***The Lost World*** by Arthur Conan Doyle, which is about a group of explorers finding a hidden plateau in South America where dinosaurs are still alive. (UBG 149)
• Or what about a modern traveller? Bill Bryson has written some hilarious stories. Try ***Notes from a Small Island*** first.

AROUND THE WORLD IN EIGHTY DAYS Jules Verne

➡ In the introduction to this gripping story, Englishman Phileas Fogg bets his stuffy friends at the Reform Club £20,000 that he can travel around the world in eighty days – an incredibly short time for a voyage like this when the book was written (trains still ran on steam then). Setting off with his calm valet Passepartout, Fogg travels for much of the time under the baleful eye of Detective Fix, who has been sent out by Scotland Yard to investigate a mysterious bank robbery. This is a terrific story about travel, science and adventure – that first gave me a taste for travel.

11+

Sara Wheeler

If you're looking for Kevin Crossley-Holland's Arthurian trilogy, turn to p. 216

ARTEMIS FOWL Eoin Colfer

➨ I first had to read *Artemis Fowl* when I worked at Puffin. It was late, I was tired and all I thought I wanted to do was watch television. But, in fact, reading *Artemis Fowl* was what I really needed – the closest possible reading experience to watching a big budget action film.

Artemis Fowl is fantasy, but is closer to James Bond than to *The Lord of the Rings*. It is also very funny. In the first book, Artemis Fowl, a twelve-year-old criminal mastermind who isn't satisfied with robbing banks, sets his sights on the ultimate treasure – fairy gold. What he doesn't realise is that the fairies he is up against aren't soft and pretty with sparkly wings. These fairies are smart, armed and dangerous and one of the smartest, Captain Holly Short of the LEPrecon Unit, is going to do everything she can to make sure Artemis doesn't succeed. And so begins a fantastic battle of wits and weapons, with plenty of action and larger-than-life characters, including my personal favourite Mulch Diggums, the dwarf with the amazing bum-flap.

9-12

Philippa Milnes-Smith

Next?
- The sequels so far are ***Artemis Fowl: The Arctic Incident*** and ***Artemis Fowl: The Eternity Code***.
- For other Bond-like action, try Anthony Horowitz's Alex Rider books, starting with ***Stormbreaker***. (UBG 228)
- If you enjoy the madly unexpected, try ***Piratica*** by Tanith Lee. (UBG 190)
- If you enjoy fast-paced fantasy, try Terry Pratchett's ***Truckers***. (UBG 36)

THE ARTHUR RACKHAM FAIRY BOOK Arthur Rackham

➨ For me, Arthur Rackham was the greatest children's illustrator of them all. He looked like an Edwardian bank clerk – such a contrast to most of the people and creatures depicted in his illustrations. Rackham's astonishing goblins, trees, wizards, genies and giants enthralled the eye and mind of this young lad through childhood. For this particular book he chose around two dozen popular tales from various countries and illustrated them with line drawings, silhouettes and full colour paintings.

9-11

Michael Lawrence

Next?
- Some other books brilliantly enhanced by Arthur Rackham are Kenneth Grahame's ***The Wind in the Willows*** (UBG 265), Charles Dickens's ***A Christmas Carol*** and Aesop's ***Fables*** (UBG 75).
- There are loads of great versions of classic fairy tales – turn to p. 76 for a selection.
- Or for a more modern take, try ***A Necklace of Raindrops*** by Joan Aiken. (UBG 174)

AS GOOD AS DEAD IN DOWNTOWN Neil Arksey

✓ Here

➨ Kai is a street-boy; tough, edgy, full of confidence – and full of a great need to escape the dirt and restrictions of life in Downtown.

Phoebe and Phoenix are perfect, genetically-enhanced twins who have risked everything to escape from their laboratory home in Nebula.

When Kai is used as a tool to hunt the escapees, all the plots of the master-manipulator come to nothing. For Phoebe remembers the legends told among the lab kids, stories of hope, that one of their number was already free, living in the crammed streets and tenements of Downtown. And she recognises something in Kai that is very similar to herself …

Then the kids have another serious problem to deal with – a huge tidal wave is set to destroy the city, and somehow they have to survive.

This is a complex, fast-paced and exciting story about the need for freedom and the value of hope.

10-12

Leonie Flynn

Next?
- More Neil Arksey? Try ***Playing on the Edge***. (UBG 191)
- Also about genetic engineering is Nicholas Fisk's ***A Rag, A Bone and a Hank of Hair***. (UBG 197)
- Or for a really dark, futuristic story, read ***Why Weeps the Brogan?*** by Hugh Scott. (UBG 263)

ASTERIX

René Goscinny and Albert Uderzo

Next?
- If you like the ***Asterix*** books, try the **Tintin** series by Hergé. (UBG 244)
- Jeremy Strong is a writer known for packing his stories with silly jokes and puns. Look out for ***Krazy Kow Saves the World – Well, Almost*** (UBG 138) and ***My Mum's Going to Explode!*** (UBG 170).
- Or read the ***The Rotten Romans*** in the **Horrible Histories** series, where you get puns, jokes and real history too! (UBG 116)

➨ Adventures, warriors, quests, magic potions and the funniest bad jokes ever to come out of Gaul. These are the ingredients of the **Asterix** cartoon series. Asterix, a cunning little warrior, and his mountainous best friend, Obelix, are the heroes of over twenty stories about the last Gaulish tribe to remain undefeated by the Roman legions, thanks largely to the magic potion brewed by the druid Getafix.

The heroes' adventures take them to many distant lands, and on different missions, but the recipe remains the same – a fantastic mix of thrills and laughs. Highlights include the fondue orgy scenes in *Asterix in Switzerland*, the constant nose jokes in *Asterix and Cleopatra*, and the great feast at the end of every adventure, when Cacofonix the bard (geddit?) is invariably gagged and tied to a nearby tree to prevent him from performing. The illustrations are a joy – full of slapstick moments, while the stories themselves leave no pun unpenned.

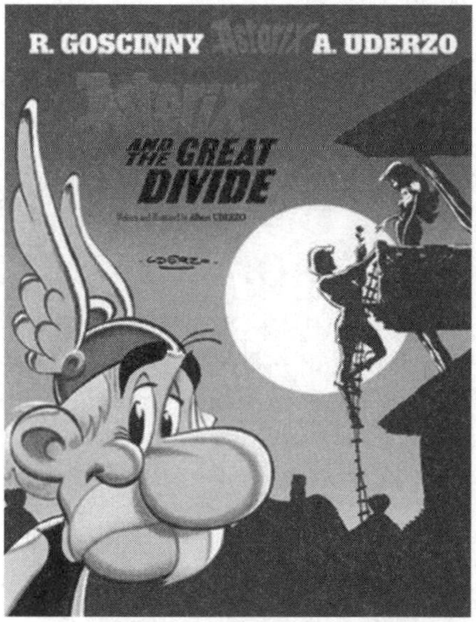

Originally written in French, much effort has been made to ensure that all the wonderful jokes and joke names (and there are lots of them) lose nothing in the translation.

You might not learn much (accurate) history reading them, but you'll certainly enjoy the adventures of Asterix.

8+

Marcus Sedgwick

AUGUST '44

Carlo Gébler

➨ Saul and his family are Jewish. It's the Second World War and they're hiding out in the forest to escape from the Nazis. Living in a cave, and in constant danger of being found, their lives are harsh and incredibly hazardous. To cheer them all up, Claude, who is a family friend, tells the story of the Golem – a legendary creature created out of clay to help the Jews in Prague, long, long ago.

Carlo Gébler weaves together two amazing stories: both of Jewish people living under terrible persecution – but they are ultimately hopeful. By retelling the legend of the Prague Jews, who at least had the Golem to protect them, he brings to the fore just how vulnerable the Jewish people hiding from the Nazis really were. This is a very powerful and very thoughtful book.

11+

Susan Reuben

Next?
- ***The Devil's Arithmetic*** by Jane Yolen is a deeply moving story set in Poland during World War Two. (UBG 60)
- ***The Star Houses*** by Stewart Ross is about how one family of Hungarian Jews survived the war.
- Donna Jo Napoli's ***Stones in Water*** is a beautifully-told story of two Italian boys who are taken as slave-labourers into Eastern Europe. What happens to them, and how they try and hide the fact that one of them is Jewish, is a moving testament to friendship and is loosely based on a true story.
- ***Doctor Illuminatus*** by Martin Booth is a fantasy story in which a golem plays an important part.

If you're looking for Lemony Snicket's *The Bad Beginning*, turn to p. 217

BADGER ON THE BARGE Janni Howker

Next?
• Janni hasn't written a huge number of books, but if you found this as amazing as I hope you will then you really must read her other longer stories. Try ***The Nature of the Beast*** first.
• ***Flying with Icarus*** by Curdella Forbes is a set of short stories all set in the Caribbean. (UBG 86)
• Or try David Almond's moving collection, ***Counting Stars***. (UBG 52)

➨ In my humble opinion, collections of short stories just don't get enough fuss. They're perfect for reading at bedtime, or on trains and buses, or anywhere where a long story gets interrupted too often. And a good short story can say far more than any three-part epic could *ever* say ... especially when that story is written by Janni Howker.

There are five stories in this collection, and each one deals in a different way with a relationship between a child (or children) and a much older person. Do you ever think you know something for *certain* and then find out you've got it all backwards? Well, these stories are about exactly that kind of experience ... and they're the kind of stories you can read a zillion times and each time discover something new and profound and mind-stretching. A book to keep for ever.

11+

Vivian French

THE BAGTHORPE SAGA
(Book 1: Ordinary Jack) Helen Cresswell

Next?
• The series continues with ***Absolute Zero***, ***Bagthorpes Unlimited*** and ***Bagthorpes v the World***.
• For more boys who outwit most adults, try ***Aquila*** by Andrew Norriss (UBG 18) or Elizabeth Honey's ***Don't Pat the Wombat*** (UBG 66).

➨ If you suffer from low esteem – and who doesn't sometimes? – read this hilarious and uplifting book. Jack Bagthorpe feels low because unlike the rest of the large Bagthorpe family who all excel at something, he isn't particularly good at anything. And it's not for want of trying. Uncle Parker, married to ravishingly beautiful Aunt Celia who typically excels at poetry and pottery and can do *The Times* crossword in ten minutes flat, decides to help Jack out. He says Jack must *pretend* to excel at something and he has a plan to make Jack immortal. The Bagthorpes are like lots of families, where achievement is the thing, so the story rings true at the same time as being fantastical and farcical, rollicking and rumbustious, and sometimes quite moving.

9-11

Julia Jarman

BAMBERT'S BOOK OF MISSING STORIES Reinhardt Jung

Next?
• ***Dreaming in Black and White*** is another book by Reinhardt Jung.
• ***Love That Dog*** by Sharon Creech will keep you thinking long after you've closed it. (UBG 150)
• ***Where Were You, Robert?*** by Hans Magnus Enzenburger is the story of a boy who travels through time, collecting new stories and telling his own.
• For another beautiful story about stories, try Salman Rushdie's ***Haroun and the Sea of Stories***. (UBG 104)

➨ There is something rather sad about Bambert. A small man, he lives alone in his attic flat. He finds moving around difficult because of the pains in his joints. His only contact is with Mr Bloom, his landlord, who sends food and drink from the ground floor to Bambert in a specially fitted lift. But Bambert's life isn't constrained or lonely – because he writes stories about worlds he imagines and feels he knows. His world is actually as big as his dreams allow, and because he dreams such fabulous dreams, the stories he writes don't reflect his physical life.

This is a book which seems very simple, but long after you've finished it you will still be thinking about Bambert letting his stories float off into the distance in search of their own setting.

9+

Lindsey Fraser

Here

EVERYBODY'S FAVOURITE...

BALLET SHOES Noel Streatfeild

➡ I must have read *Ballet Shoes* at least ten times when I was young. I longed to have ballet lessons myself. I pretended my pink bedroom slippers were real ballet shoes and pranced round our flat, pointing my toes and whirling round and round. I must have looked a total idiot!

Ballet Shoes is the story of three adopted girls, Pauline, Petrova and Posy Fossil. They're sent to a London stage school and manage to earn their own livings appearing in plays and films. Pauline is a brilliant actress. Posy is an outstanding dancer. Petrova hates acting and dancing – she loves cars and wants to fly her own aeroplane.

Ballet Shoes seems a little old-fashioned now, and you might roll your eyes at the Fossil sisters' idea of their own poverty, given that they live in a big house in London with servants – but it's still a riveting story.

Jacqueline Wilson

Next?

- There are many more Noel Streatfeild 'Shoes' stories – try ***Dancing Shoes***, ***Theatre Shoes*** and ***Tennis Shoes***, then look out for all the others. Her **Gemma** books are about being in the movies; and there's also ***White Boots***, which is about ice-skating.
- Another lovely story about wanting to perform on the stage is ***The Swish of the Curtain*** by Pamela Brown. (UBG 233)
- Or try ***Cuckoo in the Nest*** by Michelle Magorian, about a boy who wants to be an actor. It is a harder read but well worth it.
- Or ***The Collins Book of Ballet and Dance***, edited by Jean Ure.

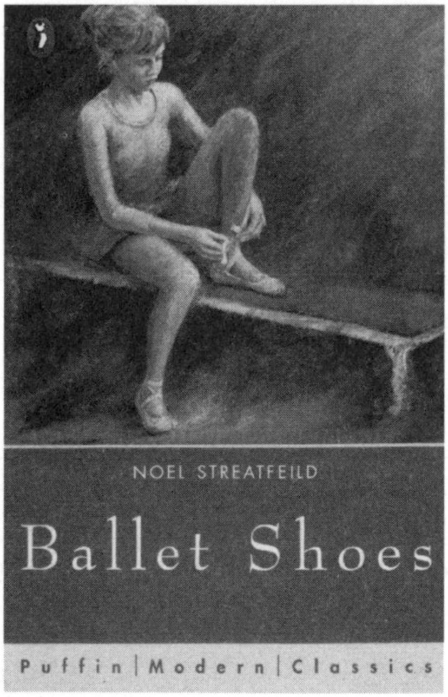

➡ At the drab end of the Second World War, ballet exploded across Britain. Before I ever saw a performance I knew it was my thing. The brilliant stage, the stories, the music, the dance, I found them irresistible. Ballet became my passion. When companies came to the Empire Theatre I saw every production, racing from school to queue in a back street and do my homework sitting on the pavement.

The only ballet books I could find were grown-up histories and biographies, and I read them all. *Ballet Shoes* was the exception, a lovely fantasy about three orphans at a stage school which I read and re-read.

I was never teased, but I knew that at that time boys in Sunderland did not become ballet dancers. I didn't know how to go about it. Trying a different form of romanticism, I went to sea instead.

9-11

Alan Temperley

THE BATTLE OF BUBBLE AND SQUEAK **Philippa Pearce**

➨ Philippa Pearce is a brilliant storyteller – this story will have you gripped from beginning to end; she sees and understands real life and knows how to involve her readers in it.

Life for the Sparrow family changes with the arrival of two gerbils: Bubble and Squeak. The Sparrow children, especially Sid, are passionate about the gerbils. Their dad doesn't mind them, but Mrs Sparrow simply wants them out of her house. So the family conflict begins.

The gerbils survive many threats – being returned to the pet shop, being given away, being put out for the dustbin men to collect and being attacked by Ginger the cat. Mr Sparrow tries to keep everyone happy, and of course the story does have a satisfying ending and leaves readers smiling.

Wendy Cooling

8-10

Next?

- Read about Jack the dog who tells his own story in Patricia Finney's ***I, Jack***. (UBG 120)
- Try the wonderful fantasy stories of Hermux Tantamoq the mouse by Michael Hoeye. Start with ***Time Stops for No Mouse***. (UBG 243)
- For another very short story of families and pets, read Anne Fine's ***The Diary of a Killer Cat***.
- Or try ***Frank and the Black Hamster of Narkiz*** by Livi Michael. (UBG 87)

A BEAR CALLED PADDINGTON

Michael Bond

➨ The hapless Paddington is my all-time favourite children's book character. He never fails to make me laugh. This book introduces him and his new family, the Browns (having been adopted by them on Paddington Station after his trip there from Darkest Peru), as well as the regulars who appear in the series, including the grouchy Mr Curry, Paddington's horrible neighbour, and gentle Mr Gruber, his friend from the antiques shop on Portobello Road.

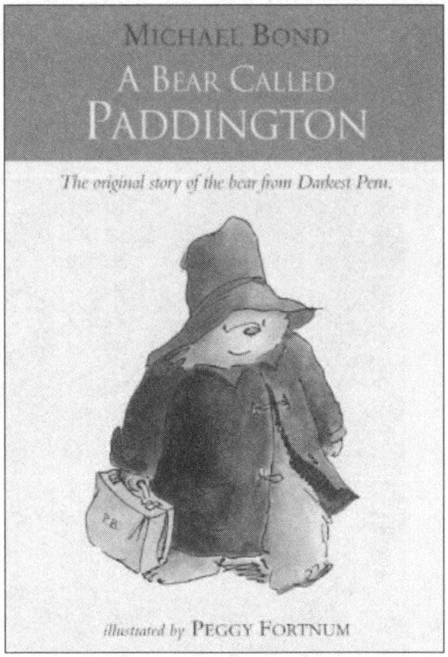

MICHAEL BOND
A BEAR CALLED
PADDINGTON
The original story of the bear from Darkest Peru.
illustrated by PEGGY FORTNUM

Paddington himself is a walking disaster area, always getting into some desperate scrape or other. Yet, once the mayhem has been sorted out (usually by the long-suffering Browns, or their housekeeper, Mrs Bird), he never fails to come out of it well; often better than he began.

In this book, having a bath, going on the London Underground and visiting the theatre are just some of the events that get the inimitable Michael Bond touch. Timeless, hilarious and essential reading – for readers of all ages!

Chris d'Lacey

6-8

Next?

- There are far too many books in the **Paddington** series to mention them all. If you liked ***A Bear Called ...***, then none of the others will fail to amuse you. My favourite Paddington adventure comes in the book ***Paddington at Large***, when Paddington appears on a game show and has an hilarious run-in with the host, Ronnie Playfair.
- Of course, another classic bear book is ***Winnie-the-Pooh*** by A.A. Milne. (UBG 266)
- I must also put a word in here for another of my favourite authors, Allan Ahlberg. His young fiction is brilliant. Read ***Ten in a Bed*** – you won't stop laughing.

BEAUTY Robin McKinley

Next?
- If you'd like to see what McKinley does with this same story twenty years later, try ***Rose Daughter***, which is a harder read.
- Donna Jo Napoli has done very different retellings of ***Beauty and the Beast***, ***Rapunzel*** and others.
- Sleeping Beauty has been the starting point for Jane Yolen's ***Briar Rose***, Sophie Masson's ***Clementine***, and Robin McKinley's ***Spindle's End***.
- Gillian Cross's tense, atmospheric ***Wolf*** takes a different spin on another well-known story. (UBG 270)
- And try the wonderful, older **Egerton Hall Trilogy** by Adèle Geras.

➨ When her wealthy family loses all its money, Beauty and her horse, Greatheart, work hard to help out. Having moved far away from their home, the family is just starting to get settled when her father runs foul of a wizardly Beast in an enchanted castle. Beauty and Greatheart go to the castle to live in exchange for her father's life, and find tiny, sly magics everywhere, invisible servants, plenty of books, and a Beast who only distresses her when he asks his nightly question, 'Will you marry me?'

The story is familiar, but McKinley makes it magical again, with a Beauty who redeems a wistful Beast, a magical library and obliging table settings (created long before the Disney movie), and a hundred grace notes that give this unique retelling a pleasure all its own.

Tamora Pierce

10+

BECAUSE OF WINN-DIXIE

Kate DiCamillo

➨ Funny and moving, *Because of Winn-Dixie* tells the story of ten-year-old Opal Buloni, recently arrived with her father, the preacher, at a trailer park in Naomi, Florida. Opal befriends a dog running amok through the local supermarket, calling him Winn-Dixie (like naming a dog Tesco). Winn-Dixie helps Opal and her father deal with the loss of Ruby, Opal's mother, and enables Opal to make friends with many of the town's more interesting citizens, dispelling both their loneliness and her own.

This book deals with big themes: love, loneliness, loss and reconciliation, with a sureness of touch beyond all but a few. The story is told in the absolutely authentic voice of its charming heroine. Every sentence rings true.

9-11

Celia Rees

Next?
- Try Kate DiCamillo's next book, ***The Tiger Rising***, and anything else she ever writes.
- Like DiCamillo, Mark Twain writes in the Southern tradition of seeing the adult world through a child's eyes. You might like to try his ***The Adventures of Tom Sawyer***. (UBG 9)
- Another story about how finding a stray dog helps a child through life is ***Dog Friday*** by Hilary McKay.

BECKY BANANAS Jean Ure

Next?
- Other Jean Ure books to look for are ***Daisy May*** (UBG 55), an easier read, and ***Shrinking Violet***.
- You'll find certain similarities to Jacqueline Wilson's older ***Vicky Angel.*** (UBG 255)
- ***Harvey Angell*** by Diana Hendry is an upbeat, lighter tale that still makes you think about people. (UBG 107)

➨ Don't even think about reading *Becky Bananas* if you're embarrassed when books make you cry. Even the toughest, meanest, most cold-hearted monster among you will be sniffling loudly by the end of this …

And you'll love it, of course. Becky Banaras ('Bananas') is a very loveable character, and the story she's telling you about her own life, and about a girl called Bryony who has leukaemia, is funny and moving and uplifting and lots of other good things.

Of all Jean Ure's great books (and there are loads), this one's definitely my favourite. You'll love all the characters – little brother Danny, Mum, gorgeous Uncle Eddy, but especially the wonderful, lively Becky, of course. And once you've started you'll probably end up reading it in one sitting, as I did. But remember, hankies at the ready …

Daniel Hahn

7-10

BEDKNOB AND BROOMSTICK

Mary Norton

Next?
- For more sibling adventures, try ***The Saturdays*** by Elizabeth Enright. (UBG 210)
- Mary Norton also wrote ***The Borrowers***, which you can read all about on p. 33.
- Or try ***Mary Poppins*** by P.L. Travers, another story of magic intruding on humdrum lives! (UBG 156)

➡ Have you ever heard about some amazing place and thought, 'I wish I could go there!' But you couldn't, because it was too far, or too dangerous, too expensive or just plain impossible? Everyone has dreams like that.

Carey and her brothers, summering at their aunt's dull house in Bedfordshire, are given a magic bedknob by kindly neighbourhood witch-in-training, Miss Price. The bedknob will take them (and their bed) anywhere they want to go. They can think of loads of places – but which to try first? Should they go to explore a beautiful desert island? Or to London to visit their mother? Or perhaps into the past? But Carey, Charles and Paul soon discover that magical adventures are never as simple as they first seem ...

This is 'a classic' – not just because it's very old and your grandparents loved it, but because it's genuinely a brilliant read – exciting, funny, lively ... everything you could want in a book.

9-11

Daniel Hahn

BENNY AND OMAR Eoin Colfer

➡ This story follows Benny, a popular, outgoing Irish boy with a fast tongue and a witty manner, as he moves to Tunisia. His favourite sport, hurling, isn't played there, and all his friends will be left behind. Will it be the end of life as he knows it?

This is where Omar comes in. He is a wild local boy living on his own. He speaks in broken English garnered from TV, and has a skill for making do with the little that he has. The two soon become inseparable friends and form a terrifying duo, raising havoc in the tiny village which Benny grows to love.

I really enjoyed this book when I was ten. I had to move countries and make new friends, so this was something that I could relate to.

9-12

Chris Cross

Next?
- If you like this you might also like the sequel, ***Benny and Babe***. Back with his grandfather, Benny meets Babe, the local tomboy.
- ***Ruby Holler*** by Sharon Creech is a very different book about adjusting to a new life situation. (UBG 205)
- Eoin Colfer is most famous for ***Artemis Fowl*** (UBG 20), but why not try ***The Wish List*** too? See p. 267.

BEOWULF: DRAGONSLAYER

Rosemary Sutcliff

Next?
- If you want to know more about the original story, try reading some Norse Myths (UBG 175), or the Icelandic Sagas.
- Another Sutcliff that is based on legend is ***Hound of Ulster***, about the great Celtic hero, Cuchulain.
- Or for something lighter, try ***Fabulous Monsters*** by Marcia Williams – monsters can be funny too! Read more about Marcia's books on p. 166.

➡ This is the oldest Anglo-Saxon story in existence. And it might just be the best. It's got everything: Beowulf, a valiant young hero; Grendel, a beast who has been pulling warriors apart for fun; and an even more powerful creature, Grendel's mother, a hideous seahag who lives at the bottom of a lake. Not content with facing these terrors, Beowulf also has a pop at a vicious dragon before he is acclaimed the bravest warrior of all.

Originally written in Old English, the story of Beowulf has been told round the evening fire for generations. Rosemary Sutcliff's retelling brings it to life for our own time, but captures the guts and courage of the dark days that stand at the head of our history.

9-11

Marcus Sedgwick

adventures – just like the children (shipmates) in ***Swallows and Amazons***.

BETSY-TACY series Maud Hart Lovelace

➡ Where were Maud Hart Lovelace's books when I was growing up? I guess they were around, but somehow I missed them. High school would have been so much easier if I'd been prepped for it by reading these books! And even though Betsy, Mrs Lovelace's heroine, went to high school in 1910 Minnesota, things haven't really changed at all since Betsy's day. There were popular girls who weren't especially nice to her, and cute boys to have huge crushes on, and best friends to fight with, and parties and dances and popular music and pretty new clothes, and even a few things I didn't have growing up – like sleigh rides and onion (blech!) sandwiches.

Start with Betsy's first year in high school – *Heaven to Betsy*. This is the book where she first meets Joe, her one true love … or *is* he?

Maud Hart Lovelace based the Betsy books on her own high school years. There is even a museum in Minnesota where you can go and see photos of her and her friends and all of the people and places in her stories. I hope you'll like them as much as I do!

8-10

Meg Cabot

Next?
- Look for: ***Betsy in Spite of Herself, Betsy Was a Junior, Betsy and Joe, Betsy and the Great World*** and ***Betsy's Wedding***.
- Another great American series about growing up is Laura Ingalls Wilder's **Little House** books. (UBG 142)
- For something more modern, try ***Simone's Letters*** by Helena Pielichaty. (UBG 220)

THE BFG Roald Dahl

➡ The special friendship between the little orphan girl Sophie and the BFG, and their adventures together as they save the world from less-than-friendly giants (with a little help from the Queen), make the most wonderful of stories. It's one of those rare books that sweeps you away from the very beginning of chapter one – The Witching Hour – when the reader immediately knows that magic and mystery is at work. Roald Dahl really does weave his own individual magic in this book, which is also particularly good on tape or read aloud, not least because of the BFG's own delicious (or indeed 'scrumdiddlyumptious') mixed-up language. The story combines excitement, humour and unforgettable characters, including the BFG himself with his trademark ears, sandals and dramatic cloak.

8-10

Philippa Milnes-Smith

Next?
- Read all of Roald Dahl's children's books (you'll find some listed on p. 285).
- Try Philip Ridley's ***Meteorite Spoon*** and ***Scribbleboy*** (UBG 211), which also feature extraordinary characters.
- If you like the combination of humour and magic, try Jeremy Strong's ***Krazy Kow Saves the World – Well, Almost***. (UBG 138)

THE BIG BAZOOHLEY Peter Carey

➡ Sam has extraordinary parents: his mum, Vanessa, paints masterpieces the size of a matchbox and his dad, Earl, is a professional gambler down on his luck. They're broke, really broke; yet Earl insists they check into the luxurious King Redward Hotel. It's Toronto in a blizzard and there's a lot going on! The story has more twists than a pretzel and great characters that conjure up the most hilarious images in your imagination.

Sam gets locked out of his room, then kidnapped, and after all this has to enter a 'perfect child' competition (the prize is lots of money!). 'Am I dreaming?' you laugh, and wonder, 'How on earth can Sam win the big bazoohley to save them? He hasn't got a chance.' You'll have to read the book to find out if he does!

10-12

Elizabeth Honey

Next?
- Try one of Elizabeth Honey's own books: ***Don't Pat the Wombat***. (UBG 66)
- Another book about a parent who makes life exciting is Roald Dahl's ***Danny, the Champion of the World***. (UBG 56)
- For another daffy dad in need of sorting out, try Pete Johnson's ***Rescuing Dad***. (UBG 202)

BIGGLES series Captain W.E. Johns

➡ Flying ace, Squadron Leader James Bigglesworth, ducks and weaves through countless thrilling adventures, invariably escaping disaster by a whisker and leaving his dastardly enemies gasping for mercy. Biggles is always ready for anything and everything. In one book, *Biggles: Foreign Legionnaire*, he enlists in the infamous French Foreign Legion, bravely casting fears aside and plunging in to whatever dangers might present themselves (plenty do). He capers about all over the globe, chomping Chinese fried rice one minute and garlic snails the next.

The author allows him to wander freely through the decades: several of the books are set during the First World War, during which our hero boldly defends the goodies' supply route between Calcutta and China, and on another occasion, scraps with his old German enemy in the wilds of Palestine. The Second World War finds Biggles battling away deep in the jungle of Japanese-occupied Malaysia.

I never tired of Biggles and his breathtakingly hazardous antics, and from him I learnt that with a bit of initiative and a dash of courage you can think your way out of anything. Chocks away!

10-12

Sara Wheeler

Next?
- If you want to read books that blend truth with fiction, try the **Warpath** series by J. Eldridge.
- For more action-packed adventure, try ***Cannibal Adventure*** and sequels by Willard Price. (UBG 39)
- And don't forget ***Stormbreaker*** by Anthony Horowitz for more up-to-date thrills. (UBG 228)

BILL'S NEW FROCK Anne Fine

➡ 'When Bill Simpson woke up on Monday morning, he found he was a girl.'

Bill's mother puts a frilly pink dress over his head, and he is horrified. After all, he's a boy. But there doesn't seem to be anything else for him to wear, so off he goes to school, in his frilly pink dress.

It's the beginning of the worst day of Bill's life, but for the reader it's incredibly funny. Gradually, Bill is made aware of all the injustices a girl has to suffer. The boys won't let him play football, and he has to model for the art class. He is even wolf-whistled. Bill can't help being a boy, and by the end of the day the pink dress is in a mess: ripped, muddied and covered in paint. But as the school day draws to a close, we begin to wonder if Bill will ever return to what he was before.

Although this story is about a boy, both boys and girls will find it hilarious. It brings into focus some of the funniest differences between us.

7-10

Jenny Nimmo

Next?
- Read some more of Anne Fine's shorter stories: ***The Angel of Nitshill Road*** for instance (UBG 14), and ***The Country Pancake***. Both are school stories with a difference.
- Or Allan Ahlberg's ***Woof!*** about a boy who is transformed into a Norfolk terrier! (UBG 271)

BILLY ELLIOT Melvin Burgess

Next?
- For more about boys and ballet, see Alan Temperley's recommendation of ***Ballet Shoes*** by Noel Streatfeild. (UBG 23)
- What about another book by Melvin Burgess? Try ***Kite*** (UBG 136) or ***The Ghost Behind the Wall*** (UBG 90).
- ***Cuckoo in the Nest*** by Michelle Magorian is about a boy wanting to be an actor.

➨ If you don't know this story, it's about a twelve-year-old boy in County Durham who discovers he has a talent for ballet. Not the sort of thing northern boys are meant to dream about, frankly – just ask Billy's dad, on-strike miner, Jackie. He's not amused. Billy should be boxing or doing something else 'manly' like that. But Billy has a real gift, and his ballet teacher, Mrs Wilkinson, is determined that he shouldn't waste it. It's a story about conflict between what different people think about things; Melvin Burgess dramatises this conflict really effectively by switching between points of view – parts of the story are told by Billy himself, parts by Jackie, Billy's brother Tony, his friend Michael.

Book adaptations of films are often (usually?) rubbish. But you can trust a writer like Melvin Burgess to produce something this good – not just a good film-transformed-into-a-book, but a really good book in itself. Don't read this instead of seeing the film, nor the other way round; both are great. See which you prefer – I'm still not sure ...

10-12

Daniel Hahn

Here (YA)

EVERYBODY'S FAVOURITE...

BLACK BEAUTY Anna Sewell

➨ Stories can be exciting, mysterious, frightening or funny. But they can also be sad, as much of *Black Beauty* is. One scene in it is among the most moving in all of children's literature.

Cruelty to horses was commonplace in Victorian times, and one thing that Anna Sewell fought against was the use of a bearing rein, a device designed to pull a carriage horse's head right up. It looked smart but it was agony for the animal.

The story isn't all gloom. Admittedly, the black horse with the white star on his forehead has an accident – a fall when driven by a drunkard – but his early life with Squire Gordon, John Manly the coachman and Joe Green the stableboy is a happy one. By the end we can smile, though we may have shed some tears along the way.

Next?
- To find out more about Anna Sewell, read Naomi's foreword in the new Kingfisher Classics edition of ***Black Beauty***.
- ***The Silver Brumby***, by Elyne Mitchell, about a wild stallion and his struggles to protect his herd. (UBG 218)
- Read ***National Velvet*** by Enid Bagnold, about a girl with ambitions to ride in the Grand National. (UBG 171)

Dick King-Smith

➨ I read this story often as a child, and whenever I came to a hill (London has plenty), it always made me think of horses carrying heavy loads. And I can't help noticing how horses are treated in, say, Dickens or Sherlock Holmes. I owe this, and much more, to Anna Sewell. But since she died soon after her book's publication, she never knew that she had created a major all-age bestseller, never out of print, still rated as the most influential work of fiction on animal welfare ever written.

Black Beauty is the self-told tale of a horse whose many changes of work and owner tell us much. Remember – there was no motorised transport when this was written, but horses were all too cheap and plentiful. There were no traffic rules in the hideously crammed streets, where sick and overworked creatures daily died in harness. The highbred carriage horses fared no better. Quickly ruined by fashion's cruelties, they were sold off for rough street use. It's all in Anna's book.

10-12

Naomi Lewis

BLACK JACK Leon Garfield

Next?
- Other Leon Garfield books you may enjoy are ***Smith*** (UBG 221) and ***Devil-in-the-Fog***.
- If you like historical novels, try Rosemary Sutcliff – ***Knight's Fee*** is wonderful. (UBG 137)
- If you're feeling braver, why not dip into Charles Dickens with ***Great Expectations*** or ***Oliver Twist***?

➨ A boy, Tolly, is in a moonlit room. With him, the dead body of a huge man who has just been hanged. Then, 'Those eyes! They were wide open! They were moving! They were staring at him!'

So begins an eighteenth-century adventure, with villainy afoot on every page. Interwoven with Tolly's story is that of Belle, a girl who is thought mad and sees visions: 'A tall tower with a golden top – higher than the sky. There are white angels flying with white wings. And all the world's singing a lullaby – for the sun's gone to bed in a blanket.' Leon Garfield uses words as if they are alive and will draw you into a strange, dangerous world – and it's a sort of love story too. Read it.

10-12

Helen Cresswell

BLACK MARIA

Diana Wynne Jones

➨ Although *Black Maria* is set in a quiet (maybe *too* quiet?) seaside town, the story speeds along, twisting and turning as it goes. This is because nothing and no one in Cranbury-on-Sea is quite what they seem. Mig and Chris go there to stay with apparently-lovely Aunt Maria. They soon discover that the doddery old lady has deadly gifts. Before long they are trapped into staying with Black Maria and her sinister friends.

Nobody comes to their rescue; the men are all biddable zombies, the women in thrall to Maria, and the children all strange creatures kept in an orphanage. Perhaps the green ghost who visits Chris's bedroom every night will help?

10-12

Gill Vickery

Next?
- Diana Wynne Jones's ***Power of Three*** opens with a murder. ***The Time of the Ghost*** features a ghost who isn't sure which one of a family of sisters she is. (UBG 242)
- For one of the most sinister families ever, read Neil Gaiman's ***Coraline***. (UBG 51)
- Try Penelope Lively's funny, enchanting ***The Revenge of Samuel Stokes***. (UBG 203)

BLACK SHIPS BEFORE TROY

Rosemary Sutcliff, illustrated by Alan Lee

Next?
- Odysseus was one of the bravest and most cunning heroes. His story is told in ***The Wanderings of Odysseus***. The series continues with ***The Aeneid***, retold by Penelope Lively.
- You will probably also like ***Troy*** by Adèle Geras, though it's a slightly more challenging read. (UBG 248)
- Or try ***The God Beneath the Sea*** by Leon Garfield and Edward Blishen, for more Greek myths. (UBG 95)

➨ Long, long ago Paris, a Trojan prince, fell in love with Helen, wife of the Greek king Menelaus and sailed with her back to Troy. Helen's is the famous 'face that launched a thousand ships' – the black ships of the Greeks who set sail for Troy to wreak vengeance on the Trojans and get Helen back.

Nineteen stories, each one ending with a cliff-hanger, tell the tale of the ten-year-long war which followed. You'll meet heroes and villains and gods and goddesses in many disguises. There's gruesome realism and there are amazing magical feats. You'll read about a golden apple that could be said to have caused the war, the famous Wooden Horse of Troy that brought it to an end, and what was probably the first cloak of invisibility in literature.

These are some of the oldest stories in the world – and so good that writers have been pinching from them ever since! Rosemary Sutcliff brings them vividly to life in this stunning re-telling.

10-12

Julia Jarman

songs and such magic in them, and I loved the idea of being thrown into such a different world.

BLITZ BOYS Linda Newbery

➡ Ronnie's experiences in London during the Blitz make an exciting and interesting novel. While exploring a bombed-out house, he meets Dusty Miller, a boy who's hiding out there. Dusty tells Ronnie that his father is an RAF pilot.

The descriptions of the sounds and smells of wartime London, characters who come across to the reader as real people, and the relationships of the two boys with one another and with the adults in their lives, make this one of those books that contains a great deal in the space of relatively few pages. One of Newbery's main themes is courage: the different kinds of bravery that people exhibit in time of danger and difficulty. There's also a horse, an air raid, a fire and a satisfying ending.

10-12

Adèle Geras

Next?
- Try ***Carrie's War*** by Nina Bawden, about a girl evacuated to Wales during the Second World War. (UBG 41)
- Or ***Blitzed*** by Robert Swindells, in which a boy finds himself going back in time to the Blitz.
- Or ***A Candle in the Dark*** by Adèle Geras, about a Jewish brother and sister who escape from the Nazis. (UBG 38)

BLITZCAT Robert Westall

Next?
- Robert Westall wrote many acclaimed books about the war. ***The Machine Gunners*** is a good place to start. (UBG 150)
- If you're interested in reading about the Second World War, try ***The Blitzed Brits*** in **Horrible Histories.** (UBG 116)
- Or try ***Fireweed*** by Jill Paton Walsh, in which two children survive in London during the Blitz.

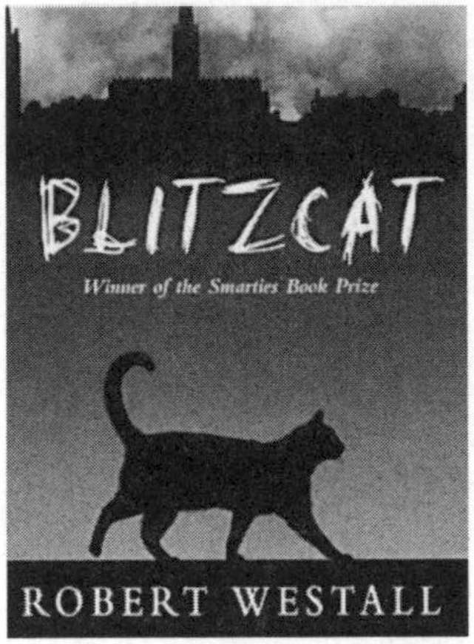

➡ *Blitzcat* is an animal book with a difference. The heroine is a black cat, Lord Gort, who decides to go in search of her absent person, an RAF pilot. Set in the darkest hours of the Second World War, Lord Gort's quest takes her first to bomb-torn Dover, then to Coventry, just as the city is being destroyed by fire. The cat then travels across country where she becomes the lucky mascot at an RAF station – and that's just for starters. *Blitzcat* is an exciting, action-packed read, highly realistic and informative about the life of RAF fighter pilots. Be warned – although a cat is the central character, this book is not at all soft or sentimental. It's a breathtaking, vividly-told adventure.

10+

Sherry Ashworth

THE BLOBHEADS
Paul Stewart and Chris Riddell

➡ Billy Barnes is in his bathroom when he hears strange noises coming from the toilet. Three purple and red blobby things with tentacles emerge. Once Billy Barnes has got over his shock, the blobs introduce themselves as Zerek, Kerek and Derek, and say they are on a very important mission to save the High King of the Universe from the evil Sharon and her followers. The High King of the Universe just happens to be Billy Barnes' baby brother Silas. The Blobheads want to take Silas away but Billy won't let them. The Blobheads are supposed to be super-intelligent beings, but things never seem to go quite to plan. Billy has to deal with talking fridges, kettles and toasters, and that is just for starters …

10-12

Julia Lytollis

Next?
- There are lots of Blobheads books, though they are now available as one collection. My favourite individual title is ***An Alien Ate My Homework***.
- Try ***There's an Alien in My Classroom*** by Bruce Coville.
- Or for something very funny – and very nasty – read Raymond Briggs's ***Fungus the Bogeyman***. (UBG 88)

THE BLOOD STONE **Jamila Gavin**

➡ Filippo never knew his father, Venetian jeweller Geronimo Veroneo who embarked for Hindustan seeking riches before Filippo was born. But Geronimo's presence lingers over the family home, and the dazzling diamond pendant Ocean of the Moon remains a token of his adoration for his wife Theodora.

Now, twelve years have passed. Geronimo has not returned and malevolent merchant, Bernardo Pagliarin, is scheming to destroy the family. When a message arrives that Geronimo has been imprisoned for ransom, Filippo knows he must use the diamond to save him. But as he embarks on a dangerous voyage, whom can he trust?

A marvellous, exotic quest for missing fathers and sons, *The Blood Stone* is a magical story of adventure across continents.

Helen Simmons

10-12

Next?
- Track down some other titles by Jamila Gavin; **The Wheel of Surya Trilogy** is my favourite. (UBG 261)
- You might also like William Nicholson's **The Wind on Fire Trilogy**; another epic adventure. (UBG 266)
- Another great story about unveiling family secrets is Thomas Bloor's ***The Memory Prisoner***. (UBG 158)

THE BOGGART **Susan Cooper**

➡ Boggarts are invisible most of the time. But just because they can't be seen doesn't mean no one knows they're there. They're mischievous little sprites who love playing tricks on humans, especially ones who don't believe in them.

Emily and Jessup's parents inherit an ancient Scottish castle, but when they pack up the contents, it's more than just a few bits of furniture they take home with them to Canada – for the Boggart, who has been trapped in the castle for centuries, comes along too.

The children's lives are suddenly intertwined with that of the ancient Boggart, but ironically, it's the modern world in the form of computers that comes to their aid.

Marcus Sedgwick

9-11

Next?
- Try the sequel, ***The Boggart and the Monster***.
- If you liked this, why not try Susan Cooper's **The Dark Is Rising** sequence? It consists of five books stuffed with ancient magic. (UBG 57)
- For stories about more unusual beings, try ***The Little Grey Men*** by B.B. (UBG 142)

THE BOOK OF THREE

(Book 1 of The Chronicles of Prydain) Lloyd Alexander

➡ Taran is a very ordinary teenager, dreaming of heroism, swords and magic in the land of Prydain. He works for Dallben, an ancient enchanter given to taking naps. The orphaned Taran yearns for glory, a title and a place in life, but the only title he has is the inglorious one of Assistant Pig-Keeper.

Then Dallben's prophetic pig, Henwen, escapes her pen and runs into the forest with Taran trying to catch her. Taran's search introduces him to the heroic Prince Gwydion and the evil sorceress, Achren. He draws companions to him along the way, such as the hapless would-be bard Fflewddur, cursed with a harp that breaks a string every time he colours the truth, and the chatterbox princess Eilonwy, and the furry, odd Gurgi – simple, loyal, cowardly, and clever. Nothing is as it seems: a scruffy stranger can be a prince, a stout, bald smith can be a retired hero, and a pig-keeper may defy the Horned King, who is bent on the conquest of Prydain. Taran is very real, inexperienced, foolhardy, but willing to admit when he makes a mistake. Every reader can identify with him and live with him through his adventures.

Tamora Pierce

9-11

Next?
- Look out for the sequels: ***The Black Cauldron***, ***The Castle of Lyr***, ***Taran the Wanderer*** and ***The High King***.
- For another series full of magic and adventure, try the **Chronicles of Narnia** by C.S. Lewis. (UBG 141)
- ***See our FANTASY STORIES selections on pp. 79-81.***

If you're looking for Catherine Fisher's The Book of the Crow, turn to p. 201

THE BORRIBLES Michael de Larrabeiti

➡ Borribles are curious and interesting creatures indeed – humanoid children that live as outcasts and runaways in the dark alleys, disused buildings and overgrown canals of London. They live forever unless their ears are clipped back to proper shape by the S.B.G. – Special Borrible Group – a dedicated London police division bent on unearthing them.

One night, the Battersea Borribles discover that they're under threat from their ancient enemy, the Rumbles. The Borribles' elite fighters set off on what will become The Great Rumble Hunt.

There is so much in this first adventure for the Borribles: excitement, a long and dangerous journey, bravery, treachery, violence and devilish cunning – it's got the lot. An often overlooked but much-appreciated modern fantasy classic, recently given a new lease of life.

11+

John McLay

Next?
- Read the rest of the trilogy: ***The Borribles Go For Broke*** and ***Across the Dark Metropolis***.
- ***Oliver Twist*** by Charles Dickens tells of street urchins in London, too.
- Try Leon Garfield's ***Smith*** for another evocative and adventurous slice of London life in days gone by. (UBG 221)

THE BORROWERS

Mary Norton

➡ This is a must-read. The Clock family – Pod, Homily and their daughter Arriety – are only thirteen centimetres high and live under the grandfather clock in the Old Rectory. They live by 'borrowing' from 'human beans' upstairs, and their greatest fear (apart from the cat!) is of discovery, or 'being seen'. Pod goes on expeditions to borrow – a silver thimble for a cooking pot, match boxes for chests of drawers, a champagne cork for a stool. When my daughters were small and something went missing they would say, 'The Borrowers have got it!' – and they'd believe it, too.

Arriety is tired of the lonely life under the floorboards and longs to go into the wider world. She breaks the rules by talking to a human bean, a boy, and disaster strikes when the housekeeper sends for the ratcatcher to smoke them out. The Borrowers have to flee their home and set off in search of relatives – Uncle Hendreary, Aunt Lupy and Eggletins and the others who live in the countryside about …

9-11

Helen Cresswell

Next?
- We can follow the Clocks' adventures in: ***The Borrowers Afield***, ***The Borrowers Afloat***, ***The Borrowers Aloft*** and ***The Borrowers Revenged***.
- You might enjoy my own book ***The Piemakers***, about the Danby Rollers who make a steak and kidney pie in a dish big enough for them to sail in down the river. (UBG 185)
- Try ***Charlotte's Web*** by E.B. White, a book about a world that is quite impossible and yet entirely real. (UBG 45)

THE BOX OF DELIGHTS

John Masefield

Next?

- If you enjoyed this you will want to read ***The Midnight Folk***, also about Kay Harker, who hunts for lost treasure, is bedevilled by a wicked-witch governess, and is helped by his faithful cat, Nibbins.
- You may then want to go on to read Masefield's ***The Bird of Dawning***, about a shipwrecked sailor and his mates who find an abandoned ship and sail it home.
- Or what about ***Corbenic*** by Catherine Fisher, also about a train journey that turns into something more exciting? (UBG 52)

➨ Kay Harker is in a train going home for the Christmas holidays. The landscape he sees through the window is snowy and threatening. Two crafty men cheat him out of some money and seem to have bad intentions towards an old Punch-and-Judy showman. Kay helps the showman to escape them, and he gives Kay the Box of Delights, which has magic properties. Wild adventures follow ...

This is one of my very favourite books. I read it first when I was twelve, in the train, taking it home for the Christmas holidays. Snow was falling outside as I read the first chapter. It was a truly magical experience.

(But I think Masefield should have left off that last paragraph. Do you agree?)

10-12

Joan Aiken

BOY

Roald Dahl

Next?

- ***Going Solo*** is a sort-of sequel. (UBG 96)
- There are so many brilliant Roald Dahl books, but among my favourite reads are ***Danny, the Champion of the World*** (UBG 56), ***The Twits*** (UBG 250) because it's so daft, and ***Matilda*** (UBG 157).
- Or for another author's childhood, try ***The Vicarage Family*** by Noel Streatfeild. (UBG 254)
- ***My Family and Other Animals*** by Gerald Durrell is the wonderful true story of a very unusual childhood. (UBG 169)

➨ It's clear, even inevitable, from this amazing and eclectic set of real-life memories from his early childhood, how Roald Dahl would grow up to draw on these often grotesque experiences to people his fiction with such quirky and eccentric characters and bizarre situations. Here we meet Mrs Pratchett, the bad-tempered, filthy-fingered sweet-shop lady who gets her comeuppance with a dead mouse surreptitiously placed in her jar of Gobstoppers; Corkers, the maths master who hates figures, so teaches his pupils how to solve *The Times* crossword instead; and Dahl's 'ancient half-sister' (aged a mere twenty-one) who nearly caused the young Roald to lose his nose in an accident whilst driving the family's newly-acquired car. Weird ... but absolutely wonderful reading.

9-12

Chris d'Lacey

BOY OVERBOARD Morris Gleitzman

➨ This vivid, comical and lively story details the life of Jamal, an Afghani boy whose undying enthusiasm for football greatly perks up the war-torn life that he leads. As in most of Morris Gleitzman's books, the story is hilarious in places, but the subject of this particular one means that it has a more serious note to it too.

When Jamal, his rather violent nine-year-old sister, and his parents are forced to flee from Afghanistan, they must undertake a dangerous and crowded (and often comical!) journey which forces them through such horrors as separation, wild seas, corrupt policeman and pirates. The aim of the journey is to reach Australia, where they believe they will be able to harvest a share of the never-ending wealth that they have heard about.

The book combines a splendid blend of humour, recent news, football and such issues as war and emigration which together form an action-packed adventure, funny but with a more serious side to it as well. It gives a real insight into the sort of lives other people lead, and is a must for all young readers!

Tim Cross

9-11

Next?
- More Gleitzman? They all have the formula of serious issues handled with great humour. Try ***Bumface*** (UBG 37) and ***Two Weeks with the Queen*** (UBG 251).
- ***Benny and Omar*** by Eoin Colfer is about an Irish boy who has to go and live in Tunisia. (UBG 26)
- Or try some of the books Morris Gleitzman has written with Paul Jennings, such as ***Wicked!*** (UBG 264) and ***Deadly!***

THE BOY WHO LOST HIS FACE

Louis Sachar

➨ 'He only did it to be accepted as part of a gang, but stealing from an old lady? It never seemed right. Especially this cane. From this old lady ...'

... because she puts a curse on him. From that day, David cannot do anything right. Everything he does turns into a disaster, and his life turns from sort-of-all-right to completely and absolutely miserable. And worse may happen if he can't make things better, because he believes the old lady to be a witch – one who can steal faces to hang on her living-room wall.

Funny, sad, sharp and fast-paced, this is a story about guilt, friendship – and not being rude to your mother.

Leonie Flynn

9-11

Next?
- More Sachar! Try ***Holes*** (UBG 113) and ***There's a Boy in the Girls' Bathroom*** (UBG 237).
- Another story about wanting to be popular is ***Stargirl*** by Jerry Spinelli. (UBG 225)
- Even spookier is ***The Haunting*** by Margaret Mahy. (UBG 107)
- ***The Wish List*** by Eoin Colfer has more terrible consequences of stealing from the elderly. (UBG 267)

THE BREADWINNER Deborah Ellis

➨ Parvana is eleven years old and lives in Afghanistan. Under Taliban law, girls are forbidden from going to school and all women must stay at home. For more than a year, Parvana's family has been trapped in their one-roomed flat. But when their father is arrested, the family faces starvation unless Parvana disguises herself as a boy and tries to earn a living. It's a dangerous plan, but it's their only chance of survival.

We've all heard the phrase 'living under the Taliban', but few of us understand what it really means. This book opens our eyes to the chilling truth, but Parvana's courage and determination to survive against all the odds is truly inspiring and there is hope at the end.

Kathryn Ross

11+

Next?
- In the sequel ***Parvana's Journey***, Parvana becomes separated from her mother and sisters.
- For more about the devastating effects of war on young people, read ***Zlata's Diary*** written by Zlata Filipoviç, a young girl living in Sarajevo during the civil war.
- For a story about an Afghan child with a lighter touch, try Morris Gleitzman's ***Boy Overboard***. (UBG 35)

Here

BREAK IN THE SUN Bernard Ashley

➡ This book is a realistic account of how Patsy Bligh's life is changed when she sees the theatre boat in the creek. You see, Patsy has a bed-wetting problem that started the night her mum came home with her new boyfriend Eddie Green. Running away and joining the theatre group is Patsy's way of making a new life for herself, away from the pressures at home – of making her own break in the sun.

How Patsy meets the challenges that are presented and the ill-judged actions she takes make this story as exciting and as relevant today as it was when written over twenty years ago. Bernard Ashley creates an environment in which everyone feels they can belong and, whilst moving the action from London through the Kent countryside to end up at Margate, he nourishes this sense of belonging.

9-11

David Blanch

Next?
• Another Bernard Ashley is ***Freedom Flight***, about Tom, who finds a runaway girl on the beach. She turns out to be an illegal immigrant from Poland. Tom is very determined – but can he save her? This book takes a tough look at both immigration and families. Also try his older, tougher ***Little Soldier***. (UBG 144)
• For another, older book about trying to escape from reality, try ***Tightrope*** by Gillian Cross. (UBG 242)

BRIDGE TO TERABITHIA

Katherine Paterson

Next?
• Another great book by Katherine Paterson is ***The Great Gilly Hopkins***, or try one of her novels set in Japan, such as ***The Master Puppeteer***.
• If you like this sort of book, try ***Walk Two Moons*** (UBG 256) and anything by David Almond – maybe start with ***Skellig*** (UBG 220) or ***Kit's Wilderness*** (UBG 135).

➡ I love this book. It's about joy and sorrow, friendship and grief and it's about learning what really matters in life.

Jess is intrigued by his new neighbour, Leslie. She reads books, doesn't have a television, doesn't give a hoot what the small-town kids think of her, and she can beat them all at running, hands-down.

Soon they're the best of friends, Jess and Leslie, and together they create Terabithia, a secret kingdom in the woods. It becomes their sanctuary until tragedy strikes. But, however sad, Jess knows that Leslie has opened him up to the joys of imagination, learning and true friendship.

My favourite books are the ones that move me – that make me feel deeply sad, deeply happy, and preferably both. This is one of the very best.

10-12

Malachy Doyle

THE BROMELIAD TRILOGY

TRUCKERS • DIGGERS • WINGS Terry Pratchett

➡ For as long as anyone can remember, a race of tiny beings called Nomes has lived under the floors of a huge department store. It is their whole world. As far as they are concerned, there is no Outside, no Night and Day, no Sun or Rain. When they discover the store is going to be demolished, it's up to two of the Nomes, Masklin and Grimma, to use all their ingenuity and help them escape and overcome their fears of the Outside. They get away to a deserted quarry but are forced to leave there, too …

These books are supposed to be children's books, but like so many good books, they can be enjoyed by all ages. I love them now I'm sixty just as much as I did when I first read them.

10 +

Colin Thompson

Next?
• More Pratchett! There's the **Johnny Maxwell Trilogy** (UBG 129) and then the **Discworld** series to entertain you (UBG 51).
• Douglas Adams's ***The Hitchhiker's Guide to the Galaxy*** has to be one of the funniest books ever. (UBG 109)
• More about little people? Try ***Mistress Masham's Repose*** (one of Terry Pratchett's own choices) by T.H. White. (UBG 162)

BUMFACE Morris Gleitzman

➡ This novel has the funniest, and to some the most outrageous, opening page in all of today's children's books. It indicates that there is humour to come, but what it doesn't show is that this is also a wonderful and serious story of a young boy forced to take on huge family responsibilities.

Angus is a great character. His mum calls him Mr Dependable and leaves him to care for his brother and sister, and he longs for her to behave like a proper mother. He dreams of being free, wild and bold, but he is caught up in a world of nappies.

Angus's story is a moving one, yet it's told with great humour, making this a book that is impossible to put down. Just open it at the first page, start reading, and you'll see …

9-12

Wendy Cooling

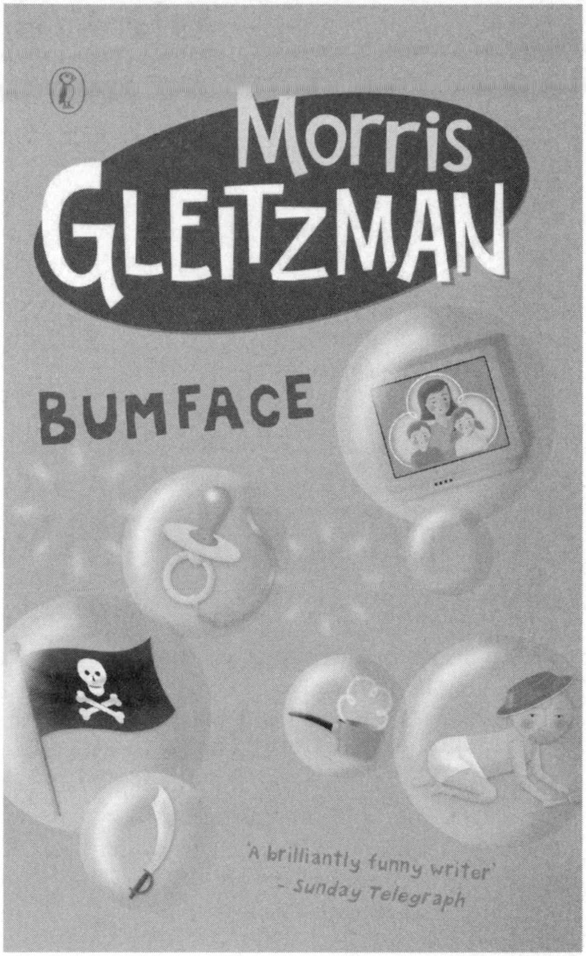

Next?

- Humour is Gleitzman's trademark however serious the subject. ***Boy Overboard*** is a good one to read next (UBG 35), or try ***Two Weeks with the Queen*** (UBG 251).
- At times Angus is very alone, but he is not as alone as Stanley in Louis Sachar's brilliant book ***Holes***. (UBG 113)
- Elizabeth Honey, also Australian, writes funny books about real things – try ***Don't Pat the Wombat***. (UBG 66)

THE BUTTERFLY LION

Michael Morpurgo

➡ A lonely boy runs away from boarding-school where he is being bullied. It begins to rain, and the boy notices a car following him. He slips through a gate into the garden of a large house. An old lady appears and invites him in for tea. As the boy eats his scones, he looks out of the window and sees the shape of a white lion, cut into the chalky hillside. The sun comes out and when the lion is suddenly covered in blue butterflies, the old lady begins to tell the boy an extraordinary story. A story about a boy called Bertie who lived in Africa, and the white lion cub he rescued.

This is a beautifully-told sad/happy story that makes you think a little deeper about past events every time you read it. It also shows that the end of a story does not always have to be what you expect, in order to be called happy.

7-10

Jenny Nimmo

Next?

- Try ***The Dancing Bear*** or ***Why the Whales Came*** (UBG 264), both by Michael Morpurgo.
- Of if you enjoy books that bring the past and the present together, and you're up for a more challenging read, then try ***An Angel for May*** by Melvin Burgess. (UBG 14)
- Willard Price wrote brilliant adventure stories about African lions – look out for ***Lion Adventure***. His **Adventure** series is recommended on p. 39.

THE CALL OF THE WILD

Jack London

'He had never seen dogs fight as these wolfish creatures fought ...'

The year is 1897 and men are heading to Alaska, looking for gold. But they need big dogs to haul the sledges there, and they don't care where they get them from. Buck is stolen from his sunny home and forced to work as a sledge dog.

This book was written in 1907, and you might think that would make the language somewhat dated. Not so. The story of what happens to Buck is quite simply one of the most powerful and intense animal tales ever told.

11+

Cliff McNish

Next?
- If you enjoyed this book, try Jack London's companion novel, ***White Fang***. (UBG 263)
- For another tale of an animal surviving great odds, why not try Melvin Burgess's ***Kite***? (UBG 136)
- Or if you want to know what it would be like for a child to survive alone in heartbreaking conditions, go to the simply-written and simply wonderful ***Hatchet*** by Gary Paulsen. (UBG 107)

CALLING A DEAD MAN

Gillian Cross

Wrap up warm and immerse yourself in this gripping novel, set mostly in a freezing Russian winter. Hayley just wants to see the place where her older brother, John, died suddenly – but when she and John's fiancée, Annie, arrive in Siberia, they find themselves solving the mystery of his disappearance. Meanwhile, in another thread of the story, we meet a man on the run, who has no memory but an awful sense that he is somehow dangerous. He is helped by generous Russian families but he can't get close to any of them. This is a truly tense and unputdownable story.

11+

Jon Appleton

Next?
- Start with more Gillian Cross books, especially the wonderful ***Wolf***. (UBG 270)
- For more action and suspense, read the historical novels of Philip Pullman: ***The Ruby in the Smoke*** is excellent. (UBG 205)
- Alison Prince's ***Oranges and Murder*** is an exciting mystery, set in the London of the early nineteenth century. (UBG 177)

A CANDLE IN THE DARK

Adèle Geras

This unusual, moving wartime story tells of Clara, a young German Jewish girl, who is sent to England for safety in 1939. With her five-year-old brother, Maxi, she moves in with Phyllis and her family in a Leicestershire village. It's bad enough leaving her home and parents, but Clara finds that not everyone in Long Easterby is friendly – Phyllis's friend Eileen regards Clara as odd and strange, coming from Germany, the enemy country. Phyllis wants everyone to be friends, but has to cope with Eileen's spitefulness, as well as helping Clara through a dilemma – if she sings 'Stille Nacht' for the school Nativity play, is she being disloyal to her Jewish parents and upbringing? Do read the afterword to learn more about what happened to the children sent out of Germany for safety.

9-11

Linda Newbery

Next?
- Another short novel which takes an unusual look at wartime is Ann Jungman's ***Resistance***, set in occupied Holland.
- ***When Hitler Stole Pink Rabbit*** is the first in a classic set of stories by Judith Kerr, telling of her wartime childhood when, as a German-Jewish girl, she was forced to flee her native land. (UBG 261)
- For more stories about the Second World War, try the **World War II Flashbacks**, such as Linda's ***Blitz Boys***. (UBG 31)

out, that I was held safe in Aslan's mighty but gentle paws.

CANNIBAL ADVENTURE

Willard Price

➡ Hal and Roger Hunt, two teenage brothers, are off on another of their improbable adventures – this time in pursuit of crocodiles, sharks and death adders for their father's zoo.

Willard Price got me reading when I was eleven, and I think it's just great that his books are still so popular today. They may have aged a little (cablegrams instead of e-mails) and capturing animals in the wild may no longer be politically correct, but the stories are action-packed, mixing vicious animals and even more vicious crooks with huge energy and attention to detail. In what other stories would the hero sit down to a meal of 'a large broiled bat garnished with fried beetles'?

The **Adventure** series is a wonderful way to explore the world and to learn about natural history. The stories are also surprisingly gory. When Roger is attacked by a crocodile, he can count the wounds made by every one of its seventy teeth ...

Anthony Horowitz

10-12

Next?

- There's ***African Adventure, Diving Adventure, Volcano Adventure, Whale Adventure*** and many more!
- Anthony Horowitz's **Alex Rider** books are some of the most exciting adventure stories of recent years – see ***Stormbreaker***. (UBG 228)
- There's **Biggles** by Captain W.E. Johns, about a pilot during the wars. (UBG 28)
- Or try the **Hardy Boys** stories by Franklin W. Dixon, about a pair of boy detectives. (UBG 104)

THE CANTERVILLE GHOST

Oscar Wilde

➡ When an American called Hiram B. Otis buys Canterville Chase, he laughs at the notion that the house is haunted by Sir Simon de Canterville. He uses 'Champion Stain Remover' to get rid of the ghostliest of bloodstains. Then he offers Sir Simon some 'Rising Sun Lubricator' to stop his chains creaking. No matter what the poor ghost gets up to, his new victims are not impressed. This is bad news for a ghost. Soon, he wants Otis out on a permanent basis, but first someone has to take pity on him. This story is funny and moving, but above all the writing is elegant and eccentric, and you'll find that each reading reveals something new and exquisite. A true delight.

10-12

Karen Wallace

Next?

- You might also like Oscar Wilde's ***Fairy Tales***. (UBG 77)
- For modern gothic humour, try Debi Gliori's ***Pure Dead Magic***. (UBG 195)
- If you want a good ghostly spoof, read ***Something Slimy on Primrose Drive*** by Karen Wallace.

THE ULTIMATE READERS' POLL

YOUR TOP TEN FAVOURITE BOOKS

1. The Harry Potter series by J.K. Rowling
2. The Lord of the Rings by J.R.R. Tolkien
3. The Princess Diaries by Meg Cabot
4. Matilda by Roald Dahl
5. Charlie and the Chocolate Factory by Roald Dahl
6. The Story of Tracy Beaker by Jacqueline Wilson
7. The BFG by Roald Dahl
8. Goodnight Mister Tom by Michelle Magorian
9. Black Beauty by Anna Sewell
10. Double Act by Jacqueline Wilson

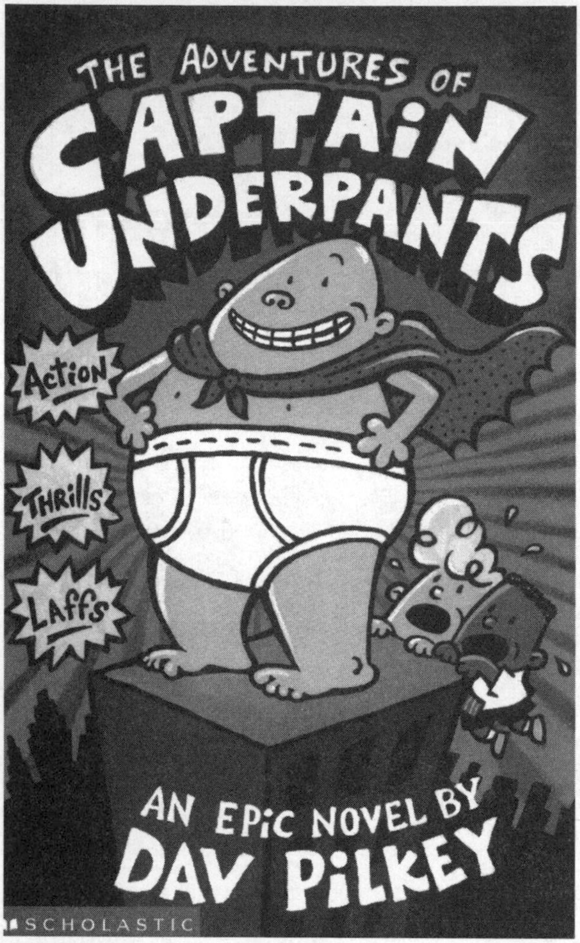

CAPTAIN UNDERPANTS Dav Pilkey

➡ Let's not beat about the bush … If you're the sort of person who thinks it's funny when someone farts during school assembly, then *Captain Underpants* is for you!

George and Harold use a 3-D Hypno-Ring to hypnotise their mean old head teacher, Mr Krupp, and turn him into the amazing Captain Underpants!

Will the evil Dr Nappy destroy the earth or will our heroes defeat him? Can you really shoot a pair of underpants? Will a plastic doggy-doo foil Doctor Nappy's plans? I know you want to find out … get reading now!

6-8

Shoo Rayner

Next?
- You'll probably want to read the other Captain Underpants stories and ***Captain Underpants Extra Crunchy Books of Fun***.
- If you've not had enough poo, then try Roddy Doyle's ***The Giggler Treatment*** (UBG 92) and don't forget my own, wonderful ***Craig M'nure***!
- Or what about the **Jiggy McCue** books by Michael Lawrence? (UBG 127)
- Two other fun series (with great pictures) are Keith Brumpton's **The Kung Fu Pigs** and Shoo Rayner's **Dark Claw** stories (UBG 56).

CAPTAINS COURAGEOUS

Rudyard Kipling

➡ This book was written over a hundred years ago and uses words and language that are not always easy to read, but – make no mistake – it's one of the best stories ever written.

Fifteen-year-old Harvey Cheyne is the spoilt son of a multi-millionaire, who accidentally falls off the stern of an ocean liner one night, and gets picked up by a fishing boat, the *We're Here*. As a result, he has to spend four months fishing for cod on the Grand Banks in the middle of the Atlantic – an adventure that changes his life for ever.

The work is hard and dangerous, and Harvey has to learn that qualities such as friendship, hard work and courage are needed simply to stay alive. But he does learn, and when the *We're Here* finally returns to America, he is no longer a boy, but a strong and confident young man.

Brilliant!

11+

Andrew Norriss

Next?
- Rudyard Kipling wrote several books for children. The most famous are ***The Jungle Books***. (UBG 130) My favourite is probably ***Puck of Pook's Hill***. (UBG 195) He also wrote a book of school stories called ***Stalky and Co.*** – you wouldn't believe what school could be like a hundred years ago!
- A very different story about surviving in the wilderness is ***Hatchet*** by Gary Paulsen. (UBG 107)

William Golding, because it is an extraordinary story of survival.

CARBONEL Barbara Sleigh

➨ Rosemary buys her broom and Carbonel the cat (who costs three precious Queen Victoria farthings) in a London market. Carbonel tells her he is under a binding spell, and she and her friend John race to free him before his kingdom is lost to a vicious rival. But, it is silent magic that binds the great cat: no one can tell the children what it is or how to break it. They must, somehow, discover it for themselves.

When I was small, children were allowed to roam the streets on their own, like Rosemary and John do. In my wanderings I daydreamed of buying a magic broom, like Rosemary did, that would help me talk to the king of cats. It's easy to daydream about Carbonel: the story moves along quickly and the characters could – just – be the kind you might meet – even disreputable Mrs Cantrip, the retired witch.

Gill Vickery

9-11

Next?
- ***Carbonel*** is the first in a trilogy. Why not go on to read ***The Kingdom of Carbonel*** and ***Carbonel and Calidor***?
- Another writer who understands cats is Adèle Geras. Try her stories told by Ozymandias the cat, in ***The Fabulous Fantora Files*** and ***The Fabulous Fantora Photographs***. (UBG 75)
- If you like books about animals, read Dodie Smith's ***The Hundred and One Dalmatians***. (UBG 119)

CARRIE'S WAR Nina Bawden

➨ When the Second World War began, thousands of children were moved out of British cities and sent to live with people in small towns or the country, for fear of enemy bombing. Imagine how it would feel, suddenly being dumped among strangers who might or might not want to have you. Actually, most of the children were kindly treated, though they must have missed their homes and families terribly. But some were out of luck and had a miserable time.

Carrie and her younger brother Nick are among the unlucky ones, sent to stay with mean old Councillor Evans ('Up and down the stairs, soon as my back's turned, wearing out the stair carpet,' he complains) and his downtrodden sister, 'Auntie Lou'. Serious, thoughtful Carrie has a hard time, one of her problems being to keep irresponsible Nick out of trouble. But the children survive, find friends in their new surroundings, and even bring about a happy ending for Auntie Lou. *Carrie's War* tells you how they did it. It's a book you'll never forget. And it makes you wonder how you would have managed if all this had happened to you.

John Rowe Townsend

9-12

Next?
- Another evacuee story is ***Goodnight Mister Tom*** by Michelle Magorian. (UBG 97) Or try Robert Leeson's younger ***Tom's Private War***. (UBG 245)
- Still on the Home Front is ***The Machine Gunners***, by Robert Westall. (UBG 150)
- ***Stones in Water*** by Donna Jo Napoli is a heartbreaking story about an Italian boy taken to work as slave labour by the Nazis.

A CASTLE OF BONE Penelope Farmer

➨ If you buy a cupboard, you don't expect it to change things. But Hugh's new cupboard has amazing powers of transformation. If you place an object inside, out it comes again, altered – changed back into its original elements, or processed further into something new. This is a book full of intriguing ideas about growth and change – in people, not just things. And what is a castle of bone? It lingers throughout the whole story, and it's so satisfying when Penelope Farmer explains just what it is. Everything makes sense in a Penelope Farmer story, which makes them such a pleasure to read. Above all, this is a gripping story: especially when Hugh's friend, Penn, stumbles into the cupboard himself ...

Jon Appleton

10-12

Next?
- Don't miss Penelope Farmer's other classic, ***Charlotte Sometimes*** (UBG 45), or Diana Wynne Jones's wonderful **Chrestomanci** books. (UBG 272)
- The **Narnia** books by C.S. Lewis have magic – and the world's most famous wardrobe! (UBG 141)
- ***The Castle of Dark*** by Tanith Lee is another great book about magic and mystery. (UBG 42)

THE CASTLE OF DARK

Tanith Lee

Next?
- Want to read another Tanith Lee book? Try ***East of Midnight***. (UBG 69)
- Another eerily atmospheric book is Jenny Nimmo's ***Griffin's Castle***. (UBG 101)
- **Young Wizards** by Diane Duane is a great series about learning to become a wizard. (UBG 275)
- Or try Garth Nix's ***Sabriel***, a fabulous mix of fantasy, magic, good and evil, for older readers. (UBG 207)

➨ Magic comes into lots of fantasy stories, and so do the forces of good and evil. Tanith Lee has them all operating at the same time in this powerfully memorable book.

Lir has the gift of musicianship, and his life is transformed when he fashions a unique, magic harp. The harp leads him from town to town, and as he plays he earns his keep. But is it only magic that lures him to the Castle of Dark, or something more sinister? There he meets Lilune, the girl in the tower, a prisoner of darkness. Lilune believes Lir has been called to lead her to freedom. Lir wants to oblige, but his pledge to help Lilune may lead to his destruction.

9-12

Jon Appleton

THE CAT ATE MY GYMSUIT

Paula Danziger

➨ This isn't a book about cats or about gymsuits, but it is a wonderful feel-good read about a thirteen-year-old girl called Marcy, who thinks she's hopeless at absolutely everything. She's frightened of her father, convinced she'll never, ever find a boyfriend, bored to death by school ... In fact, everything in her life is a big problem ... until she meets the trendy young new teacher, Ms Finney. But just as life starts to look up again, Ms Finney is banned from the school for ever. Does Marcy have the confidence to fight to win her back?

9-11

Eileen Armstrong

Next?
- Why not try one of Paula's other family stories? Lauren shares her teenage traumas with you in ***Can You Sue Your Parents For Malpractice?***
- Helena Pielichaty's **Simone** books look at the problems of starting a new school, parents splitting up, new partners and new babies. (UBG 220)
- The **Ally's World** stories by Karen McCombie are every bit as enjoyable – all about family and friends. (UBG 12)

CATHERINE, CALLED BIRDY

Karen Cushman

Next?
- You might like to try Karen Cushman's ***The Midwife's Apprentice***, about a mediaeval orphan rescued from a dung heap.
- Another good diary story, set in recent times, is Sue Townsend's hilarious ***The Secret Diary of Adrian Mole aged 13 ¾***. (UBG 214)
- For a mediaeval fantasy in which a girl disguises herself as a boy so she can become a knight, try the **Protector of the Small** series by Tamora Pierce. (UBG 194)

➨ Birdy is the spirited, inquisitive daughter of a mediaeval knight, living in England in 1290. She is thirteen when she starts to write this diary – and is determined not to let her father marry her off. So what does she do? She blackens her teeth, puts mouse bones in her hair and sets fire to the outside toilet. And that's just the beginning. Her diary romps along, full of details about feasts and horrible medicines and saints like Saint Juthwara, who wore cheeses on her chest.

Birdy's diary gives a rich, funny picture of Birdy's life, but it's not just a joke. As she moans about the tasks she has to do and her father's plans to marry her to the atrocious Shaggy Beard, she is puzzling over life and death as well. And some of the things she learns are just as important now as they were then.

11+

Gillian Cross

THE CELLAR LAD Theresa Tomlinson

➨ It's Sheffield in 1842 – a city of industry, poverty and revolution. The crucible workshop is noisy, dirty and dangerous, but Ben is soon to take his place there as a cellar lad, doing odd jobs and fetching ale for the men, who need it to survive beside the raging heat of the furnace. There is anger in Sheffield, too, as new inventions put more and more people out of work, the Corn Laws keep the price of bread high and none of the poverty-stricken workers have the right to vote. As the unions take action to protect the people, Ben begins to question the mysterious events in the factories and to take his place in the adult world. *The Cellar Lad* is a gripping story, full of warmth and family love. It's also the most interesting and exciting history lesson I've ever had.

Antonia Honeywell

9-11

Next?
- If you liked the historical setting and want to read more stories about working conditions in factories, try Joan Aiken's ***Midnight Is a Place***. (UBG 159)
- If you want to read more about people fighting to get the vote, try ***A Question of Courage*** by Marjorie Darke.
- Theresa Tomlinson also wrote ***The Herring Girls*** (UBG 109) and ***The Forest Wife***.

THE CHALET SCHOOL series
Elinor M. Brent-Dyer

➨ With their parents dead and twelve-year-old Joey Bettany suffering poor health in the damp English climate, Joey's older sister, Madge, decides to start up a school for girls in the Austrian Tyrol, where they begin the adventure of a lifetime. The stories are full of excitement, but it's the author's love of her characters and the Tyrol that makes them so special.

The series spans the Second World War, when the school has to flee to Switzerland, and follows Joey and her friends' lives from their eventful schoolgirl years until she is the mother of nine and a successful author.

Once you read one **Chalet School** story you might end up, as I did, reading the whole series. In my mind, I lived a parallel existence as a Chalet School girl, with Joey Bettany and her gang as my imaginary friends. I had a special bond with Jo as, just like me, she suffered endlessly from bronchitis, was a bit hot-headed and we both grew up to be writers!

10-12

Julie Bertagna

Next?
- Try the **Malory Towers** series by Enid Blyton if you like school stories. (UBG 153)
- Try ***Anne of Green Gables*** by L.M. Montgomery (UBG 17); or ***Little Women*** by Louisa May Alcott (UBG 146) for a wonderful story that follow the lives of four adventurous girls, one of whom grows up to be a writer.
- Angela Brazil wrote many school stories, such as ***The Youngest Girl in the Fifth***. (UBG 275)

THE CHANGEOVER Margaret Mahy

➨ Laura Chant is content with her family the way it is – her, her mum, Kate and her little brother, Jacko. She misses the dad who left them but doesn't want any more changes in their lives. Laura is psychic and, on the morning the book begins, she has a Warning: something is about to change for the worse.

Little Jacko gets his hand branded by the sinister Carmody Braque, owner of a novelty shop that wasn't there before. Jacko falls ill and slips into a coma, the life being drained from him by Braque. Only Laura can save him, with the help of dishy sixth-former, Sorensen Carlisle, who turns out, like her, to be a witch.

An intoxicating mix of magic, danger and romance.

11+

Mary Hoffman

Next?
- You might also like ***The Haunting*** by the same author. (UBG 107)
- For magic, you might enjoy Diana Wynne Jones's books, particularly ***Howl's Moving Castle*** and ***A Tale of Time City***. (UBG 235)
- Or try the eerie novel ***Whispers in the Graveyard*** by Theresa Breslin. (UBG 262).

THE CHANGES TRILOGY

THE DEVIL'S CHILDREN • HEARTSEASE • THE WEATHERMONGER

Peter Dickinson

➡ These three novels take us into an England in the near future, but one in which something terrible has happened. A strange madness has spread across the country, causing people to hate machines; in fact any technology invented more recently than the Middle Ages is regarded as evil. As a result, civilisation has come crashing to ruin, and only a handful of children, such as Nicky in *The Devil's Children*, and Margaret and Jonathan in *Heartsease*, seem to be immune from the machine-hatred. But it is only in the last book, *The Weathermonger*, that Geoffrey and Sally uncover the awful reason underlying The Changes, and only they have the chance to restore England to the way it once was.

Marcus Sedgwick

11+

Next?
- Try some of Dickinson's other books, such as ***The Gift***, about a boy with second sight, or ***A Bone from a Dry Sea***, which mixes the modern day with prehistory in a gripping archaeological adventure.
- Or **The Book of the Crow** by Catherine Fisher, also about a society where there is no technology and machines are seen as magic. (UBG 201)
- If you fancy more science fiction, try the very unsettling ***A Rag, a Bone and a Hank of Hair*** by Nicholas Fisk. (UBG 197)

CHARLIE AND THE CHOCOLATE FACTORY

Roald Dahl

➡ Charlie Bucket lives with his parents and grandparents in a tiny wooden house. They are so poor, all they have to eat every day is weak cabbage soup. Then, one day, Charlie finds the last of five golden tickets that allow the winners to spend a whole day inside Willy Wonka's chocolate factory. Apart from Charlie, the other golden ticket winners are either spoilt, greedy or already rich. Only Charlie still has the magical innocence of childhood. And that is what Willy Wonka is looking for …

This is a wonderful book that anyone of any age can enjoy. Read it and then see the movie, which is so good you've probably already seen it three times. I certainly have.

Colin Thompson

8-10

Next?
- ***Danny, the Champion of the World*** which is wonderful Roald Dahl at his brilliant best. (UBG 56)
- Or try Jenny Nimmo's ***Midnight for Charlie Bone***, another book about a young boy on a magical adventure. (UBG 159)
- Or what about ***Aquila*** by Andrew Norriss, in which two boys' lives are changed for the better after something extraordinary happens? (UBG 18)
- For more realistic, but equally fun, stories try ***The Quigleys*** by Simon Mason. (UBG 196)

Illustration by Kirstie Evans, age 11, Menstrie Primary School

COMPETITION WINNER ★ COMPETITION WINNER

CHARLIE AND THE CHOCOLATE FACTORY

Roald Dahl

➨ I really love this book because it's got so much imagination put into it. I always seem to like the book much better than the film. With a book you can let your mind imagine how everything looks – like a big fountain of chocolate surrounded by a dense forest of lollipop trees and other incredible things – but with a film you just have to let someone else imagine it. I love the characters and the simple but effective words, but most of all I love how Roald Dahl has made it seem quite normal that a boy can go to school every day, but then it all changes ...

Mollie Alcott, age 11, Charters Ancaster College

CHARLOTTE SOMETIMES

Penelope Farmer

➨ A famous timeslip story. Charlotte, at boarding school in the 1950s, changes places with Clare, who slept in the same bed towards the end of the First World War. Sometimes, it's just good to feel like a whole person, even if it's the wrong person; other times it's plain confusing. Alarmingly, details of being Charlotte slip away, but she must return to her own time – which becomes even harder when she and her sister, Emily, are sent away from the school and the magic bed. You read this book for its gripping dilemma and when you get to the end, you realise it's about so many other things, and there's an extra, deeper pleasure.

10-12

Jon Appleton

Next?
- There are lots of excellent timeslip books – one of my favourites is ***Playing Beatie Bow*** by Ruth Park. (UBG 190)
- In his legendary novel ***Earthfasts***, William Mayne brings the past to the present. (UBG 68)
- If you like the idea of a magic bed, try ***Bedknob and Broomstick*** by Mary Norton! (UBG 26)

CHARLOTTE'S WEB

E.B. White

➨ This is a story about a pig called Wilbur, a rat called Templeton, a spider called Charlotte, plus various other animals. But it is also about a girl called Fern, who saves Wilbur when he is the unwanted runt of the farmyard pig litter, and it is about life on the farm seen from the point of view of the animals. It is funny, and sad, and you become completely involved with all the characters – human and animal. This is a book that I have loved for years and years, and each time I open it I have to read it all through again, from the opening words: 'Where's Papa going with that axe? said Fern to her mother ...'

8-10

Penelope Lively

Next?
- You might also enjoy ***The Borrowers*** by Mary Norton, about the mysterious tiny people who live under the floorboards. (UBG 33)
- Another book about a pig is ***The Peppermint Pig***, by Nina Bawden. (UBG 184)
- For something different, and rather harder, but equally lovely, try ***Mistress Masham's Repose*** by T.H. White. (UBG 162)

CHEWING THE CUD: An unexpected life from farmyard to Hollywood Dick King-Smith

➨ Dick King-Smith's stories are compelling, original, full of incidents and packed with lively characters. His delightful animal tales sprang from the twenty years he spent as a farmer in Gloucestershire and were inspired by the many unusual creatures he encountered. What I so love about his books is the warmth. *Chewing the Cud* is his own story – about his early childhood, his growing up, his parents and family and, of course, about the many extraordinary animals in his life.

9-11

Gervase Phinn

Next?
- Another real favourite author of mine is Michael Morpurgo. Read ***The Marble Crusher*** (UBG 154), or ***Why the Whales Came*** (UBG 264) – both cracking good stories.
- For a heart-warming tale about interesting animals and lively people, read ***Dog's Journey*** by Gene Kemp.
- Or more of Dick King-Smith's books – try ***The Crowstarver***. (UBG 54)

CHILD X Lee Weatherly

➨ Lots of people dream of being famous, being recognised for doing something brilliantly – singing maybe, or acting. Jules wants to act and when she's given the starring role in a theatre production of *Northern Lights* she's ecstatic, even if she does have to work alongside nerdy Adrian, from whom she'd normally run a mile.

But there's another kind of fame, and when Jules's beloved father, a TV scriptwiter, publicly rejects her and her mother, the paparazzi pursue her everywhere and, despite news reports calling her 'Child X', everyone knows they mean her. Jules quickly learns who her real friends are.

What makes Lee Weatherley's book special is that Jules is exactly like you and your friends – a normal, believable school student.

10+

Gill Vickery

Next?
- You might also enjoy Linda Kempton's ***Who'll Catch the Nightmares?***, in which Gemma, like Jules, juggles with a burning ambition to act, whilst dealing with a totally unexpected, high-profile family crisis.
- If you've been intrigued by Jules's role in ***Northern Lights*** you may like to try the original novel by Philip Pullman. (UBG 176)

THE CHILDREN OF GREEN KNOWE Lucy M. Boston

➨ In this, the first of the **Green Knowe** series, we meet young Toseland (Tolly for short) on his way to live with his great-grandmother, Mrs Oldknow, at her ancient house by the river. Her first greeting to him is: 'So you've come back!' When questioned, she explains that he's very like his grandfather, who bore the same name.

Tolly soon learns that time means little at Green Knowe, and he makes the acquaintance of others who have lived there over the centuries. In the six **Green Knowe** books we meet several different children at different time periods. They all have one thing in common: the house itself and their love for it. In one, *The Stones of Green Knowe*, we are present at its construction in the twelfth century.

I didn't discover the **Green Knowe** series until I was in my twenties. I enjoyed them then, but I'm sure I would have got so much more out of them at the age of nine, ten or eleven. Green Knowe is based on the author's own house, which I have visited several times. Lucy Boston first saw it as a young woman in 1915, and eventually purchased it in 1937. As owner, Lucy at once set about uncovering the various histories of the house, and discovered far more than she had ever imagined. It was these discoveries as much as anything that led to her writing the series.

9-11

Michael Lawrence

Next?
- Lots of books deal with the possibilities of going back in time – one classic is ***A Traveller in Time*** by Alison Uttley (UBG 246); another is ***Tom's Midnight Garden*** by Philippa Pearce (UBG 245).
- ***Charlotte Sometimes*** by Penelope Farmer is another timeslip story, this one about a girl who finds herself somewhere very different than she expected. (UBG 45)

THE CHILDREN OF THE NEW FOREST Captain Marryat

➡ This story is set during the English Civil War. King Charles I has recently escaped from the Parliamentarians who are searching the New Forest, where they believe he is hiding. Edward, Humphrey, Edith and Alice, the orphaned children of a cavalier, live in a large house in the forest. When Jacob, an elderly forester, overhears the Parliamentarians (or 'Levellers') plotting to burn down the house, he rescues the children and takes them to live in his cottage, deep in the forest. Here, they have to hunt, catch wild ponies and grow their own food.

The children's lives are always exciting, not least because they are in constant danger from the Levellers, and the tension mounts when Edward leaves the forest to join the Cavalier army.

Captain Marryat wrote the book in 1847 when many people considered the cavaliers to be heroes. Today we have a very different view of the king and his men, but the children themselves are all extremely likeable characters who never fail to engage our sympathy.

10-12

Jenny Nimmo

Next?
• You could go on to ***Mr Midshipman Easy*** and ***Masterman Ready***, both written by Captain Marryat but this time set at sea. Or try R.L. Stevenson's ***Treasure Island*** (UBG 247) and ***Kidnapped*** (UBG 133).
• Rosemary Sutcliff's ***Simon*** is an historical novel, set at around the same time as ***The Children of the New Forest***.

CHILDREN ON THE OREGON TRAIL

A. Rutgers van der Loeff

➡ This book is based on the true story of John Sager, who, in the summer of 1844, aged thirteen, set off with his family to the wild west in America. John is the keeper of his father's dream. When his parents die of fever on the gruelling journey, John refuses any easy options. He wants to go the way his father had planned. This is the story of a remarkable journey – crossing rivers with horses, listening to the rumble of thousands of buffalo hooves. The courage of John Sager and his brothers and sisters is inspiring. I liked reading this as a child, coming across place names like Green River Rendezvous. This was a way of travelling across the frontier towns I'd never seen, with the Blue Mountains ahead. Sleeping through the howling of the wolves. A great adventure story that perhaps makes uncomfortable reading now as an adult when you consider that the land the Sagers went to conquer belonged to the Native Indians …

Jackie Kay

9-11

Next?
• Lots of books deal with what it was like to be a pioneer. Try the true stories by Laura Ingalls Wilder, ***Little House on the Prairie*** and sequels. (UBG 142)
• Geraldine McCaughrean has written a powerful and gripping book about the coming of the railroads in ***Stop the Train***. (UBG 227)
• A different sort of survival goes on in J.D. Wyss's ***The Swiss Family Robinson***, in which a family is shipwrecked. (UBG 234)

COMPETITION WINNER★ COMPETITION WINNER

CHINESE CINDERELLA Adeline Yen Mah

➡ I loved *Chinese Cinderella* because it made me realise how lucky I am to have a loving and caring family, unlike Adeline. *Chinese Cinderella* is an autobiography, written by an unwanted girl, whose mother died giving birth to her. The book taught me that if I really try, I can do anything. I wanted to turn each page to read on, but I knew that it would be more sad and terrifying than the page before. I felt as if I were in the scene, watching. The author tells the story in a way that is simply superb.

Selina Parmar, age 10,
North London Collegiate School

If you're looking for Darren Shan's *Cirque du Freak*, turn to p. 208

THE ULTIMATE READERS' POLL

YOUR TOP TEN MOST EXCITING BOOKS

1. The Harry Potter series by J.K. Rowling
2. The Lord of the Rings by J.R.R. Tolkien
3. The Lion, the Witch and the Wardrobe by C.S. Lewis
4. The Hobbit by J.R.R. Tolkien
5. The Story of Tracy Beaker by Jacqueline Wilson
6. Journey to the River Sea by Eva Ibbotson
7. Charlie and the Chocolate Factory by Roald Dahl
8. Northern Lights by Philip Pullman
9. Point Blanc by Anthony Horowitz
10. The Secret Seven series by Enid Blyton

CHINESE CINDERELLA

Adeline Yen Mah

➨ This book, subtitled 'The Secret Story of an Unwanted Daughter', tells the true story of the author's childhood in China in the 1940s. Adeline is considered bad luck because her mother died giving birth to her and she is always made to feel unwanted. Her stepmother is particularly cruel to her; her brothers and sisters are often mean and her father even forgets her real name! But Adeline is a clever girl and does have some happy, and very successful times at school, and strong relationships with her aunt and her grandfather.

This is a moving autobiography, the story of a girl's struggle for acceptance, and it offers a real look at life in another country over fifty years ago. It is unforgettable.

10+

Wendy Cooling

Next?

- For another true and moving story try ***The Diary of of a Young Girl*** by Anne Frank. (UBG 61)
- For fictional stories of young people coping with difficult times, try Jacqueline Wilson's books, such as ***The Illustrated Mum***. (UBG 122)
- Try ***The Girl in Red*** by Gaye Hiçyilmaz, the challenging story of a Romanian girl coming to live in the UK and meeting great prejudice.

CITY OF GOLD Peter Dickinson

➨ These are no ordinary retellings of Bible stories. Peter Dickinson has a great gift for bringing things to life, and by imagining himself telling the stories before *The Bible* was ever written down, the tales feel like they happened yesterday. There are thirty-three stories, full of drama on a big scale as well as the small details of human life that make them utterly convincing. All are from the Old Testament, and are so far removed from the dryness of biblical versions that you will have to remind yourself that's what you're reading. Fantastic stories, wonderfully told, and accompanied by illustrations by acclaimed artist Michael Foreman.

11+

Marcus Sedgwick

Next?

- Dickinson has written too many good books to list them all, but one with an ancient theme is ***A Bone from a Dry Sea***. A list of others in the ***UBG*** appears on p. 285.
- Try some other ancient tales, like the Norse (UBG 175) or Greek myths.
- ***Tales of the Early World*** by Ted Hughes is another retelling of early legends. (UBG 236)
- Or for a simply told and beautifully illustrated Bible story, read Jane Ray's ***The Story of Christmas***. (UBG 229)

CLEVER POLLY AND THE STUPID WOLF Catherine Storr

Next?
- The clever sequel, ***Polly and the Wolf Again*** by Catherine Storr.
- Or ***A Necklace of Raindrops*** by Joan Aiken – a collection of fairy tales where all sorts of weird and wonderful things go on. (UBG 174)
- Or try ***I Was a Rat!*** by Philip Pullman, about a boy who was once a rat! (UBG 121)

➨ One day, a wolf appears at Polly's front door and quite politely asks if he may eat her. Polly, understandably enough, says 'No, thank you. I'd rather not be eaten.' It's a simple idea, but this hilarious book spins it out into twelve deliciously intelligent and well-crafted stories. The Wolf's stupidity knows no bounds. He ends up being quite an endearing character and Polly finds it so easy to run rings round him that we enjoy sharing in her cleverness. My favourite bit is the poem Wolf produces as an example of 'proper poetry': 'Monday's child is fairly tough/ Tuesday's child is tender enough/ Wednesday's child is good to fry ...' and so on through the week. This book is pure pleasure.

7-9

Adèle Geras

CLIFFHANGER Jacqueline Wilson

➨ Tim is absolutely hopeless at any kind of sport, so when his dad decides to toughen him up by sending him on a week-long, activity-packed holiday, he just *knows* it'll be hell – and that's before he's even met his big-headed, bullying bunkmate Giles. But as the week goes on, with the help of his biscuit-chomping friend and his understanding instructor, Jake, he finds he quite enjoys the challenges of canoeing and cliff-climbing and actually excels in the final crazy bucket race. Every chapter ends in a cliffhanger with a clever postcard cartoon from Tim to his parents charting his adventures and new-found confidence. This is an exciting easy read about facing up to your very worst fears and doing it anyway. Tim is such a likeable, easy-to-understand hero, you'll be dying to see what he and Biscuits get up to in the sequel, *Buried Alive*.

7-9

Eileen Armstrong

Next?
- In the **Ramona** books by Beverly Cleary, Ramona is a bit of a pest, but her mischief makes for fantastic reading! (UBG 198)
- ***Bill's New Frock*** by Anne Fine is a wonderfully funny story of a boy who has to spend a day as a girl. (UBG 28)
- Try Anne's ***How To Write Really Badly*** too; it's about another kid who has to overcome his own problems. (UBG 119)

THE CLOCK TOWER GHOST

Gene Kemp

Next?
- Track down some other books by Gene Kemp. ***The Turbulent Term of Tyke Tiler*** is a particular favourite. (UBG 249)
- ***The Ghost of Thomas Kempe*** by Penelope Lively (UBG 91) and Helen Cresswell's ***Moondial*** and ***Stonestruck*** are other intriguing and ghostly novels you might enjoy.

➨ You wouldn't exactly call King Cole a contented ghost, but at least he feels at home in the clock tower he haunts: after all, he built it! However, his uneventful routine is shattered when a demon moves in. The demon is Amanda Phillips, who 'from the day she was born, was awful'. As Amanda's family settles into their new home, Amanda becomes increasingly unpopular, in her new school and with the ghost. Does the family actually belong to Amanda? If so, how come she's a demon?

A tumultuous battle of wills rages between King Cole and Amanda, until Amanda realises how the ghost might find contentment – and how she might lay to rest a few ghosts of her own. This is a funny, quirky ghost story with a difference.

Helen Simmons

9-11

CLOCKWORK or All Wound Up

Philip Pullman, illustrated by Peter Bailey

➡ This is one of the best-named books ever. It has been put together as carefully as an intricate piece of machinery and even though you could take it apart to see what makes it tick, it's more fun to enjoy the story Pullman has created. He's wound it all up tight, and opening it starts the tale unwinding through the pages.

It's a strange story, with another two or three stories contained within it, and they all have the dark, wintry and Gothic atmosphere associated with European fairytales: inns, forests, clock towers and a heroine named Gretl.

One of the most original and delightful things about this book is the way the author adds his own commentary to the action. His remarks are presented in capital letters at the side of the page, reminding you that you're reading a story. The act of reading is almost as important as what's being read.

8-11

Adèle Geras

Next?

- Try some other Philip Pullmans, for instance ***Count Karlstein*** or ***The Firework-Maker's Daughter*** (UBG 84).
- Read some much older European fairy tales by the Brothers Grimm – they're terrifying! (UBG 76)
- A modern storyteller who is quirky enough to be a writer of fairy tales is Philip Ridley – try ***Krindlekrax***.

COLD TOM

Sally Prue

➡ This is a very unusual story. Tom is on the run from his own kind. He takes shelter among the Demons who live alongside the Tribe. One of the best things about the story is the way Prue uses Tom's point of view to show us what our own world might be like to someone who isn't one of our species. Sometimes the effect is very funny. Anna, one of Tom's protectors, has a pet guinea pig called Sophie. Tom thinks 'a sophie' is what she is, and to him, she's no more than meat.

On one level a chilling story of danger and adventure (with a very exciting first chapter) the book is really about love: the different ties that bind us together if we call ourselves human. Prue is a writer of strong but elegant prose. Every word is chosen, thought about, considered and the result is a moving and fascinating novel.

10-12

Adèle Geras

Next?

- Read Sally Prue's second book, ***The Devil's Toenail*** – a story of a boy under pressure who turns to something he thinks of as magic for help.
- ***Skellig*** by David Almond is a wonderful story about a boy who finds a mysterious creature in the broken-down garage at the bottom of his garden. (UBG 220)
- For another, gentler story about relating to an alien, try Vivien Alcock's ***The Monster Garden***. (UBG 163)

THE COLOUR OF MAGIC

Terry Pratchett

➨ On the back of four vast elephants standing on a turtle floating through space, sits ... the Discworld, whose geography and characters have become more real to millions of readers than most of Earth.

In *The Colour of Magic* we meet Rincewind, the worst magician ever, who lives in the city of Ankh-Morpork. You can buy a street map of Ankh-Morpork in the shops in our world – that's how seriously people take all this. Rincewind is given the job of looking after a clueless tourist called Twoflower, who is always trying to take pictures with his camera – a box containing a little elf who can draw very quickly. We meet the Luggage, relentlessly following its master on little legs. We meet Death, who rides a horse called Binkie and always talks in capital letters ...

I am one of the many people who buy everything Terry Pratchett writes, and one of the best things about discovering this brilliantly funny series is knowing that there are another twenty-seven titles to go (and counting ...), and every one of them seems better than the last!

Andrew Norriss

11+

Next?
- My favourite **Discworld** books include ***Mort*** and ***Guards, Guards!*** and ... Well, all of them, really.
- He's written some books for children as well, such as ***The Carpet People*** and ***Truckers*** – see **The Bromeliad Trilogy**. (UBG 36)
- For another different and hilarious set of fantasy stories, try Douglas Adams's ***The Hitchhiker's Guide to the Galaxy***. (UBG 109)

THE CORAL ISLAND R.M. Ballantyne

➨ What did we do before TV, radio and cinema? We curled up with a good book – especially one that took us off on exciting adventures in the South Seas.

In the company of Ralph Rover and his friends, Jack Martin and Peterkin Gray, we sail away on a merchant ship. The ship is wrecked on a coral reef, and so begins the Robinson Crusoe-like adventures of the three friends, surviving on their desert island and making their home on a captured schooner. But in between times they have many scary encounters with pirates, cannibals and missionaries – who all want bits of their body or their soul.

Though many of the ideas about morality are outdated today, we can still thrill to the adventures and Ballantyne's description of the natural history of the South Seas. He makes readers wonder how we would fare shipwrecked on a desert island, with no way of communicating with the outside world. Come to think of it ...

James Riordan

11+

Next?
- Other classic adventures are R.L. Stevenson's ***Treasure Island*** (UBG 247) and Daniel Defoe's ***Robinson Crusoe***.
- ***The Swiss Family Robinson*** by J.D. Wyss is a terrific story of a family shipwrecked on a tropical island. (UBG 234)
- ***Plundering Paradise*** by Geraldine McCaughrean is a wonderful story about pirates and the fabulous island of Madagascar.

CORALINE Neil Gaiman

➨ Coraline is bored. She's just moved into a new house and can't think where to explore next. Then she finds a door in one of the walls. It leads along a dark corridor. It leads her to another home, almost identical to hers but not quite. It leads her to another mother, almost identical to her own but not quite. What does this other mother want? And why has she got buttons instead of eyes?

This is an imaginative and genuinely scary story that starts off innocently and ends up frightening you half to death.

Cliff McNish

10+

Next?
- If this book excites you, try other psychological chillers such as Tim Bowler's ***Midget***, about a boy whose brother is out to get him.
- Or John Brindley's ***Rhino Boy***, the unusual story of a boy with a rhino horn growing right out of the middle of his head!
- A weird and wonderful tale that always deserves re-reading is ***Alice's Adventures in Wonderland*** by Lewis Carroll. (UBG 11)

It was exciting and gave me a view of a wider, more glamorous world than anything my quiet,

CORAM BOY Jamila Gavin

➡ In her introduction, Jamila Gavin says, that 'the highways and byways of England were littered with the bones of little children.' Her book is set in the eighteenth century and is about the 'Coram Man' who toured the country supposedly collecting unwanted babies to take to the Coram Hospital in London. But this newly-founded hospital never employed such a man, so exactly what was he doing with all those babies?

This is a thrilling, spellbinding book full of gothic mystery, which had me reading long after I should have been asleep. The historical tone is authentic and the tension is held throughout.

11+

Mary Hooper

Next?
- Other great books by Jamila Gavin include ***The Wheel of Surya*** (UBG 261) and ***The Blood Stone*** (UBG 32).
- A classic that is largely about the horror of life for poor Victorian children is ***Oliver Twist*** by Charles Dickens.
- And look out for the wonderful ***Smith*** (UBG 221) and ***Black Jack*** (UBG 30), both by Leon Garfield, set in the same period.

CORBENIC Catherine Fisher

➡ Desperately insecure, unhappy Cal leaves his mother (and her drinking) to go and live with his Uncle Trevor, who likes things neat, tidy and the more expensive the better. But Cal gets off the train at the wrong stop and ends up at Corbenic and a castle in the middle of nowhere. Or does he ...?

Finally getting to his uncle's, Cal tries to adjust to his new life. Then he meets up with a group of young travellers, including Arthur, Kai, and the beautiful Shadow – and everything changes again.

Woven through with Arthurian legend, from the Fisher King to the grail itself, this book will keep you guessing and wondering and breathlessly wanting to know more. The story uses real places to make you rethink legend – and if you ever visit the town of Caerleon in South Wales, stand in the centre of the Roman amphitheatre and think of this story.

11+

Leonie Flynn

Next?
- If you loved the legends hinted at here, read ***The Crystal Cave*** by Mary Stewart.
- Or any of the Arthurian myths retold by Roger Lancelyn Green. (UBG 134)
- Or Kevin Crossley-Holland's ***The Seeing Stone***. (UBG 216)
- Try Catherine Fisher's **The Book of the Crow**, set in a world that seems like fantasy, but might not be. (UBG 201)

COUNTING STARS
David Almond

➡ If you, like me, prefer to read novels rather than short stories, lay aside your prejudice for Almond's beguiling collection of tales from his Catholic childhood.

Here walks Miss Golightly, the seamstress who keeps her unborn baby in a jar; and David's mam, who strokes behind his shoulder blades to let him know where his angel wings once joined; and David's sister Barbara, who died and really did become an angel, because Mary Byrne, resident of Watermill Lane, saw her out walking, so it must be true.

Almond writes with a brutal beauty and there is real magic in these stories – not the sort to do with wizards but the sort you feel when you look up into a night sky drilled with stars.

11+

Nicky Singer

Next?
- You might like to see how these true stories develop into David Almond's fiction – try his amazing ***Skellig***. (UBG 220)
- Or see how another great writer's childhood affected his novels, in Roald Dahl's ***Boy***. (UBG 34)
- Or if it's Almond's spare style you like, or the point where the real slips into the unreal, then you might also enjoy books such as ***The Owl Service*** by Alan Garner. (UBG 179)

THE COUNTRY CHILD Alison Uttley

➡ Susan Garland, the country child, walks through threatening woods on her daily four-mile trek to a village school. This book tells of her childhood and describes not only the woods and the school but also the farmhouse in which Susan lives, and describes seasons, festivals, gardens and many other aspects of her life. The book reminds readers that, with the help of a strong imagination, everyday life can become fascinating and mysterious.

Alison Uttley is best known for her **Little Grey Rabbit** stories for young children. However she also wrote a series of non-fiction books recording a remembered but vanishing British country life, and *The Country Child* is probably the most haunting and unforgettable of these. Certain readers, particularly girls, will enjoy this account of a past life which is made remarkable by the imagination of the writer remembering it.

9-11

Margaret Mahy

Next?

- You might also enjoy William Mayne's ***The Twelve Dancers*** or ***A Grass Rope*** (UBG 99) – stories in which the countryside has a powerful presence.
- ***The Diddakoi*** by Rumer Godden is about an outsider coming to live in a rural community. (UBG 61)
- Karen Wallace's ***Raspberries on the Yangtze*** is about growing up in the wilds of Canada. (UBG 198)

A CRICKET IN TIMES SQUARE

George Selden

➡ When Chester, a cricket from Connecticut, finds himself lost and alone in the underground station of New York's Times Square, he quickly becomes the pet of young Mario Bellini, who helps his parents run a news stall. He also makes friends with Tucker Mouse and Harry Cat, and learns to play the most wonderful music. But cricket, mouse and cat are dogged by disaster!

This is a beautiful story of city life, rich with the sort of detail that comes from good writing. The mix of secondary characters adds extra nooks and crannies to the plot.

9-11

Simon Puttock

Next?

- You might like ***Charlotte's Web*** by E.B. White – another lovely story of eccentric animals and humans. (UBG 45)
- For a story of (again, eccentric) characters afloat in a great and unnoticing city, try ***The Thief Lord*** by Cornelia Funke. (UBG 238)
- Similarly, check out the **Hazel Green** books by the wonderfully-named Odo Hirsch.

CRISPIN: THE CROSS OF LEAD

Avi

➡ At thirteen, Crispin doesn't even know his real name. Everyone in the village calls him Asta's Son – that is, when they bother talking to him at all. Living in mediaeval England, Crispin and his mother are subjects of Lord Furnival, and after paying all the taxes they are left with barely enough to eat. When his mother dies, Crispin's miserable life takes a turn for the worse. He is falsely accused of stealing and is pursued by the Lord's steward, who declares him a Wolf's Head – an outlaw to be killed on sight. Crispin must escape, and he takes with him his only valued possession – a lead cross, given to him by his mother. On the road, Crispin joins Bear, a jolly juggler who is not all that he seems to be. Things look up for Crispin, but as he has never learned to read, he is unaware that the writing on his cross reveals a dark secret that will soon catch up with him.

11+

Noga Applebaum

Next?

- ***The Seeing Stone***, the first in Kevin Crossley-Holland's trilogy about a squire's son in mediaeval England who discovers his true identity. (UBG 216)
- ***The Wool-pack*** by Cynthia Hartnett is another mediaeval adventure in which a boy sets out to save his father from a plot to ruin him. (UBG 271)
- Try one of Rosemary Sutcliff's exciting historical adventure stories such as ***The Eagle of the Ninth*** (UBG 68) or ***Sword Song*** (UBG 234).

THE CROWSTARVER Dick King-Smith

Here

➡ Dick King-Smith's poignant, finely-controlled writing demonstrates everything that is best about books for children. This can certainly be said for *The Crowstarver*. But in other ways, this is not a typical Dick King-Smith book.

Setting his story on a farm in the 1930s and 1940s, King-Smith writes with expert knowledge and straight from the heart. He tells the story of Spider, a special boy, who is brought up by a shepherd and his wife after being left in the lambing-pen as a newborn baby. A slow learner, he has amazing gifts, including a magical ability to imitate the sounds made by birds and animals. Most of the characters treat Spider sympathetically, but in spite of the ridicule he faces from some, and a complete lack of understanding from the local headmaster, his warm, gentle personality shines through in some deeply moving moments.

9-11

Jenny Blanch

Next?

- Another Dick King-Smith similar in tone is ***Godhanger***, about a ferocious battle of wills between some woodland birds and a gamekeeper.
- Another book about survival in the countryside is Richard Adams's classic ***Watership Down***, about the epic adventures of a group of rabbits. (UBG 259)

THE CUCKOO SISTER Vivien Alcock

➡ On the surface, Kate has a good life. She lives in a lovely house with her well-to-do parents and wants for nothing. But a shadow hangs over the family. Before Kate was born, her parents had another baby, Emma, who was snatched from her pram and never seen again.

One day, a teenage girl turns up with a note saying that she is the long-lost Emma! There follows a time of huge turbulence for the family. The girl isn't like them at all. Is she really Emma? How can they prove it? Everyone is distressed and disorientated – and no one more so than the girl herself.

This is a very entertaining and also rather uncomfortable book about class, identity, and the complicated things that are families.

9-11

Susan Reuben

Next?

- Other Vivien Alcock titles to look for are: ***The Monster Garden*** (UBG 163), ***The Trial of Anna Cotman***, ***The Sylvia Game*** and ***The Haunting of Cassie Palmer***.
- Another book about finding your place in a family is ***Saffy's Angel*** by Hilary McKay. (UBG 207)

CUE FOR TREASON Geoffrey Trease

➨ The day Peter Brownrigg falls foul of the local squire, his life changes for ever. Forced to go on the run, he joins a company of travelling players and becomes an actor, taking girls' parts, as boys always did in Elizabethan days, when real girls were not allowed on stage. He proves quite good at it, but there is another boy in the company, Kit Kirkstone, who is totally brilliant and out-acts them all. How does he do it? The scene where Peter discovers Kit's secret used to be one of my all-time favourites when I was young!

Together, the two of them make their way to London, where they bump into William Shakespeare and read his new play, *Romeo and Juliet*; act in a performance before the Queen; uncover a treasonous plot and are sworn into the Secret Service.

This is a book which brings history vividly to life, complete with romance, intrigue, high adventure – and lots of lovely swashbuckling.

10-12

Jean Ure

Next?
• Susan Cooper's ***King of Shadows*** (UBG 134) and Jan Mark's ***Stratford Boys*** (UBG 230) both involve Shakespeare.
• A great adventure story set in mediaeval England is ***Knight's Fee*** by Rosemary Sutcliff (UBG 137), as is ***The Gauntlet*** by Ronald Welch (UBG 89).

DADDY-LONG-LEGS Jean Webster

➨ My father sent me *Daddy-Long-Legs* (I was at boarding school) when I whinged about being miserable and lonely and in bed with chicken pox. The book is a series of letters from an orphan (i.e. more lonely and miserable than me) to the anonymous benefactor who pays for her to go to college on the understanding that she writes to him at least once a month. I was eleven and laughed for three days.

It's a tender tale of growing up, the story of an asylum kid with 'an all-inclusive ignorance', discovering the wider world with an astonished frankness and freshness ('Have you ever read *Hamlet*? It's perfectly corking!') and gradually allowing herself to form a relationship with the man who moves from 'Daddy-Long-Legs' to 'Daddy'. Read it and weep.

10-12

Nicky Singer

Next?
• My next chicken pox read (chicken pox can drag on for weeks) was ***The Rose and the Ring*** by W.M. Thackeray. Don't be put off by the fact that it was published in 1855. The fantastical tale of Prince Bulbo of Crim Tartary is a 'fireside pantomime' and a good laugh.
• If you want to stay in the family you could try Mark Twain's ***The Adventures of Tom Sawyer***. (UBG 9). Twain was Jean Webster's great-uncle.
• If it's the personal letter format that appeals, you might also like a real diary – ***The Diary of a Young Girl*** by Anne Frank. (UBG 61)

DAISY MAY Jean Ure

➨ This book is set in the reign of Queen Victoria and is a good indication of what life was like then. Good old days? Not a bit of it! Not if you were as poor as little Daisy May, found abandoned in a daisy field. Pushed from pillar to post, downtrodden and bullied, Daisy May strives for a better life and to rise above her bad start.

Everyone loves a Cinderella story, and this is a great one which also has a spine-tingling, supernatural element to it. As with all good stories, for most of the book everything is as bleak as can be – but then quite wonderfully, it all comes right in the end. You'll be rooting for Daisy May every inch of the way!

Mary Hooper

6-8

Next?
• If you like Jean Ure's books, you'll find plenty more on the library shelves. She writes historical, funny, animal and character-based stories. Look out for ***Dazzling Danny***.
• ***Daisy May*** is one of the **Roaring Good Reads** series – look out for others including ***Witch in Training*** by Maeve Friel.
• Or for something a bit spooky, try Jan Mark's ***Long Lost***, about a boy and his long-lost relatives. (UBG 147)

DAKOTA OF THE WHITE FLATS

Philip Ridley

➡ '"I hope it is a monster," said Dakota softly. "Really I do."'
Dakota likes hanging around with her best friend Treacle. She's always starting off on some new adventure or other, and this time she's determined to uncover the secret of Medusa: a strange, green-haired woman who always walks around with a supermarket trolley. There's a rumour Medusa has a baby monster hidden in that trolley. Dakota is determined to find out ...

This is a typically clever, funny, unpredictable and delightfully weird tale by Philip Ridley.

9-11

Cliff McNish

Next?
• If you like this story, Philip Ridley has created many more wonderfully zany characters in books such as ***Mercedes Ice*** and ***Scribbleboy***. (UBG 211)
• Or, if you haven't yet tried it, why not dip into the classic weird and wacky world of ***Alice's Adventures in Wonderland*** by Lewis Carroll? (UBG 11)

DANNY, THE CHAMPION OF THE WORLD

Roald Dahl

➡ As a boy, what I loved most about this book was the wonderful relationship between Danny and his fabulous father, and the fact that they lived in a gypsy caravan. I stared for a long time at the pictures of the inside of that cosy caravan, and could imagine no better place in the world to live.

Danny discovers his father's deep dark secret: he loves poaching pheasants from the boorish Victor Hazell's woods. Together, father and son come up with an ingenious scheme to poach every single one of Hazell's pheasants the night before his big pheasant shoot. This book combines thrilling night-time excitement and humour, and is certainly one of Dahl's most realistic and warm-hearted books.

8-11

Kenneth Oppel

Next?
• You may want to read about the author's own childhood in ***Boy***. (UBG 34)
• Or try his ***The BFG***, about an orphan girl's adventures with a dream-catching giant. (UBG 27)
• Another great book about fathers and sons is Pete Johnson's ***Rescuing Dad***. (UBG 202)
• Or try ***Result!*** by Neil Arksey – and find out what it's like when your dad is also one of your teachers.

DARK CLAW series TUNNEL MAZERS • ROAD RAGE • RAT TRAP • BREAKOUT! • GUIDING PAW • BLACK HOLE

Shoo Rayner

➡ If you're looking for something with wacky speech bubbles and pictures that will really make you laugh, then try this hilarious *Star Wars* spoof. Don't expect Luke Skywalker, though – the cast are mice and rats, with the hideously evil Dark Claw looking remarkably like next door's moggy with toothache.

Onlee One, Hammee and Chin Chee are fighting to save the Muss from extermination by Dark Claw, and they riot through space never knowing when danger will strike. Fortunately Onlee One has an extra specially wonderful sense of smell (the result of a quick sniff of a piece of Fworgonzola) and this helps the intrepid adventurers on their way ...

6-8

Vivian French

Next?
• When you've read all six books, you might like to try anything by Jeremy Strong – he's *great*. Try ***The Hundred-Mile-an-Hour Dog***.
• And look out for ***The Twits*** (UBG 250) or ***Fantastic Mr Fox*** (UBG 82), both by Roald Dahl.
• ***Captain Underpants*** by Dav Pilkey is another series that is totally wacky and full of the most hilarious illustrations! (UBG 40)

EVERYBODY'S FAVOURITE...

THE DARK IS RISING sequence

OVER SEA, UNDER STONE • THE DARK IS RISING • GREENWITCH • THE GREY KING • SILVER ON THE TREE

Susan Cooper

➡ The five books in the **The Dark Is Rising** sequence are some of the best fantasy ever written. Each book interlocks with the others, and as the sequence unfolds we are taken from one mystical adventure to another. The first, *Over Sea, Under Stone*, introduces us to Simon, Jane and Barney, and their great-uncle Merry, around whom strange things seem to happen. Sure enough the children are swept into a perilous quest for an ancient Grail.

The Dark Is Rising, the second book, is the most haunting, focusing on young Will, the seventh son of a seventh son, who discovers he is the last of the powerful Old Ones. *Greenwitch* moves down to the Cornish coast, and features pagan magic. *The Grey King* takes us to the mysterious mountains of North Wales, and a secret lying inside them. The series comes to an epic climax in *Silver on the Tree*, when all the threads are finally drawn together.

Susan Cooper drew on many different aspects of British folklore and legend to create this wonderful set of five connected novels, and the result is worthy of the heritage from which she took inspiration.

Marcus Sedgwick

➡ It's almost Christmas, but Will Stanton isn't thinking about presents this year. Radios buzz with static when he comes near them and animals seem afraid of him. On Midwinter's Day, he wakes to find everyone in his house fast asleep. But it is not a normal sleep, and the heavy snow that blankets the surrounding countryside is no ordinary snow. Will is the seventh son of a seventh son, one of the Old Ones, who has come into the world to protect it from an evil force. But time is rapidly running out ...

This story is the second book in Susan Cooper's fantasy series, **The Dark Is Rising**. Susan Cooper writes brilliantly, contrasting warm funny scenes of a rural family preparing for Christmas, with Will's lonely, terrifying struggle against the Dark.

Annie Dalton

10+

Next?

- Read **The Changes Trilogy** by Peter Dickinson, which travels similar territory, with equally powerful writing. (UBG 44)
- **The Book of the Crow** by Catherine Fisher is a dark adventure set in a world that might be the past and might be the future. (UBG 201)
- If you'd prefer a more demanding fantasy read, try Alan Garner's ***The Owl Service***, a gripping supernatural thriller set in a Welsh village. (UBG 179) In fact, anything by Garner is worth reading.
- You might enjoy John Masefield's Christmas fantasy ***The Box of Delights***, in which Kay Harker has to protect a wonderful box from evil governess Miss Pouncer and her sinister coven of male and female witches. (UBG 34)

If you're looking for Darren Shan's creepy stories, turn to p. 208

THE DARK HORSE Marcus Sedgwick

➠ *The Dark Horse* drew me into a strange, primitive world. Sigurd and his adopted sister Mouse (whom he rescued from wolves) are children of the Storn, a tribe led by superstition and fear which is struggling for survival. As the Storn fights within itself, dark forces they know only from legends gather around it. It falls to Sigurd to question his assumptions, rise to the challenge of leadership and face the terrible fate which awaits his people at the hands of the Dark Horse.

This isn't a comfortable novel to read, but I loved it. In most novels, you know that things are going to work out well. In this novel, you can never be sure, so the story is genuinely unpredictable. It's powerful, too, and made me think about how often we make our minds up without thinking, and about how important it is not be ruled by fear.

10-12

Antonia Honeywell

Next?

- If you like the bleak, intriguing setting of this novel, try ***Heaven Eyes*** by David Almond. (UBG 108)
- If you want to read another novel about a young boy forced to become an adult, try ***The Sword in the Stone*** by T.H. White. (UBG 234)
- Marcus Sedgwick has written three other novels – ***Floodland*** (UBG 86), ***Witch Hill*** and ***The Book of Dead Days***.
- Rosemary Sutcliff is always worth a read; try ***Warrior Scarlet*** and ***Dawn Wind***.

THE DAY MY BUM WENT PSYCHO

Andy Griffiths

➠ OK, I bet you're thinking – how can a *bum* go psycho? Well, it can … and when all the bums in the world get fed up with their lot and start the Great Bum Rebellion, someone has to take a stand! Zack is just the guy for the job. His bum has run off, and he doesn't see why he should take that lying down.

To find out about stinks, poos, pongs and how to use a pink fluffy toilet seat cover as bait for a feral bum – read this book. You'll laugh, you'll cry – you'll probably never look at your bum in the same way again. (And if you've never looked at your bum at all, you'd better get two mirrors and check it's still there …)

9-11

Leonie Flynn

Next?

- More toilet humour? Try ***The Killer Underpants*** by Michael Lawrence (UBG 127), or ***The Giggler Treatment*** by Roddy Doyle (UBG 92).
- Another really funny book – possibly with the best opening chapter ever – is ***Bumface*** by Morris Gleitzman. (UBG 37)
- For more hilarious stories about weird goings-on, try the **Buster Bayliss** books by Philip Reeve. (UBG 175)

THE DAY OF THE TRIFFIDS John Wyndham

➠ Ever thought about how the world might end? In this thought-provoking novel, John Wyndham shows us just how quickly civilisation as we know it would fall apart if most of humanity woke up to find that they had gone blind overnight. Throw in man-eating plants walking around, making survival even harder, and you have the basic premise of the novel.

This book was written at a time when most people were worried about the very real possibility of nuclear war, and you may want to skip the more political bits. What will keep you reading is the way in which it tempts you to imagine how you would cope in such circumstances. If you had to keep a small group of people alive, where would you go and what would you do? From its famous opening line to its nail-biting conclusion, this is a book that will keep you hooked and you'll find yourself thinking about it long after you've finished it.

11+

Laura Hutchings

Next?

- John Wyndham wrote lots of other novels, such as ***Chocky***, ***The Midwich Cuckoos*** and ***The Kraken Wakes***. All of these books involve aliens affecting things on Earth.
- If you enjoyed the theme of surviving after a great catastrophe, why not read ***Z for Zachariah*** by Robert C. O'Brien, or Hugh Scott's ***Why Weeps the Brogan?*** (UBG 263)

DEATH AND THE ARROW

Here ✓

Chris Priestley

➡ It's London, 1715. Another murder has taken place, and again the murder victim is found with a 'death and the arrow' card on him – a card showing the figure of death, pointing, and brandishing an arrow, about to hurl it …

When his friend, Will, becomes involved with these terrible murders, Tom Marlowe just has to do something about it. Tom has some serious sleuthing to do – and fast, before the murderer strikes again … But what do all these victims have in common? And how is Will implicated? And who is the shadowy, caped figure on the roof?

Chris Priestley's detailed creation of eighteenth-century London is totally convincing, and captivating (it's quite a shock to come to the end of the book and find yourself back in the twenty-first century), and the story is absolutely gripping. Here's hoping for more Tom Marlowe adventures like it!

9-11

Daniel Hahn

Next?
• Tom Marlowe returns in the brand-new sequel, entitled *The White Rider*.
• Alison Prince writes really good historical mysteries; try *Oranges and Murder*. (UBG 177)
• Or what about Sophie Masson's *The Tempestuous Voyage of Hopewell Shakespeare*? Apprenticed to a boring trade, Hopewell envies his distant and famous cousin Will. Given the chance to join the crew of *The Golden Dragon* he jumps at it, and ends up embarking on a adventure that may feel curiously familiar.

THE DEMON HEADMASTER

Gillian Cross

Next?
• The series continues with *The Prime Minister's Brain*, *The Revenge of the Demon Headmaster*, *The Demon Headmaster Strikes Again*, *The Demon Headmaster Takes Over* and *Facing the Demon Headmaster*.
• The origin of *The Demon Headmaster* is in another Gillian Cross book, *Save Our School*, where there is a reference to a story about a wicked headmaster.
• The Demon Headmaster is reminiscent of some of the villains from the classic TV series *Doctor Who*. There are many Doctor Who novels by various writers, among whom Terrance Dicks is a stalwart. Amongst other titles, *Doctor Who: The Web of Fear* is a classic.
• For a more gothic take on the misuse of power, try Stephen Elboz's *The House of Rats*.

➡ 'What's the worst thing you can imagine in a school?' For new girl, Dinah Hunter, the answer to this question is as unexpected as it is chilling. She realises something is wrong before lessons have even begun. The pupils stand around in the playground, quietly chanting the times tables and testing one another on geography questions. The prefects' word is law, and they are obeyed without question. A large poster in the corridor proclaims: 'The man who can keep order can rule the world'. And soon she will meet that man, the mysterious and terrifying demon headmaster himself. What is the nature of the hold he has over the school? And is there any limit to his craving for power?

9-11

Thomas Bloor

The Demon Headmaster

GILLIAN CROSS

THE DEPTFORD MICE TRILOGY

THE DARK PORTAL • THE CRYSTAL PRISON • THE FINAL RECKONING

Robin Jarvis

➨ Don't be put off by the fact that the main characters in this trilogy are mice. There's nothing cute about these creatures! In *The Dark Portal*, Arthur and Audrey's father has gone missing in the sewers that lie beyond the grating in the hall. Believing rats have captured him, they go looking for him. But something terrifying dwells deep in the sewers – it's the lair of the evil sorcerer, Jupiter. As the trilogy progresses, the mice battle again and again to repel the dark magic of Jupiter, and in *The Final Reckoning* he returns to exact his revenge.

This is a fantastically exciting trilogy, fast-paced and tense; but there is humour too and you'll be kept guessing by the twists in the plot.

10-12

Kathryn Ross

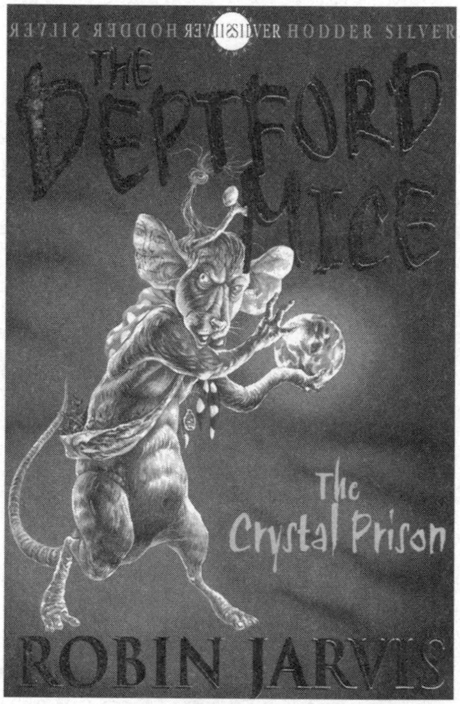

Next?

- You'll want to read the prequels, **The Deptford Histories**, which provide fascinating detail about many of the characters in **The Deptford Mice.**
- Brian Jacques's famous **Redwall** series has a huge fan-base – his heroes are also mice. (UBG 199)
- ***Silverwing***, ***Sunwing*** and ***Firewing*** are the titles of Kenneth Oppel's thrilling series set in the world of silverwing bats. (UBG 219)
- Back to mice ... don't miss the adventures of the affable watchmaker mouse, Hermux Tantamoq, hero of Michael Hoeye's highly original detective story, ***Time Stops for No Mouse***. (UBG 243)

THE DEVIL'S ARITHMETIC

Jane Yolen

➨ It is Passover, and Hannah is tired of her family constantly dwelling on the past. What does it mean? What is the point? But then, by some strange twist of time, Hannah finds herself in Poland, in 1942, and on her way to a concentration camp. And much as she tries to remember her 'real' family and the future from which she came, she is soon lost in the awful reality of this new 'now'.

This beautifully-told story focuses on a fragment of one of the most despicably vile passages in human history: the Holocaust. But Hannah, out of place, out of time, is not alone. She is bound to those around her through suffering and humanity, and through the devil's arithmetic; counting yourself among the living, one day at a time.

10+

Simon Puttock

Next?

- Read something quite different next. Something upbeat that'll reassure you that humans can be nice too ... Or maybe just go and talk to someone you really like.
- And if you then want to come back to this subject, try ***In My Hands: Memories of a Holocaust Rescuer*** by Irene Gut Opdyke. Look for Anne Frank's ***The Diary of a Young Girl*** for the real diary of a girl living through these terrible experiences. (UBG 61)
- Or ***The Star Houses*** by Stewart Ross, based on the memoirs of a survivor.
- ***August '44*** by Carlo Gebler is another deeply moving World War Two story. (UBG 21)

If you're looking for the Diamond Brothers adventures by Anthony Horowitz, turn to p.77

THE DIARY OF A YOUNG GIRL Anne Frank

➡ I first read this as a teenager in South Africa. I knew that Anne's family had been discovered in their hideout in Amsterdam by Nazi soldiers. I knew she had died in a concentration camp. Her diary gripped me because her voice was so alive, so honest. She was also a fantastic observer of people!

This was the first book that told me that literature was real. If I had been born in Europe, I knew that I, too, would probably have been killed because my mother was Jewish. But it was only years later that I realised that my own country was, in many ways, a vast concentration camp for most of its people – black South Africans. I had cried over Anne without seeing the racism all around me.

I still love the freshness of Anne's voice. I am convinced she would have stood up for all people equally – Jews, Muslims, Christians, Arabs, Africans, everyone: 'Why do some people have to starve, while there are surpluses rotting in other parts of the world? Oh, why are people so crazy?'

9+

Beverley Naidoo

Next?
- There is nothing else quite like Anne's diary, but try ***Zlata's Diary*** by Zlata Filipoviç, written during the war in Bosnia. Like Anne, Zlata sees the madness and stupidity of war.
- Can a cartoon make you cry? Read Art Spiegelman's ***Maus***, where the Jews are mice and the Nazis are cats, and see. (UBG 157)
- Another book about growing up somewhere very different is ***Chinese Cinderella*** by Adeline Yen Mah. (UBG 47)

COMPETITION WINNER ★ COMPETITION WINNER

THE DIARY OF A YOUNG GIRL Anne Frank

➡ There are two reasons why I chose this book. The first reason is, I keep a diary. I like to put my thoughts and feelings in it, just like Anne did. The second reason is that my grandfather was the same age as Anne Frank and he was living in Poland when the Germans invaded.

I liked this book because it is about true life. Anne Frank expressed her feelings whether she was upset, happy, sad or angry. When the bombs and guns went off she tried her best to be brave. Anne Frank was a bit mean in parts, especially when she talked about her mother and Mrs Van Dyke. They bossed her about a lot because she was the youngest.

After I read the book I felt I knew Anne very well and I thought she was a bit like me when she wrote about her mother. I felt sad when Anne and her sister Margot died because I would have loved Anne to have been my best friend.

Emma Louise Baczkowski, age 9, Oakley House School

THE DIDDAKOI Rumer Godden

➡ Kizzy Lovell and her gran live in a horse-drawn wagon in Admiral Twiss's orchard. When her gran dies, Kizzy has to adapt to living in a house and going to school, where she is bullied mercilessly by the other girls for being a diddakoi – a half-gypsy.

It's a great read, this, and very moving, but it's also an important book, because it shows how very hard it can be to live your life as an outsider. Kizzy is determined not to conform – she is proud of her background, proud of being different. The book gives an insight into the lives of gypsies and travellers and is a plea for tolerance – it asks us to respect and cherish difference, rather than fear and despise it.

9-11

Malachy Doyle

Next?
- Other strong stories that capture the nature of rural England are Philippa Pearce's ***Tom's Midnight Garden*** (UBG 245), and the very powerful ***Badger on the Barge*** (UBG 22) and ***The Nature of the Beast*** by Janni Howker.
- A great story about a boy meeting an outsider is the wonderful ***Stig of the Dump*** by Clive King. (UBG 226)

DETECTIVE AND SPY STORIES

'I spy ...'

BY CAROLINE LAWRENCE

When I was a kid, I was amazed by other people. How did they know how to live in the world? I read books to find out.

My favourite books were detective stories. The detective was an observer – like me – and often a loner. Detectives didn't have to be athletic or good-looking; they just had to be clever.

STORMBREAKER
ANTHONY HOROWITZ
"Alex Rider – you're never too young to die..."

Sherlock Holmes, for example. He was a brilliant Victorian detective who could look at a person and tell all about them from their gestures, plus the little clues on their hands and clothes.

Or take Nancy Drew, an ordinary American girl who lived in the 1950s and always caught the culprit. I devoured her mysteries. Nancy was clever and brave and could embark on lots of exciting cases because she had no mother and her father was quite absent-minded.

The boy versions of the **Nancy Drew** stories are the **Hardy Boys** or **Biggles** books. Enid Blyton's **Famous Five** books are for boys and girls. The stories in these series are all quite similar, so if you like one you can be sure you'll like the others.

When I decided to write the **Roman Mysteries**, my first thought was, 'The Nancy Drew books meet *Gladiator* the movie.' My girl detective Flavia is clever and brave, with an absent-minded father and no mother, so she can also have exciting adventures. And like the Famous Five, she has some clever friends and a dog.

Agatha Christie had two great detectives: Miss Marple (an old lady) and Hercule Poirot (a short Belgian). These books are classics and many writers steal from them. Although written for adults they are easy to read and suitable for kids, if somewhat old-fashioned.

For something more modern, try Cornelia Funke's *The Thief Lord*. Or Anthony Horowitz's **Diamond Brothers** series. For a good laugh, try Michael Hoeye's stories about a mouse private eye, starting with *Time Stops for No Mouse*. Or Shoo Rayner's hilarious **The Rex Files**, about a dog detective agency.

Here are some authors of detective and spy stories. Your mission? Find a book you like!

★ DETECTIVES

- Arthur Conan Doyle: try ***The Hound of the Baskervilles***
- Agatha Christie: try ***The Murder of Roger Ackroyd***
- Sax Rohmer – start with ***The Insidious Fu-Manchu***
- Erich Kästner: try ***Emil and the Detectives***
- Carolyn Keene: any of the **Nancy Drew** mysteries
- Enid Blyton: **The Famous Five** or the **Secret Seven** mysteries
- Franklin W. Dixon: any of the **Hardy Boys** mysteries
- Captain W.E. Johns: the **Biggles** stories
- Michael Hoeye: ***Time Stops for No Mouse***
- Shoo Rayner: ***The Rex Files 1: the Life-snatcher***
- Cornelia Funke: ***The Thief Lord***
- Philip Pullman: ***The Ruby in the Smoke***
- Anthony Horowitz: the **Diamond Brothers** series
- Caroline Lawrence: **The Roman Mysteries**: start with ***The Thieves of Ostia***

Did you know that Philip Pullman has written some historical mysteries with a girl detective? Try *The Ruby in the Smoke*, set in Victorian London, like the Sherlock Holmes stories. Historical novels (books set in the past) like these make the perfect mystery stories because while the detective is solving the crime, the author is solving the mystery of what it was really like to live in another age.

Then there are spy stories. If the detective is 'the hero who thinks' the spy is 'the hero who acts'. Spies tend to rely on gadgets rather than friends.

The most popular kids' spy series are the **Alex Rider** books by Anthony Horowitz. But there is also a great new series by ex-SAS member Chris Ryan, called **Alpha Force**. Or try the **Outernet** series by Steve Barlow and Steve Skidmore; their space spy stories tie in with a website: you have to go online to get clues and passwords. Finally, there is a good historical novel called *The Spanish Letters* by Mollie Hunter, about a girl spy in sixteenth-century Scotland.

★ SPIES

- Anthony Horowitz's **Alex Rider** spy stories: start with ***Stormbreaker***
- Chris Ryan – start with ***Survival: Alpha Force 1***
- Steve Barlow and Steve Skidmore – **The Outernet** series: start with ***Friend or Foe?***
- Mollie Hunter – ***The Spanish Letters***

DIMANCHE DILLER series

DIMANCHE DILLER • DIMANCHE DILLER IN DANGER • DIMANCHE DILLER AT SEA

Henrietta Branford

➡ What a tragic loss to children's literature was the untimely death of Henrietta Branford! She wrote some of the most captivating and original books in the canon. The three Dimanche Diller books anticipate the all-the-rage series by Lemony Snicket, **A Series of Unfortunate Events**. A baby, orphaned ('and don't hope her parents will turn up alive at the end') when her rich parents are drowned at sea, is adopted by a ghastly villainess called Valburga Vilemile, posing as her aunt.

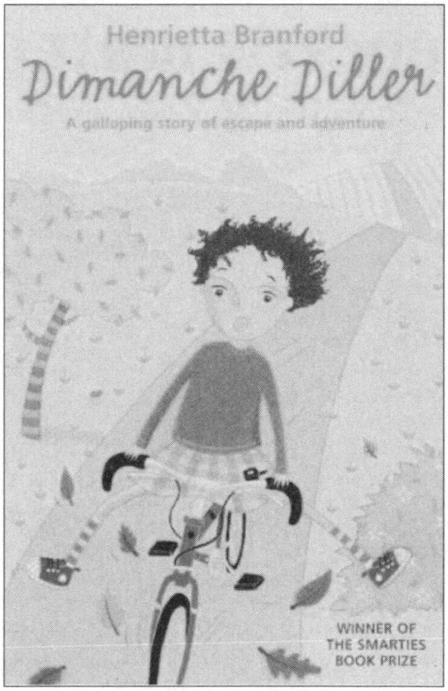

Henrietta Branford
Dimanche Diller
A galloping story of escape and adventure
WINNER OF THE SMARTIES BOOK PRIZE

VV, who leaves Cruella de Vil at the post, does her best to have the child meet with a fatal accident so she can get her evil hands on her money. Happily, Dimanche – adventurous, sparky and bursting with life – survives, with help from her many friends. In fact, all who meet her become her devotees, and I greatly hope an endless stream of new readers will feel the same.

7-9 **Lynne Reid Banks**

Next?

- **A Series of Unfortunate Events** by Lemony Snicket, about another three children whom life treats very badly. (UBG 217)
- ***Harry and the Wrinklies*** by Alan Temperley – a story about an orphan, with a wonderfully evil Nemesis, Gestapo Lil. (UBG 105)
- Jean Ure's ***Daisy May*** is about an abandoned child in Victorian times who struggles for a better life. (UBG 55)
- For a very different story about children being apart from their parents, try ***The Owl Tree*** by Jenny Nimmo. (UBG 181)

If you're looking for Terry Pratchett's Discworld series, turn to p. 51

Next?
- Another book about dreams, illness and the blurring of the real world is ***Marianne Dreams*** by Catherine Storr. (UBG 154)
- A series of books also about fantasy and reality Susan Cooper's **The Dark Is Rising** sequence. (UBG 57)
- Or for a realistic and terrifying look at life-threatening illness, try Malorie Blackman's ***Pig-heart Boy***. (UBG 187)

THE DIVIDE Elizabeth Kay

➨ Elizabeth Kay's first book is a great parallel-world adventure starring Felix, a young boy suffering from a life-threatening illness. As he falls asleep, he is taken to another world where he encounters all sorts of strange and mystical beasts that could only have sprung from the furthest corners of his imagination.

Slowly, Felix becomes involved in a race to stop the evil Snakeweed from dominating this fantasy world. With the help of numerous other fantastical beasts, he simultaneously battles evil and manages to find a temporary cure for his illness.

The book has a gripping and exciting storyline, the plot is brilliant and the characters are vivid. It is very original and I certainly haven't read any book quite like it before.

10-12

Tim Cross

DOCTOR DOLITTLE Hugh Lofting

➨ Doctor John Dolittle lives in the seaside town of Puddleby-on-the-Marsh. He is not very successful as a 'people' doctor; he prefers looking after his animals. His pet parrot Polynesia persuades him to become a vet and teaches him to talk to his animal patients in their own languages.

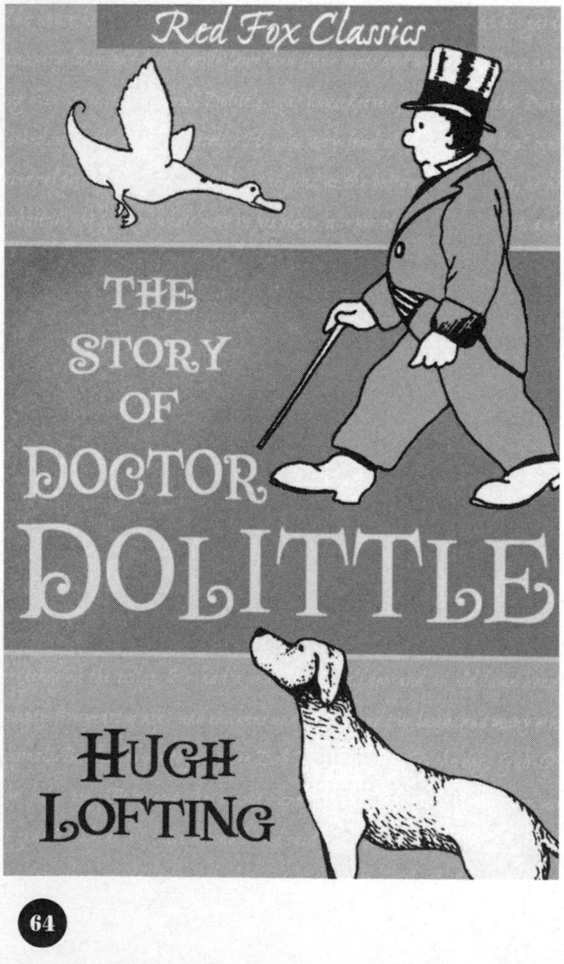

Gradually his fame spreads, as the animals pass on the good news to one another that at last there is a vet who can understand and treat the needs of his patients!

The doctor's adventures take him all over the world, and even to the moon. His many animal friends, including Polynesia, Jip the dog, Dab-Dab the duck, and a pushmi-pullyu (the rarest animal in all of Africa), are loveable characters in their own right.

There is a whole series of books chronicling the warm and funny adventures of Doctor Dolittle.

8-10

Ian Beck

Next?
- More animals? Try ***The Jungle Book*** by Rudyard Kipling, about a boy brought up by animals. (UBG 130)
- Or the delightful ***Mr Popper's Penguins*** by Richard and Florence Atwater. (UBG 165)
- Another series about wonderful goings-on – this time with a tin man, scarecrow and cowardly lion – is L. Frank Baum's ***The Wizard of Oz*** series. (UBG 269)
- ***Read our ANIMAL STORIES selections on pp 16-17.***

A DOG SO SMALL

Philippa Pearce

➨ Have you ever wanted something so badly it seems to take over your life? Everything that happens in this book is connected with Ben Blewett's wish for a dog. But in a busy family household in busy London, it just isn't possible even to have the smallest dog. At the start of the book, Ben is convinced that his grandparents will give him a dog for his birthday. Instead, he gets a picture of a dog; but not just any old picture. Written on the back are the magic-sounding words *Chiquitito chihuahua* – and magic they are. But Ben discovers that sometimes fantasies can go too far, in this engaging, warm and wonderful book.

9-11

Jon Appleton

Next?
- Try ***The Lady with Iron Bones*** by Jan Mark (UBG 139) and ***The Twelve and the Genii*** by Pauline Clarke (UBG 250) – terrific stories about the good and bad things that can happen when you really want something to be true.
- ***Tom's Midnight Garden*** is a wonderful and more challenging, story by Philippa Pearce. (UBG 245)
- For another book with a great dog, read ***I, Jack***, by Patricia Finney. (UBG 120)

DOGSBODY

Diana Wynne Jones

➨ Imagine if stars were living beings! Sirius is the dog-star, and he has a terrible temper. As punishment for apparently killing a lesser star whilst in a rage, he is banished to Earth and reborn as a dog. Once on Earth, he is cared for by Kathleen, a lonely, bullied orphan whom he comes to adore.

Dogsbody has wonderfully vivid characters: there are resourceful children like Kathleen; mighty stars like Sol; villains like cruel Aunt Duffy who makes vile ceramics; and hilarious animals like the stupid Hello Dogs.

Best of all is Sirius himself, with his powerful star nature, struggling within his humble dog's body as he tries desperately to prove his innocence and return to his place in the heavens.

9-11

Gill Vickery

Next?
- Try ***Black Maria***, another of Diana Wynne Jones's books where people are turned into animals. She really makes you understand what it would be like to feel as if you were a wolf or a cat but still thought like a human. (UBG 30)
- If you enjoy books like these you will also enjoy Allan Ahlberg's ***Woof!***, about a boy who keeps turning into a dog and back again without warning. (UBG 271)
- For a more serious tale, read Henrietta Branford's ***Fire, Bed and Bone***, a novel set in the Middle Ages told from the point of view of a dog. (UBG 83)

THE DOLL'S HOUSE

Rumer Godden

➨ This story, by one of the most sensitive of writers, is about a mismatched family of dolls longing for a settled home. Their owners, sisters Emily and Charlotte, restore a house for them, and within its wooden walls unfolds what Godden's biographer Anne Chisholm calls 'a miniature melodrama of love and murder among dolls'. The characters of the dolls are wonderfully described – sensible, loving Tottie, eccentric, vulnerable Birdie and the sinister and manipulative Marchpane. Contrasting with the lives of the dolls is the relationship between Emily and Charlotte themselves.

This is a delightful book – moving, thoughtful and perceptive.

8-10

Jane Ray

Next?
- You may like to try ***The Borrowers*** by Mary Norton, about a family of tiny people who live under the floorboards and 'borrow' the things that go missing in our day-to-day lives. (UBG 33)
- Or try Sylvia Waugh's ***The Mennyms***, about another unusual family. (UBG 158)
- Or what about Elizabeth Goudge's delightful fantasy, ***Henrietta's House***? It is a little older, but it's really worth reading. (UBG 109)

THE DOLPHIN CROSSING

Jill Paton Walsh

Next?
- In ***Grace***, Jill Paton Walsh explores a true story, this time that of Grace Darling, who became a national heroine after saving some drowning sailors.
- Or try Paton Walsh's ***A Parcel of Patterns*** about when plague visited the Derbyshire village of Eyam. (UBG 182)
- Another story of friendship is Philippa Pearce's ***Minnow on the Say***. (UBG 161)

➨ In 1940, John's comfortable life has been disrupted by the War. His father is in the Merchant Navy and his brother is away in Birmingham. The army has requisitioned their home so he and his mother are living in a gardener's cottage. But at least John is luckier than Pat – an evacuee from London who has to live in a derelict railway carriage with his pregnant stepmother, and who is bullied by the local children. John goes out of his way to help Pat, but when John realises the significance of the small boats and pleasure steamers being taken by the navy over the horizon towards Dunkirk in France, he finds it is Pat's turn to help him.

The British evacuation of Dunkirk was one of the turning points of the Second World War. The Little Ships helped save 300,000 soldiers – including my great-uncle – by sailing to the French coast and taking on board as many soldiers as they could. Some of the boats were so small that only a few could be rescued at a time, but because hundreds of boats made the dangerous crossing, thousands of men survived.

10-12

Barbara Wright

DON'T PAT THE WOMBAT

Elizabeth Honey

➨ This is a funny, rude and sometimes moving book about an Australian school camp. It's told by Mark, one of a group of friends called the Coconuts, who are shocked when the worst teacher of all (the Bomb – so-called because you never know when he might explode) suddenly joins them on their annual summer trip. It's full of the gory details of children left almost to their own devices, but has a more serious heart to it – the story of how the Bomb persecutes a strange boy called Jonah, and how Jonah is victorious in the end.

9-11

Marcus Sedgwick

Next?
- If you liked this, why not try ***45 and 47 Stella Street***, or ***Fiddleback***, also by Elizabeth Honey.
- Or some classic stories about young trouble-makers, such as ***Just William*** by Richmal Crompton (UBG 131) or the **Jennings** stories by Anthony Buckeridge (UBG 126).

THE DOOMSPELL

Cliff McNish

Next?
- Rachel's battle is continued in two equally readable sequels called ***The Scent of Magic*** and ***The Wizard's Promise***.
- If you've got the witch twitch, try the most famous witch story of them all, L. Frank Baum's ***The Wizard of Oz***. (UBG 269)
- Battling a witch in a faraway land, via the back of an unassuming wardrobe, is the theme of C.S. Lewis's classic ***The Lion, the Witch and the Wardrobe***. (UBG 141)

➨ When Rachel and her brother, Eric, are sucked unexpectedly through a terrifying portal to the faraway frozen ice world, Ithrea, they know they are in trouble. A seriously unhappy witch called Dragwena – a loathsome creature with blood-red skin, tattooed eyes, four sets of teeth and a writhing snake-mouth filled with purple-eyed, armoured spiders – has been seeking her perfect slave for centuries and thinks Rachel is it.

This book bulges with a classic big battle between good and evil. McNish creates an entertaining story that is by turns magical and gripping, yet full of danger and treachery. It's a page-turner, and sometimes a stomach-churner, but its breakneck excitement never fails to enthral.

9-11

John McLay

DOUBLE ACT Jacqueline Wilson

➡ Ruby and Garnet are identical twins. They do everything together. But although they look exactly alike, Garnet is a lot shyer, so Ruby's used to getting her own way all the time.

When their dad finds a new girlfriend, they are absolutely *disgusted*, and even more so when they all have to move together to the countryside and become a brand new family. Ruby and Garnet are determined to hate their new life and not make any friends.

This is one of Jacqueline Wilson's most enjoyable books. You'll come to love the twins, even though you'll feel like slapping them sometimes – Ruby for being so bossy and Garnet for being so timid!

8-11

Susan Reuben

Next?

- Try ***Lotte and Lisa*** by Erich Kästner, another very funny story about identical twins.
- Enid Blyton's **St Clare's** books are stories that feature in ***Double Act***. (UBG 209)
- ***Goggle-eyes*** by Anne Fine is another story about getting used to a step-parent, this time a stepfather. (UBG 95)
- ***The Prince and the Pauper*** by Mark Twain is a classic story about two boys who look like twins. (UBG 193)

DOWN WITH SKOOL

Geoffrey Willans, illustrated by Ronald Searle

Next?

- The **Jennings** series, by Anthony Buckeridge is a set of very funny stories about boys at boarding school. (UBG 126)
- Or try ***Three Men in a Boat*** by Jerome K. Jerome. This is a humour classic. Just read a bit of it, and if you like it, devour the whole thing.
- Or what about Gene Kemp's ***The Turbulent Term of Tyke Tiler***, for another child who gets into trouble at school. (UBG 249)

➡ The hero of this book is Nigel Molesworth. The first thing you notice is how he spells. Because mostly he doesn't. Also, his world view is refreshingly straightforward. 'My skool is nothing but kanes, lat. French, geog. Hist. Algy, geom., headmasters, skool dogs, skool sossages, my bro molesworth 2 and MASTERS everywhere.' There it is, the world as we all know it (though hopefully not the cane any more!) reduced to essentials: Us (noble brave fearless) and Them (oiks et al.).

Political correctness is probably one of the reasons we couldn't create Molesworth these days, as he is very un-PC. He is disrespectful and anarchic to the core, a plotter and troublemaker, over-opinionated, irreligious, mean to his little brother, wily ('Aktually the trick is to look dopey and then the Latin master will do all the translation himself'), a smoker, and completely uninterested in that most important thing, Doing Well at School. He is also hilarious – and the illustrations by Ronald Searle are worth the price of the book on their own!

9+

Diane Duane

DRAGONQUEST Anne McCaffrey

➡ Lessa is the last of the line of Ruatha Hold. Her enemy, Fax, has killed all the rest of her family, and she is now hiding from him by pretending to be a drudge in the huge kitchens. And then the dragons arrive …

These huge, beautiful, intelligent beasts, with telepathic powers and the ability to breathe fire, are the only defence the people of Pern have against the terrible flesh-eating Threads that fall from the sky. But there are so few of them left and F'lar, the chief dragonrider, is desperately searching for someone strong-willed and telepathic enough to ride the last female dragon. Will Lessa get her revenge on Fax, and will F'lar find the right girl?

After this, you'll always want your own dragon!

11+

Patricia Finney

Next?

- There are plenty more books by Anne McCaffrey, many of them continuing the story of the dragons.
- You'll find the same ingredients – strong girl hero, revenge, dragons – in ***The Shamer's Daughter*** by Lene Kaaberbol.
- For much more 'human' dragons, try ***The Fire Within*** by Chris d'Lacey. (UBG 84)

THE EAGLE OF THE NINTH Rosemary Sutcliff

➨ A brilliantly exciting story set in Roman Britain. Marcus's father was in the lost Ninth Legion, which marched north and was never seen again. After a serious injury, Marcus has to leave the army, so joins up with his British slave, Esca, and sets off on a quest to retrieve the Ninth's Eagle and restore his father's honour. Battles, wild landscapes and strange tribal rituals fill the book with action, and Sutcliff's dense prose makes you feel you're living in Marcus's world.

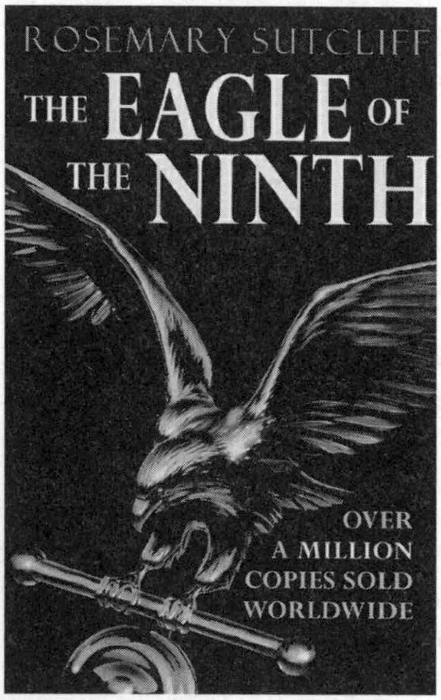

Two other books continue the story of Marcus' descendants. In *The Silver Branch* the eagle is rediscovered and used against the cruel emperor, Allectus, and in *The Lantern Bearers*, one of Rosemary Sutcliff's best books, Aquila has to choose between leaving Britain with the Roman army or searching for his lost sister.

Sutcliff's books are about friendship and loyalty, about overcoming pain and difficulty. They are not easy, and she doesn't flinch from showing the cruelty and violence of the time. But if you enjoy history and exhilarating adventure you'll find her books immensely satisfying, and won't rest till you've read them all.

10-12

Catherine Fisher

Next?
- Try Sutcliff's ***The Mark of the Horse Lord***, where a boy becomes a gladiator and then, after many adventures, the Horse Lord of a strange tribe. (UBG 155) Or ***Outcast***, a story set in the latter part of the Roman empire, which is about a journey into slavery.
- For other tough, uncompromising history novels try Henry Treece's ***The Horned Helmet***.
- If you like Romans, try the hugely enjoyable ***The Thieves of Ostia*** in Caroline Lawrence's **Roman Mysteries** series. (UBG 239)

EARTHFASTS William Mayne

➨ Nellie Jack John, the drummer boy, marched into a tunnel in the earth of Yorkshire two hundred years ago and was never seen again. So when David and Keith hear the drum and see him emerge into the modern world, they realise something very strange is beginning. A candle that doesn't go out, mysterious moving stones and the theft of all the pigs in the town puzzles them even more. And then David vanishes in a mysterious shaft of lightning, and Keith is left alone.

William Mayne is a wonderful writer, and this has to be one of my favourite books. It's full of loving description of a small rainy Yorkshire town and the fells that surround it, their legends and the area's odd brusque dialect. David and Keith are both very real, and their friendship for each other is clearly conveyed in Mayne's deadpan style. But you'll need to be alert, because this writer often slips things past you without you noticing, and the most astonishing things are told simply. For Mayne the landscape is riddled with its past, and past and present often mesh. This is true also for the two sequels to *Earthfasts* which Mayne wrote many years later.

11+

Catherine Fisher

Next?
- Try the sequels: ***Cradlefasts*** and ***Candlefasts***.
- There are many other great stories by William Mayne; they include ***It***, about a girl troubled by a spirit, and ***A Grass Rope***, where Mary finds a unicorn's horn which leads her to treasure. (UBG 99)
- For other timeslip books, try the brilliant ***Tom's Midnight Garden*** by Philippa Pearce (UBG 245) or ***A Stitch in Time*** by Penelope Lively (UBG 226).

THE EARTHSEA TRILOGY

A WIZARD OF EARTHSEA • THE TOMBS OF ATUAN • THE FARTHEST SHORE

Ursula Le Guin

➨ Earthsea is a vast group of islands ruled by kings and warlords, but the real power is held by mages – great wizards. These are not beardy types with pointed hats, but immensely wise men who spend years, perhaps their whole lives, learning their craft. Ged, also known as Sparrowhawk, is a wild and arrogant youth with a gift for magic that he does not understand and cannot control. A dangerous challenge almost costs him his life. Someone else dies in his place and he learns that his gift is also a huge responsibility.

As he grows older, he journeys throughout Earthsea, from island to island, meeting with many adventures, and finally becomes Archmage, the supreme wizard. A young prince from a distant kingdom comes to seek his help when a renegade wizard finds a way to cheat death and upsets the balance of nature. Ged must travel to the land of the dead and give up his own powers to make things whole again.

There are hundreds of novels about magic and spells and wizards, but if you were asked what magic actually is you might find the answer by reading the Earthsea tales.

10+

Jan Mark

Next?

- After this trilogy there are two further novels in the Earthsea cycle, ***Tehanu*** and ***The Other Wind***, and a book of Earthsea stories, ***Tales from Earthsea***.
- Another trilogy is **His Dark Materials** by Philip Pullman. (UBG 176)
- ***The Blue Hawk*** by Peter Dickinson begins with a strange ritual in a far-off land long ago, and tells the story of a boy who dares to break with tradition.

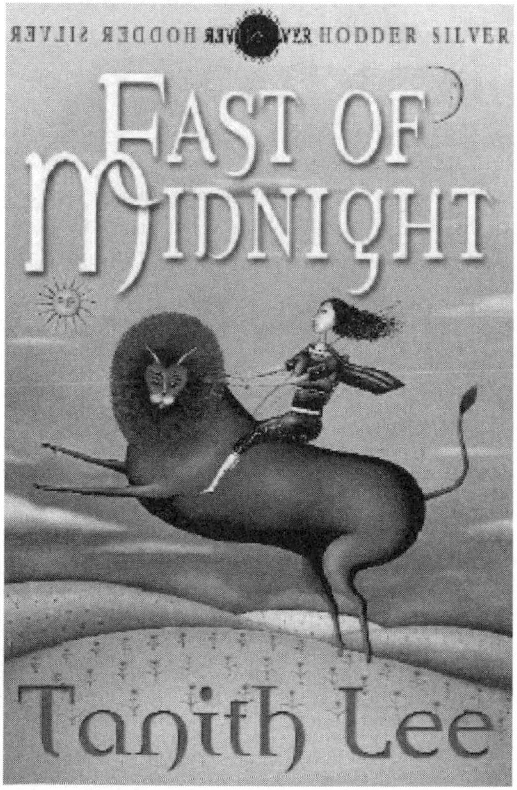

EAST OF MIDNIGHT

Tanith Lee

➨ Tanith Lee's fantasy worlds are so vivid and original that reading her work always feels like an exciting, brand-new experience. This story begins with Zaister, who is the privileged consort to Izvire, the female King. But it's time for someone new to take over, and for Zaister to die. He desperately wants to live and uses magic to swap places with Dekteon, a slave. It seems an easy plan, but the trouble is that Dekteon has kept his own mind, too – and he is stronger than Zaister could ever be. Daringly, he brings huge disruption to Izvire's court. A struggle of identity breaks out between Dekteon and Zaister. Who will triumph, and what will it mean for Izvire's future?

9-11

Jon Appleton

Next?

- Look for Tanith's ***The Castle of Dark*** (UBG 42) and the slightly tougher (but utterly brilliant) ***Piratica*** (UBG 190).
- Don't miss Catherine Fisher's books, such as **The Book of the Crow** series (UBG 201) and ***The Snow-walker's Son*** trilogy (UBG 222).
- ***Check out the special FANTASY STORIES feature on pp. 79-81.***

Aussie, is a very funny writer – all of his books are good because they are so real.

THE EDDIE DICKENS TRILOGY

AWFUL END • DREADFUL ACTS • TERRIBLE TIMES

Philip Ardagh

➡ This hilarious series chronicles the bizarre adventures of eleven-year-old Eddie Dickens, and is set in a nineteenth-century world that is a madcap mix of fact and Philip Ardagh's off-the-wall imagination. In *Awful End*, Eddie's parents contract a strange disease that turns them yellow and crinkly round the edges, and he's sent to stay with Mad Uncle Jack (who has a treehouse built of dried fish) and Even Madder Aunt Maud.

Eddie's adventures continue in *Dreadful Acts*, where he narrowly avoids being blown up and arrested, but falls into the clutches of a desperate gang of escaped convicts. Needless to say, he survives, only to be sent to America in the third book to save the family's *Terrible Times* newspaper business – although whether he will actually make it across the Atlantic is another matter …

Philip Ardagh's writing style is unmistakable. He talks directly to you, the reader, and constantly interrupts his own story to tell you amazing facts, awful jokes and share interesting thoughts. Even stranger, his characters know they are in a book and wonder aloud if the author has it in for them. These books are incredibly daft, fantastically funny and completely addictive. You have been warned!

8-11

Kathryn Ross

Next?

- Philip Ardagh has begun a new series of Eddie Dickens's adventures, starting with ***Dubious Deeds***.
- Debi Gliori's ***Pure Dead Magic*** is the first of three very funny books about the Strega-Borgia family, who live in an ancient castle in Scotland. (UBG 195)
- And if reading Eddie Dickens has made you want to try some Charles Dickens, then Marcia Williams's ***Mr Charles Dickens and Friends***, a lively comic-strip retelling of five of Dickens's best-known tales. Turn to p. 166 to read about all of Marcia's great books.

THE EDGE CHRONICLES

Paul Stewart and Chris Riddell

➡ This fabulous fantasy series takes readers into new and amazing worlds. *Beyond the Deepwoods*, the first title, tells the story of Twig, abandoned at birth and brought up by wood trolls, who sets out into the wild world in search of his past.

The story is fast and action-packed and the characters are extraordinary – goblins, trogs, flesh-eating trees and more. The books move on to tell of Twig's dangerous adventures as a sky pirate and of the mysteries, evils and intrigues always to be found in the dangerous floating world of Sanctaphrax.

These books continue to surprise and entertain as new and brilliantly imagined characters join in with the stories. They're given extra wonder by Chris Riddell's intricate and fascinating black and white line drawings. The books are a compelling read and great to look at too!

9-12

Wendy Cooling

Next?

- The titles so far include ***The Curse of the Gloamglozer*** (a prequel), ***Beyond the Deepwoods***, ***Stormchaser***, ***Midnight Over Sanctaphrax***, ***The Last of the Sky Pirates*** and ***Vox***.
- ***Muddle Earth*** is by the same team, and is a wicked parody of a certain other well-known fantasy classic … (UBG 168)
- If you loved the fantasy element, try ***Artemis Fowl*** by Eoin Colfer (UBG 20), or ***Mortal Engines***, the start of another brilliant fantasy series by Philip Reeve (UBG 164).

EIGHT DAYS OF LUKE

Diana Wynne Jones

➨ David's summer holiday looks like it's going to be grim from day one, as he has to spend it with his ghastly relatives who constantly tell him he's horribly ungrateful. Then, accidental magic brings Luke into the picture. Everybody likes Luke, even the ghastly relatives, and David only has to strike a match for Luke to appear. Unfortunately, Luke's family also begins to turn up and events take a sinister turn.

The characters include some seriously eccentric people such as Uncle Bernard and Astrid who have illness competitions, and Mr Chew, the unnaturally huge gardener with a streak of pure malice. All Diana Wynne Jones's books are full of marvellous humour and this is one of her funniest.

10-12

Gill Vickery

Next?

- This book is based on the Norse legend of Loki, the mischievous trickster god. For another story that uses the same legend, read Patricia Elliott's ***The Ice Boy***. (UBG 121)
- For books based on other myths, try Peter Dickinson's ***The Weathermonger*** (see **The Changes Trilogy** – UBG 44).
- To find out which of Diana Wynne Jones's other books are recommended in the *UBG*, turn to p. 288.

THE EIGHTEENTH EMERGENCY

Betsy Byars

➨ This American story is set in a landscape of gritty sidewalks, apartment blocks and basketball hoops on walls. Benkie the hero has a habit of labelling things in very small writing. He labels a picture of Neanderthal Man after the school bully. Nobody can help him then – not even his best friend Ezzie, with whom he has already found solutions to seventeen life threatening situations.

Read this book if you have ever been frightened or bullied. You will find it full of useful information and encouragement. Do not read it if you are a bully yourself. It will not increase your self respect, and you may find yourself having to change your ways.

9-11

Hilary McKay

Next?

- Betsy Byars has written dozens of books. Try ***The Seven Treasure Hunts***, ***The Midnight Fox*** (UBG 159), or ***The Pinballs*** (UBG 189).
- If you like books with an American flavour you might also enjoy ***Dogs Don't Tell Jokes*** by Louis Sachar, or his **Wayside School** stories.

ELIDOR Alan Garner

➨ This is a book with fear in it. It's like the dark corner in which something terrible may be lurking; you want to run away, and yet you can't resist having a closer look …

Nicholas, David, Helen and Roland go wandering through Manchester. They find a church that's about to be demolished; hear strange high music; kick a ball into the church … and it falls into a different world, a threatened, desperate world called Elidor. The four of them are expected in Elidor, and they save four Treasures, a sword, a spear, a cauldron and a stone, by taking them back into their own world. But danger and sorcery go with them, and the two worlds terrifyingly intermesh. The story leaps between reality and fantasy, as does the magnificent unicorn Findhorn who can save Elidor only through the children, and the climax is as electrifying and heartbreaking as anything you'll ever read.

10-12

Susan Cooper

Next?

- Try Alan Garner's earlier fantasies ***The Weirdstone of Brisingamen*** (UBG 260), ***The Moon of Gomrath*** or the wonderful ***The Owl Service*** (UBG 179).
- ***The Dark Is Rising*** sequence by Susan Cooper is another brilliant fantasy. (UBG 57)
- Or for something really scary, try ***The Stones of Muncaster Cathedral*** by Robert Westall. (UBG 227)

EMIL AND THE DETECTIVES

Erich Kästner

➡ It all starts because young Emil Tischbein – the name means 'table-leg'! – is robbed while he sleeps on board a train. He was right in the middle of a nightmare in which he was facing the consequences of having painted the face on the statue of Grand Duke Charles. He's on the train because he's off to stay with his Aunt Martha in Berlin.

Losing the money is, of course, a disaster, but it's the trigger for the adventure of trying to catch the thief and for us to discover a gangsworth of resourceful young characters setting up the trap. Behind all this, we are treated to an introduction to a Berlin, reminiscent of a painter like George Grosz. 'The underground railway rumbled and the noise from the trams and buses and cycles joined together in a wild concert'. Just think, he was celebrating the city even as British children's literature was stuck firmly in Wild Woods, Hundred Acre Woods and Old Brown's Island! Kästner not only gives us line drawings of the city, but droll touristic interludes, so there he was pioneering new narrative techniques too.

8-10

Michael Rosen

Next?

• Emil is the first appearance in children's literature of the child detective. For more, try Enid Blyton's **The Famous Five** (UBG 78) and **The Secret Seven** (UGB 216) series.

• Anthony Horowitz's Alex Rider series – start with ***Stormbreaker***. (UBG 228)

• For something old and atmospheric, try and find Cecil Day Lewis's ***The Otterbury Incident***. (UBG 178)

• ***Bambert's Book of Missing Stories*** by Reinhardt Jung is another quirky, totally captivating book by a German writer. (UBG 239)

• ***And don't miss our DETECTIVE AND SPY STORIES recommendations on pp. 62-63.***

EMILY OF NEW MOON L.M. Montgomery

➡ This story is set on an island off the east coast of Canada, about a hundred years ago. So it is going to be old-fashioned – you will have to live with that.

Emily, aged ten, is an orphan, taken to live with her relations. They don't particularly want her, but they are stuck with her. Not an unfamiliar plot, especially as Emily is beautiful, talented, charming, etc.

But this is a good book! (Just skip as much as you like of the first five chapters – I have summed them up for you in the paragraph above.) Emily and her wild and gorgeous friend Ilse are a funny, witty, unsentimental pair. The descriptions of the island are vivid and entrancing. And there is a bit of a tingle, too, an unexplained death and an eerie moment of second sight.

This is a book to read when you are ill, and the weather is bad, and there is nothing but educational documentaries on TV. It is a book to hurl across the floor (Emily's mysterious smile and cloudy hair get a little too mysterious and cloudy now and then), but after you have hurled it do pick it up again, and straighten out the pages. One rainy day you will want to read more.

9-11

Hilary McKay

Next?

• If you want to know what happens to Emily next, read ***Emily Climbs*** and ***Emily's Quest***. And the ***Anne of Green Gables*** books are by the same author (but Hilary doesn't think they are as good). (UBG 17)

• Try the classic **Katy** books that begin with ***What Katy Did*** by Susan Coolidge. (UBG 260)

• Or for something of Hilary's own, try ***The Exiles***, which isn't sentimental at all! (UBG 75)

> **Next?**
> • You might like to try E. Nesbit's ***Five Children and It*** and ***The Phoenix and the Carpet***. (UBG 85)
> • Or what about the classic ***The Cuckoo Clock*** by Mrs Molesworth, in which lonely Griselda is taken into strange worlds by the cuckoo from the cuckoo clock?
> • Two contemporary novels about statues coming to life are Vivien Alcock's gripping ***The Stone Walkers*** and Jenny Nimmo's haunting ***Griffin's Castle*** (UBG 101).

THE ENCHANTED CASTLE E. Nesbit

➡ Gerald, Kathleen and Jimmy discover a tunnel near the dull little town where they are spending the summer holidays. They follow it into mysterious parkland, where statues come alive at night – including a stone dinosaur – and a great house holds a magic ring in a room of jewels.

The ring can grant wishes and make its wearer invisible. But, as the children discover to their cost, it also has a mind of its own ...

This story, first published a hundred years ago, may take a little more getting into than stories written today, but it's worth the effort – all E. Nesbit's fantasies sparkle with brilliant, original ideas and unpredictable plots. They are funny as well as magical, and sometimes touched by horror and the surreal. Here, the hideous 'Ugly Wuglies', made from a collection of old clothes, coat-hangers and umbrellas that come alarmingly to life, are amongst the creepiest creations in fiction. And though the children use old-fashioned slang like 'Crikey!' and 'Oh, rot!', they behave just like children nowadays.

10-12

Patricia Elliott

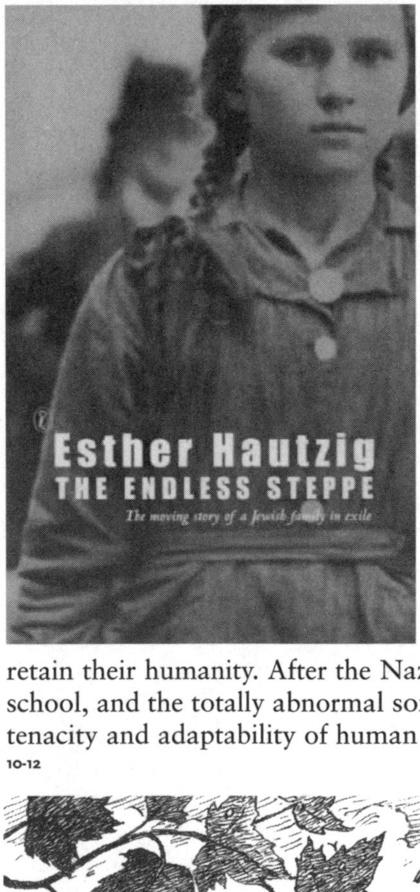

Esther Hautzig
THE ENDLESS STEPPE
The moving story of a Jewish family in exile

THE ENDLESS STEPPE

Esther Hautzig

➡ Apart from *The Diary of a Young Girl* by Anne Frank, this is probably the finest true account of a war-disrupted childhood ever written. Esther's family lives in happiness and luxury in pre-war Poland, until the Russians take over and banish such 'capitalists' to Siberia. She, her mother, father and grandmother arrive on the Steppe after weeks of comfortless travel by cattle-train. They all have to do hard manual labour in bleak and often freezing conditions, living a life of utter deprivation – yet they somehow survive and retain their humanity. After the Nazis invade Russia, they're no longer prisoners. Esther can go to school, and the totally abnormal somehow comes to seem normal. An astonishing testament to the tenacity and adaptability of human beings, and especially children.

> **Next?**
> • ***The Diary of a Young Girl*** by Anne Frank, if you haven't read it already. (UBG 61)
> • Try ***Carrie's War*** by Nina Bawden (UBG 41), or ***When Hitler Stole Pink Rabbit*** by Judith Kerr (UBG 261), both set during the Second World War.
> • ***The Devil's Arithmetic*** by Jane Yolen is another moving book centred on this subject. (UBG 60)

10-12

Lynne Reid Banks

Next?
- If you like books that make you think, with characters you believe in and care about, read ***The Eclipse of the Century***, also by Jan Mark.
- For other books set in a future afflicted by environmental abuse, you could read Julie Bertagna's ***Exodus*** (a much harder and older read) or Marcus Sedgwick's ***Floodland*** (UBG 86), both of which are concerned about the effects of global warming and worlds set adrift in rising seas.
- ***The Giver*** by Lois Lowry is another science fiction story to make you think. (UBG 93)

THE ENNEAD Jan Mark

➡ Imagine a world where unemployment is illegal, where you are deported the moment you lose your job. This is fifteen-year-old Isaac's world, Erato, and his job as a Steward is a precarious one. He works out a plan to make himself indispensable. Unfortunately, the plan has to include Eleanor, a sculptor on contract from violent, overpopulated Euterpe, and she seems determined to break all the laws that Isaac knows they have to keep in order to survive.

This brilliant book is full of unpredictable, sometimes bitter, twists: the plot turns when you least expect it and the characters, like real people, spring surprises when it suits them. *The Ennead* will haunt you long after you've finished reading.

11+

Gill Vickery

✓ Here YA

ETHEL AND ERNEST Raymond Briggs

➡ Raymond Briggs's strip cartoon evocation of his parents' life together, from their first meeting in the 1920s when Ethel was a housemaid, through the 1930s, the Second World War, to their deaths in old age is an extremely touching and warm-hearted story, full of humour and pathos, illustrated with exquisite detail. Let me tell you, it's not often that I finish reading a book hardly able to see it for tears.

Given the popularity and fame of Briggs's other books I expected to find this in the children's section of my local library when looking for a copy to refresh my memory, but was directed to 'adult autobiographies'. Nothing wrong with that, but I feel children would get just as much out of it as adults. It should definitely be on your shelves too.

10+

Michael Lawrence

Next?
- For a rather different family story, with more words and fewer pictures, seek out ***The Family from One End Street***, by Eve Garnett. (UBG 78)
- There are other books by Raymond Briggs. Try ***When the Wind Blows***, ***Fungus the Bogeyman*** (UBG 88) and ***Ug*** (UBG 251).
- Another book that makes you think about the past is ***Farm Boy*** by Michael Morpurgo. (UBG 81)

Next?
- If you like stories about brave, resourceful orphans, try ***A Little Princess***, by Frances Hodgson Burnett. (UBG 144)
- And of course, for more unfortunate events, read ***The Bad Beginning***, by Lemony Snicket. (UBG 217)

EVERYTHING ON A WAFFLE
Polly Horvath

➡ Cross Pippi Longstocking with Anne of Green Gables, and you get Primrose Squarp, the vibrant, funny, and frank eleven-year-old narrator of this novel. Newly-orphaned, Primrose moves in with her Uncle Jack, a former navy man turned estate agent who has his sights set on developing Coal Harbour into a chic tourist town. Convinced that her parents are still alive, Primrose must cope with a brief stint in jail, the loss of a toe, and encounters with various bizarre, and sometimes scheming, townsfolk. It sounds heavy, but it's more often hilarious.

What makes this a truly fantastic book is not simply its heroine and comic, unfortunate events; it's also the fabulous cast of supporting characters whom Horvath refuses to render as clichés. Horvath's writing crackles with energy. This is a funny, wise, big-hearted novel about the unquenchable nature of hope and joy, and the nourishing power of storytelling.

10-12

Kenneth Oppel

THE EXILES Hilary McKay

➡ Everyone feels sorry for the Conroy sisters. Their parents don't have a car, won't buy a TV and can never afford to go on holiday. But pity is the last thing in the world that Ruth, Naomi, Rachel and Phoebe want. They march defiantly through life, devouring books, arguing constantly and rebelling against every form of authority.

But when they are sent off to stay with Big Grandma for the summer, that is the last straw. 'Big Grandma doesn't like us!' they cry – and they set off mutinously, certain that they're going to have a miserable time.

The Conroy sisters are four of the funniest, most likeable and infuriating characters you're ever likely to read about. And as soon as you've finished *The Exiles*, you'll want to go straight out and find *The Exiles at Home* and *The Exiles in Love*.

9-11

Susan Reuben

Next?
- You must read the wonderful books about the Casson family also by Hilary McKay, starting with ***Saffy's Angel*** (UBG 207); and her book ***Dog Friday*** – the Robinsons will remind you very much of the Conroys ...
- Another very different book about four sisters is ***Little Women*** by Louisa M. Alcott. (UBG 146)
- Try the **Ally's World** series by Karen McCombie, for stories about another chaotic family. (UBG 12)

FABLES Aesop

Next?
- Try a jazzy version of the fables in a retelling by Vivian French called ***Aesop's Funky Fables***. (UBG 9)
- Find a good, short version of the oldest written story, the Epic of Gilgamesh (try the one by Geraldine McCaughrean, ***Gilgamesh the Hero***).
- Or the more modern, and equally wonderful, ***How the Whale Became*** by Ted Hughes.

➡ Want to read some of the oldest stories ever told? These fables, written down by Aesop as long ago as the sixth century BC, were probably being told long before that. Ancient they may be, but these stories about the antics of animals and men are every bit as relevant today. Many of them impart a moral, or simple message, usually about foolishness and wisdom. Some of them are amongst the best-known stories of all time: 'The Hare and the Tortoise', 'The Boy who cried "Wolf!"', 'The Wolf in Sheep's Clothing'. They are all very short – most only a couple of paragraphs, some as short as a line or two – but the best thing about them is their number. There are hundreds of them, and many of the less well-known fables are gems, such as the one about the Tortoise who wanted to fly.

8-11

Marcus Sedgwick

THE FABULOUS FANTORA FILES

Adèle Geras

There's a "Fabulous Fantoras. Book one, family files" in VPL ∅ ✓

➡ Adèle Geras has written lots of entertaining books and if you haven't sampled them yet, this is an excellent place to start. She seems to love writing about complicated, extended families and here we have the Fantoras – three children, two parents, a grandmother, and an aunt who happens to be a vampire. Watching their every move (and recording it faithfully for posterity) is Ozymandias, the talking, reading-and-writing family cat. (I don't think I can do justice to his powers of perception and cleverness in this review, so you will just have to take my word for it.)

This very funny book recounts the adventures of the Fantora family, and Ozzy, of course, in a series of linked chapters, with revealing excerpts from the files in between.

8-11

Jon Appleton

Next?
- Another enterprising cat features in Julia Jarman's ***The Time-travelling Cat***. (UBG 244)
- For the revelations of a dog, look no further than ***I, Jack*** by Patricia Finney. (UBG 120)
- And for a terrific series which also features letters and things other than conventional chapters, try Ian Whybrow's ***Little Wolf's Book of Badness***. (UBG 145)

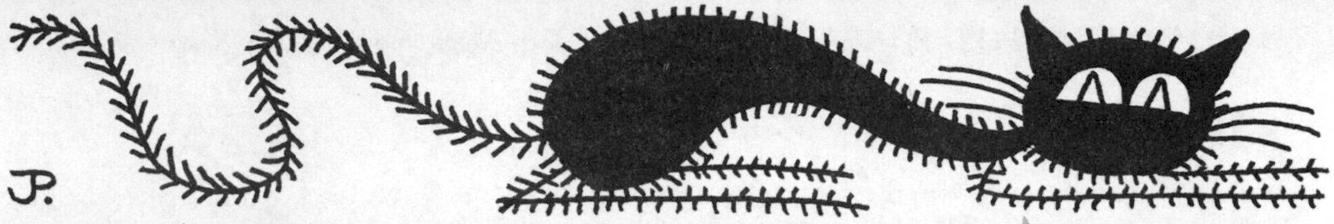

EVERYBODY'S FAVOURITE…

The World of FAIRY TALES

Hans Christian Andersen

There are hundreds of collections of fairy tales, both classic and modern, and if you like reading them it is worth trying to find a variety of collections, as they are all different, and all fascinating.

➡ The fairy tales of Hans Christian Andersen were intensely important to me, and have been a huge influence throughout my life. Mine was a real book: large and heavy with a thick dark cover and decorative lettering embossed in gold. The pages were thick and creamy white, with clear black print, which seemed to complement the numerous pen and ink drawings scattered throughout.

The illustrations by William Heath Robinson were absolutely as much a part of the thrill of this book as the stories themselves. Beneath each illustration, whether a small corner one or a panel in the middle, or a full-scale one in glossy, glorious colour, was always a quote from the story. 'She understood the speech of birds', or '"Yes, I will go with thee," said Tommelise.' These so inspired me, that long before I started writing I used to draw my own illustrations and write quotes beneath from my non-existent stories.

But it is the power of Andersen's tales which still moves me; I was inspired in childhood to compose an opera about 'The Red Shoes'; I agonised and wept with the Little Mermaid, and was awe-struck by Kay's search for Gerda, which took him to the land of ice and snow and the Northern Lights.

There was never anything cosy about Hans Andersen, but I think he should be a rite of passage which every young reader should experience. It will mark them for life – and for the better.

Jamila Gavin

8-11

Next?

- The Puffin edition is probably the best collection of Hans Christian Andersen's tales.
- Try Alan Garner's ***Fairy Tales of Gold***.
- Another interesting book to try is ***Kate Crackernuts*** by K.M. Briggs – a novel based on one of the folk tales in ***English Fairy Stories*** collected by Joseph Jacobs.
- For a twist on some well-loved tales, try ***I Was a Rat!*** by Philip Pullman (UBG 121), and Roald Dahl's ***Revolting Rhymes***.
- You might also enjoy ***The Light Princess*** (UBG 140) and other collections by George Macdonald.

Jacob Ludwig Carl Grimm and Wilhelm Carl Grimm

➡ These are the best-known stories in the history of folk tale and children's reading. Many of the stories, for example 'Rumpelstiltskin', and 'Snow White and the Seven Dwarfs' have become children's classics. People tend to forget that originally the stories were not strictly for children, but belonged to a whole community with connections across Europe and Asia. Among the tales are stories of death and cruelty, but there are also many stories in which the least-regarded child (often a 'simpleton') triumphs through kindness to an old person or an animal, and the simple narratives give power to the good-hearted hero or heroine. By now the tales, often selected and edited, exist in many editions and take many forms.

Margaret Mahy

8-11

- For more folk tale collections, look at those by Kevin Crossley-Holland, such as ***British Folk Tales*** and ***Enchantment***, or the coloured fairy books by Andrew Lang.
- Or try some new, and very funny, fairy tales by Terry Jones in ***Fairy Tales*** and ***Fantastic Stories***.
- Other tales that may feel the same are ***The Arabian Nights***, and as you read you'll recognise stories that are now used in pantomime. (UBG 19)

Oscar Wilde

I loved these beautiful, tender stories when I was young, and I still do. Stories such as 'The Happy Prince' and 'The Selfish Giant' have stayed with me all my life, and never fail to move me. In them, Oscar Wilde presents us with people who think they are better than everyone else, and then shows us, in wonderfully imaginative ways, how it is the people who are able to show pity, the ones who are better at giving than at taking, who are the truly blessed. In 'The Happy Prince', for example, the statue of a prince is so moved by the human misery in the streets below that he persuades a swallow to take his jewels and gold leaf and give it to the poor.

There is much sadness in these stories – they are about beauty and sorrow, friendship and love, pity and suffering – but there is happiness too, and poetry, wonder and joy. If you like stories that make you think, stories that let your imagination soar, then these are for you.

8-10

Malachy Doyle

Oscar Wilde was very influenced by the stories of Hans Christian Andersen. If you like one, you're sure to like the other ...

FAERIE WARS **Herbie Brennan**

➨ I loved *Faerie Wars* from the first sentence. It starts, 'Henry got up early on the day that changed his life,' and just gets better. *Faerie Wars* is a brilliant mixture of fantasy, adventure story and real-life drama.

After being told that his dad's leaving because his mum has met another woman, Henry goes to Mr Fogarty, the cantankerous elderly man he works for, only to find a fairy in the shed. The fairy, Pyrgus, is a full-sized and wingless prince in his own world. He's brave, but never thinks before he acts. (Thankfully, his sister does!) Henry has to defend the faerie world from a diabolical plot, which becomes darker and more sinister as the story unfolds. Henry's parents worry about him, but it's difficult to open up when you've got a world to save, a prince to restore to his throne, and the devil hanging over your very existence.

11+

Antonia Honeywell

Next?

- Try ***Mighty Fizz Chilla*** by Philip Ridley: a book where, once again, stories interlock and together make something far more exciting. (UBG 160)
- Joan Aiken's ***Midnight is a Place*** is another exciting adventure with more horrible happenings. (UBG 159)
- ***Ryland's Footsteps*** by Sally Prue is another book in which parents aren't always perfect ...

THE FALCON'S MALTESER

Anthony Horowitz

➨ It all begins when a dwarf leaves a package for safe-keeping at the detective agency run by Nick Diamond's extremely dim older brother, Tim. Hours later, the dwarf is dead, Tim is being held at the police station and our hero has to outwit a string of ruthless villains, all in search of the key to Henry von Falkenberg's hidden diamonds.

I can guarantee that you will enjoy this very funny detective thriller in which there is never a dull moment, with laugh-aloud, irreverent jokes on every page. Anthony Horowitz never lets the reader have even the tiniest dull moment – you really do have to keep turning the page (and laughing).

8-11

Kate Petty

Next?

- There are four more stories about Nick Diamond: ***Public Enemy Number Two***, ***The French Confection***, ***The Blurred Man*** and ***I Know What You Did Last Wednesday***.
- Another funny Horowitz story is ***Granny*** – about the most horrible gran in the universe.
- Some more detection? Try **The Invisible Detective** series by Justin Richards. (UBG 123)

THE FALL OF FERGAL

Philip Ardagh

➨ Any story that begins with the hero falling out of a window and definitively dying is bound to be a touch different – and this is *very* different. It's one of those books where a lot of the humour lies in the authorial jokes and comments on Fergal's adventures (before he's dead, in case you were wondering); by the end you feel you know Philip Ardagh (and his beard) even better than you know Fergal. (And a very fine thing that is too.) The first time I read one of Big Phil's books I got hiccups because I laughed so much. A word of warning, though. This book ends with the hero's brain being … No. Read it yourself and find out!

8-10

Vivian French

Next?
• When you've chortled your way through ***The Fall of Fergal***, you'll be thrilled to hear there's another in the series, ***Heir of Mystery***. Then read Big Phil's hilariously offbeat **Eddie Dickens Trilogy**, beginning with ***Awful End***. (UBG 70)
• Another clever, comic writer is Terry Pratchett. If you don't know his work already, why not try **The Bromeliad Trilogy**? (UBG 36)
• Enter another world where anything can happen in **The Spiderwick Chronicles** by Holly Black and Tony DiTerlizzi.

THE FAMILY FROM ONE END STREET

Eve Garnett

➨ The family from One End Street is the Ruggles – Mum, Dad, and seven children: Lily Rose (stout and helpful), Kate (the brainy one), Jim and John (twins), Jo, Peg and baby William. With a family as big as that, it's not surprising they get up to all sort of adventures.

Mr Ruggles is a dustman, Mrs Ruggles is a washerwoman, and they live in the little town of Otwell, somewhere between London and the sea. You'll not only love the characters and the humour in this classic, but you'll also enjoy finding out about how ordinary people lived in the 1930s, and the trouble the children managed to get into. Each chapter tells a story in itself. Find out what Lily Rose did when she managed to destroy an artificial silk petticoat, or what happened when Jim and John join the Gang of the Black Hand.

9-11

Sherry Ashworth

Next?
• There are two more books about the Ruggles – ***Further Adventures of the Family from One End Street*** and ***Holiday at Dew Drop Inn***.
• If you like books set in the not-too-distant past, try Bill Naughton's ***The Goalkeeper's Revenge***. (UBG 94)
• Or ***Stig of the Dump*** by Clive King, which is a bit less old-fashioned, and very readable. (UBG 226)

THE FAMOUS FIVE Enid Blyton

➨ It was Enid Blyton who got me hooked on books. People can be a bit snotty about her now, but she helped me escape from a drab room in a drab house. She smuggled my imagination down secret passageways. With her help I discovered hidden tunnels and mysterious caves. I spied on robbers and solved mysteries the grown-ups were too dim even to know about! Enid Blyton washed what seemed to me to be mundane reality aside.

Her writing might have been awful, repetitive and clumsy, but I didn't know that back then, and if I had I wouldn't have cared. She sat down with her battered typewriter; her prejudices; her unsophisticated formulae for stories; her unrealistic, wooden, middle-class characters; her stereotyped villains; and she did what far better writers failed to do. She transported us kids beyond the reaches of school time and bedtime and the thou-shalt-not world of the grown-ups. Would I have become addicted to books without her? I very much doubt it.

8-10

Brian Patten

Next?
• Other Blyton? Along with the **Famous Five** and the **Secret Seven** books (UBG 216) there is an **Adventure** series (UBG 124), the **Malory Towers** series (UBG 153) and the **St Clare's** series (UBG 209)
• Don't miss Louise Fitzhugh's ***Harriet the Spy*** for a different kind of detective. (UBG 104)
• Want a change? ***The Saturdays*** by Elizabeth Enright is perfect. (UBG 210)

FANTASY STORIES

Hobbit feet and fairy dust

BY SUSAN COOPER

Like a lot of us, I don't write fantasy on purpose, but because it won't go away. Every time I start a story, sooner or later it goes off the tracks of reality into the world of imagination. A realist friend of mine once said, about *The Dark Is Rising*, 'This is a very good book until that horse starts to fly.' But in fantasy, the horse of the imagination always flies.

It flies in all the old myths and fairytales we're told when we're very small; in ancient poems like 'Beowulf' and 'The Faerie Queene' and all the way down to Harry Potter (where of course the horse morphs back into a magic broomstick). In the 1800s and early 1900s only a few writers took off from reality, like Lewis Carroll (*Alice in Wonderland*), George Macdonald (*The Princess and the Goblin*) and E. Nesbit (*Five Children and It*). But as the 1900s went on, the two world wars gave everyone such an overdose of reality that the fantasy writers have been multiplying ever since. Maybe they took to it, as I did, because it was the kind of thing they loved to read, but couldn't find.

In Britain, our imaginations are soaked in history whether we like it or not, so our fantasy novels tend to grow out of it, like amazingly weird trees sprouting out of compost. C.S. Lewis's children go through a wardrobe from real England into Narnia, Phillip Pullman's from real Oxford into a parallel world. J.R.R.Tolkien's hobbits start in the extremely English countryside of the Shire and walk off into fantasy. For Alan Garner, William Mayne and others (including me) the unworldly power of magic invades everyday English life, bringing amazement and terror with it.

★ FIVE WORKS OF CYBERFICTION:

- **The Legendeer Trilogy** by Alan Gibbons
- ***Hacker*** by Malorie Blackman
- **The Johnny Maxwell Trilogy** by Terry Pratchett
- ***The Transfer*** by Terence Blacker
- ***Space Demons*** by Gillian Rubinstein

★ SUSAN COOPER'S TOP TEN FANTASY LIST

Take note: these are ***not*** the books I think are the best ten fantasies ever written (there are about thirty of those). But they are – in alphabetical order by author – the ten I would certainly take if I had to be marooned on a desert island. In a waterproof bag, please.

- ***Skellig*** by David Almond
- ***Tuck Everlasting*** by Natalie Babbitt
- ***The Children of Green Knowe*** by L.M.Boston
- ***The Owl Service*** by Alan Garner
- ***The Mouse and his Child*** by Russell Hoban
- ***A Wizard of Earthsea*** by Ursula LeGuin
- ***Earthfasts*** by William Mayne
- ***Tom's Midnight Garden*** by Philippa Pearce
- ***The Three Little Wolves and the Big Bad Pig*** by Eugene Trivizas, ill. Helen Oxenbury
- ***The Nargun and the Stars*** by Patricia Wrightson

The Hobbit **– illustration by Jai Bhambra, age 11, Quainton Hall School**

Other fantasy authors (especially Americans, whose country is so much younger, and lacks compost) invent totally new worlds, like Ursula Le Guin's Earthsea, and Anne McCaffrey's Pern. Tolkien did that once his hobbits had left the Shire, filling his **The Lord of the Rings** trilogy with invented geography, creatures and languages. Or there's the type of fantasy story that plays with time, like Philippa Pearce's classic *Tom's Midnight Garden*; or the animal fantasies, such as Kenneth Grahame's *The Wind in the Willows*, E.B. White's *Charlotte's Web* or Richard Adams's *Watership Down*.

If you've read a lot of fantasy, you'll know which author belongs in which category. It doesn't matter, of course; all fantasy stories belong to the same family in the end. They're books of escape; books that take you to places you'll never see; books in which the impossible happens, making the hair stand up on the back of your neck. They may not deal with facts and reality, but you know in your heart that they are true.

And d'you know why so many authors write a whole series of fantasy books? Sometimes it's because we know you want to read book after book set in the same imaginary world – but more often, it's because we live there while we're writing about it, and we can't bear to leave.

★ TWENTY BOOKS THAT SLIP BETWEEN WORLDS:

- ***Piggies*** by Nick Gifford
- ***Coraline*** by Neil Gaiman
- ***The Homeward Bounders*** by Diana Wynne Jones
- **His Dark Materials** trilogy by Philip Pullman
- **The Chronicles of Narnia** by C.S. Lewis
- ***The Dark is Rising*** by Susan Cooper
- ***Corbenic*** by Catherine Fisher
- ***The Owl Service*** by Alan Garner
- ***Elidor*** by Alan Garner
- ***The BFG*** by Roald Dahl
- ***Five Children and It*** by E. Nesbit
- ***The Secret of Platform 13*** by Eva Ibbotson
- ***Harry Potter and the Philosopher's Stone*** (and sequels) by J.K. Rowling
- ***Marianne Dreams*** by Catherine Storr
- ***Midnight for Charlie Bone*** by Jenny Nimmo
- ***Mary Poppins*** by P.L. Travers
- ***The Weirdstone of Brisingamen*** by Alan Garner
- ***Alice's Adventures in Wonderland*** by Lewis Carroll
- ***An Angel for May*** by Melvin Burgess
- ***Shadow of the Minotaur*** by Alan Gibbons

Northern Lights **– illustration by David Bard, age 9, Arnold House School**

★ SIX 'LITTLE PEOPLE' BOOKS:

- ***The Borrowers*** by Mary Norton
- ***The Indian in the Cupboard*** by Lynne Reid Banks
- ***Mistress Masham's Repose*** by T.H. White
- ***The Mennyms*** by Sylvia Waugh
- ***The Little Grey Men*** by B.B.
- ***The Hobbit*** by J.R.R. Tolkien

FANTASTIC MR FOX Roald Dahl

➨ This book is my favourite Dahl because our children adored it. It's got something very important to the success of any book: a really horrible villain, multiplied by three. Boggis, Bunce and Bean are farmers, and they are truly revolting. They're described in loving detail, right down to things like earwax. Mr Fox, his wife and the small foxes do battle with all three of them, and guess who comes out a winner in the end?

The book finishes with a splendid banquet in which the Foxes invite the other animals to join the feast. The illustrations by Quentin Blake add greatly to the fun and there are many moving and exciting moments along the way. This book is rightly known as a classic.

6-8

Adèle Geras

Next?

- ***George's Marvellous Medicine*** (UBG 89) and ***The Twits*** (UBG 250), which are both Dahl classics.
- You also might enjoy ***How Tom Beat Captain Najork and his Hired Sportsmen*** by Russell Hoban.
- Ian Whybrow's ***Little Wolf's Book of Badness*** is spot on for laughs and a great story. (UBG 145)

FARM BOY Michael Morpurgo

Illustrated by Michael Foreman

➨ On a farm in Devon, Grandpa recalls the stories his father told him about life on the land in the first half of the twentieth century. He remembers a favourite horse sold as a warhorse in the First World War, tells the tale of a ploughing match between a tractor and a horse-and-plough, and confesses his own 'shameful secret' of many years – that he has never learned to read and write.

Michael Morpurgo is a superb storyteller and he knows about farming. You believe completely in the characters he creates and Michael Foreman's wonderful illustrations bring the whole thing vividly to life. This is a short, easy read, but it's full of information and entertainment.

8-10

Kathryn Ross

Next?

- ***Out of the Ashes*** also by Michael Morpurgo is a hard-hitting look at the recent outbreak of foot-and-mouth disease. (UBG 179)
- Another moving and exciting Morpurgo story is ***Toro! Toro!*** (UBG 245)
- The farm horse sold to the cavalry in ***Farm Boy*** is the inspiration for Michael Morpurgo's ***War Horse***. (UBG 258)
- In ***War Boy***, Michael Foreman looks back on his own wartime childhood.

★ MAGIC!

- ***Witch Trade*** by Michael Molloy
- ***Pure Dead Magic*** by Debi Gliori
- ***Half Magic*** by Edward Eager
- ***Carbonel*** by Barbara Sleigh
- **The Chronicles of Narnia** by C.S. Lewis
- ***The Weirdstone of Brisingamen*** by Alan Garner
- ***The Book of Three*** by Lloyd Alexander
- ***Groosham Grange*** by Anthony Horowitz
- ***Puck of Pook's Hill*** by Rudyard Kipling
- ***A Handful of Magic*** by Stephen Elboz

★ EIGHT SCI FI BOOKS

- ***Mortal Engines*** by Philip Reeve
- **The Book of the Crow** series by Catherine Fisher
- ***A Rag, a Bone and a Hank of Hair*** by Nicholas Fisk
- ***The Giver*** by Lois Lowry
- **The Changes Trilogy** by Peter Dickinson
- ***Playing on the Edge*** by Neil Arksey
- ***Why Weeps the Brogan?*** by Hugh Scott
- ***The Day of the Triffids*** by John Wyndham

★ A DOZEN TIMESLIP BOOKS:

- ***A Traveller in Time*** by Alison Uttley
- ***King of Shadows*** by Susan Cooper
- ***The Children of Green Knowe*** by Lucy M. Boston
- ***A Stitch in Time*** by Penelope Lively
- ***Puck of Pook's Hill*** by Rudyard Kipling
- ***Earthfasts*** by William Mayne
- ***Tom's Midnight Garden*** by Philippa Pearce
- ***A Wrinkle in Time*** by Madeleine L'Engle
- ***The Time-travelling Cat*** by Julia Jarman
- ***Charlotte Sometimes*** by Penelope Farmer
- ***The Ghost of Thomas Kempe*** by Penelope Lively
- ***Stravaganza: City of Masks*** by Mary Hoffman

Next?
- You should try L. Frank Baum's ***The Wizard of Oz*** (UBG 269) and Lewis Carroll's ***Alice's Adventures in Wonderland*** (UBG 11), two classics with brave, bright heroines who set out on incredible journeys.
- If tomboys appeal, you may like Jo March in Louisa May Alcott's ***Little Women*** (UBG 146), Princess Amy in M.M. Kaye's ***The Ordinary Princess*** (UBG 177) or Petrova Fossil in ***Ballet Shoes*** by Noel Streatfeild (UBG 23).
- Another story by Lynne Reid Banks to try is the much-loved ***The Indian in the Cupboard***. (UBG 105)

THE FARTHEST-AWAY MOUNTAIN Lynne Reid Banks

➨ Dakin is nearly fifteen and lives happily with her family in the valley of the farthest-away mountain. Dakin is determined to have adventures. From her bedroom the mountain looks quite close, its peaks capped with green, purple and pink snow. No one knows why the snow isn't white, and when the mountain summons her, Dakin does not know why she is wanted. But she understands that the mysterious journey is her destiny, and sets off on a terrifying adventure, encountering trolls, gargoyles and an ogre, before uncovering the evil secret that enslaves the mountain and all who live there ...

There are chilling baddies, loveable goodies, passwords and poems, a wicked wood and a sea of spikes. Dakin is a feisty, no-nonsense heroine who embraces her challenges with refreshing good humour.

9-11

Francesca Lewis

FATTYPUFFS AND THINIFERS

André Maurois

➨ Two brothers discover a secret escalator that takes them to the Country Under The Earth, land of the Fattypuffs and Thinifers. The Fattypuffs are easygoing, lazy and adore food. The Thinifers on the other hand, are tetchy, hard-working and scarcely eat a thing. Sad to say, these two contrasting nations are both foolish and stubborn enough to let a silly dispute between them develop into a full-scale war. Can Edmund and Terry find a way to bring it to an end?

André Maurois tells a clever, witty and thought-provoking tale, but what makes this book extra special are Fritz Wegner's glorious illustrations which, with their detail, humour and charm, bring alive the eccentric Fattypuffs and Thinifers in a way that means you'll never ever forget them.

7-10

Nick Sharratt

Next?
- To see more of Fritz Wegner's wonderful illustrations, try ***The Giant Baby*** by Allan Ahlberg. (UBG 92)
- For something equally hilarious, try the **Professor Branestawm** books by Norman Hunter, about an absent-minded professor who always gets into terrible scrapes. (UBG 194)
- Or the totally wild and wacky ***Great Piratical Rumbustification and The Librarian and the Robbers***, from the wonderful Margaret Mahy. (UBG 100)

Next?
- You might like ***Skellig*** by David Almond. There's a lot going on in Michael's life, too. He's just moved house and found someone strange living in the garage! Angel or devil – who knows? (UBG 220)
- How about ***Holes*** by Louis Sachar? Stanley Yelnats is not very lucky and he's dug himself into deep trouble. (UBG 113)
- Or if you'd like to read another Nicky Singer, try the darker and tougher ***Doll***.

FEATHER BOY Nicky Singer

➨ Robert is a tormented boy. In school, the mean and clever bully, Niker, is always on his case. Outside, he's troubled by the ghosts of an old lady's childhood. The ghosts lead Robert and Niker to Chance House, an old haunted ruin, scene of their chilling showdown.

And there are the feathers! If Robert makes a coat of feathers, he thinks the old lady won't die. But life is not that simple.

This book will make you laugh and cry as well as giving you the creeps. You have to read it, if only to find out what happened during the grape incident! You might end up running to the toilet to be sick!

11+

Shoo Rayner

FIGHTING FANTASY

Steve Jackson and Ian Livingstone

➡ Do you ever wish you could choose the way a story goes? Well, with the **Fighting Fantasy** books you are the main character, and you can do just that – though be warned: although you can decide where to go and what to do next, you can't predict what will happen once you've done it!

In each book you are an explorer, setting off on an intrepid adventure. You have constant choices, ('Will you: Drink the red liquid? Turn to p. 98. Or leave the chamber to continue west? Turn to p. 83.') Each decision could bring instant death, or the accumulation of riches that will help you further along the route.

Next?

- For other books that use gaming as part of their plots, read Diana Wynne Jones's ***The Homeward Bounders*** (UBG 114) and Terry Pratchett's ***Only You Can Save Mankind***. (UBG 129)
- For more sword and sorcery, try ***Dragonquest*** by Anne McCaffrey. (UBG 67)
- Or for space and wars between planets, try ***Midshipman's Hope*** by David Feintuch – a harder read, but a great adventure story.

There are many monsters to battle on the way (with throws of the dice predicting who wins) and only one true path to the end of your quest. You'll have to embark on the adventure again and again before you find the way through!

Susan Reuben

9-12

FIRE, BED AND BONE Henrietta Branford

➡ To a fourteenth-century peasant farmer, a dog was a very important possession. Taking one such dog – an old hunting bitch – as its central character, this story views the world from her perspective, as a revolt against the tyranny of the Church and powerful landlords sweeps through England's poorest communities.

The old bitch's faithfulness to the family she grew up with proves stronger than anything circumstance can hurl at her. Her pregnancy, the arrest of her owners, being kidnapped and forced into service by evil people, and much, much more – through it all her instinct and unerring sense of loyalty carries her through. A masterpiece of storytelling – powerful and deeply moving.

Neil Arksey

9-11

Next?

- Henrietta Branford also wrote about a wolf, in ***White Wolf***.
- Another brilliant book is Melvin Burgess's ***The Cry of the Wolf***, in which the hunter and the hunted shift roles.
- Or perhaps you want more fantasy mixed with your animals? Try the **Redwall** series by Brian Jacques. (UBG 199)
- ***And see our HISTORICAL STORIES selections on pp. 110-111.***

THE FIRE-EATERS David Almond

Next?
• You might like a breather after finishing this, but when you're seeing the world without flames again, try other David Almonds, especially ***Skellig*** (UBG 220) and ***Kit's Wilderness*** (UBG 135).
• Then? Aidan Chambers is a much harder and more demanding read, but if you loved ***The Fire-Eaters*** it is worth looking out his books and trying one, such as ***The Toll Bridge***.

➡ This is not an easy book. Violence is there on every page: in the imminent threat of nuclear war; in a fawn harried by dogs; in a school where pain and humiliation are everyday; in friendship; in the wheezing breath of Bobby's dad; and most of all in the story of McNulty, who came home from the war in Burma a broken man, and who eats fire, wraps himself in chains and runs skewers bloodily through his own cheeks for money.

Set in October 1962, when the world expected to be blown to smithereens in a single night, this is the story of Bobby and those around him. In some ways it is a history book, but in reality it is timeless. And more harrowing than the printed word has the right to be.

12+

Leonie Flynn

THE FIRE WITHIN Chris d'Lacey

➡ Do you believe in dragons? David had never thought that dragons could be real – never in a million years. Not ever. Until he went to live with Mrs Pennykettle and her daughter Lucy and found out that all kinds of things could be true.

The Pennykettles, you see, make pottery dragons. Very beautiful dragons with intelligent faces and spines and wings and big padded feet. In their house there are dragons everywhere, on every shelf, even on the cistern (David has to turn that one away before he can use the loo). Some of the dragons are very special, as David finds out when the Pennykettles make him his own pottery dragon (whom he calls Gadzooks), and he learns how to find the spark of light in the heart of the dragon that responds to being loved.

9-11

Leonie Flynn

Next?
• If you liked the idea of something becoming real, try ***Manxmouse*** by Paul Gallico.
• Or try ***Pinocchio***, a very well-known film but an even better book by Carlo Collodi. (UBG 189)
• Another great title by Chris d'Lacey is ***The Salt Pirates of Skegness***, hilariously funny and very touching too. (UBG 209)
• Or for a very different sort of dragon, read J.R.R. Tolkien's ***The Hobbit***. (UBG 112)

THE FIREWORK-MAKER'S DAUGHTER Philip Pullman

Next?
• Read more Philip Pullman – try ***Spring-Heeled Jack: a Story of Bravery and Evil***, a fast and funny tale of three defenceless little orphans or his ***I Was a Rat!*** (UBG 121)
• Other stories about spirited characters who do not give up on their dreams are ***Matilda*** by Roald Dahl (UBG 157), and the funny, feel-good ***Saffy's Angel*** by Hilary McKay (UBG 207).

➡ Lila lives 'a thousand miles ago, in a country east of the jungle and south of the mountains'. Motherless, she has grown up among the fizz and crackle of her Firework-Maker father's work. Lila's greatest wish is to become a Firework-Maker too, but her father thinks it's no job for a girl. So Lila must undertake a quest to discover the secrets of the sacred art of firework-making for herself; a difficult, dangerous quest which brings her face to face with Razvani the terrifying Fire-Fiend ...

The world of a Firework-Maker explodes from the page in this exciting story – you can almost smell the gunpowder! Lila's adventure will inspire you to have the courage to fight for the life that you want and to live your own dream.

9-11

Julie Bertagna

what a book was till I was twenty. I think I would have to say ***Danny the Champion of the World***

FIVE CHILDREN AND IT E. Nesbit

➡ Edith Nesbit's novels were among the great solaces and imagination-stirrers of my childhood. I read most of her books before the age of twelve (I seem to remember regretting having to put her behind me because I was getting 'too old'). Of all her books, *Five Children and It* and its two sequels, *The Phoenix and the Carpet* and *The Story of the Amulet*, are the ones I loved best. Amongst the most truly 'magical' stories ever written, these three may be read in any order, but they really constitute a trilogy, in which the same five Edwardian siblings embark upon a series of astonishing adventures in time and reality – themes which fascinate me to this day.

E. Nesbit's stories will seem very old-fashioned to modern readers, but they are as much of their time as books currently being produced, which will inevitably seem just as dated a century hence. And those who enjoy eccentric, wholly original characters need look no further than the opinionated Phoenix and Psammead in these three books. They're evocatively illustrated in the versions I have by the great H.R. Millar.

C.S. Lewis was a fan, too. In his book *The Magician's Nephew*, the sleeping Queen Jadis is awakened and conveyed to Edwardian London. In *The Story of the Amulet* (also by E. Nesbit), the 'Babylonian Queen' comes to the London of that same era – and both queens make use of a horse-drawn cab. In addition, on the first page of *The Magician's Nephew*, Lewis acknowledges his debt to the earlier author in a reference to 'the Bastables', another of Nesbit's fictional families.

9-11

Michael Lawrence

Next?
- Another wonderful E. Nesbit tale is ***The Story of the Treasure Seekers***.
- ***The Magician's Nephew*** by C.S. Lewis is worth reading whether you knew of the link with ***Five Children and It*** or not. (UBG 141)
- If you are of a mind to do so, take a look at my new book, ***The Griffin and Oliver Pie***. My favourite E. Nesbit stories were very much in my mind when I created my griffin (whom I love to bits).

FLAT STANLEY Jeff Brown

➡ Stanley Lambchop is squashed flat when a noticeboard falls on top of him. Surprisingly, Stanley is none the worse for his accident; in fact, he can now do all sorts of things that he couldn't do before. He can squeeze under doors and down manholes, and he even pretends to be a picture on the wall and helps to catch two art thieves.

But then things go wrong. People start laughing at Stanley, and he gets very depressed. He longs to be normal again. But how can he achieve his former shape? It's Arthur, Stanley's younger brother, who eventually solves the problem.

Flat Stanley is extremely funny. It makes you wonder about all the things you could do if you were flat. And then you begin to think about other ways of being different, and how they would make you feel.

6-8

Jenny Nimmo

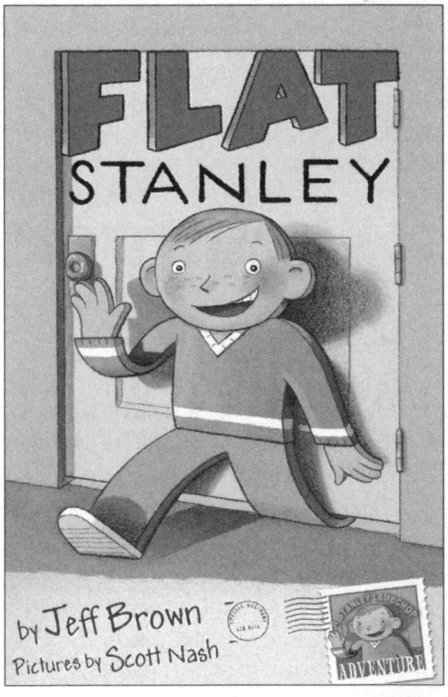

Next?
- There are more Stanley books! Look out for ***Stanley and the Magic Lamp*** or ***Stanley, Flat Again!***
- ***Bill's New Frock*** by Anne Fine is another very funny story that makes you think about what it's like to be different, just for a while. (UBG 28)
- Or what about Ursula Moray Williams's ***The Adventures of the Little Wooden Horse***, which is warm and wonderful?

FLOODLAND Marcus Sedgwick

➠ In this science-fiction story, a disastrous flood leaves most of England underwater and turns Norwich into an island. Zoe, left behind in the confusion when her parents are rescued, finds an old rowing boat and bravely sets out on a quest to find her lost family. Her journey takes her to Eel Island, run entirely by children, from which she realizes she must escape if she is to succeed in her quest.

I first came across this book while judging the Branford Boase Award 2001 (which it won!), and I was immediately drawn into Zoe's adventure. You'll find a Flood story in almost every people's history (there's one in the Bible – Noah's Ark). The difference here is that Zoe's flood happens in our future.

10-12

Katherine Roberts

Next?

- ***Floodland*** was Marcus's first novel. He has gone on to write three other excellent novels: ***Witch Hill***, ***The Dark Horse*** (UBG 58) and ***The Book of Dead Days***.
- Or you might like to track down the old Biblical and Mesopotamian legends about famous floods. (Do you believe any of them actually happened?)
- Try Jill Paton Walsh's ***Gaffer Sampson's Luck***, which is set in the same region. (UBG 89)
- Another story set in a disrupted future is Neil Arksey's ***As Good as Dead in Downtown*** (UBG 20), or why not try the challenging ***The Ennead*** by Jan Mark? (UBG 44)

FLOUR BABIES Anne Fine

➠ Simon Martin belongs to class 4C. How to describe class 4C? Let's just say they are the class that has trouble focusing, working, or even listening.

When the science fair arrives, 4C pick the project called 'Flour Babies'. Each child must have his own six-pound flour baby, and care for it at all times. The 'baby' can't get heavier or lighter and must be kept clean. As time goes on Simon (who has never got involved in anything at school before) becomes very attached to his flour baby, and he starts asking his mum questions about himself as a baby. He realises how difficult it must have been for his mum being single with all the responsibility.

Flour Babies is riotously funny, perceptive and moving. At the end of the book, my son and I both wanted our own flour baby.

9-11

Jackie Kay

Next?

- Anne Fine is one of the best and least compromising writers around. Look out for her titles in bookshops and libraries and read a selection, there's bound to be something you'll adore. Start with ***The Book of the Banshee*** or ***Goggle-eyes*** (UBG 95).
- If you liked ***Flour Babies***, you might enjoy ***There's a Boy in the Girls' Bathroom*** by Louis Sachar. (UBG 237)

FLYING WITH ICARUS Curdella Forbes

➠ 'I don't know if you have an aunt like Mildred, but if you haven't, give thanks and behave yourself, because there are some me-e-e-an beings somewhere who dish out relatives.'

This is Curdella Forbes's first book for children, and she's the most exciting new author that I've come across for ages. Her use of language is just wonderful; she swoops from the lyrical to the streetwise with a wonderful ease and confidence. The seven different stories are set in the Caribbean (the author grew up in a small village in Jamaica), but the themes – truth, bullying, love, loneliness, misunderstanding, joy, grief – will ring true wherever you come from. My favourite story is 'Slater Minnifie and the Beat Boy Machine' – what's yours?

9-11

Vivian French

Next?

- If you like short stories, try Janni Howker's ***Badger on the Barge***. (UBG 22)
- If you like stories about different places, read ***Journey to the River Sea*** by Eva Ibbotson. (UBG 129)
- And try ***Starring Grace*** by Mary Hoffman for a collection of stories about the feisty Grace, and what she gets up to with her friends in the school holidays.

teaches you how to do naughty things and get one over on horrible grown-ups.

FOLLOW ME DOWN Julie Hearn

➨ Tom comes to stay at his grandmother's house by Smithfield Market, in the City of London. Down in the cellar he discovers 'the gap', a way into the past, and when he crosses it he finds himself in eighteenth-century London with a group of people who are exhibited as monsters in a freak show. Although they are wretched and ill-treated, they need Tom's help not for themselves but to rescue the bones of a 'Giant' from a doctor who will put them on public display.

Tom's mother is suffering from cancer. She may recover, but not because of anything he can do. Still, he can help his new friends, who may look strange, but are ordinary people – kind and generous.

10-12

Jan Mark

Next?

- William Mayne wrote three novels about people who travel through time: ***Earthfasts*** (UBG 68), ***Cradlefasts*** and ***Candlefasts***.
- A writer who makes you very glad to live now and not then is Leon Garfield, whose books about low life in eighteenth- and nineteenth-century London include ***Smith*** (UBG 221), ***Jack Holborn*** and ***Mr Corbett's Ghost***.
- Try two of Sally Prue's novels. ***Cold Tom*** (UBG 50) and ***Ryland's Footsteps*** are both wonderfully strange stories about outsiders.

FOOTBALL FEVER ed. Tony Bradman

➨ Here are three volumes of excellent football stories. It is the variety and broad range of authors that makes the *Football Fever* books such a pleasure to read (and I declare an interest here – there's even one by me!). The emphasis is on good original stories, well told, so in addition to the expected names there are, refreshingly, writers you won't find anywhere else.

Football-mad boys and girls will gobble up this feast of stories about others like them around the world, playing their favourite sport. The variety and power of the stories in these three volumes is such that even those who do not consider themselves fans of football may find themselves won over by the magical allure of the beautiful game.

8-10

Neil Arksey

Next?

- Try other collections of football stories – there are good ones by Gary Lineker, Michael Hardcastle, Alan Durant, Tony Bradman, Rob Childs and Terence Blacker.
- Try Neil Arksey's ***MacB***, in which an old Scottish legend gets re-enacted on the football pitch. (UBG 150)
- Or ***The Table Football League*** by Chris d'Lacey – a light, fun read.

FRANK AND THE BLACK HAMSTER OF NARKIZ Livi Michael

➨ There are all kinds of hamster, just like there are all kinds of person. Some hamsters are friendly and some are fierce, some are loyal and some are treacherous, some are courageous and some (like poor, trembling George) are very nervous indeed. Frank is definitely the brave sort of hamster – probably the bravest of the four that live on Bright Street. But will he able to live up to his motto ('Courage!') when the mysterious Black Hamster starts calling him? Will he be brave enough to follow? Even if it means leaving his cage and venturing out into The Wild?

Livi Michael has a hamster called Frank and wrote this first brilliant book introducing him and his friends to us; she thought Frank's exciting adventures were worth telling us about, and personally I think she's right – I'm delighted to have met him! I'm sure you will be too. I'm off to read the sequel now …

8-10

Daniel Hahn

Next?

- Frank's story continues in ***Frank and the Chamber of Fear***.
- Try ***Hannibal's Rat*** by Geoffrey Guy for yet more rodent adventure.
- We have a list of rodent books on p. 202. Of these, perhaps start with ***The Rescuers*** by Margery Sharp, which is the same sort of mix of humour and adventure. (UBG 202)

FRINDLE Andrew Clements

➡ Of all the books I've read this past year (and let me tell you – I read a lot of books), *Frindle* is the best. Simple as that. It just is. I loved the hero, Nick, the other characters (his friends, his teacher Mrs Granger), the story, the ending – everything. It's priceless.

It all begins with Nick's school report on how dictionaries are made. He pesters Mrs Granger: 'I still don't get the idea of why words all mean different things. Like, who says that d-o-g means the thing that goes 'woof' and wags its tail? Who says so?' She answers: 'Who says dog means dog? You do, Nicholas. You and me and everyone in this class and this school and this town and this country. We all agree.' And from that moment Nick is determined that he can get people using a new word if he tries. By calling a pen a 'frindle', and persuading his friends to do the same, and more people, and more, he's sure he can do it. The school isn't amused, though …

I laughed loads as I read this, and really, really wanted Nick to make it. And I readily confess to a big old lump in my throat at the end … I really can't begin to convey how good, how unique it is in a few words, but just try it and you'll see.

9-11

Daniel Hahn

Next?
- ***School Story*** is another good Andrew Clements title, as is ***A Week in the Woods***.
- Or you could try ***Loser*** by Jerry Spinelli. (UBG 149)
- Don't miss my most favourite troublemaker story of them all – Gene Kemp's ***The Turbulent Term of Tyke Tiler***. (UBG 249)

FUNGUS THE BOGEYMAN

Raymond Briggs

➡ Fungus the Bogeyman lives deep underground in a damp slimy place called Bogeydom. Bogeys love the things that humans hate. They like to be cold and wet and smelly. They like their bedclothes to be dirty. They eat things like Flaked Corns and Golden Waxy Bits. They brush their teeth with stuff to make them go black and they wear wellies full of dirty water to stop their feet drying out. At night, Bogeymen come up into our world to frighten us. They make tiles fall off the roof, they hide under our beds and pull the covers off.

This is a wonderful picture book that is even *more* wonderful because when it came out a lot of adults thought it was disgusting and some schools even banned it. Of course, that was a while ago, but it is still a really funny, wonderfully disrespectful book that you should read over and over again.

8+

Colin Thompson

Next?
- There are more Raymond Briggs books to look out for: ***Ug*** (UBG 251), about a caveman, or ***Father Christmas*** (about Father Christmas – but not as anyone else has ever seen him) are both great.
- The **Asterix** books by Goscinny/Uderzo are hilarious, with some of the best puns – and names – around. (UBG 21)
- Or what about Colin Thompson's ***How to Live Forever***? It's one of the best picture books you'll ever see. (UBG 118)

GAFFER SAMSON'S LUCK

Jill Paton Walsh

➡ James and his parents have just moved from the Yorkshire Dales to the bleak, flat East Anglian Fens – a contrast that does not at first appeal. But then James makes a friend of Gaffer Samson, an old local man who, believing himself to be on his last legs, asks him to find his 'luck' (an ancient stone) which the Gaffer has lost and without which he feels unable to die peacefully. So James's adventure begins. In the company of village outcast Angey he goes in search of Gaffer Samson's luck, and in so doing learns more about the village and the landscape than he thought at the start he would ever want to know. The descriptions of the Fens are evocative, vivid and true. An undervalued classic.

9-11

Michael Lawrence

Next?
- I also recommend ***Tom's Midnight Garden*** by Philippa Pearce. (UBG 245) This, too, is set in the Fens, and like ***Gaffer Samson's Luck*** includes a visit to Ely.
- Another very good Jill Paton Walsh book is ***The Dolphin Crossing***, about two boys and the retreat from Dunkirk. (UBG 66)

THE GAUNTLET

Ronald Welch

➡ On holiday in South Wales, Peter Staunton finds a gauntlet which, local legend claims, can raise six hundred-year-old ghosts. But the gauntlet does more than that; it transports Peter to the fourteenth century, where he is Peter de Blois, son of Lord Roger de Blois, with a lot to learn. (His modern ideas about spelling leave much to be desired.) As time goes by, it all seems less and less like a dream ...

This is a thrilling story, bursting with fascinating mediaeval detail and great adventure, and seen, often humorously, through the eyes of a twentieth-century boy who cannot help but make the odd comparison and find 'the fourteenth century an evil-smelling world at the best of times'. I loved it as a boy, and still do!

Simon Puttock

10-12

Next?
- For another dream-like time travelling story, try ***Tom's Midnight Garden*** (UBG 245). Like ***The Gauntlet***, it is a beautiful mixture of feelings of discovery and loss. Or try the spooky ***Earthfasts*** series by William Mayne. (UBG 68)
- If you like feeling as though you are back in time, try ***The Wool-pack*** by Cynthia Harnett (UBG 271), or ***Cue for Treason*** by Geoffrey Trease (UBG 55).

GEORGE'S MARVELLOUS MEDICINE

Roald Dahl

➡ Most grandmothers are lovely, kind and helpful ... but not this one.

Poor George, aged eight, is left alone with his 'grizzly grunion of a grandmother'. Hoping to get her to explode, he mixes up his Marvellous Medicine. You'll need to read the book to find out the very funny list of ingredients, but it includes 'NEVERMORE PONKING DEODORANT SPRAY' and horse pills 'FOR HORSES WITH HOARSE THROATS'. The drawings of what happens to Grandma when she drinks the Medicine are hilarious.

And the story doesn't end there. What happens when George tries out his concoctions on the farmyard animals will make you laugh out loud.

Jane Darcy

7-9

Next?
- When I was young I really loved the ***Nurse Matilda*** books by Christianna Brand. Nurse Matilda is a stern nanny who comes to look after some very naughty children. It too has hilarious lists of exactly what they're getting up to.
- Roald Dahl's funny lists also reminded me of the Emergencies in Betsy Byars' ***The Eighteenth Emergency***. (UBG 71)
- Something that happens to Grandma may remind you of what happens to Alice in ***Alice's Adventures in Wonderland*** by Lewis Carroll. (UBG 11)
- A very different (but equally gruesome) sort of gran is in Anthony Horowitz's ***Granny***.

GEORGIE Malachy Doyle

➨ Georgie is in care. Life has robbed him of a voice. He shuts people out, shrinking into a brutal world of his own. In the novel, another boarder and a care worker try to get through to Georgie. In other hands this story would sound preachy but Malachy Doyle pulls it off triumphantly. It is sensitively written and exciting, classic storytelling.

Malachy himself says it was difficult to give a voice to someone who is voiceless. By concentrating on Georgie and allowing the reader to see through his eyes, he succeeds in giving his readers a tautly-written, emotional masterpiece.

11+

Alan Gibbons

Next?

- Malachy Doyle's second novel is ***Who Is Jesse Flood?*** (UBG 263)
- ***Up on Cloud Nine*** by Anne Fine is a deeply moving story of two friends. (UBG 252)
- Want something very different? Try ***Martyn Pig*** by Kevin Brooks, about a boy who ... no I can't spoil it for you. Just go ahead and read it – you won't be disappointed. (UBG 156)

THE GHOST BEHIND THE WALL

Melvin Burgess

➨ It is a Tuesday when twelve-year-old David, bored and at home on his own after school, first discovers he can get behind the walls of the very ordinary tower block he lives in with his dad. The ventilation shaft gives him the perfect opportunity to have a bit of fun; from then on, he leads a secret life, getting up to lots of mischief spying on his neighbours and discovering their secrets – old Mr Hadrian, Miss Turner the teacher, baby Georgie and old Mr Alveston who has Alzheimer's and thinks David is a ghost. But when Mr Alveston's flat is vandalised David gets the blame – and comes face to face with a ghost himself ...

This is a gripping, absolutely original page-turner about the developing friendship of a young boy and an old man. It's frightening and funny and makes you understand how people with Alzheimer's must really feel. It'll change the way you think about old people for ever and leave you with plenty to think about.

9-11

Eileen Armstrong

Next?

- Try Melvin Burgess's ***The Earth Giant*** about a half-human, half-animal giant, and the two children who do everything to help her escape to another planet. In ***An Angel for May***, Tam is zoomed back in time to the Second World War. (UBG 14)
- Another story about relationships between different generations is Nina Bawden's ***Off the Road***.
- Another book to make you think about your relationship with your grandma and what happens when she can't cope on her own is Anne Fine's ***The Granny Project***.

THE GHOST DRUM Susan Price

➨ Told almost like a folk-tale by a learned storytelling cat, and set in the freezing snow of the far north, this is the story of the young son of the Czar Safa who is kept imprisoned in a tower room. Only the witch-girl Chingis can hear his cries and help him.

But two people threaten them: Margaretta, Safa's evil aunt, who wants to rule the Czardom herself, and Kuzma, the wicked old shaman, who is jealous of Chingis's powers.

Some stories grab you by the collar from the very first page and propel you into an entirely new experience. With this novel you enter a brooding, mysterious world of myth, magic and adventure that's so extraordinarily vivid, you'll feel it's more real than your own.

10-12

Patricia Elliott

Next?

- There are two other novels in this trilogy: ***The Ghost Song*** and ***The Ghost Dance***.
- For a similar winter-myth-world setting, try Catherine Fisher's atmospheric ***The Snow-walker's Son*** sequence. (UBG 222)
- Alan Garner's ***The Weirdstone of Brisingamen*** (UBG 260) and its sequel, ***The Moon of Gomrath***; these remarkable novels combine myth, magic and desperate danger.

the first book that reduced me to a jabbering mass of uncontrollable giggles. N. Molesworth is

THE GHOST OF THOMAS KEMPE

Penelope Lively

➡ This is a brilliant story. James and his family move into an old house and things soon start going wrong. Objects are being smashed in the house and everybody blames James. Why is someone advertising as an apothecary? And whose are the broken pipe and spectacles he and Tim the dog dig up in the garden? It is only when James learns about poltergeists and calls in the local ghost-catcher that things really start to get alarming.

Funny and sad, scary and cosy, the story of bad-tempered Thomas Kempe's return to his old home is a great read. Penelope Lively loves to mingle the past with the present, and show how one makes the other.

9-11

Catherine Fisher

Next?

- Try Penelope Lively's other stories, such as ***The Driftway***, about a boy and his sister running away, or ***A Stitch in Time*** where a girl staying in Lyme Regis on holiday finds a Victorian sampler and is fascinated to know who sewed it. (UBG 226)
- Lively's ***The Revenge of Samuel Stokes***, also has an irritable ghost – this time one whose garden is having houses built on it. (UBG 203)
- For another troublesome creature, look for ***The Boggart*** by Susan Cooper. (UBG 32)

GHOST WRITER Julia Jarman

➡ You may know someone who struggles with reading and writing, or maybe you have difficulties yourself. Frankie Ruggles knows all too well what it's like. Joining a new village school, he tries to hide his problems by clowning – and always heads straight for the reading group with the thinnest books! It's unlucky for him that his unsympathetic new teacher makes no effort to understand – but there is one person who knows exactly how he feels: the ghostly boy who emerges from the classroom cupboard and leaves messages on the board. What is the boy trying to tell Frankie? In the effort to find out, Frankie makes new friends, learns not to feel left out just because he's new, and ends the story triumphantly D.B.N.T. – Dyslexic But Not Thick! Julia Jarman writes very well about school and village life in this unusual mystery story.

Linda Newbery

8-10

Next?

- Julia Jarman's many books include ***Ollie and the Bogle***, about a spiteful sprite and **The Time-travelling Cat** series, set largely in ancient Egypt. (UBG 244)
- Another book about the trials of writing is ***How to Write Really Badly*** by Anne Fine. (UBG 119)
- A really good series about a hilarious school, are the **Wayside School** stories by Louis Sachar, including ***Wayside School Is Falling Down***.

THE GIANT BABY Allan Ahlberg

➨ Alice is an only child, and she badly wants a baby brother. Her parents don't agree at all. But they end up not having very much choice in the matter, because one day, a giant baby arrives on their doorstep. And we're talking *giant*. The baby is bigger than Alice's dad.

Alice is delighted with the new member of the family; her parents less so. But the town is stuffed with dastardly characters who want to kidnap the amazing baby to make their fame and fortune.

Alice's adventures as she tries to keep the baby safe are extremely amusing, and Fritz Wegner's illustrations add vividly to the fun. Allan Ahlberg doesn't flinch at the detail of looking after a baby of such a great size – can you imagine changing its nappy?! Read and discover ...

7-9

Susan Reuben

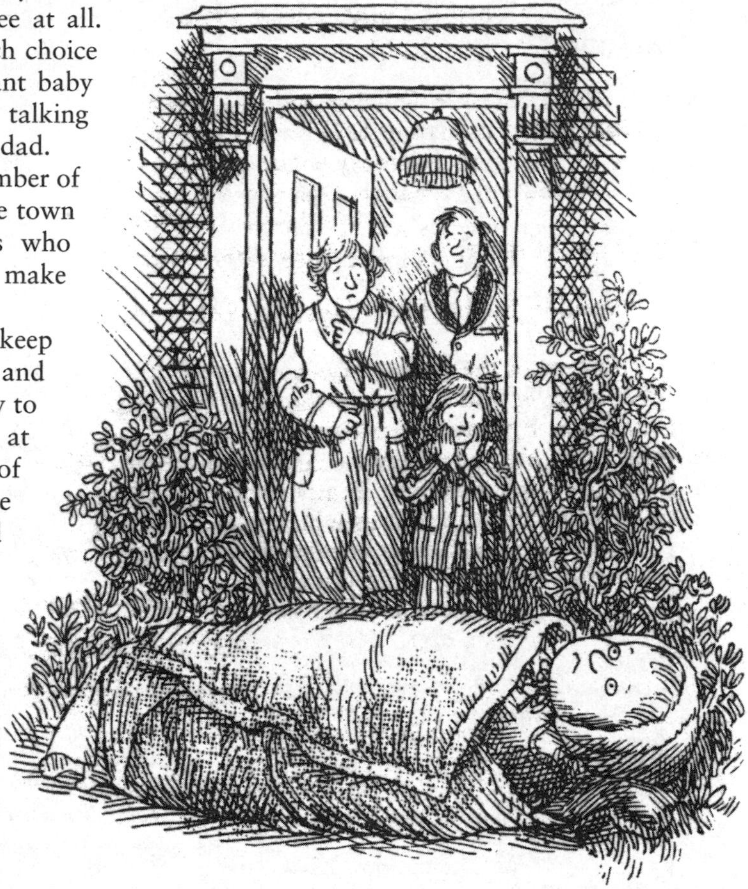

Next?
- ***Woof!*** is another Ahlberg that you should love. (UBG 271)
- Or try J.P. Martin's ***Uncle***, about a delightfully polite and well-educated elephant. (UBG 252)
- Or what about the Moomins? Read Tove Jansson's wonderful books, starting with ***Finn Family Moomintroll***. (UBG 163)

THE GIGGLER TREATMENT
Roddy Doyle

➨ This is a story all about poo. Honestly. Dog poo, in fact. In this case, a dog called Rover's poo. I'll explain a bit. First let me introduce you to the Gigglers, baby-sized furry creatures who can change colour. Their job is to look after children and punish adults who treat them unfairly. Their main weapon is dog poo which they leave in the way of any misbehaving adult. Next, you need to meet the Mack family: there's Mister Mack, a taster in a biscuit factory, his wife Billie Jean, Jimmy, Robbie and little baby Kayla. The book tells the story of why the Gigglers left Rover's poo for Mister Mack on his way to the train station and the heroic efforts of his family, the smaller-than-smallest Giggler and Rover, to save him from his fate.

Even the chapter titles are hilarious. Definitely try this if you like silly jokes and being naughty.

7-9

Abigail Anderson

Next?
- There is an equally pooey sequel, ***Rover Saves Christmas***.
- A series of books about another heroic dog are Patricia Finney's **Jack** books, starting with ***I, Jack***. (UBG 120)
- For a story as disgusting as any you can imagine, read Raymond Briggs's ***Fungus the Bogeyman***. (UBG 88)

THE GIVER Lois Lowry

➡ This is a powerful story about a future society that has forgotten love. When Jonas reaches the vital age of twelve, instead of being assigned a life-task, he finds himself selected to be apprenticed to The Receiver. This old man must pass to Jonas all the memories, beautiful and hideous, of the distant past, a time before the Community found ways to keep the population calm, polite, stable – and heartless. When Jonas learns how unwanted members are 'released', he is driven to try to escape. A gripping, and at times shocking, book, which cries out for a sequel.

10-12

Lynne Reid Banks

Next?
- Do you like thinking about the way the future might unfold? Try ***Playing the Field*** by Neil Arksey, or ***A Rag, a Bone and a Hank of Hair*** by Nicholas Fisk (UBG 197).
- ***Mortal Engines*** by Philip Reeve is set after the world as we know it has been destroyed. (UBG 164)
- ***Why Weeps the Brogan?*** by Hugh Scott is another powerful – and disturbing – vision of the future. (UBG 263)
- More haunting visions of the future occur in Peter Dickinson's **The Changes Trilogy**. (UBG 44)

GLORY IN THE CUP (Glory Gardens series) Bob Cattell

➡ Hooker, Azzie, Erica and their friends all love cricket, but it isn't until one of their teachers suggests that they make a team that things get serious. With diagrams, score sheets, tips and tests spread all through the story, you'll follow every twist of every game – and be cheering for our mismatched heroes (and heroines!) to win.

These are some of the best books about cricket you can buy. OK, there may be more serious factual ones about real teams, but if you want a story that is funny, fast and yet also manages to teach you all about those fiddly field placings and when exactly to get your fast bowler off the field and your spin bowler on, these are the books for you.

9-11

Leonie Flynn

Next?
- ***Hurricane Hamish the Calypso Cricketer*** by Mark Jefferson is the first of another good cricket series. (UBG 119)
- Or for football, try Gary Lineker's ***Favourite Football Stories***. Also check out ***Football Fever*** edited by Tony Bradman. (UBG 87)
- Stories about a gang of good friends? Try the **Jennings** books by Anthony Buckeridge! (UBG 126)

GO SADDLE THE SEA Joan Aiken

➡ Meet Felix, otherwise known as Little Tiger, a feisty and mischievous twelve-year-old living in Spain shortly after the end of the Napoleonic Wars. Since his parents died when he was a baby, Felix has lived on his grandfather's estate with a collection of mean, elderly relatives.

But everything changes drastically the night that Bernardina, the warm-hearted family cook, dies. Just before dying, Bernardina gives Felix a little bundle that once belonged to his father. 'Leave this place and find your father's kin,' she says. 'You know what I always say – go saddle the sea—' And so Felix runs away and starts the long journey to the coast …

This is a high-paced adventure story. There will be moments where your hair will stand on end and you won't be able to put the book down. Felix forms some wonderful new friendships. He also learns one or two valuable life lessons, and finds out quite a bit about his family. By the time you finish the book Felix will seem very different from the Felix you met in Chapter One, or will he …?

Candida Gray

10+

Next?
- This is the first in a series, which continues with ***Bridle the Wind*** and ***The Teeth of the Gale***.
- For other Joan Aiken, try the James III series, starting with ***The Wolves of Willoughby Chase***. (UBG 270)
- Why not check out the books Joan Aiken herself has recommended? There's John Masefield's ***The Box of Delights*** (UBG 34) and on pp. 10-11, Joan has created her own selection of adventure stories.

weedy. Chiz chiz – hurrah for St Custard's!

THE ULTIMATE READERS' POLL

YOUR TOP TEN FAVOURITE AUTHORS

1. J.K. Rowling
2. Jacqueline Wilson
3. Roald Dahl
4. J.R.R. Tolkien
5. Tamora Pierce
6. Dick King-Smith
7. Enid Blyton
8. Anthony Horowitz
9. Lucy Daniels
10. Michael Morpurgo

THE GOALKEEPER'S REVENGE

Bill Naughton

➡ *The Goalkeeper's Revenge* is a book of short stories based on the author's childhood memories, all set in the north-west of England in the olden days. Every one of these short stories is special. Some are very funny, such as 'A Bit of Bread and Jam'; others are a little more serious, such as 'The Well-off Kid' and 'The Goalkeeper's Revenge'.

Best-known among these stories is 'Spit Nolan'. It's about a boy suffering from tuberculosis who challenges one of his friends to a trolley race. Spit is the champion trolley rider of the district, but his friend has a brand-new, specially-made trolley. What happens at the end of the race is unexpected, and unforgettable.

10-12

Sherry Ashworth

Next?

- If you like Bill Naughton's short stories, there are other collections, such as ***My Pal Spadger***.
- ***The Family from One End Street***, by Eve Garnett, is an enjoyable collection of tales about a family of children growing up in the south of England in the 1930s. (UBG 78)
- You might also like ***The Otterbury Incident*** by Cecil Day Lewis, which is a funny adventure set in the post-Second World War years in England. (UBG 178)

GOBBOLINO THE WITCH'S CAT

Ursula Moray Williams

➡ Gobbolino's mother Grimalkin is a witch's cat and his sister, Sootica, promises to be just like her. They are both pure black. But Gobbolino has blue eyes, one white paw and a trace of tabby in his coat. This kitten is no use to a witch, so he's abandoned and has to make his own way in the world.

Each chapter of this enchanting book is a story in itself. Gobbolino is always finding a home, and then losing it because he is a witch's cat. The children he meets always love him because he is playful, kind and selfless, but he will have to prove that he is no longer a witch's cat before he can find the home he deserves, and become the kitchen cat that he has always longed to be.

8-10

Jenny Nimmo

Next?

- You might enjoy ***The Adventures of the Little Wooden Horse*** and ***The Further Adventures of Gobbolino and the Little Wooden Horse*** by Ursula Moray Williams. Or you could try ***The Snow Kitten*** by Nina Warner Hooke, another enchanting kitten story.
- Try ***The Worst Witch*** by Jill Murphy, about a girl who isn't very good at being a witch. (UBG 272)
- Or ***Carbonel*** by Barbara Sleigh, in which a girl buys a stray cat at the market and ends up with much more than just a house-cat! (UBG 41)

THE GOD BENEATH THE SEA

Leon Garfield and Edward Blishen, illustrated by Charles Keeping

➨ Beginning with a fiery baby being hurled out of heaven, this book brilliantly retells the legends of the Greek gods, weaving them all together into a continuous story which reads like a novel, and includes the making of the world, the war between the gods and their powerful enemies the Titans and the creation of mankind.

It's sometimes beautiful, sometimes funny and often really horrific, as the authors don't shy away from the darkness and violence of the original stories. The pictures, by the great illustrator Charles Keeping, fit the words perfectly, and help to make this a book that will linger in your mind for a long time after you've read it.

10+

Philip Reeve

Next?

• You'll find more Greek myths re-told in the sequel, ***The Golden Shadow***, which deals with the twelve labours of Hercules.

• Look out for Rosemary Sutcliff's ***Black Ships Before Troy*** (UBG 30) and ***Troy*** by Adèle Geras (UBG 248); each tell the story of the Trojan war and the wooden horse in very different ways.

• Or try Geraldine McCaughrean's ***Gilgamesh the Hero*** which reworks an even older story, from ancient Mesopotamia.

GOGGLE-EYES Anne Fine

➨ A top story by a top writer who knows how to make you laugh and feel like crying at the same time. 'Goggle-eyes' is what Kitty Killin calls her mum's new boyfriend. She hates him – to start with. Worse, her kid sister Jude seems to like him. Kitty tells the story to her schoolmate Helly, who's also having problems with her mum's boyfriend, Toad-shoes.

Anne Fine writes brilliantly on family life – the trade-offs, the rows, the jealousies. Everyone who reads this is going to recognise something about their own family. Her characters live and breathe. Kitty's mum is not a cardboard cut-out, as mums so often are in children's books. And you'll love Kitty – she's the least perfect of heroines but one of the funniest and feistiest ever.

10-12

Helen Cresswell

Next?

• Read ***Madame Doubtfire***, even if you've seen the film – the book's much better. (UBG 151) Then go on to discover the rest of Anne Fine's work. There's a list of books in the ***UBG*** on p. 285.

• Or ***The Mum-minder*** by Jacqueline Wilson about a girl who is very capable, out of necessity.

• ***The Mum Hunt*** by Gwyneth Rees takes a different look at being in a one-parent family. (UBG 168)

GOING SOLO **Roald Dahl**

➡ Billed as 'the thrilling sequel to *Boy*', this book continues Roald Dahl's idiosyncratic trip down memory lane, from age twenty, and the start of his life in East Africa as an employee of Shell, to being invalided home to Britain after becoming a fighter pilot in the Second World War a bare handful of years later.

It is indeed thrilling, from the drama of meetings with poisonous snakes to being shot at in a dogfight whilst aloft in a plane of a type in which he had only seven hours' flying experience. There are so many odd, barmy and downright peculiar characters in this journey that it makes you wonder if Dahl wasn't some kind of madness-magnet. A brilliant read and a must for true fans of the great man's books.

9-12

Chris d'Lacey

Next?

- There's ***Boy***, of course, if you haven't tried it already. (UBG 34)
- Try Roald Dahl's collection of stories for older readers, ***The Wonderful Story of Henry Sugar***. (UBG 271)
- If you like the part of this book about flying, try the **Biggles** books by Captain W.E. Johns (UBG 28) or ***Thunder and Lightnings*** by Jan Mark (UBG 242).

GOLD DUST **Geraldine McCaughrean**

➡ One day, someone starts digging a hole outside Inez and Maro's home in Serra Vazia, in the forests of Brazil. No one really knows why, but soon a *fofoca* (a rumour) begins, of a seam of gold ...

This is a book full of wonderful things – comedy, tragedy, excitement, and a whole community beset by poverty and ambition. As the holes get bigger, and miners, criminals, the teacher, the priest and even Maro fall under the lure of gold, it's only Inez who has the will to put things right. But the football pitch has already been eaten away, and the houses are beginning to tremble. What can Inez do?

An utterly brilliant story, set in an extraordinary and fascinating place.

10-12

Sally Prue

Next?

- Try another of Geraldine McCaughrean's books, ***Stop the Train***, about a character-filled community in the USA. (UBG 227)
- If you enjoyed the South American jungle setting, then try ***Journey to the River Sea*** by Eva Ibbotson – a splendid tale of mistaken identities and inheritance. (UBG 129)
- Michael Morpurgo writes terrific adventure stories. Look out for ***Kensuke's Kingdom*** (UBG 133) and ***Waiting for Anya***.

Dick King-Smith
The Golden Goose
By the creator of BABE the Sheep-Pig

THE GOLDEN GOOSE

Dick King-Smith

➡ Sorrow and Misery, a goose and a gander, belong to Farmer Skint of Woebegone Farm. Just from the name, you can tell at once what kind of a state the farm is in! But one day, Farmer Skint's luck changes. Sorrow lays a golden egg that hatches into a golden goose. She is a beautiful creature who brings happiness and luck to anyone who touches her. Her name is Joy. For all the ways Joy transforms life on Woebegone Farm you'll have to read the book.

This is a happy story that brings a smile to your face – just as if you had been able to touch Joy in person! It's a lively, quick read and there are some good hidden jokes for on-the-ball readers.

Abigail Anderson

6-8

Next?

- The **Animal Crackers** series by Rose Impey is charming and funny.
- Or try Dick King-Smith's **Sophie** books, about a young girl determined to grow up to be a farmer. Try ***Sophie's Snail*** and ***Sophie's Lucky***.
- Michael Morpurgo's ***The Dancing Bear*** is a tear-jerking animal story. For something lighter, try ***Harry the Poisonous Centipede*** by Lynne Reid Banks. (UBG 105)

Next?
- The rest of the **Tales of the Dark Forest**: ***Trollogy***, ***Whizzard*** and ***Knightmare***, so far.
- Or try the same authors' very funny ***The Lost Diary of Shakespeare's Ghostwriter*** in the **Lost Diaries** series.
- Or for another wacky and fantastical tale, try Paul Stewart and Chris Riddell's ***Muddle Earth***. (UBG 168)
- Or look out for Debi Gliori's very funny **Pure Dead** series that begins with ***Pure Dead Magic***. (UBG 195)

GOODKNYGHT! (Tales of the Dark Forest)

Steve Barlow and Steve Skidmore

➨ *Goodknyght* is the wacky tale of the fantastical city of Dun Indewood, where young Willum the swineherd can only dream of going to the famous knyght school. Life has become one long chore for him, as he must serve as the whipping boy for Symon (the son of the city ruler, Lord Gordin). It's all rather strange, but a great read with a rich plot and a totally original idea.

Alongside our friend Willum, you also meet such bewildering characters as Humpfrey the Boggart, Luigi the Pastafarian and the crossbow-toting forest maiden, Rose. They are a stunning group of characters who, coupled with a great storyline, contribute to the amazing atmosphere of the book.

Grab this book if you like a fast and furious read with all the makings of a classic.

Chris Cross

9-11

GOODNIGHT MISTER TOM

Michelle Magorian

➨ A moving and heart-warming tale about a timid young boy and a gruff old man who form an unlikely bond that transforms both their lives.

At the beginning of the Second World War, eight-year-old Willie Beech is evacuated to the countryside. He is billeted on the curmudgeonly Mister Tom Oakley, who is less than pleased to be landed with the responsibility of looking after the scrawny, awkward little city boy. However, the old man soon begins to realise that Willie is hiding an unhappy secret. Gradually, under Mister Tom's care, Willie begins to forget his sad, deprived past and grows in strength and confidence. But when a summons comes from London, Willie is forced to leave his new home and return to the war-torn city to face his mother again.

Goodnight Mister Tom is one of the most gentle, touching and powerful stories ever written.

Victoria Webb

10+

Illustration by Julie Beamond, age 11, Oakleigh House School

Next?
- If you want to read more by Michelle Magorian, try the wonderful ***Back Home***, about another evacuee, a young girl called Rusty, who returns home to England after being sent to America for five years – and finds a very different place from the one she left. You might also enjoy ***A Spoonful of Jam*** by the same author.
- For more stories about children in the Second World War, you might like to try ***Carrie's War*** by Nina Bawden (UBG 41) and ***When Hitler Stole Pink Rabbit*** by Judith Kerr (UBG 261).

GOOSEBUMPS series R.L. Stine

➠ 'Reader beware – you're in for a scare ...' is the slogan on the cover of each of these books, and each spooky story is guaranteed to give you goosebumps ... if you dare pick one up in the first place! There's *Monster Blood*, about an evil green slime that grows and grows and sucks up everything in its path; later in the series, you'll meet a new kind of slime that's blue, the most dangerous substance on Earth, with eyes and the sharpest of sharp teeth ...

Or try *The Haunted Car*, about a top-of-the-range, super-cool, shiny sports car, which has every extra you can imagine: CD-changer, power windows, cruise control ... and an evil spirit ...

Then there's *The Attack of the Mutant*, about Skipper who's obsessed by a comic superhero The Masked Mutant and falls into trouble with the most evil superhero of them all ...

These ridiculous and spine-tinglingly, hair-raisingly spooky stories are far too silly to be really scary – the best bit is that there are hundreds of titles to keep you reading – and laughing!

8-10

Eileen Armstrong

Next?

- There are lots more tense moments, unguessable plot twists and cliffhangers in store in ***Horowitz Horror*** by the master of the short story chiller (UBG 115).
- In Robert Westall's ***The Wheatstone Pond*** evil is at work with drowned motorbikes, fatal accidents and corpses.
- Or try Darren Shan's funny, freaky, fast-paced vampire saga starting with ***Cirque du Freak***. (UBG 208)
- For horror that's a bit more heavy-going, try the older **Point Horror** series. If you dare! (UBG 191)

GORILLA Anthony Browne

➠ One of the best things about growing up and becoming a parent is that you get to read all the good children's books you never read when you were a child. When my son was five we discovered Anthony Browne's amazing surrealistic picture books. *Gorilla* is my favourite.

Gorilla-obsessed Hannah lives alone with her preoccupied father. Things can be scary when you're the only child of an only parent.

She ends up spending the night before her birthday on the town with a gorilla: they go to the zoo, see a film, eat sundaes and dance in the moonlight among gorilla-shaped topiaries. Hannah has never been so happy. Then she wakes up. It was only a dream ... Or was it?

Ten years after I first bought this book, I caught my fifteen-year-old son sitting cross-legged on his top bunk, computer games forgotten, re-reading it. *Gorilla* is that kind of book. A classic.

6+

Caroline Lawrence

Next?

- There are lots of Anthony Browne books to look out for. Two favourites are ***My Dad*** and ***I Like Books***.
- Want something else quirky? Try ***Utterly Me, Clarice Bean*** by Lauren Child. More words, but they are totally wound up in the pictures. (UBG 253)
- Another strange and wonderful picture book is Shaun Tan's ***The Rabbits***. (UBG 196)
- ***And don't miss our PICTURE BOOKS selection on pp. 186-187.***

do things that Little Black can't. Little Black is very unhappy and eventually runs away. I love this

Next?

- You might also like other books by Berlie Doherty. In ***Holly Starcross***, Holly finds out who she really is when she unlocks her family's untold stories. (UBG 114)
- You might also like ***Kezzie*** by Theresa Breslin, another story of an 'ordinary' family facing hard times, set in Scotland in the 1930s. (UBG 133)
- You can see how people relate to the past of a particular place in the ***The Children of Green Knowe*** by Lucy M. Boston. (UBG 46) Or, for a very different story, why not try Theresa Tomlinson's ***The Herring Girls***? (UBG 109)
- ***And ook out for our HISTORICAL STORIES recommendations on pp. 114-115.***

GRANNY WAS A BUFFER GIRL

Berlie Doherty

➡ Jess is off to study in France for a year. Before she sets off for her new life, leaving Sheffield behind, her family share the stories that make their history: of Grandma Dorothy dreaming of escaping from her hard, dirty job buffing up Sheffield cutlery; of Grandpa Jack and Grandma Bridie finding love in spite of deeply divided families. And they all have something to add to the story of Danny, Jess's disabled brother, who died.

An ordinary family, perhaps, but *Granny Was a Buffer Girl* quietly proves that behind everyday appearances, nobody's story is really ordinary. Such stories make us who we are, giving us a sense of our past and our place. Knowing these stories makes Jess stronger as she sets off on the next chapter of her family's history. By turns funny, sad and surprising, this is a book you will remember.

10-12

Helen Simmons

A GRASS ROPE William Mayne

➡ This is a story from one of our very best writers. Mary lives in a remote Yorkshire dale on a working farm with no neighbours in view. She believes so strongly in the 'legend of the unicorn and the hounds' that she forces them to be real through the sheer power of her imagination. This may be against all known laws of science, but it happens. The plot unfolds slowly, but as you read you will come to share Mary's belief, and be not at all surprised when the unicorn is suddenly there, unmistakably real in that everyday setting.

9-11

Helen Cresswell

Next?

- You will probably want to read other books by William Mayne. Try ***Earthfasts*** (scary! – UBG 68), ***Cuddy*** (yup, scary too) and ***A Year and a Day*** (slightly younger and quite magical).
- Helen Cresswell's own ***The Night-Watchmen*** is along similar lines, and is also very scary.
- Elizabeth Goudge also writes about a lonely girl, a strange house and a magic horse in ***The Little White Horse***. (UBG 145)

Next?

- Gillian Cross has written many books, all of them good. Try ***The Demon Headmaster*** (UBG 59), or ***Wolf*** (UBG 270), or the slightly older ***A Map of Nowhere*** and the heart-stopping ***On the Edge***.
- ***Black Hearts in Battersea*** by Joan Aiken would be a good adventure to move on to. Find out about the book that precedes it, ***The Wolves of Willoughby Chase***, on p. 270.
- For another book in which a characterful elephant features, read ***Uncle*** by J.P. Martin. (UBG 252)

THE GREAT ELEPHANT CHASE Gillian Cross

➡ Imagine a two-thousand-mile journey across America with an elephant! Cissie and Tad, alone in the world and forced together by necessity, have no alternative if they're going to reach the safety of Cissie's only friend, Ketty. Cissie believes the elephant, Khush, belongs to her, but sinister Mr Jackson and his accomplice Esther believe he's theirs and pursue Tad and Cissie all the way.

Khush feels so real you could reach into the book and stroke his long trunk. He's frustrated and playful and totally unpredictable. Unpredictable – that's a good word to describe this heart-stopping story.

Jon Appleton

9-11

story so much because of the message that it portrays: that you shouldn't think of yourself as

THE GREAT PIRATICAL RUMBUSTIFICATION and THE LIBRARIAN AND THE ROBBERS

Margaret Mahy

➡ Mr and Mrs Terrapin (who are delightfully odd, as parents go) are out for the night – and what a night! All over town, retired pirates are feeling restless – they are longing for a party to steal. Three small boys are restless, too, longing for adventure. All it needs is for the wrong babysitter to arrive, and wild and yo-ho-ho-ish chaos is set to follow.

The second story, 'The Librarian and the Robbers', is one of the funniest I have ever read. It is a tale of Love! Lunacy! Lives of Crime! a Lurgy! and, of course, Librarianship! 'Unglamorous!' do I hear you cry? Nonsense! If all librarians were as quick-witted, daring, delightful and dashing as Miss Laburnum, I for one would set up home on my local library's doorstep.

7-9

Simon Puttock

Next?

- Another wonderfully silly book is ***Flat Stanley*** by Jeff Brown. (UBG 85)
- Or try ***Bob and the House Elves*** by Emily Rodda, in which a tough, manly builder finds that his house is taken over by dainty elves ...
- And of course, more Margaret Mahy, especially ***The Blood and Thunder Adventure on Hurricane Peak*** and ***The Riddle of the Frozen Phantom.***
- For more than you ever really needed to know about pirates, try ***Pirate Diary*** by Richard Platt and Chris Riddell.
- Or for a very different library, seek out Colin Thompson's ***How to Live Forever***. (UBG 118)

THE GREAT PYRAMID ROBBERY

Katherine Roberts

➡ This exciting adventure story is set in The Two Lands (ancient Egypt), when the pyramids were being built. Senu longs to work with his father in the temple, but can't pass the tests. He has strange powers which he is forced to face as he is drawn into a dark, secret plot. His father is kidnapped and his tasks become more serious and more deadly than he could ever have guessed. Can Senu challenge the evil Nemheb, save the treasure and determine his own future in The Two Lands?

If you're interested in ancient Egypt, you'll love this novel. The story is based on real history, so although it's fiction you'll learn a great deal about Egyptian life and beliefs. Senu, his clever friend Reonet, and his mischevious *ka*, or spirit companion, are wonderful characters – and the story keeps you guessing right to the very end.

9-12

Antonia Honeywell

Next?

- If you enjoyed this, you'll be glad to know it's the first in the **Seven Fabulous Wonders** series, each set in a different one of the Seven Wonders of the World. Two more are ***The Mausoleum Murders*** and ***The Babylon Game***.
- If you liked the strong, clever character of Reonet, try ***Faerie Wars*** by Herbie Brennan (UBG 77) or the **The Song of the Lioness** series by Tamora Pierce. (UBG 223)
- ***Mara, Daughter of the Nile*** by Eloise McGraw is a wonderful story set in ancient Egypt. (UBG 154)

THE GREAT TWIN TRICK Mary Hooper

➡ Jenny and Jasmine are twins. 'The outside of us,' says Jenny, 'is identical, the inside is different.' But being twins they always do things together, so it comes as a bit of a shock when Jenny wins a competition to go on holiday to Paradise Park without Jasmine. It's Jaz who comes up with the bright idea: why don't they both go? They can wear the same clothes and take it in turns to be seen, and people will think there's just one of them. 'You go swimming while I stay in, I go skating while you stay in. Easy! No one will ever find out.' The great twin trick! Well, that's the theory. But there's trouble ahead, as the twins soon discover. Two into one just won't go ... Read this book for lots of fun!

Jean Ure

7-9

Next?
- Want to try another Mary Hooper book? Look out for ***Spook Summer***. (UBG 224)
- For other books about twins try ***Lotte and Lise*** by Erich Kästner – although it is a little harder, it is very funny. Or try ***Shrinking Violet*** by Jean Ure or ***Double Act*** by Jacqueline Wilson. (UBG 67)

GRIFFIN'S CASTLE Jenny Nimmo

➡ When Dinah comes to live in the old house she calls Griffin's Castle, she is determined to stay there for ever. And after the stone lioness from the wall of the real castle follows her there, she knows it will guard her and the house from the threatening world outside.

But one by one the other creatures from the wall join the lioness in the garden. Dinah, all alone in her fortress, wonders if they are turning the world to stone. Not only the world, but herself as well ...

All Jenny Nimmo's books have a dreamy, magical feel. I think this is her best, an extraordinarily imaginative fantasy that is as gripping as a thriller, yet says serious things about the danger of cutting yourself off from other people.

Patricia Elliott

10-12

Next?
- In Robert C. O'Brien's classic ***The Silver Crown***, Ellen's early morning walk takes her on a journey through sinister unknown territory.
- Catherine Fisher writes powerful fantasies. In ***The Lammas Field***, Mick's flute-playing calls a stranger, who offers a terrible choice.
- In Sally Prue's ***Cold Tom***, Tom runs from the other members of the Tribe – but he has to avoid the demons as well. (UBG 50)
- If you like your fantasy light-hearted and fun, read Stephen Elboz's ***A Handful of Magic***. (UBG 103)

here

GROOSHAM GRANGE Anthony Horowitz

➡ When David Eliot is expelled from Beton College, his cruel and ambitious parents are in despair. Then a prospectus arrives for Groosham Grange: 'an old-fashioned school which still believes in discipline'. Determined to tame David, his parents dispatch him instantly, in the middle of the Christmas holidays.

Groosham Grange is a school for witchcraft. Staff include a vampire, a werewolf, a one-eyed dwarf and a two-headed headmaster. The punishments for non-conformity are dire, but David, a natural rebel, doesn't want to be a witch. Can he outwit the staff, with their supernatural powers? Can he escape before the initiation ceremony on his thirteenth birthday which is only days away?

This book is edge-of-your-seat exciting and hilariously funny in lots of different ways. There's satire, witty word play, and larger than life characters including David's only friend at school, plucky Jill. You'll be gripped and grinning from the first page to the last.

Julia Jarman

8-11

Next?
- There's a sequel, ***Return to Groosham Grange*** (it used to be ***The Unholy Grail,*** and you may find it with either title) and lots of other books by Anthony Horowitz. His **Diamond Brothers** books are funny, too. (UBG 77)
- Want more about wizards? Try **Harry Potter** (UBG 106); or for a more serious look at a wizard school, ***A Wizard of Earthsea*** by Ursula Le Guin. (UBG 69)
- For another child who has to survive in unlikely and hilarious ways, try Alan Temperley's ***Harry and the Wrinklies***. (UBG 105)

GULF Robert Westall

➡ Robert Westall is one of my very favourite authors – he wrote with power, passion and superb control. You can read this short book in one sitting, yet it might just stay with you for the rest of your life.

Tom, the narrator, watches his extraordinarily sensitive younger brother Andy, a.k.a. Figgis, become more and more strange. Figgis identifies so closely with the suffering of others that he seems to take on their pain, and in fact almost become them. It is the time of the first Gulf War and Tom watches in horror as Figgis starts to live out the life of a young Iraqi soldier, lying in wait for the American onslaught. Can Tom help Figgis back into the real world before it is too late?

Westall had the uncanny ability to tell a rattling good yarn and yet at the same time make you think long and hard about the issues that matter – in this case, the human cost of war. Long may his books continue to be read.

10-12

Malachy Doyle

Next?

- Westall's ***The Kingdom by the Sea*** and ***The Machine Gunners*** (UBG 150) are both exciting and thought-provoking stories about war.
- Other books about war or its effects are the harrowing ***The Fire-Eaters*** by David Almond (UBG 84) and the terrifying ***When the Wind Blows*** by Raymond Briggs.

GUMBLE'S YARD John Rowe Townsend

➡ Kevin and Sandra have been abandoned by the grown-ups. With no cash, and their two small cousins to look after, they find an old, run-down row of cottages to live in.

They're absolutely determined that no one should find out where they are, as they don't want to be split up and put into care. But when they discover that the cottages they're living in aren't as deserted as they'd thought, things get very hairy indeed ...

This book was written forty years ago, and it was one of the first to talk about children with family difficulties and not much money. Kevin and Sandra's problems are just the same as the problems of some children today – but the way the authorities deal with them is fascinatingly different. It's a really good, gripping read.

9-11

Susan Reuben

Next?

- For a modern child who has problems with her parents, try ***The Suitcase Kid*** by Jacqueline Wilson.
- For another story about children having to cope alone, read ***The Wolves of Willoughby Chase*** by Joan Aiken. (UBG 270)
- ***The Children Who Lived in a Barn*** by Eleanor Graham is about five very independent siblings who do actually live in a barn.
- A brother and sister are forced apart in Jacqueline Woodson's ***Locomotion***. (UBG 146)

HACKER Malorie Blackman

➡ Vicky thought she was in trouble when she was threatened with suspension from school for cheating in her maths exam. But this is nothing compared to the trouble her father is in, accused of stealing a million pounds from the bank where he works. Vicky and her half-brother, Gib, know he is innocent – but how do they prove it?

Doggedly, they delve into the maze of the bank's computer system, to discover an audacious crime – and a shocking surprise!

You don't need to be a computer nut to follow the fast-moving plot: *Hacker* will keep you in suspense and give you a lump in your throat, as Vicky realises that even though she is adopted, this family is where she truly belongs.

10-12

Helen Simmons

Next?

- You might also like to try some other books by Malorie Blackman, who often bases her stories around unusual ideas. ***Tell Me No Lies*** (UBG 237) and ***Pig-heart Boy*** (UBG 187) are well worth a read.
- Check out some novels by Gillian Cross. ***The Demon Headmaster*** (UBG 59) and ***The Great Elephant Chase*** (UBG 99) are both exciting books full of adventure with wonderfully wicked baddies.
- Anthony Horowitz is also another author you might enjoy if you like a storming good yarn; ***Stormbreaker*** and its sequels are well worth tracking down. (UBG 228)

If you're looking for *Hans Brinker* by Mary Mapes Dodge, turn to *The Silver Skates* on p. 219

HALF MAGIC series Edward Eager

➡ I was nine or ten when I discovered Edward Eager's fantastic books about a group of children's magic adventures. In the first, *Half Magic,* Katharine, Jane, Mark and Martha pick up a coin on the way to the library. They think it's an ordinary nickel, but gradually discover, through a series of misadventures, that it's a magic coin. The catch is, it only grants half your wish. So when the youngest, Martha, is sick of being bossed around by her siblings and wishes she wasn't there, half of her remains, while the other half flits about wreaking ghostly havoc. I was intrigued by the idea that magic might not be controllable. I also loved the range of adventures the children have, from fighting pirates to meeting their future offspring.

The children fight and argue, their widowed mother has big money troubles, they are bookish and imaginative. If magic could happen to them, an ordinary family, it could happen to anyone. Perhaps even to me.

8-10

Francesca Simon

Next?

- You should try some of the others in the series. ***The Knight's Castle***, ***Magic by the Lake*** and ***Time Garden***.
- Beverly Cleary is well known for her great series about Ramona (UBG 198) and you also shouldn't miss her slightly older, but still wonderfully funny books ***Henry Huggins*** and ***Henry and Beezus***.
- There's more sibling adventure in ***The Saturdays*** by Elizabeth Enright. (UBG 210)

A HANDFUL OF MAGIC Stephen Elboz

➡ Kit lives in a London of magic, wizards and witches. Kit's father is a witch doctor; in fact, the personal witch doctor to Queen Victoria. Stafford Sparks, 'The Royal Superintendent of Scientific Progress', dislikes magic being used. Kit's secret friend is Prince Henry, Queen Victoria's grandson. They have adventures all over London using Kit's magic carpet. For a dare they go to the Royal Zoo in the Tower of London where Henry gets poisoned by a werewolf bite. Queen Victoria discovers their friendship and Kit is sent to live with his aunt. Stafford Sparks persuades the Queen that magic is bad. Children in London start to go missing. Kit goes to the palace to try and help Prince Henry who is still ill but they get captured and taken underground to dig tunnels. Who is in charge down there? Where are the tunnels going? Will Kit be able to cure Henry from the werewolf poison and save him and all the children? Read on and find out …

8-10

Julia Lytollis

Next?

- ***A Land Without Magic*** and ***A Wild Kind of Magic***, more fast-paced Henry and Kit adventures. Also try Stephen Elboz's ***The Tower at Moonville***, about orphans who swap places. For a scarier read, try ***The House of Rats***, about children trapped in a mysterious house who find help from an unusual place.
- ***The Lion, the Witch and the Wardrobe*** by C.S. Lewis (UBG 141).Whilst playing hide and seek, Lucy hides in the wardrobe and finds her way to the magical world of Narnia …

HANDS UP! Paul Magrs

➡ *Hands Up!* is an amazing book: a zany, fast-paced and funny story (which is very unusual!) combined with interesting characters and a real gem of an idea. Our hero Jason Lurcher must overcome all sorts of problems, including an obsessive, practically insane father, a fantastically rich (and very pompous) brother, and an aggressive long-eared bat puppet. This really isn't very easy, as Jason's only thirteen!

It is forbidden in the Lurcher household to mention the golden days when Jason's father Frank was king of entertainment with his cloth sidekick, Tolstoy the Long-eared Bat. Disaster strikes when Jason is forced to pick up the family glove and become a puppeteer himself, with hideous results.

You are guaranteed to find this book interesting. And slightly disturbing.

9-11

Chris Cross

Next?

- Another twisted tale is ***Coraline*** by Neil Gaiman. (UBG 51)
- Or read Anthony Horowitz's series called **Horowitz Horror**. Especially apt is the story 'Killer Camera'. (UBG 115)
- Darren Shan writes nasty, unsettling stories – you'll love them! Start with ***Cirque du Freak***. (UBG 208)

THE HARDY BOYS

(Book 1: The Tower Treasure) Franklin W. Dixon

➡ Like many teenagers, Frank and Joe Hardy have always fancied the idea of being detectives. Unlike most teenagers, the Hardy Boys get the chance to solve a real mystery when old Mr Applegate's safe is broken into. Once the mystery of the Tower Treasure is solved, there's another, and another … No sooner have the boys solved a case and returned to the life of a normal American schoolboy, something else crops up – another case, another clue …

The Hardy Boys books are perhaps a little old-fashioned these days; the plots are all fairly similar, the heroes are a bit too clever and athletic and resourceful and kind-hearted to be true (yeuch); oh, and there are lots and lots of exclamation marks! Yes, lots! Wow!! But they're fun reads, and each will keep you hooked till you find out whodunnit.

9-12

Daniel Hahn

Next?

- ***Emil and the Detectives*** by Erich Kästner is a good old-fashioned detective story. (UBG 72)
- Or for something more up-to-date, read Anthony Horowitz's brilliant ***Stormbreaker***. (UBG 228)
- Two brothers travel the world with their naturalist father and have amazing adventures, in Willard Price's **Adventure** books. (UBG 39)
- For a girl doing the adventuring, try Carolyn Keene's **Nancy Drew** mysteries. (UBG 171)

HAROUN AND THE SEA OF STORIES Salman Rushdie

➡ Salman Rushdie's career was interrupted when one of his novels caused great offence to sections of the international Muslim community. *Haroun and the Sea of Stories* was his first novel after he was forced to withdraw from public life, and it is about a father – a storyteller in India – who loses his ability to create stories. It is up to his son to help his father, and this novel is all about their struggle to overcome those who want to stop the storyteller sharing his stories. Although it is sad in places, it is also very funny and hugely inventive. If you enjoy complicated, ingenious plots – this is the book for you.

10-12

Lindsey Fraser

Next?

- Try David Almond's collection of short stories, ***Counting Stars***. (UBG 52)
- And for something completely different, but still all about storytelling, try ***The Stinky Cheeseman and Other Fairly Stupid Tales*** by Jon Scieszka and Lane Smith – it may seem like a picture book for younger children, but look closely and you'll discover all kinds of treasures.
- Another wonderful book about storytelling is ***Bambert's Book of Missing Stories*** by Reinhardt Jung. (UBG 22)

HARRIET THE SPY Louise Fitzhugh

➡ Harriet M. Welsch is a New Yorker: her best friends are Sport, who wants to be a famous baseball player, and Janie, who blows things up with her chemistry set. Harriet's passion is her notebook where she records her innermost thoughts about her friends and her secret life as Harriet the Spy.

After school, in her spy uniform and with notebook in hand, Harriet pounds her spy route, coolly observing the lives of 1960s Manhattan dwellers. Harriet has never been caught – until now. When her friends find her notebook – and read it – Harriet is suddenly totally alone.

I am a big fan of Harriet; she is funny, eccentric and thoughtful, even as she learns some painful truths about herself and friendship.

8-11

Helen Simmons

Next?

- If you want to read more about Harriet, track down ***The Long Secret***, also by Louise Fitzhugh.
- In Lois Lowry's **Anastasia Krupnik** series you can meet another quirky heroine with a mind of her own. (UBG 13)
- You might like ***The Eighteenth Emergency*** by Betsy Byars, which is about what happens to Mouse when, despite all his plans, he gets on the wrong side of school bully, Marv Hammerman. (UBG 71)

HARRY AND THE WRINKLIES

Alan Temperley

➡ Harry hates everything about his home. So much so that he even loves his boarding school! He dreads holidays when he has to return to his vile nanny (Harry secretly calls her Gestapo Lil), who makes him do all the housework and spends his allowance on herself. Then, one day, he is told that his parents are dead. Orphaned and penniless, Harry is packed off unceremoniously, with just a few old clothes in one battered suitcase, to live at Lagg Hall with his great-aunts, Florrie and Bridget.

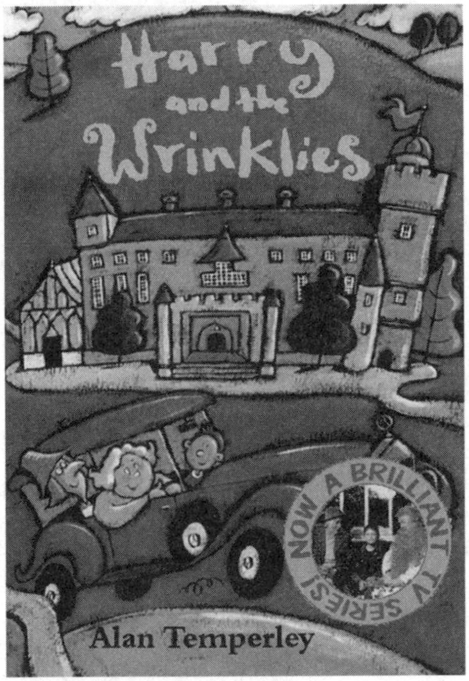

But that isn't the last he sees of Gestapo Lil. And the sweet old aunts are not your usual knitting-crazy, doddery old ladies. In fact Harry finds himself deep in plots, crime and capers with The Wrinklies, the best band of thieves since Robin Hood and his Merry Men. Like Robin's gang, Florrie and Bridget only steal from those who deserve it. Mostly. And, dropped like a lost parcel into their lives, Harry soon discovers that being a Wrinkly is huge fun – but very dangerous too ...

This is a book you'll want to read up super-fast. Full of puns and rip-roaring excitement, it'll speed you from page to page faster than Great-Aunt Florrie's Norton Commando.

Leonie Flynn

9-12

Next?
- If you want to read more of the magical Mr Temperley's books, try the sequel to this book, ***Harry and the Treasure of Eddie Carver***, and the novel ***The Magician of Samarkand***.
- If you liked the mad adventures and the truly terrible jokes, try the **Diamond Brothers** books by Anthony Horowitz – see ***The Falcon's Malteser***. (UBG 77)
- If you want to read about another orphan who finds a new life somewhere unexpected, try **Harry Potter**. (UBG 106)

HARRY THE POISONOUS CENTIPEDE

Lynne Reid Banks

➡ 'A story to make you squirm' is the subtitle to this story about Harry, a cheerful, if poisonous, centipede. In the jolly language of centipedes his name is HXZLTL. He lives with his mother in a cosy burrow underground.

Harry isn't particularly brave, but egged on by his naughty friend George, he begins to explore. We learn a lot about real life creepy crawlies from his many adventures under and on the surface. The greatest danger he faces are 'giant twolegses' or 'hoomans' (humans, of course). There's lots of fun as he and George insult each other in centipede-speak – George calls him a 'sissyfeeler' and a 'dry sandbed' (what we'd call a 'wet blanket').

Jane Darcy

7-9

Next?
- If you enjoyed this, you might like a funny book about woodlice by Penelope Lively called ***A House Inside Out***.
- For stories of a boy who always does the wrong thing, try Francesca Simon's **Horrid Henry** series. (UBG 116)
- Jeremy Strong's books often feature madcap animal adventure – try ***Krazy Kow Saves the World – Well, Almost***. (UBG 138)

HARRY POTTER AND THE PHILOSOPHER'S STONE series

J.K. Rowling

➡ It's hard to believe, with all that has happened since these books first started to climb the bestseller lists, that when I first started *Harry and the Philosopher's Stone*, I didn't even know that Harry was a wizard. Now people across the world know about Harry, his miserable early childhood and the exciting new freedom resulting from his enrolment in Hogwarts School of Witchcraft and Wizardry. Harry and his friends are familiar to us all, and their stories are enjoyed by millions of people of all ages throughout the world.

The success of the Harry Potter books is due to their popularity with children. Adults certainly enjoy them, and the publisher has even published editions with 'adult-friendly' jackets – but it was children who got there first. Their enthusiastic recommendations to friends in classrooms and playgrounds throughout the country drew the attention of their parents – and the rest, as they say, is history. Just as Harry is growing up, so are his readers. By the time the promised seventh book in the series reaches our eager hands, we will all be a good bit older. But we'll still want to know how things work out – Harry, Ron and Hermione have become good friends to us and we couldn't ever imagine losing touch.

9+

Lindsey Fraser

Next?

- Of course, there are the sequels, if you haven't already read them. So far, there is ... ***HP and the Chamber of Secrets***, ***HP and the Prisoner of Azkaban***, ***HP and the Goblet of Fire*** and ***HP and the Order of the Phoenix***.
- You might enjoy ***The Witches*** by Roald Dahl. Like J.K. Rowling, Dahl likes to keep his readers guessing right to the end. (UBG 268)
- How about Diana Wynne Jones's wonderful alternative world in the **Chrestomanci** series? A must-read for all HP fans. (UBG 272)
- ***Midnight for Charlie Bone*** by Jenny Nimmo is the story of another boy with special powers. (UBG 159)
- A smaller series that's just as inventive begins with Debi Gliori's ***Pure Dead Magic***. (UBG 195)
- Anthony Horowitz's ***Groosham Grange*** features a school as surprising as Hogwarts. (UBG 101)
- Or try some classic boarding school stories, such as Elinor Brent-Dyer's **The Chalet School** series (UBG 43); **Malory Towers** by Enid Blyton (UBG 153); or Anthony Buckeridge's **Jennings** (UBG 126).
- Or what about other kids learning to be wizards? Try Ursula Le Guin's ***A Wizard of Earthsea*** (UBG 69), or Diane Duane's **Young Wizards** series (UBG 275).

Harry Potter and the Chamber of Secrets **– illustration by Gillian Rennie, age 11, Charleston School**

HARVEY ANGELL Diana Hendry

➡ This terrific story starts very quietly, but soon explodes into an extravaganza of a book with loads going on.

Let's start with the house. As one of the long-suffering tenants remarks, no one would live at 131 Ballantyre Road unless they had to. Sadly, Henry *does* have to, and must suffer at the hands of miserly Aunt Agatha. Then along comes the irrepressibly cheerful Harvey Angell, who's some sort of electrician (researching energy fields, apparently), and everything changes. Underneath the house's gloomy exterior is the potential for fun – but there's sadness to be revealed and a mystery to be unravelled too, that might just explain why Aunt Agatha is so miserable, and might just tell Henry a thing or two about himself.

Jon Appleton

9-11

Next?

- ***MapHead*** by Lesley Howarth is another fizzing story about self-discovery. (UBG 153)
- If you like quirky fantasy, why not try ***The Hitchhiker's Guide to the Galaxy*** by Douglas Adams? (UBG 109)
- One of my favourite fantasy worlds is found in Charlotte Haptie's ***Otto and the Flying Twins***. (UBG 178)
- For books about angels, why not read the **Angels Unlimited** series by Annie Dalton? (UBG 14)

HATCHET Gary Paulsen

➡ A plane has crashed. Brian, a thirteen-year-old city boy is the sole survivor. But he has landed in the middle of the Canadian wilderness, and no one knows he is there. Brian has only one tool to help him: a hatchet. As the night closes around him on his first day alone, the hatchet seems of little use. How will he eat? How will he keep warm and evade the wild animals all around him?

This is a terrific survival story, simply written, and all the more powerful because the author, Gary Paulsen, has actually lived like Brian. He knows exactly what is required to stay alive in the cruel north.

Cliff McNish

10-12

Next?

- For another brilliant story of survival, try the classic ***I Am David*** by Anne Holm, about a boy who escapes from a prison camp and travels across Europe to find his mother. (UBG 120)
- Or, for perhaps the greatest story of animal survival ever written, why not try ***The Call of the Wild*** by Jack London. (UBG 38)
- If you want to know what happens next to Brian after ***Hatchet***, you'll want to get the sequels, starting with ***Hatchet: The Return***.

THE HAUNTING Margaret Mahy

➡ Imagine what it would be like to hear a voice in your ear, telling you that you – or someone with your name – is dead. That is what happens to Barney. He even sees the owner of the voice, a small golden-haired boy, who he believes must be a ghost.

At first Barney doesn't tell anyone about his distressing experience, but then the ghost-boy starts to write the chilling message down, and Barney's sister Tabitha notices what's happening. Tabitha wants to be a journalist, and she sets out to find the source of poor Barney's haunting.

Gradually we learn the history of Barney's family – a family that hides its strange magical talents. *The Haunting* is a beautifully-written story that never lets you go. You just have to find out who is trying to reach Barney, and why.

Jenny Nimmo

10-12

Next?

- You might want to read more by Margaret Mahy. She has great insight into the way families work, and the way she writes is always different and surprising. ***Aliens in the Family*** has a lot in common with ***The Haunting*** but for the more ambitious, ***The Changeover*** is my favourite. (UBG 43)
- A ghost story that becomes a timeslip one is Melvin Burgess's ***An Angel for May***. (UBG 14)
- For more really scary stuff, try Theresa Breslin's ***Whispers in the Graveyard***. (UBG 262)

THE HAUNTING OF ALAIZABEL CRAY **Chris Wooding**

➨ Seventeen-year-old Thaniel Fox is the best wych-hunter in London. Every night he prowls the deserted streets in search of the wych-kin – dangerous demons and spirits in every terrifying form imaginable. The city, shaken and shattered after a recent war, is brimming with evil, and the wych-kin are not the only ones to be afraid of. Behind the scenes a secret powerful cult makes a deadly pact that may have disastrous consequences.

But what does the delirious young woman that Thaniel finds in the Old Quarter have to do with any of this? Who is haunting the mysterious Alaizabel Cray?

There's horror, adventure, suspense and plenty of gore and blood around every corner– the descriptions will make your hair stand on end! You will never walk alone in the dark without thinking of Stitch-face … Read it and you'll see what I mean.

Noga Applebaum

10+

Next?
- How about ***Poison,*** also by Chris Wooding? (UBG 191)
- Try ***Mortal Engines*** by Philip Reeve, which is set in London, but not London as we know it. (UBG 164)
- You might enjoy Marcus Sedgwick's ***The Book of Dead Days*** – a chilling novel, set long ago.
- Travel with Lyra, the heroine of Philip Pullman's **His Dark Materials**, through a parallel world. (UBG 176)
- Or for something else to keep you awake at night, try ***The Watch House*** by Robert Westall. (UBG 258)

HEAVEN EYES **David Almond**

➨ Step into a David Almond book and there's no mistaking where you are – there isn't another world like it. The filter through which he sees things is quite unlike anything else you'll ever experience.

Three children run away on a raft and come across Heaven Eyes, an extraordinary girl, and her fierce and protective Grampa. They cannot help but get drawn into the lives of this strange pair, and they find out some extraordinary secrets.

Don't worry that the story might be soppy – it's not at all. It's quite dark and disturbing in places. It talks of mysteries which you only half understand. It may change, just a little bit, the way you look at the world.

Susan Reuben

10-12

Next?
- David Almond has written some of the most unusual and brilliant books for kids ever. Try ***Skellig*** (UBG 220) and the disturbing ***The Fire-Eaters*** (UBG 84).
- ***Cold Tom*** by Sally Prue is mysterious, haunting and beautifully written. (UBG 50)

HEIDI **Johanna Spyri**

➨ Orphaned Heidi is taken to live with her gruff, unfriendly grandfather in an alm hut in the Swiss mountains. Heidi has fears and unhappiness to overcome, yet she transforms the lives of her grandfather and of Peter the goatherd and his blind grandmother with her love and bright spirit. When Heidi is forced to leave and live in a grand house in Frankfurt as a companion to Klara, an invalid girl, she is overcome with homesickness.

Heidi was the first book I ever read on my own, and I read it so often I felt as if the characters were my own family. Even now, when I hear the wind in the pine tree outside my bedroom window, I think of Heidi in her hay-loft bed, eating fire-toasted cheese and listening to the music of the mountain pines outside her window. This book gave me a love of lakes and mountains – and toasted cheese!

Julie Bertagna

8-11

Next?
- Try ***Heidi Grows Up*** to read what happens next.
- Other fantastic stories of orphan girls who make good are ***Anne of Green Gables*** by L.M. Montgomery (UBG 17) and ***Pollyanna*** by Eleanor H. Porter (UBG 192).
- ***James and the Giant Peach*** by Roald Dahl is an another story about an orphan sent to live with unwelcoming relations (UBG 126), as is the more challenging ***Journey to the River Sea*** by Eva Ibbotson (UBG 129).

If you're looking for Philip Pullman's His Dark Materials, turn to p. 176

HENRIETTA'S HOUSE Elizabeth Goudge

➨ If you like dreams coming true, this is for you – I'm very much in favour of this myself. In this story, everyone gets their heart's desire, though not until there has been a magical quest that takes place on a picnic held on St Hugh's Day.

Henrietta is motherless and her father, a poet, is often away, so she lives with the family of her cousin Hugh. Her own dream is a house of her very own where everyone she loves can stay, and she has imagined it down to the tiniest detail. On the way there you will pass through sinister stone pillars guarded by an Old Man, visit a spectacular grotto and be lost in an impenetrable wood. This was one of my favourite books as a child, and as a grown-up I wrote to tell Elizabeth Goudge so. I received a lovely letter from her, and wished I'd written sooner.

10-12

Helen Cresswell

Next?
- Another classic from this author is ***The Little White Horse***. (UBG 145)
- A modern book about a different, lonely child trying to find her place is ***Rain*** by Paul May.
- E. Nesbit wrote many magical books. Why not try ***Five Children and It***? (UBG 85)

THE HERRING GIRLS

Theresa Tomlinson

➨ The setting for this story is the Yorkshire fishing port of Whitby a hundred and fifty years ago. When her mother falls ill, thirteen-year old Dory leaves her small village to live the tough life of a Whitby herring girl, gutting fish from morning till night so she can earn enough money to keep her family from the workhouse. Though the work is gruelling, the fishing community Dory lives in is warm and close-knit. This interesting novel, illustrated with contemporary photographs, shows you what life was like for a teenage girl at that time.

9-11

Kate Petty

Next?
- Read more by Theresa Tomlinson. ***The Flither Pickers*** is another story about fisher-girls in the north-east of England. Like many of her other novels, ***The Rope Carrier*** is set in her home-town of Sheffield.
- A wonderful book about growing up in a rural community is ***Granny Was a Buffer Girl*** by Berlie Doherty. (UBG 99)
- Another book about working children is Leon Garfield's ***The Apprentices***. (UBG 18)

THE HITCHHIKER'S GUIDE TO THE GALAXY series Douglas Adams

➨ A few minutes before Earth is destroyed to make way for a hyperspace bypass, Arthur Dent, an ordinary, unassuming man, is whisked away to an alien spaceship by his friend, Ford Prefect. Although Ford looks like a human, he comes from a distant planet and had been visiting Earth as a writer for *The Hitchhiker's Guide to the Galaxy*.

What follows is a series of incredible, hilarious, weird adventures where anything can happen and usually does. Our heroes discover that the planet Earth was not a planet at all but a giant super-computer built by a race of aliens. They even discover the answer to the meaning of Life, the Universe and Everything.

The best books for young readers were often not written specially for children. Once you have read this series and bought the tapes and DVDs, you will find you keep going back to them over and over again for the rest of your life!

11+

Colin Thompson

Next?
- The sequence continues with ***The Restaurant at the End of the Universe***; ***Life, the Universe and Everything***; ***So Long and Thanks for All the Fish*** and ***Mostly Harmless***.
- Not very much in the human book world comes close to Douglas Adams's series, but try Terry Pratchett's **Discworld**. Start with ***The Colour of Magic***. (UBG 51)
- For serious sci-fi – and great adventure – read the **Hope** books, starting with ***Midshipman's Hope***, by David Feintuch or ***Citizen of the Galaxy*** by Robert Heinlein.
- If you like ***Doctor Who*** there are lots of good tie-in novels around.

HISTORICAL STORIES

Past lives

BY JAMES RIORDAN

Good writers bring history to life, teach us about the lives of others, and help us understand ourselves better.

When I was a boy (my children hate me saying that!), I grew up on Stevenson's *Treasure Island*, Ballantyne's *Coral Island*, Rider Haggard's *King Solomon's Mines*, Rudyard Kipling's *Gunga Din* (it was my grandfather's party piece at Christmas), not to mention Defoe's *Robinson Crusoe*. Even though my childhood years were spent under a chimney-sweep's roof, it never entered my head to ask why all the young heroes of these novels lived in rich and conservative social settings, where women were absent and black people were slaves or servants.

How far we've come in fifty years! There are still historical novels that continue the crusading tradition (where black people and women are second-rate citizens), but they have mostly given way to a view of history that respects girls as well as boys, black as well as white, miners and peasants as well as nobles and kings.

Rosemary Sutcliff was one of the first to set a new standard for history stories by being deeply concerned about ordinary people, especially the Romans and the Britons (in **The Eagle of the Ninth** series). She also brings history vividly to life, as with the Celtic Queen Boudicca (*Song for a Dark Queen*) and the Vikings (*Blood Feud*). Terry Jones is another who gives us a vivid picture of the Vikings (*The Saga of Erik the Viking*).

Although Kevin Crossley-Holland deals with the mythical King Arthur (*The Seeing Stone* and its sequels), he provides a clear and exciting insight into British history after the Romans left. The Middle Ages are well covered by Henrietta Branford (*Fire, Bed and Bone*, on the peasants' revolt of 1381), Geoffrey Trease (*Bows against the Barons*), Cynthia Harnett (*The Wool-pack*) and Geraldine McCaughrean (*A Little Lower Than the Angels*), while

★ TWELVE SECOND WORLD WAR BOOKS

- ***Blitzcat*** by Robert Westall
- ***The Machine Gunners*** by Robert Westall
- ***Prisoner*** by James Riordan
- ***The Silver Sword*** by Ian Serraillier
- ***The Diary of a Young Girl*** by Anne Frank
- ***Carrie's War*** by Nina Bawden
- ***Music on the Bamboo Radio*** by Martin Booth
- ***When Hitler Stole Pink Rabbit*** by Judith Kerr
- ***Dolphin Crossing*** by Jill Paton Walsh
- ***August '44*** by Carlo Gébler
- ***Goodnight Mister Tom*** by Michelle Magorian
- ***The Snow Goose*** by Paul Gallico

★ MORE BRILLIANT WAR BOOKS

- ***Lord of the Nutcracker Men*** by Iain Lawrence
- ***War Game*** by Michael Foreman
- ***War Horse*** by Michael Morpurgo
- ***Little Soldier*** by Bernard Ashley
- ***Gulf*** by Robert Westall
- **Biggles** series by Captain W.E. Johns
- ***I Am David*** by Anne Holm
- ***Black Ships Before Troy*** by Rosemary Sutcliff
- ***A.K.*** by Peter Dickinson

★ FIVE FROM ANCIENT ROME

- ***Eagle of the Ninth*** by Rosemary Sutcliff
- **The Roman Mysteries** series (***The Thieves of Ostia*** etc.) by Caroline Lawrence
- ***The Mark of the Horse Lord*** by Rosemary Sutcliff
- ***Asterix*** by René Goscinny and Albert Uderzo
- ***Aquila*** by Andrew Norriss

Susan Cooper sets her *King of Shadows* in Shakespeare's time.

The lives of young people during the Industrial Revolution in both Britain and the United States are amply covered by celebrated writers like Joan Aiken (*Midnight is a Place*), Ann Turnbull (*Pigeon Summer*) and Geraldine McCaughrean (*Stop the Train*), while Theresa Breslin (*Kezzie*) and Robert Swindells (*A Candle in the Night*) recreate the hard lot of child coal miners.

Both Melvin Burgess (*The Copper Treasure*) and Leon Garfield (*Smith* and *The Apprentices*) write of youngsters growing up in Victorian London, while Laura Ingalls Wilder's autobiographical **Little House** books describe her own childhood in the Big Woods of Wisconsin, USA.

★ LOOKING AT BRITISH HISTORY - A DOZEN BOOKS:

- ***Black Jack*** by Leon Garfield
- ***Smith*** by Leon Garfield
- ***Coram Boy*** by Jamila Gavin
- ***The Ruby in the Smoke*** by Philip Pullman
- ***The Mark of the Horse Lord*** by Rosemary Sutcliff
- ***A Parcel of Patterns*** by Jill Paton Walsh
- ***A Little Lower Than the Angels*** by Geraldine McCaughrean
- ***The Apprentices*** by Leon Garfield
- **Horrible Histories** by Terry Deary
- ***Knight's Fee*** by Rosemary Sutcliff
- ***Midnight is a Place*** by Joan Aiken
- ***The Wool-pack*** by Cynthia Harnett

... or look at Joan Aiken's ***The Wolves of Willoughby Chase***, for an alternative version of history.

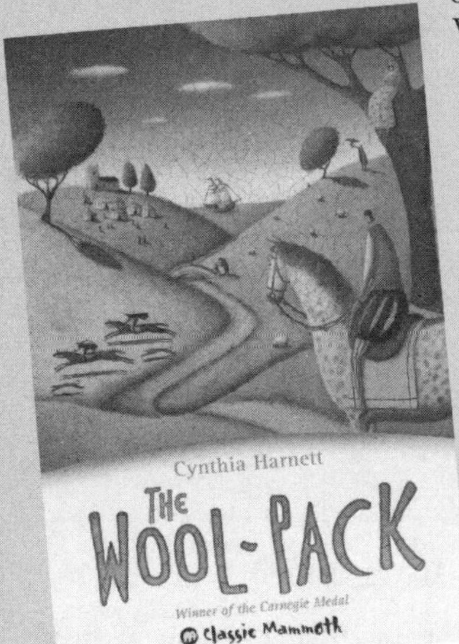

War is a theme taken up by many authors who have written books dealing with the heroic, and sometimes tragic, lives of children. Nothing can match, of course, Anne Frank's moving *The Diary of a Young Girl*. But books like Anne Holm's *I Am David*, Ian Serraillier's *The Silver Sword*, Jill Paton Walsh's *The Dolphin Crossing*, my own *Match of Death*, Michael Morpurgo's *War Horse* and several others describe war itself; while Robert Westall (*The Machine Gunners* and *Blitzcat*) and Robert Swindells (*Hurricane Summer*) mainly focus on the effects of war on young people at home in Britain. Michelle Magorian (*Goodnight Mister Tom*) and Nina Bawden (*Carrie's War*) write of the lives of children evacuated during the war – the most traumatic years of my own life!

★ MORE PIRATE STORIES!

- ***The Last of the Sky Pirates*** by Paul Stewart and Chris Riddell (from **The Edge Chronicles**)
- ***Plundering Paradise*** by Geraldine McCaughrean
- ***Treasure Island*** by R.L. Stevenson
- ***The Salt Pirates of Skegness*** by Chris d'Lacey
- ***Piratica*** by Tanith Lee
- ***Pirates!*** by Celia Rees

Here

HITLER'S DAUGHTER Jackie French

Next?
- Everyone should read ***The Diary of a Young Girl*** by Anne Frank. (UBG 61)
- Another book about the war is ***Number the Stars*** by Lois Lowry, set in Nazi-occupied Denmark.
- Or for another fictional daughter, this time a character from a Shakespeare play, read ***Shylock's Daughter*** by Mirjam Pressler, which is a slightly tougher read but well worth trying.

➡ (And she's no relation, although I'd be hugely proud if she was ...) This is a bit of a one-off book – I've not read anything quite like it. It's strange and unusual and absolutely fascinating; a story within a story about Hitler's daughter – could it be true? Anna tells Heidi's story to Mark and little Tracey, and their reactions mirror those of the world at large. If Hitler really had had a daughter would anybody have ever looked at her as a person in her own right, or would his shadow always have darkened the way she was seen? Could you love a man like that if he was your father? It's a wonderfully thought-provoking idea, and this is genuinely one of the most beautifully written books I've come across ... do, do, *do* try it.

10+

Vivian French

THE HOBBIT J.R.R. Tolkien

➡ This was a book that I can honestly say changed my life!

The Hobbit was my first introduction to Middle Earth, Tolkien's mediaeval world of magic, monsters and fantastic quests. Up until then, 'fantasy' had always implied fairy tales – charming bedtime stories for young children. But Tolkien's characters, the stories, the plots, the intrigues – the story of Bilbo's travels made a huge and lasting impression on me (though when I read the book I was twenty years old!).

Gandalf the Grey, Smaug the Dragon, Shelob the Giant Spider and, of course, Gollum have all become household names. With *The Hobbit* and *The Lord of the Rings*, the whole fantasy genre gained a maturity and authenticity it never had before. Tolkien's universe was a huge influence over all the role-playing games to come, from Dungeons and Dragons to Warhammer and of course, Fighting Fantasy. But let's not forget that *The Hobbit* is also a jolly good read, too!

10+

Steve Jackson

Next?
- If you're ready to graduate to the grandfather of all fantasy fiction, plunge straight into the massive and magnificent ***The Lord of the Rings***. (UBG 148)
- You might appreciate Paul Stewart and Chris Riddell's very funny parody fantasy, ***Muddle Earth***. (UBG 168)
- If you haven't tried **Fighting Fantasy** (written by Steve in collaboration with Ian Livingstone), you can find out more about it on p. 83.
- Try some Robin Jarvis – fantasy in a rather different vein. There's **The Deptford Mice Trilogy** (UBG 60) and **The Whitby Witches Trilogy** (UBG 262).
- ***And don't miss our FANTASY STORIES choices on pp. 79-81.***

Here

THE HODGEHEG Dick King-Smith

Next?
- Any other Dick King-Smith book, though ***The Sheep-Pig*** is probably my favourite. (UBG 218)
- Colin Dann's **The Animals of Farthing Wood** series is great. (UBG 17)
- Or for the story of a shipwrecked mouse, try ***Abel's Island*** by William Steig. (UBG 8)

➡ If you are very lucky you might have hedgehogs living in your garden. This charming story shows you life from their point of view. The hero is a young hedgehog called Victor Maximilian St George ('Max' for short). After yet another hedgehog's tragic death, brave Max sets out to find a way to cross the road safely. His explorations lead him into great danger, including a close encounter with a bicycle, which gives him a nasty bump on the head and makes him get all his words muddled up. That's when he starts calling himself a 'hodgeheg'. The solution he finally finds will make you laugh and wish you could be there to see it. This is a fun, quick read which will show you familiar things in an unfamiliar way.

9+

Abigail Anderson

The Hobbit by J.R.R. Tolkien. I loved it because my father read it to me. He used lots of different

HOLES Louis Sachar

➡ *Holes* really is a miracle of a book – a fast, involving read that seems very simple on the face of it, but which conceals an incredibly clever structure that's packed with surprises.

It tells the story of the oddly named Stanley Yelnats, who finds himself arrested for stealing a pair of trainers and sent to a terrible American prison where he is condemned to dig endless holes in a huge, dried-up lake. Stanley comes to realise that there's a reason for this seemingly pointless task. His survival, his friendship with the other prisoners (all brilliantly characterised) and his eventual salvation provide the main thrust of the narrative, as secrets, buried in the past, come to the surface in the most unexpected of ways.

I read this short novel in the same week as my twelve-year-old son and we both enjoyed it equally. Like all the best children's books, it has enormous adult appeal. I thought it quite simply amazing.

9+

Anthony Horowitz

Next?

- Everything Louis Sachar has written, including ***Stanley Yelnats' Survival Guide to Camp Green Lake***, ***The Boy Who Lost His Face*** (UBG 35) and ***There's a Boy in the Girls' Bathroom*** (UBG 237).
- Jerry Spinelli is another American who spins a mighty tale; try ***The Mighty Crashman*** (UBG 160), and ***Stargirl*** (UBG 225).
- Natalie Babbitt's ***Tuck Everlasting*** is about a girl who finds herself in a strange place which leads her to making an extraordinary decision. (UBG 248)

COMPETITION WINNER

HOLES Louis Sachar

➡ *Holes* is about a poor boy called Stanley Yelnats who has really bad luck. After being falsely accused of stealing a pair of trainers, he is sent to Camp Green Lake for boys who have done something wrong.

Stanley and the other boys have to dig holes every day. Now, I know you're thinking, 'Oh, so what? It's just a hole.' But would you like to dig holes that are five feet wide and as long as your shovel? So what would you do? I know you're probably thinking, 'I would just run away,' but there's nothing for miles.

You can't help but read and read. Before you pick up the book make sure you allow lots of time to read before your normal 'lights out'. The book is so funny and extremely serious. It's got the cleverest plots and problems. Let's hope something good happens to Stanley.

Gemma Owens, age 10, St Paul's School

THE ULTIMATE READERS' POLL

YOUR TOP TEN SAD BOOKS

1. Vicky Angel by Jacqueline Wilson
2. Goodnight Mister Tom by Michelle Magorian
3. A Series of Unfortunate Events: The Bad Beginning by Lemony Snicket
4. The Lord of the Rings by J.R.R. Tolkien
5. Black Beauty by Anna Sewell
6. Out of the Ashes by Michael Morpurgo
7. The Cat Mummy by Jacqueline Wilson
8. Chinese Cinderella by Adeline Yen Mah
9. The Suitcase Kid by Jacqueline Wilson
10. The Diary of a Young Girl by Anne Frank

HOLLY STARCROSS

Berlie Doherty

➡ With three step-siblings and a step-father who tries hard – perhaps too hard – to be the perfect father, the one constant in teenaged Holly's life is her cold, troubled mother. When her father reappears, she proves a willing, and then delighted abductee and they run away. With him she feels loved and free to love. She also meets members of his family she didn't know existed and begins to learn how she is connected to them, through her talents and interests. Holly has a big decision to make – which of her parents should she live with? In the end, her parents learn as much about their roles in Holly's life as she does about where she wants to be.

11+

Lindsey Fraser

Next?
- Try Anne Fine's ***Flour Babies***, about a boy who is given responsibility for a bag of flour and has to treat it with all the care he would treat a baby. (UBG 86)
- ***The Snake-Stone*** also by Berlie Doherty, tells of another complicated family set-up, triggered by a boy's curiosity to find out who his real mother is. (UBG 221)
- In Tim Bowler's ***Starseeker***, the loss of a father casts shadows over the life of both the son and the mother.

HOMECOMING Cynthia Voigt

➡ This is one of those books – the best sort of books – where the author creates real characters that you care about and puts them slap bang in the middle of a crisis. You're willing them to succeed, you're scared stiff they won't, and the book is just about the most important thing in your life until you find out what happens.

Dicey, aged thirteen, is left in a car park with her younger brothers and sister. When her mentally-disturbed mother fails to return, Dicey sees no alternative but to set off across America to try to find a long-lost aunt and a place to call home. The children sleep rough, go hungry, have many near-disasters, and walk, mile after mile after mile.

The characters are beautifully drawn – they're so different and yet so close. There is humour, sadness and wisdom in this story, and my whole family loved it. It's a long book but stick with it, because the ending is tremendous.

10-12

Malachy Doyle

Next?
- There are six more books about the Tillerman family: try ***Dicey's Song*** and ***A Solitary Blue***.
- Another very moving American novel is ***Bridge to Terabithia*** by Katherine Paterson. (UBG 36)
- A wonderful novel set in the middle of nowhere in America is ***Stop the Train*** by Geraldine McCaughrean (UBG 227)
- Another excellent book about trying to find a home is ***I Am David*** by Anne Holm. (UBG 120)

THE HOMEWARD BOUNDERS Diana Wynne Jones

➡ Jamie loves life in his dirty, slummy city. He loves football, and exploring – but one day he blunders into a place where 'They' are playing a game. 'They' make Jamie a Homeward Bounder, fated to be dragged from one world to another until he finds Home again. But there are a multitude of different worlds, and it looks as though Jamie's search will go on for a long, long time.

This is a marvellous adventure, full of extraordinary characters and worlds that you'll remember for a long time. It's perhaps the most powerful and haunting of Diana Wynne Jones's children's books, and Jamie's journey through so many different worlds – some fun to live in and some most definitely not – will keep you transfixed to the end.

11+

Sally Prue

Next?
- Diana Wynne Jones carries the multi-world idea through many books. For a really hilarious story, try ***Charmed Life***, or read any of her other **Worlds of Chrestomanci** books. (UBG 272) Diana's ***Eight Days of Luke*** is a great read too. (UBG 71)
- ***The Wish List*** by Eoin Colfer is about struggling with life – and death. (UBG 267)
- Or if the gaming appeals to you, how about ***Only You Can Save Mankind*** by Terry Pratchett? (UBG 129)

on and read *The Lord of The Rings*.

HOOT Carl Hiaasen

➡ Carl Hiaasen has long beguiled older readers with stories about the havoc being wrought by avaricious, land-hungry property developers on the flora and fauna of his beloved Florida. Not an obvious subject for a children's novel, but by bringing into his story pupils from a local school – Dan, the loathsome bully; Roy, his long-suffering victim; an unlikely maiden in shining armour in the Amazonian form of Beatrice Leep; not to mention some burrowing owls, he bridges the gap as though it were the most natural thing in the world. Exciting and thought-provoking from the word go, *Hoot* is full of twists and cliff-hangers, spiced overall with Hiaasen's unique brand of humour. It will stay in your mind long after you have finished it.

11+

Michael Bond

Next?
• Louis Sachar's *Holes* is amazing and equally twisty. (UBG 113)
• For another book about conserving wildlife, read *Kite* by Melvin Burgess. (UBG 136)
• Peter Carey is another author who usually writes for adults; his funny, snappy book for younger readers is *The Big Bazoohley*. (UBG 27)

HORNBLOWER series C.S. Forester

➡ Horatio Hornblower is an unlikely hero. He's a 'weedy youth' who is clumsy, stutters, blushes bright pink and gets seasick before his ship has even left the harbour. But he has always dreamed of going to sea. As a 'lonely little boy' he'd sit in an empty pig trough pretending he was captain of his own ship.

Horatio's first trip to sea starts badly. Homesick, seasick and bullied, he challenges his tormentor to a duel, secretly hoping the bully will kill him and end his misery. But the plan doesn't work and Horatio survives. After that, adventures come so fast that he doesn't have time to be homesick. He has lots of challenges to face, from climbing the rigging when he's scared of heights to his first shocking experiences of warfare.

This book is a terrific adventure story. But it's more than that. It's the story of a shy, thoughtful teenager who's plunged into some nightmare situations and has to grow up, far too quickly, but who discovers qualities in himself he never knew he had.

9-12

Susan Gates

Next?
• Read more of Horatio's adventures in *Hornblower and the Hotspur*. If you're really hooked, follow his naval career right up to Admiral!
• There's a story about C.S. Forester himself in Roald Dahl's *The Wonderful Story of Henry Sugar*. (UBG 271)
• For adventure set at sea and in places foreign, try *Treasure Island* by R.L. Stevenson (UBG 247), or *Plundering Paradise* by Geraldine McCaughrean.
• For brilliant action at sea read the *Sharpe* books by Bernard Cornwell, starting with *Sharpe's Rifles*.

HOROWITZ HORROR

Anthony Horowitz

➡ If you like sweet happy stories that ease you to sleep with images of lambs gambolling in the fields and butterflies fluttering – don't read this book!

But … if you like to be scared, if you like the shivery fear of wondering what might be lurking under the bed or what nasty things might be hiding in the most innocent of objects, then these are the stories for you.

There are nine in the first collection, all short, sharp and shocking. Don't read them if you get nightmares easily – and be careful about lending them to grown-ups – they might not be able to cope!

9-12

Leonie Flynn

Next?
• If you want these stories in handy, bite-sized chunks, each is available as a slim book on its own. And you'll find even more horror from Mr Horowitz in *More Horowitz Horror*.
• If you like being scared, read the spine-chilling *Saga of Darren Shan* – and try to work out if the story really is true … (UBG 208)
• Or for a different sort of scary, try the slightly older *The Thief of Always* by Clive Barker. (UBG 239)

HORRIBLE HISTORIES series

Terry Deary, illustrated by Martin Brown & Philip Reeve

➡ How could anyone not love Terry Deary's books? The pictures are funny, the puns are awful, the facts are fascinating – and it's all rough and gory and hilarious. What's not to love?

Not that they're not sort-of-serious in their way too, and really well-researched, and all factually correct; it's just that it's really easy to forget that it's all useful and educational (etc., etc.) when you're enjoying yourself this much. After all, how many history books do you know that will tell you about glass eyes and earwax and bodysnatchers and lots and lots of toilets?

I think my favourites are *The Measly Middle Ages* and *The Terrible Tudors*, but I've not yet found one that hasn't made me laugh out loud. You can start with *The Savage Stone Age* and work your way through them chronologically, chuckling right through to the twentieth century (I'm sure that if you start you'll want to read them all ...), or just pick one at random and throw yourself in!

8-11 **Daniel Hahn**

Next?
- Try some of Terry Deary's historical fiction, such as ***The King in Blood Red and Gold*** or ***The Prince of Rags and Patches***, both in the **Tudor Terror** series.
- There is also a **Horrible Histories** quiz book: ***The Awesome Ancient Quiz Book***. Or perhaps you want a diary with important dates to impress your history teacher already filled in? Look out for a ***Desperate Diary***.
- ***And don't miss our HISTORICAL STORIES recommendations on pp. 110-111.***

HORRID HENRY Francesca Simon

➡ Do you have a brother or sister who is perfect, while you never do anything right? If so, then *Horrid Henry* is for you.

Poor Henry suffers dreadfully. His brother Peter is 'perfect' but Henry somehow manages to get things wrong. It's not Henry's fault that he doesn't tidy up, or that when he wants to buy something he has spent all his money, or that things just seem to 'happen' when he is around.

Horrid Henry is a must for everyone. Mum and Dad will enjoy him too and count their blessings that you are not like Henry (or not *very* like Henry). Henry does all the things that you would never dream of doing, but sometimes wish you could.

6-9 **Julia Lytollis**

Next?
- In ***George's Marvellous Medicine*** by Roald Dahl, George cooks up a medicine to make his grandma nicer. (UBG 89)
- Or try ***Mr Majeika*** by Humphrey Carpenter. Mr Majeika is a schoolteacher who used to be a wizard. (UBG 165)
- In ***The Worst Witch*** by Jill Murphy, Mildred is in her first year at Miss Cackle's Academy for Witches. Like Henry, she can't seem to get anything right. (UBG 272)
- For something a little harder, try ***Jimmy Zest*** by Sam McBratney, about another boy who tries hard but can't stay out of trouble. (UBG 128)

THE HOUND OF THE BASKERVILLES Sir Arthur Conan Doyle

Next?
- If your hair is not already standing on end after this, maybe you could venture to open the ***Collected Ghost Stories of M.R. James***.
- Try Agatha Christie's page-turners, such as ***The Pale Horse*** (UBG 182) and ***And Then There Were None*** (UBG 13).
- A more modern sort of horror is collected in ***Horowitz Horror*** by Anthony Horowitz. (UBG 115)

➨ Try this for size: a vast, deserted moor full of deadly quagmires. The howling of a nightmare beast. A lonely house whose owner has been frightened to death. And two servants who creep about the candle-lit corridors in the dead of night. Dr Watson is left alone to solve the mystery of the Hound of the Baskervilles, while Sherlock Holmes, the greatest detective of all time, is busy on another case.

The Hound of the Baskervilles is perhaps the finest detective story ever written. It mingles logic and the supernatural in a bewildering package that even Sherlock Holmes hesitates to unwrap ...

11+

Hugh Scott

THE HOUNDS OF THE MORRIGAN

Pat O'Shea

➨ One day, Pidge goes into a used bookstore in Galway and finds an old manuscript in which the serpent Olc-Glas lies hidden. And so an amazing adventure begins. Pidge is an ordinary boy, so when the magic starts it is all the more magical. His relationship with his sister, Brigit, has the same matter-of-fact reality about it, making the dangers they encounter all the more exciting and scary. They're real: you care.

Lots of people help – and hinder – Pidge and Brigit in their battle to help keep the Morrigan from regaining her old power over the world, and probably destroying it in the process.

10+

Diane Duane

Next?
- Try some Irish legend. There is a wonderful collection by Marie Heaney – ***The Names Upon the Harp***.
- Another story that uses an Irish legend is Nicholas Stuart Gray's ***The Seventh Swan***.
- Or try one of the books in Diane Duane's the **Young Wizards** series. (UBG 275)

HOW TO EAT FRIED WORMS

Thomas Rockwell

Next?
- More Thomas Rockwell! Try ***How to Fight a Girl*** and ***How to Get Fabulously Rich***.
- ***Chocolate Fever*** by Robert Kimmel Smith or ***Freckle Juice*** by Judy Blume are both really good.
- Try Paul Jennings's ***Uncanny!*** (UBG 251) The 'Un-' books make up a series that is fast, funny and unpredictable.
- And look out for *anything* by Jeremy Strong! ***My Mum's Going to Explode!*** is recommended on p. 170.

➨ Would you do anything for money? In this delightfully disgusting tale, Billy accepts a bet from his friends to eat fifteen worms in fifteen days – if he wins, he'll earn enough for a new bike.

When my son was nine he abandoned 'proper' books for computer magazines and graphic novels such as *Asterix* and *Tintin*.

Then, one day on holiday in California, I discovered this book. What nine-year-old boy could resist such a title? I didn't suggest he read it; I merely left it in a prominent position. He read it. I can't swear it was this particular book that got him reading 'proper' books again, but a year later – aged ten – he had finished the entire **Lord of the Rings** trilogy.

If you think books are boring, this'll definitely change your mind!

7-10

Caroline Lawrence

Here ✓

HOW TO LIVE FOREVER
Colin Thompson

➡ I'd already reached the ripe old age of twenty-two when this book came out, so I didn't get the chance to read it when I was your age. And come to think of it, if someone had given it to me then, I would probably have taken one look at it and said 'But it's a picture book! That's for babies!'

I would have been so wrong. I loved _How to Live Forever_ when I was twenty-two, and still do at an elderly twenty-nine – and if I'm not too old for picture books, then you certainly aren't.

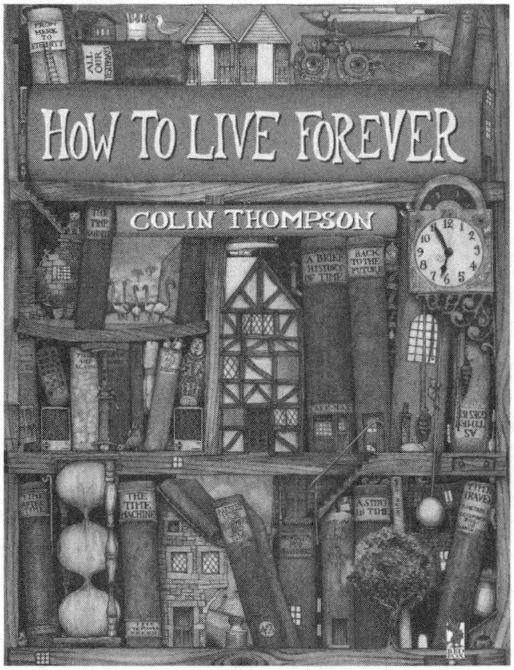

Colin Thompson's pictures are just the cleverest you'll see: chock-full of clever little jokes (and some truly awful puns) hidden away for you to discover. The story itself is lovely, and very simple (a library that comes to life, and a boy who lives there going on a quest for a missing, magical book), but it's really the pictures you'll find delightful and fun, each one jam-packed with brilliant, witty detail. Don't miss out!

Daniel Hahn

7+

Next?
• This is one of those stories that is pretty much unique, but another book with a similar feel is **The Little Prince** by Antoine de Saint-Exupéry. (UBG 144)
• Colin Thompson has written and illustrated other books – look out for **Falling Angels**, **The Paperbag Prince**, **Looking for Atlantis** and **The Tower to the Sun**.
• _And don't miss our selection of comics and PICTURE BOOKS featured on pp. 186-187._

HOW TO TRAIN YOUR PARENTS Pete Johnson

➡ Twelve-year-old Louis (pronounced 'Lou-ee') wants to be a stand-up comic. Trouble is that 'Swotsville', where he lives, is hooked on educational competitiveness – that is, exams! And worse still, it seems that Louis's parents have caught the bug, even to the extent of removing the telly from his bedroom!

Enter Maddy, his new and resourceful friend and self-styled 'talent scout', who not only guides him along his 'career' path but enrols him in her sure-fire parent-training programme.

Related through the pages of Louis' personal diary, the book is observant and very funny. Pete Johnson has an amazing ability to portray resolutely individual characters, and his story takes a revealing sideways look at over-ambitious and pushy parents. (Your own parents could probably learn something from this book too ...)

8+

Chris Stephenson

Next?
• If you like the diary form, try **Simone's Diary** by Helen Pielichaty. (UBG 220)
• Or you might want to follow Louis' example and read the book Todd lends him, **Joy in the Morning**, one of P.G. Wodehouse's funniest stories about Jeeves and Bertie Wooster. Read about the Jeeves and Wooster series on p. 203.
• For something else by Pete Johnson, you can do no better than read **Rescuing Dad**, another extremely funny and emotionally true novel, and sort of companion-piece to this one. (UBG 202)

and my heart still soars at the descriptions of Heidi and Peter running over the mountains, free as

HOW TO WRITE REALLY BADLY

Anne Fine

➡ Chester Howard has been to some terrible schools in his time, all of them a thousand times worse than yours; but Walbottle Manor is the most awful of them all. Now he's been buddied up to help the bottom-of-the-class boy who sits next to him.

Joe Gardner isn't a total loser – he can build the most intricate models; he's just hopeless at schoolwork. Until the day Miss Tate sets another one of her 'How to' projects. Wickedly, Chester sets to work with Joe on a project to 'write really badly', something Joe is naturally very good at.

Anne Fine writes the most brilliantly witty, make-you-stop-and-think stories that really keep you reading – and thinking – beyond the last page.

7-10

Eileen Armstrong

Next?

- ***Joey Pigza Swallowed the Key*** by Jack Gantos is about a loveable troublemaker. (UBG 128)
- ***Utterly Me, Clarice Bean*** by Lauren Child is a story within a story about a class project that turns out to be more lively than expected! (UBG 253)
- Part poem, part story-to-make-you-smile, ***Love That Dog*** by Sharon Creech is about Jack who learns that writing poetry isn't difficult after all. (UBG 150)

THE HUNDRED AND ONE DALMATIANS

Dodie Smith

➡ When Pongo and his mate Missis Pongo become the proud parents of fifteen dalmatian puppies, they think their happiness is complete. But the sinister Cruella de Vil, lover of all things black and white, also wants their puppies – to make a fur coat! When the puppies are kidnapped, Pongo and Missis set out on a quest to rescue them, helped by the dogs they contact through the mysterious 'Twilight Barking'.

This truly magical story has lingered in my mind since I first read it, aged nine. Cruella de Vil (devil – get it?) makes a wonderful villainess with her half white, half black hairstyle and her taste for pepper on everything. But there are tender moments too – my favourite scene is where the Spaniel's old master thinks Pongo and Missis are ghosts of his old dogs, and makes them hot buttered toast over an open fire with his toasting-fork.

9-11

Katherine Roberts

Next?

- You might also want to read ***Starlight Barking***, Dodie Smith's sequel.
- For a story written from the point of view of a dog, try Henrietta Branford's ***Fire, Bed and Bone***. (UBG 83)
- Or if you like magical stories about animals, look for ***Watership Down*** by Richard Adams (UBG 259) or, for an easier read, ***The Sheep-Pig*** by Dick King-Smith (UBG 218).

HURRICANE HAMISH, THE CALYPSO CRICKETER

Mark Jefferson

➡ Hurricane Hamish has always been special – ever since he was found washed up on a Caribbean beach as a baby, wrapped in an MCC towel. Now he's twelve, and his origins are still a mystery – but one thing's for sure: he can bowl fast. Really fast. So fast there's talk of him playing against England in the Test series. As long as villainous Rich Vermin doesn't find a way to stop him …

If you enjoy cricket and especially the fun and excitement of West Indian cricket, you'll follow Hurricane's crazy life with rapt attention.

9-11

James Riordan

Next?

- There are more adventures in ***Hurricane Hamish: the Cricket World Cup***.
- Football books abound. Some of the best are by Bill Naughton: ***The Goalkeeper's Revenge and other stories*** (UBG 94) and Michael Hardcastle: ***Dog Bites Goalie and other stories.***
- Try the Caribbean landscape in Curdella Forbes's beautiful collection of stories, ***Flying with Icarus***. (UBG 86)

HURRICANE SUMMER

Robert Swindells

➨ Robert Swindells is an amazing storyteller. His novels and short stories, which frequently deal with issues fundamental to growing up and learning how to cope, are invariably funny, sad, exciting and totally compelling. *Hurricane Summer*, set at the time of the Second World War, has a challenging and fast-moving plot centering on Jim, who worships the brave, dashing, dare-devil fighter pilot, Cocky, who lodges at his house.

Words are used sparingly but to great effect, characterisation is strong and Swindells weaves a gripping story guaranteed to captivate his readers.

10-12

Gervase Phinn

Next?

- Try ***Goodnight Mister Tom*** by Michelle Magorian. It's an extraordinary book. I once sat in a classroom and saw thirty children spellbound as they listened to this moving story. (UBG 97)
- ***The Silver Sword*** by Ian Serraillier is also about war, but described in a very different way. (UBG 219)
- ... as are the **Biggles** stories by Captain W.E. Johns. (UBG 28)

I AM DAVID Anne Holm

➨ A boy escapes from a nameless camp in a nameless country. With nothing but a map and a compass, he crosses Europe to find the mother he has never known. He is wary, distrustful, older than his years. And yet in many ways he is an infant. His journey across Europe is a kind of rebirth; he discovers new colours, such as the colour of the sea under a summer sun; new tastes, like the taste of an orange; he learns to trust: people, a dog, God.

This is a timeless story of the triumph of persistence and courage over a truly evil opponent. There is one scene of self-sacrifice which is unforgettable. And the ending is moving beyond belief.

10-12

Caroline Lawrence

Next?

- There are a lot of very good stories about children surviving against the odds. Try ***Stones in Water*** by Donna Jo Napoli, or ***The Silver Sword*** by Ian Serraillier (UBG 219).
- ***The Diary of a Young Girl*** by Anne Frank is a classic memorial to children who did not survive. (UBG 61)
- A modern story is that of Zlata Filipoviç, in ***Zlata's Diary,*** about a Bosnian girl living through the recent conflict in her country.

I, JACK

Jack Perry (as told to Patricia Finney)

➨ Jack is a very clever yellow labrador who likes to pretend he is very thick – that way, he gets more pats and more food (more food? Yes, yum, slurp, lick ...). He tells his story himself.

Jack lives with his pack, the standing-up apedogs, Front Paw (Dad), Other Front Paw (Mum), Back Paw (Terri), Other Back Paw (Pete) and Tail (Mikey). There are also other normal-walking-with-fur-and-tail (cats, ouch!) called Remy, Maisie and Muskie, slimies in the pond and flying featheries. Jack has a great life (food!) and loves everyone and everything, especially his food bowl.

He also has adventures – not always ones his pack approves of ... To find out what and how, read Jack's books. No one can write like Jack, and if you like dogs, animals, or just very funny books, you will love this.

8-10

Leonie Flynn

Next?

- If you liked ***I, Jack***, read the other Jack book, ***Jack and Police Dog Rebel***.
- If you liked it because it was funny, try ***Jimmy Zest*** and the rest of Sam McBratney's stories about that super pest. (UBG 128)
- Or for a book about a boy and a dog, try ***Because of Winn-Dixie*** by Kate DiCamillo. (UBG 25)

Heidi has with her grandfather and the tenderness he shows her.

I WAS A RAT!

Philip Pullman

➡ An absolute must for anybody who has ever considered the implications of the sort of things that fairy godmothers get up to. Our hero is a little boy in a coachman's outfit who is convinced that he used to be a rat. Many people try to use him for their own gain as he tries to sort out what has happened to him and return to the kindly couple who adopted him.

The best thing about the book is the regular use of the front page of the fabulously tabloid *Daily Scourge*, which provides both the voice of the people, and an advertisement for a heavily armed garden gnome, costing only £299.99!

8-11

Anthony Reuben

Next?

• Other books that take a different view of fairy stories include ***Clever Polly and the Stupid Wolf*** by Catherine Storr (UBG 49), ***Revolting Rhymes*** by Roald Dahl, ***The Three Little Wolves and Big Bad Pig***, by Eugene Trivizas and Helen Oxenbury, and Jon Scieszka's ***The True Story of the Three Little Pigs***.

• Other Philip Pullmans to find: ***Spring-Heeled Jack***, ***Clockwork*** (UBG 50) and ***The Firework-Maker's Daughter*** (UBG 84).

THE ICE BOY

Patricia Elliott

➡ Edward and his brother Matt have always spent summer holidays with their uncle in his seaside home, but this year they are without their father who drowned at sea the year before.

One day, Edward mistakes a stranger for his father. Close to, the man is nothing like him, but he has a job for Edward, to pass on a message to his son. Edward has never met his son, but 'He will know you,' the man tells him.

Edward begins to notice that there are other strangers in town, and even the locals may not be quite what they seem. Something very ancient is being re-enacted and Edward's father is at the heart of it.

Jan Mark

9-11

Next?

• To know more about the mythology the story is based on, try Rodney Matthews' ***Norse Myths and Legends***, or ***Axe-Age, Wolf-Age*** by Kevin Crossley-Holland. Read more about the Norse myths on p. 175.

• ***Eight Days of Luke*** by Diana Wynne Jones is very different, but you'll find many of the characters in it familiar. (UBG 71)

• ***The Weirdstone of Brisingamen*** by Alan Garner is an engrossing and exciting story about magic in the everyday. (UBG 260)

• For ancient evil invading the present, try **The Magician's House Quartet** by William Corlett. (UBG 225)

• ***And don't miss our MYTHS AND LEGENDS selection on pp. 172-173.***

ICE CAT Linda Newbery

➡ After a heavy snowfall, Tom begins to make a snowman. Gary, his friend who lives next door, is making one too, with his father's help. Tom's dad is lying upstairs in the bedroom, and he's very different from the father Tom is used to. He's extremely ill and the book doesn't try to hide from its readers exactly how serious the situation is. Tom's snowman turns out to be a cat, and he's not quite sure how this happened ... I won't give away the ending, but the Ice Cat is a personification of Tom's fear and anger at his father's illness. This is an easy book to read on one level, but it talks about complicated feelings of love, resentment and awe very movingly.

7-9

Adèle Geras

Next?

• You might also like Linda's ***Star Turn*** (a touching story about a Nativity Play), and ***Smoke Cat*** (a ghost story with a cat in it).

• Another book about caring is ***The Owl Tree*** by Jenny Nimmo. (UBG 181)

• Don't miss the wonderful ***Storm*** by Kevin Crossley-Holland. (UBG 228)

• A Jacqueline Wilson story you might like to try is ***The Cat Mummy***, though beware – it is very sad!

If you're looking for The Illmoor Chronicles by David Lee Stone, turn to p. 198

THE ILLUSTRATED MUM

Jacqueline Wilson

➨ Dolphin and Star's mother Marigold doesn't behave like other mothers: she spends the food money on ingredients for cakes that go wrong; wears bizarre clothes; stays out late or lies in bed, drinking vodka. Jacqueline Wilson shows how Marigold's manic depression means she sometimes cannot take care of her daughters and that there are no magic solutions, although Star hopes a boyfriend or her long-lost father will provide one.

An important aspect of this sometimes very sad story is how Dolphin, in particular, still loves her mother and how much she appreciates her creative, playful side, and admires her tattoos that cover her body, each one inspiring its own chapter. Dolphin herself finds refuge in drawing when life gets tough, and Nick Sharratt's artwork is cleverly worked into the structure of the book.

Geraldine Brennan

11+

Next?
- More Jacqueline Wilson! You've probably read masses of her books, but it is worth checking that you've found them all. Try ***Vicky Angel*** (UBG 255) and ***Secrets***.
- A book about a troubled girl who finds hope in an unusual way is ***Green Fingers*** by Paul May.
- A very disturbing Anne Fine book about families and friendship is ***The Tulip Touch***. (UBG 248)

INCREDIBLANIA stories Norman Hunter

➨ Welcome to Incrediblania, the wackiest, most eccentric country in non-existence!

If only our country could be run as well as Norman Hunter's incredible royal family runs theirs. Having fun with disasters is the King and Queen's speciality, with a dollop of help from their daughters, Princesses Sonia and Rosy and their husbands. The despicable gloater Count Bakwerdz is always on the carpet for his misdeeds.

I loved illustrating these stories. Norman really was a conjuror and the madness that fizzed out of his pen makes such outrageously funny pictures in your imagination that you will discover the real magic of reading.

6-8

Babette Cole

Next?
- Read every Norman Hunter book you can find, including all the **Professor Branestawm** books. (UBG 194)
- You could also try – ***Mrs Pepperpot*** by Alf Prøysen (UBG 167), ***Vlad the Drac*** by Ann Jungman (UBG 256) and ***Mr Majeika*** by Humphrey Carpenter (UBG 165).

THE INDIAN IN THE CUPBOARD Lynne Reid Banks

➨ This is a classic story of the dangers and temptations that surround magic. Omri is given an old plastic Indian, an old plastic cupboard and an old, strange-looking key. When he decides to put the Indian in the cupboard, the tiny plastic figure comes alive and suddenly, Omri is responsible for the life and safety of a tiny human being. When he lets his best friend Patrick in on the secret, things suddenly become very complicated.

This story is about temptation, and honesty and above all, the welfare of others. At the end of the book, the two boys have to make a grown-up, selfless decision. Will they be able to do it?

More adventures are in store with *The Return of the Indian* and *The Secret of the Indian*.

Karen Wallace

9-11

Next?
- Another great Lynne Reid Banks book is ***The Farthest-Away Mountain***. (UBG 82)
- Try ***Five Children and It*** by E. Nesbit, another classic about the temptations of magic. (UBG 85) And try ***The Phoenix and the Carpet***, by the same author – what would happen if a phoenix hatched in your house and took you off on a magic carpet?
- Hans Christian Andersen's fairy tales include lots of stories of toys coming to life. (UBG 76)
- ***Pinocchio*** by Carlo Collodi is another classic in the same vein. (UBG 189)

THE INVISIBLE DETECTIVE
(Book 1: The Paranormal Puppet Show)
Justin Richards

➡ Arthur Drake is an ordinary boy living in the London of today. One day he buys an old notebook dated 1936 – weird enough that his own name and address are inside it, but even more spookily, the handwriting is exactly like his own.

Of course, our Arthur has to find out more. And so he learns about the mysterious Invisible Detective who used to help ordinary people with their problems back before the war; and he also learns about the 'other' Arthur – of 1936 – who is investigating Professor Bessemer's Exhibition of Paranormal Puppets, a display so amazing that you'd think the puppets were alive ...

Two mysteries, two Arthurs, four friends and masses of clues all add up to a gripping, scary and brilliant story.

9-11

Leonie Flynn

Next?
- The series continues with ***The Shadow of the Beast*** and ***Ghost Soldiers***.
- Try some Arthur Conan Doyle. His character Sherlock Holmes was the greatest of all detectives – start with ***The Hound of the Baskervilles***. (UBG 117)
- Or for another great mystery, try ***Death and the Arrow*** by Chris Priestley. (UBG 59)

THE INVISIBLE MAN H.G. Wells

➡ A gruff stranger arrives at the Coach and Horses, demanding a room, food and warmth. He is an alarming sight, with his head and face completely covered. His name is Griffin, and he's a scientist who has discovered the secret of invisibility and used it on himself. Finding it more of a curse than a triumph, Griffin's temper and sanity unravel and he becomes increasingly violent and dangerous.

Wells's fertile imagination really hit the spot for me, and led me to imaginative works by other writers. This book was intended for adults, but I'm sure that confident young readers who love adventure and unusual goings-on (and don't need their reading to be 'modern') will enjoy this as much as I did.

11+

Michael Lawrence

Next?
- If you like ***The Invisible Man***, you should enjoy ***The Time Machine*** and ***The War of the Worlds*** also by H.G. Wells. Also try his ***Short Stories***. (UBG 218)
- Wells's books were a huge influence on dozens of authors who came after H.G., including another early favourite of mine, John Wyndham, who wrote ***The Day of the Triffids***. (UBG 58)
- A much easier book about the perils of being invisible is ***... Invisible!*** by Robert Swindells.
- Another classic about an experiment gone wrong is ***Dr Jekyll and Mr Hyde*** by R.L. Stevenson.

THE ULTIMATE READERS' POLL

YOUR TOP TEN FAVOURITE CHARACTERS

1. Harry Potter
2. Tracy Beaker (from The Story of Tracy Beaker by Jacqueline Wilson)
3. Ron Weasley (from Harry Potter by J.K. Rowling)
4. Hermione Granger (from Harry Potter by J.K. Rowling)
5. Legolas (from The Lord of the Rings by J.R.R. Tolkien)
6. Aragorn (from The Lord of the Rings by J.R.R. Tolkien)
7. Horrid Henry (from the books by Francesca Simon)
8. Matilda (from the book by Roald Dahl)
9. Alex Rider (from Stormbreaker by Anthony Horowitz)
10. Ruby (from Double Act by Jacqueline Wilson)

If you're looking for the Ironfist Chinmi books by Takeshi Maekawa, turn to p. 139

THE IRON MAN

Ted Hughes

➨ The impact of the first page is instant and unforgettable. 'The Iron Man stepped forward off the cliff into nothingness.' He pieces himself together, most of himself anyway. And then he feels hungry. The problem is, he only eats iron. Understandably, the farmers don't want him eating all their tractors and machinery and barbed wire fences, so they dig a trap for him.

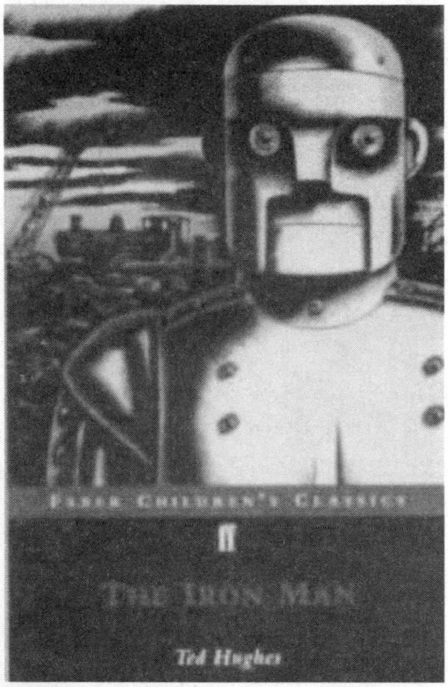

Hogarth, a farmer's son, sees him fall in the trap and takes pity on him. So begins the touching alliance between the two, where trust replaces fear. Wonderfully told by the greatest poet/storyteller of our times, you would think that was good enough. Not for Hughes. From this point on the story takes off, literally, into space, and is transformed into a pulsating battle in which the Iron Man has to save the Earth itself. Yet, essentially, despite all the frantic cosmic fireworks this remains a story with a heart – the heart of the Iron Man, who proves (as his friend Hogarth knows) that he has a kind and noble spirit.

8-10

Michael Morpurgo

Next?

- Read the follow-on, ***The Iron Woman***. Also try another Ted Hughes book, ***Tales of the Early World***. (UBG 236)
- For something totally different, that somehow feels the same (both of this world and also totally alien), try Antoine de Saint-Exupéry's ***The Little Prince***. (UBG 144)
- There are other stories about things coming to life – such as Ursula Moray Williams's ***The Adventures of the Little Wooden Horse***, or ***Pinocchio*** by Carlo Collodi. (UBG 189)

ISLAND OF ADVENTURE

Enid Blyton

➨ Jack, his parrot Kiki and sister Lucy-Ann are staying for the summer holidays with their new friends, Philip and Dinah, in a rambling, half-ruined house on top of the cliffs. When they spot strange lights at night out at sea on the supposedly deserted Isle of Gloom, they become determined to sail to the island and discover its secret.

Inevitably, they are soon up to their necks in danger – and quite literally – as the old mine tunnels beneath the island, where they have been imprisoned by a gang of criminals, start to flood with sea water …

Enid Blyton was the first professional writer for children, and I think the stories in her **Adventure** series were her best. They crack along at the same amazing pace as her **Famous Five** books (see p. 78), but though they are just as compulsively page-turning, they are longer, more satisfying reads and often have more imaginative settings. *Island of Adventure* is the first in the series.

7+

Patricia Elliott

Next?

- The books in Willard Price's **Adventure** series (***Cannibal Adventure***, for instance) have plenty of thrills too. (UBG 39)
- An excellent series of mystery adventures by Caroline Lawrence, set in ancient Rome, begins with ***The Thieves of Ostia***. (UBG 239)
- Malorie Blackman writes up-to-the-moment, cliff-hanging thrillers. Check out ***Hacker*** (UBG 102) or ***Operation Gadgetman*** for starters.

THE ISLAND OF BLUE DOLPHINS

Scott O'Dell

➠ This is the story of Karana, a twelve-year-old Native American who is abandoned on an island off the coast of California. Alone except for a pack of wild dogs, Karana shows astonishing bravery and resourcefulness.

Scott O'Dell shows us a world of great beauty: otters eating abalone molluscs in their kelp beds, a skirt made of shimmering cormorant feathers, a white dog howling in a grotto, a tidal wave – blood red in the setting sun. And dolphins, of course.

When O'Dell died, his family scattered his ashes over the glittering blue Pacific, and as they turned for home, a dozen leaping dolphins escorted the boat back to shore. A fitting end for the masterful storyteller of this classic.

10-12

Caroline Lawrence

Next?
- ***Hatchet*** by Gary Paulsen is the story of a boy surviving alone in the wilderness. It is gritty and exciting and totally realistic. (UBG 107)
- ***Walk Two Moons*** by Sharon Creech has a heroine of Native American descent. (UBG 256)
- And ***Journey to the River Sea*** by Eva Ibbotson is another story about travelling to a strange and exotic place. (UBG 129)

THE IVY CROWN Gill Vickery

➠ Megan's father rents a remote Gothic house for three months while he works on a graphic novel. Her brother Brand has not played his violin since their mother died; Megan has something on her conscience and cannot forgive herself.

The house and the woodlands around it are full of secrets. A woman was burned there as a witch, and once the great virtuoso Paganini gave a recital in the house. There is a painting of his violin on one of the doors, but the real instrument has been lost. And something very odd is happening to the pictures in Dad's graphic novel …

This is part-mystery, part-ghost story, set in a present where the past has never quite gone away.

Jan Mark

10-12

Next?
- You may enjoy ***The Ghost of Thomas Kempe*** (UBG 91) or ***The Wild Hunt of Hagworthy*** by Penelope Lively, stories where the past has a powerful effect on the present.
- In ***Tom's Midnight Garden*** by Philippa Pearce, the clock strikes thirteen and Tom opens the door into the life of someone who lived many years ago. (UBG 245)
- ***The Little White Horse*** by Elizabeth Goudge is another story about a remote house with a secret. (UBG 145)

JAKE'S TOWER

Elizabeth Laird

➠ Jake's mother has a very violent boyfriend. Trying to escape from the real world, Jake takes refuge in his imagination. There he creates a fantasy tower on an island where he will have complete control over who is allowed in. But when he and his mother have to escape from the boyfriend, Jake finds that imagination and reality can sometimes meet.

A harrowing and disturbing story that is finally uplifting. It is as compelling as it is distressing to read. Jake is a brave and inspiring boy whose imagination is his saviour.

11+

Jackie Kay

Next?
- Why not try Elizabeth Laird's story of the African boys, Mamo and Dani, two runaways whose stories are told in ***The Garbage King***? Though be warned, this is a tough, terrifying story. Her other brilliant books include the very moving ***Red Sky in the Morning*** and ***Kiss the Dust*** (UBG 135).
- A very different book about the way children can be misused is Jamila Gavin's ***Coram Boy***. (UBG 52)
- Other tense, thought-provoking novels about bullying and violence include Aidan Chambers' ***The Present Takers*** (UBG 192) and, for older readers, ***Tightrope*** by Gillian Cross (UBG 242).

JAMES AND THE GIANT PEACH

Roald Dahl

➡ Because of a terrible accident (if you can call being eaten by a rhinoceros an accident) James Henry Trotter is left an orphan. One minute he's a happy child with two wonderful parents and a lovely seaside home. The next he's sent to live with his awful aunts, Aunt Sponge and Aunt Spiker. Then one day the Aunts are suddenly run over by an enormous peach, as big as a house, and James is free to go on the adventure of his life – with a wonderful group of overgrown garden insects. They travel across the world in the peach, by land and sea and air, always one step ahead of danger.

8-10

Jane Yolen

Next?
- Try Roald Dahl's bizarre and wonderful ***George's Marvellous Medicine***. (UBG 89)
- If you want more outrageous fun, try ***Aquila*** by Andrew Norriss. (UBG 18)
- For something spookily weird, try ***Long Lost*** by Jan Mark. (UBG 147)

JENNIE Paul Gallico

other title "The Abandoned" (discard only)

➡ This is, quite simply, absolutely, the best book about cats ever written. It is also a story about a great friendship, daring adventures, violent fights and exploring new worlds.

Peter is a lonely boy living in London. One day he is in an accident and when he wakes up he has turned into a cat! He is chased out of the house by Nanny and runs out into what is now a very big, noisy, frightening world. Luckily, he meets Jennie, a kindly stray tabby cat who becomes the kind of best friend everyone wishes they could have. Jennie teaches Peter the rules about being a cat, which everyone who has ever lived with a cat will recognise. Be warned – have hankies ready for the ending; I have never met anyone who didn't cry!

10-12

Abigail Anderson

Next?
- Try other books by Paul Gallico: ***The Snow Goose*** (UBG 221), ***A Small Miracle*** and ***Mrs Harris Goes to Paris***.
- ***Old Possum's Book of Practical Cats***! Poetry, yes, but what amazing cats – the poet T.S. Eliot must have known a feline or two.
- ***Lionboy*** by Zizou Corder is also about a boy befriending cats – *big* cats! (UBG 142)

JENNINGS series Anthony Buckeridge

➡ This classic, much-loved series looks on the sunny side of life at a boys' boarding school. In *Jennings Goes to School*, our young hero goes off (in some trepidation) to Linbury Court Preparatory School, with its traditional dormitories, a common room, tuck-boxes, Matron, and squabbles ended by a cry of 'Pax!'

Here, Jennings becomes best friends with the dusty-spectacled Darbishire, son of a vicar. With each book in turn we watch the enthusiastic, and always well-meaning, pair get into one scrape after another and fall in and out of trouble, usually because of some accident or misunderstanding. There is a host of amiable and eccentric characters of all ages, notably the cool-headed but sympathetic teacher Mr Carter and the huge-voiced and explosive Mr Wilkins (Old Wilkie) who was clutching his head and saying 'Doh!' years before Homer Simpson took to the habit.

One of the joys of these books is the sheer range of language, from the lofty and involuted sarcasm of some of the teachers to the bizarre invented slang used by the pupils. The stories are varied and, though easy enough to read, are extremely well written, offering simple, cheering escapism of the finest sort. Old-fashioned as the books appear, they still deservedly have fans worldwide.

9-12

Anne Fine

Next?
- The **Just William** stories by Richmal Crompton mine a similar vein of humour (UBG 131).
- Or try ***Down With Skool*** by Geoffrey Willans and Ronald Searle, which is one of the funniest looks at school life you can find. (UBG 67)
- ***And don't miss our SCHOOL STORIES selections on pp. 212-213.***

boxed set and it looked very smart on my bookshelf!

JESSICA HAGGERTHWAITE: WITCH DISPATCHER Emma Barnes

➡ Are your parents really embarrassing? No, I mean *really* embarrassing? I bet they're not as bad as Jessica Haggerthwaite's mum, who has decided she's going to set herself up as a professional witch! Jessica wants to be a great scientist when she grows up, so having a witch in the family isn't exactly something to be proud of. Her brother, Midge, has started being teased about it at school. Even their Dad can't take any more …

Jessica has to do something. But what? She cooks up a plan, which begins with her becoming a Professional Witch Dispatcher (using only the most scientific methods, naturally). The results are hilarious. By the end, all the characters will have learnt to think about what's best for each other, and not just themselves – but will Mrs Haggerthwaite be able to keep her peculiar new job?

A lovely, funny story about a family that may seem strange, but in all the important ways is just like any other; all brought to life by Tim Archbold's great pictures.

Daniel Hahn

8-10

Next?
- There's a sequel! ***Jessica Haggerthwaite: Media Star***.
- Mary Norton's ***Bedknob and Broomstick*** is another great story about a witch-in-training. (UBG 26) And there's ***Carbonel*** by Barbara Sleigh. (UBG 41)
- There are lots of books about what it's like having different or difficult parents. Turn to p. 200 for a list.

JIGGY McCUE series

THE POLTERGOOSE • THE KILLER UNDERPANTS • THE TOILET OF DOOM • MAGGOT PIE • THE SNOTTLE

Michael Lawrence

➡ Jiggy McCue is just an average boy, but he feels like the unluckiest kid in town. Strange things are always happening to him and his best mates, Pete and Angie. He's been haunted by a dead goose, been plagued by a hideous pair of non-removable underpants and fallen foul of a computerised toilet that flushed his life away and gave him another, much worse than his own. When he finally stumbles on a teenage genie willing to grant him three wishes, he thinks his luck has finally changed, but of course nothing could be further from the truth …

With laugh-out-loud humour, wacky plot-lines and a light sprinkling of rudeness, the Jiggy McCue books have got the lot.

7-10

Kathryn Ross

Next?
- For another boy who can't stay out of trouble, try the **Buster Bayliss** stories by Philip Reeve. (UBG 175)
- In ***The Gizmo*** by Paul Jennings, Stephen is talked into stealing a troublesome toy called a gizmo and then he can't get rid of it, no matter how hard he tries. You might also like Paul's weird and wonderful collection of stories, ***Uncanny!*** (UBG 251)
- And although he's not as unlucky as Jiggy, strange things certainly happen to Johnny Maxwell, in Terry Pratchett's excellent trio of novels beginning with ***Only You Can Save Mankind***. (UBG 129)
- Another terrific, fun series is Bruce Coville's **The Magic Shop** series. (UBG 152)

COMPETITION WINNER • COMPETITION WINNER

JIGGY McCUE: THE TOILET OF DOOM Michael Lawrence

➡ This book is about a boy called Jiggy McCue and his friends. They play a computer game called 'The Toilet of Life'. Jiggy hits 'f' for 'flush' and they all switch bodies. They spend the rest of the book trying to get their own bodies back. I really liked this book because of all the wacky adventures. It was very funny and some bits even made me gasp. I always wanted to turn the page and see what happened next. I knew this book would be good because of the title and the front cover. I was right!

Alec Jenkins, age 9, The Perse Preparatory School

JIMMY ZEST Sam McBratney

➡ Jimmy Zest is a boy who is always dreaming up schemes. Sometimes they involve egg-boxes, sometimes dinosaurs, and sometimes worms. But they nearly always involve upsetting all the adults around him, especially his parents and his teachers. The plans often get his friends into trouble too, but whatever else Jimmy does, he certainly makes life for everyone around him interesting.

I love Jimmy. He's kind and warm and completely oblivious to the mayhem he causes around him. He loves his mum, but he still sold her old teddy in exchange for an egg-box (just the one, as Teddy wasn't in very good condition). These stories are hilarious – and strangely very true to life ... though I've not seen an eight-foot dinosaur being towed down the High Street – not yet, anyway.

7-9

Leonie Flynn

Next?

- Other books include ***The Jimmy Zest All-Stars*** and ***Jimmy Zest, Super Pest.***
- The **War Diaries of Alastair Fury** by Jamie Rix is a very funny series about seeking vengeance against brothers.
- Or try Henrietta Branford's hilarious books about Dimanche Diller, possibly the unluckiest girl in the world. (UBG 63)

JOEY PIGZA SWALLOWED THE KEY Jack Gantos

➡ Joey knows he is 'wired'. When he doesn't take his 'meds' he can't keep still, but must race around frenetically, getting into every kind of trouble. His home-life is chaotic, with a 'sometimes' mother, a crazy grandmother and an absent father. The other adults around him try their best to help him overcome his difficulties, but sometimes it seems to Joey that nothing will ever stop his headlong rush to disaster. His adventures are both heartbreaking and horribly funny, like the time he cuts the tip of a girl's nose off by accident ... Gantos is a master of mixing misery with bizarre comedy and this is a little masterpiece.

7-9

Lynne Reid Banks

Next?

- Read the sequels! ***Joey Pigza Loses Control*** and ***What Would Joey Do?***
- For the story of one boy's adventures when he gets sent to a place for 'troublesome kids', read Louis Sachar's ***Holes***. (UBG 113)
- Another book about triumphing over adversity is the brilliant ***Locomotion*** by Jacqueline Woodson. (UBG 146)

children's book when I was very small was ***Ned the Lonely Donkey***. I can't remember much about

THE JOHNNY MAXWELL TRILOGY

ONLY YOU CAN SAVE MANKIND • JOHNNY AND THE DEAD • JOHNNY AND THE BOMB Terry Pratchett

➡ Twelve-year-old worrier Johnny Maxwell is addicted to computer games, especially *Only You Can Save Mankind* in which an alien fleet from the Mighty ScreeWee empire thunder across the screen to be shot into a million pieces. But one day, the aliens surrender, leaving trigger-happy Johnny and his weird and wonderful friends to save Mankind from the Galactic Hordes – and the Galactic Hordes from Mankind – by getting inside the game and making themselves the targets, which leaves you, the reader, wondering what reality really is!

Pratchett's wickedly funny, completely mad and amazingly imaginative action-packed adventures are easy to get into, but these laugh-a-page stories also make you think, asking important questions about the world and our place in it and our attitudes to the people around us.

9-11

Eileen Armstrong

Next?
- For more fabulous Pratchett books, look for ***The Colour of Magic*** (UBG 51) and ***The Carpet People***.
- ***Space Demons*** by Gillian Rubinstein is a fast-paced computer game adventure. (UBG 223)

JOURNEY TO JO'BURG Beverley Naidoo

➡ Thirteen-year old Naledi and her little brother Tiro live in a Tswana village in South Africa. Like most village children, their parents work far away in the city. When their baby sister falls ill, they decide to walk the three hundred kilometres to Johannesburg to find their mother. On the way they discover a land where black people are servants and white people their masters.

They can only travel on a jam-packed bus for Blacks Only; they watch helplessly as police check the passes that all blacks must carry; they hear about the shooting of hundreds of black schoolchildren in Soweto as they marched for freedom. Naledi decides to become a doctor, not a maid like her mother.

Nine years after this book was published, Nelson Mandela became President of South Africa and black people were free.

9-11

James Riordan

Next?
- Beverley Naidoo's other books about children from Africa: ***The Other Side of Truth*** (UBG 178) and ***Out of Bounds***.
- Try ***Roll of Thunder, Hear My Cry*** by Mildred D. Taylor. (UBG 204)
- ***See our feature on books about OTHER CULTURES on pp. 180-181.***

JOURNEY TO THE RIVER SEA

Eva Ibbotson

➡ Maia is unbelievably brave when she discovers that her parents have died and that she must go and live with her aunt and uncle in their home on the banks of the River Amazon. Accompanied by her trusted nanny, she leaves London for South America.

There Maia discovers a completely different world, and tries hard to make her new life work. But she can't ignore the fact that her aunt and uncle, and their horrible daughters, loathe her and will never make her part of the family.

Even so, Maia begins to build friendships with some of the extraordinary people she meets, and through them, and her nanny, she finds herself almost enjoying life by the Amazon. Enjoyment, however, is not what her relatives have in mind for the girl, and they try everything they can to ensure that she is as miserable as they are.

Lindsey Fraser

10+

Next?
- Try ***Stop the Train*** by Geraldine McCaughrean – about starting a new life far away. (UBG 227)
- ***A Little Princess*** by Frances Hodgson Burnett is the story of Sara Crewe who returns from India to go to boarding school. (UBG 144)
- ***Boy Overboard*** by Morris Gleitzman tells the story of an Afghan family forced to become refugees. (UBG 35)

EVERYBODY'S FAVOURITE...

THE JUNGLE BOOKS Rudyard Kipling

➡ A tiger springs into the firelight of an Indian woodcutters' camp. The Indians run, but their baby is left behind, and crawls into a wolves' den. When the tiger comes, seeking his dinner, the wolves defend the baby. They adopt him and call him Mowgli – 'little frog'.

Throughout the two *Jungle Books*, short stories tell how Mowgli grows up in the jungle. The tiger Shere Khan hates him, but Mowgli is protected by the wolves, by the great black panther Bagheera, by the wise bear Baloo, and by Kaa, the python. Mowgli himself is no easy prey – he's tough, courageous, resourceful and intelligent. Does Shere Khan kill him? Read the books and find out.

Not all the stories are about Mowgli. Rikki-Tikki-Tavi the mongoose battles cobras in *The First Jungle Book*, and Quiquern, a monstrous Arctic ghost, haunts the *Second*. There are other wonderful stories too, which I leave you to discover for yourself.

My dad loved these books, and bought them for my seventh Christmas. I loved them too. Still do. If you love them as well, you can pass them on to your children.

Susan Price

➡ In *The First Jungle Book* Rudyard Kipling, that great teller of tales, offers us the choice of seven wonderful stories. My favourite is 'Tiger! Tiger!' in which Mowgli, the boy who was adopted by wolves, finds that his mortal enemy, the lame tiger, Shere Khan, is lying up in the big dry ravine of the Waingunga that is steep and sheer-sided. With the help of the wolves, Akela and Gray Brother, Mowgli separates the herd of buffaloes, leaving the cows to block the bottom of the ravine and taking the bulls to the top. Then, mounted on the great bull Rama, he leads the buffaloes in a headlong charge down the narrow gorge ...

Dick King-Smith

➡ I don't much care for talking animals, but the book I loved most when I was young is full of them. The jungle creatures in *The Jungle Books* are still real to me: Baloo the wise old bear, Bagheera the beautiful black panther, Hathi the elephant and Kaa the rock python. They all defend Mowgli, the human baby rescued by Mother Wolf, against Shere Khan, the terrifying lame tiger who intends to kill him if he can. From the moment Mother Wolf takes Mowgli to the Council Rock where Akela the Lone Wolf introduces new cubs to the pack with the haunting cry, 'Look. Look well O wolves,' this is a marvellously exciting story.

Nina Bawden

9+

Next?

- Anyone who enjoys ***The Jungle Books*** will almost certainly love the ***Just So Stories***, also by Rudyard Kipling. They are funny, extravagant tales told in beautifully rhythmic language. (UBG 132)
- Then you could try Kipling's ***Puck of Pook's Hill*** (UBG 195) and ***Rewards and Fairies***. In these short stories, the goblin Puck magically summons people from the past to tell the stories of their lives.
- Another animal classic is ***Stuart Little*** by E.B.White, though this time it's about an animal adopted by people.
- ***See our ANIMAL STORIES selections on pp. 16-17.***

a premonition of the number of things I was going to lose in my life rather than for the actually

EVERYBODY'S FAVOURITE…

JUST WILLIAM Richmal Crompton

➨ William Brown first appeared in 1922 and has never been out of print since. There has arguably been no greater spirit – celebrated in the most exquisite comic prose – in children's literature.

William is always eleven. At his muddy heel is his ardently faithful dog, Jumble. The Outlaws – Ginger, Henry and Douglas – are William's blood brothers; not scruffy schoolboys at all, but pirates, cowboys and Indians, ancient Greeks or cannibals. William, with his artist's soul and imagination, his passionate sense of justice, his tactless honesty and indefatigably clumsy bravery, is their beloved leader.

Through these wonderful stories, peopled by pompous or misguided adults, thwarted sweethearts, baffled teachers and relatives, William stomps with his home-made placards ('RONGS RITED: 1 penny'), his helpful inventions which strew chaos in their wake, his bow and arrow and his catapult – the patron saint of childhood.

Carol Ann Duffy

➨ William Brown, the eternal eleven-year-old epic hero, never fails to startle with his bold genius at the expense of those grown ups unlucky enough to cross his path.

William and his three friends call themselves The Outlaws. They meet in a dilapidated old barn where they plan their exploits. These frequently go wrong and get them into hot water. As a result of William having these ideas and doing dreadful things, his long-suffering family are left to pick up the pieces.

Into an orderly world, William brings unexpected, entertaining, never-ending chaos.

Jan Pienkowski

➨ William is one of the most famous and best-loved characters in children's fiction. Socks round his ankles and cap awry, he roams the countryside round his home village leaving a trail of chaos, while his long-suffering mother sighs, his father makes distantly disparaging remarks, his snooty older sister incessantly complains about him and his nervy brother Robert frets that William is ruining his love life.

Each of the forty-odd William books is a collection of short stories that take in a remarkable range of characters and settings. The plots are clever and the dialogue superb. Highlights are William's declamatory sarcasms from the scenes of mayhem ('I was only tryin' to help. S'pose you don't want me to try helpin' in future.'), and the ghastly, lisping, spoilt Violet Elizabeth Bott's threats – 'I'll thcweam and thcweam and thcweam until I'm thick! I can, you know.'

Anne Fine

8-11

Next?

- A more modern story of a child who just can't help getting into trouble is ***The Turbulent Term of Tyke Tiler*** by Gene Kemp. (UBG 249)
- Or you could try Anne Fine's own ***Flour Babies***, about a school project with a difference. (UBG 86)
- Or what about the **Jennings** books, by Anthony Buckeridge? They're about boys like William, and just as funny? (UBG 126)
- ***Frindle*** by Andrew Clements is about a boy who finds a reason to start enjoying school. (UBG 88)
- Or try the classic, hilarious **Molesworth** books by Geoffrey Willans and Ronald Searle and that begin with ***Down with Skool***. (UBG 67)

literary quality of the book. Later I loved Enid Blyton's **Malory Towers** books. I read them feverishly

THE ULTIMATE READERS' POLL

YOUR TOP TEN SCARY BOOKS

1 Harry Potter series by J.K. Rowling

2 Goosebumps series by R.L. Stine

3 The Lord of the Rings by J.R.R. Tolkien

4 A Series of Unfortunate Events: The Bad Beginning by Lemony Snicket

5 The Witches by Roald Dahl

6 Clockwork by Philip Pullman

7 The Demon Headmaster by Gillian Cross

8 Room 13 by Robert Swindells

9 Skeleton Key (the Alex Rider series) by Anthony Horowitz

10 Coraline by Neil Gaiman

JUST SO STORIES

Rudyard Kipling

➡ This is a collection of twelve short stories, for the most part telling how certain creatures achieved their characteristics: how the leopard got his spots, how the camel got his hump and so on. What makes the stories outstanding is not only their fantastic inventiveness but also the lively words in which they are told.

Stories read in silence are still heard by the inner ear of the reader, but these stories somehow demand to be heard in the outside world. If you hear them read aloud, the storyteller's voice comes through with humour, excitement and powerful explosions of language (as in 'The Sing-Song of Old Man Kangaroo'). Whether it is through the exclamations of the elephant's child (with a crocodile clinging to his trunk) or through the chanting account of the kangaroo who flees from the dingo and learns to jump in the process, these stories are definitely stories to be heard aloud.

9+

Margaret Mahy

Next?

- Try ***English Folk Tales*** by Joseph Jacobs or ***A Bag of Moonshine*** by Alan Garner – stories based on British folklore and told in an idiomatic storyteller's voice.
- Less direct, rather incoherent at times, yet verbally astonishing, are the ***Rootabaga Stories*** by Carl Sandburg.
- And, of course, Rudyard Kipling's ***The Jungle Books***. (UBG 130)
- Or try Ted Hughes's ***Tales of the Early World*** for more folklore. (UBG 236)

KENSUKE'S KINGDOM

Michael Morpurgo

➡ This book has all the best ingredients: a faithful dog, a strange but magical world, hardship, and the struggle to survive in an inhospitable place. Michael is washed overboard and stranded on a desert island with nothing but his dog, Stella, for company. Or so he thinks. The first night he almost gives up hope, and curls up to sleep, not caring if he lives or dies. Then, when he wakes in the morning, he finds a bowl of food by his side ...

This is an exciting story that has you reading faster and faster to find out what happens. You might also find yourself with an interest in learning Japanese!

8-11

Caroline Lawrence

Next?

- You'll find ***The Last Castaway*** by Harry Horse a nice easy read next; it's a very different take on the 'stranded on a desert island' sort of story.
- Or you might try ***Swiss Family Robinson*** by J.D. Wyss, about a family marooned on an island for many years. (UBG 234)
- And of course, you must read more Michael Morpurgo! ***Why the Whales Came*** (UBG 264) and ***The Butterfly Lion*** (UBG 37) are both wonderful stories.

KEZZIE Theresa Breslin

➡ Set in Scotland in the 1930s, this is a story of fourteen-year-old Kezzie, and her courage and determination in the face of really tough times.

It's the Depression and jobs are scarce. First Kezzie's mother dies and then her father, leaving her to look after her six-year-old sister Lucy and her crippled grandad. But there's worse to come. When Kezzie becomes ill, Lucy is taken into care and sent to Canada by an adoption agency – a common practice at the time. When she recovers, Kezzie is determined to get Lucy back. Her quest makes for a plot that's moving and thrilling.

This is realistic fiction at its best, mixing powerful ideas with high adventure and a touch of romance.

8-11

Julia Jarman

Next?

• More Theresa Breslin? Try her very scary ***Whispers in the Graveyard***. (UBG 262)

• For a gentler story of adoption, try either Hilary McKay's ***Saffy's Angel*** (UBG 207), or Sharon Creech's ***Ruby Holler***? (UBG 205). Both are quite different, as is the equally wonderful ***The Story of Tracy Beaker*** by Jacqueline Wilson. (UBG 229)

KIDNAPPED R.L. Stevenson

Next?

• You've probably already read ***Treasure Island***, if not, read it now! (UBG 247) You might also try Stevenson's scary ***Dr Jekyll and Mr Hyde***.

• There are some other old-time adventure stories: R.M. Ballantyne's ***The Coral Island*** (UBG 51) or Rider Haggard's ***King Solomon's Mines*** (UBG 135).

• Or for a book about a different sort of kidnapping, try Tim Bowler's ***Storm Catchers***. (UBG 228)

➡ Like *Treasure Island*, *Kidnapped* is an adventure story: a classic page-turner. David Balfour is a seventeen-year-old Scot who, in the year 1751 (his parents being dead), sets out to find his uncle and perhaps his fortune. Before we're into Chapter Five, his uncle has tried to murder him. Another few chapters, and David has been kidnapped and carried off to sea, has met the most complicated friend of his life, and has killed a man. And we're turning the pages, turning ...

I remember not being able to understand half the Scottish dialect words in *Kidnapped*, and I still can't. But I've never forgotten the fear and excitement that Stevenson makes us feel along with David, and the brilliant characters, such as weaselly, haunted Uncle Ebenezer and above all David's prickly, arrogant, dangerous companion Alan Breck. This is a story about friendship, and about growing up. And anyone who thinks it's a book just for boys (as its author did) doesn't know much about girls.

10-12

Susan Cooper

KILLER MUSHROOMS ATE MY GRAN

Susan Gates

➡ Maggot's gran wants some answers. When Jack Dash, her 'gentleman-friend', first returned from his amazing fungus-finding botanical adventure, he was keen to settle down and become a button mushroom farmer. So why, on the morning of their wedding day, does he disappear?

When Gran and Maggot cycle round to Jack's mushroom farm, they discover he has been fungified! The huge, monstrous, blood-red, brain-like mushrooms want to take over the world!!

Maggot is left alone as – KERRAK! – a ripe mushroom explodes and the spores invade Gran's brain too. Can he save her – and the rest of the world?

A word of warning – you do run the dangerous risk of learning many mushroom facts and becoming a fungus freak if you read this book!

10-12

Elena Gregoriou

Next?

• If you enjoyed this strange and wacky adventure try ***Revenge of the Toffee Monsters*** and ***Attack of the Tentacled Terror*** also by Susan Gates.

• Other hilarious and weird goings-on: ***There's an Alien in My Classroom*** by Bruce Coville; ***The Killer Underpants*** and the other **Jiggy McCue** books by Michael Lawrence. (UBG 127) out what lacrosse was – something to do with a net?

KING ARTHUR AND HIS KNIGHTS OF THE ROUND TABLE

Roger Lancelyn Green

➨ I guess I was nine when I tugged this lovely book from my stocking on Christmas morning. It won me over straight away and caused ripples in me that have never settled. Arthur pulls the sword from the stone on the fourth page, he's king by the fifth, and by the time Merlin speaks of Logres, God's Kingdom upon the Earth, I was quite ready to agree that 'all who heard him felt that they were at the beginning of a time of wonders.' Strong and sinewy storytelling. Bloody accounts of heads and limbs being hacked off sit side-by-side with haunting descriptions of magic and miracle. Beautiful illustrations by Lotte Reiniger. A true classic, by a wonderful writer.

10-12

David Almond

Next?

- There are many versions of these legends; try Marcia Williams's, which are hilarious and brilliantly illustrated. (UBG 166)
- For a more challenging read on the same theme, try T.H. White's ***The Sword in the Stone*** (UBG 234) or ***The Seeing Stone*** by Kevin Crossley-Holland (UBG 216).

THE KING MUST DIE Mary Renault

➨ When the Cretans come for the annual tribute that is owed to their god, Theseus, son of the Athenian King, insists on going with them. Among his imprisoned people, he finds strength and the ability to lead, and to keep all of his friends alive. But when the volcano Mount Thera erupts, he must journey into the labyrinth to fight and hopefully kill the Minotaur – a monster, half man and half bull.

Mary Renault takes an old Greek myth, set just before the Trojan War, and brings it brilliantly and convincingly to life. But this is more than an adventure story: it's about the responsibilities of power in ancient Pagan religion, for in the last resort, even the King may have to die to save his people.

Following Theseus from childhood, this is a very sophisticated read, but one that really lets you understand the reality behind the myth.

12+

Patricia Finney

Next?

- You might enjoy the sequel, ***The Bull From the Sea***.
- For other stories of the ancient world, work your way through Rosemary Sutcliff, especially ***The Eagle of the Ninth*** (UBG 68) and ***The Mark of the Horse Lord*** (UBG 155).
- ***The God Beneath the Sea*** by Leon Garfield and Edward Blishen is a wonderful collection of retellings of Greek myths. (UBG 95)
- For another interpretation of the Greek myths, try Adèle Geras's wonderful novel ***Troy***. (UBG 248)

KING OF SHADOWS Susan Cooper

➨ Nathan Field is a young American actor, who travels to London with his theatre company to stage a version of *A Midsummer Night's Dream* in the newly-reconstructed Globe theatre. A few days after his arrival he is taken seriously ill and when he wakes up, finds himself in a very different London – that of four hundred years earlier. Even stranger is that everyone seems to know him, and are expecting him to play the part of Puck in a special performance at the Globe. Imagine his surprise when he learns who he will be acting alongside – none other than William Shakespeare himself.

Susan Cooper weaves past and present together skilfully in this gripping and moving story, rich in the detail of Elizabethan life.

9-12

Marcus Sedgwick

Next?

- Why not try Susan Cooper's powerful ***The Dark Is Rising***? (UBG 57)
- Or if you like timeslip stories, try ***Charlotte Sometimes*** by Penelope Farmer. (UBG 45)
- ***Death and the Arrow*** by Chris Priestley is a great historical detective story. (UBG 59)
- Go back to the original Shakespeare stories in collections by Ian Serraillier or Leon Garfield.

If you're looking for *The Killer Underpants* by Michael Lawrence, turn to p. 127

KING SOLOMON'S MINES

H. Rider Haggard

➨ Three Englishmen – Allan Quartermain, Sir Henry Curtis and Captain John Good R.N. – guided by a primitive map, set out into an unexplored part of Africa, searching not only for King Solomon's treasure but for Sir Henry's lost brother. They cross a desert and climb a mountain, suffering but surviving, then encounter an unknown tribe and become involved in local wars. They do find treasure ... but the discovery is more complicated and dangerous than they had imagined it would be.

While this book is rather more straggling than *Treasure Island*, it is still a classic adventure story. A modern reader may wince at the slaughter of elephants (Quartermain is an ivory hunter, a respectable profession in Rider Haggard's day) but the African characters are imaginatively vital.

Margaret Mahy

10+

Next?
- The the sequel ***Allan Quartermain***, and also look out for ***Treasure Island*** by R.L. Stevenson. (UBG 247) You also might like ***The Coral Island*** by R.M. Ballantyne. (UBG 51)
- Gary Paulsen's ***Hatchet*** is a good read for anyone looking for adventure stories. (UBG 107)
- Or try William Nicholson's ***The Wind Singer***. (UBG 266)

KISS THE DUST Elizabeth Laird

➨ When this book was first published in 1991, it was right on the button. It is the story of a Kurdish Iraqi family who, in 1984, have to flee their home.

From Sulaimaniya to the mountains, from the mountains to terrible refugee camps in Iran, and from there to England – and a containment centre. It sounds grim. It *is* grim, but there is so much more! From the beautiful descriptions of place, to the uncrushable spirits of the characters in the story, this is a wonderfully life-affirming book.

Sadly, with all that has happened since, with the issues over asylum seekers today, this book has not shifted one millimetre from the button.

If you are sitting comfortably, then read this story – it is a brilliant insight into a situation no one wants to be in, but so many are.

Simon Puttock

10-12

Next?
- Elizabeth Laird has written many other wonderful books; try ***The Garbage King*** or ***The Listener***.
- Beverley Naidoo's ***The Other Side of Truth*** is about two refugees from Nigeria who are abandoned in London. (UBG 178)
- ***The Breadwinner*** by Deborah Ellis looks at life in Afghanistan under the Taliban. (UBG 35)

KIT'S WILDERNESS David Almond

➨ For over four years I've had a running argument with Susan (fellow editor) about which David Almond book is best. She thinks it's *Skellig*, I'm sure it's *Kit's Wilderness*. (I'm right, incidentally.) In fact, I think it's one of the best books *anyone* has written in years.

Set in the north-east, it's the story of Kit Watson, and the bonds he forms with classmate Allie Keenan, wild boy John Askew and the spirits of the past, and the game they all play. The game called Death.

This book is just as dark as it sounds, absolutely suffused with death and menace; but there's also great beauty in this wilderness, in Kit's relationship with his old grandfather and his friendships with Askew and Allie, in Kit's storytelling and Allie's acting and Askew's extraordinary drawings.

Kit's Wilderness will do something only the greatest books can – it will change the way you see the world. Trust me. Read it.

Daniel Hahn

10+

Next?
- Read ***Skellig*** and see if you agree with me or Susan. (UBG 220)
- Susan has recommended another of David Almond's great books, ***Heaven Eyes***. (UBG 108)
- Sally Prue's ***Cold Tom*** has a similarly eerie feel (UBG 50); or for something else that's mysterious but totally unsentimental, try Julie Hearn's ***Follow Me Down***. (UBG 87)

KITE Melvin Burgess

➨ Taylor Mase is hand-rearing a red kite – a bird of prey. He shouldn't be. They're endangered. And this particular bird is in more danger than most. No one seems to want it to live. The local landowner, the brutal Harris, wants it dead. Even Taylor's own dad wants it dead.

This is a wonderful, nail-biting tale of a bird's incredible will to live and a boy who will do anything to help it.

10-12

Cliff McNish

Next?

- If you enjoyed this, you may wish to try another of Melvin Burgess's animal-centred stories, such as ***The Cry of the Wolf***.
- Or why not read the brilliant classic ***The Call of the Wild*** by Jack London – a fantastic story of one dog's fight for survival in the ice and snow of Alaska? (UBG 38)
- ***The Midnight Fox*** by Betsy Byars is another popular animal story. (UBG 159)
- ***And don't miss our ANIMAL STORIES selections on pp. 16-17.***

THE KITE RIDER

Geraldine McCaughrean

➨ To escape from his father's murderer, twelve-year-old Gou Hayou joins the travelling Jade Circus, flying high into the skies of mediaeval China, strapped to gigantic silk and paper kites. But circus master Miao Jie has a deadly secret, and Hayou's scheming Uncle Bo has plans of his own for the kite rider …

This is a rich and exciting book, full of strange sights, sounds, smells and superstitions. The fast-moving story has more twists and turns than a snake doing yoga, and you can never be sure that Hayou and his friends will escape from the terrible predicaments which Geraldine McCaughrean keeps dumping them in.

10-12

Philip Reeve

Next?

- Geraldine McCaughrean has written lots of books, each very different and all very good. Try her modern-day gold-rush tale, ***Gold Dust*** (UBG 96) and ***A Little Lower Than the Angels***, set in the Middle Ages (UBG 143).
- If you liked the Oriental parts of the story, try ***The Master Puppeteer*** by Katherine Paterson, which (along with the mysterious art of Japanese puppet theatre) is about famine, survival and family secrets.

Illustration by Hannah Moxon, age 10, Charlton House School

was young were all those by Alistair Maclean. I'd never heard of him until my dad took me to see a

> **Next?**
> • Terry Jones has also written ***The Saga of Erik the Viking***, about the voyage of a band of Vikings to the land where the sun sets. (UBG 207) His ***Fantastic Stories*** are also well worth a read.
> • If you enjoy fantasy combined with humour, try Eoin Colfer's ***Artemis Fowl***. (UBG 20)
> • Or for a girl who disguises herself in order to become a knight, try **The Song of the Lioness** series by Tamora Pierce, set in a mythical Middle Ages where magic is real. (UBG 223)

THE KNIGHT AND THE SQUIRE

Terry Jones

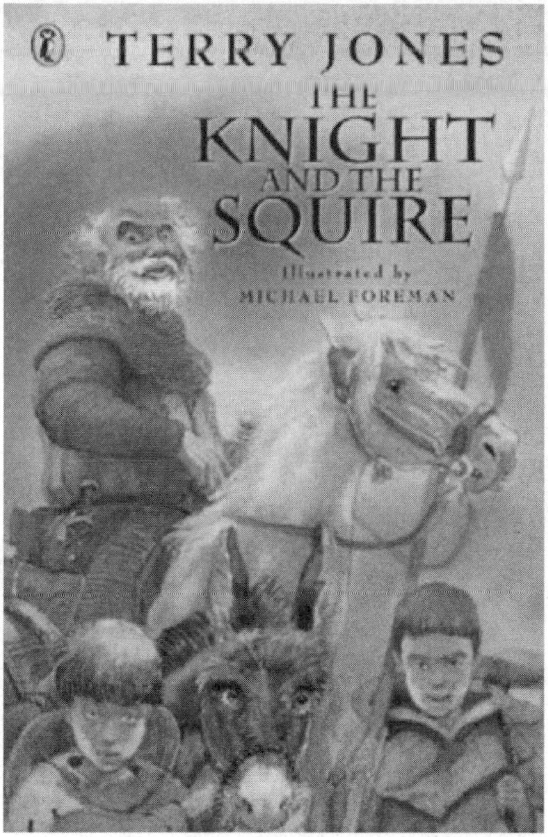

➡ When Tom decides to run away from home, he knows life won't be easy. Tom lives in the fourteenth century where wolves are on the loose, there are dangerous characters in pursuit and threats all around. But Tom is urged on by his desire for adventure, and he travels across the channel to France and right into the middle of a siege – and that's just for starters. *The Knight and the Squire* is fast-moving, a little bloodthirsty, packed with detail about the past and also – and this is important – very funny. It's not without one final, dramatic twist, too.

Tom's adventures continue in *The Lady and the Squire*, when he travels as the Duke of Lancaster's squire in France and life gets even more exciting – and perilous. If you think you've heard of Terry Jones, it might be because he was also one of the Monty Python team.

9-11

Sherry Ashworth

KNIGHT'S FEE Rosemary Sutcliff

➡ It could have been the worst day of his life, the day he dropped a half-eaten fig on to the nose of his Lord and Master's horse. For Randall is a dog boy, the lowest of the low, and he knows he is certain to be beaten. But chance intervenes, and after being saved by the castle's minstrel, he ends up packed off as companion to a young Lord, called Bevis.

The Saxon dog boy and the Norman lordling grow up together to become soldiers fighting for King Henry against his brother Robert. It is Bevis's destiny to become a knight, but Randall has no family, land or money – and certainly no way to pay his knight's fee. Can the friendship survive? Set at a time when the Saxons and Normans were just beginning to come together as one people, this is a terrifically exciting story.

10+

Barbara Wright

> **Next?**
> • Another Rosemary Sutcliff about an unlikely friendship is ***The Eagle of the Ninth***. (UBG 68) For a mediaeval setting, look out for ***The Witch's Brat***.
> • ***A Little Lower Than the Angels*** by the wonderful Geraldine McCaughrean is also set in the Middle Ages. (UBG 143)
> • What about a fantasy adventure? Try Lloyd Alexander's ***The Book of Three***. (UBG 32)

KON TIKI: Across the Pacific by Raft

Thor Heyerdahl

➨ Sailing on a balsa wood raft across the ocean? Wow! I can still feel the sense of adventure I experienced when reading *Kon-Tiki* as a teenager. The warm Pacific seas, the wind in the sails, even the hardships and relentless sun seemed like exotic fun to me.

Everything from building the boat to planning the journey, along with all of the hardships Heyerdahl and his crew experience, make this more exciting than most works of fiction. Heyerdahl was trying to prove that Polynesian islands could have been settled by sea-faring natives from South America. What he proved to *me* was that words in a book could take me along as a fascinated member of the crew.

11+

Jerry Spinelli

Next?

- Other Thor Heyerdahl adventures, such as ***The Ra Expeditions*** or ***Aku Aku***.
- If you fancy another true story of suffering, exploration and endurance, read one of the most amazing ever written, ***The Worst Journey in the World*** by Apsley Cherry-Garrard, about his own experiences on an ill-fated Antarctic journey.
- For a lighter, fictional account of survival, try ***The Swiss Family Robinson*** by J.D. Wyss. (UBG 234)
- Want more perilous sea adventure? Try ***Captains Courageous*** by Rudyard Kipling (UBG 40) and ***The Sea Wolf*** by Jack London (UBG 211).

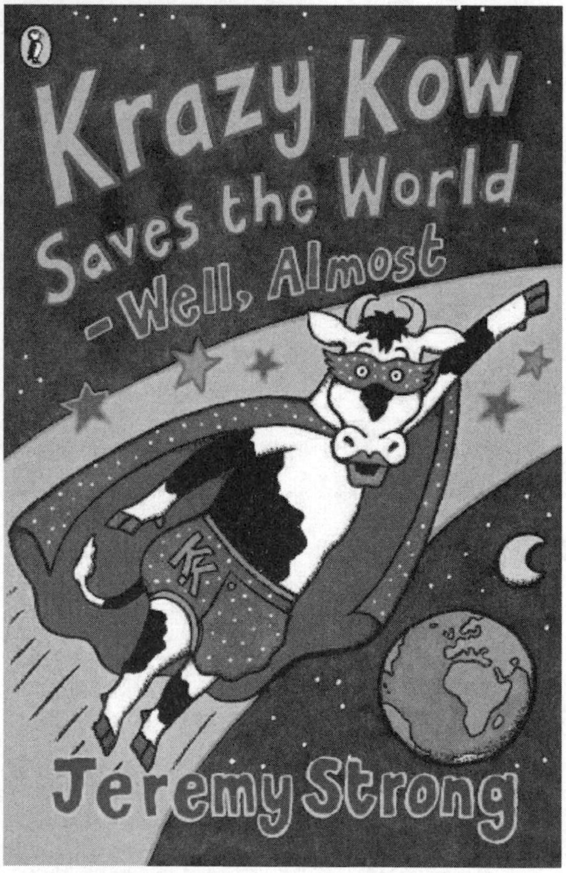

KRAZY KOW SAVES THE WORLD - WELL, ALMOST

Jeremy Strong

➨ If you like long and weighty books about serious issues, then this is not for you. However, if you like daft, rollicking reads, preferably involving flying cows and evil villains, then get hold of *Krazy Kow* immediately.

Jamie Frink's great desire in life is to be a film-maker, and when he invents Krazy Kow (a bovine superhero and eco-warrior) there's hope of his dream coming true.

The plot switches constantly between the world of Jamie and his problems, and the world of Krazy Kow and her very different problems (the main one of which is avoiding nuclear chickens). Jeremy Strong whizzes through the story at his usual madcap pace. You won't get bored – I guarantee it!

7-9

Susan Reuben

Next?

- The equally silly ***Captain Underpants*** by Dav Pilkey is about another very different sort of superhero. (UBG 40)
- More good Jeremy Strong books include ***The Indoor Pirates***, ***The Shocking Adventures of Lightning Lucy*** and ***My Mum's Going to Explode!*** (UBG 170).
- Or why not try Michael Lawrence's wacky and hilarious **Jiggy McCue** books, starting with ***The Killer Underpants***? (UBG 127)

KUNG FU BOY (Ironfist Chinmi series)

Takeshi Maekawa

➡ These stories are told with pictures. Lots of pictures. In fact, they are comics! But don't let anyone tell you that this makes them less good than books with lots of words and no pictures at all, because it doesn't. If you like fast stories about warrior monks, kung fu, ancient Chinese mysteries and lots and lots of adventure (not to mention lots of fights), read about all those things and more in the Chinmi series.

One vital thing – these books have to be read back to front. Confusing? Yes, but that's how Japanese books are read, and these were all originally Japanese manga (their word for comics). And if you like these, there are many other manga in translation, plenty to keep you going for years and years!

7-9

Leonie Flynn

Next?
- More Manga? ***Mobile Suit Gundam Wing***, ***Cardcaptor Sakura*** and ***Sailor Moon*** all have great books to buy that tie in to TV series.
- Want a change from Japanese comics? Try the Americans – ***Superman***, ***Batman*** and ***X-Men*** are all classics and all boringly have to be read from front to back (be careful when you're choosing, as some are more violent and are aimed at adults).

THE LADY WITH IRON BONES

Jan Mark

➡ Kasey needs a big favour and the magical lady with iron bones grants it in exchange for the gift of a rose. Or at least, Kasey thinks that is what has happened, but her friend Ellen knows that Kasey is wrong – the lady hidden in her neighbour's garden doesn't really have special powers at all.

Kasey starts to leave more presents for the lady, more valuable things, because she's scared that if she doesn't her good luck will come to an end. Even worse, bad things might start to happen. Ellen doesn't want to hurt her friend's feelings but she's got to make Kasey see the truth. You won't be able to put this book down until you find out how she does it!

9-11

Gill Vickery

Next?
- Look out for more Jan Mark. ***Thunder and Lightnings*** was her first book and it is a brilliant story of friendship (UBG 242), and the wonderful ***Handles*** is all about fitting in somewhere new.
- Another top story about testing your beliefs is Jackie French's ***Hitler's Daughter***. (UBG 112)

THE LAND OF GREEN GINGER

Noel Langley

➡ I love funny books based on traditional tales. This is the story of Aladdin's son, Prince Abu Ali, whose only fault is being too nice. He is sent by the genie of the lamp to free a magician from a nasty spell which has turned him into a button-nosed tortoise. He sets off in search of the flying back garden known as The Land Of Green Ginger. On the way, he has some very daft adventures and meets all kinds of weird characters, some good and some Very Bad. They all have wonderfully silly names like Rubdub Ben Thud, Sulkpot Ben Nagnag and Boomalakka Wee. It made me giggle over thirty years ago and it still does now. Gentle reader, I now leave you with the words of Vapid, Villainous, Vindictive, Vengeful, Wilfully Wicked Prince Tintac Ping Foo: 'Ho there, Slaves! My camels! My retinue! My Magic Sword! My Jellybeans! I leave at once for Samarkand!'

9-11

Kaye Umansky

Next?
- ***The Magician of Samarkand*** by Alan Temperley is a wonderful, magical story about a far-away place.
- Or for another book about a place that might exist under our noses (or at the back of King's Cross) try ***The Secret of Platform 13*** by Eva Ibbotson (UBG 213).
- A classic, and totally brilliantly weird story, is that of ***Alice's Adventures in Wonderland*** by Lewis Carroll (UBG 12).

THE LAST VAMPIRE Willis Hall

➡ Fancy a camping holiday with your parents in the shadow of a mysterious castle in Transylvania? Blood-sucking bats, ravenous wolves and a village full of raging imbeciles who threaten the very lives of you and your family are all part of the fun.

Henry Hollins befriends the misunderstood, vegetarian vampire, Count Alucard, who arranges their escape with no help from his own relatives! He accompanies the Hollins family back to England in search of a new home. After trouble with immigration officers, he foxes them by turning himself into a bat and flies off to search for Henry.

A fine romp and a good twist on a vampire story that you can't put down. Stake your heart on it … you'll die laughing!

8-10

Babette Cole

Next?
- Do read more of the books about the Hollins family and Count Alucard. Look out for ***Vampire Park*** and ***The Vampire Vanishes***. The Hollins family also feature in ***The Inflatable Shop***.
- Try Kaye Umansky's great ***Prince Dandypants and the Masked Avenger*** – very funny. Or how about her best-loved creation, ***Pongwiffy***? (UBG 192)
- For more vampire fun, try Ann Jungman's ***Vlad the Drac***, about another vegetarian vampire. (UBG 256)

THE LEGENDEER TRILOGY

SHADOW OF THE MINOTAUR • VAMPYR LEGION • WARRIORS OF THE RAVEN
Alan Gibbons

➡ When Phoenix's computer-whiz dad invents a virtual reality game based on the Greek legends, Phoenix can't wait to try it out. He's being bullied at his new school and Legendeer seems like the perfect escape from his troubles, until something goes horribly wrong and suddenly he's facing the Gorgon and the Minotaur for real. In the next two titles Phoenix confronts vampyrs, werewolves and the evil gods of Norse mythology. *Shadow of the Minotaur* is an all-action roller-coaster ride, as Alan Gibbons cleverly interweaves Phoenix's terrifying computer adventures with his less immediately dangerous, but

10+

Next?
- Find out about the myths in ***The Orchard Book of Greek Myths*** by Geraldine McCaughrean. (UBG 177)
- ***Troy*** by Adèle Geras is a totally fresh take on the Trojan wars that's brutal and bloody, but full of passion. (UBG 248)
- ***Hacker*** by Malorie Blackman is another fast-paced story that uses computers as an important part of the plot. (UBG 102)
- **The Saga of Darren Shan** will give you insights into the lives of vampires and will make you laugh. (UBG 208)

THE LIGHT PRINCESS
George MacDonald

➡ *The Light Princess* has all you'd expect from a fairy story, and more. A king and queen have a much-longed-for daughter. A witch who isn't invited to the christening puts a curse on the baby princess. It's an unusual curse – the witch has taken her sense of gravity. So the baby floats up to the ceiling! The story is funny at the beginning, but grows dark as the princess grows up and the witch's magic grows stronger.

But will this fairytale have a fairytale ending?

10+

Julia Jarman

Next?
- For another unusual fairytale, try Elizabeth Goudge's ***The Little White Horse***. (UBG 145)
- For another princess with a strange christening gift, read M.M. Kaye's warm and wonderful ***The Ordinary Princess***. (UBG 177)
- Or E.D. Baker's ***The Frog Princess***, which is about a clumsy, unhappy princess who hates the prince she is meant to marry. One day she kisses a frog … and is turned into a frog too!
- Or what about a very, very modern princess? Read Meg Cabot's ***The Princess Diaries***. (UBG 193)

THE LION, THE WITCH AND THE WARDROBE

(The Chronicles of Narnia) C.S. Lewis

➡ When Peter, Susan, Edmund and Lucy stumble through a magic wardrobe into the wondrous world of Narnia, they find themselves caught up in a battle against the White Witch, who has placed a wintry curse on the land. Edmund is separated from his brother and sisters, meets the Witch and, under her spell, makes a secret pact that puts all their lives in danger. Great courage is needed as the other children lead the creatures and talking beasts of Narnia into battle. With them is Aslan, true ruler of Narnia, and the most powerful enemy of the Witch. But Edmund still belongs to the Witch, who demands a terrible price for his freedom.

Narnia has a long history, told through seven books called *The Chronicles of Narnia*. Each book is a gripping adventure on its own, yet together they make one long and glorious story – a story of brave people and extraordinary creatures struggling to protect Narnia from the evil forces against it; a story of courage and loyalty; of battles and betrayals; of amazing travels and magical places; a story of the wildness and warmth of the lion, Aslan, whose presence shines in all the stories like a light.

9-11

Sherryl Jordan

Next?

• You'll be enthralled by the magic of all the **Chronicles of Narnia**. They are best read in the following order:

The Magician's Nephew – a tale of magic and mayhem, and the beautiful beginning of Narnia.

The Lion, the Witch and the Wardrobe

The Horse and his Boy – adventures in Calormen, an enemy land to Narnia.

Prince Caspian – about a young king who must lead all of Narnia to freedom.

The Voyage of the Dawn Treader – the most marvellous sea voyage ever!

The Silver Chair – a thrilling story of evil enchantment, captivity, faithfulness, and rescue.

The Last Battle – the greatest story of all, about deceit and truth, and the glory that goes on for ever.

• And after all that? Try the **Worlds of Chrestomanci** books by Diana Wynne Jones, which are all about magic and adventure. (UBG 272)

• Or **Harry Potter**. You might know J.K. Rowling's classics already – but if you don't, go and introduce yourself right now. (UBG 106)

Illustration by Chloe May Smith, age 10, Charters Ancaster College

LIONBOY Zizou Corder

➨ This is the first book in a trilogy and I think it's fair to say that it isn't totally complete in itself because of that. But it's still great fun and hugely imaginative and original.

Since he was small, Charlie has had the amazing ability to speak Lion. It's not the only unique thing about Charlie, but it stands him in excellent stead when he needs the lions' help to track down his beloved scientist parents, who have been kidnapped and taken from London to Paris and beyond.

Although it is set in London in the future, there's something old-fashioned about the feel of the writing and shape of the story that reminded me of classic fantasies I've enjoyed and re-read. Maybe Lionboy's magic seeps into everyone who reads it?

Jon Appleton

9-12

Next?
- If you're looking for another epic read to enjoy then try Pat O'Shea's spellbinding ***The Hounds of the Morrigan***. (UBG 117)
- If you haven't read the enchanting tales of ***Doctor Dolittle*** by Hugh Lofting, there's a treat in store for you. (UBG 64)
- For more fantasy that begins in the real world and sweeps you away, try Alan Garner's brilliant ***Elidor***. (UBG 71)

THE LITTLE GREY MEN B.B.

➨ When spring comes to the Folly Brook, it's time to get moving. Among the animals and birds starting out on the year are Dodder, Baldmoney and Sneezewort, the last gnomes in Britain. Normally they live quiet lives, comfortable in their homes in the roots of an oak tree, but this year is different. Their brother Cloudberry, who went exploring to find the source of the Folly Brook, has gone missing. So they build a boat and set off to find him. It is a dangerous venture, for when you are so small the wilderness has many hazards: weasels, herons, pike and lots of others – including gamekeepers.

This is an adventure story, packed with incident and details of nature. B.B. (Denys Watkins-Pitchford) was art master at Rugby School and illustrated his own book, with colour, scraperboard and pen and ink drawings.

Alan Temperley

9-11

Next?
- ***Down the Bright Stream*** recounts the further adventures of our three heroes, when people invade the secret places that are their home.
- ***Brendon Chase***, also by B.B., is the story of three boys who don't want to return to boarding school, and so go to ground in a great forest.
- Or try the hilarious ***Uncle*** by J.P. Martin, about a millionaire elephant who lives in a labyrinth and has dwarfs, ghosts and lunatics as neighbours. (UBG 252)

LITTLE HOUSE ON THE PRAIRIE

Laura Ingalls Wilder

➨ This is the story of a pioneering family in the late nineteenth century. The story centres round Laura, the second daughter and, although her life is sometimes harsh and certainly far removed from our own experiences, it makes you long to be out there, sleeping in a log cabin under the boundless stars and hundreds of miles from anywhere. There are adventures with cowboys, wolves, bears and American Indians. And all the while, Laura's wonderful Pa is sawing and hammering and building, to keep the family and their animals safe and warm.

(A word of warning to fathers. If you fancy yourself as a D.I.Y. specialist, don't read this story to your children. My husband did and he says it left him feeling permanently inadequate.)

Jenny Nimmo

9-11

Next?
- Laura Ingalls Wilder wrote six more books about her life in the American West. ***Little House in the Big Woods*** is the first in the series, but is much less well known. For older readers, there's ***The First Four Years***, about Laura's early married life.
- For other true stories of people's lives, look for Adeline Yen Mah's ***Chinese Cinderella*** (UBG 47), or ***Boy*** by Roald Dahl (UBG 34).
- ***Sarah, Plain and Tall*** by Patricia MacLachlan is also set on the American prairies in the nineteenth century. (UBG 210)

LITTLE LORD FAUNTLEROY

Frances Hodgson Burnett

➡ This is the story of Ceddie, a seven-year-old American boy, brought back to England at the request of his bad-tempered, much hated old grandfather the Earl of Dorincourt, to become Lord Fauntleroy, heir to a great fortune.

Ceddie is a sweet-natured child who only wants to use his new-found wealth to do good. As a warm relationship develops between the old man and the little boy, the Earl's icy heart gradually thaws as he grows to love his grandson. But there are obstacles in the way. The Earl refuses to have anything to do with Ceddie's beloved widowed mother, and when a rival heir appears, it looks as though Ceddie might not be the real Lord Fauntleroy after all …

If you like the idea of being taken back to Victorian times to follow the journey from rags to riches of a character you're bound to love, then look out for this book!

Gwyneth Rees

9-11

Next?

- If you want to try another children's classic by the same author, then go for Frances Hodgson Burnett's ***The Secret Garden*** (UBG 215) or ***A Little Princess*** (UBG 144).
- If you'd like to read a book about a different character who also goes to live with a daunting relative and changes everyone's lives for the better, try Eleanor H. Porter's ***Pollyanna***. (UBG 192)
- ***Journey to the River Sea*** by Eva Ibbotson is about a girl journeying to South America to start a new life with distant relatives. (UBG 129)

A LITTLE LOWER THAN THE ANGELS

Geraldine McCaughrean

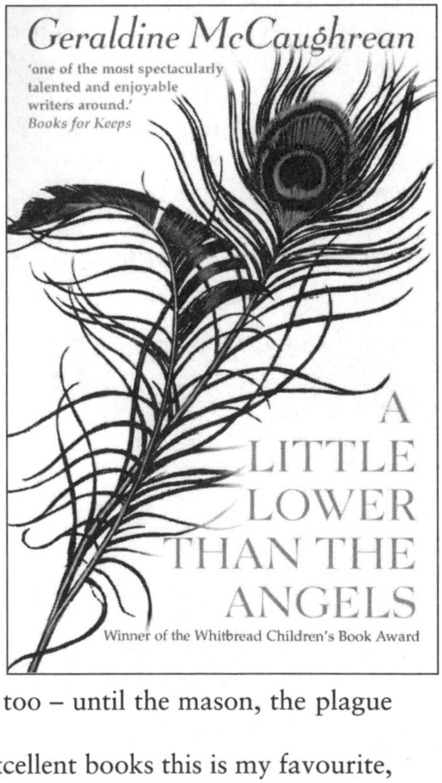

➡ 'Gabriel jumped into the Mouth of Hell. The smell of burning pricked the back of his nose. He wriggled into the red gullet of Hell. Two hands from beyond reached into his armpits and pulled him through. It was God.'

How about that, eh? Well, it's not actually God, it's the leading actor of the Mystery Players, who have turned up in the mediaeval English town where miserable golden-haired Gabriel is apprenticed to a bullying mason. Gabriel, instantly stagestruck, runs away with them. He's a natural to play an Angel. The peasant audiences think he works miracles, and for a while he thinks so too – until the mason, the plague and the devil take over his life …

Of all Geraldine McCaughrean's excellent books this is my favourite, perhaps because I've always been as stagestruck as Gabriel.

Susan Cooper

10+

Next?

- Look for other vivid pictures of a past England in Rosemary Sutcliff's ***The Eagle of the Ninth*** (UBG 68), or – coming forward to the eighteenth century – Leon Garfield's ***Smith*** (UBG 221).
- You can find twentieth-century stagestruck characters in Pamela Brown's ***The Swish of the Curtain***. (UBG 233)
- Or for a wonderful story that is about theatre, history and time-travel, try Susan's own ***King of Shadows***. (UBG 134)

Next?
• I am supposed to suggest to you what to read next, but I can't. There is no book quite like this. So instead, go outside and feel the wind. Look at the stars if there are any. Make a wish. Wait till tomorrow to start another book. That would be best.

THE LITTLE PRINCE

Antoine de Saint-Exupéry

➨ A lone aircraft pilot crashes his plane in a desert, and there he meets a traveller from another world – a little prince. While the pilot struggles to mend his plane, the little prince describes his life.

Read this book! Read the first page, anyway! That will be enough because it is unputdownable. What happens to the little prince an intelligent reader will discover. What happened to the pilot is more of a mystery, because the author, himself a pilot, disappeared. His plane was lost a year after his story was published.

Hilary McKay

8+

A LITTLE PRINCESS

Frances Hodgson Burnett

➨ This is the story of Sara Crewe, whose mother died when she was a baby and who has lived in India all her life with her father, Captain Crewe. At the start of the book, Captain Crewe brings Sara to England, to Miss Minchin's Select Seminary for Young Ladies. Sara's papa is very rich, and Sara is very privileged. The other girls call her 'Princess' and Miss Minchin is as nice as pie to her. But when Sara is eleven, tragedy strikes. Her beloved papa dies, and all his money is gone. Poor Sara is left a pauper.

Everyone turns against her. She is put to work as a drudge and sent to live in the attics. Her whole life has collapsed – but Sara is not a girl to give way to despair. She may be cold, and starving, and exhausted, but still she manages to keep her spirits up. And at the end ...

This book was written over a hundred years ago, but is as magical now as it was then.

Jean Ure

9-11

Next?
• Other terrific Frances Hodgson Burnett stories are ***Little Lord Fauntleroy***, about a boy who discovers he is a lord and ***The Secret Garden***, in which a girl is sent to a lonely, rambling old house in the country to live with her uncle. (UBG 215)
• ***The Railway Children*** by E. Nesbit is an enchanting story, guaranteed to make you cry! (UBG 197)
• ***See our list of PRINCESS STORIES on p. 193.***

LITTLE SOLDIER Bernard Ashley

➨ Kaninda is rescued from a brutal attack on his East African village and joins a rebel army, where he learns to use deadly weapons and vows to take revenge on the enemies that killed his mother, father and sister. Aid workers bring him to London to start a new life with a well-meaning family, but the bullet-scar in his arm is a constant reminder of his traumatic past.

His rundown comprehensive school and shabby inner-city estate are rife with violent and dangerous 'tribal' conflicts between rival gangs, and together with his only friend, Laura Rose, Kaninda finds himself drawn into another kind of power struggle which spins out of control.

With its stomach-churning descriptions, street dialogue and fighting, this is not an easy read, but it is exciting, edge-of-the-seat stuff about human conflict, pride and friendship, and a book you just won't be able to put down.

Eileen Armstrong

11+

Next?
• Try other moving stories about child asylum seekers in Britain, such as ***The Other Side of Truth*** by Beverley Naidoo (UBG 178) or rap poet Benjamin Zephaniah's ***Refugee Boy***.
• ***A.K.*** by Peter Dickinson is the gripping story of modern civil war in a fictional African country. (UBG 8)
• ***Boy Overboard*** by Morris Gleitzman is about refugees from Afghanistan trying to find a new home in Australia. (UBG 35)

CELEBRITY QUOTES! Kathy Lette (author): My favourite author as a child ... hmmmm. It *has*

THE LITTLE WHITE HORSE

Elizabeth Goudge

➨ Orphan Maria is that unusual combination – a practical girl, who is also completely open to magical possibilities.

Sent to the mysterious, beautiful estate of Moonacre, she finds a place where history, myth and fairytale mingle with her own Victorian world. What is the ancient quarrel that haunts the Merryweather family and makes the vast, dark pine forest so sinister and full of trouble? What is the fatal repeated mistake that has broken so many hearts?

Helped by several astonishing animals and humans, not to mention her own true love, Maria must still call on all her own bravery and determination. But then, she has glimpsed the magical white horse – the horse with the single silvery horn; to see him again, she will risk almost anything.

10-12

Tanith Lee

Next?

- Tanith Lee has written some wonderfully dark stories. Try ***The Castle of Dark.*** (UBG 42)
- Why not try Susan Cooper's ***The Dark Is Rising*** and the others in the sequence? (UBG 57)
- Catherine Fisher's ***The Lammas Field*** is another fantastical story with a white horse.
- Or ***The Enchanted Castle*** by E. Nesbit, which has a similar atmosphere of magic. (UBG 73)

LITTLE WOLF series

- **LITTLE WOLF'S BOOK OF BADNESS**
- **LITTLE WOLF'S HALL OF HAUNTED HORRORS**
- **LITTLE WOLF'S DIARY OF DARING DEEDS**
- **LITTLE WOLF, FOREST DETECTIVE**
- **LITTLE WOLF, PACK LEADER**

Ian Whybrow, illustrated by Tony Ross

Next?

- If you liked this series, you might also love the **Molesworth** books: ***Down with Skool*** (UBG 67) and ***How to be Topp*** by Geoffrey Willans and Ronald Searle. Although they are older reads, you will enjoy tasting bits of them – and marvelling at both the spelling and the illustrations.
- A book about a boy who gets into lots of trouble is ***Jimmy Zest*** by Sam McBratney. (UBG 128)
- If you're looking for another funny and a bit silly series, try the **Dark Claw** books by Shoo Rayner. (UBG 56)

➨ In the *Book of Badness*, Little Wolf is sent to Cunning College. You'll laugh out loud at his letters home. 'I know you want me to be wild and wicked just like Dad, but why do I have to go so far away? I told you I only cleaned my teeth last week for a joke.'

In *Forest Detective*, Little Wolf, Yeller, Normus and Smellybreff start up a detective agency. 'We are good solvers,' he writes, 'but not Smells. His brane is 2 small.'

They locate the seventy-two missing football boots of Ants United FC: a centipede confesses, 'I just wanted to do loud riverdancing and get faymus.' But Little Wolf's parents don't trust him. They send along Mister Furlock Homes-Wolf, Private Investigator. Whose detection methods will be better?

8-10

Jane Darcy

LITTLE WOMEN Louisa May Alcott

➨ Ask women writers of forty or over to name their favourite children's book and you'll find many of them say '*Little Women*'. This is because they identify closely with Jo, one of the March sisters. She's the tomboyish one, the unconventional one and most importantly, the one who wants to be a writer when she grows up. She also resembles Alcott herself.

The book is about the four sisters and how they cope while their father is away fighting in the American Civil War. Meg, the eldest, is good and domestically competent. Jo is next in age, then Beth, who's dreamy, musical and delicate. Amy, the youngest, is a vain little madam who is also very charming.

I adored *Little Women* because I'm an only child and the idea of having sisters fascinated me. By the time you come to the end of the book, you've made four friends. You live through everything that happens to the March girls, and you really feel you're right there in that house. You will definitely cry during the course of the novel but you'll laugh as well.

10+

Adèle Geras

Next?

- The story continues in: ***Good Wives*, *Little Men*** and ***Jo's Boys***.
- Most people who grow up with the stories of the March family also love L.M. Montgomery's **Anne of Green Gables** books (UBG 17) or the **What Katy Did** books by Susan Coolidge (UBG 260).
- ***The Exiles*** by Hilary McKay, and its sequels, are very different stories about four sisters. (UBG 75)
- ***The Brontë Girls*** by Garry Kilworth is a book about the sisters who *all* became famous authors.

LIZZIE DRIPPING Helen Cresswell

➨ Lizzie Dripping is always in trouble and never quite tells the truth, so of course no one believes her when, one day, she says she has seen a witch in the village. Not that this bothers Lizzie – she knows it's true and life is suddenly much more exciting. The witch (who lives in the graveyard) becomes her best friend, and leads her into all kinds of unexpected mischief!

You can follow Lizzie's wonderfully silly and just a little bit spooky adventures in *Lizzie Dripping Again*, *Lizzie Dripping and the Angel*, *Lizzie Dripping and the Witch* and *Lizzie Dripping on Holiday*.

8-10

Eileen Armstrong

Next?

- Try Helen Cresswell's hilarious **The Bagthorpe Saga**. (UBG 22)
- Belladonna in Eva Ibbotson's ***Which Witch*** longs to be a bad, fiendish old hag instead of a beautiful enchantress.
- Miss Cackle runs an Academy for Witches intent on mischief in Jill Murphy's ***The Worst Witch*** (UBG 272), and ***Pongwiffy*** by Kaye Umansky (UBG 192) has to be the smelliest witch ever!
- If you prefer wizards, Diana Hendry's ***Harvey Angell*** will have you smiling till the very last page. (UBG 107)

LOCOMOTION Jacqueline Woodson

➨ 'So this whole book's a poem because poetry's short,' says Lonnie Collins Motion (Lo Co Motion). Though he's only eleven, he has a lot that needs saying ... About his parents, who died in a fire; his sister Lili, who now has a 'new mama'; Miss Edna, with whom he lives; his fellow students.

His teacher's suggestion, writing poetry, releases Lonnie's imagination. Using a variety of forms – sonnets, haiku, free verse – he reveals his story in poetic snapshots expressing his sorrow, hope, fear, pent-up fury and, ultimately, a quiet but barely-suppressible joy and confidence.

This is a powerful and gentle novel about the emerging dignity and social awareness of a sensitive boy.

10-12

Chris Stephenson

Next?

- Delve into Anne Fine's splendidly personal three-volume collection of her favourite poems, ***A Shame to Miss***.
- A book about a boy's discovery of poetry is Sharon Creech's ***Love That Dog***. (UBG 150)
- Discover the way another boy handles his troubles at school in Jack Gantos' ***Joey Pigza Swallowed the Key***. (UBG 128)
- A tougher read about a boy in care is ***Georgie*** by Malachy Doyle. (UBG 90)

LONG LOST Jan Mark

➡ Have you ever run fast to avoid a patch of darkness at the bend of a staircase? Or wondered what the shadows crawling in firelight really are? George Bassett has. And his fears are made worse when he meets his cousins – particularly the elegant and very unpleasant Bertie.

Is there a curse on the eldest Bassett son? George is sure there isn't. He's the eldest after all, and besides, it is the beginning of a new century, and curses are just scary stories ... or are they?

Set in the early 1900s, this is scary enough to keep you awake at night – and to make sure you keep an eye on the shadows. Even your own.

7-9 **Leonie Flynn**

Next?
Long Lost is part of a great series of scary stories called **Shock Shop**, all by different authors. Try these ... if you really think you're up to it.

Hairy Bill by Susan Price is about a very tidy ghost.

You Have Ghost Mail by Terence Blacker is a spooky story with a startling twist.

The Bodigulpa by Jenny Nimmo contains creepy plants, horror and humour!

Goodbye Tommy Blue by Adèle Geras is about a ghostly soldier.

Wicked Chickens by Vivian French. Chickens are sweet ... aren't they?

- Try Chris Mould's comic-book adaptation of the spooky classic ***Dr Jekyll and Mr Hyde***.
- Had enough chillers? For something as different as you can imagine, look for ***Daisy May*** by Jean Ure. It's a lovely, very easy, happy-making book. (UBG 55)

LORD OF THE NUTCRACKER MEN Iain Lawrence

➡ Johnny Briggs is excited when the Great War starts. His father has carved him wooden soldiers – his Nutcracker Men. Evacuated to his Auntie Ivy's, Johnny turns her garden into a muddy battlefield for them, re-enacting the raids and attacks his father describes in letters home from the trenches.

But the letters become grim. Johnny cannot escape the fact that war is frightening. He learns more from a wounded deserter on the run. He begins to wonder if his mock attacks might be influencing what's really happening in France.

You will read of things that are horrifying, but you'll be fascinated. And there's a cheering side to this story, with a wonderful ending based on the extraordinary real-life truce in the trenches at Christmas 1914.

10+ **Jane Darcy**

Next?
- I don't think you'll find a more brilliant book about the First World War, but ***War Game*** by Michael Foreman is a moving story of two friends' experiences in the trenches, which also has something about the Christmas truce. (UBG 257)
- Iain Lawrence also wrote the **High Seas Trilogy**, beginning with ***The Wreckers***.
- Or try Rosemary Sutcliff's ***Simon***, about a boy in the English Civil War.

THE LORD OF THE RINGS J.R.R. Tolkien

➨ You've seen the movie – now read the book!

This is the story of Frodo the hobbit's adventures as he struggles to take the terrible Ring to Mount Doom to destroy it, and of his friends as they try to help him. There's Sam, his faithful servant who also becomes a Ringbearer; Merry and Pippin, fellow hobbits who fight their way through capture by Orcs, sieges and massive battles; Gandalf the wizard who is a great deal more powerful than he seems; and Aragorn, the warrior and Ranger who must find his own powerful destiny. There are elves, dwarves, hideous Black Riders and the evil all-seeing Sauron who intends to conquer all of Middle Earth.

This is the Big Daddy of all sword-and-sorcery fantasy and it's still one of the best. Tolkien invented an entire world, complete with mythologies and languages. The huge epic sweep of his imagination picks you up and carries you to the final thundering battle of wills on Mount Doom.

Warning: obsession can strike at any time.

11+

Patricia Finney

Next?

- After you've finished, do read the Appendices (the passages at the end which are almost a book in themselves) and learn the history of Middle Earth.
- Other sword-and-sorcery fantasies might seem a little thin after Tolkien, but try Anne McCaffrey's **Dragonquest** books. (UBG 67)
- Or read Philip Pullman's **His Dark Materials** – the only children's fantasy sequence that really matches ***The Lord of the Rings*** for scale and epic appeal. (UBG 176)
- To find out how Bilbo got the Ring of Power, read ***The Hobbit***. (UBG 112)
- Tolkien also wrote some other short tales that are worth hunting out – such as ***Farmer Giles of Ham***. For the real fan, there's also a multi-volume companion to ***The Lord of the Rings***, compiled by Tolkien's son Christopher, compiled from notes his father made: ***The History of Middle Earth***.

COMPETITION WINNER

THE LORD OF THE RINGS J.R.R. Tolkien

➨ It took me all the summer holidays to read the three books of *The Lord of the Rings*. Once I started I could not put them down – I was gripped. It was the first book I ever read on the beach.

You might say that a story about little hobbits trekking their way across the world to destroy evil for ever is boring. It is not. In this epic there is action and there are thrills and one of the greatest heroes of all time, Aragorn. In between the huge battles there are stories of hidden worlds, lost secrets and one of the saddest villains I know – Gollum.

This is an adventure s with a difference and a sting-in-the-tail finale. It says a lot about human qualities – the best and the worst – and I thought it was very reflective. It is the ultimate book.

James Male, age 11, Arnold House School

LORNA DOONE R.D. Blackmore

➨ John Ridd is a young man of prodigious strength who lives on Exmoor. It is 1676 and robbers and highwaymen are a part of life. John wanders on to the land of the Doones, a notorious and much-feared family of outlaws. There he meets Lorna, a beautiful little girl who begs him to escape before her violent relatives find him. Years later, John and Lorna meet again and fall in love, but Lorna is now betrothed to the most brutal of all the Doones.

Eventually Lorna discovers her true identity and John rescues her, only to lose her again and again. Published in 1869, the language may seem a little old-fashioned today, but once you get used to it, you'll find it well worth the effort. There are wonderful descriptions of the West Country, great character sketches and brilliantly realised fights where John's great strength proves irresistible.

11+

Jenny Nimmo

Next?

- You might want to read ***Wuthering Heights*** by Emily Brontë. Written in 1847, it tells of a passionate and ill-starred relationship, this time set on the Yorkshire Moors.
- ***Kidnapped*** by R.L. Stevenson is a classic adventure. (UBG 133)
- ***The Children of the New Forest*** by Captain Marryat is another classic story, set during the English Civil Wars. (UBG 47)

hammer. He can make you cry (waterproof mascara a must) and laugh out loud simultaneously.

LOSER Jerry Spinelli

➨ 'Yahoo!' is Donald Zinkoff's first recorded utterance. Happiness, enthusiasm, laughter – that's his natural habitat. Ever the optimist, he finds pleasure in everything, loves school so much he gets there early, considers his father's job as a mailman the most important in the world, and is friends with everyone (particularly the opposing soccer team).

Trouble is, others don't view it that way; to them he's just a loser, someone you avoid picking to play in your team. But Zinkoff's eternal optimism remains intact, even after narrowly avoiding an unnecessary but characteristically unselfish demise.

The story of the irrepressible Zinkoff's progress through elementary school is funny, warm, occasionally heart-wrenching; a celebration of individuality and non-conformity.

Chris Stephenson

9-11

Next?

• You might like to try more of Jerry Spinelli's books about individuals whose behaviour makes them stand out from the crowd. Try ***Stargirl***, a novel as exuberant as a firework display (UBG 225), or the darker-toned ***Wringer***.

• For a real outsider's impact on everyday family life (in this case, an alien), read about the hilarious complications arising from Pascal's visit with the Castles in Pat Thomson's ***Strange Exchange***. It's one of the funniest books around.

THE LOST WORLD

Arthur Conan Doyle

➨ *The Lost World* was written nearly a hundred years ago, and was one of the first books to explore the excitement and possibilities of adventure in encountering dinosaurs. Conan Doyle knew all about telling a story (he was the creator of Sherlock Holmes) and I think the exploits of the extraordinary Professor Challenger and his companions are still gripping today. As a boy's story for men, or a man's story for boys of its time (as the author admits), women hardly get a look-in at all – but perhaps part of the interest of reading the book is also to note the differences of behaviour and expectation between then and now. In that way, too, it is a description of a lost world.

Quentin Blake

11+

Next?

• Try Arthur Conan Doyle's Sherlock Holmes classic, ***The Hound of the Baskervilles***. (UBG 117)

• Read some more classic adventure, such as ***Twenty Thousand Leagues Under the Sea*** (UBG 250) or ***Journey to the Centre of the Earth***, both by Jules Verne.

• Or one of the all-time great dinosaur books, Michael Crichton's ***Jurassic Park***.

• Or what about something completely different? Raymond Briggs's cartoon story of the caveman ***Ug*** will make you laugh. (UBG 251)

THE LOTTIE PROJECT

Jacqueline Wilson

➨ Have you ever been given a school project that you thought was going to be *really* boring? Well Charlie ('*Don't* call me Charlotte'), the most popular girl in her class, thinks that the project she has to do on the Victorians is going to be deathly dull. But then she dreams up the character of Lottie, a Victorian servant girl the same age as her, and when she starts to write Lottie's diary a whole new world comes to life in her head.

This book is one of Jacqueline Wilson's very best. It's a sparkling read that deals with friendships, single mums, boyfriends, school and lots else as well. Charlie's a great character – she's the sort of girl anyone would want as their best friend, and her only fault is ... she knows it!

Susan Reuben

8-11

Next?

• Try ***Double Act***, another story by Jacqueline Wilson. (UBG 67)

• Or ***A Little Princess*** by Frances Hodgson Burnett, about a girl who is orphaned and ends up as a servant. (UBG 144)

• Or try ***The Story of the Treasure Seekers*** by E. Nesbit, about a family of Victorian children.

• In Anne Fine's ***A Pack of Liars***, Laura and Oliver are surprised by their new pen-pals ...

LOVE THAT DOG

Sharon Creech

➡ This book is very difficult to categorise. It's like a diary, that's a collection of poems, that tell a story with some help from William Blake and Robert Frost. It's just unique. Jack is a boy who thinks poems are for girls until he begins to find his own voice through writing poetry and starts appreciating the poetry around him. A quick read, this is perfect for those who find big novels hard going, and those who find poetry difficult. Following Jack on his journey is easy, and fun, and as you turn the pages you get gently drawn into the mind of a little intellectual.

This book is yellow, but it's not afraid to go the way no other book has gone before it. It's a great example of how the rules can be broken by staying true to a simple idea that works.

8+

Benjamin Zephaniah

Next?
- Poetry! You'll get good ideas for a few poets to look for in ***Love That Dog***.
- You might also like collections by Michael Rosen, Roger McGough or ***Heard It in the Playground*** by Allan Ahlberg.
- Or try the tougher ***Locomotion*** by Jacqueline Woodson (UBG 146).
- More Sharon Creech? Try ***The Wanderer*** for a more challenging read in which you have to piece together the story as you go along. (UBG 257)

MACB Neil Arksey

➡ A confession first: I don't like football. So why am I telling you about a book that features football big-time? Because it's such a fantastic story – it's exciting, creepy, fantastically fast moving – and it gripped me from the first page. I finished it at four in the morning – and when I didn't know what 'Snaking left, then right, he bypassed two' meant it didn't matter a hoot. It's an incredibly clever book because it echoes the story of *Macbeth*, with a fortune-teller promising an unlikely promotion ... but if you don't know any Shakespeare that's fine. And don't think that the Shakespeare connection makes it a 'posh' book; it's full of real kids who chew gum and kick beer cans – and get caught up in a literally deadly rivalry.

9-11

Vivian French

Next?
- If it's another grab-you-by-the-throat read you want, then I'd go for ***Playing on the Edge***, also by Neil Arksey. (UBG 191)
- If you want more ways of finding out about Shakespeare, try the illustrated books by Marcia Williams, starting with ***Mr William Shakespeare's Plays***. (UBG 166)
- Or for something else that's fast and gripping, try ***Piggies***, by Nick Gifford. (UBG 188)

THE MACHINE GUNNERS

Robert Westall

➡ It is 1940, the most dangerous moment of the Second World War. Britain is alive with rumours of a German invasion. Thirteen-year-old Chas McGill and his friends spend their time scavenging for souvenirs: bits of aircraft, bombs. One day, Chas finds a working machine gun in a crashed bomber. But what happens when he finds a German gun, along with a German gunner, Rudi?

This is a thrilling adventure about outwitting adults, making friends and a war so real you'll imagine you lived through it.

10-12

Alan Gibbons

Next?
- Another great book by Robert Westall is ***The Kingdom by the Sea***.
- Westall's ***Gulf*** is set during the first Gulf War in the early nineties. It features the strange relationship between a British boy and an Iraqi soldier far away. (UBG 102)
- ***Blitzcat*** features two of Westall's themes – war and cats – in a terrific adventure. (UBG 31)
- Or read ***Blitzed*** by Robert Swindells, about a boy going back in time to the Blitz.
- Linda Newbery's ***Blitz Boys*** is another great story set during the Second World War. (UBG 31)

MADAME DOUBTFIRE Anne Fine

➡ Out-of-work actor, Daniel Hilliard, is divorced from his businesswoman wife, Miranda; the two of them do not see eye to eye. So in order to spend more time with his children, Daniel disguises himself as a woman and applies for the position as their nanny. And, of course, hilarious situations follow. Will Miranda discover Madame Doubtfire's true identity? As always, Anne Fine resolves the story in an unexpected way.

This clever book is as insightful as it is funny. Out of the misery of an all too common situation – a broken family, and children tugged between warring parents – is plucked love and humour. A well-told tale that is warm and real without sentimentality. A classic with heart.

10-12

Neil Arksey

Next?
- Try Anne's ***Goggle-eyes*** about a girl who hates her mother's new boyfriend. (UBG 151)
- Or what about Pete Johnson's ***Rescuing Dad***, about two kids who try to 'improve' their dad in order to persuade their mum to take him back? (UBG 202)
- In Gwyneth Rees's ***The Mum Hunt***, a girl tries to find her dad a new girlfriend. (UBG 168)
- ***Granny the Pag*** by Nina Bawden is a powerful story of a girl's fight to live with whom she chooses.

THE MAGIC FARAWAY TREE

series

THE ENCHANTED WOOD • THE MAGIC FARAWAY TREE • THE FOLK OF THE FARAWAY TREE

Enid Blyton

➡ These books were written in 1943. I read them as a child and loved them, my daughter read them (they used to be her favourite books) and you will read them now and enjoy them just as much. Although dated in tone and background (the girls 'help mother in the house' and the boy, Jo, 'helps his father in the garden'), the stories remain marvellously ingenious and entertaining, combining magic, fantasy, excitement and adventure together with a cosy homeliness. If only life were really like that!

There are several **Faraway Tree** books, all containing lots of adventures. They are quite long, so are not a quick read. Although the content is suitable for those aged eight and upwards, I think you'd find them enjoyable at any age – they are the sort of lovely, comfortable stories you could always turn to if you're feeling frazzled.

8-10

Mary Hooper

Next?
- When you've read all the **Magic Faraway Tree** books, you can move on to Enid Blyton's other magic series. And then her **Adventure** books (UBG 124), **The Famous Five** (UBG 78) and **The Secret Seven** (UBG 216). And then ... but it will probably take you until you are grown up to get through them all!
- But if you want to try something not by Enid Blyton, read ***Half Magic*** by Edward Eager. (UBG 103)

COMPETITION WINNER★ COMPETITION WINNER

THE ENCHANTED WOOD Enid Blyton

I loved this book because it was really exciting, magical and interesting. This book made me feel all tingly inside and it made me feel like I couldn't stop reading it and it made me feel like I couldn't do anything but read. Because of this book I keep looking for more. I absolutely loved it!

Jessica Shafique, age 9, Heathfield Junior School

especially ***Naughty Amelia Jane***.

THE MAGIC FINGER

Roald Dahl

➡ Have you ever felt so angry with someone that you wished something really awful would happen to them? Not because you really meant it, but because just for a moment you were in such a temper with them? How would you feel, then, if that dreadful thing were actually to come true?

The heroine of *The Magic Finger* has just this strange power: 'It always happens when I see red … Then I get very, very hot all over … Then the tip of the forefinger of my right hand begins to tingle most terribly …' So when she points at her neighbours the Greggs, we know something terrible will happen to them … And because this is a Roald Dahl story, we know that it'll be something funny, and very strange …

Daniel Hahn

7+

Next?

- Another Roald Dahl book that's great (well, they *all* are really, but this one is particularly so) is ***The Twits***. (UBG 250)
- Or try his poems, which are very funny; my favourites are the ***Revolting Rhymes***.
- Another book about strange things happening, this time at school, is Paul Stewart's ***The Blobheads***. (UBG 31)

THE MAGIC SHOP series

RUSSELL TROY, MONSTER BOY • JEREMY THATCHER, DRAGON HATCHER • JENNIFER MURDLEY'S TOAD • CHARLIE EGGLESTON'S TALKING SKULL

Bruce Coville

➡ Four children – three boys and a girl – find Mr Elives's magic shop with its scary owner, talking owl, magician's tools and books. Each takes one special thing away with them. Russell doesn't read the instructions on his monster ring properly, and it turns him into a winged, clawed, monster. Will he be stuck like that for ever? Jennifer's toad turns out to be embarrassingly talkative. Charlie's skull makes him far too truthful when before he was never honest, and Jeremy's dragon – well, these things *will* eat – and they *are* meat eaters … Each child has to try to pretend that life is normal, and find ways to deal with their very conspicuous new possessions, and some mistakes, once made, can't be erased.

Tamora Pierce

8-10

Next?

- Read them again! Whatever your age, you'll find something new to think about.
- Or try Patrice Kindl's ***Owl in Love***, the story of a perfectly normal young shapeshifter named Owl, who eats mouse sandwiches and has a crush on her science teacher.
- Patricia Wrede's **Enchanted Forest** books (starting with ***Dealing with Dragons***) have more of a fairytale setting, but they introduce a very practical princess dealing with extraordinary things.
- Other Bruce Coville books are a must, too. Try ***There's an Alien in My Classroom*** and its sequels.
- Also look for the slightly harder **Young Wizards** series by Diane Duane. (UBG 275) Or for something easier, how about the **Half Magic** series by Edward Eager? (UBG 103)

If you're looking for The Magician's House Quartet by William Corlett, turn to p. 225

MALORY TOWERS Enid Blyton

Next?
- If you like school stories you might try the 'boy' sort, such as ***Billy Bunter of Greyfriars School*** by Frank Richards. Or try **Jennings** by Anthony Buckeridge. (UBG 126)
- You might also like Enid Blyton's ***Adventure*** series. My favourite was ***Island of Adventure***. (UBG 124)
- For the next stage up girls' rite-of-passage book, try ***Daddy-Long-Legs*** by Jean Webster. (UBG 55)
- ***Don't miss our SCHOOL STORIES selection on pp. 212-213.***

➨ As a child, I adored Enid Blyton's books and **Malory Towers** had two profound impacts on my life: it convinced me to go to boarding school (a mistake) and taught me the value of page-turning narratives (a gift).

The six-book series follows the fortunes of a group of girls from their first to their last term at the school. Even now, thirty-five years on, when I open a **Malory Towers** book, the characters leap off the page: spoilt and spiteful, golden-haired Gwendoline; sharp talking Alicia; steadfast Sally and our brave, hot-tempered heroine, Darryl Rivers.

Blyton's stories follow a strict moral code: they are about owning up to faults, recognising loyalty and kindness, accepting the need for the full and frank apology. Blyton is particularly strong on issues of female peer-group rivalry and the difficulty of changing social allegiances. But her books are also compelling, funny, warm and surprisingly twenty-first century stories about girls growing up and discovering who and what they are.

7-10

Nicky Singer

THE MAN IN THE IRON MASK

Alexandre Dumas

➨ The spirit of the Three Musketeers lives on, though wrinkled with the years. Here the story revolves around a mysterious masked prisoner, doomed to a ghastly fate. Who is he? The twin brother of the king? The king's illegitimate son?

The 'man in the iron mask' is based on a true character brought to the dreaded Paris prison, the Bastille, in 1698. He was kept masked at all times and never had his name spoken. After his death, five years later, he was buried in an unmarked grave.

Whoever he is, the idea of enclosing a man in an iron mask has its own grisly glamour. No wonder he became a star of stage and screen, and hero of many more novels. But though the purists may carp at Dumas's sprawling unmade bed of a novel (over six hundred pages), few storytellers can spin a better yarn or make history come to life so vividly.

11+

James Riordan

Next?
- Try Charles Dickens's ***A Tale of Two Cities***. The cities are London and Paris, although Paris is where the action takes place.
- Baroness Orczy's ***The Scarlet Pimpernel*** tells of a band of Englishmen pledged to rescue victims of the post-revolutionary reign of terror in Paris. (UBG 211)
- And, of course, try ***The Three Musketeers*** also by Alexandre Dumas if you've not read it already. (UBG 241)
- ***See my HISTORICAL STORIES selections on pp. 110-111.***

MAPHEAD Lesley Howarth

Next?
- ***Flour Babies*** (UBG 86) and ***Up on Cloud Nine*** (UBG 252), both by Anne Fine, will keep your spirits buoyed after ***MapHead***.
- If you're seeking more other-worldly visitors, check out ***Harvey Angell*** by Diana Hendry. (UBG 107)
- ***Stargirl*** by Jerry Spinelli is another great story about enjoying life. (UBG 225)

➨ MapHead, who comes from the Subtle World, is facing his twelfth birthday – the Dawn Power Year. Usually he roams the world with his Dad, but this year they've come to Cornwall to find MapHead's mother, and to find MapHead's own true self.

No one who meets MapHead will ever forget him, and neither will you. He is a true original and his story is one of the sunniest, most cheerful books you'll ever read. It celebrates life – three cheers for Lesley Howarth! Don't forget to look out for the sequel, *MapHead 2*.

Jon Appleton

9-11

MARA, DAUGHTER OF THE NILE Eloise McGraw

➡ Mara, an Egyptian slave under the rule of the female pharaoh Hatshepsut, is hired as translator to the princess Inanni, who is meant to be a bride to the captive co-pharaoh Thutmose. Mara is being blackmailed by a handsome nobleman who wants her to slip Thutmose messages about a plot to take Hatshepsut from the throne and set Thutmose there as sole ruler of Egypt. Mara has to worry about her master's spies and Inanni's homesickness, tomb robbery and treason, love and freedom. She needs her quick wits as she goes from master to blackmailer, spy to rebel, with death as a reward if she is caught. She's spirited, clever, and strong – one of my favourite literary heroes!

9-11

Tamora Pierce

Next?
• If you want more stories with an Egyptian theme, try ***The Great Pyramid Robbery*** by Katherine Roberts (UBG 100) or ***The Time-travelling Cat*** by Julia Jarman(UBG 244).
• Or some comics: Goscinny/ Uderzo's ***Asterix and Cleopatra*** (read about Asterix on p. 21) and Hergé's Tintin in ***Cigars of the Pharaoh***. (You'll find the **Tintin** books recommended on p. 244.)
• For strong heroines, try Tamora Pierce's own **Song of the Lioness** series, which starts with ***Alanna, The First Adventure***. (UBG 223)

THE MARBLE CRUSHER Michael Morpurgo

➡ Albert starts a new school when his parents move from the countryside to the town. There, streetwise Sid Creedy takes advantage of Albert's innocence and tells him all sorts of fibs. Without batting an eyelid, Sid informs Albert that their PE teacher Mr Cooper is an escaped monk (bald head: complete giveaway) and that the headmaster has six wives. And Albert believes him. After getting into serious trouble for playing marbles in school, Albert confronts his wicked teachers with their misdeeds and fun and games follow (but sadly, no games of marbles).

I first came across this story when my class and I were feeling particularly fed up at the prospect of the return of our head teacher, Dangerous Doris. Two minutes after starting it we were falling about with laughter and had forgotten all about Doris.

Michael Cox

7-9

Next?
• ***Ging Gang Goolie, It's an Alien*** by Bob Wilson is an hilarious story about Boy Scouts encountering an extra terrestrial!
• Anne Fine's ***How to Write Really Badly*** is a school story with a difference. (UBG 119)
• ***The Marble Crusher*** is also available with the stories 'Colly's Barn' and 'Conker' in one book. For something like these, try Dick King-Smith's books – see p. 286 for a list.

MARIANNE DREAMS Catherine Storr

➡ I didn't have my own copy of *Marianne Dreams* when I was a child. I had about fifteen scruffy paperbacks on my bedroom shelf in those days – a little different from the fifteen thousand books crammed into my tiny house now! I borrowed *Marianne Dreams* from the library many times. It was a book that haunted me. Now I've just re-read it I still find it strange, beguiling and frightening, and I'm more aware of the psychological depth of the story.

The plot is simple. Marianne is recovering from a long illness and is confined to bed. She doodles a house in her drawing book and then dreams she is there. She draws a boy looking out of the window and the next night dreams he is there, too. She gets angry with him and scribbles over the window and then in this weird dreamworld he is trapped behind bars. She draws eyes on the rocks in the garden and they become real sinister beings, watching the two children ... I'm not going to tell you what happens next. Read it yourself!

9-12

Jacqueline Wilson

Next?
• Try another Catherine Storr book: ***The If Game***, a scary story about the blurred edges of reality.
• For another unsettling story, try ***Coraline*** by Neil Gaiman. (UBG 51)
• Or there is ***Kit's Wilderness*** by David Almond, about fear and hope. (UBG 135)

eight was ***Our Island Story*** by H. E. Marshall. Almost all the historical subjects I have written about

THE MARK OF THE HORSE LORD Rosemary Sutcliff

➨ This wonderful book is full of classic storytelling devices. There is the gladiator who wins his freedom, the ex-slave who looks enough like a prince to be able to swap roles with him and, of course, a wicked queen.

When Phaedrus the Gladiator finally puts life in the arena behind him, he quickly finds himself caught up in a plot to overthrow Liadham, treacherous queen of the Dalriad tribes, and to restore the Lord of the Horse People. Phaedrus has to learn how to carry out his new role successfully, and gradually he grows into the part. I won't tell you how the story ends but be warned – it reduced me to tears on the bus home from school when I first read it!

This is an adventure story, a history lesson and a trip to Scotland all in one. I can't recommend it highly enough.

Laura Hutchings

10-12

Next?

- I'm tempted to say anything by Rosemary Sutcliff, but some of her books are better than others. Most highly recommended is ***The Eagle of the Ninth*** and the books that follow it. (UBG 68) ***Frontier Wolf*** is another one set in Scotland.
- If you enjoy learning about history through fiction then try the following: ***The King Must Die*** by Mary Renault (UBG 134); ***King of Shadows*** by Susan Cooper (UBG 134) or ***The Crown of Violet*** by Geoffrey Trease.

MARTIN FARRELL

Janni Howker

➨ The eponymous hero of *Martin Farrell* is a lad caught between two great feuding families in the north of England. He belongs to both of them, but is loved by neither. They are a fierce, barbaric people, and many of the scenes of the story are truly horrific. But the wicked deeds do not go unobserved. There is a spiritual battle going on for peace in the 'debatable lands', a searching for the time when the killing will cease. And Martin, newly-orphaned, is the fulcrum.

Janni Howker's book is a genuine favourite of mine. It ought to be just an historical novel, but it is not. The tale is told as a Border Ballad; the rhythm is perfect, and the lilt of northern speech is interspersed with lovely old dialect words. The proper way to read it is to let the words sing inside your head.

Sylvia Waugh

10-12

Next?

- You might also like ***The Border Ballads***, a collection of mediaeval song and verse, all about war, thieving, jealousy and revenge!
- Try reading a version of ***Sir Gawain and the Green Knight***; there is a good one by Selina Hastings.
- Janni Howker's other books include ***Badger on the Barge*** (UBG 22) and ***The Nature of the Beast***.
- ***The Dark Horse*** by Marcus Sedgwick deals with an equally barbaric threat. (UBG 58)

THE ULTIMATE READERS' POLL

YOUR TOP TEN FUNNY BOOKS

1. The Twits by Roald Dahl
2. Captain Underpants by Dav Pilkey
3. George's Marvellous Medicine by Roald Dahl
4. Horrid Henry by Francesca Simon
5. The Story of Tracy Beaker by Jacqueline Wilson
6. The BFG by Roald Dahl
7. Charlie and the Chocolate Factory by Roald Dahl
8. The Dare Game by Jacqueline Wilson
9. The Giggler Treatment by Roddy Doyle
10. Harry Potter and the Chamber of Secrets by J.K. Rowling

ever since have their origins in chapters in that wonderful, vivid book.

MARTYN PIG Kevin Brooks

➨ This is a darkly funny, gripping thriller that will keep you completely hooked right up to the final twist.

Martyn Pig is a fifteen-year-old boy trapped in a miserable, dreary world with a horrible, drunken father and a seriously embarrassing name. His only means of escape are his obsession with murder mysteries, and his friendship with Alex – the beautiful, talented and enigmatic girl who lives down his street. Then, one grey evening just before Christmas, a horrible accident happens. Events spiral out of control, with breathtaking and chilling consequences – and Martyn finds himself caught up in the centre of his very own 'whodunnit'.

Tense, fast-paced and at times hilarious, *Martyn Pig* is the sort of book that will make you want to stay up all night and keep turning the pages, just to find out what happens!

Victoria Webb

11+

Next?
- If you want to read more by Kevin Brooks, you might like to try the slightly older ***Lucas***.
- Or try K.K. Beck's thriller ***Fake***, about two boys on the run from a 'wilderness survival camp' that was meant to improve them.
- John Brindley's ***Rhino Boy*** is also about a boy dealing with unexpected and freaky events.
- ***Holes*** by Louis Sachar is a novel about another teenager in big trouble. (UBG 113)
- Malachy Doyle's ***Who Is Jesse Flood?*** is another great book about a boy finding his place in the world. (UBG 263)

MARY PLAIN series Gwynedd Rae

➨ This series about 'an unusual first-class bear' (as she describes herself) is delightfully witty, well-written and original. Mary lives in the famous Bear Pits in Berne, Switzerland, with her twin cousins and other relatives, until her favourite visitor the Owl Man takes her out to compete in a contest to find the most unusual animal, which she easily wins. Her white rosette goes straight to her head and after that there's no holding her back. With the Owl Man in tow, she struts her way from one hilarious adventure to another, full of bounce and conceit, with only occasional bouts of 'pit-sickness' ('Do you think the twins are happy without me?'). Long may she stay in print to delight new generations!

Lynne Reid Banks

7-9

Next?
- Michael Bond created another wonderful character, who is also a bear, in his famous stories about **Paddington**. (UBG 24)
- More bears? A.A. Milne's ***Winnie-the-Pooh*** is possibly the nation's favourite! (UBG 266)
- E.B. White's ***Charlotte's Web*** is a story that will make you laugh, cry and just about everything in between. (UBG 45)

MARY POPPINS series P.L. Travers

➨ Believe me, the book is far better than the film. It's stranger, and nothing is quite as you expect. Mary Poppins is a governess to Jane and Michael, and a figure with odd, supernatural powers. Whether dining out in a chalk drawing, pasting stars on the sky, having a birthday at the zoo or going Christmas shopping with one of the Pleiades, Mary P. is always starchy and prim, but secretly wise underneath. Hilariously funny, sometimes piercingly sad and full of a surreal magic that is never explained, this is a book you'll never forget.

Catherine Fisher

8-10

Next?
- Try others in the series (though I think the first is the best): ***Mary Poppins Comes Back*** and ***Mary Poppins in Cherry Tree Lane***.
- A book about the doorways that can lie between worlds is ***The Lion, the Witch and the Wardrobe*** by C.S. Lewis. (UBG 141)
- Another peculiar nanny? Try the harder, but really great, ***Madame Doubtfire*** by Anne Fine. (UBG 151)
- A book with a similar sense of whimsy is the classic ***The Hundred and One Dalmatians*** by Dodie Smith. (UBG 119)

MATCH OF DEATH James Riordan

➡ This is based on a true story. And like many true stories, it is far more shocking and terrifying than anything made up.

Vova is fifteen and loves football. He lives in the Ukraine, and is powerless to stop the German army invading his country, although he joins the resistance and fights as best he can. He survives suffering and hardship, until one day he is given the chance to play football again – though the stakes are unbelievably high. Lose and live, or win and die.

Starkly told and heartbreaking in the way the lives of so many people are shown to be so casually destroyed by war, this book made me cry. I'll always remember Vova, and his choice. And I'll never think of football in quite the same way again.

Leonie Flynn

11+

Next?

- For another surprising appearance of football in the midst of war – this time in a more upbeat context – try Iain Lawrence's ***Lord of the Nutcracker Men.*** (UBG 147)
- A much easier read about another football game in a different war – also based on a true story – is ***War Game*** by Michael Foreman (this made me cry too!). (UBG 257)
- Another James Riordan novel to try is ***The Prisoner***. (UBG 194)
- If you were interested in reading about the war, try ***Music on the Bamboo Radio*** by Martin Booth. (UBG 168)

MATILDA Roald Dahl

Next?

- Try ***The BFG*** (UBG 27) and ***The Witches*** (UBG 268), also by Roald Dahl. Or you may prefer his shorter books such as ***The Twits*** (UBG 250) and ***George's Marvellous Medicine*** (UBG 89); both are outrageously funny.
- J.K. Rowling's **Harry Potter** books have enough jokes, adventures and independent children outwitting adults to keep you happy for a long time. (UBG 106)

➡ By the time Matilda is three she has taught herself to read. She's tiny and extremely brainy, but her awful parents hate her for her cleverness. When she goes to school, she finds that the headmistress, Miss Trunchbull, is even worse than her parents. She's a huge bully, who throws children about whenever she feels like it. One day, Miss Trunchbull goes too far and Matilda is so angry she makes something happen to her. Matilda finds that she has an extraordinary magical power.

Luckily, Matilda is befriended by her teacher, Miss Honey, and when she learns about Miss Honey's sad past, Matilda decides to use her new power to help her. But as well as helping Miss Honey, Matilda's brilliant plan changes her own life in a way she never thought possible.

This brilliant story is so entertaining and funny, and so cleverly resolved, that readers of all ages can't fail to enjoy it.

Jenny Nimmo

8+

MAUS I and II Art Spiegelman

➡ *Maus* is another survivor's story of life under the Nazis, as told to his son, Art Spiegelman. All the characters, including Art and his dad, are depicted as animals – mice for the Jews, cats for the Germans, and pigs for the Polish. The pictures are tiny and scratchy and look innocent enough, but the story is so overwhelming that even these tiny little characters made me cry at one point. The animal viciousness of the Nazis is worse than any cat-and-mouse game ever was. There are two volumes of this book, both of which are in print and may not be in your library's history section because there are still a few people out there who think anything in comics form isn't a 'proper' book. Wait till you see this.

Ted Dewan

11+

Next?

- ***The Diary of a Young Girl*** by Anne Frank is a riveting and heartbreaking read. (UBG 61)
- Raymond Briggs's ***Ethel and Ernest*** is a biography of his mum and dad. Although theirs is a more ordinary tale than Spiegelman's, it's a great story, and told in words and pictures with a lot of love and affection. (UBG 174)
- ***Witnesses to War: Eight True Life Stories of Nazi Persecution*** edited by Michael Leapman is a harrowing and yet uplifting book.
- ***Look out for Ted Dewan's selection of comics and PICTURE BOOKS on pp. 186-187.***

my current favourite kids' books are the **Harry Potter** series and the Lemony Snicket books.

THE MEMORY PRISONER Thomas Bloor

➡ Maddie is one of the most fascinating characters you'll ever come across: clever, brave and with an extraordinary photographic memory. But her memory holds back one vital piece of information: what was the terrible thing she saw thirteen years ago? Try as she might to recover the lost memory, all Maddie can recall is that it was so utterly terrifying she hasn't dared to leave her house since it – whatever 'it' was – happened. Until, that is, she's forced to go in search of the truth hidden in the sinister Tower Library, control centre of everything that happens in Pridebridge City.

Thomas Bloor's book has a bizarre, scary atmosphere yet it will also make you laugh with its dark, off-beat humour.

9-12 **Gill Vickery**

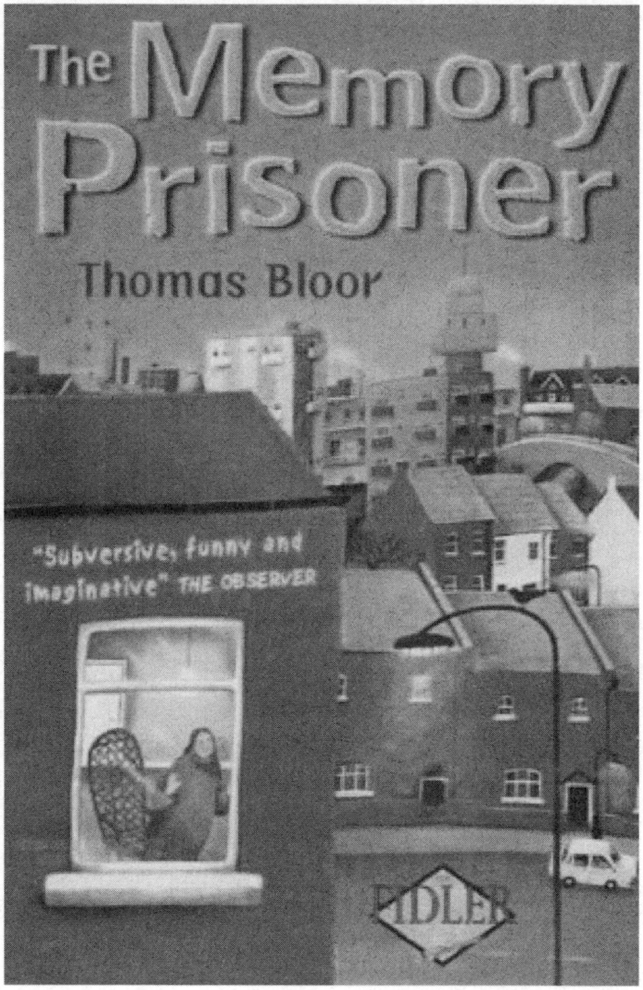

Next?
- For more of this author's quirky novels, read the prequel to this book, ***The House of Eyes***, and also ***Factory of Shadows*** and ***Blood Willow***.
- Gillian Cross's ***The Demon Headmaster*** is also about a sinister manipulator who, like Lexeter in ***The Memory Prisoner***, is set on controlling everyone and everything. (UBG 59)
- If you like to read about the real world made mysterious by cruel circumstances, read David Almond's ***Heaven Eyes*** (UBG 108) and Anne Merrick's ***Someone Came Knocking***.

THE MENNYMS Sylvia Waugh

➡ The Mennyms are a family of human-sized rag dolls, unchanged since life was breathed into them by their maker, forty years ago. They can deceive the world into thinking they're real people but they can't deceive themselves; they enjoy their 'pretends' but they know their limitations. Suddenly, over the course of a year, the family faces challenges like never before – from both inside and outside their home. You fear for their safety from chapter to chapter and at the end of the book you sigh with delight and trepidation – because there are four more books in this brilliant, compelling series and I guarantee you won't want to leave the Mennyms till you've finished the very last word written about them.

9-12 **Jon Appleton**

Next?
- When ***The Mennyms*** was published, it reminded people of Mary Norton's classic tale, ***The Borrowers***. (UBG 33)
- ***Mistress Masham's Repose*** by T.H. White is a classic tale of discovering a family of strange and different people. (UBG 162)
- Or try Rumer Godden's story about the inhabitants of a doll's house – ***The Doll's House***. (UBG 65)

MIDNIGHT FOR CHARLIE BONE (Book 1 of Children of the Red King)

Jenny Nimmo

➡ Charlie is an ordinary boy living with his mum, two grandmas (nice and nasty) and Uncle Paton. Charlie's life changes for ever when, one afternoon, something peculiar happens.

By mistake he gets someone else's family picture from the photo shop and hears the people in the photo talking. He manages to find its owner Miss Ingledew who tells him about her niece, Emma Tolly, the baby in the photo. Baby Emma was exchanged for a box and Miss Ingledew has never stopped looking for her since. Charlie decides to try and help Miss Ingledew find Emma (who would now be Charlie's age). In his quest, Charlie makes new friends and enemies.

I didn't want to put this exciting book down. I really wanted to find out what happened to Charlie. Will Miss Ingledew ever see her niece again? You must read it and find out for yourself.

Julia Lytollis

9-11

Next?
- Move on to the sequel, ***The Time Twister***. Charlie's powers have developed. He meets his great-uncle who has travelled forwards in time. Will Charlie be able to help him?
- ***Matilda*** by Roald Dahl is about a girl whose parents do not appreciate her. When trying to teach her father a lesson, she learns that she has extraordinary powers. (UBG 157)
- ***Charmed Life*** in the **Worlds of Chrestomanci** series by Diana Wynne Jones is a hugely enjoyable story of a boy who finds his destiny. (UBG 272)

THE MIDNIGHT FOX Betsy Byars

➡ To begin with, Tom is not interested in going to live on a farm for two months – he wants to stay in the city. When his mum tries to entice him with tales of cows and horses, he says 'Animals hate me.' But then he goes off to his Aunt Millie's farm. Here time slows down for Tom; he's bored and hangs out by the pond. Then, one day, Tom sees a black fox and is absolutely electrified. He is more excited than he has ever been. *The Midnight Fox* follows Tom's sightings of the fox through to him actually fighting to save its life. It is a thrilling adventure story, tense and exciting, that keeps you gripped to the very last page.

Jackie Kay

9-11

Next?
- For a quite different Betsy Byars, read ***The Eighteenth Emergency***. (UBG 71)
- For a slightly more demanding read, try Matthew Sweeney's ***Fox*** about a boy who becomes friends with a homeless man and his pet fox.
- ***Don't miss our ANIMAL STORIES recommendations on pp. 16-17.***

MIDNIGHT IS A PLACE Joan Aiken

➡ Well, the place is Blastburn, and the hero and heroine are Lucas and Anna-Marie, both beset by wicked relations, lost fortunes and all the trimmings of awful weather and astonishing luck (bad and good). And the time is an industrial age, when children in England worked in dreadful conditions in factories (as they still do in some parts of the world).

All the adventure in this brilliant book is *outrageously* adventurous. The horrible places are about as horrible as they come (wild, pig-infested sewers and the slippery rims of boiling vats of glue). No characters are more likeable than the brave and resourceful Lucas, or the sparkling Anna-Marie. And listen for the song that runs through the story, wistful and beguiling. That's where the title comes from.

Hilary McKay

10-12

Next?
- Now read everything else by Joan Aiken – all her books are superb. Start with ***The Wolves of Willoughby Chase*** (UBG 270) or ***The Shadow Guests***.
- ***The Midnight Folk*** by John Masefield is a classic about magical possibilities. Also look for his ***The Box of Delights***, which Joan Aiken recommends on p. 34.
- Another book centred around the mills is ***The Cellar Lad*** by Theresa Tomlinson. (UBG 43)

THE MIGHTY CRASHMAN

Jerry Spinelli

➨ Friendships are forged in the strangest of ways. Crash Coogan is the coolest kid at school. He's the star of the football team; he's big, tough and all the other kids adore him. And then there is Penn Webb. Penn is … different. He's a vegetarian. His parents are odd. He even wants to be a cheerleader – anybody'd think he *wanted* to be bullied!

And Crash is happy to oblige …

This story, though told through the eyes of a bully, is about a lot more than just bullying. You learn as Crash learns, and when his life takes a dip, and even all his brute strength and football skill can't help him, then you really do take a new look at what it means to be strong.

9-11

Leonie Flynn

Next?

- Two other great stories that look at friendship, school and families in a very different way ***Stargirl*** (UBG 225) and ***Loser*** (UBG 149) both by Jerry Spinelli.
- Also look out for two Louis Sachar books: ***Holes*** (UBG 113) and ***The Boy Who Lost His Face*** (UBG 35), both by Louis Sachar. They're both about surviving whatever life throws at you.
- For a great story with a footballer as the hero (this time UK football, not the American kind) try ***Playing on the Edge*** by Neil Arksey. (UBG 191)

MIGHTY FIZZ CHILLA

Philip Ridley

➨ Milo Stick (Ridley names are always tasty) is thirteen with sensitive lips and a mohican haircut. His mum, unable to handle him, sends him off to a defunct boarding house by the sea, run by two women: Cressida Bell who is overweight, blind and emotional, and Dee Dee Six who is mannish and 'fact-crazy'. Outside, a dangerous Scotsman Captain Jellicoe, armed with an eye-patch and a kilt, rages and rampages on the shore. Through a set of interlocking stories told by Cressida, Dee Dee and the Captain, an awful lot is concealed and bit by bit things are revealed. These are little masterpieces of weirdness, feeling and suspense. As the book progresses the tales interweave and by the end magically merge. A clever book from a very clever writer.

10-12

Michael Rosen

Next?

- Read more Philip Ridley, such as ***Vinegar Street***, ***Dakota of the White Flats*** (UBG 56) and ***ZinderZunder***.
- ***Muddle Earth*** by Paul Stewart and illustrated by Chris Riddell is hilarious fun. (UBG 168)
- Or try Theresa Breslin's **Dream Master** books, about dreams that can take you back in time.

MILLY-MOLLY-MANDY stories

Joyce Lankester Brisley

➨ I first read *Milly-Molly-Mandy* when I was a girl and enjoyed the stories then. After re-reading them, I can still give them a big thumbs up!

Milly-Molly-Mandy lives with her father, mother, grandma, grandpa, uncle and aunty in a white cottage with a thatched roof. Her real name is Millicent Margaret Amanda, but as that is a real mouthful, her family and friends call her Milly-Molly-Mandy for short. Each chapter in the book tells you about Milly-Molly-Mandy's adventures with her friends Billy Blunt and Susan in the village where she lives.

This is a very enjoyable book to read by yourself or to have read to you. You are sure to have fun with Milly-Molly-Mandy.

7-9

Julia Lytollis

Next?

- ***My Naughty Little Sister*** by Dorothy Edwards is just as charming and funny. (UBG 170)
- Or try Enid Blyton's ***Folk of the Faraway Tree*** (see p. 151 for the ***Magic Faraway Tree***).
- Or read the delightful **Mrs Pepperpot** stories by Alf Prøysen. (UBG 167)

MINNOW ON THE SAY

Philippa Pearce

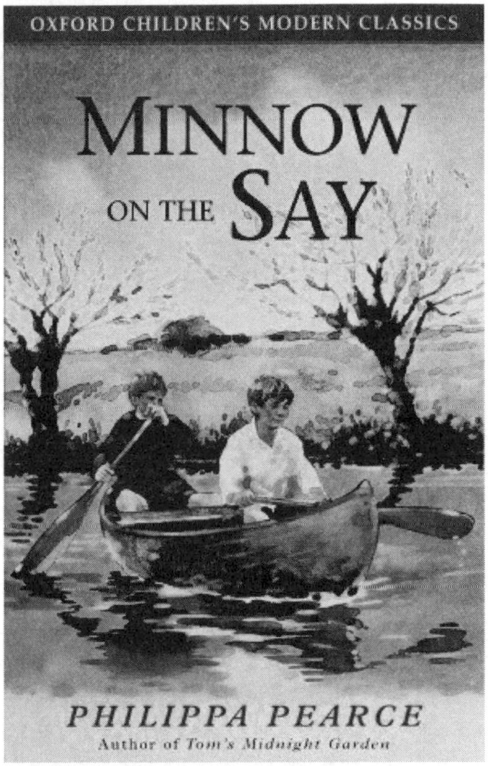

➡ The *Minnow* is an old canoe which David and Adam restore together to make her riverworthy again. The Say is the river on which they go canoeing. They have a treasure hunt to undertake, a riddle within a riddle to solve, a stranger to name and a home to save, all in a race against time.

This is my favourite Philippa Pearce book. I like the smells of summer that come floating from the pages: clean green river water, flower wine and baking cakes. I like the way the reader solves the puzzle almost side by side with David and Adam. I like the people in the background of the story – they seem so alive. Best of all I like the description of the prickly, stubborn friendship that grows between the boys. It is one of those books that 'feels like real'.

Hilary McKay

10-12

Next?
- Another wonderful Philippa Pearce book is ***Tom's Midnight Garden***. (UBG 245)
- A book with a similar feel is Jan Mark's ***Thunder and Lightnings***. (UBG 242) Then again, you can't really go wrong with Philippa Pearce and Jan Mark!
- ***The Eagle of the Ninth*** by Rosemary Sutcliff is another great adventure story about friendship and a quest. (UBG 68)

MISSING series

(Book 1: When Lightning Strikes)

Jenny Carroll

➡ Jessica Mastrani is just a normal sixteen-year-old girl, living in a small town in Indiana. Until she gets struck by lightning!

With the electricity comes the sudden ability to dream the whereabouts of missing people, and all of a sudden Jess's life gets really complicated. Not only do the FBI want her to work for them but she also acquires a boyfriend, someone her parents definitely won't approve of, and she finds out the hard way that not everyone who is missing wants to be found.

Jess's abilities help her solve a variety of crimes and each book deals with a different mystery. However, it's the details of life in the very strange Mastrani household and the story of her developing relationship with Rob that will keep you going back for more.

Fast-paced, funny and full of great dialogue – I can't wait for the next one!

Laura Hutchings

11+

Next?
- Jenny Carroll also writes under the name Meg Cabot – try the very popular ***The Princess Diaries***. (UBG 193)
- If you enjoy the mix of American high-life and something a little out of the ordinary, why not try some of the TV tie-in novels written for both **Buffy** and **Smallville**.
- Want something weirder? Try ***Piggies*** by Nick Gifford. (UBG 188)

EVERYBODY'S FAVOURITE...

MISTRESS MASHAM'S REPOSE T.H. White

➡ Young Maria's an orphan who lives with her spiteful, kitten-drowning governess in a decaying mansion so huge that Cook uses a bicycle to get along the corridors. In tangled grounds round the lake, Maria discovers a secret island. In the crumbling summerhouse where Mistress Masham used lazily to 'repose', she finds the Lilliputians (from *Gulliver's Travels*) – folk so tiny a frog's leg will do them for Christmas dinner.

Maria's brave attempts to keep this fascinating miniature world safe, and a secret, leads to dangers, chases, imprisonments, a hidden will, a sneaky and grasping vicar, and in the end, splendid secrets revealed.

It's a rich read. You'll find yourself trailing the nearest adult to ask things like 'What's fichu?' and 'Did the Duke of Orleans really shoot larks with corks from champagne bottles?'

But hey, what's wrong with learning swathes of odd stuff during a rattling good story?

Anne Fine

➡ I'm amazed to see that *Mistress Masham's Repose* is back in print. Grab it. It's one of my favourites. In this book the events of *Gulliver's Travels* really happened, and some Lilliputians (the small people) are living in secret in England. I thought that was such a great idea when I was a boy. I still do. And there's a huge old stately home where you need a bike to get along the corridors, hidden treasure, artful villains, moonlight chases – it's all there. What more do you need? Some adults think parts of it are too difficult for children. Hah! They really mean that the author sometimes enjoys himself so much that he forgets you don't know as much as him – but he is clever enough to make you think you do.

Terry Pratchett

10+

Next?

- Terry Pratchett's own ***The Amazing Maurice and his Educated Rodents*** (UBG 12), or ***The Wee Free Men*** (UBG 259).
- ***Harry and the Wrinklies*** by Alan Temperley has more chases, wicked villains and hidden secrets. (UBG 105)
- For another story of a mysterious place and an enchanting world, look for Elizabeth Goudge's ***The Little White Horse***. (UBG 145)
- Also by T.H. White, try the classic story of the young King Arthur, ***The Sword in the Stone***. (UBG 234)
- Or do you want to read about more 'little people'? Try ***The Borrowers*** and its sequels by Mary Norton. (UBG 33)
- Or read the ripping adventure, ***Artemis Fowl*** by Eoin Colfer. (UBG 20)

THE MONSTER GARDEN

Vivien Alcock

➡ Frankie Stein has a mad scientist for a father and, with a name like that, it is hardly surprising when, one day, she accidentally creates life from a blob of something she thinks has been rejected by her father's laboratory. But has she created a monster?

This clever and thoughtful book is based on some of the ideas in Mary Shelley's *Frankenstein*, but has its own bubbles and ripples of humour running all the way through. Frankie goes from horror at this abrupt accident of life to an almost maternal love and protection of her (fast growing) creation, which she calls Monnie – short for 'Monster' ...

This is a story about relationships, friendship, family and that unexpected, uninvited, unlooked-for thing called responsibility. And love. It left my mind feeling a lot bigger!

Simon Puttock

10-12

Next?

- Anne Fine's ***Flour Babies*** is about a boy having to look after a bag of flour as though it were a human baby. (UBG 86)
- Genetic engineering is a difficult subject to write about, but Nicholas Fisk's ***A Rag, a Bone and a Hank of Hair*** deals with the topic in an uncompromising way. (UBG 197)
- The original ***Frankenstein*** is a hard read, so why not try Chris Mould's great comic-book retelling?

THE MOOMINS (A Comet in Moominland)

Tove Jansson

➡ *A Comet in Moominland* is the very best of the totally brilliant **Moomin** books. They're all excellent but I was only allowed to choose one, and this is it. This is a wonderful introduction to life in Moomin Valley, inhabited by an extraordinary array of creatures, not least the Moomins themselves: large-snouted, silky smooth and brave. I've never read books quite like them. They're funny, sad, exciting and – dare I say it – even make you think. In this race-against-time tale, young Moomintroll and his friend Sniff set off for the Observatory on Lonely Mountain to find out if a comet really is on a collision course with Earth. Along the way, they have some nail-biting adventures, with everything from angry crocodiles to a Snork-eating bush, and meet some wonderful characters, too.

Philip Ardagh

7-9

Next?

- You might enjoy the other full-length Moomin books: ***Finn Family Moomintroll***, ***Moominsummer Madness***, ***Moominland Midwinter***, ***The Exploits of Moominpappa*** and ***Moominpappa at Sea***. Younger Moomin fans should look out for the rhyming picture books, ***The Book About Moomin, Mimble and Little My*** and ***Who Will Comfort Toffle?***
- For something different, try ***Mr Popper's Penguins*** by Richard and Florence Atwater. (UBG 165)

MOONFLEET John Meade Falkner

➡ A storm is raging. Smugglers wait with their ponies while a great sailing ship is smashed to pieces by the waves. Worshippers fly in terror as a sound of knocking comes from the crypt beneath the church where the notorious Blackbeard lies in his rotted coffin. Is there any truth in the legend of a priceless diamond with a curse upon it?

This is the village of Moonfleet, where lonely, fifteen-year-old John Trenchard sits on a gravestone staring out to sea. He is saved from death by Elzevir Block, the brooding, powerful landlord of the Why Not? Inn, who becomes like a father to him.

I love this story: strong characters, powerful action, beautifully written. A classic smuggling adventure!

Alan Temperley

10-12

Next?

- For more adventures that involve pirates and skulduggery, read Tanith Lee's ***Piratica***, about a girl whose mother was a pirate – or was she? (UBG 190)
- R.L. Stevenson's ***Kidnapped*** is another classic story of adventure. (UBG 133)
- For a scary chase story, read John Buchan's ***The Thirty-Nine Steps***.

MORTAL ENGINES Philip Reeve

Next?
- Check out its sequel, ***Predator's Gold***, in which Tom and Hester's adventures continue.
- You might also like the James III series by Joan Aiken, starting with ***The Wolves of Willoughby Chase*** (UBG 270), but particularly ***Black Hearts in Battersea*** – also about a London that is recognisable, but only just.
- Another brilliant series is **The Edge Chronicles** (where you get reality and surreality) by Paul Stewart and Chris Riddell. (UBG 70)
- For more science-fiction – try Catherine Fisher's **The Book of the Crow**. (UBG 201)

➠ It's the far future and London is now a Traction City – a seven-tiered metropolis mounted on enormous treads, rolling over the wastes of Europe, searching for smaller cities to gobble up. Fifteen-year-old Tom Natsworthy has his life turned upside-down when he stumbles upon a sinister secret concerning the city's beloved hero, archaeologist Thaddeus Valentine. Pushed off the city, and left for dead in the barren Out-Country, Tom teams up with Hester Shaw, a disfigured girl who has her own dark reasons for getting back to London. As Tom and Hester try to catch up, London rolls on, armed with a powerful weapon from the past and intent on world domination.

This is a sensationally exciting book, well written, with a plot that continually surprises. There are airships, cyborg assassins, floating cities, and swashbuckling on a grand scale. Reeve's vision of the future is mesmerizing and original, and Tom, in his breakneck quest, is constantly forced to rethink all his beliefs and assumptions about his home, and the people and world around him. A fabulous adventure story.

10+

Kenneth Oppel

THE MOUSE AND HIS CHILD Russell Hoban

➠ When he is wound up, the clockwork mouse of the title tosses his tin child up and down until the clockwork runs down again. Small wonder that they both want to escape from this clockwork life and become 'self-winding'. Thrown out when their clockwork breaks down, they are gathered up by the scavenging villain Manny Rat, but they escape and move on through a series of encounters and adventures, with Manny Rat following after them, determined to catch them and reduce them to clockwork rubble.

Next?
- Pod, Hominy and Arriety, characters in ***The Borrowers*** by Mary Norton, also have to struggle in a world dominated by alien giants. (UBG 33)
- Why not have a look at ***Pinocchio*** by Carlo Collodi? There are some surprising connections! (UBG 189)
- You might also enjoy ***The Glassblower's Children*** by Maria Gripe.

This is the sort of book that grows with the reader, who will be able to enjoy it in different ways as he or she gets older. Some of the ideas in it certainly connect with adult literature and one of the final conclusions ('that no one is completely self-winding') is something that adults as well as children can appreciate. Read this book when you are – say – eleven, and you will be able to re-read it every now and then for the rest of your life.

10+

Margaret Mahy

too, weeping at those sad stories. Just thinking about the books brings back my childhood vividly.

MOUSE ATTACK Manjula Padma

➡ Arvee is a very educated and sophisticated mouse. He likes nothing better than to read and have a nice cup of cocoa before bed. But one day he is given to a young girl as a pet! Even though he is well-treated (he has a doll's house to live in, complete with electricity, running water and a kitchen), he longs for other mice for company. But then he finds a tiny sandal on the floor, which leads him to an amazing adventure, in which he meets brown mice, ants who are messengers (especially when you polish them, which they love), and he discovers that the fastest way to travel is by flying – on the back of a praying mantis!

But the story is more than just wonderful whimsy, because there are bullying rats who are enslaving the mice, and Arvee's friends are in terrible danger. Can Arvee, with all his education, help them?

7-9

Leonie Flynn

Next?

- Try **The Welkin Weasels** by Garry Kilworth, in which animals of all sorts live, more or less, as humans.
- Or you might enjoy ***The Song of Pentecost*** by W.J. Corbett. (UBG 223)
- For something funny, where the animals are like humans, try ***The Salt Pirates of Skegness*** by Chris d'Lacey. (UBG 209)
- If you want to read more about the festival of Diwali (which has an important role in this book), try ***Monkey in the Stars*** by Jamila Gavin.

MR MAJEIKA Humphrey Carpenter

➡ From the very first moment that Class Three see their new form teacher, they know there's something funny about him. For one thing, he arrives through the window on a flying carpet!

Mr Majeika is a wizard – well, he *was* a wizard, but now he's given up magic for good. Now he just wants to be a normal teacher, and never do magic again. Except that sometimes he just can't help himself – especially when class brat, Hamish Bigmore, is involved …

Between the flying potion, the magic carpet and the turn-Hamish-into-a-frog charm, is there any way Mr Majeika will be able to keep his magic a secret from Mr Potter the Headmaster?

This book is just the first in an hilarious series of twelve. So if you enjoy this one as much as I did – which I'm sure you will – you can read them all!

6-8

Daniel Hahn

Next?

- Try Jill Murphy's stories about ***The Worst Witch*** – who has trouble controlling her magic. (UBG 272)
- Or for more classroom mayhem, try **The Pickle Hill Primary** books, each of which has a magic teacher who can explain a subject brilliantly.
- Try Terence Blacker's ***Ms Wiz***. Another magical teacher for another Class Three! (UBG 167)

MR POPPER'S PENGUINS

Richard and Florence Atwater

➡ My battered copy of this book contains an inscription from my grandmother on the occasion of my eighth birthday. Almost forty years on, I still remember Mr Popper, the house painter (an untidy man, according to his wife), who yearned for a little arctic excitement and got sent a penguin which obviously had to go in Mrs Popper's fridge. The story tells how one penguin becomes twelve (pressure on the fridge) and the twelve become the performing sensation of America. All American associations were totally lost on me as child; I thought it very English.

The charm of this book is its deadpan humour, its heartbreaking illustrations (you'd give Mr Popper a penguin, too), and its simple joyfulness.

Nicky Singer

7+

Next?

- If you like your animals to say a bit more than 'gook', try Hugh Lofting's ***Doctor Dolittle*** books. (UBG 64)
- If you're big on birds, try Dick King-Smith's ***Harry's Mad***. This heart-warming tale of a parrot is a favourite with all three of my children.
- If you enjoyed the humour, but prefer it a bit more spiky, try Roald Dahl's ***The Twits***. (UBG 250)

MR WILLIAM SHAKESPEARE'S PLAYS and other cartoon-strip stories

Marcia Williams

Marcia Williams has retold lots of classic stories in her unique cartoon-strip style. Here's a look at some of them ...

➨ Some of the greatest stories ever told are captured in just a few pages of bright and colourful cartoon strips, packed full of funny details to make you look closer, pull you into the action and really bring the stories alive again. Legend lovers should start with *Greek Myths*, to discover the truth about Pandora's box, meet Theseus and the dreaded Minotaur, daring highfliers Daedalus and Icarus, and many more. For heroes closer to home try *The Adventures of Robin Hood* and meet Little John, Friar Tuck and Maid Marian; or go journeying with *The Iliad* and *The Odyssey*, meeting the lovesick Helen of Troy and the Trojan Horse, the one-eyed Cyclops and the six-headed Scylla, or travel across mediaeval Spain in *Don Quixote* with the would-be knight and his ever-patient sidekick, Sancho Panza.

Charles Dickens and Friends lets you make friends (or enemies!) of Dickens's colourful goodies and baddies like Mr Fagin, Uriah Heep, Pip and Estella, Tiny Tim, Oliver, Ebenezer Scrooge and many more. Best of all are *Mr William Shakespeare's Plays* and *Bravo, Mr William Shakespeare!* which mix Shakespeare's words with Marcia Williams's cartoon captions to tell the story. The noisy comments of the audience in the clever page borders make you one of the spectators, too, as the curtain goes up on comedies and tragedies like *Hamlet, Macbeth, Romeo and Juliet, A Midsummer Night's Dream* and *The Merchant of Venice*.

And do look out for Marcia's *King Arthur and the Knights of the Round Table, Sinbad the Sailor* and *Bible Stories*, too, which use the same winning formula of large format pages, funny handwritten dialogue based on the words of the original, jokes, bright action-packed frames and easy-to-read captions to capture the sense of the story and all the excitement of the originals.

8-10

Eileen Armstrong

Next?

- Terry Deary's ***Top Ten Shakespeare Stories*** mix comic strips and comic humour to bring the stories to life, and include fascinating fact sections too, which you won't find in any history book! Others in the series include ***Top Ten Greek Legends, Top Ten Arthurian Legends, Top Ten Bible Stories*** and ***Top Ten Dickens Stories***.
- Some of the liveliest retellings of traditional stories are by Geraldine McCaughrean, who captures the thrill and drama of the originals but makes them much easier to read. In ***The Orchard Book of Greek Myths***, she brings the adventures and magic of the flying Icarus, gold-fingered King Midas, fast-of-foot Atlanta and many more vividly and unforgettably back to life. (UBG 177)
- Roger Lancelyn Green wrote more expanded versions of ***Robin Hood*** (UBG 8) and ***King Arthur*** stories (UBG 134), and you can try the Lambs' ***Tales*** (UBG 235) or Leon Garfield for more wonderful Shakespeare retellings.

MRS FRISBY AND THE RATS OF NIMH Robert C. O'Brien

➨ I read this to my daughter in 1975 (or thereabouts) at bedtime, and she couldn't wait for the next instalment; she'd hide the book when we finished for the night so I couldn't read ahead. (I wanted to, very badly.) Just recently, I read it again, and it's still great, although I now feel that the boy rats in the story get the best of the action – the girls are more in the background. Still, Mrs Frisby is one fantastically brave and daring mouse mother; she's determined to get help for her son Timothy when he falls dangerously ill – and her bravery opens up the extraordinary world of the rats of NIMH. If you're interested in defending animals from experimentation you'll be deeply intrigued by this book – and who knows? Those rats could well be out there in real life ...

9-11

Vivian French

Next?

• I'd suggest looking out for ***Watership Down*** by Richard Adams if you want a similar kind of book (UBG 259), but if you're a rat enthusiast (I am!) then grab Terry Pratchett's ***The Amazing Maurice and his Educated Rodents***, and enjoy! (UBG 12)

• ***Mouse Attack*** by Manjula Padma is another tale of a mouse – this one likes hot chocolate! (UBG 165)

MRS PEPPERPOT Alf Prøysen

➨ Mrs Pepperpot is an old lady who lives a quiet life with her husband. She's very ordinary, except for one small thing – she keeps shrinking to the size of a pepperpot! She never knows when it's going to happen, or for how long.

Each story in *Mrs Pepperpot* describes a different day when she shrinks to the size of a pepperpot, and how she gets done all the things she needs to do. Find out how she delivers a doll she promised to a little girl – when the doll is bigger than she is; and what happens when her husband takes her to the shops in his pocket, and she gets stuck inside a bag of macaroni!

7-9

Susan Reuben

Next?

• Another nice easy read about magic is Jill Murphy's classic series ***The Worst Witch***. (UBG 272)

• If you liked Mrs Pepperpot, you'll probably like Astrid Lindgren's ***Pippi Longstocking***, about a girl with special powers – it has the same mix of normal life and weird goings-on. (UBG 189)

• ***Mrs Pepperpot*** and ***Pippi Longstocking*** are both Scandinavian. The other really great Scandinavian series is **The Moomins** by Tove Jansson; if you liked Mrs Pepperpot, I'm sure you'll love these too. (UBG 163)

MS WIZ series Terence Blacker

➨ With long black witchy hair, glossy black nail polish, a china cat, a magic rat up her sleeve, an owl in her handbag and a vacuum cleaner to travel around on, Ms Wiz isn't your average teacher! She is, in fact, the strangest, cleverest teacher Class 3 has ever had, and the minute she walks into St Barnabas' school, they're under her spell – and you will be too. Weird and wonderful things start happening and life for these pupils will never be boring again. You'll wish she worked in your school!

Scribbly black and white sketches add hugely to the fun and excitement in these laugh-out-loud funny reads. They're just the thing to curl up with in winter.

Once you've met Ms Wiz you'll never want her mad adventures to end – and luckily she has lots more. Try *Ms Wiz Loves Dracula*, *Ms Wiz Smells A Rat*, *Ms Wiz Goes To Hollywood*, and *Ms Wiz, Millionaire*: each adventure madder than the one before!

Eileen Armstrong

7-9

Next?

• For books about 'real' witches, don't forget ***Lizzie Dripping*** by Helen Cresswell. (UBG 146)

• ***Groosham Grange*** by Anthony Horowitz is a very funny series about a school for magic, though it is a bit longer – try it and see. (UBG 101)

• And though they are very young, go and read the **Meg and Mog** stories by Helen Nicoll and Jan Pienkowski. They are wonderful, and the illustrations are brilliant!

MUDDLE EARTH

Paul Stewart and Chris Riddell

➡ Let's get the obvious out of the way first: yes, this epic novel is a bit of a spoof on the legendary world created by J.R.R. Tolkien, but it's absolutely a class act in its own right. Our hero Joe Jefferson is a schoolboy who finds himself transported to Muddle Earth (a world with three moons) by Randalf, the wizard, who requires Joe's services as a warrior hero to help defeat various villainous individuals. There's a particularly nasty spoon to beware of, too.

Yes, it is totally weird, but wonderful and very funny and in the hands of the creators of the wonderful **The Edge Chronicles**, you can't go wrong. And you won't!

Jon Appleton

9-12

Next?

- At least have a peek at ***The Lord of the Rings*** by J.R.R. Tolkien. (UBG 148)
- Other excellent Paul Stewart/ Chris Riddell collaborations include ***The Blobheads*** (UBG 31) and **The Edge Chronicles**, of course, which start with ***Beyond the Deepwoods***. (UBG 70)
- For another brilliantly realized world of good and evil, try ***The Ratastrophe Catastrophe*** by David Lee Stone. (UBG 198)

THE MUM HUNT

Gwyneth Rees

➡ Esmie's dad is a single and overworked police detective, who just seems too busy to date anybody. However, Esmie has other plans! Together with her brother Matthew, and Juliette their French au-pair, she conspires to use a newspaper lonely hearts column to set him up with a new girlfriend. Matthew records the phone message, because he can sound like his dad sometimes, and they wait for the replies to roll in. It's all a disaster of course but helps to bring the family back together after a few years of drifting apart.

Everything about this book is warm and good intentioned, confident and easy to read. It's sometimes witty, sometimes sad and sometimes uplifting. Very realistic too.

John McLay

9-12

Next?

- Try Anne Fine's ***Goggle-eyes*** for another fun, but poignant, story about finding new partners for your parents – this time for your mum. (UBG 95)
- Adjusting to a new family make-up is also under the spotlight in Mimi Thebo's ***Wipe Out***.
- If you want to read about a family drama, look up ***Child X*** by Lee Weatherly – a very exciting novel about a complex family situation. (UBG 46)

MUSIC ON THE BAMBOO RADIO

Martin Booth

➡ In December 1941 Hong Kong falls to the invading Japanese army. Left alone, English boy Nicholas has no idea where his parents are – or even whether they are alive or dead. All the Europeans are being rounded up and imprisoned, but Nicholas is rescued by the Chinese house servants and smuggled out of the city.

Disguised as a Chinese boy, Nicholas survives as best he can. Looked after by Ah Kwan and Ah Mee, he becomes like their son, but he never forgets his own parents. So, when the chance comes to do something to help the resistance – even though that something is very dangerous – he leaps at it.

Taut and scary, this is an adventure set in a real war. Horrible things happen, and you're never sure – right until the end – if Nicholas's story will end in tragedy or happiness.

Leonie Flynn

10-12

Next?

- More from Martin Booth? Try ***P.O.W.*** about a boy held as a prisoner of war in Germany in 1915.
- More on what it was like to be a child when the Japanese invaded? Try J.G. Ballard's amazing memoir, ***Empire of the Sun***, though be warned – this is a very tough book, and it was written for adults.
- ***Gulf*** by Robert Westall is a story about war affecting ordinary people in an extraordinary way. (UBG 102)

MY DARLING, MY HAMBURGER
Paul Zindel

➡Liz is smart, brash and beautiful, and is dating Sean, the coolest boy at school. The two engineer it so that their less-beautiful, less-cool best mates Maggie and Dennis date each other too; something Maggie and Dennis aren't too happy about – at first. This is a tale of American teens, peer pressure, rocky relationships and flawed friendships, all wrapped around familiar settings such as the prom and graduation. Yep, there are plenty of movies and books around that cover similar themes, but this was one of the first, and when it comes to describing feelings and emotions Paul Zindel does it very subtly, and manages to avoid corny clichés. This book deals with tough stuff, and doesn't exactly have a fairytale ending, but that makes it all the more realistic.

11+

Karen McCombie

Next?
- Try the lighter – but just as moving – ***Pardon Me, You're Stepping On My Eyeball!*** also by Paul Zindel.
- If you want more humour-mixed-with-issues stuff, you can't beat Paula Danziger. Life after your parents' divorce is the subject of ***It's An Aardvark-Eat-Turtle World*** or try ***The Cat Ate My Gymsuit*** (UBG 42).
- Or try one of Judy Blume's books – maybe ***Are You There, God? It's Me, Margaret.*** (UBG 19)

MY FAMILY AND OTHER ANIMALS
Gerald Durrell

Here but- ADULT NFIC only.

➡ Probably my favourite book of all time. And it's not even fiction. (Well, maybe just a little ...)

Gerald Durrell was ten when his family moved to Corfu. Thanks to a photographic memory, he remembers every detail of each glorious day spent on the colour-saturated, sun-soaked island. Full of the sights, sounds, tastes, smells and animals of a Greek island, this book alternates between being uproariously funny and deliciously descriptive.

Gerald's older brother Lawrence is the one who claims literary greatness, but for my money Gerald beats him hands down! An early scene about the Durrell family's hilarious entry into Corfu town still leaves me helpless with laughter. I steal from this book constantly and unashamedly. Durrell is one of my heroes.

10+

Caroline Lawrence

Next?
- Gerald Durrell's other books about animals are all great. Look out for ***Birds, Beasts and Relatives*** or ***A Zoo in My Luggage***.
- ***Chewing the Cud*** is Dick King-Smith's story of his own childhood – a must if you like real stories and animals. (UBG 46)
- Or ***All Creatures Great and Small*** by James Herriott, a great book about his life as a vet in Yorkshire before – and during – the war.

MY FRIEND FLICKA
Mary O'Hara

➡ Ken McLaughlin lives on his family's ranch in wild and wonderful Wyoming, USA. Ken's a bit of a wimpy daydreamer and his dad would like him to be more like his tough big brother. Ken wants to tame Flicka but the wild and wilful young horse has got other ideas. After all sorts of adventures involving barbed wire and mountain lions and lots more horses, Ken and Flicka become firm friends and Ken's dad realises his son is no wimp after all.

After reading this brilliant horse book I actually became half-boy, half-palomino pony for a while and, as a result, spent many happy afternoons cantering around the streets of Nottingham and being fed sugar lumps by the local shopkeepers.

9-11

Michael Cox

Next?
- The follow-up to Flicka: about her son, ***Thunderhead***, a huge white stallion. The third book in the Flicka trilogy is ***The Green Grass of Wyoming***.
- ***The Silver Brumby*** by Elyne Mitchell – more about horses, this time wild ones in Australia. (UBG 218)
- ***Billy Elliot*** by Melvin Burgess is another book about standing up for your dreams. (UBG 29)

MY FRIEND'S A WEREWOLF

Pete Johnson

Next?
- ***The Undertaker's Gone Bananas*** or ***The Pigman*** by Paul Zindel.
- Try ***My Best Fiend*** by Sheila Lavelle for a next-door neighbour who isn't as good a friend as she seems.
- ***Rescuing Dad*** is also by Pete Johnson, but it's very different. (UBG 204)
- For a more serious book about friendship, try Elizabeth Laird's ***Secret Friends***. (UBG 214)
- For something gorier, try **The Saga of Darren Shan** by none other than Darren Shan himself! (UBG 208)

➡ When Simon moves in next door to Kelly, she thinks she has found a new best friend. He is fun to hang out with and brilliant at sport, but why does he always wear those naff black gloves? Does he think they're cool? And what is the truth about the howling from next door at night? The events that follow are very scary in places, but the scariest thing is that the book is written like a story that could happen to you – or your next door neighbour. You'll learn a lot about werewolves and about being a true friend. It is also a story about challenging prejudice and learning that being different can be a good thing, and not something to be afraid of.

9-12

Abigail Anderson

MY MUM'S GOING TO EXPLODE! Jeremy Strong

➡ What would you do if your mum was expecting a baby, made you and your dad take 'baby lessons' by looking after her old doll (bald and legless), and refused to feed you anything but sausages?

Nicholas is in just this situation. He manages to cope with the help of his dad (who's as fed up about the new baby as he is) and his granny (who's married to a Hell's Angel and has her belly button pierced).

This story is really funny – you'll very probably laugh out loud. But it's quite touching too – especially as Mum's tummy grows bigger and bigger and Nicholas realises there's soon going to be a real baby in the house. Well – that last bit's not quite accurate – but find out why for yourself!

Susan Reuben

6-8

Next?
- Another Jeremy Strong you might like is ***The Hundred-Mile-an-Hour Dog***.
- What's it like when your brother or sister is perfect – and you're not? Try Francesca Simon's ***Horrid Henry***. (UBG 116)
- Another great tale of mayhem – read ***The Great Piratical Rumbustification*** by Margaret Mahy. (UBG 100)

MY NAUGHTY LITTLE SISTER series

Dorothy Edwards, illustrated by Shirley Hughes

Next?
- What about a naughty older brother? Try Francesca Simon's ***Horrid Henry*** (UBG 116); or Sam McBratney's ***Jimmy Zest***. (UBG 128)
- Or try Alf Prøysen's stories about the small but feisty Mrs Pepperpot. (UBG 167)

➡ There are lots of books in this series and it doesn't matter which order you read them in. Each chapter in each book is a self-contained story about something My Naughty Little Sister did. The stories are about everyday things, like your first wobbly tooth, drawing pictures at school, planting an acorn, and are told by the naughty little sister's older sister who half-thinks what her sister gets up to is naughty and half-thinks it's brilliant fun.

The stories might seem a little old-fashioned at first and our idea of naughty behaviour might be very different now, but there is still something magical about My Naughty Little Sister's way of looking at the world – and there's a lot to learn about how to get your own way!

Abigail Anderson

7-9

NANCY DREW FILES Carolyn Keene

➡ Nancy Drew is a girl detective with attitude, a real American 'tough cookie' who inherited the mystery-solving gene from her lawyer father and seems to find a brain-bafflingly complicated mystery lurking around every corner of her neighbourhood! It's impossible not to be drawn into the trickiest of situations with her, picking up clues, desperate to solve the case before she does – and until it's solved you'll find it impossible to put the book down. Nancy herself gets older and wiser the more crimes she solves. Whether you like spooky stories (*The Secret of Candlelight Inn*), scientific crimes (*The Crime Lab Case*), all-action adventure (*The Mystery at the Ski-Jump*), or mind-bogglingly complex thrillers (*The Case of Capital Intrigue*) there's a Nancy Drew mystery to suit you – and another and another!

9-11

Next?
- For fast-moving mystery adventures with boy 'heroes', try **The Hardy Boys** series by Franklin W. Dixon. (UBG 104) Don't forget **The Secret Seven** (UBG 216) and **The Famous Five** (UBG 78) by Enid Blyton and her wonderful ***Island of Adventure*** (UBG 124), with a dark and sinister twist.
- A good historical detection series is **The Invisible Detective** by Justin Richards. (UBG 123)

NATASHA'S WILL Joan Lingard

➡ When a family discovers that they may be thrown out of the house they regard as home, they are shattered. Surely its owner, Natasha, the lady they'd loved and cared for so carefully until her death, wouldn't have left them without a roof over their heads? The search for her will begins, and with it a literary treasure hunt.

In fact, many years previously, Natasha had escaped from St Petersburg at the time of the Russian Revolution and this novel also tells her story, about her daring escape and about the way in which she came to set up home in Scotland.

This is a lovely mixture of mystery, adventure and history. You can enter into the spirit of the story by solving the puzzle of the treasure hunt.

Lindsey Fraser

10+

Next?
- ***Hitler's Daughter*** by Jackie French will make you think about our relationship with the past. (UBG 112)
- ***Raider's Tide*** by Maggie Prince is set in Elizabethan England and tells of a young girl's fight against the life planned for her by her parents.
- ***Control-Shift*** by Nick Manns tells the story of a family's move to the country and how the story of the house and its surroundings infiltrates their lives until it almost ruins them.
- Other terrific Joan Lingard books include the famous Kevin and Sadie books, beginning with ***The Twelfth Day of July***.

NATIONAL VELVET Enid Bagnold

➡ When *National Velvet* was first published, a critic called it 'a super day-dream', but it's much, much more than that. Every time I think about the story, it's as if light bulbs pop in my head; it's one of those books that lights up your life and makes you truly believe that anything is possible. Basically, it's a thrilling adventure about a girl and a horse, but even if you hate horses you'll still love the story; the world in which Velvet Brown lives is so warm it glows, and so real you can't believe that Edwina, Malvolia, Meredith, Velvet and Donald don't exist.

'The Browns loved Jacob as they loved each other, deeply, from the back of the soul, with intolerance in daily life.' It reads as if it was written yesterday, even though it was first published in 1935; it's so fresh and funny and profound that it'll always be one of my most favourite books of all time.

Vivian French

10+

Next?
- What to read after this? I'd suggest Debi Gliori's ***Pure Dead Magic***. It's totally different in almost every way – but there's another wonderfully warm close family at the heart of the story. (UBG 195)
- ***My Friend Flicka*** by Mary O'Hara is about a friendship between a horse and a boy. (UBG 169)
- Or there is the famous horse story, ***Black Beauty*** by Anna Sewell. (UBG 29)
- Or for *wild* horses, try ***The Silver Brumby*** by Elyne Mitchell. (UBG 218)

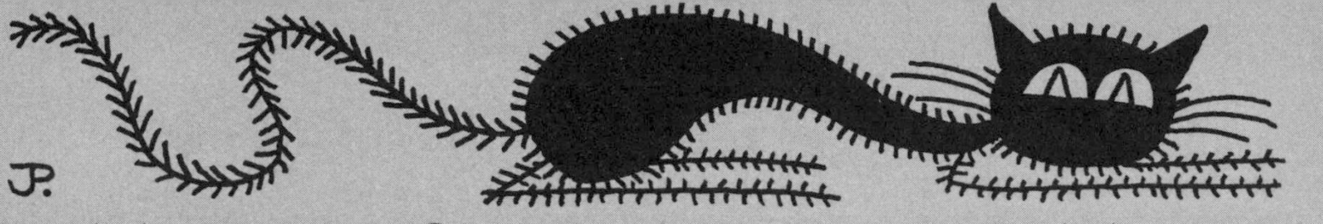

MYTHS, LEGENDS & FAIRY TALES

Legendary!

BY CATHERINE FISHER

Myths and legends lead us deep into humanity's oldest fears and dreams. We come across them first in fairy tales. Dark forests, third sons, devious dragons, magic swords – such motifs recur throughout this simple, savage world, fascinating in their power over our imagination. The classic collection is Grimm's *Fairy Tales*, available in many modern versions. The Grimm brothers collected traditional stories; from their dark forests emerge 'The Frog Prince', 'Rumpelstiltskin', 'Snow White', and from that terrifying house of gingerbread, 'Hansel and Gretel'. Not originally intended for children, they were tales for any age. Hans Christian Andersen may have been the first children's writer to use traditional stories as a basis for his own, to make biting satires like 'The Emperor's New Clothes', 'The Ugly Duckling', and the haunting tale of 'The Little Mermaid'.

Myths are older, and so re-embroidered that no one knows who began them. The ancient tales of Greece and Rome crawl with grotesque creatures and are breathless with epic journeys; they also show us men and women tormented by destiny. Odysseus spends years coming home from Troy for offending the wrong god, and Jason searches the world for the Golden Fleece. For modern versions try *The God Beneath the Sea* by Leon Garfield and Edward Blishen, Geraldine McCaughrean's *The Orchard Book of Greek Myths*, or *Black Ships Before Troy* by Rosemary Sutcliff. For novels set in this world there is the wonderful *Troy* by Adèle Geras or Mary Renault's fantastic story of Theseus and the Minotaur, *The King Must Die*.

Welsh and Irish stories have a Celtic strangeness that has influenced many modern

★ EDITORS' CHOICES:

- ***The Just So Stories*** by Rudyard Kipling
- ***Tales of the Early World*** by Ted Hughes
- ***The Arthur Rackham Fairy Book***
- ***The Snow-walker's Son*** by Catherine Fisher
- ***Norse Myths***
- ***How the Whale Became*** by Ted Hughes

★ EIGHT BOOKS OF (OR INSPIRED BY) GREEK AND ROMAN MYTHS:

- ***The God Beneath the Sea*** by Leon Garfield and Edward Blishen
- ***The King Must Die*** by Mary Renault
- ***Black Ships Before Troy*** and its sequels by Rosemary Sutcliff and Penelope Lively
- ***Troy*** by Adèle Geras
- ***The Orchard Book of Greek Myths*** by Geraldine McCaughrean
- ***Greek Myths for Young Children*** by Marcia Williams
- ***Tales of the Greek Heroes*** by Roger Lancelyn Green
- ***Tales of Troy and Greece*** by Andrew Lang

★ EIGHT 'SORT-OF' FAIRY TALE BOOKS

- ***Cold Tom*** by Sally Prue
- ***Artemis Fowl*** by Eoin Colfer
- ***Faerie Wars*** by Herbie Brennan
- ***The Little Grey Men*** by B.B.
- ***One Thousand and One Arabian Nights*** retold by Geraldine McCaughrean
- ***I Was a Rat!*** by Philip Pullman
- ***Clever Polly and the Stupid Wolf*** by Catherine Storr
- ***Incrediblania*** by Norman Hunter

And don't miss our selection of real FAIRY TALES on pp. 76-77.

writers; try *Tales from the Mabinogion* by Gwyn Thomas and Kevin Crossley-Holland, for the story of the woman made of flowers, or the crazy list of Arthur's men who help woo the giant's daughter. In *The Owl Service*, Alan Garner makes brilliant use of Welsh myth, as does Susan Cooper in **The Dark Is Rising** sequence.

King Arthur is an offshoot of a Welsh story that has electrified the imagination of many. For a good version of the classic, try *King Arthur and the Knights of the Round Table* by Roger Lancelyn Green. Few legends have been retold so often; the powers of Merlin, the search for the mysterious Grail, the betrayal of the perfect court from within, are themes that still obsess us. T.H. White's *The Sword in the Stone* explores this world wonderfully; more recently, Kevin Crossley-Holland in *The Seeing Stone* sets it in mediaeval Shropshire; and in my own *Corbenic*, it becomes a struggle of modern times.

Another fascinating set of myths comes from the North – the Viking stories of Thor and treacherous Loki, of dwarfs, dragons and trolls. Crossley-Holland's *Norse Myths* retells these in jewelled prose. J.R.R. Tolkien uses Norse images and names in *The Hobbit* and *The Lord of the Rings*, as does Alan Garner in *The Weirdstone of Brisingamen*.

Constantly re-interpreted by writers, myths never die. Jenny Nimmo's *The Snow Spider* uses Mabinogion stories, Susan Price's *The Ghost Drum* has Siberian elements, and William Mayne writes of boggarts in *Earthfasts*. Myths remain a haunting backdrop to great stories by Pauline Fisk, Adèle Geras, Peter Dickinson and many, many more.

★ HALF A DOZEN ARTHURIAN STORIES:

- ***Corbenic*** by Catherine Fisher
- ***King Arthur and his Knights of the Round Table*** by Roger Lancelyn Green
- ***King Arthur and the Knights of the Round Table*** by Marcia Williams
- ***The Dark Is Rising*** by Susan Cooper
- ***The Sword in the Stone*** by T.H. White
- ***The Seeing Stone*** by Kevin Crossley-Holland

THE ULTIMATE READERS' POLL

YOUR TOP TEN BOOK HEROES

1. Harry Potter
2. Legolas
3. Frodo
4. Captain Underpants
5. Aragorn
6. Alex Rider
7. Tracy Beaker
8. Robin Hood
9. Gandalf
10. Bilbo

be ***The Lorax*** by Doctor Seuss, because it is a beautiful book with a carefully disguised moral.

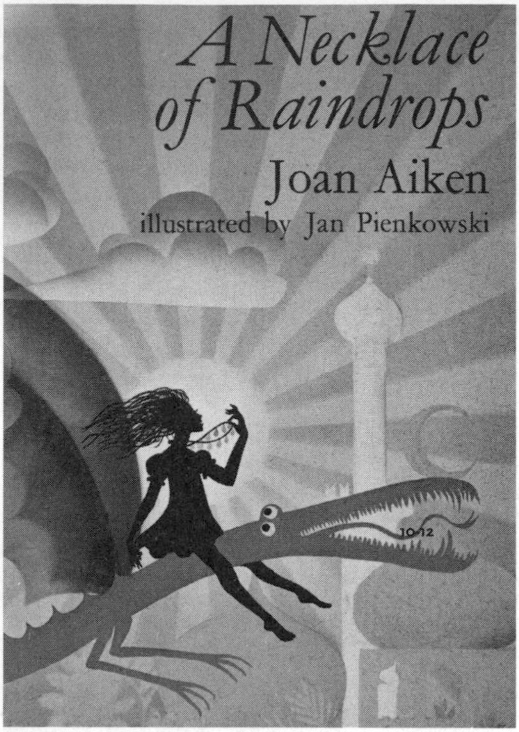

A NECKLACE OF RAINDROPS

Joan Aiken, illustrated by Jan Pienkowski

➨ Baby Laura's father finds the North Wind caught in a tree and helps to disentangle him. In return, the North Wind offers to be Laura's godfather and makes the baby a gift of a magic necklace of raindrops. But Meg, a nasty girl from Laura's school, becomes jealous of Laura's special powers and is determined to steal the necklace for herself …

Other stories in this collection feature a cat that swells to an enormous size after eating too much yeast, a giant flying apple pie with a bit of the sky baked into it, and a feathered house that lays an egg. And in 'The Elves in the Shelves', Janet can't believe it when the characters in her books come to life in the night. This wonderful book will make your imagination soar and may well inspire you to write some stories of your own!

7-9

Francesca Lewis

Next?

- You will also love ***The Kingdom Under the Sea***, a collection of eleven fairy tales from eastern Europe and the Soviet Union, retold by Joan Aiken.
- Joan Aiken is probably best known for her James III series, beginning with ***The Wolves of Willoughby Chase***. They're aimed at slightly older readers, but do give them a try; they're brilliant. (UBG 270)
- Another collection of new stories in the fairy tale mould is ***Singing to the Sun*** by Vivian French.

THE NEVERENDING STORY

Michael Ende

➨ Bastian Balthazar Bux is the sort of boy other kids pick on. One day, he takes a copy of a book called *The Neverending Story* from a secondhand bookshop and, locking himself in a deserted attic above his school, he reads it. It is a story of a fantastical world that is disintegrating. As he reads, he becomes more and more involved in the story until he is part of it. He becomes the hero who alone can save this magical place from destruction.

This is a great storybook full of wonderful ideas and amazing characters. It's a little old-fashioned but well worth reading as it will draw you right into its magic. (Oh, and don't see the movie, it's awful.)

11+

Colin Thomson

Next?

- Another book about being drawn unwillingly into magic is Catherine Fisher's powerful ***Corbenic***. (UBG 52)
- Diana Wynne Jones's wonderful ***The Homeward Bounders*** is about a boy who becomes a pawn in a god-like game. (UBG 114)
- Or try ***Only You Can Save Mankind*** by Terry Pratchett, another story about life, the universe and gaming. (UBG 129)

THE NIGHT OF THE LIVING VEG

Philip Reeve

➡ Buster Bayliss likes a quiet life; just getting on with his hobbies, like getting out of doing homework and being late for school. But when his mum goes away on a lollipop lady retraining course in Belgium, Buster gets sent to his Fake Aunty Pauline's and life suddenly becomes very busy. You see, there are these plants that are trying to take over. I can hear you thinking – hey! Plants can't do that! But these are no ordinary veg – they eat meat, hypnotise their owners and grow very big very, very fast.

If you want to find out how a French horn and a bathroom sink can save the world, you need to read this book. Packed with jokes, puns and hilarious happenings, it's a fast, fun read.

Leonie Flynn

11+

Next?

- The rest of the Buster Bayliss books! – ***The Big Freeze, Day of the Hamster*** and ***Custardfinger***.
- For more puns and daft things happening, try ***Killer Mushrooms Ate My Gran*** by Susan Gates (UBG 133) or the **Jiggy McCue** stories, such as ***The Killer Underpants***, by Michael Lawrence (UBG 127).

NORSE MYTHS

➡ We were pagans in this country once. The stories of the gods we worshipped were common knowledge, but now few remember their names. Only the days of the week give us a clue to how important they were. Tyr's day – Tuesday; Wodin's day – Wednesday; Thor's day – Thursday.

If you like fantasy stories, then you'll love these old tales. It's all there – the dragons and warriors, the elves and dwarfs, the mystery and darkness, the tricks and the treasure, the struggle of good against evil. But on top of that, you have the gods themselves. My favourites are Odin, who loved death and poetry, war and wisdom, and knew how to make the dead speak; and Loki, the model for the Christian devil, who loved to twist things out of shape.

Try these stories. As with all great religious stories, there's something here for everyone.

Melvin Burgess

9+

Next?

- Roger Lancelyn Green's retellings have been published as ***Myths of the Norsemen***. Look for his other retellings: ***Robin Hood*** (UBG 8) and ***King Arthur*** (UBG 134).
- Another great collection of Norse myths is Kevin Crossley Holland's ***Axe-age, Wolf-age***.
- A story that is based around the god Loki is Diana Wynne Jones's ***Eight Days of Luke***. (UBG 71)
- Look for the myths of other countries, such as: India – ***Seasons of Splendour*** by Madhur Jaffrey; Egypt – ***Tales from Ancient Egypt*** by Roger Lancelyn Green; and China – ***Tales from China*** by Cyril Birch.

NOTHING TO BE AFRAID OF

Jan Mark

➡ No one writes short stories better than Jan Mark, and no one can create more wickedly cunning characters whom you just can't help but like. All the children in these ten stories, which are set fifty years ago, live out their own realities, because they're far more interesting than anything the adults care to tell them. But somehow, each of them gets a little too carried away – with unfortunate consequences for themselves and innocent (and often a bit drippy) bystanders. The results make for crackingly funny reading. So, prepare yourself for Anthea's tales of leopards and fever pits in the local gardens, Alice's dubious potions or Anthony's hideously freakish bonfire-night guy, and much more – and enjoy!

Jon Appleton

9-11

Next?

- Like short stories? Here are some more collections to try: ***Badger on the Barge*** by Janni Howker (UBG 22), ***Flying with Icarus*** by Curdella Forbes (UBG 86) and any of Philippa Pearce's stunning collections: start with ***The Shadow Cage*** and ***The Rope***.
- ***The Giant Baby*** by Allan Ahlberg is funny, eccentric and all about children getting into scrapes. (UBG 92)

EVERYBODY'S FAVOURITE…

NORTHERN LIGHTS (Book 1 of His Dark Materials)

Philip Pullman

➡ Fantasies don't come more magnificent than this. This first book in Pullman's **His Dark Materials** trilogy introduces Lyra, an impulsive and adventurous girl, whose search for her missing friend Roger takes her to the far north, and launches her on a quest in which the fate of the human race hangs in the balance. Roger is just one of numerous children kidnapped by the beautiful Mrs Coulter, a sinister agent of the Church, who is using the children in terrible experiments to try and understand the nature of a mysterious substance known as Dust. Armed with a golden compass which can divine the truth, and aided by a colourful cast of characters which includes an armoured polar bear, broomstick-riding witches, and Gyptians, Lyra tries to rescue the imprisoned children and put an end to the dark experiments.

Pullman has created an alternate world in which magic and technology coexist, and everyone is born with a daemon – an animal familiar that accompanies them through life, and is a sort of manifestation of their soul. The book is thought-provoking, fabulously exciting, and chilling. Pullman introduces a great cast of characters, including the powerful scientist Lord Asriel and the sinister Mrs Coulter – both of whom have motivations which are alternately admirable and evil. *Northern Lights* is not simply an epic adventure tale, but a reconsideration of good and evil, God and religion.

Kenneth Oppel

➡ Lyra, the heroine of **His Dark Materials**, lives in Oxford. Though this is not the Oxford we might think we know, because Lyra lives in an alternate world. In her Oxford and her world, you will meet armoured polar bears and flying witches, and everyone has a daemon.

Lyra travels on a huge journey of discovery through these books. She meets the boy Will, who cuts through to her Oxford using the Subtle Knife which can literally cut holes between the joins of any number of possible worlds. Their adventure eventually takes them into the land of the dead and further.

Inspired by Milton's famous poem *Paradise Lost*, these books are an inspiring and exciting read, full of challenging ideas and unforgettable images. In the end, though, they are simply one enormous and entertaining story told by a master storyteller. They have become modern classics and have captured the imagination of a whole generation of both children and grown-ups. Read them soon before the epic Hollywood films are made, and use your own imagination, rather than relying on others to visualise these worlds for you. Then you, too, will live through Lyra and Will's story in these remarkable books.

11+

Ian Beck

Next?

- You'll doubtless want to read the next two books in the trilogy, ***The Subtle Knife*** and ***The Amber Spyglass***. And try ***Lyra's Oxford*** – a new short story, plus a fantastic map and other stuff all in one little book.
- For a fantasy sequence just as powerful in ideas as this, try Ursula Le Guin's **Earthsea** books. (UBG 69)
- ***The Owl Service*** by Alan Garner works dark mythology into the everyday. (UBG 179)
- Or for a huge, sprawling adventure, try J.R.R. Tolkien's ***The Lord of the Rings***. (UBG 148)
- Or you might want to look at what's on offer for grown-ups, as there isn't anything very like this for kids. Try C.S. Lewis's **Perelandra** books, which start with ***Out of the Silent Planet***.
- If you're a fantasy buff, try Kenneth Oppel's brilliant bat fantasies, ***Silverwing***, ***Sunwing***, and ***Firewing***. (UBG 219)
- As you read on through the Pullman series, you might find you want to know more about his source material, so look at John Milton's epic poem, ***Paradise Lost*** (difficult but amazing), and also a good, comprehensive book of mythology, such as ***Bulfinch's Mythology***.

want to be.

ORANGES AND MURDER

Alison Prince

Next?
- Try some other books by Alison Prince. ***The Sherwood Hero*** is my favourite: a modern-day take on the Robin Hood story – with a twist!
- You might also like ***Coram Boy*** by Jamila Gavin, which is set in the same historical period and is another story of lost parents and mystery. (UBG 52)
- You could also try ***The Wolves of Willoughby Chase*** by Joan Aiken (and the books that follow): great, pacy historical adventures, although set in an imaginary period of history that never actually happened! (UBG 270)

➨ Although Joey has always lived with Poll and Curly, he knows they aren't his real parents. At thirteen, he decides it's time to leave home and become a costermonger, selling fruit and vegetables in Whitechapel market. Life is hard and Joey spends his first few nights in a doss house. Then, just as he is starting to make a life of his own, he is accused of murder!

Joey fights to clear his name and unravels the secret of his birth as well as a web of deceit and corruption. *Oranges and Murder* is packed with the sights, smells and bustle of eighteenth-century London; the pace is fast, the characters are fascinating and there's plenty of mystery.

Helen Simmons

10-12

THE ORCHARD BOOK OF GREEK MYTHS

Geraldine McCaughrean

➨ Beautifully and concisely retold, these sixteen favourite Greek myths are brought to life with all the excitement, magic, intrigue and drama you could ever hope for. The heroic exploits of Jason; Theseus and Odysseus; Icarus, who flies too close to the sun; Perseus; Heracles and King Midas, whose touch turns everything into gold – all these stories are enhanced by the magnificent illustrations of Emma Chichester-Clark. Lesser known myths are also included: Atlanta the fleet-footed goddess; Arachne the spinner, who boasts so much that she is turned into a spider; and Narcissus the vain shepherd boy who stares at his own beautiful reflection and pines away in hopeless love until at last he takes root, and all that remains are 'the tissuey petals and a bending stalk'.

Next?
- Try Ted Hughes's colourful collection of creation stories, ***Tales of the Early World*** is recommended by Geraldine McCaughrean on p. 236.
- For more myths brilliantly retold, try ***Black Ships Before Troy*** by Rosemary Sutcliff and Penelope Lively. (UBG 30)
- Or for an easier, and really funny take on them, try ***Helping Hercules*** by Francesca Simon.

Gervase Phinn

8-11

THE ORDINARY PRINCESS

M.M. Kaye

Next?
- If you like Princess Amy's no-nonsense attitude, you might also like Dakin, the heroine of Lynne Reid Banks's ***The Farthest-Away Mountain*** (UBG 82) or Maria Merryweather in Elizabeth Goudge's magical and witty ***The Little White Horse*** (UBG 145).
- ***Don't miss our list of PRINCESS STORIES on p. 193.***

➨ When Princess Amethyst Alexandra Augusta Araminta Adelaide Aurelia Anne is born, excitement is high, for everyone knows that the seventh daughter of a king is the most gifted and beautiful of all. A lavish christening is arranged and all the fairy godmothers in the kingdom are invited. But the fairy Crustacea arrives in a foul mood and makes the baby an unusual gift: a spell that she should be ordinary! So Princess Amy grows up with freckles instead of lily-white skin and prefers climbing trees to attending royal balls. She soon realises that drastic action must be taken to avoid being married to a pompous prince, and that's when her adventures really start.

Princess Amy's story makes you think about what is really important in life, about what you need to make you happy.

Francesca Lewis

9-11

THE OTHER SIDE OF TRUTH

Beverley Naidoo

➡ After witnessing their mother's murder, twelve-year-old Sade and her younger brother Femi are forced to flee Nigeria and are smuggled into England – where they are cruelly abandoned. Penniless and homeless, unsure of where to go or whom they can trust and at the mercy of the English system for refugees, they make friends and enemies, are forced to move homes, struggle with official bureaucracy, school bullies and bewildering grief. This is a tense and tragic, gripping but hopeful book which allows the reader to see the world through Sade and Femi's eyes and share their hopes, fears and troubles. It's about injustice, asylum, bullying and family love – somehow it feels like much more than just a good story.

10+

Eileen Armstrong

Next?
- Naidoo's ***No Turning Back*** tells the story of a street child in Johannesburg; and don't miss the page-turning ***Journey to Jo'burg***. (UBG 129)
- ***Bound for America*** by Elizabeth Lutzeier is a painfully honest story of a family fleeing to America after struggling to survive the Irish potato famine.
- ***The Endless Steppe*** by Esther Hautzig is another story of children caught up in war. (UBG 73)

Here

THE OTTERBURY INCIDENT

Cecil Day Lewis

➡ When Nick Yates accidentally breaks a school window, he and his friends have to raise the money to pay for the repairs – and so Operation Glazier is born. But it turns out that Operation Glazier is only the beginning of the boys' adventures, which will involve them in some pretty nifty detective work, and end up with a huge pitched battle with air-guns, brick-throwing, cut-throat razors, and some really nasty villains. As George (the boy telling us the story) says, 'This is a really super story – I should know, I wrote it.'

And it is *indeed* a super story – though also quite an old-fashioned one. That doesn't mean it isn't every bit as exciting and funny as anything written in the twenty-first century; just that the language the author uses sounds a bit different from the way people talk today (the slang and swearing, especially). You'll get used to it quickly, and soon won't mind at all – and it adds a lot to the atmosphere!

Daniel Hahn

8-11

Next?
- For another great tale of old-fashioned boy detectives, try ***Emil and the Detectives*** by Erich Kästner. (UBG 72)
- ***Frindle*** is about a schoolboy and his friends making trouble of a different kind. (UBG 88)
- Another story of schoolyard conflict is ***The War of Jenkins' Ear*** by Michael Morpurgo. (UBG 258)

OTTO AND THE FLYING TWINS

Here

Charlotte Haptie

➡ Otto lives in a city with bouncing pavements, two-foot-tall butterflies and magical people who can do impossible things. But the city authorities want to control the magic for their own purposes – and they'll stop at *nothing* to achieve this.

Open up this book and get ready to plunge into a world unlike any you've ever dreamed of, peopled with extraordinary characters: Mab, the waif of a girl who travels on a flying carpet; Elfina, cold and arrogant with a bitter past; Mr Six and Mr Eight – policemen with empty hearts, who seem to be everywhere at once.

This book clings to you after you've reached the end; once you've read it, you'll probably never forget it.

Susan Reuben

9-12

Next?
- ***Pure Dead Magic*** by Debi Gliori, for hilarious and magical adventures. (UBG 195)
- Try ***The Wind Singer*** by William Nicholson, for another fantastic and fantastical adventure story. (UBG 266)
- ***Midnight for Charlie Bone*** by Jenny Nimmo is about a boy who discovers he has magical powers. (UBG 159)

OUT OF THE ASHES

Michael Morpurgo

➨ Do you remember the foot-and-mouth disease outbreak? Well, this (fictional) story is about what it was like for one girl, Becky Morley, who lived on a farm hit by the disease. The book is in diary form, and as you read her entries day after day, you are guaranteed to cry. But don't be put off by the story sounding too sad. It has hope in it as well, and it shows how people can come closer together in difficult times.

Michael Morpurgo experienced the effects of foot-and-mouth disease directly – he had to close his Farms for City Children during the outbreak. *Out of the Ashes* is his way of getting behind the pictures on the news and showing people what that awful time was really like.

Susan Reuben

10-12

Next?
• Try ***Farm Boy*** (UBG 81), ***Kensuke's Kingdom*** (UBG 132) and ***Friend or Foe*** – also by Michael Morpurgo.
• For a story about a family whose world falls apart in a very different way, read ***When Hitler Stole Pink Rabbit*** by Judith Kerr, and its two sequels. (UBG 261)

THE OUTSIDE CHILD

Nina Bawden

➨ Jane and her friend Plato feel like outside children because they both come from families that are out of the ordinary. Jane's mother is dead and she lives with her two eccentric aunts and only sees her seafaring father occasionally. Then she discovers her father has a whole other family she didn't know about. Jane's quest to find her half-brother and -sister leads her to uncover some family secrets and, in doing so, come to terms with who she is.

Jane and Plato are very appealing characters and the story has plenty of twists and turns as Jane discovers the truth about her past. This book is a great read – and if you sometimes feel like an outside child yourself, you might enjoy it even more!

9-12

Gwyneth Rees

Next?
• Don't miss Nina Bawden's other story featuring these characters, ***The Real Plato Jones***.
• Two other great Nina Bawden books are ***Carrie's War*** (UBG 41) and ***The Peppermint Pig*** (UBG 184), so if you liked this book why not try these two next?
• The main characters in the ***The Pinballs*** by Betsy Byars are a bit like 'outside' children when they meet at the start of the book. (UBG 189)
• A terrific high-action, seafaring quest story is Joan Aiken's ***Go Saddle the Sea***. (UBG 93)

THE OWL SERVICE Alan Garner

➨ A very scary and complex fantasy. When Alison's family moves to Wales and she finds the owl-patterned plates in the loft, and when her brother feels the invisible spear whistle past him, they don't know that they have become part of the terrible legend of Blodeuwedd, the woman of flowers, and her ancient destruction. Gwynn, who lives in the valley, is drawn in too, by his resentment and envy of the newcomers.

A book about legend lingering in the soul of a place, about class, and about teenagers becoming adults, *The Owl Service* is a great read for those who like their fantasy full of secrets. Garner teases and riddles with his readers. This is a book that inspires your imagination.

10+

Catherine Fisher

Next?
• Try Alan Garner's ***Elidor***, a tale about children bringing the four Hallows from the land of Elidor to urban Manchester. (UBG 71)
• If you enjoyed the Welsh legends in ***The Owl Service***, read more about them in ***The Mabinogion***, available in various retellings. Gwyn Jones and Thomas Jones's version is especially good.
• Other books using Welsh legend include Susan Cooper's ***The Dark Is Rising*** (UBG 57) and Catherine Fisher's ***Corbenic***. (UBG 52)

OTHER CULTURES

Out there in the big, bad world

BY ELIZABETH LAIRD

Don't tell me – you're a fantasy freak. No? But you love the spooky stuff. Thriller-chillers. Broomsticks and spells. Or is it animal stories you like? What about real life, then? Out there in the big bad world?

It's the big bad world, the real one out there beyond our shores, that gets me going. Every day, when I see the TV news, amazing tales unfold: true stories of terror and courage, adventure and survival. But TV only shows the tip of the iceberg. I always want to know more. To feel what it's like for the people to whom momentous things are happening. To climb inside their skins. And when I do, I find stories that are just as exciting as the chilliest thriller or the wildest fantasy.

Novels can transport you to places you're never likely to visit, and let you live, for a little while, the lives of people you'll never meet. Perhaps you've seen short clips about child soldiers in Africa – boys and girls as young as nine or ten, who carry guns, and fight and kill. If you read *Little Soldier* by Bernard Ashley, you'll really get an idea of how those children feel. Peter Dickinson's wonderful novel, *A.K.*, is on the same theme. Now try to imagine what it's like for two African children, torn away from home, arriving in the chill of London and labelled 'asylum seekers'. If you read *The Other Side of Truth* by Beverley Naidoo, you'll find out what it might really be like.

Tired of Africa? Then let's move on to India, to the enthralling trilogy by Jamila Gavin, beginning with *The Wheel of Surya*. You can travel with two children as they survive a civil war and undertake a daring journey alone, across the sea, to find their father. If you want a gentler tale of India, Anita Desai's beautiful story, *The Village by the Sea*, will fill your mind with new sights and sounds.

It's great to read about distant places, but it's even more fun to write about them. As a writer, I seek people out and immerse myself in their lives. When I lived in Baghdad, I visited the Kurds in their high mountain villages and the story of their struggles gripped me. I wrote about them in *Kiss the Dust*.

★ EIGHT VERY DIFFERENT BOOKS THE EDITORS RECOMMEND:

- ***Chinese Cinderella*** by Adeline Yen Mah
- ***The Village by the Sea*** by Anita Desai
- ***The Breadwinner*** by Deborah Ellis
- ***Journey to the River Sea*** by Eva Ibbotson
- ***Little House on the Prairie*** by Laura Ingalls Wilder
- ***Journey to Jo'burg*** by Beverley Naidoo
- ***Flying with Icarus*** by Curdella Forbes
- ***Roll of Thunder, Hear My Cry*** by Mildred D. Taylor

(You should also keep an eye out for Floella Benjamin's ***Coming to England***, a memoir of her coming over from Trinidad as a young girl.)

Ethiopia's a country I've always loved. I've lived there, and travelled to every corner of it, teaching, writing and collecting folk stories. While I was there, I got to know a gang of kids who lived on the streets of Addis Ababa. They told me about themselves, showed me the place where they sleep and introduced me to their dog. They let me write about their incredible lives in *The Garbage King*.

How did we get back to Africa? I wanted to tell you about Turkey, and Gaye Hiçyilmaz's great book, *Against the Storm* (read it and find out!). And I wanted to tell you something about the host of wonderful books of myths and legends there are to be found, from every part of the world. But I've run out of space – so it's over to you. Find out for yourself. Go on. Try a slice of the big, bad world for a change. You won't be disappointed.

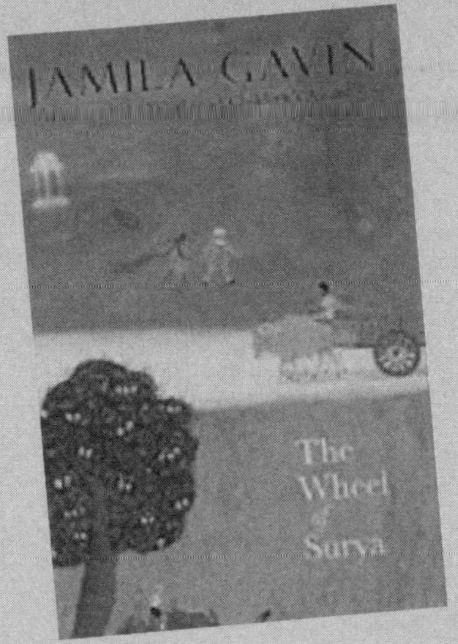

THE OWL TREE Jenny Nimmo, illustrated by Anthony Lewis

➡ Jenny Nimmo is such a wonderful author. Here, in under a hundred pages, she gives us a story of such beauty and wisdom that I find myself close to tears each time I read it.

Joe and Mina go to stay with their great-grandmother while their mother is expecting a baby. Granny Diamond becomes ill because her neighbour wants to cut down the beautiful old tree which overhangs her garden. Joe is terrified of heights, but decides to climb the tree to prove that a rare barn owl is nesting at the top, and then has to convince the crabby old man next door to change his mind.

With echoes of one of my favourite childhood stories, *The Selfish Giant* by Oscar Wilde, Jenny Nimmo gives us an enchanting book that readers of any age will find meaningful.

6+

Malachy Doyle

Next?

- If you want to read a spooky story about the countryside, try ***Storm*** by Kevin Crossley-Holland. (UBG 228)
- Or what about ***Ice Cat*** by Linda Newbery, about building a snowcat that is distinctly creepy? (UBG 121)
- Or, have you ever thought about what it is like to be an animal in a cage? In ***Countdown*** by Anne Fine, Hugo wants a gerbil. His dad agrees, but only if Hugo can spend seven hours alone in his newly-painted bedroom, with just three toys for company.

of. It's a fantastic story with a great moral: not to be scared of the dark.

A PACK OF LIES

Geraldine McCaughrean

➡ Ailsa first meets M.C.C. Berkshire as he is about to be thrown out of the library. She rescues him and he comes to work in her mother's antique shop, where M.C.C. reveals a wholly unexpected talent for charming customers into purchasing things by telling fantastical stories. The telephone engineer buys a harpsichord; a nun takes an umbrella stand ... Everything and everyone has a tale in this funny, thought-provoking story-filled story.

Does it matter that M.C.C.'s stories are all lies? Or are they true? How do you know? In this game of a book, Geraldine McCaughrean really makes you think about what's happening when stories are told. I won't spoil the final twist but this is a darn good story!

10-12

Helen Simmons

Next?

• Track down some more of Geraldine McCaughrean's novels. I would recommend ***Stop the Train*** (UBG 227) and ***The Kite Rider*** (UBG 136).

• If you enjoyed having fun putting the relationship between reader and narrator under the microscope, you might also like ***They Do Things Differently There*** (UBG 238) and ***Nothing to be Afraid of*** by Jan Mark (UBG 175).

• ***Haroun and the Sea of Stories*** by Salman Rushdie is a book full of stories, but it is also *about* stories. (UBG 104)

THE PALE HORSE Agatha Christie

➡ Mark Easterbrook is a young man who finds mysterious happenings popping up all around him. The worst of these are strange deaths, apparently caused by something called the Pale Horse. Investigating these deaths is Detective Inspector Lejeune, helped by an eager witness, Zachariah Osborne, who accuses a man in a wheelchair – a very rich man, called Venables – of being behind the murders; but Mark is more interested in Thyrza Grey, who claims to have killed people by witchcraft!

This creepy murder mystery is one of Agatha Christie's weirdest stories and has one of her cleverest solutions. If you enjoy stories of the days when London was thick with fog and amateur detectives helped the police, then *The Pale Horse* is just for you!

11+

Hugh Scott

Next?

• If your brain needs another puzzle to solve, then grab ***Mrs MacGinty's Dead***. This is a favourite Christie of mine, with Monsieur Hercule Poirot suffering dreadful of fates in the name of justice.

• For another great detective in foggy old London, try ***A Study in Scarlet*** by Arthur Conan Doyle. (UBG 231)

• ***And Then There Were None*** is another Christie classic. (UGB 13)

• Here's a good word: 'ratiocination'. If you want more brain-bending logic – that is, ratiocination – step even further back in time than Christie and try a volume of short stories by Edgar Allan Poe. But you may have to sleep with the lights on.

A PARCEL OF PATTERNS Jill Paton Walsh

➡ Like every child growing up in Derby, I knew about what happened in the village of Eyam. It's so peaceful there now it's hard to imagine what it was like when the plague came, and the little grey houses were full of people dying.

Mall tells us how the plague arrived, how the villagers vowed not to leave Eyam until the disease had burnt out, so as not to let it spread any further. And she tells us about these terrified, courageous people – like terrible Marshall Howe, who dragged the dead bodies away with a hook and Emmot Sydall, who dreamed of her own death.

Mall's story burns as fiercely and relentlessly as the plague she describes with such bitter accuracy while, sometimes one by one, sometimes in dozens, her friends and neighbours and family die around her.

11+

Gill Vickery

Next?

• Try other historical novels by Jill Paton Walsh. ***The Dolphin Crossing*** (UBG 66) and ***Fireweed*** take place during the Second World War.

• Berlie Doherty's ***Children of Winter*** is also concerned with the plague in Derbyshire.

• ***Check out our HISTORICAL STORIES choices on pp. 110-111.***

A PATTERN OF ROSES
K.M. Peyton

➡ This isn't one of K.M. Peyton's best-known novels, but it's one of her best (and I know she thinks so, too). It's a mystery story, in which Tim Ingram, recovering from glandular fever, finds sketches drawn by a boy living in the same house in Victorian times, who happens to share his initials – T.R.I. When Tim learns from a gravestone that T.R.I. died tragically young, he enlists the help of the vicar's daughter in trying to discover what happened. How did T.R.I. die? Who was the mysterious Netty? Does Tim, with his expensive education, have anything like T.R.I.'s talent for drawing? The reader is allowed to experience both past and present in this clever, atmospheric story, which shows Tim sorting out his own priorities in life and defying his parents' expectations.

11+

Linda Newbery

Next?
- If you like this, there are many other K.M. Peyton titles to enjoy. I particularly recommend the **Pennington** books, but anything written by her is well worth reading.
- A compelling mystery, complete with a ghost, is Margaret Mahy's fabulous ***The Haunting***. (UBG 107)
- Or try reading ***The Watch House*** by Robert Westall, a very, very scary book about the past sliding nastily into the present. (UBG 258)

THE PENGUIN IN THE FRIDGE Peter Dixon

➡ Peter Dixon is my favourite children's poet. I love his humour, cleverness of language and his brilliantly original verse. Wild, wonderful and exaggerated characters abound on page after page.

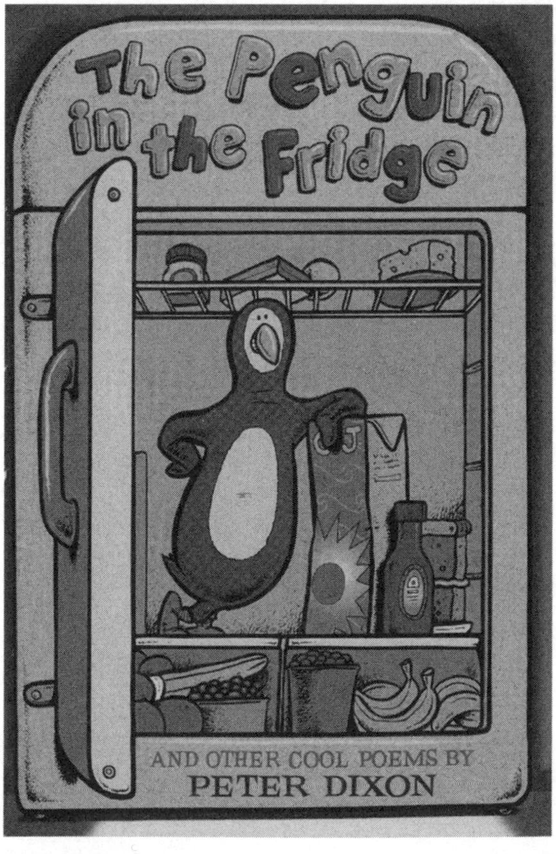

There's Reggie the Roman, strutting down the street calling, 'Hail Caesar', and Silly Kitty who caught a condor, and Brett who 'likes being daft and having laughs'.

Some of the poems, such as 'Hospice', 'Lost Rainbow' and 'Uncle Charlie' are thoughtful and poignant.

Offbeat, often amusing and great to read aloud, this collection is enhanced by the quirky and endearing illustrations of David Thomas.

8-11

Gervase Phinn

Next?
- Try ***Ask a Silly Question*** by Irene Rawnsley. I laugh out loud every time I read her poem, 'Nut up my Nose'. And ***Third Time Lucky*** by Mick Gowar, ***Thawing Frozen Frogs*** by Brian Patten and ***The Jungle Sale*** by June Crebbin are all cracking collections with much to entertain and amuse.
- For more penguins in fridges? ***Mr Popper's Penguins*** by Richard and Florence Atwater is lovely. (UBG 165)
- For some more serious (well, less silly) poems try ***Under the Moon and Over the Sea*** edited by John Agard and Grace Nichols. (UBG 252).

THE ULTIMATE READERS' POLL

YOUR TOP TEN FILMS BASED ON BOOKS

1. The Lord of the Rings
2. Harry Potter and the Philosopher's Stone
3. Matilda
4. The Princess Diaries
5. Charlie and the Chocolate Factory
6. 101 Dalmatians
7. The Story of Tracy Beaker
8. The BFG
9. Black Beauty
10. Goodnight Mister Tom

THE PEPPERMINT PIG

Nina Bawden

➡ The 'peppermint pig' has nothing to do with candy. He's so-called because he's so tiny when he arrives in the Greengrass household. He's a very real pig, his name is Johnnie, and Poll Greengrass's mum is going to rear him. Dad's gone to America to seek his fortune, and Mum and the four children are having a hard time. Johnnie grows up clean and well behaved, and is almost like one of the family. He can even be taken out to tea at the house of a great lady.

This story is set in your great-grandparents' day, but it's as bright and fresh as if it were yesterday.

9-12 **John Rowe Townsend**

Next?
- You may like to look for some other stories about pigs. Try Gene Kemp's ***The Prime of Tamworth Pig*** and Dick King-Smith's ***The Sheep-Pig*** (UBG 218). And Wilbur the pig is the hero of ***Charlotte's Web*** by E.B. White. (UBG 45)
- Pigs also are very important in Lloyd Alexander's ***The Book of Three***. (UBG 32)
- For a different animal, try one of the best dog stories, ***A Dog So Small*** by Philippa Pearce. (UBG 65)
- Another story of a family falling on hard times and how the children cope is ***The Silver Skates*** by Mary Mapes Dodge. (UBG 219)

PETER PAN

J.M. Barrie

➡ *Peter Pan* is truly one of the classics – in the original play, the subsequent book, pantomime and film. Ever since Peter first flew in through Wendy Darling's nursery window and took the three children to Neverland, Barrie's story of the boy who never grew up has thrilled young readers – from your great grandparents to your mum and dad.

Peter loses his shadow, sprinkles fairy dust over the children and flies with them to a magical island. There the real adventures begin: meeting the lost boys and the jealous little fairy Tinkerbell, swimming in the mermaids' lagoon, and fighting pirates led by the evil Captain Hook ...

Do you believe in fairies? You must if you are to save Tinkerbell's life ... Which brings us to the present: before he died, Barrie gave all future money from *Peter Pan* to saving lives at London's Great Ormond Street Children's Hospital.

8-10 **James Riordan**

Next?
- For other great adventure stories from a time before radio, TV and cinema, take a look at L. Frank Baum's ***The Wizard of Oz*** (UBG 269), and Lewis Carroll's ***Alice's Adventures in Wonderland*** (UBG 11) – unusually for their times, both have a female hero.
- Another boy who is always inventing schemes and getting into trouble features in ***Jimmy Zest*** by Sam McBratney. (UBG 128)

THE PHANTOM TOLLBOOTH

Norton Juster

➡ I first read this wonderful book when I was nine – then again and again and again ... I've since read it to both my children, who loved it (almost) as much as me!

For Milo, 'everything is a waste of time'. This changes when a small car appears, and whisks him away to the Kingdom of Wisdom. He is sent on a quest to rescue the princesses of Rhyme and Reason from the Castle in the Air. On his journey he encounters some of the weirdest characters ever created: Doctor Dischord and the terrible Dynne; Faintly Macabre, the not-so-wicked Which; the Gelatinous Giant; the Threadbare Excuse, and the Dodecahedron with its twelve faces, each with a different expression – to save wear and tear!

The book has a map, wonderful line drawings by Jules Feiffer and more puns, jokes and brain-teasers than anything I've read before or since. Simply fantastic!

Paul Stewart

10-12

Next?

- You will probably enjoy Lewis Carroll's ***Alice's Adventures in Wonderland***. Though written a long time ago, the humour is just as wacky, and the language isn't difficult. (UBG 11)
- More modern, but equally wacky, are the adventures of Eddie Dickens by Philip Ardagh, beginning with the splendidly eccentric ***Awful End***. (UBG 70)
- And don't forget the wonderful ***Muddle Earth*** by Paul Stewart and Chris Riddell. (UBG 168)

THE PIEMAKERS Helen Cresswell

➡ What a pie! It must be the biggest in the history of the world: a pie to feed two thousand people. The Roller family, who have been piemakers in Danby Dale for generations, are making it in the hope of winning a prize for the best and biggest pie, awarded by the King. Their daughter Gravella (whose name comes from 'gravy'), is helping.

What a recipe! Two hundred pounds of steak, seventy-five pounds of kidney, fifty pounds of onions, to say nothing of all those teaspoonfuls of water, pinches of salt and handfuls of herbs. What a voyage, when a pie-dish as big as a barge has to be steered down the river! But in the end the pie is a gorgeous, golden-crusted triumph, wheeled out into the sunshine to roars of applause. What a feast!

8-10

John Rowe Townsend

Next?

- Helen Cresswell has a light hand with comedy. You'll also savour the stories about an eccentric family in **The Bagthorpe Saga**. (UBG 22)
- I don't always like Roald Dahl's books myself, but ***The BFG*** is crammed with rich, occasionally slightly rude, humour. (UBG 27)
- Michael Rosen's weird ***You're Thinking About Doughnuts*** will definitely make you smile. (UBG 274)

PIG IN THE MIDDLE Sam Llewellyn

➡ When Alex Whean rescues and befriends a stranded seal pup, he finds himself in the middle of a furious row between a group of wrong-headed conservationists and a fisherman with a shotgun. This is a brilliantly moving book about divided loyalties and family breakdowns, set against the wild landscape of the West Coast of Scotland. The scene in which Alex's father is out in a rowboat, desperately searching for his son as the tide rises and the night draws in, is almost unbearably moving and makes this a book that will live long in the memory, well after you've turned the last page.

8-10

Karen Wallace

Next?

- Try ***Wonder Dog*** by the same author. What happens when Dai Evans has eleven months to turn the runt of a litter into a champion sheep dog?
- What about more seals? Try Aidan Chambers' ***Seal Secret***, another story about the rights and wrongs of how we treat animals. (UBG 214)
- Or try Michael Foreman's ***Seal Surfer***. Complete with his own wonderful illustrations, it is a great story about a boy rescued by a seal.

PICTURE BOOKS

'No TV for you anymore – from now on, it's only radio!'

BY TED DEWAN

Imagine what it would be like if a grown-up said this to you: 'Now that you're ten years old, you should stop watching TV and only listen to the radio. You don't need the TV pictures anymore ... when you listen to the radio, the pictures you make in your head are better anyhow!' This is just what some parents and teachers say about picture books and comics.

When I was about ten years old, I still enjoyed reading picture books long after I could read 'properly'. The school librarian was a bit worried about this, and gently persuaded me to give up the picture books, introducing me to science-fiction (which I liked) and some children's classics that just weren't right for me (which misled me into thinking that most books without pictures were boring). Luckily it didn't work, and I now make and read picture books for a living.

I was also hooked on *MAD* magazine, which, in the 1960s and 1970s, was very political and constantly made fun of advertising. *MAD* was almost entirely comic strips or words and pictures put together. I learned nearly everything I knew about politics, social status, and consumerism by reading it. My mum must be the only mother in the world who didn't throw out my collection of *MAD* magazines; in fact, she went out of her way to preserve them for me, and even rescued them from a cellar flood. They are in my studio to this day.

So why are some people snobby about words? David Fickling, the famous children's book editor, thinks the 'word snobs' were at their peak in the Middle Ages when most people couldn't read or write. The people in control, the upper classes and especially the church, kept the secret of

★ A FEW PICTURE BOOKS RECOMMENDED IN THE UBG:

- ***Fungus the Bogeyman***, ***Ethel and Ernest***, ***Ug*** – all by Raymond Briggs; also look out for his ***When the Wind Blows*** and ***Father Christmas***
- ***Maus*** by Art Spiegelman
- **Asterix** series by René Goscinny and Albert Uderzo
- **Tintin** series by Hergé
- ***Gorilla*** by Anthony Browne
- ***The Rabbits*** by Shaun Tan and John Marsden
- ***How to Live Forever*** by Colin Thompson; also try his ***Falling Angels***
- ***Mr William Shakespeare's Plays*** and other books by Marcia Williams
- ***Ironfist Chinmi*** by Takeshi Maekawa

written language to themselves (writing in Latin, like a secret code), in order to maintain power over the illiterates. Most people could, of course, understand pictures, which is how the stories of the Bible were told in stained-glass windows for people to 'read' over and over again. But words ruled over pictures, as they still do today in the world of books.

So don't let anyone make you think that learning to read means having to give up the pictures. Nowadays, school librarians are much more aware of good books with words and pictures for older kids. One book you might want to read, *Understanding Comics*, was written by Scott McCloud, a childhood friend of mine who also refused to give up the pictures. It's the best book around that shows how words and pictures work together. After reading it, you'll be able to run rings around any word snob who tries to take your pictures away.

And, of course, it's all done as a comic!

★ MORE PICTURE BOOKS NOT TO BE MISSED:

- ***Where the Forest Meets the Sea*** and other torn-tissue collages by the wonderful Jeannie Baker.
- ***Clown*** by Quentin Blake
- ***The Three Little Wolves and the Big Bad Pig*** by Eugene Trivizas and Helen Oxenbury.
- ***The Kiss that Missed*** by David Melling
- ***Castle Diary*** by Richard Platt and Chris Riddell (and look out for *Pirate Diary*, too)
- ***Zoo*** and ***Voices in the Park*** by Anthony Browne – in fact, any of Anthony Browne's picture books will delight you and make you think twice.
- ***Smelly Jelly, Smelly Fish*** by Michael Rosen and Quentin Blake
- ***Amazing Grace*** and its sequels by Mary Hoffman and Caroline Binch
- ***Where the Wild Things Are*** by Maurice Sendak
- ***East of the Sun and West of the Moon*** by P.J. Lynch
- The **Grinch** books by Dr Seuss – in fact, read *everything* by Dr Seuss.

PIG-HEART BOY

Malorie Blackman

➡ A viral illness a couple of years ago has left thirteen-year-old Cameron Kelsey with a failing heart. He's faced with a stark choice – either an early death or a heart transplant, but the only available donor is a pig. Despite his mother's misgivings and his own fear, Cameron opts for the transplant. *Pig-heart Boy* tells the moving, sometimes funny, and deeply thought-provoking story about a boy who undergoes a pioneering operation. We see his friends' reactions, the stresses and strains on his family and how Cameron bravely tries to cope with the consequences of living with his new heart. This book is an unforgettable 'real-life' read that will keep you thinking long after you've turned the last page.

8-10

Sherry Ashworth

Next?

- Malorie Blackman has written a number of other exciting books for children – older readers might like to try ***Thief!*** (UBG 238). Or try ***Hacker***, about a girl determined to prove the innocence of her father, accused of stealing over a million pounds (UBG 102).
- If you are interested in reading other books that talk about illnesses, you could try Judy Blume's ***Deenie***, about a teenage girl with a spinal deformity.
- Another brilliant book that deals in a totally original way with a baby having a heart problem is David Almond's ***Skellig***. (UBG 220)
- ***Becky Bananas*** by Jean Ure is a younger, very moving and unforgettable book about illness that may make you cry. (UBG 25)

still reading them today! My number one fan sends me a Pooh calendar for Christmas each year.

PIGEON SUMMER

Ann Turnbull

➠ You might find the idea of a story about racing pigeons slightly peculiar – but think again! In *Pigeon Summer*, Mary's family are facing hard times. Her father has left home looking for work, her sister's wages help to make ends meet, but whatever Mary herself does is wrong: as her mother says, 'You're that different.' While she is looking after her father's racing pigeons, she thinks of a way to help, even if it means going against her mother – and convention.

Mary is determined to find solutions her way. The pigeons bring dreams of distant places far above the dark mineshafts, and when her father and his winning pigeon finally come home, there is hope of a better future.

10-12

Helen Simmons

Next?

- Ann Turnbull has written two more books about the Dyer family. Look out for ***No Friend of Mine*** and ***Room for a Stranger***.
- You might like ***The Peppermint Pig*** by Nina Bawden; another family story with a determined heroine – and an unlikely animal character. (UBG 184)
- Or try one of Michael Morpurgo's books that have animal as well as human characters, such as ***Mr Nobody's Eyes***, about a boy who befriends a chimp who has escaped from the circus, or ***Why the Whales Came*** (UBG 264). And don't miss his terrific book, ***Toro! Toro!*** (UBG 245)

PIGGIES

Nick Gifford

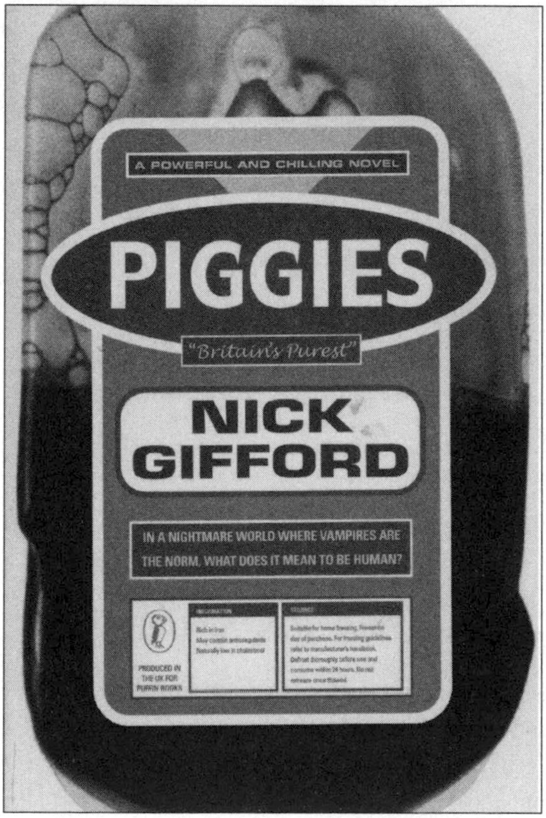

A POWERFUL AND CHILLING NOVEL
PIGGIES
"Britain's Purest"
NICK GIFFORD
IN A NIGHTMARE WORLD WHERE VAMPIRES ARE THE NORM. WHAT DOES IT MEAN TO BE HUMAN?

➠ Imagine a world where the norm is being a vampire, and humans are seen as nothing more than walking blood-banks. How would you cope if you suddenly found yourself thrust into this parallel universe? In Nick Gifford's original take on traditional vampire stories, this is precisely the situation that his hero, Ben, finds himself in. Victim of a freak accident that transports him to such a place, he quickly finds himself running for his life, desperately searching for fellow humans. The trouble is, once he does find them they are reluctant to trust him and his problems are far from over …

This clever book is fast-paced and full of suspense (and includes a great surprise ending). Not only that, but it makes you think twice about the way our world works, and I guarantee that you'll never look at meat in quite the same way again!

10-12

Laura Hutchings

Next?

- If you enjoy reading about vampires then **The Saga of Darren Shan** is highly recommended. (UBG 208)
- Someone else who writes about vampires is the American author L.J. Smith (I particularly enjoyed ***The Secret Vampire***).
- Another book about finding yourself in a kind of parallel universe is Neil Gaiman's terrifying ***Coraline***. (UBG 51)

Next?
- Try others by Betsy Byars: ***After the Goat Man, The Cartoonist, The TV Kid***, or ***The Eighteenth Emergency*** (UBG 71).
- ***Ruby Holler*** by Sharon Creech is about two orphaned children adjusting to a new home. (UBG 205)
- Morris Gleitzman's ***Bumface*** (UBG 37) and ***Two Weeks with the Queen*** (UBG 251) are both great, and deal with *real* issues.

THE PINBALLS Betsy Byars

➡ Three young people from broken families find themselves in the same foster home. Harvey arrives with two broken legs – he's been run over by his dad, driving his new car. Thomas J., abandoned like an unwanted puppy, has been taken in by the eighty-year-old Benson twins, until they both break a hip on the same day. The third is a girl called Carlie – cynical, and as hard to crack as a coconut.

But if you think that all sounds a bit heavy, you'd be wrong. The dynamo of the story is wise-cracking Carlie. 'We're just like pinballs,' she tells Mrs Mason, the foster mother. 'Somebody put in a dime and punched a button and out we came, ready or not.'

This is a small treasure that will make you laugh out loud on one page and cry on the next. What else could you possibly want?!

9-12

Rose Impey

PINOCCHIO Carlo Collodi

➡ Mr Cherry, a carpenter, finds a piece of wood that begs him not to strike it too hard with his axe, and when he planes it it laughs and says that he's tickling it. The unnerved Mr Cherry gives the wood to his friend Geppetto, who makes a living puppet of it – Pinocchio – who promptly decides that he would like to be a real boy. Pinocchio leaves home to try and find a way to achieve this, and the adventures that follow are many and colourful.

My introduction to this story was the Disney film. On subsequently reading the book I found that a great deal had been written out of the film, or completely changed. The book tends to moralise, and isn't entirely devoid of sentimentality, but it has a much harder edge than the film, and a far more complex and rewarding storyline.

9-11

Michael Lawrence

Next?
- Try ***The Adventures of the Little Wooden Horse*** by Ursula Moray Williams, which owes an awful lot to ***Pinocchio*** but is gentler and younger.
- Another wonderful story of a something coming to life is Ted Hughes's ***The Iron Man***. (UBG 124)
- Lynne Reid Banks's hugely popular series about something similar starts with ***The Indian in the Cupboard***. (UBG 122)

Next?
- Look out for ***The Amazing Pippi Longstocking, Pippi Longstocking in the Park*** and ***Do You Know Pippi Longstocking?***
- Another really funny series about a wild little girl is ***My Naughty Little Sister*** by Dorothy Edwards. (UBG 170)
- Or there is always Beverly Cleary's **Ramona** series, all about a girl who never means to get into trouble, but somehow ... (UBG 198)

PIPPI LONGSTOCKING Astrid Lindgren

➡ Pippi is a nine-year-old with very long feet and bunches that stick horizontally out of her head. She lives alone in her own house, with a horse and a monkey for company. Although Pippi looks like a scarecrow, she turns out to be very clever, outwitting any adult who crosses her path. During the course of the many **Pippi Longstocking** books, this strange girl wins the battle of wits with lots of grown-ups. I remember being terribly impressed by that, and wondering why I couldn't do the same.

Pippi's friends, Tommy and Annika, envy her as she never has to do boring things like go to school, or go to bed early, or eat vegetables instead of sweets. I envied her, too, as to me she was always so free, especially when she went zipping off to exotic places on her own!

7-10

Sara Wheeler

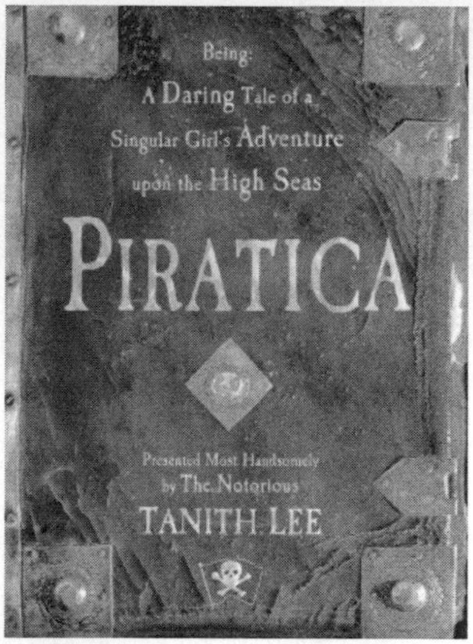

PIRATICA

Tanith Lee

➡ For six years, Artemesia (or 'Art') has forgotten everything about her mother Molly, and in that time has been all that her father wanted her to be – demure, biddable and sweet. But after a crack on the head, all her memories come flooding back, and everything changes.

What Artemesia remembers is that Molly was a pirate, and Molly taught her daughter everything she knew. Escaping from a locked room, Art disguises herself as a boy and flees to 'Lundon'. She meets up with her mother's old crew, a shambling bunch of rapscallions. And there, after a while, she learns that her memories are a twisted variation on the truth; for Molly was only a pirate of sorts – she was really an actress who played the part of a pirate queen, Piratica, on the stage.

Would that stifle your piratical ambition? It doesn't even dent Art's. She steals a ship, persuades her crew that they can actually do for real all they acted on stage, and heads out to sea.

Art's adventures are outrageous, amazing and exhilarating. She is, of course, beautiful, and she meets a young man called Felix Phoenix, who is mysterious, and even more beautiful than she. With a parrot, tempestuous piratical villains, jewels, fights, duels, treasure maps, betrayal and a finale that is so exciting you have to remind yourself to breathe while reading, this is a fantastic story.

11+

Leonie Flynn

Next?

• Tamora Pierce writes about strong women too. Read the **Song of the Lioness** series (UBG 223) and **Protector of the Small** (UBG 194).

• Or try some more Tanith Lee. ***The Castle of the Dark*** (UBG 42) and ***East of Midnight*** (UBG 69) are both exciting fantasies.

PLAYING BEATIE BOW Ruth Park

➡ A girl is drawn from the past into modern day Sydney by children calling her name. They are playing a scary game: Beatie Bow. Fourteen-year-old Abigail Kirk, intrigued by the appearance of this odd-looking child, decides to follow her. She quickly becomes confused by the maze of unfamiliar streets in one of the oldest parts of the town and eventually realises, to her horror, that she is not only lost, but back in another time: the Sydney of 1873.

Abigail's adventures are exciting, heart-warming and terrifying by turns. Her experiences in this strange world turn this shy, prickly, self-centred child into a more mature, generous, tough-minded young woman.

I love the mix of reality, fantasy and history that make up timeslip books. The best (and I'd put *Playing Beatie Bow* up there) are exciting unputdownable reads that make you think. In my opinion, there is no better way of bringing history to life.

10-12

Celia Rees

Next?

• More timeslips? Some classics include: ***Tom's Midnight Garden*** by Phillipa Pearce (UBG 245), ***Moondial*** by Helen Cresswell, ***Charlotte Sometimes*** by Penelope Farmer (UBG 45), ***A Stitch in Time*** by Penelope Lively (UBG 226).

• Another terrific timeslip, published more recently, is ***An Angel for May*** by Melvin Burgess. (UBG 14)

• What about some straight history? Try Rosemary Sutcliff's ***The Armourer's House***, or for something else Victorian, try ***The Ruby in the Smoke*** by Philip Pullman.

PLAYING ON THE EDGE Neil Arksey

➡ Football in 2064 has changed dramatically from today's game. There are now only two leagues playing in Britain – the British Premier League, amalgamations of current top teams, and the Corporates League, owned by the world's biggest companies. However, the underground Unaffiliated Football League is growing in popularity and there is a big swing by the public away from the official teams.

The plot thickens when Todd Linker, a scout for super-team Gunman Reds, finds damning evidence that the performance-enhancing drugs being fed compulsorily to their players are having deadly side-effects. When he is arrested to stop him speaking out, it is left up to his son Easy to escape with the evidence and save the day ...

10-12

Chris d'Lacey

Next?

- What I like about Neil Arksey's books is the different slant they take on football. Try ***Flint***, about a lad whose dad is a thief. Or try ***MacB***, a clever twist on a Shakespearean drama. (UBG 150)
- Or what about ***The Angel Factory*** by Terence Blacker, about a world where nothing is as it seems? (UBG 13)

POINT HORROR series

➡ If you are looking for a fun, light, page-turner to scare you pleasantly before you turn off your bedside lamp, then **Point Horror** is perfect. Because many authors have written for this series, the books tend to be varied in style and quality – in short, some are better than others. My favourites are the ones written by authors who write other stuff besides **Point Horror**. They tend to be a bit more original and therefore, interesting.

Blood Sinister by Celia Rees tells the story of a girl suffering from a mysterious disease who comes across personal diaries of her Victorian ancestor. What begins as an entertaining pastime turns into a close encounter with supernatural horror. Chris Wooding's *Catchman* revolves around Davie, a boy slumming it in a communal squat, who is running away from a pretty disturbing past. But secrets are no longer safe when an unknown serial killer is on the lookout for victims. Brrrr ... this is the stuff that nightmares are made of.

9-12

Noga Applebaum

Next?

- Celia Rees's gripping ***Witch Child*** is more challenging than most of the **Point Horror** books – but a lot better, too! (UBG 267)
- How about a supernatural murderous hound? Try Arthur Conan Doyle's ***The Hound of the Baskervilles***! (UBG 117)
- For something easier than that, try R.L. Stine's **Goosebumps** series. (UBG 98)
- A more challenging read is Chris Wooding's ***The Haunting of Alaizabel Cray***. (UBG 108)

POISON Chris Wooding

➡ I don't much like fantasy books, frankly. I've never really liked them. All those made-up names and fake maps and languages just annoy me. Am I the only person in the world who just couldn't get into *The Lord of the Rings* at all? But every once in a while a book comes along that makes me wonder, 'Hmm, maybe there's something in this fantasy stuff after all ...' *Poison* is such a book.

It's the sinister story of a girl (Poison) from the Black Marshes, and her quest to rescue her little sister from the Phaerie Lord, facing numerous chilling threats along the way ...

But for all the fantasy, the imagined worlds etc., it's really just a great human story, beautifully written, with excitement and emotion and plenty of evil and everything a good story should have. A few pages into it I'd already forgotten that I wasn't meant to be enjoying it, and was hooked.

10+

Daniel Hahn

Next?

- I suppose you should probably try ***The Lord of the Rings*** (so should I). (UBG 148)
- If you don't want to brave that just yet, try ***The Hobbit***, which I *have* read and loved. (UBG 112)
- Try Chris Wooding's ***The Haunting of Alaizabel Cray***. (UBG 108)
- Or how about Lene Kaaberbol's ***The Shamer's Daughter*** about a girl who discovers a gift for making others admit their weaknesses.

POLLYANNA

Eleanor H. Porter

➡ If you feel like reading something old-fashioned and heartwarming, you'll enjoy the story of Pollyanna. Although her parents have no money, Pollyanna's childhood is full of love. Even when her mother dies, her father manages to keep their spirits up by playing the famous 'glad game'.

Then, when Pollyanna is eleven, her father also dies and she goes to live with her cold Aunt Polly, who takes her in simply because she considers it to be her duty. Somehow Pollyanna manages to win over all the eccentric inhabitants of the village, and eventually her aunt too.

This moving story makes you stop and think about your own life, and your own reasons to be glad.

Kate Petty

9-11

Next?
- There is another Pollyanna story by Eleanor H. Porter, called ***Pollyanna Grows Up***, and several more by other authors.
- Frances Hodgson Burnett's ***The Secret Garden*** (UBG 215) and ***A Little Princess*** (UBG 144) are also classics which feature determined heroines.

PONGWIFFY

Kaye Umansky

Next?
- If you're into witches and spells, turn immediately to p. 272, and read about Jill Murphy's ***The Worst Witch***.
- For downright outrageous fun, seek out Margaret Mahy's ***The Great Piratical Rumbustification***. (UBG 100)
- Or try Willis Hall's series about ***The Last Vampire***. (UBG 140)
- Bruce Coville's **The Magic Shop** books are funny, clever stories that will make you think twice. (UBG 152)

➡ Kaye Umansky's madcap stories are always all-singing, all-dancing affairs. Why not try her most famous book of all, and meet her best-loved character, Pongwiffy, 'a witch of dirty habits' (and the star of several books and even a TV show).

Pongwiffy has a bit of a personal hygiene problem, and doesn't always think before she acts, but she's extremely likeable. You'll love her long-suffering friend Sharkadder too, and even the goblins (although they're quite stupid). In the first story, Pongwiffy finds a new place to live, a new familiar to keep her company, and gets involved in a talent competition and in planning an extra special birthday. Nothing ever quite goes to plan, but it's a lot of fun to read about!

Jon Appleton

8-10

THE PRESENT TAKERS

Aidan Chambers

➡ Sometimes people can make you feel very young indeed by acting really grown up – and that's part of Lucy's problem when she becomes the latest victim of school bully, Melanie Prosser and her gang. Lucy's no pushover, but the bullies are fierce. Angus wants to help, but Lucy thinks he's a bit off the wall. But they have to find a way to stop Prosser, once and for all. This is a fast-paced, edge-of-your-seat book, with lots of short, sharp scenes like a film, and windows into all the characters' minds, just like clever camera work. It was written twenty years ago, but still feels up-to-date. It makes you think not just about bullying, but the way we see other people.

Jon Appleton

9-12

Next?
- Bridget Crowley's ***Step into the Dark*** is a gripping story about bullying, among other things. (UBG 225)
- ***The Mighty Crashman*** by Jerry Spinelli is a story that is seen from the point of view of a bully. (UBG 160)
- And Nicky Singer's ***Feather Boy*** tackles the same subject. (UBG 82)
- A more cheerful story with a school background is ***How to Eat Fried Worms*** by Thomas Rockwell. (UBG 117)

THE PRINCE AND THE PAUPER

Mark Twain

➡ Edward Tudor is heir to the throne and spoiled rotten. Tom Canty is poor – a half-starved beggar who, more often than not, gets beaten by his drunken father. The only thing the two boys have in common is that they look identical, and that one day, by strange chance, they swap lives.

Written a long time ago, and set even further back in time, this is a classic story of mistaken identity. You'll soon get the hang of the way it is written – words like prithee and perchance crop up a lot – and be reading just to find out what happens to the boys. For will they ever get their own lives back – and will they want to?

10-12

Leonie Flynn

Next?

- Another wonderful Mark Twain story is ***A Connecticut Yankee at King Arthur's Court*** – one of the first time-travel stories. Twain also wrote ***The Adventures of Tom Sawyer***. (UBG 9)
- ***Lotte and Lisa*** by Erich Kåstner is a story of identical twins who play a trick on their separated parents.
- ***Double Act*** by Jacqueline Wilson is a very modern story of twins. (UBG 67)
- ***And don't miss our feature on HISTORICAL STORIES on pp. 110-111.***

THE PRINCESS DIARIES

Meg Cabot

➡ Just because you've seen the movie, don't deny yourself this treat. Like all the best children's fiction, this series can be enjoyed by adults as well as kids.

Brilliantly written in the form of an ongoing diary with lots of fun pop culture references, these books are delectable! Mia Thermopolis is fourteen when she discovers that her Jean-Luc-Picard-lookalike father is really the crowned prince of a small European country. And as his only daughter, she is a princess!

Meg Cabot makes you feel you really know what being a high school student in New York is like. And besides being funny, well-written and totally unputdownable, this book has lots of delightful lists. For example, here is a list of Mia's favourite books: *IQ 83*, *Jaws*, *The Catcher in the Rye*, *To Kill a Mockingbird* and *A Wrinkle in Time* ('only we never get to find out the most important thing: whether or not Meg has breasts ...')

10+

Caroline Lawrence

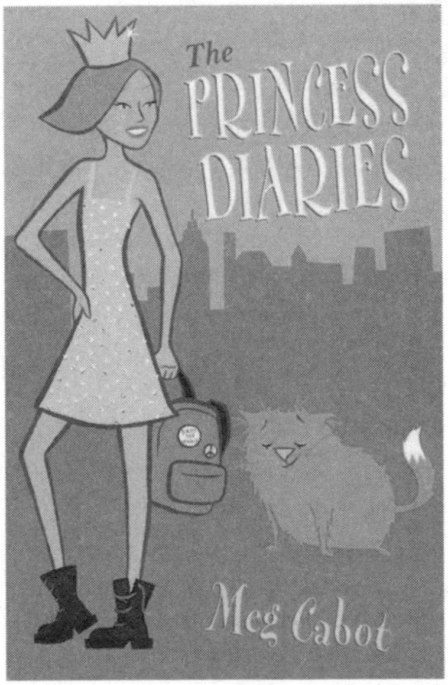

Next?

- Try Annie Dalton's great series, **Angels Unlimited**. (UBG 14)
- Or there are Hilary McKay's brilliant stories about the Conroy sisters in ***The Exiles***. (UBG 75)
- ***Simone's Diary*** by Helen Pielichaty offers another kind of journal. (UBG 220)
- For more surprises about parents, try Nina Bawden's absorbing ***The Outside Child***. (UBG 179).
- Want to read another New York-based story? Try Louise Fitzhugh's ***Harriet the Spy***. (UBG 104)

Mia's diaries continue in ***Take Two***, ***Third Time Lucky***, ***Mia Goes Fourth***, ***Give Me Five***, etc. And if you're looking for some more princess stories, why not try ...

- ***A Little Princess*** by Frances Hodgson Burnett (well, it's sort-of a princess story).
- ***The Ordinary Princess*** by M. M. Kaye
- ***The Light Princess*** by George Macdonald
- **The Princess Tales** series by Gail Carson Levine
- ***The Frog Princess*** by E.D. Baker
- **The Egerton Hall Trilogy** by Adèle Geras (for much older readers)

them again.

THE PRISONER James Riordan

➡ It is 1943, and the world for Tom and Iris is full of air-raids, bombings and war. They hate the Germans, and when one day they find a downed enemy bomber, they take the wounded pilot and imprison him in an old railway shed. He's theirs. Their responsibility. Theirs to interrogate …

But the pilot isn't quite what they expect. He speaks English, and seems very young. He has pictures of his girlfriend, and talks of loved ones who have died. Suddenly he isn't a monster any more, he is human. Just like them.

Full of things that make you think very hard about the nature of good and evil, this book brings the war evocatively to life.

Leonie Flynn

10-12

Next?

- Two Robert Westalls: ***Blitzcat*** paints a vivid picture of Britain at war (UBG 31), while ***The Machine Gunners*** is about a downed plane (UBG 150).
- Another book about friends and enemies is Donna Jo Napoli's ***Stones in Water.***
- Iain Lawrence's ***Lord of the Nutcracker Men*** is about learning to see your enemies as real people. (UBG 147)

PROFESSOR BRANESTAWM

Norman Hunter

➡ Professor Branestawm is the inventor of, amongst other things, a powerful elixir of life. There are extraordinary results when the potion is accidentally spilt on to the rubbish in his wastepaper bin, culminating in the Professor being chased up into the pear tree by a gigantic postcard. Illustrated throughout by W. Heath Robinson, an artist whose name has become a byword for outlandish, imaginary inventions, this collection contains fourteen stories involving the Professor, his housekeeper the often-traumatised Mrs Flittersnoop, and his friend Colonel Dedshott of the Catapult Cavaliers. There are encounters with screaming clocks, spring-cleaning machines and living photographs and there is a great deal of trouble with the local libraries over a book about lobsters.

7-9

Thomas Bloor

Next?

- You may want to read more Professor Branestawm books – ***The Peculiar Triumph of Professor Branestawm***, for instance.
- If you like short stories that are funny and full of weird and wonderful ideas, but with a more modern setting, then try Paul Jennings's ***Uncanny!*** (UBG 251) or ***Wicked!*** (UBG 264).
- Or if you really like science? Try Russell Stannard's ***The Time and Space of Uncle Albert.*** (UBG 243)

PROTECTOR OF THE SMALL

FIRST TEST • PAGE • SQUIRE • LADY KNIGHT

Tamora Pierce

➡ Tamora Pierce writes fantasy that is earthy, colourful and fun. What's more, the strong heroes of her tales of adventure and chivalry are girls.

Keladry wants to emulate her great hero Alanna (from **Song of the Lioness**, another Tamora Pierce series), and win a knight's shield. It is very unusual for a women to train with the boy pages, but despite much opposition and struggle, she survives the hardships to rise to squire.

In *Squire*, Kel learns to joust, goes into battle, falls in love and acts as a foster parent to a baby griffin – a fascinating, bird-like creature with a fearsome beak, that demands attention twenty-four hours a day. She also builds towards her final tests on the road to becoming a knight.

In *Lady Knight* Kel tries to fulfil a quest, deal with a camp full of refugees and wage a war, all the while trying to be certain that she is deserving of her knight's shield.

Kate Petty

10+

Next?

- You might enjoy Tamora Pierce's other series about a female knight: **The Song of the Lioness.** (UBG 223)
- Alanna the Lioness also appears in **The Immortals Quartet**, about a girl discovering both an ability to communicate with animals and her own magic.
- Or try Tamora Pierce's books set in a different universe: **The Circle of Magic** quartet.
- Another great book about strong and absolutely no-nonsense women is ***Piratica*** by Tanith Lee. (UBG 190)

PUCK OF POOK'S HILL Rudyard Kipling

Next?
- Try two other very English fantasies: John Masefield's ***The Midnight Folk*** and ***The Box of Delights*** (UBG 34).
- Or try Kipling's ***The Jungle Book***. (UBG 130)
- Susan Cooper's **The Dark Is Rising** uses English folk tales and history. (UBG 57)
- Why not try Julie Hearn's brilliant timeslip, ***Follow Me Down***? (UBG 87)

➡ The best chapter of all in *Puck of Pook's Hill* is called 'Dymchurch Flit', but to read it you must first read how Una and Dan act their own version of *A Midsummer Night's Dream*, three times running, on Midsummer's Eve, in a field near their Sussex home. Since they happen to be standing inside one of those dark grass circles called a fairy ring, they unwittingly call up Puck, Robin Goodfellow, oldest of the Old Things – and that leads to all kinds of stories from the past, of a kind you don't find in history books. A very English kind of magic echoes through all of them. Kipling was really good at tapping into that, even though he's better known for *The Jungle Books* and his other stories about India.

Susan Cooper

10+

PUNCHBOWL FARM stories

THE BLACK HUNTING WHIP • PUNCHBOWL MIDNIGHTS • THE SPIRIT OF PUNCHBOWL FARM • THE CATS OF PUNCHBOWL FARM and more

Monica Edwards

➡ I loved these books as a child, and read each one several times. Punchbowl Farm seemed so real to me – a feeling helped by the hand-drawn maps inside the book covers – that it was no surprise to learn it was a real place, and that Monica Edwards lived there. Seen mainly from the viewpoint of quiet, animal-loving Lindsey, the stories follow the Thornton family, who first appeared in an early book, *No Mistaking Corker*. Beginning with *The Black Hunting Whip*, in which the family moves to the derelict farm, the books span several years, and cover various adventures and dilemmas – including fire, a shooting accident, and a conflict when Dion, the schoolboy farmer, wants to fell the ancient yew tree, summoning a warning ghost. Monica Edwards wrote wonderfully about animals, countryside, weather, and all the things that make Punchbowl Farm a living, breathing place.

Linda Newbery

9-11

Next?
- If you like series about the same characters, try the **Romney Marsh** books by Monica Edwards – through ***Wish for a Pony*** and ***The Summer of the Great Secret*** to the last books, ***No Going Back***, ***The Hoodwinkers*** and ***A Wind is Blowing***. Tamzin, Meryon, Rissa and Roger, besides having adventures of their own involving ships and smuggling, become friendly with the Punchbowl Farm characters and even go to stay with them in ***The Outsiders***.
- If you enjoy books about the countryside, try ***Farm Boy***, by Michael Morpurgo. (UBG 81)
- Or for a very funny book about families, animals, friends and trying to make a living, look out for ***Dog Friday*** by Hilary McKay.

PURE DEAD MAGIC Debi Gliori

Next?
- There are another two books about the same family – ***Pure Dead Wicked*** and ***Pure Dead Brilliant***.
- If you like wild and wacky you could try Philip Ardagh's ***Fall of Fergal*** (UBG 78) or his **Eddie Dickens Trilogy** (UBG 70).
- Philip Ridley writes off-the-wall books too. Try ***ZinderZunder*** and ***Mighty Fizz Chilla***. (UBG 160)

➡ Any book that has a baddie called Don Lucifer di S'Embowelli has to be pretty extraordinary, and when you throw in a Gothic castle, a hero called Titus Strega-Borgia, a baby called Damp and a spider who *loves* scarlet lipstick, it all adds up to a fantastic package of weird and wonderful plots and counterplots – and a great read. The story rattles along at breakneck speed, and it's completely mad, but there's a really warm heart behind all the activity; the Strega-Borgias may have beasts in the cellars, but they are a gloriously loving and affectionate family when they're not wanting to murder each other – and isn't that just like all the best sorts of families?

Vivian French

8-11

Next?
- I think you'll enjoy Philippa Pearce's ***The Battle of Bubble and Squeak*** (UBG 24) and also her brilliant set of stories, ***Lion at School***.
- Anne Fine writes about a funny family in ***Crummy Mummy and Me***, and about a family Christmas from hell in the hilarious ***The More the Merrier***.
- For more unexpected adventures, check out Francesca Simon's **Horrid Henry** stories. (UBG 116)

THE QUIGLEYS Simon Mason

➡ Everything we learn in the first few pages of this delightful book makes us think it's going to be fairly ordinary – but that's exactly what makes the book so special! In writing about everyday people and events, Simon Mason shows just how interesting – and funny – family life can be (and he makes a fair case for believing that no one really is 'ordinary' after all).

Here are four stories about the Quigleys: one each about Mum, Dad, Will and Lucy. Lots happens, both planned and unexpected, such as an evening's babysitting which goes disastrously wrong and a wedding in which the bride might be upstaged by a bee!

I loved the humour and observations in this book, but best of all I loved the characters. If you do also (and I think you will) look out for more adventures in the sequel, *The Quigleys at Large*.

8-10

Jon Appleton

THE RABBITS

Illustrated by Shaun Tan with text by John Marsden

➡ Australian illustrator Shaun Tan and author John Marsden have created a remarkable story about colonisation and slavery. European rabbits were introduced to Australia centuries ago, and since they had no predators there, the rabbit population went nuts. In this book, the rabbits are dressed as British colonising troops who ride roughshod over the native possums, carving up the land, building cities and displacing the possums.

Shaun Tan's marvellous storytelling is strangely beautiful and frightening. This amazing book is as visually loaded as a Terry Gilliam film despite its slender thirty-two pages (no, you're never too old for picture books, especially if they're like this one). *The Rabbits* deserves to become a classroom classic alongside Orwell's *Animal Farm*.

8+

Ted Dewan

Next?
- Look for more of Shaun Tan's picture books. You can spend hours searching for different meanings and little stories in the pictures. I've read all his books many many times and I keep seeing new things. Look especially for ***Red Tree***.
- Get a book on the artists Bosch or Brueghel. Both of them lived hundreds of years ago but their paintings are still inspiring today's artists and filmmakers.
- ***How to Live Forever*** by Colin Thompson is another Australian picture book. Only for little kids, eh? Take a good look at it and see what you think. (UBG 118)

If you're looking for *The Arthur Rackham Fairy Book*, turn to p. 20

A RAG, A BONE AND A HANK OF HAIR Nicholas Fisk

➡ Brin is twelve, and at the end of the twenty-second century that makes him a very important person. The birth rate has plunged following an environmental disaster. The human race could be facing extinction. Brin, with his super-high IQ, receives a request from the Western Council of Seniors to help them with their plans to repopulate the world. His mission is to observe the Reborns, new humans recreated from dead tissue. He meets Brian, Mavis and Mrs Mossop, all Reborns who believe they're still living in 1940. Will they ever be able to adjust to a new world – two centuries on from the one they knew? And why can't Brin shake the feeling there's something he's not being told?

Thomas Bloor

10-12

Next?

- Try more of Nicholas Fisk's science fiction, such as ***Trillions*** or ***Grinny***.
- If stories set in the future appeal to you then Philip Reeve's ***Mortal Engines*** is a good choice. (UBG 164).
- For a story set in the past, try Nina Bawden's ***Carrie's War*** which looks back to a child's life in the 1940s. (UBG 41)
- 'A rag, a bone and a hank of hair' is a quotation from a poem called 'The Vampire' by Rudyard Kipling, who wrote a number of famous stories, including ***The Jungle Book*** (UBG 130) and ***The Just So Stories*** (UBG 132).
- ***The Giver*** by Lois Lowry also looks at the future, and sees something not very nice. (UBG 93)

EVERYBODY'S FAVOURITE…

THE RAILWAY CHILDREN E. Nesbit

➡ Bobbie, Peter and Phyllis have a comfortable suburban life in Edwardian England until their father mysteriously goes away. Nobody will explain where he's gone, or why, and suddenly they find themselves poor, living in a bleak little country house near a railway line. But the chuffing steam trains bring danger and adventure into their lives, and in the end solve the mystery and change their lives again.

Don't be put off by the old-fashioned language of this book; before you know it, you'll be deep inside that family, hardly noticing when Peter calls something excellent 'perfectly ripping'. Edith Nesbit was a crafty storyteller who can make you laugh and cry at the same time – and feel good afterwards.

Susan Cooper

➡ Definitely a Desert Island book. You probably know the story already from the film, but you simply must read the book. Then you'll really come to know the family – Roberta (Bobby) the eldest, and Peter and Phyllis. Their father mysteriously goes away and their mother takes them to Three Chimneys, a tumbledown house in the country.

Suddenly they are poor and have to learn a new, harder way of life. Mother becomes ill and Bobby is now the carer. They have to discover what poverty, heartbreak and injustice are, but also what kindness and friendship there is in the world. They fight and squabble like any other family, but are brave and honest and funny and never lose hope that one day, if they play their part, everything will come right again. And of course it does, in the most wonderful way possible. I know how this book ends, but every time I read it, I cry. And so will you.

Helen Cresswell

10-12

Next?

- You might want to try E. Nesbit's fantasies, ***Five Children and It*** (UBG 85) and ***The Phoenix and the Carpet***. Same vintage, same engaging kind of family, but with magic thrown in.
- Or try the autobiographical story ***A Vicarage Family***, by Noel Streatfeild. (UBG 254)
- Or what about another family coping while father's away? Try Louisa M. Alcott's ***Little Women***. (UBG 146)

RAMONA THE PEST **Beverly Cleary**

➨ Ramona Quimby is one of the most engaging characters in children's fiction. In this book, we follow her through her first days at school, from her joyful start, through her time as a kindergarten drop-out, to her triumphant return. We also get to know the other characters in Ramona's world: her mother and father, her sister Beezus, her friend Howie and her teacher Miss Binney.

Beverly Cleary is an acute observer of ordinary, everyday family and school life. She makes Ramona's world instantly recognisable to anyone under ten (or anyone who remembers being under ten). The **Ramona** books are funny, witty and touching by turns. I read them to my daughter, and we both delighted in them. It is impossible not to share the author's enormous affection for her heroine.

Celia Rees

8-10

Next?

- You will have to read the others, which include: ***Ramona Forever***; ***Ramona and her Mother***; ***Ramona and her Father***; ***Ramona Quimby, Aged 8***; and ***Ramona the Brave.***
- You might also like Judy Blume's ***Tales of A Fourth Grade Nothing*** (UBG 236), ***Superfudge*** and the rest of the Fudge series; Paula Danziger's **Amber Brown** stories; and **Ally's World** by Karen McCombie (UBG 12).

RASPBERRIES ON THE YANGTZE **Karen Wallace**

➨ *Raspberries on the Yangtze* is one of those books that suck you into the story right from the first sentence – 'It all began the day my brother and I decided to poison our mother.' In spite of this promising beginning, it isn't a crime novel. It's a sweet, funny, tender family story about Nancy, her brother Andrew and friends Amy and Clare. They live in the Canadian backwoods and during the summer holidays they're free to roam around all day, swinging on the wire fence, picking wild raspberries, searching for the perfect cave, visiting their kindly neighbour Mr Chevrolet, and peeking at precocious Tracy Wilkins with her boyfriend ...

Nancy is lively and funny and wildly imaginative. She's so real you feel she could be your sister or your best friend.

Jacqueline Wilson

10-12

Next?

- Read the sequel, ***Climbing a Monkey Puzzle Tree***, in which Nancy has to leave for boarding school in England.
- For another book set in the past about a brother and sister, try ***Carrie's War*** by Nina Bawden. (UBG 41)
- For something else about growing up in the country, try the **Punchbowl Farm** books by Monica Edwards (UBG 195), or for a country story with a darker twist, Dick King-Smith's ***Godhanger***.

THE RATASTROPHE CATASTROPHE

(Book 1 of The Illmoor Chronicles) David Lee Stone

➨ This book pits mercenaries Groan and Gordo (together with a rather decrepit sorcerer), against an evil pied piper, Diek Wustapha, who leads the children of Illmoor (the fantastical continent in which all of this occurs) down to a series of suitably dank and endless caves for his evil master's gain.

As you may well have guessed from the title, the book features another theme: rodents. In fact, the whole cause of the disappearing children scenario is due to our piper not being paid, owing to deficiencies in the treasuries. The furry beasts completely overcome Illmoor's capital city Dullitch and swiftly become a plague to its inhabitants.

The Ratastrophe Catastrophe combines vivid, comic, vibrant characters with a refreshing and original plot. Well, almost original ...

Tim Cross

10-12

Next?

- If you enjoyed this, try ***The Edge Chronicles*** by Paul Stewart and Chris Riddell. (UBG 70) And don't miss their ***Lord of the Rings*** spoof, ***Muddle Earth***. (UBG 168)
- The **Redwall** stories are all about talking animals. (UBG 199)
- Or try Terry Pratchett's very funny ***The Amazing Maurice and his Educated Rodents***. (UBG 12)

REDWALL series Brian Jacques

➡ Brian Jacques's famous **Redwall** series combines a vivid blend of characters with a fascinating plot to provide an enthralling read. Jacques has incorporated a whole range of songs and poems as well, creating original, lively and hugely enjoyable books.

The series follows the mammalian inhabitants of Redwall Abbey, where a community of animals are entirely self-sufficient and behave in many human ways – cooking, fishing etc. The book's bad guys are the 'vermin', consisting of foxes, stoats, weasels, polecats etc.

In *Redwall*, the first book in the series, a young mouse, Matthias, must take up a prophecy of the Abbey's famous warrior, and wield his sword in battle against evil. It's a great war/adventure story, but minus most of the gore!

Tim Cross

9-11

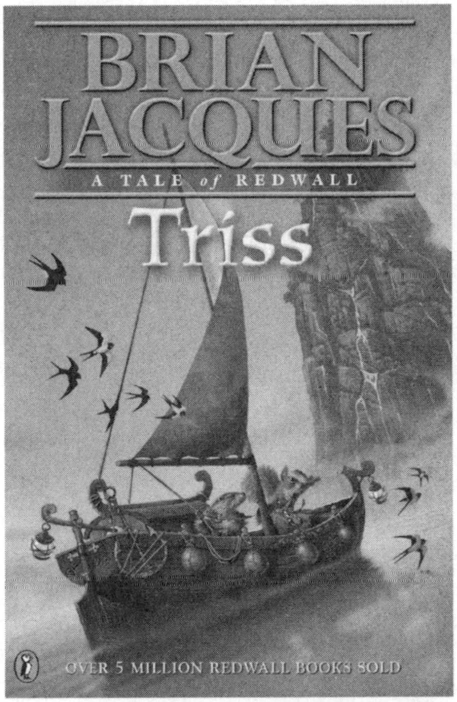

Next?

- Some of the many titles in the series are: ***Lord Brockwell***, ***Mossflower***, ***The Legend of Luke***, ***Mariel of Redwall***, ***Mattimeo***, ***The Taggerung***, ***The Long Patrol*** and ***Triss***.
- Another popular series about animals is Garry Kilworth's ***Welkin Weasels***.
- Robin Jarvis writes wonderfully intense, engrossing books, that are slightly tougher. **The Deptford Mice Trilogy** is in the same vein, with talking animals. (UBG 60) Jarvis has also written **The Whitby Witches**, another great series. (UBG 262) You might also enjoy his ***Tales from the Wyrd Museum***.
- For animals behaving more like animals, try Kenneth Oppel's wonderful bat saga that starts with ***Silverwing***. (UBG 219)
- Or how about the **Sharpe** books (beginning with ***Sharpe's Rifles***) by Bernard Cornwell? Not animal stories, but a first-class war adventure series!
- ***And don't miss our ANIMAL STORIES recommendations on pp. 16-17.***

COMPETITION WINNER ★ COMPETITION WINNER

REDWALL series Brian Jacques

➡ I had to choose the whole series because they are all so brilliant. I could not pick the best one.

Some people might laugh at stories about mice and woodland creatures but I think they are fascinating. From the first page, every story is gripping and exciting. I even read one book in the bath because I just could not stop for one moment.

All the **Redwall** stories have similar storylines and always end the same way: the mice and woodlanders kill the evil villain in a bloodthirsty battle which can be very scary. Sometimes it is so scary I cannot get to sleep and I have to keep reading on past my bedtime until the battle is over. I often feel sorry for the villains because although they are cruel, they are clever and brave and they are always dogged by bad luck.

Alexander Male, age 8, Arnold House School

REAL LIFE: FAMILY STORIES

Parents, siblings and other sorts of trouble

BY HILARY McKAY

Oh, am I a family story writer? I am so sorry to hear that. It sounds so dull. No fantasy. No dragons. No magic. No escape from this place that we call the real world.

Well, although it was never my intention to be such a thing, I suppose it is true. This essay should be entitled 'My Excuse For Inadvertently Writing Family Stories'.

We begin in families. It is the thing we all have in common. A mother, adequate or otherwise. A father, absent or present. Brothers and sisters, or a lack of them. Some place to sleep at some sort of base. A jumble of people wished upon us from birth.

In fairy stories you get gifts, good or bad. Hair as black as ebony, lips as red as blood. A fatal attraction for spinning wheels. The (dubiously useful) talents of being able to detect peas under mattresses and to kiss frogs into handsome princes. In families you get relations. Some of them are blessings, and more of them are curses. You (the hero or heroine of your own epic) must rub along with them as best you can, being (at the start of the story anyway) as helplessly bound to them as any princess to her fate.

That is how it has happened with me. I have given my blessings and curses human form, bound them as tightly as I could to my principal characters, and written down my observations of the results. And thus (I reluctantly admit) I have created a family story.

It is time I changed all this, but I know it will be hard. I could write about an orphan in an unknown land, but he would inevitably find a fatherly wizard. I could try a love story, but we all know what happens at the end of love stories.

★ Some suggestions...

There are many writers, like Hilary, who write books full of excitement, drama, magic, emotion and adventure, without ever leaving the real world. And they're all so different! Here are just a few of their books:

- ***Goggle-eyes*** by Anne Fine
- ***The Illustrated Mum*** by Jacqueline Wilson
- ***My Mum's Going to Explode!*** by Jeremy Strong
- ***The Mum Hunt*** by Gwyneth Rees
- Anything by Judy Blume
- ***What Katy Did*** by Susan M. Coolidge
- ***Little Women*** by Louisa May Alcott
- ***Gumble's Yard*** by John Rowe Townsend
- ***Swallows and Amazons*** by Arthur Ransome
- ***Feather Boy*** by Nicky Singer
- ***Stargirl*** by Jerry Spinelli
- ***Danny, the Champion of the World*** by Roald Dahl
- ***The Railway Children*** by E. Nesbit
- ***The Vicarage Family*** by Noel Streatfeild
- and of course Hilary's own ***Saffy's Angel***, its sequel ***Indigo's Star***; and **The Exiles** series

★ A DOZEN 'PROBLEM PARENT' BOOKS

People are always talking about 'problem children'. Well, how about a list of a dozen books about 'problem parents'?

- ***Hands Up!*** by Paul Magrs
- ***The Illustrated Mum*** by Jacqueline Wilson
- ***Rescuing Dad*** by Pete Johnson
- ***Madame Doubtfire*** by Anne Fine
- ***Jake's Tower*** by Elizabeth Laird
- ***Goodnight Mr Tom*** by Michelle Magorian
- ***The Mum Hunt*** by Gwyneth Rees
- ***Jessica Haggerthwaite: Witch Dispatcher*** by Emma Barnes
- ***Double Act*** by Jacqueline Wilson
- ***Goggle-eyes*** by Anne Fine
- ***Gumble's Yard*** by John Rowe Townsend
- ***Holly Starcross*** by Berlie Doherty

I could send my heroes and heroines off into the wild, on ships or horses or interstellar spacecraft. They could be shipwrecked on islands, or fight dragons or discover new civilisations. But I know what would come next. They would set up little camps on those islands. They would grow tired of the needless and painful slaughter of endangered species and long for a bed for the night, and someone to admire their wounds. They would look at the civilisations on those distant planets and they would think, how like (or unlike) Planet Earth.

So we return. To our blessings and curses. To the ones we love most, and the ones we would obliterate first. To our families. That is the truth of it. We live in our little worlds, spinning our little lives. Hair into rope, straw into gold, dreams into stories.

Personally, I plan to write no more family stories. The next one will be pure fantasy. Battle scenes. Shining friendships. Lonely quests in strange lands. And I will cunningly conceal from my heroes and heroines why they are fighting and what they are searching for. And I will make sure they do not get too close to those shining friends, and I will never, ever, ever, let them come home …

★ TEN BOOKS ABOUT DEALING WITH ILLNESS

- ***Pig-heart Boy*** by Malorie Blackman
- ***Becky Bananas*** by Jean Ure
- ***Up on Cloud Nine*** by Anne Fine
- ***Skellig*** by David Almond
- ***Two Weeks with the Queen*** by Morris Gleitzman
- ***Pollyanna*** by Eleanor H. Porter
- ***The Secret Garden*** by Frances Hodgson Burnett
- ***The Fire-Eaters*** by David Almond
- ***What Katy Did*** by Susan Coolidge
- ***Heidi*** by Johanna Spyri

★ AND WE MUSTN'T FORGET SIBLINGS …

- ***The Exiles*** by Hilary McKay
- ***Saffy's Angel*** and ***Indigo's Star*** by Hilary McKay
- ***Little Women*** by Louisa May Alcott
- ***The Cuckoo Sister*** by Vivien Alcock
- ***Double Act*** by Jacqueline Wilson
- ***Storm Catchers*** by Tim Bowler
- ***Ballet Shoes*** by Noel Streatfeild
- ***Tales of a Fourth Grade Nothing*** by Judy Blume
- The **Ramona** series Beverly Cleary
- ***My Naughty Little Sister*** by Dorothy Edwards
- ***The Family from One End Street*** by Eve Garnett
- ***Horrid Henry*** by Francesca Simon

THE RELIC MASTER

(Volume 1 of The Book of the Crow)

Catherine Fisher

➡ Raffi, apprentice to the bitter and unpredictable Relic Master Galen, lives from moment to moment. Outlawed, living on charity and hope, Raffi and Galen wander a hostile and dangerous land, using their magic and their wits to survive. Forced into searching for a Sekoi – one of a race of cat-like people – they begin a journey that takes them deep into the most terrible danger, but also towards an understanding of what their magic is, why their world is as it is and what the strange relics they hoard really are.

There are four main travellers in these books, and I fell in love with all of them. Following every painful step of their journey, I chewed my nails and urged them on through every page, desperate for them to find some answers – and some happiness.

9-12

Leonie Flynn

Next?

- The other books in this series are ***The Interrex***, ***Flain's Coronet*** and ***The Margrave***.
- If you like the magic here, read **The Dark Is Rising** sequence by Susan Cooper. (UBG 57)
- Or the **Earthsea** books by Ursula Le Guin. (UBG 69)
- If you liked the quest, try J.R.R. Tolkien's ***The Hobbit*** (UBG 112) and ***The Lord of the Rings*** (UBG 148).

THE RESCUERS

Margery Sharp

Next?
- Look out for the sequel – ***Miss Bianca.***
- Try ***Mrs Frisby and the Rats of NIMH*** by Robert C. O'Brien about a mouse, her family and some very interesting rats. (UBG 167)
- Feeling a bit moused-out? Try some more human adventure with ***The Big Bazoohley*** by Peter Carey (UBG 27) or maybe ***The Demon Headmaster*** by Gillian Cross (UBG 59).

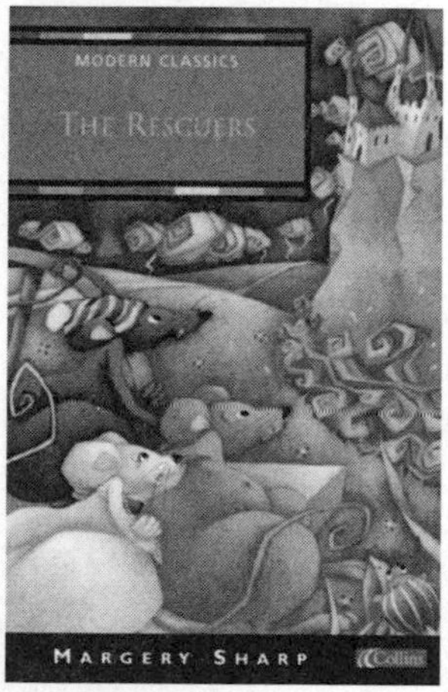

➡ Bernard, Nils and Miss Bianca have been given the terrifying task of rescuing a Norwegian poet imprisoned in the grim, windowless Black Castle. The Castle is heavily guarded, and there's no way in or out.

Will our heroes be strong enough to overpower the castle jailers? Well, no, actually. The thing is, you see, shy, well-meaning Bernard, unflappable Nils and beautiful (but vain) Miss Bianca are, well, mice. (Though they're so human you'll forget this detail for most of the book.) Their only hope is to outwit the jailers instead. But there's another problem, much scarier than the jailers: the biggest test for our friends will be keeping out of the clutches of Mamelouk, the jailers' evil cat, who is 'twice natural size, and four times as fierce!'

I saw the Disney version of this long before reading the book, and really enjoyed it. The book and the film are very different, though; and though I do like the film, I think the book is more exciting, more dangerous, and funnier. The story is quite different too. I think I prefer the book, but I'm not sure – what about you?

8-11

Daniel Hahn

Here are some other rodent books the Editors like:
- **The Deptford Mice trilogy** by Robin Jarvis
- ***Abel's Island*** by William Steig
- ***The Battle of Bubble and Squeak*** by Philippa Pearce
- ***Frank and the Black Hamster of Narkiz*** by Livi Michael
- ***The Ratastrophe Catastrophe*** by David Lee Stone
- ***The Amazing Maurice and his Educated Rodents*** by Terry Pratchett
- ***The Mouse and His Child*** by Russell Hoban
- ***Mouse Attack*** by Manjula Padma
- ***Time Stops for No Mouse*** by Michael Hoeye
- ***The Song of Pentecost*** by W.J. Corbett

RESCUING DAD Pete Johnson

➡ When Mum and Dad start acting suspiciously nice all of a sudden, Joe knows what's up. Huge smiles, roast chicken and massive slices of chocolate cake can mean only one thing. It's worse than being packed off to boarding school or borstal or the local zoo ... Mum is chucking Dad out!

Joe and his sister Claire want life to return to how it used to be when Mum would explode with laughter at Dad's jokes. They have to work fast as Dad's appearance is deteriorating and he needs urgent training for his bad habits, which are too many to be listed. To make matters worse, the slimy Roger Salmon is sniffing around Mum.

Joe and Claire have a matter of weeks to retrain Dad (without him knowing!). All runs relatively smoothly – there's no hitch too big for this determined pair. How will Mum be able to resist 'Dad Mark Two'?

This book tackles a sensitive topic in a humorous and down-to-earth way. You'll love the jokes and Pete Johnson's realistic and funny observations of life through Joe's eyes.

8-11

Elena Gregoriou

Next?
- If you enjoyed Pete Johnson's style of writing, why don't you try some of his other books, which you may find rather spooky? Read ***My Friend's a Werewolf*** (UBG 170), ***How to Train Your Parents*** (UBG 118) or ***The Phantom Thief.***
- Karen McCombie's funny and moving series **Ally's World** is a series about a girl living with her dad. (UBG 12)

THE REVENGE OF SAMUEL STOKES Penelope Lively

➨ When Tim and family move on to a new estate to be near Grandad it is soon clear that something is not right. The washing machine smells of roast venison, tobacco smoke comes out of the television, cabbage seeds grow into hedges, glass houses turn into Greek temples and then a lake suddenly appears out of nowhere. No one has a clue what it means or what to do.

With Grandad's help, Tim and Jane manage to solve the mystery that puzzles the town council and press.

A charming book about how the past can invade the present, the nature of change and progress and how useful a lot of knowledge and 'not thinking in straight lines' can be.

9-11

Ann Jungman

Next?

• You might enjoy Penelope Lively's ***The Ghost of Thomas Kempe***, in which the past finds its way into the present in a different but equally enjoyable way. (UBG 91)

• How past and present come together in a garden is beautifully realised in Philippa Pearce's classic novel ***Tom's Midnight Garden***. (UBG 245)

• ***Playing Beatie Bow*** by Ruth Park tells of a girl who finds herself moving back a century. She has to find what it is she has to bring back to the present. (UBG 190)

RIGHT HO, JEEVES!

P.G. Wodehouse

➨ Bertie Wooster is an upper-class young gentleman with a manservant called Jeeves. Bertie, who is not very bright, gets into all sorts of trouble with all sorts of people. He relies on Jeeves, a solemn man of high intellect, to rescue him. The adventures the pair of them have are hilarious.

Now, humour is a personal thing and what makes me laugh might not make you laugh, but I've never met anyone who didn't find this book funny. It's set in an old-fashioned and out-of-date Britain, but the writing is so smooth and easy, reading it is like getting in a warm bath and just soaking in laughter. Tempting?

10+

Garry Kilworth

Next?

• The twenty or so other Bertie Wooster books get better and better!

• Same world as Jeeves? Try the great detective stories written by Dorothy L. Sayers. The first is ***Clouds of Witness***.

• Otherwise, there's ***The Admirable Crichton*** by J.M. Barrie, about a helpless upper class family shipwrecked with their very capable butler.

• Jan Mark is another writer with a very unique sense of humour. Her brilliant book ***They Do Things Differently There*** is set in an 'alternate' modern Britain. (UBG 238)

THE RINALDI RING Jenny Nimmo

➨ Eliot is being haunted. Since the death of his mother in America, he has come to stay with his cousins in an English country town. What links his frightening experiences with the mad girl once imprisoned in his room?

To discover the truth about the long-ago tragedy of the Rinaldi ring, Eliot must confront the sinister Freya Greymark. It is only then that his own troubles can come right. But Freya Greymark has guarded her dreadful secret for a long time.

This is a compelling ghost story about loss and redemption, in which events that happened in the First World War cast their shadow over the present day. Eerie and atmospheric, it has plenty of shivery moments …

Patricia Elliott

9-12

Next?

• Read Caroline Pitcher's powerful and moving novel, ***Mine***, in which Shelley finds that she is being haunted by the voices of two girls from the past.

• Gill Vickery's ***The Ivy Crown*** is a richly atmospheric novel, set in a strange old house in remote woodland. (UBG 125)

• In Magdalen Nabb's ***The Twilight Ghost***, Carrie's attempts to find out the identity of the ghost at the window draw her into time-travel.

• K.M. Peyton's ***A Pattern of Roses*** is a slightly harder mystery blending past and present. (UBG 183)

THE ULTIMATE READERS' POLL

YOUR TOP TEN BOOK VILLAINS

1. Voldemort (from Harry Potter)
2. Count Olaf (from A Series of Unfortunate Events)
3. Cruella de Vil (from The Hundred and One Dalmatians)
4. Saruman (from The Lord of the Rings)
5. Draco Malfoy (from Harry Potter)
6. Captain Hook (from Peter Pan)
7. The White Witch (from the Chronicles of Narnia)
8. Miss Trunchbull (from Matilda)
9. The Grand High Witch (from The Witches)
10. The Demon Headmaster

RIVER BOY Tim Bowler

➡ Jess has a special bond with her grandfather. He is an artist and she is his inspiration, his muse. Jess has her own talent, swimming, and her ambition is to finish a long-distance swim that will really challenge her.

When her grandfather suffers a heart attack and insists on a final holiday in his boyhood home, Jess finally gets her wish. With her grandfather growing weaker every day and struggling to complete his picture of the 'River Boy', she finds herself becoming fascinated by the stranger she keeps glimpsing swimming in the river near their holiday cottage.

This amazing book is about obsession and love and death. The ending is both heartbreakingly sad and yet 'right' at the same time – months after reading it, I'd find myself thinking about Jess and her swim, and what it all meant.

10-12

Laura Hutchings

Next?

- ***Storm Catchers*** (UBG 228), ***Dragon's Rock*** and ***Midget*** are all Tim Bowler books you might like to read.
- ***Kit's Wilderness*** by David Almond is dark, scary and amazing. (UBG 135)
- Gillian Cross writes gripping stories often featuring life-changing encounters with mysterious people. Try ***Wolf*** (UBG 270) or, for older readers, ***Calling a Dead Man*** (UBG 38).

ROLL OF THUNDER, HEAR MY CRY Mildred D. Taylor

➡ Nine-year-old Cassie Logan is one of the most feisty characters I know in fiction. The kind of person who makes you think, 'Amazing! She doesn't take any nonsense!'

There's a lot of nonsense in Mississippi, America, in the 1930s. The Logans are the only black family who own land in the district. However much Mama, Papa and Big Ma try to protect Cassie and her three brothers from the hateful racism they experience, nothing can stop the children's instinct to fight injustice. And that means trouble.

Mildred D. Taylor is a wonderful storyteller, though she also thanks her father for the gripping family stories he passed down to her. They show the underside of the 'Land of the Free' and show how the human spirit can survive (has to survive!) with strong values in a world where powerful people tell so many lies.

11+

Beverley Naidoo

Next?

- If you enjoyed this, you will be desperate to read the sequel, ***Let the Circle Be Unbroken***.
- To discover the extraordinary story of how Cassie's grandfather got his own land fifty years earlier, read ***The Land***.
- Look out for ***White Socks Only***, by Evelyn Coleman. Yes, this is a picture book, but don't be put off, it encapsulates everything that's wrong about racism.
- ***And see our stories from OTHER CULTURES selections on pp. 180-181.***

If you're looking for The Roman Mysteries by Caroline Lawrence, turn to p. 239

RUBY HOLLER Sharon Creech

➨ Florida and Dallas have just about given up hope. Every time they are adopted their new parents end up deciding they're just too much trouble, and they find themselves thrown back to the Boxton Creek Home for Children, and the custody of not-very-nice Mr and Mrs Trepid. Florida and Dallas don't mean to be 'trouble twins'; they just see the world differently from everyone else!

So when elderly couple Tiller and Sairy ask to have the twins spend the summer with them in their house in Ruby Holler, Florida and Dallas can't help assuming it'll be just another disaster. But they love the magical Holler, and soon discover that Tiller and Sairy are different too, in their way. Before long all four have become fonder of each other than they'd expected to. And as you read this charming, warm-hearted book, you'll grow fond of them all too.

Daniel Hahn

8-11

Next?

- For another hard-hitting story of a girl in a children's home, try ***Locomotion*** by Jacqueline Woodson (UBG 146) or ***The Story of Tracy Beaker*** by Jacqueline Wilson (UBG 229).
- For something quite different by the wonderful Sharon Creech, try ***The Wanderer*** (UBG 257) or ***Walk Two Moons*** (UBG 256). My favourite (and an easier read is) ***Love That Dog***. (UBG 150)
- Lemony Snicket's **A Series of Unfortunate Events** is a very different! story of orphaned siblings! (UBG 217)

THE RUBY IN THE SMOKE Philip Pullman

➨ Sally Lockhart is sixteen, living on a grudging relative's charity at a time when middle-class young women were thought incapable of most things and in need of protection. But Sally, being a financial wizard and a sharp-shooter, is spared a future as a governess or lady's companion. Instead, she makes loyal friends including office-boy Jim and pioneer photographer Fred, joins Fred's ramshackle household and solves the mystery of who killed her father in the South China Sea. The Victorians we meet here are all on the fringes of society because of poverty, criminal tendencies or an interest in stepping outside conventions, and they make intriguing characters.

The later Sally Lockhart books, *The Shadow in the North* and *The Tiger in the Well*, will appeal more to older teenage readers, but this one can be read alone, and it will keep you on the edge of your seat.

11+

Geraldine Brennan

Next?

- Philip Pullman is also author of the acclaimed **His Dark Materials** trilogy. (UBG 176)
- Another great Victorian detective is Sherlock Holmes. Try Arthur Conan Doyle's ***The Hound of the Baskervilles***. (UBG 117)
- Julie Hearn's ***Follow Me Down*** is another gripping tale showing London's seedier side. (UBG 87)
- ***Don't miss our DETECTIVE AND SPY feature on pp. 62-63***

RULES OF THE ROAD Joan Bauer

➨ In the United States you can get a driving licence at sixteen. Jenna Boller is still at school but works part-time in a shoe store. One day, the elderly owner, Mrs Gladstone, hires Jenna to drive her from Chicago to company headquarters in Dallas, visiting Gladstone's shops on the way.

As they travel, Mrs Gladstone reveals that her weasel of a son is planning to sell the neighbourhood stores to a giant retail chain. Jenna has plenty of troubles of her own, but she is never afraid to fight for what she believes is right and she soon finds that all the best people are on her side.

If you are tired of drippy girls who whinge and witter about clothes and diets and boys, you will love big, strong, funny Jenna. She could sell shoes to a mermaid – but she wouldn't. That would be cheating, and Jenna never cheats.

10-12

Jan Mark

Next?

- Joan Bauer's ***Squashed*** is very different but still really great. (UBG 224)
- If you would like to meet other strong, intelligent young women, why not try ***Breakers*** by Julia Clarke, whose heroine has to look after her sister and their actress mother, who still behaves like a teenager.
- Ordinary people take on the big guys in ***Stop the Train*** by Geraldine McCaughrean. (UBG 227)

Next?
Since reading the literature of a period is one of the best ways of entering another age, I recommend you try:
- Three books by E. Nesbit: ***The Railway Children*** (UBG 197), ***Five Children and It*** (UBG 85) and ***The Phoenix and the Carpet***.
- Brian Fairfax-Lucy's ***The Children of the House***, retold by Philippa Pearce: a really good read about the adventures of four children who lived in a great house at the end of the nineteenth century.
- Or for another book about a lonely girl, try ***The Little White Horse*** by Elizabeth Goudge. (UBG 145)
- And, of course, don't forget ***Alice's Adventures in Wonderland*** by Lewis Carroll. (UBG 11)

THE RUNAWAY

Elizabeth Anna Hart

➨ This is a delightfully funny story about a lonely girl called Clarice who discovers a girl called Olga – the runaway – and agrees to hide her in her bedroom. The plot is closely woven and reflects the age in which it was written – 1872 – and since the author was a cousin of Lewis Carroll it is not surprising that there are echoes of *Alice in Wonderland* in the writing.

Gwen Raverat says in her preface that this is the sort of book which will always be liked because it is such fun and she feels that no heroine, however modern, ever climbed trees or walls as well as Olga did. I have only just discovered the book but I was quite captivated by it.

10-12

Anthony Buckeridge

THE RUNAWAYS

Ruth Thomas

➨ What would you do if you found a stash of money, had no friends at school and were in trouble with your head teacher? Brought together by accident, Nathan and Julia decide the only thing to do is to run. But running away is hard. Where do you go? How do you get there, then fool grown-ups into not noticing you're on your own? How do you become invisible?

An unlikely friendship develops between Nathan and Julia as their roller-coaster journey takes them from Brighton to a dream-like campsite on Exmoor. One minute happy and free, the next scared and running, they can never quite forget their homes and families. A novel that keeps you guessing to the very last page!

10-12

Helen Simmons

Next?
- You could try ***Treasure Island*** by R.L. Stevenson. It's Nathan's favourite book and one of the best books ever about runaways of all ages. (UBG 247)
- ***We Didn't Mean to go to Sea*** by Arthur Ransome is one of my top books about runaways, even though, in this case, they didn't mean to! Very tense and full of excitement. Read about all of Ransome's ***Swallows and Amazons*** books on p. 232.
- ***The Thief Lord*** by Cornelia Funke is another excellent book about a gang of 'runaways' in Venice; it's a thriller and a great story about the way an unlikely group of children become friends. (UBG 238)

SABRIEL Garth Nix

➡ Sabriel is a young woman who lives in Ancelstierre, close to the Old Kingdom. In this mythical world, Charter magic keeps the inhabitants safe, but Free Magic is an ever-present threat. Sabriel discovers that her father, Abhorsen, is in peril in the Old Kingdom, and she must leave the safety of her boarding school to find him and discover the nature of the danger he is in. Be warned: this unusual and gripping fantasy is quite gruesome in places, and terrifying too, as the Dead leave their Kingdom to prey on the living. All is so vividly imagined you'll think you're in the midst of battles and fleeing for your life. *Sabriel* is a must, and not just for fans of fantasy.

11+

Sherry Ashworth

Next?
- There are two sequels to ***Sabriel***, which will be essential reading: ***Lirael*** and ***Abhorsen***.
- You might also love J.R.R. Tolkien's ***The Lord of the Rings*** (UBG 148) and Philip Pullman's **His Dark Materials** trilogy (UBG 176). Both are classic fantasy stories, but in very different ways.
- You should also sample ***A Wizard of Earthsea*** by Ursula Le Guin. (UBG 69)

SAFFY'S ANGEL Hilary McKay

➡ This is a far more recent book than my other choices and it was recommended by my ten-year-old daughter – we both loved it. Saffy believes herself to be the second of the four Casson children. The other three are all named after colours on their painter parents' colour charts, and when Saffron realizes she is not a colour on the chart, she learns that she is not actually their child, but their adopted niece. When her beloved grandfather dies he leaves Saffy a lost angel in his will.With her friend Sarah, Saffy goes in search of her angel in a journey that takes her from a garden in Italy to a hillside in Wales. And in the course of her search she also comes to understand her place in the chaotic but loving family that has adopted her.

This is a lovely book, funny and moving – a very satisfying read!

9+

Jane Ray

Next?
- There's a sequel, ***Indigo's Star***, which is just as wonderful!
- If you enjoyed Saffy you might also enjoy ***When Marnie was There*** by Joan G. Robinson. This has a similar theme of a lonely child (I've just realised that nearly all my choices are about lonely children – what a sad little soul I must be!) (UBG 262)
- Or try Hilary McKay's **The Exiles** – a series of books which capture exactly what it is like to be part of a big family. (UBG 75)

THE SAGA OF ERIK THE VIKING Terry Jones

➡ Erik and his band of loyal followers set sail on an almost impossible quest – to find the land where the sun goes at night. He takes his sword, Blueblade, and his ship, Golden Dragon, and says farewell to his wife and son. What follows is a series of exciting, fantastic and vivid adventures, each one more dramatic than the next. Travel with Erik and you will meet Enchanters, Dogfighters, the Old Man of the Sea and even see the Edge of the World. But will you find the land where the sun goes at night? And will the crew survive? Anyone who enjoys adventure, fantasy and suspense in equal mixture will love this book and read it again and again.

8-10

Sherry Ashworth

Next?
- You could try more books by Terry Jones, including the funny ***The Knight and the Squire*** (UBG 137), and ***Fairy Tales***. You might also enjoy ***The Yellow Fairy Book***, a collection of traditional tales by Andrew Lang.
- Or for a very funny pet book, try ***How to Train Your Dragon*** by Cressida Cowell, in which a young Viking learns everything he can about the care of dragons.
- There are the Norse Myths, if you want to read about the gods the Vikings worshipped. A very modern version is ***Top Ten Viking Legends*** by Michael Cox. Turn to p. 175 for Melvin Burgess's recommendations of some Norse myths.

Next?
- You might be interested in Chris Wooding's ***The Haunting of Alaizabel Cray*** – a longer, more sophisticated horror novel that begins in the deserted back alleys of London. (UBG 108)
- ***Piggies*** by Nick Gifford takes a different look at vampires – and their prey. (UBG 188)
- Interested to see which books Darren Shan chose as his favourites? Look for his entries on Roald Dahl's ***The Witches*** (UBG 268) and ***The Secret Garden*** by Frances Hodgson Burnett (UBG 215).

THE SAGA OF DARREN SHAN

CIRQUE DU FREAK • THE VAMPIRE'S ASSISTANT • TUNNELS OF BLOOD, etc.

Darren Shan

➨ Darren Shan is not only the author of this horror series, but also the main character. A regular kid, Darren likes football, hanging out with his mates, and spiders. Unfortunately, this latter hobby will land him in enough trouble to last a whole saga. Together with his best friend Steve, Darren sneaks out of his house to visit the mysterious and forbidden Cirque du Freak. Among the many creepy acts in the show is the amazing spider, Madam Octa. Darren cannot resist the temptation – he must have the poisonous creature all to himself, even if that means stealing the spider from her owner, who is (how shall I put it?) a member of the living dead. This foolish deed ends in a nightmare and Darren must pay the price with his own blood ... and this is just the first volume!

You certainly need guts to read these books, because many of the characters end up with theirs hanging out of their bodies, half-chewed, if you catch my drift ...

9-11

Noga Applebaum

COMPETITION WINNER ★ COMPETITION WINNER

THE SAGA OF DARREN SHAN: Killers of the Dawn

➨ I loved Darren Shan's *Killers of the Dawn* because it has lots of action and fighting. There is a lot of suspense which keeps you going through the story. The description is brilliant. Darren Shan describes every character down to the last hair on their head. There is a good bit of humour to keep you at it.

The thing I loved most about it is the great fighting scenes and the suspense. I chose this book to write about because apart from the rest of the series there is no other book as good as it that I have read. There are so many characters such as Vancha, Harkat Mulds, Mr Crepsley and Darren Shan. They are all really well imagined.

I more than recommend this book. I insist you go to the shops and hassle the owner to give you a copy right away.

Review and illustration by James Peter Thorp, age 11, Heathfield Junior School

ST CLARE'S series Enid Blyton

➡ Twins Pat and Isabel O'Sullivan were the most popular girls at their old school and are determined not to like St Clare's one little bit. They'll stop at nothing to be noticed and are always in trouble. But they soon come to love the new school, and the St Clare's stories follow their mad adventures year by year.

You'll make friends with the unpopular telltale Margery, suspected of starting a terrible fire; too-good-to-be-true teacher's pet, Prudence, who causes trouble by revealing the secret past of new girl Carlotta; wayward Claudine who thinks rules are just there to be broken; and sad Scottish Morag, who's only happy when she can escape to the nearby riding stables. Then there are the hilarious school plays where everything that can go wrong does, the head girl elections, mad jokes and mayhem – even when the twins are in the sixth form and don't ever want to grow up. Although these stories are a bit old-fashioned now, they're still fun to read and give the reader a fascinating look at what boarding school life can be like!

7-10

Eileen Armstrong

Next?

- When you've read all the **St Clare's** books, why not try **Malory Towers**, also by Enid Blyton, set in a castle-like school with a real rebel of a main character? (UBG 153)
- Try **The Chalet School** stories by Elinor M. Brent-Dyer set in Switzerland in the 1950s (UBG 43), or the more up-to-date **Trebizon** stories by Anne Digby.
- For boarding school stories with a touch of magic, look for J.K. Rowling's **Harry Potter**. (UBG 106)
- Sinister school goings-on are on the timetable with Gillian Cross's ***The Demon Headmaster*** (UBG 59), while the characters at **Grange Hill** by Robert Leeson seem so real they could almost go to your school!

THE SALT PIRATES OF SKEGNESS

Chris d'Lacey

➡ When is a dog not a dog? When it's a pirate!

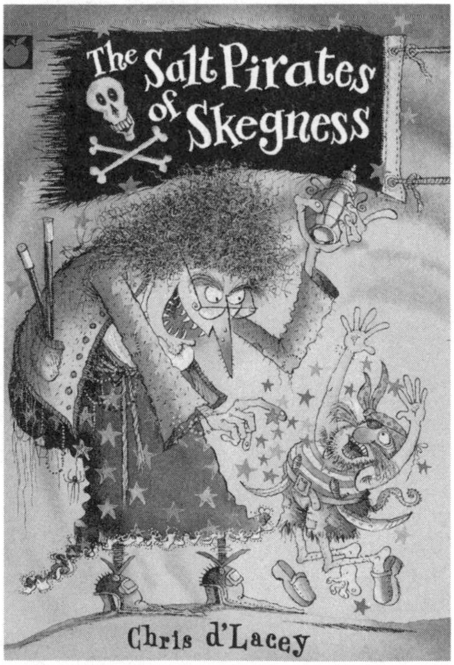

Well, it may *look* like a scrawny, wire-haired terrier that's about ten baths away from fragrant, but it is really Scuttle the pirate, who was trapped in a bottle that Jason accidentally opened. Like a genie, but smellier and saltier and with a distinctly nautical turn of phrase and …

… a deep need to go to Skegness. Which, luckily, is exactly where Jason is heading for his holidays, to stay with his Aunt Hester. Now, Aunt Hester is tetchy, difficult, grouchy (you get the picture) – but can she be the evil Skegglewitch? To find out, read this book – which will have you laughing and groaning (the puns are awful!) from the first page.

8-11

Leonie Flynn

Next?

- For another Chris d'Lacey book, though this time slightly (very slightly) more serious, try ***The Fire Within***. (UBG 84)
- For more terrible (but equally funny) puns and jokes, try ***The Killer Underpants*** by Michael Lawrence. (UBG 127)
- Susan Gates is a writer who makes readers laugh. Why not try her ***A Brief History of Slime*** or ***Killer Mushrooms Ate My Gran***? (UBG 133)
- For more Pirates, try ***Pirate Diary*** by Richard Platt and Chris Riddell.
- Or have a read of the **Sam Hawkins, Pirate Detective** series by Ian Billings.

SAM PIG Alison Uttley

➨ My favourite pig. I don't remember when I first came across Sam, but he is as much a part of my childhood as any visit to an aunt in the country or journey into a ditch on the crossbar of my father's bike. Like all the best stories, the sense of place and character in these tales draws the reader in and carries him or her along. Sam's adventures are usually quite slight – writing a letter, going to a country fête, taking a stroll in the moonlight – but always there are incidents and encounters along the way, and the warmth of the language makes the stories a joy to read aloud. A.E. Kennedy's exquisite illustrations (in early versions) perfectly complement the magical text.

7-9

Michael Lawrence

Next?

- If you like Sam Pig you have another treat in store in Barbara Euphan Todd's **Worzel Gummidge** series, which is also humorous, inventive and completely original. (UBG 273)
- Another great story about a pig is ***Charlotte's Web*** by E.B. White. (UBG 45) Or for a different animal, try White's ***Stuart Little***, about a mouse.

SARAH, PLAIN AND TALL

Patricia MacLachlan

➨ When Sarah comes as a mail-order bride all the way from Maine to the prairie to marry Anna's father, the motherless Anna isn't at all sure it's a good idea. But her little brother, Caleb, whose birth caused their mother's death, has no one to compare Sarah with. Slowly, both children – and their father – come to appreciate Sarah's gentle strength, her good humour, her wisdom. They become a family in the deepest sense of the word.

This gentle, persuasive story is filled with humour, adventure, and an understanding of the practical considerations that made up life on the American prairies in the nineteenth century.

8-10

Jane Yolen

Next?

- There are two sequels. The first is ***Skylark***, in which Anna and Caleb and their parents live through a terrible drought on the prairie which forces many of their friends to desert their homes. The next is ***Caleb***, the first to be told from a boy's point of view.
- For stories about growing up at a similar time in America, try Laura Ingalls Wilder's autobiographical **Little House** series. (UBG 142)
- For a look at country life in Britain, try Berlie Doherty's memorable books, such as ***Deep Secret***, ***Jeannie of White Peak Farm*** and her younger book, ***Willa and Old Miss Annie***. (UBG 264)

THE SATURDAYS Elizabeth Enright

➨ It's Saturday afternoon. It's raining, and the four Melendy children are stuck indoors. None of them has enough pocket-money to do anything exciting. The radio's broken, and Mona, Randy and Oliver don't feel like reading or listening to their brother Rush on the piano playing Bach – again. Yawn ...

Until Randy has an idea: why don't they pool their pocket-money, and take it in turns to spend all of it, one Saturday a month each, doing something really special? Think of all the possibilities! And so begin the adventures of the Saturdays.

Even if you don't have loads of brothers and sisters of your own, Elizabeth Enright makes you feel like you're really part of this family, and that you know them all just as well as any real people. And when it's over you'll be ever so sorry to have to say goodbye to them; but never fear, you won't have to just yet – there are three great sequels!

8-11

Daniel Hahn

Next?

- Well, you won't want to do anything till you've read the sequels, so first things first: they're ***The Four-Storey Mistake***, ***Then There Were Five*** and ***Spiderweb for Two***.
- For another great book about siblings, schemes and friendships, try Hilary McKay's fast and very real ***Dog Friday***.
- ***Ballet Shoes*** by Noel Streatfeild is about three sisters. (UBG 23)
- Or the fun and easy ***Tales of a Fourth Grade Nothing*** by Judy Blume. (UBG 236)

THE SCARLET PIMPERNEL

Baroness Orczy

➡ Don't worry if you don't know anything about history – this is a fantastic spy story set at the time of the French Revolution, and everything you need to know is explained as part of the action. A mysterious man, code-named the Scarlet Pimpernel, makes it his task to rescue as many French aristocrats as possible from the deadly peril of the Guillotine. Nobody knows the identity of this audacious and cunning Englishman, but this won't deter the evil Chauvelin who will stop at nothing to hunt him down. Has the Scarlet Pimpernel met his match?

Filled with seemingly impossible escapes, brilliant disguises and twists in the story that keep you guessing right to the end, this book is great fun. And the grand finale leaves you breathless!

11+

Abigail Anderson

Next?
If you liked the historical and romantic aspect, try books by Georgette Heyer who wrote about Georgian and Regency England. Start with ***Powder and Patch*** which has always been my favourite.
• If you liked adventurous twists and turns, try R.L. Stevenson's ***Treasure Island*** (UBG 247) or ***The Master of Ballantrae***, or Alexandre Dumas' classic ***The Count of Monte Cristo***, ***The Three Musketeers*** (UBG 241) and ***The Man in the Iron Mask*** (UBG 153).

SCRIBBLEBOY Philip Ridley

➡ Philip Ridley's stories are the most wild and wacky you'll ever see – and see them you must because the wonderfully detailed illustrations with the words themselves whirling and whizzing and zipping across the pages are crucial to the way these exciting, sad-but-happy stories work their magic.

Scribbleboy, a magical character we may never actually meet, brightens up his boring grey, concrete neighbourhood with scribblefabulous scribbles, then mysteriously disappears, leaving Ziggy Fuzz to keep up his good work by starting the Scribbleboy Fan Club – and recruiting new boy Bailey Silk as a member. The racy, pacy adventures of these larger-than-life characters, with memorable names like Hip-Hop and Pa Punkrock, who somehow manage to make the best of everything, will open your eyes to the magic in the world around you too. Watch out for the breathtakingly inventive twist at the end!

9-11

Eileen Armstrong

Next?
• If you enjoy meeting mad characters, why not try some of Philip's other books? There's Lassiter Peach who lives behind the barbed wire fortress with its mutant killer eels in ***Dakota of the White Flats***, for starters! (UBG 56)
• Paul Jennings is another first-class author of imaginative and surprising tales. The books are addictive – so it's just as well there are lots of them – nearly all with titles beginning with 'Un-'. Start with ***Uncanny!*** (UBG 251)

THE SEA WOLF Jack London

➡ Humphrey Van Weyden is a rich American who falls overboard from a ferry in San Francisco Bay. He is rescued in thick fog by Wolf Larsen, the captain of a seal-hunting ship. Instead of putting Humphrey ashore, Larsen forces him to become a cabin boy on a sailing ship where life is very tough, even for experienced sailors.

This is a great sea story, set in the early 1900s, which will have you gripped in a reading-vice. You will feel the same anger, frustration and helplessness as Humphrey, as he battles psychologically with Wolf Larsen, a bully with great physical strength and a cruel mind. Books this tense often seem to stop my heart in mid-beat.

11+

Garry Kilworth

Next?
• Try one of Jack London's animal adventure stories, such as ***White Fang*** (UBG 263) or ***The Call of the Wild*** (UBG 38).
• Anther terrific sea story is ***Moby Dick*** by Herman Melville (difficult, but there are abridged versions).
• Or try the **Hornblower** series by C.S. Forester – all set on ships, but in an atmosphere as different as you can imagine. (UBG 115)

SCHOOL STORIES

Top of the class!

BY ANDREW NORRISS

School is something we all had to go through, and it's always good to read how other people did it, or how it might have been if your parents had sent you somewhere else! Personally I always enjoyed reading 'school stories' much more than I enjoyed actually being at school. The children in them seemed to have such a good time. They outwitted sneaky masters, found hidden treasure (there was a lot of it about) and always scored the winning runs in vital cricket matches. But the thing I liked best was the friendship. However bad things were on the outside, the hero had his friends (usually two of them) and together they would battle through. That's the real point of school stories. They're about winning through with your mates.

★ TWELVE BOARDING SCHOOL BOOKS

- The **Jennings** series by Anthony Buckeridge
- ***Boy*** by Roald Dahl
- ***Point Blanc*** (in the **Alex Rider** series) by Anthony Horowitz
- The **Malory Towers** series by Enid Blyton
- The **St Clare's** series by Enid Blyton
- The **Chalet School** series by Elinor Brent-Dyer
- ***The Youngest Girl in the Fifth*** by Angela Brazil
- ***The War of Jenkins' Ear*** by Michael Morpurgo
- ***Down with Skool/How to be Topp*** by Geoffrey Willans
- ***Daddy-Long-Legs*** by Jean Webster
- ***The Little Princess*** by Frances Hodgson Burnett
- ***The Time of the Ghost*** by Diana Wynne Jones

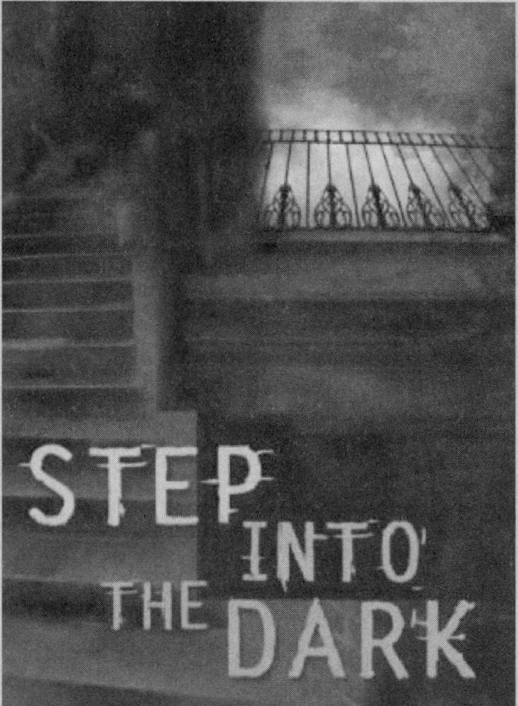

It's a formula that was begun in the first school story ever written – *Tom Brown's School Days* – and has continued ever since. One of my own favorites was *Stalky and Co.* by Rudyard Kipling (written at a time when the older boys had guns and the only subject anyone ever studied was Latin) but I also read several dozen of the books about Billy Bunter at Greyfriars School, and I loved the **Jennings** stories.

The girls had their stories as well of course and though I've not read them myself, if you mention the **Chalet School** or Enid Blyton's **Malory Towers** or Angela Brazil, a lot of girls go all misty-eyed at the memory. And one of the nice things about finding you like one of these books is the knowledge that there's a dozen more like it in the same series.

By the time my own children had arrived, I noticed that school stories were changing. They weren't all about posh kids sent to boarding school any more, they were about real children in real schools and what really happened to them. I thought it was much more interesting. So Anne Fine writes about bullying in *The Angel of Nitshill Road* (brilliant!) and about understanding other people's viewpoints in *Flour Babies*. Roald Dahl writes about weird teachers in his autobiographical *Boy*, and Gene Kemp describes the trials of a troublemaker in *The Turbulent Term of Tyke Tiler*.

When I wrote *Aquila*, one of the things I wanted to describe was what it was like to be in school when you weren't very clever or good at sport, and how that made you feel. It was a subject I felt I knew something about.

But the old type of school story is still around – though these days it comes in the form of fantasy. **The Demon Headmaster** books by Gillian Cross are great, or there's Bruce Coville's series set in an American high school that begins with *My Teacher Is an Alien*. Anthony Horowitz has created *Groosham Grange*, where the children learn magic, and of course there's the most famous school of them all, Hogwarts, where Harry Potter battles against evil and wins through with his mates: the original magic formula.

★ HALF A DOZEN MAGIC SCHOOL BOOKS

- The ***Angels Unlimited*** series by Annie Dalton
- **The Harry Potter and the...** by J.K. Rowling
- **The Worst Witch** series by Jill Murphy
- ***A Wizard of Earthsea*** by Ursula Le Guin
- The **Young Wizards** series by Diane Duane
- ***Groosham Grange*** by Anthony Horowitz

★ TEN BOOKS ABOUT SCHOOLS THAT MAY BE A BIT LIKE YOURS

- ***Frindle*** by Andrew Clements
- ***Bumface*** by Morris Gleitzman
- ***The Turbulent Term of Tyke Tiler*** by Gene Kemp
- ***Flour Babies*** by Anne Fine
- ***How to Write Really Badly*** by Anne Fine
- ***The Lottie Project*** by Jacqueline Wilson
- ***Matilda*** by Roald Dahl
- ***Aquila*** by Andrew Norriss
- ***There's a Boy in the Girls' Bathroom*** by Louis Sachar
- ***The Boy Who Lost His Face*** by Louis Sachar

★ TEN BOOKS ABOUT BULLYING ...

- ***The Diddakoi*** by Rumer Godden
- ***Feather Boy*** by Nicky Singer
- ***The Tulip Touch*** by Anne Fine
- ***The Eighteenth Emergency*** by Betsy Byars
- ***Secret Friends*** by Elizabeth Laird
- ***Step into the Dark*** by Bridget Crowley
- ***The Present Takers*** by Aidan Chambers
- ***The Mighty Crashman*** by Jerry Spinelli
- ***The Angel of Nitshill Road*** by Anne Fine
- ***Indigo's Star*** by Hilary McKay

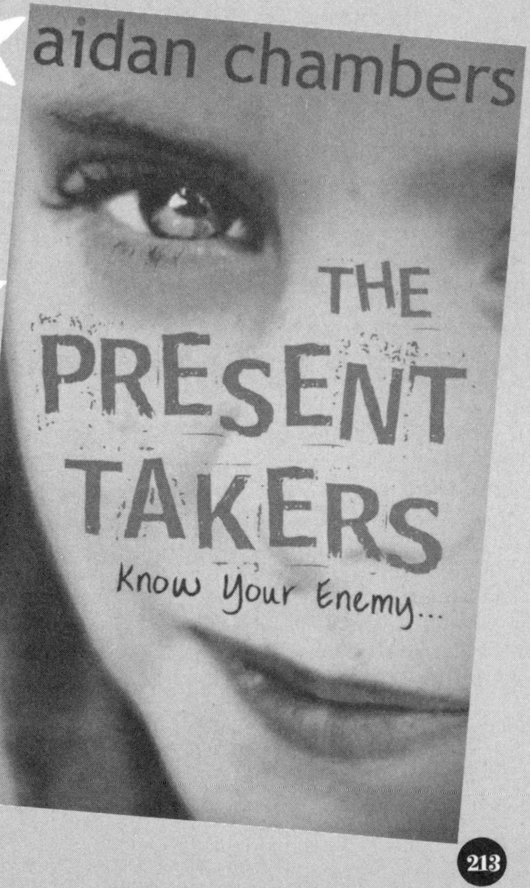

SEAL SECRET

Aidan Chambers

➡ William is not having a good holiday. For some unfathomable reason, his parents have decided to rent a farmhouse cottage instead of their usual caravan by the sea. They disappear for hours on end, his father fishing and his mother with her nose in a book, forcing William into an unwilling friendship with Gwyn, the farmer's son. Then Gwyn lets William into his secret – a seal pup kept captive in a cave – and William faces some difficult choices.

Determined and scared at the same time, William learns some hard lessons about speaking up and sticking to his beliefs, whatever the danger. There are wonderful descriptions of the Welsh countryside, the wild cliffs and, of course, the seal!

8-10

Helen Simmons

Next?
- Try ***A Dog So Small*** by Philippa Pearce; one of my favourite animal stories about an entirely imaginary animal. (UBG 65)
- If you liked this, you might also like ***Farm Boy*** by Michael Morpurgo and Michael Foreman. (UBG 81)
- ***The Seal-singing*** by Rosemary Harris is out of print but hunting down.

THE SECRET DIARY OF ADRIAN MOLE AGED 13 3/4

Sue Townsend

➡ Adrian Mole's diary begins on 1 January with a list of New Year's resolutions, including being kind to the dog, hanging up his trousers and not starting smoking. The final entry, over a year later, tells of being rushed to Casualty with a model aeroplane glued to his nose. What lies between is an hilarious account of a teenage boy's sufferings in an unkind world. What's especially funny is that Adrian takes himself very seriously indeed.

As far as I know, this was the first humorous book written in diary format. There have been many more since, but none appeals right across the age range like Adrian Mole. When it first came out, we all read it – children, teenagers, teachers, mums and dads, grandparents, everyone. And, quite rightly, we all loved it. If you like funny books, this is quite simply a must-read.

11+

Kaye Umansky

Next?
- There are several follow-ups, written as Adrian grows up. The first and best is ***The Growing Pains of Adrian Mole***.
- Do you want more diaries? Try ***The Princess Diaries*** by Meg Cabot – very different but very, very funny. (UBG 193)
- Another book about the trials of growing up is ***Bend It Like Beckham*** by Narinder Dhami. (You may have seen the film already.)

SECRET FRIENDS

Elizabeth Laird

➡ Rafaella is a new girl whose ears stick out. Such an easy target. Lucy, who tells us the story, is also nervous on her first day at Dale Road Secondary School when she meets Rafaella. She calls her 'Earwig' and raises a laugh. But the final words of Chapter One have an awful ring: 'I'm going to regret that moment till the day I die.'

When I heard that *Secret Friends* had reduced a whole class of children to tears, I wasn't surprised. I cried as well when I read this book. Perhaps our tears were something to do with recognising how easily we, too, might slip …

With its touching illustrations, this short novel is a little gem.

10+

Beverley Naidoo

Next?
- You might also like ***Jake's Tower*** (UBG 125), ***Kiss the Dust*** (UBG 135) and ***The Garbage King***, all by Elizabeth Laird. None of them is an easy read, but they are all terrific books.
- Another unsettling book, this time about friendship, is Anne Fine's ***The Tulip Touch***. (UBG 248)
- Or for something written from the point of view of the bully, try ***The Mighty Crashman*** by Jerry Spinelli – an easier read. (UBG 160)

THE SECRET GARDEN

Frances Hodgson Burnett

Next?
- ***A Little Princess***, by the same author, is about a little girl who struggles before she finds happiness. (UBG 144) Frances Hodgson Burnett also wrote ***Little Lord Fauntleroy.*** (UBG 143)
- ***Stargirl*** by Jerry Spinelli is also about an unlikely friendship. (UBG 225)
- Or try ***Tom's Midnight Garden*** by Philippa Pearce, a magical story about friendship across time. (UBG 245)
- ***The Children of Green Knowe*** by Lucy M. Boston will prove a satisfying read for anyone who enjoys ***The Secret Garden.*** (UBG 46) It is actually a ghost story but a benign one, and suffused with a dreamy, timeless atmosphere. There are several titles in this series, each as good as the first.

➡ Unloveable, unhappy little Mary Lennox arrives from India to live in her widowed uncle's huge mansion on the bleak and wind-blown Yorkshire moors. Orphaned and angry, Mary is incapable of finding any sort of comfort until she stumbles upon a walled garden, hidden in the grounds of the house. Eventually, she also discovers her cousin Colin, an equally lonely child, and along with Dickon, the bright, kindly garden boy, she sets about rescuing the overgrown garden. In the process she rescues herself and Colin from their unhappiness. I loved this book for its atmosphere, and for the descriptions of the tremendously satisfying rebuilding of the beautiful lost garden.

Jane Ray

➡ What drew me to *The Secret Garden* was that I could identify so quickly with the central character, Mary. OK, she was a girl and I was a boy, and I know boys aren't supposed to read books about girls – but who cares? Like Mary, I lived in the countryside and didn't have very many friends. I would often play games by myself, and go on quests around my house and garden in search of adventures and secrets.

I loved Dickon, the nature-boy, and his whole family. I wasn't too keen on the whining Colin, but through his spiritual and physical growth I came to like him. That's the great thing about *The Secret Garden* – it tells a wonderful, haunting, uplifting story, but it also slips in some important lessons. It shows us that we all have the potential to be better than we are and that we create our own well of happiness or misery. The book deals with childhood and friendship, of course, but so much more as well – death, religion, loneliness, the relationship between humanity and the natural world. But never in a dull, heavy way – it's a joy to read and artfully works its messages into the threads of the story, so that readers learn while they marvel. It's a remarkable, thrilling, mystical coming-of-age tale – no reader should be without it!

Darren Shan

9-11

THE SECRET OF PLATFORM 13

Eva Ibbotson

Next?
• Another world reached through a secret entrance at King's Cross Station is that of Hogwarts, so read all about it in **Harry Potter** by J.K. Rowling. (UBG 106)
• ***A Handful of Magic*** by Stephen Elboz twists the real London into a world that's quite different. (UBG 103)
• There are other Eva Ibbotsons too: ***Which Witch*** and ***The Great Ghost Rescue*** are both loads of fun.

➨ Under Platform 13 at King's Cross Station, there is a 'gump', a secret door that leads to a magical island. Children-in-the-know could tell you all about the gump, and how it opened for exactly nine days every nine years, and not a second longer.

This story begins when Lily and Violet and Rose, the triplet nurses of the young prince, are given permission by the Queen to take him on a journey off the island, all because they have become very homesick and want some fish and chips to remind them of their childhood in the shabby streets of north London. But the Prince gets stolen by the vulgarly rich Mrs Trottle and is brought up to be a vulgarly rich little boy Raymond Trottle, who has no interest in being rescued by anyone, least of all a wizard, an ogre, a fey and a hag. This is an entertaining, witty and wonderful novel, full of surprises and it's beautifully written.

9-11

Jackie Kay

THE SECRET SEVEN Enid Blyton

➨ For a really good, gallop-along adventure story, you can't beat Enid Blyton. She may not be recommended by your teacher, and your mum might turn up her nose at her – but her plots are gripping, and once you've got hooked on one book in the series, there's another, and another, and another (and another).

In the **Secret Seven** books, a group of children (you've guessed it – seven of them) form a secret society with a special badge and code. In each story they have a mystery to solve, and they do so bravely and intrepidly, finding themselves in quite a lot of danger on the way and stopping only to drink lemonade.

Susan Reuben

7-9

Next?
• After reading all the **Secret Seven** books, move on to Enid Blyton's **Famous Five** (UBG 78) ... and then the **Mystery** series, and the **Adventure** series (UBG 124). There's enough to keep you going for ages!
• ***Swallows and Amazons*** by Arthur Ransome is a slightly harder read, also about friends who have fun and solve mysteries. (UBG 232)

THE SEEING STONE Kevin Crossley-Holland

Next?
• Look out for the next two books in the trilogy: ***Arthur at the Crossing Places*** and ***King of the Middle March***.
• ***The Sword in the Stone*** by T.H. White is the story of the young Arthur (UBG 234), which is continued in ***The Once and Future King***.
• Another series that explores the Arthur legend in a modern context is **The Dark Is Rising** by Susan Cooper (UBG 57) ... as does ***Corbenic*** by Catherine Fisher (UBG 52).

➨ Here is a story to sweep you back nearly a thousand years. Arthur is growing up at Caldicot, a mediaeval manor. He longs to become a knight. Into his hands, his father's wise friend Merlin puts the seeing stone, and in its shining black depths Arthur watches unfold the story of his namesake – King Arthur of England.

We see our hero dealing with his constantly jealous older brother Serle, his outspoken friend Gatty, and a host of family and villagers, all the while becoming more and more swept along by the magic and pageantry of the world in his seeing stone.

Through his tale shines what is probably the clearest, most honest, thought-provoking and intelligent view of mediaeval life yet in a book for the young: it's not just about what people wear and how they speak, but how they think, the things that they believe, and what they know.

10+

Anne Fine

A SERIES OF UNFORTUNATE EVENTS

Lemony Snicket

Next?
• For more hideous things happening to perfectly nice children, Philip Ardagh's books are always a good bet. Try ***Awful End***. (UBG 70)
• Or ***Dimanche Diller*** by Henrietta Branford could be exactly the misery you're looking for! (UBG 63)
• Try Lewis Carroll's ***Alice's Adventures in Wonderland***, for another strange world full of particularly unusual happenings. (UBG 11)

➨Are you the kind of reader who likes to read about particularly bad, vicious and unfair things happening to a family of really very nice children, who might, let us say for the sake of argument, be called Violet, Klaus and Sunny Baudelaire? Are you the kind of reader who laughs out loud when truly terrible things happen to such pretty innocents? Are you the kind of reader who delights in identifying with really evil characters who might, say, be called Count Olaf (noble-browed and misunderstood)? Then you will laugh and thrill at the sheer spookiness and outrageousness of these wonderfully entertaining books.

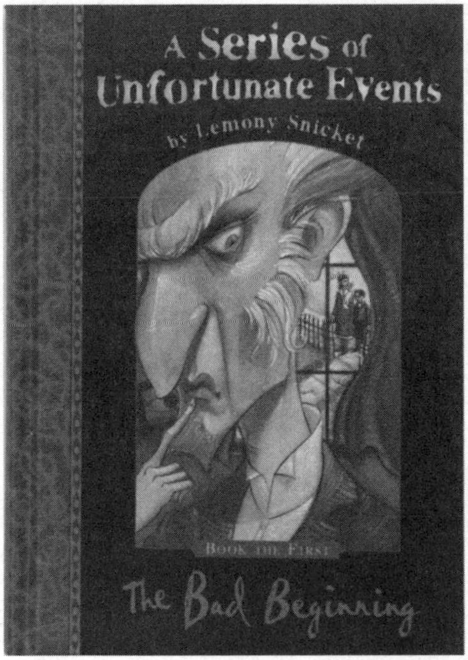

Do you like to look closely at spiky drawings made with a meticulous pencil and featuring people with beaky noses and side-whiskers? As a reader, do you like to handle a book made in the proper old-fashioned way with end papers, and an elaborate quarter binding? Do you seriously like to eat cold porridge for breakfast? Then this book and all its wonderfully clammy companion books, with their twisty plots and vile intrigues, are certainly the ones for you, gentle reader.

Ian Beck

8-12

SEVEN SPIDERS SPINNING

(The Hamlet Chronicles) Gregory Maguire

➨ Take: seven deadly baby spiders who never knew their mother, got ice-aged for several thousand years, and defrost to fall in love with (and want to bite); the Tattletales, a club of seven girls who hate: the Copycats, a club of seven boys who hate the Tattletales back, and want to beat them up; The Halloween Pageant of Horrors to which you can add: Pearl Hotchiss, a girl with a brain appreciated by: Miss Earth, a most beloved teacher, and … so much, much more! And between the laughs there are tasty morsels of spookiness and lots of excellently twisted storytelling (and some squishing)!

This story is sensational, seriously silly, and other things starting with 's'.

Simon Puttock

8-12

Next?
• Try ***Seven Haunted Hairdos***, another story of the Tattletales and the Copycats and their rivalry. And there are more in the series. Look out for ***Five Alien Elves***, ***Three Rotten Eggs*** and ***Four Stupid Cupids***.
• For something just as funny and fantastical, try Debi Gliori's **Pure Dead** series (UBG 195), or Michael Molloy's ***The Witch Trade*** and its sequels (UBG 269).

If you're looking for *Shadow of the Minotaur* by Alan Gibbons, turn to p. 140

THE SHEEP-PIG Dick King-Smith

➡ "'Mum,' the little pig said to Fly, the dog who had adopted him and was teaching him the ways of the farm. 'If you're a sheep-dog, why can't I be a sheep-pig?'"

There are many reasons: he is fat, he can't run fast enough, he is too polite to bully the sheep. But Babe, the little pig Farmer Hogget won at the fair, is determined.

This is an enchanting book. What I like particularly, though danger and even death are never far off, is the sheer niceness of the storytelling and the main characters. Dick King-Smith has given pigs the credit they deserve and which was long overdue. Basically one simple but brilliant idea and beautifully written. A modern classic.

7+

Alan Temperley

Next?
- Other Dick King-Smith books! Try ***Dragon Boy***, about a boy adopted by dragons; or ***Martin's Mice***, about a very unusual cat – he keeps mice as pets!
- ***I, Jack***, by Patricia Finney is an hilarious look at the world through an animal's eyes. (UBG 120)
- ***Look out for Dick King-Smith's ANIMAL STORIES choices on pp. 16-17.***

SHORT STORIES H.G. Wells

➡ This is a brilliant book full of terrific stories like 'The Man Who Could Work Miracles'. Many of the stories are what we would call science fiction today, but others, like 'The Country of the Blind', are just very strange tales of men or women who wander into a land where no one has been before. 'The Door in the Wall', for example, is about a man who keeps discovering a door to a beautiful place by accident, but when he purposely tries to find it, he can't.

There's a sort of unusual magic about these stories which you can't define, but which is completely fascinating. I read them when I was about twelve and I'm still re-reading them today.

11+

Garry Kilworth

Next?
- Another excellent H.G. Wells book is ***The Invisible Man***. (UBG 123)
- For something spooky, you might like M.R. James's ghost stories, such as ***O, Whistle, and I'll Come to You, My Lad***. If you can read M.R. James without being scared, you must have the courage of a cougar.
- Try Edgar Allan Poe, an American writer of weird tales from the 1800s. Start with ***The Raven***. Very scary!
- A modern writer who writes good short stories is Robert Westall. Try ***Break of Dark***.
- For something futuristic and spooky, try John Wyndham's ***The Day of the Triffids***. (UBG 58)

THE SILVER BRUMBY
Elyne Mitchell

➡ Brumbies are wild horses that roam the Australian Snowy Mountains. This is the story of Thowra, a silver brumby stallion, whose pale coat means he must learn to be very cunning because he will always be hunted for his beauty. Thowra is determined to be king of the brumbies. But first he must defeat the mighty Brolga, and then he must deal with a greater danger still – the threat of man.

I first read the **Silver Brumby** books as a child. The image of those proud silver horses, galloping like ghosts through the eucalyptus trees and leaving their footprints in the snow of the mountains, has never left me. This wonderfully atmospheric story is a must-read for horse lovers everywhere.

9-11

Katherine Roberts

Next?
- You might like to try to find ***Silver Brumby's Daughter*** about the brave filly of Thowra and Golden who must choose between her family and the Man who captures and tames her.
- Don't miss the classic horse story, ***Black Beauty*** by Anna Sewell. (UBG 29)
- If you like stories about horses with added excitement and adventure, try Walter Farley's ***Black Stallion*** and ***Island Stallion***.

If you're looking for retellings of Shakespeare's stories, look on p. 235

THE SILVER SKATES (also known as HANS BRINKER)
Mary Mapes Dodge

Next?
- Maybe it is the image of the children skating, fast and free and wild with happiness, that makes me want to suggest ***Tom's Midnight Garden*** by Philippa Pearce, with its beautiful skating scene (see my recommendation on p. 245).
- Pearce's ***Minnow on the Say*** is also about children trying to restore their family's fortune (UBG 161).
- ***White Boots*** by Noel Streatfeild is about a girl who wants to be a skater.

➨ When I was about eleven this was my favourite book. The only illustration is of a girl in a Dutch costume skating to win a race. The look of determination and eagerness on her face as she passes the other skaters is really what the book is all about: battling to win happiness against the odds.

At the beginning of the book Hans and Gretel seem to have nothing. It is Hans who manages to persuade a famous, grumpy surgeon to visit their sick father, who discovers the mystery of the doctor's past. But will Hans be able to unearth the family fortune?

I was particularly taken with the idea of the canals freezing for months every winter. Everyone skated everywhere, and even on their wooden skates Hans and Gretel managed to have fun on the ice with other children. But would they dare to enter the race, and could they even dream of winning the prize: the beautiful silver skates?

Berlie Doherty

11+

THE SILVER SWORD Ian Serraillier

➨ 'The children scrounged what food they could ...'

Your dad has been imprisoned. You don't know if your mother is alive. For years you and three other children have been surviving on your own in war-torn Europe. Only sheer courage and resourcefulness have kept you alive. And now, hungry and ill, you have a long journey ahead of you ...

This extraordinary and simply-written book is based on a true story, and is one of the most powerful novels of its kind ever written.

Cliff McNish

9-11

Next?
- For another brilliant story of wartime survival try ***I Am David*** by Anne Holm. (UBG 120)
- Esther Hautzig's ***The Endless Steppe*** is another evocative and memorable depiction of living through a war. (UBG 73)
- The best book I've recently come across about survival and hope is the short and brilliant ***Hatchet*** by Gary Paulsen. (UBG 107)

THE SILVERWING SAGA
SILVERWING • SUNWING • FIREWING Kenneth Oppel

Next?
- You might like to try ***Dead Water Zone***, an earlier, sci-fi-ish novel by Kenneth Oppel, peopled by humans.
- Or if you want another unusual animal angle, Morris Gleitzman's ***Toad Rage*** chronicles the quest of Limpy, the slightly squashed cane toad, to find out whether humans really do hate his species.
- For another epic fantasy series, read Garth Nix's trilogy, starting with ***Sabriel***. (UBG 207)

➨ Bats have generally had a bad press – think of all those vampires and haunted belfries – but in this gripping trilogy, the story of Shade the Silverwing bat, who begins life as the runt of his colony and finishes as an honoured hero, the balance is powerfully redressed.

The books have cracking stories, brimming with adventures, full of stunningly imaginative flights of invention and fabulously gothic set-pieces, and boasting a truly formidable villain in the mighty Goth. They are based on natural history and bat myths, which Kenneth Oppel plundered and expanded to create his own bat universe and mythology.

As the trilogy progresses, it becomes richer, deeper, fearless in tackling complexities. The writing is of such quality that you share their thoughts, you fly with them – but without ever forgetting they are bats.

Chris Stephenson

10-11

SIMONE series

SIMONE'S LETTERS • SIMONE'S DIARY • SIMONE'S WEBSITE

Helena Pielichaty

➨ These books are fun because they are not written in a normal storytelling kind of way. Instead, they're made up of Simone's letters to all kinds of people – as well as their replies, extracts from her school diary and questionnaires and entries from her very own website. You get to know Simone very well, in her own words, and she can really make you laugh. Each book tells a story without you noticing, about things which are recognisable and true to life: having divorced parents, changing schools, making new friends, asthma attacks and trips to toffee factories! Sometimes the writing does sound a bit like an adult writing, not that of a ten-year-old and you might find that a bit annoying – but try them and judge for yourself.

8-11

Abigail Anderson

Next?

- Another book by the same author, this time in the **After School Club** series, is ***Starring Brody as the Model from the States***.
- Try ***The Turbulent Term of Tyke Tiler*** by Gene Kemp for a funny school story. (UBG 249)
- ***Utterly Me, Clarice Bean*** by Lauren Child is another great story about a girl just being herself. (UBG 253)

SKELLIG David Almond

➨ I read this story in a day – and it took my breath away. It's a story that picks you up and swirls you around on wings of delight. In other words, it's a terrific read!

Michael's baby sister is ill and she might die. Whilst this family drama is going on, Michael finds Skellig in his garage – a down-and-out creature with a love of Chinese food. But is Skellig good or evil? Is he there to help or harm?

With the help of his friend Mina, Michael learns about life from the creature, who in turn is redeemed through his new friends. The whole story is so unpredictable – which I love. But throughout it all, you're aware that it's a story about the celebration of life, even in the midst of death. The story is moving without being maudlin, and its magic shines off each and every page. *Skellig* really is a book to savour.

Malorie Blackman

10+

Next?

- Read more David Almond: ***Kit's Wilderness*** (UBG 135), ***The Fire-Eaters*** (UBG 84), ***Heaven Eyes*** (UBG 108) and ***Counting Stars*** (UBG 52) are all wonderful.
- ***Whistle Down the Wind*** by Mary Hayley Bell is about a group of children who find a man they believe is Jesus.
- Another story of faith is Michael Morpurgo's ***The War of Jenkins' Ear***. (UBG 258)

SLEEPOVERS Jacqueline Wilson

➨ Daisy loves sleepover parties, and all the other girls in the Alphabet Club (Amy, Bella, Chloe, Daisy and Emily – get it?) are having them for their birthdays.

But Daisy has two big problems. One is that Chloe doesn't like her at all, and she's not the kind of girl who's too shy to say so. The other is that Daisy feels very unsure about whether she wants to have a sleepover party herself when her turn comes around. She has a secret at home that she hasn't told her friends – and she doesn't know what they'll do if they discover it.

You'll find yourself really rooting for Daisy as you read the book. It's a great story for anyone who has ever felt nervous about what other people might think of them – so for everyone, in fact!

7-9

Susan Reuben

Next?

- Other great Jacqueline Wilson books are ***The Cat Mummy*** and ***The Worry Website***.
- For stories of out-of-this-world friendships, try Annie Dalton's **Angels Unlimited** series. (UBG 14)
- Anne Fine's brilliant ***The Angel of Nitshill Road*** captures all the complications and fun of friendship. (UBG 14)

SMITH Leon Garfield

➨ A marvellous book. Garfield-land is eighteenth-century London, and no one knows it better.

Smith is twelve, small, filthy, sharp as a needle, top of his trade (he's a pickpocket). Pity he can't read, especially when his latest haul is a document acquired in a dark alley from a confused old gentleman. A minute later, the old man is murdered by two roughs. Enraged by the victim's empty pockets (where's the document?) they glimpse the escaping Smith. Of course! The little rat has not only nabbed the prize – but he has seen the murder. A long hunt for the boy begins …

Meanwhile, a benevolent family offers to teach Smith to read. He's cleaned up; his rags are burnt. But where's the paper? Why is Smith cast into Newgate? And more …

Naomi Lewis

10-12

Next?
- Read more Leon Garfields! Start with ***Black Jack*** (UBG 30) or ***The Apprentices*** (UBG 18).
- For more historical fiction, how about Joan Aiken's ***Midnight Is a Place***? (UBG 159)
- You might also enjoy Chris Priestley's ***Death and the Arrow***. (UBG 59)
- You could also try Charles Dickens – you'll be surprised at how readable he is! If you want pickpockets, go for ***Oliver Twist***, of course.

THE SNAKE-STONE

Berlie Doherty

➨Have you ever wondered whether your parents actually wanted you to be born? James has. Although he's always known he's adopted and loves his adoptive parents very much, he can't help wondering about his real mother and why she gave him away, leaving behind only a strange stone wrapped in a tatty old torn envelope with half an almost-illegible address on it.

When he's pushed just too hard in a top class diving competition and starts quarrelling with his family, James decides he must find out who he really is and why his mother left, using the address as a clue to where he might find her. All through the book, James's mother tells her own side of the story, making this a gripping read full of people with feelings about what makes us who we are.

Eileen Armstrong

10-12

Next?
- In Berlie Doherty's ***Holly Starcross***, Holly doesn't know who she is either, and when her father suddenly comes back into her life she must make hard decisions about where she belongs. (UBG 114)
- Anne Fine's ***Step by Wicked Step*** is a spooky story of five children thrown together in a creepy old castle, who each tell their own stepfamily stories.
- Children who run away from their care home, and survive through their friendship, are the focus of David Almond's ***Heaven Eyes***. (UBG 108)

THE SNOW GOOSE Paul Gallico

➨ I grew up on the wild marshy east coast where this extraordinary book is set. There was always wind, and the North Sea was always brown and soupy. I remember I used to watch geese fly over, and there was an old man, a recluse, who lived in a shack by the sea wall and who frightened us. Then much later I read *The Snow Goose*. It was as if Paul Gallico had grown up in my place. Here was the same strange landscape, and even a recluse who shunned the world. The story reads like non-fiction, and is utterly convincing. It's about a young girl who in the saving of a wounded snow goose breaks down the barriers and comes to know and trust the recluse. Here is a tale of tenderness, of friendship and of loss, into which war ultimately intrudes to bring sadness and absence, as it so often does.

Michael Morpurgo

10+

Next?
- Paul Gallico had a knack for writing books that have a huge emotional impact. Try ***The Small Miracle*** or the slightly longer ***Thomasina***, which, if you love animals, will have you entranced, and you can read about his novel ***Jennie*** on p. 126.
- ***The Dolphin Crossing*** by Jill Paton Walsh involves the retreat from Dunkirk. (UBG 66)
- And why not try Michael Morpurgo's own ***Why the Whales Came***? (UBG 264)

THE SNOW SPIDER Jenny Nimmo

➨ On her brother Gwyn's fifth birthday, Bethan climbed the mountain. She was never seen again. Now, four years later, as Gwyn turns nine, his grandmother announces, 'Time to find out if you are a magician!' The strange collection of objects she gives him includes Bethan's scarf, thought missing since her disappearance. But does he really have the power to get his heart's desire and bring his sister home again?

The appearance of a mysterious silver spider, Gwyn's sudden ability to floor a playground bully without touching him, and the extraordinary visions he sees on the mountain are just the beginning. Gwyn finds he must test his new found powers to the limit as he is drawn into an ancient battle against terrible evil.

10-12

Thomas Bloor

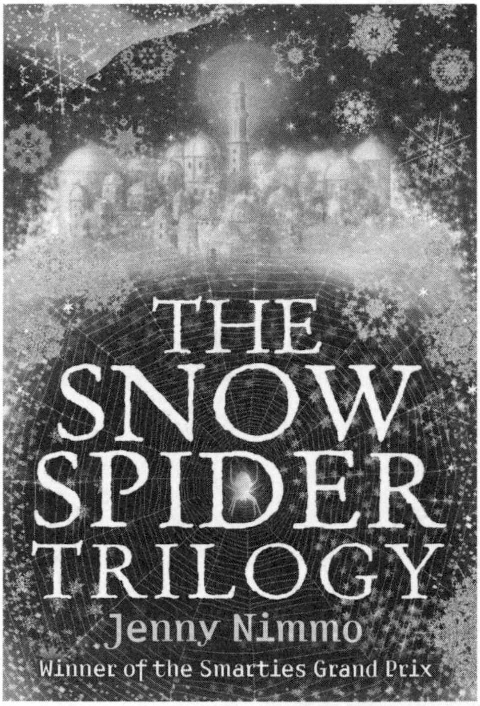

Next?

- Look for more books by Jenny Nimmo, such as ***The Rinaldi Ring*** (UBG 203) or the next titles in **The Snow Spider Trilogy**: ***Emlyn's Moon*** and ***The Chestnut Soldier***.
- Alan Garner based his book ***The Owl Service*** on an old Welsh myth, played out in modern time. (UBG 179)
- Louis Sachar's ***Holes*** also explores how family history can have an impact on the present, via a series of extraordinary twists of fate. (UBG 113)
- Kevin Crossley-Holland's ***The Seeing Stone***, set in mediaeval England, depicts a boy who, like Gwyn, has to try to balance the events of his own life with a magical parallel life, revealed to him through a magician's gift. (UBG 216)

THE SNOW-WALKER'S SON

Catherine Fisher

➨ Set in the far North, long ago, these books create a world where the everyday and the fantastic exist side by side.

Jessa's life changes dramatically when she is sent into exile by Gudrun, wicked Queen of the Snow-walker people. The books follow Jessa as she meets Kari, the Snow-walker's son who is both feared and hated by his mother. Together, Jessa, Kari and a small group of friends battle to defeat Gudrun and free Jessa's people.

These books combine the small details of everyday life in the North with references to the Norse sagas. One moment Jessa and her friends are taking part in a feast in the Jarlshold and the next they are barring the doors in a futile attempt to keep out Gudrun's magic. They encounter a man-eating monster, a ghostly army and a buried giant on their various quests. If you love stories about magic and the struggle of good over evil, then these are just the books for you.

9-12

Laura Hutchings

Next?

- The other two books about Kari are called ***The Empty Hand*** and ***The Soul Thieves***.
- Catherine Fisher has also written a wonderful quartet called **The Book of the Crow**. (UBG 201) These are fantasy books, but if you want something rooted in the real world with a hint of legend about it then try her ***Corbenic***. (UBG 52)
- You might also enjoy ***Beowulf***, retold by Rosemary Sutcliff. (UBG 26)

THE SONG OF PENTECOST

W.J. Corbett

➡ 'An astonishing achievement. I read it with delight.' That's what Roald Dahl said about this book, and he was dead right.

The hero is Pentecost, a small, strange harvest mouse, who has the huge responsibility of leading his tribe away from pollution to a new home in Lickey Top. The individuality and quirkiness of the characters really grab you and won't let you go. There's a lying frog, a highly unreliable snake, a couple of voles and a host of other animals – my favourite is the very fat owl whose life is haunted by a Dreadful Crime. There's a lot of humour, but the story's scary and touching too – and it really makes you think about why folk behave the way they do.

9+

Vivian French

Next?
- There are two sequels: ***Pentecost and the Chosen One*** and ***Pentecost of Lickey Top***.
- I thought of suggesting Robert C. O'Brien's ***Mrs Frisby and the Rats of NIMH***, an older mouse adventure; but maybe they're too alike. What do you think? (UBG 167)
- For more mice and a very involving story, read Russell Hoban's ***The Mouse and His Child***. (UBG 164)

THE SONG OF THE LIONESS series

(In the Hand of the Goddess)

Tamora Pierce

➡ *In the Hand of the Goddess*, the second book in **The Song of the Lioness** series, continues the story of Alanna of Trebond, a girl who wants to be a Knight. She switches places with her brother Thom, and she becomes Alan of Trebond. But it's not easy. To become a knight, Alanna has to learn court manners, history, algebra, how to use magic, how to fight and how to protect herself. In her first year of training she makes new friends, with the heir to the throne and the 'King of Thieves' among others – and she makes enemies too.

It's exciting to read how Alanna proves herself again and again as she struggles to achieve her goal. Then I'm sure you'll want to read the other three books, in which Alanna sees battle as a Squire and a Knight, lives among desert people and rescues a princess.

Julia Lytollis

9+

Next?
- The other books in the series are ***Alanna: the First Adventure***, ***The Woman Who Rides Like a Man*** and ***Lioness Rampant***.
- Tamora Pierce has written another series set in the same world: **Protector of the Small**. (UBG 194)
- Diana Wynne Jones is another writer who creates wonderful fantasy worlds. Try ***The Homeward Bounders***. (UBG 114)

SPACE DEMONS Gillian Rubinstein

➡ It all begins when Andrew's dad comes home from Japan and gives him a prototype of a new computer game ...

I love this thriller! When you put it down, don't think you're going to get to sleep. Your palms are sweaty and your heart is beating fast. You're like the kids in the story, so involved with the Space Demons computer game they can't leave it alone.

The twelve-year-old characters seem familiar: cool Andrew, Ben and mad Mario. Through the game you get to know them much better as the unpredictable, sinister force overtakes their lives.

Rubinstein, a masterful writer, was at the cutting edge when she wrote this story in 1986 and it's as strong as ever today. Whether you're a keen reader or not, *read this book*! But first make sure you're not alone in the house.

10-12

Elizabeth Honey

Next?
- The trilogy continues with ***Skymaze*** and ***Shinkei***.
- Or try the **Legendeer Trilogy** by Alan Gibbons, another series about gaming and its possibilities! ***Shadow of the Minotaur*** comes first. (UBG 140)
- A very funny story about two boys who find a spacecraft, is ***Aquila*** by Andrew Norriss. (UBG 18)

'Oh, one of my sons is called Gareth,' so I liked her and her books even more.

THE ULTIMATE READERS' POLL

YOUR TOP TEN BOOKS THAT SHOULD BE FILMED

1. Stormbreaker
2. A Series of Unfortunate Events
3. Horrible Histories
4. The Twits
5. Northern Lights
6. Captain Underpants
7. Sleepovers
8. Vicky Angel
9. Artemis Fowl
10. The Bed and Breakfast Star

SPOOK SUMMER

Mary Hooper

➨ Amy is a spook spotter. She looks for spooks wherever she goes! And a school camping trip in the shadow of a ruined abbey seems just the place. Where there are ruins, surely there must be ghosts! Long-dead monks, walking in the moonlight ...

Her mum suggests she might see crop circles: 'Big circles and signs left in the cornfields. Some say they're made by aliens, some say they're made by freak winds.'

Amy thinks there'll be aliens! Amy *would*. She's into mysteries in a *big way*. Her teachers tell her to stop being silly, and her best friend Hannah's more interested in bird watching, but Amy is determined to spot at least one spook before the end of the holiday. A spook, or an alien – or how about buried treasure? Surely there's got to be *something*!

There is – and it takes even Amy by surprise ...

Next?
- If you enjoy spooky fun and laughter, go on to the sequels: ***Spook Spotting*** and ***Spooks Ahoy!*** Also try Mary Hooper's ***Great Twin Trick***. (UBG 101)
- Another spooky read is ***Long Lost***, by Jan Mark. (UBG 147)
- For a funny book about aliens, read ***The Blobheads*** by Paul Stewart. (UBG 31)

7-9

Jean Ure

SQUASHED Joan Bauer

➨ This is such a fantastic book that I've never understood why it hasn't won every prize going. It makes me laugh out loud every time I read it, and it also makes me really truly feel good about myself and the world ... and it does it with a pumpkin as the main character!!! Weird? Yes.

I'd never have believed a story about growing a giant pumpkin to win a competition could be so completely unputdownable, but this is. Ellie, the girl who's doing the growing, is *so* real – and she's incredibly funny in the way she describes the dreadful Cyril Pool (her rival), her mad-as-a-chair father, her ups and downs with gorgeous Wes ... and the fact that she eats too much ice cream and her jeans are VERY stretched ...

READ IT!!! It's perfect for any reader who's looking for a hundred and eighty-six pages packed with zinging humour and a warm glow. (Well, there are a hundred and eighty-six pages in my copy ...)

Next?
- Read ***Rules of the Road*** – another great story by Joan Bauer. (UBG 205)
- ***Ruby Holler*** by Sharon Creech will get you laughing, and maybe crying, too. (UBG 205)
- If you love ***Squashed*** as much as I do, then search for Kate DiCamillo's ***Because of Winn-Dixie***. (UBG 25) They're both American; is there something in the American air that makes for brilliant writers?

9-12

Vivian French

STARGIRL Jerry Spinelli

➨ Stargirl is different. So different from all the others in her new school that she first attracts everyone's interest and admiration with her outrageous outfits and free-living style. She's everything they're not: genuinely non-conformist (not just a rebel) and a true individual. She's undeniably unique and everyone loves her. Leo Borlock, a classmate, is totally smitten.

However, no one knows what to make of her, and it doesn't take long for her very differentness to set her apart and for the admiration to turn into something nasty. In desperation and embarrassment at being seen with her, Leo tries to persuade her to become what would ultimately destroy her – a normal girl.

Chris d'Lacey

10+

Next?
- Jerry Spinelli has also written ***Loser***, about a boy who's a bit different from the crowd (UBG 149) and ***The Mighty Crashman*** which is about being a bully (UBG 160).
- ***Holes*** by Louis Sachar is simply brilliant and off-the-wall. (UBG 113)
- A book about finding out who you are – and being happy with it – is ***Saffy's Angel*** by Hilary McKay. (UBG 207).

STEP INTO THE DARK Bridget Crowley

Next?
- Bridget Crowley has also written a gripping historical novel entitled ***Feast of Fools.***
- ***The Rinaldi Ring*** by Jenny Nimmo is another book in which the past and present blur. (UBG 203)
- Another gritty, gripping bullying story is Aidan Chambers' ***The Present Takers***. (UBG 192)

➨ Bridget Crowley's brilliant first novel is a spine-tingling ghost story, a touching tale of friendship and a tough, realistic look at bullying.

Beetle (great name) lives with his mother up nine dirty, shadowy flights of tower-block stairs, but spends most of his time down at The Hall with his friends, working the lighting for the community shows. He loves it. Best of all he gets to light the spell-binding song sung by beautiful Tamar – but his friendship with her gets him into trouble. She's a Kurd, and there are people around who don't appreciate her family settling in their town …

But as if that weren't enough for Beetle to worry about, when he goes up the winding stairs to the Hall balcony to work the lighting-rig, he sees a young girl in the gallery, leaning out over the rickety handrail. Every time he goes up to the balcony, she's there too. Or is she?

Daniel Hahn

9-12

THE STEPS UP THE CHIMNEY
(Book 1 of The Magician's House Quartet)
William Corlett

➨ A remote house in a Welsh valley, an Elizabethan alchemist who can travel through time and a villain from the past who wants to control the future – when the Constant children, William, Mary and Alice, spend their holidays at Golden House, in Golden Valley, they suddenly find themselves playing a crucial role in a struggle between the forces of good and evil.

Each book in the series deals with a different threat to Golden Valley. It's only when you reach the end (which isn't entirely happy) and look back, that you realise that slowly the scale of each struggle has been increasing until the children are fighting to save the things that they treasure most.

Not only did I enjoy the time-travelling element of these books, but I also loved the way the children were able to talk to and become one with the animals that helped them.

Laura Hutchings

9-12

Next?
- Look out for the sequels: ***The Door in the Tree, The Tunnel behind the Waterfall*** and ***The Bridge in the Clouds.***
- For another story that brilliantly uses Welsh legend, read Alan Garner's ***The Owl Service***. (UBG 179)
- Or try Catherine Fisher's ***The Relic Master***. (UBG 201)
- And for magic, try ***The Box of Delights*** by John Masefield. (UBG 34)

STIG OF THE DUMP

Clive King

➡ While staying with his grandparents in the country, Barney goes exploring in the off-limits local chalk-pit. He falls over the edge and drops into the world of Stig, a caveboy living amongst the junk that has been dumped in the quarry. Despite their having no shared language, Barney and Stig become instant friends.

Though Barney speaks openly about his new friend in front of his sister and grandparents his tales are dismissed as the wild imaginings of a young boy. And so Stig remains his secret. Barney feels protective towards him, but more often than not it is the caveboy who comes to the assistance of the contemporary boy. It is a beautifully drawn friendship.

A classic tale in timeless prose, from the very beginning this story takes unexpected twists. Packed with adventure and mystery through to the end – if you're anywhere between eight and twelve, this book is a must-read for you.

Neil Arksey

8+

Next?

- ***Ug*** by Raymond Briggs is a cartoon about a caveman. (UBG 251)
- For something with a similar feel to it, try Joan Aiken's ***The Wolves of Willoughby Chase***. (UBG 270)
- Another Clive King, ***Me and My Million*** (out of print but worth hunting down a copy if you can), is really good too.
- Or for an hilarious and thought-provoking look at what it must have been like to be a caveman, read ***A is for Aarrgh!*** by William J. Brooke.

A STITCH IN TIME

Penelope Lively

A gentle and beautifully written ghost story about a girl called Maria, a quiet and perceptive only child who goes on holiday with her parents to an old – and as it turns out, very unusual – house. At first, Maria is rather overawed by the bouncy family next door. She has acute reasoning, often making the reader pause during the story and think, 'How true that is.' Penelope Lively's prose makes no concession to the fact that she's writing for children, and you finish this book knowing a lot more about trees, fossils, people's characters and life in general than when you started. A lovely book that can be returned to again and again.

9-11

Mary Hooper

Next?

- Try Penelope Lively's other, more famous timeslip story, ***The Ghost of Thomas Kempe***. (UBG 91)
- Penelope has written many other books, including ***The Revenge of Samuel Stokes***. (UBG 203)
- For more mysterious goings-on in a strange house, read Elizabeth Goudge's ***The Little White Horse***. (UBG 145)
- Or for a more modern ghostly story, try ***The Ghost Behind the Wall*** by Melvin Burgess. (UBG 90)
- And don't miss Lucy M. Boston's classic, ***The Children of Green Knowe***. (UBG 46)

THE STONES ARE HATCHING

Geraldine McCaughrean

➡ Phelim is an unusual hero with an unusual name. Living with his bossy sister Prudence, he is not sorry to leave home, but finds himself on an extraordinary quest – a monster, the Stoor Worm, is stirring from its sleep, awakened by the guns of the First World War, and Phelim, it seems, must save the world from it – even though he doesn't think of himself as even a tiny bit heroic. On his way he teams up with helpers – the Maiden, the Fool and the Horse – and encounters a series of horrifying dangers, from the Noonday Twister to the Merrows who trap fishermen's souls in lobster-pots on the sea-bed. Geraldine McCaughrean's writing is wonderfully vivid – so good that you will want to dip in again and again once you've finished. Full of twists and surprises, her story makes you feel you've accompanied Phelim on his astonishing journey.

Linda Newbery

10+

Next?
• Geraldine McCaughrean's books, which cover a wide range of subjects. Try ***Forever X***, in which it's Christmas every day, or ***The Kite Rider***, set in China (UBG 136).
• If you like books which take an unusual look at familiar stories, try ***Wolf*** by Gillian Cross (UBG 270) or the older **Egerton Hall Trilogy** by Adèle Geras.
• Another great, magical story is Alan Garner's ***The Weirdstone of Brisingamen***. (UBG 260)

THE STONES OF MUNCASTER CATHEDRAL Robert Westall

➡ Joe Clarke is a steeplejack, and one thing he isn't afraid of is heights. But when he's called upon to repair the south-west tower of Muncaster Cathedral, he loses his confidence. Why does that gargoyle give him the shivers? Why has the stone it's set in become rotten over the years? Why does his eight-year-old son Kevin start sleepwalking – and heading for the Cathedral? There are some jobs, Joe thinks, that try to kill you – and this is one of them. Read this truly chilling story, full of tension and atmosphere, and find out the terrible secret of the south-west tower, hidden since mediaeval times.

Linda Newbery

11+

Next?
• If you enjoy this, there are dozens more Westalls to find. He was particularly good at stories set during the Second World War – try ***Blitzcat*** (UBG 31), ***The Machine Gunners*** (UBG 150) and ***The Kingdom by the Sea***. If you like supernatural stories like this one, try the terrifying ***Yaxley's Cat***.
• Hugh Scott is another writer who explores supernatural themes in an unusual way; try ***The Gargoyle***.

STOP THE TRAIN

Geraldine McCaughrean

➡ It's 1893 and schoolgirl Cissy Sissney is on a steam train, excited about the new life her family is heading for in Florence, a town yet to be built in the middle of the Oklahoma prairie. They arrive and start to build, but then the railroad company decides that the train won't stop at Florence after all. This means ruin to pioneering families like Cissie's and death to the town, even before it's begun – unless the pioneers can find a way to *stop the train*. This is a joyous book based on a true story and you'll be gripped, not just by the battle, but by the characters young and old who fought it, and the adventurous language of the author as she brings it all to life.

Julia Jarman

10-12

Next?
• If you've read this story you may like ***Little House on the Prairie*** by Laura Ingalls Wilder (UBG 142), also about struggling pioneering families.
• More McCaughrean? For another historical story, try ***Plundering Paradise***. Or for something more fantastical, try ***The Stones are Hatching***. (See above)
• For another family and a train that has a huge impact on their lives, read ***The Railway Children*** by E. Nesbit. (UBG 197)

STORM Kevin Crossley-Holland

➡ Annie's sister Willa comes home to the marsh to have a baby, but when she goes into labour a terrible storm blows up and the phone line to the hospital is dead. Young Annie offers to brave the storm and run to the village to fetch the doctor, but she is terrified of the ghost of the ford. And when a strange horseman offers to help her, what will she decide to do?

Storm is exciting and haunting, and is beautifully written and illustrated. Kevin Crossley-Holland is a poet and reteller of folk tales, and his work has been a major influence on my own writing.

7-9

Malachy Doyle

Next?
- Try some of Kevin Crossley-Holland's retellings of folk tales, such as ***Enchantment***, and ***British Folk Tales.***
- Berlie Doherty has written a book which is totally different from ***Storm***, but strangely has two main characters with the same names! It's called ***Willa and Old Miss Annie***. (UBG 264)
- For more spooky stuff, read ***The Haunting of Pip Parker*** by Anne Fine or ***Ghost Writer*** by Julia Jarman (UBG 91).

STORMBREAKER

Anthony Horowitz

➡ Alex Rider is a normal fourteen-year-old schoolboy. Normal, that is, until he is recruited by MI6 to investigate the strange goings-on surrounding the famous billionaire, Herod Sayle. Sayle is planning to give a free Stormbreaker computer to every school in Britain, but there seems to be something very suspicious about it all. MI6 think that Sayle has something to hide, and only Alex Rider can find out what it is before it's too late.

This gripping adventure story introduces us to brilliant, resourceful Alex Rider, a sort of teenage James Bond – even down to the cunning gadgets! But be warned: this great new hero and the frantic, exciting plot make this a very hard book to put down …

9-12

Daniel Hahn

Next?
- If you want to read more of Alex Rider's adventures, look for ***Point Blanc***, ***Skeleton Key*** and ***Eagle Strike***.
- If you want to read about a girl detective, try ***The Thieves of Ostia*** by Caroline Lawrence. (UBG 239)
- How about R.L. Stevenson's ***Treasure Island*** – one of the greatest adventure stories of them all? (UBG 247)
- The **Biggles** books by Captain W.E. Johns are high on adventure. (UBG 28)
- For a challenging read about taking the law into your own hands, try ***Hoot*** by Carl Hiaasen. (UBG 115)

STORM CATCHERS Tim Bowler

➡ Fin should be helping his sister Ella look after their young brother Sam. But their world is safe enough – big house, nice neighbourhood – so without much thought he leaves her to it and goes off to play on his mate's PC. But even the safest-seeming places can be dangerous, and that evening, in the heart of a storm, Ella is kidnapped.

Blamed by everyone including himself for Ella's disappearance, Fin is determined to find her, even though that seems an impossibility. But young Sam is having strange dreams – even when he is awake – and the storm seems to seethe in the air even on quiet sunny days. Somehow, Fin must pull together all the things that are happening and make sense of them – for he is his sister's only real hope.

Terrifying, thrilling and heartbreaking, this book is about how secrets and lies can destroy even the happiest of families.

10-12

Leonie Flynn

Next?
- Everything by Tim Bowler. But especially ***River Boy*** (UBG 204) and ***Dragon's Rock***.
- If you liked this book for its fast-paced adventure, try ***Shadow of the Minotaur,*** the first of the **Legendeer** books by Alan Gibbons (UBG 140) or ***The Haunting of Alaizabel Cray*** by Chris Wooding (UBG 108).
- ***Kidnapped*** by R.L. Stevenson – this time it's the hero who's kidnapped. (UBG 133)

THE STORY OF CHRISTMAS

Jane Ray

➡ Jane Ray captures all the beauty, gentleness and mystery of this very special event. The reader becomes engrossed in the bustling streets of Bethlehem, journeys across the sea with the Magi in their magnificent galleon, watches with the awe-struck shepherds on the lonely hillside, stands in the stable and marvels at the miracle. This amazing tapestry of colours, highlighted in gold, illustrates the words from the gospels and is sure to delight and fascinate all who turn the pages.

8-10

Gervase Phinn

Next?
- Enjoy Jane Ray's other dazzling adaptations of Bible stories: ***Noah's Ark*** and ***The Story of Creation***. She has also illustrated ***The Orchard Book of Magical Tales*** by Margaret Mayo.
- My favourite story about Christmas is the deeply moving ***The Christmas Miracle of Jonathan Toomey*** by Susan Wojciechowski, beautifully illustrated by another amazing talent, P.J. Lynch.
- Or what about ***Father Christmas*** by Raymond Briggs? The sweet, cuddly old man will never seem the same again ...

THE STORY OF TRACY BEAKER

Jacqueline Wilson

➡ Tracy has a glamorous mum who never comes to see her. That's because Tracy lives in a children's home and her mum has disappeared. That doesn't stop her from making up wonderful stories about her, as much to comfort herself as to impress her friends. She is a tough, independent girl who wants to change her situation. She's not going to let anyone see her cry, or almost no one, and taking no prisoners along the way, she tells us her story.

It is a tribute to Jacqueline Wilson that our sympathies are not always with Tracy but our loyalty never waivers. Tracy can be just as mean and jealous as some of her house-mates. However, even though the book is very sad in parts, it never loses its humour and tackles a difficult subject with straight-up honesty.

Karen Wallace

9-11

Next?
- Read ***The Dare Game*** and find out what happens to Tracy when her dream comes true. Another lighter and easier Jacqueline Wilson book is ***The Lottie Project***. (UBG 149). Turn to p. 288 for a list of Jacqueline's other books recommended in the *UBG*.
- If you're interested in the 'children's home' that Tracy has been living in, why don't you read about a couple of others, in ***Heaven Eyes*** by David Almond (UBG 108) and ***Ruby Holler*** by Sharon Creech (UBG 205), and see how they compare?
- Look out for Adeline Yen Mah's ***Chinese Cinderella***, about a girl born into a family that doesn't want her. (UBG 47)

THE STRANGE AFFAIR OF ADELAIDE HARRIS

Leon Garfield

➡ Harris and Bostock are the kind of boys you'd go out of your way not to sit next to in class. At their school in nineteenth-century Brighton, this gruesome twosome learn about a famous Greek legend in which a baby is abandoned and brought up by wolves. With a glint in his eye, scheming Harris convinces bumbling Bostock that leaving his new baby sister Adelaide on a nearby hill would be an 'educational' experiment. But instead of wolves, Adelaide is snatched to safety by a courting couple, who then manage carelessly to lose her again. This wickedly funny tale takes in daft duels, silly skullduggery and a deeply creepy detective.

Karen McCombie

11+

Next?
- You might be in the mood for more dark doings set in the past, such as Lemony Snicket's **A Series of Unfortunate Events**, starting with ***The Bad Beginning***. (UBG 217)
- Another fascinating historical story is Theresa Tomlinson's ***The Cellar Lad***. (UBG 43)
- Or for an historical mystery, try ***Oranges and Murder*** by Alison Prince. (UBG 177)
- Leon Garfield's ***Smith*** is the exciting tale of a Victorian pickpocket. (UBG 221)

STRATFORD BOYS Jan Mark

➡ 'The Shakespeares had the builders in again.' The opening sentence sets the tone: here is the domestic Shakespeare, a growing lad at home amongst family and mates, the heady days ahead no more than a half-formed speculation.

Will, his friend Adrian Croft, plus assorted fellow Stratfordians, join together to stage a Whitsuntide play. The subsequent rehearsals – a showcase for personality clashes and for artistic insights and new alliances, described here with relish and affection – culminating in the actual performance of Will's much-amended *Fortune My Foe*, form the backbone of this brilliant, exhilarating tale of comradeship, writing, acting and maturity.

And with writing of this quality you can see, hear and smell Elizabethan Stratford, and pick its muck off your boots.

Chris Stephenson

10+

Next?

- Turn to p. 287 to see which other wonderful Jan Mark books are recommended in the UBG. Also look out for ***Something in the Air***, a recent novel set in the 1920s.
- Sophie Masson's ***The Tempestuous Voyage of Hopewell Shakespeare*** is a seafaring romp which you may enjoy.
- If you want to begin to discover the joys of Shakespeare's plays, consider first, perhaps, ***A Midsummer Night's Dream***, with its own amateur acting company, just like the one in Jan's book. You might want to start with the retelling in the Lambs' ***Tales from Shakespeare***. (UBG 235)

STRAVAGANZA: CITY OF MASKS

Mary Hoffman

➡ This book's sumptuous cover – eyes staring from a silver mask, and the Venice waterfront in the background – will attract you across a bookshop. It's a timeslip story in which present-day Lucien, diagnosed with what turns out to be brain cancer, finds that he can 'stravagate' to Bellezza, a place very like Venice – where he meets the spirited Arianna, a girl who doesn't see why being female means she can't be a gondolier (or mandolier, as they're called in Bellezza).

The story switches between past and present, with an intriguing twist when Lucien's parents take him on holiday to the real Venice – complete with McDonalds and the trappings of modern tourism. If you like a story that combines adventure, intrigue, deceptions, gloriously luxurious settings, divided loyalties and a hint of romance, this is for you – and it's only the first of three stories set in Mary Hoffman's fantasy Italy.

10-12

Linda Newbery

Next?

- Read the next in the **Stravaganza** sequence, ***City of Stars*** and look out for the third, ***City of Flowers***.
- Other novels with Venetian settings include ***The Thief Lord*** by Cornelia Funke (UBG 238), and the slightly harder ***Shylock's Daughter*** by Mirjam Pressler.
- For another series where reality and fantasy mix, read **The Dark Is Rising** sequence by Susan Cooper. (UBG 57)

STRAWGIRL Jackie Kay

➡ Molly (Maybe) MacPherson, so called because she can never answer definitely yes or no to anything, has always felt like an outsider. Her dad is from the Nigerian Ibo tribe which makes her an easy target for the bullies at her school in a tiny remote Scottish village, and she wishes she could fit in and make some real friends. When her dad is killed in a car accident, stop-at-nothing businessmen try to buy up her home Wishing Well Farm for redevelopment and, because her mum is too depressed to fight back, it's up to Maybe to save the day – and the farm – alone.

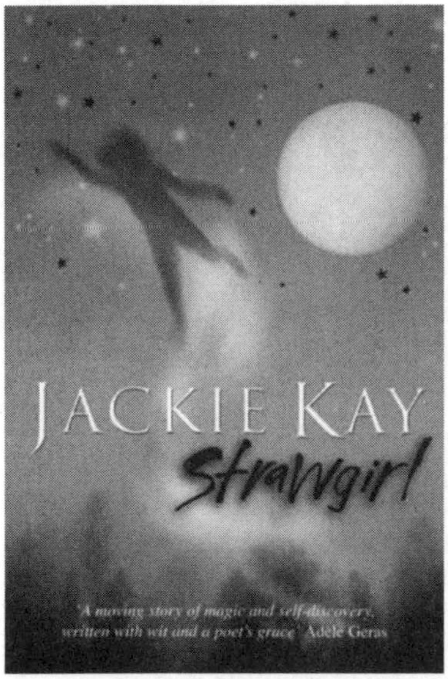

Desperate, she longs for a friend, so when the stunning Strawgirl 'with her black eyes bright and mysterious, shining like coal down a mine, like jewels' appears out of nowhere, 'the pleasure she felt was so intense the roof of her head could have flown open and thirteen beautiful blackbirds soared out'. This is a magical story, packed full of poetry which will paint pictures in your head and make you believe wishes really can come true.

11+

Eileen Armstrong

Next?
- The spirited ***Stargirl*** by Jerry Spinelli is brilliant. (UBG 225)
- Fighting to save something important to you is the theme of ***The Summer of Riley*** by Eve Bunting. Riley is a loyal and totally housetrained labrador, bought to help William get over his family's traumas and threatened with being put down for a crime he sort-of didn't commit.
- Michael finds a strange, dirty creature living in his garage in the indescribably moving and totally unique ***Skellig***. (UBG 220)

A STUDY IN SCARLET

Arthur Conan Doyle

➡ Introducing … Mr Sherlock Holmes, the world's most famous detective, and his sidekick Dr Watson. This is their first case (published in a Christmas annual in 1887). As usual it starts with a note:

'My dear Mr Sherlock Holmes. There has been a bad business during the night at 3, Lauriston Gardens … Our man on the beat … found the door open, and in the front room, which is bare of furniture, discovered the body of a gentleman … There had been no robbery, nor is there evidence of how the man met his death.'

This thrilling detective story has Holmes using his amazing powers of deduction to solve the case. How to identify someone by their footprints, long nails and one word written in blood on a wall? Off goes our intrepid detective (equipped with magnifying glass, deerstalker hat and pipe) in pursuit of the cunning villains.

How does he do it? You won't put this book down until you find out. 'Elementary, my dear Watson!' it isn't. But scary and good fun it most certainly is.

11+

James Riordan

Next?
- You'll enjoy more of Conan Doyle's adventures of Sherlock Holmes: ***The Sign of Four*** and ***The Hound of the Baskervilles*** (UBG 117) are the best known.
- You might like to try books by two authors who inspired Arthur Conan Doyle: R.L. Stevenson's ***Dr Jekyll and Mr Hyde*** and Edgar Allen Poe's ***The Murders in the Rue Morgue***.
- ***And see our DETECTIVE AND SPY STORIES selection on pp. 62-63.***

in a huge tree. I especially liked the idea of the curving slide that went right down through the

EVERYBODY'S FAVOURITE...

SWALLOWS AND AMAZONS **Arthur Ransome**

➡ 'BETTER DROWNED THAN DUFFERS,' cables distant Father to enquiring Mother, 'IF NOT DUFFERS, WON'T DROWN.' So the four Walker children are allowed to sail their little boat 'Swallow' across the lake to Wild Cat Island, and camp there, and outwit the pirates in the boat 'Amazon' who soon become their friends, and, and ...

This is the first in the series of twelve books which were my absolute favourites when I was your age. Arthur Ransome, journalist and sailor, was brilliant at pulling the reader right inside the small adventures of sturdy John, motherly Susan, the imaginative but unfortunately-named Titty, and the ship's boy, Roger. Before you know what's happening to you, you're there: sailing a boat in the dark, or trying to tell a secret code-call from the cry of an owl. They're realistic books, but with the classic absent-parents situation of fantasy. Try them. Start with this one.

Susan Cooper

➡ A series of twelve magical books to savour and love for ever. Start with *Swallows and Amazons* as John, Susan, Titty and Roger set sail for Wild Cat Island and embark on the first of their many adventures with the Amazon pirates. Move on to *Swallowdale*, and then *Peter Duck*, and on through the rest of this classic series of novels. The adventures will take you from the Lake District to the Norfolk Broads, from the Caribbean to the China Seas, from the east coast backwaters of England to the North Sea and Holland and the remote coastline of Scotland – every story packed with adventure and a cast of unforgettable characters. Part of the genius of Arthur Ransome lies in the way he allows the characters themselves to create the world of piracy and adventure through their own imaginations. It's a world so compellingly realised that we're deliciously drawn in. But there's more than just make-believe at work here. There's real action in these stories, real excitement, real danger. So what are you waiting for? Dive into the books. Soak up the world of the characters. Let the stories enrich your life just as they've enriched mine. Enjoy!

10-12

Tim Bowler

Next?

- Try some others in the series, like ***The Picts and the Martyrs***, which adds two more nautical kids to the Swallows' and Amazons' adventures in the Lake District (and will also teach you how to 'guddle' trout). Or ***The Big Six***, a kind of detective story which takes you to join Joe, Bill and Pete in their boat the 'Death and Glory' on the Norfolk Broads.
- Or (there's no stopping me) ***We Didn't Mean To Go To Sea***, in which the Walkers accidentally find themselves sailing a four-ton yacht across the North Sea to the Netherlands, in a fog and then a storm.
- If you've read all the **Swallows and Amazons** stories, move on to ***Treasure Island*** by R.L. Stevenson. It's brilliant! (UBG 247)
- Or read Philippa Pearce's ***Minnow on the Say***, another great adventure that happens over a long summer – with a boat too! (UBG 161)

middle – and that you had to dodge the dirty water coming down the tree on wash days!

Next?
- You might try ***Follow the Footprints*** or ***Summer Visitors*** by the same author. His mysteries aren't of the cops-and-robbers kind and they always lead you back into the past. For very different Maynes, try ***Earthfasts*** (UBG 68) and ***A Grass Rope*** (UBG 99).
- ***The Facts and Fictions of Minna Pratt*** by Patricia Maclachlan is about a girl living in New York who is studying to be a cellist, and her odd friends in the chamber orchestra where she plays.
- One of the first school stories ever written, and still one of the best, is ***The Fifth Form at St Dominic's*** by Talbot Baines Reed. Written over a hundred years ago, it is still a good read and still funny.
- Bridget Crowley's ***Feast of Fools*** is another gripping, cathedral school mystery.

A SWARM IN MAY and CHORISTER'S CAKE

William Mayne

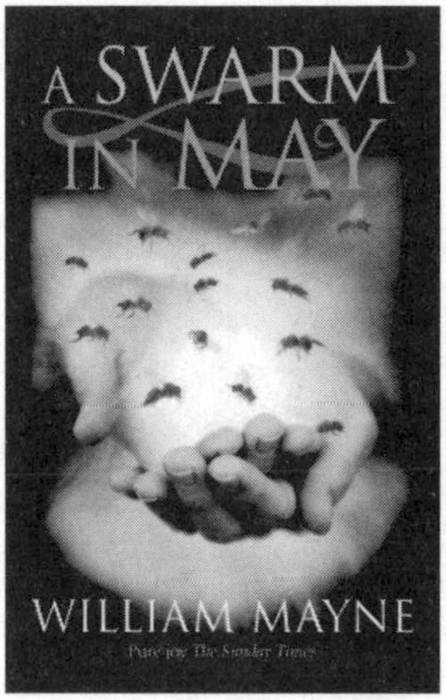

➨ Not many people go to boarding school nowadays and even fewer attend choir schools. In these books you can read about the boys who sing in the choir of a cathedral and live in the school which stands in its shadow. Their work in the choir is serious and hard but the rest of the time they are ordinary schoolboys. Sometimes the two halves of their lives are very difficult to fit together.

A Swarm in May tells how a cathedral ritual sends John Owen on a quest to solve an ancient mystery at the heart of the great building, involving hidden staircases and forgotten rooms among the stonework. In *Chorister's Cake* Peter Sandwell rebels against authority because he thinks it makes everybody the same and gives power to the wrong people. He finds out the hard way that being part of a choir is not about power but co-operation.

There are two other books about the choir school, *Cathedral Wednesday* and *Words and Music*. Although all four are fiction they are set in a real place. If you visit Canterbury, in Kent, you can go and see where it all happened.

9-11

Jan Mark

THE SWISH OF THE CURTAIN Pamela Brown

➨ One boring afternoon in sleepy Fenchester, a group of friends discover a disused theatre and decide to bring it back to life. They each have special talents and they write, design and produce every show themselves, pouring all their energy into the theatre with spectacular results.

All the problems of putting on a play are described in hilarious detail: the tantrums, collapsing sets, unhelpful parents and scrounging for props and costumes; but all the magic is there too. There are brilliant descriptions of the passion that the actors feel for their job and those special moments when the play takes off and the audience is entranced. The style might seem rather old fashioned at first, but don't be put off. You will quickly get caught up in the excitement of the friends putting on their first play.

This book will help you believe that dreams can come true. I should know – I now work in the theatre professionally, as a director, and this is the book that started it all off for me!

Abigail Anderson

9-11

Next?
- Look out for ***Ballet Shoes*** (UBG 23) and other Noel Streatfeild books about performing, such as ***Dancing Shoes*** and ***Theatre Shoes***.
- ***Billy Elliot*** by Melvin Burgess is a brilliant book (based on a brilliant film) about a boy who more than anything wants to be a ballet dancer. (UBG 29)
- Michelle Magorian's ***Cuckoo in the Nest*** is another theatrical story.

THE SWISS FAMILY ROBINSON

J.D. Wyss

➨ Abandoned on a sinking ship that is being storm-blown towards destruction, a Swiss pastor, his wife and their children find themselves ship-wrecked on a deserted tropical island. Here, through necessity, they make a new life for themselves using what they can salvage from their ruined ship and also all the wonderful things the island has to offer. No spoons to eat your soup? Use oyster shells. No cups? What's wrong with half a coconut shell?

My father read me this book when I was very young, and I can still recall the wonderful illustrations that added to the amazing story. For a long time I wanted to make my own candles and eat an iguana (apparently very tasty), but alas, I had to make do with re-reading this story.

9-11

Leonie Flynn

Next?
- If you'd like to read about another shipwreck, try the ***The Island of Blue Dolphins*** by Scott O'Dell. (UBG 125)
- If you like adventures in strange and wild places, try ***South Sea Adventure*** by Willard Price. Find out about his **Adventure** series on p. 39.
- If you want to read about a family making a new life somewhere unusual, try ***Children on the Oregon Trail*** by A.R. van der Loeff. (UBG 47)

THE SWORD IN THE STONE

T. H. White

➨ How I envy the people who have not yet read this book! They have a present still to unwrap! An unexpected piece of luck! An extra holiday! I wish that I could read this book again for the very first time.

The Sword in the Stone is the story of Arthur and his life before he heaved Excalibur from its stone, and thereby brought his fate tumbling down upon his shoulders. It describes his boyhood in a castle deep in a forest, with his foster brother Kay, his guardian Sir Ector, and his tutor, who was (of course) Merlin – the perfect wizard, owner of Archimedes, the perfect owl.

Historians say most of the legends of King Arthur are not true. Definitely, they say, no Merlin, dragons, or talking beasts. However, these are books that ought to be true. I believe them. Right from the first joke, to the last goodbye, they sound like truth to me.

10-12

Hilary McKay

Next?
- Go on to read the sequels which are collected in one volume as ***The Once and Future King***.
- And read, if you haven't already, Ursula Le Guin's **Wizard of Earthsea** sequence. (UBG 69)
- Or try ***Mistress Masham's Repose*** – it's nothing like ***The Sword in the Stone***, but interesting as it's by the same author. (UBG 162)

SWORD SONG Rosemary Sutcliff

➨Bjarni, a young Viking swordsman exiled from his home, sets out to make a life for himself among the wild seas and warring kingdoms of the Western Isles. His only companion is Hugin, the stray dog he adopts. In the course of their wanderings the pair will encounter storms and battles, shipwrecks and treachery.

Rosemary Sutcliff was brilliant at bringing history vividly to life. Her Vikings aren't just hairy warriors, but farmers, craftsmen and merchants with settlements all over northern Britain. Bjarni is a very believable hero; stubborn and headstrong, he often behaves stupidly, but he never loses the reader's sympathy; his quest to find his place in the world makes a thrilling and moving story.

10-12

Philip Reeve

Next?
- Rosemary Sutcliff wrote many great historical novels. Among my favourites are ***The Eagle of the Ninth*** (UBG 68), ***Knight's Fee*** (UBG 137) and ***Warrior Scarlet***.
- Or for a slightly different view of Viking life, try ***The Horned Helmet*** by Henry Treece.
- ***The Saga of Erik the Viking*** by Terry Jones is another brilliant story about Vikings.

A TALE OF TIME CITY

Diana Wynne Jones

➡ Jonathan and Sam kidnap Vivian Smith, thinking she is the notorious Time Lady, bent on destroying Time City and even history itself. Once they realise their mistake, Vivian helps the boys try to outwit the enemy before time runs out.

Diana Wynne Jones's story ensnares you with a dozen threads of plot all woven into a magic carpet of story that whisks you off to Time City with its habit ghosts, once ghosts and the mysterious Endless ghost who appears every day at twelve, climbing Endless Hill. Like all the author's invented worlds, Time City feels as real and vivid as your own: you will want it to survive just as much as the children who fight desperately to save it.

9-11

Gill Vickery

Next?

- You might like to read about Caprona, another city in Diana Wynne Jones's invented world where magic takes the place of technology. Try ***The Magicians of Caprona***, part of her **Chrestomanci** series. (UBG 272)
- You can find Bellezza, another Italianate city, in Mary Hoffman's ***Stravaganza: City of Masks***. (UBG 230)
- If you enjoy reading about magical adventures in real cities, try ***The Thief Lord*** by Cornelia Funke. (UBG 238)

TALES FROM SHAKESPEARE

Charles and Mary Lamb

➡ In 1807, siblings Charles and Mary Lamb published twenty of Shakespeare's most loved plays in simple prose. Mary wrote the comedies and Charles the tragedies, their intention being to make Shakespeare's tales more accessible, and in particular more readily digestible by the young. Wherever possible they have used Shakespeare's original words, and most of his better-known lines are quoted.

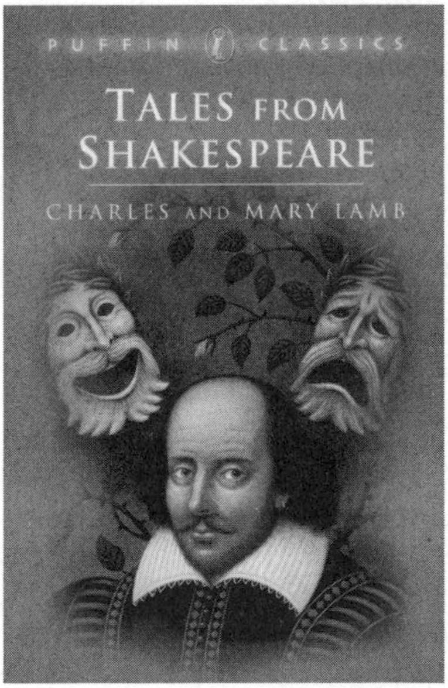

To the contemporary reader the language might seem a little old fashioned – other writers have since retold the plays in more contemporary prose. The enduring popularity of the Lambs' *Tales*, however, is testimony to the writers' skill and judgment in choosing what to extract from Shakespeare's texts and which plays to tackle. They show the bard's genius lay not just in the way he told his tales, but in the tales he picked to tell.

9+

Neil Arksey

Next?

- Compare the way other contemporary writers have retold the stories. Ian Serraillier and Leon Garfield both created wonderful retellings.
- Try Marcia Williams's funny and easy-to-follow ***Mr William Shakespeare's Plays*** (UBG 166) and its sequel ***Bravo, Mr William Shakespeare!***
- As for Shakespeare's plays themselves, don't try and read from a ***Complete Works*** but get a good edition (e.g. Arden, Oxford, Penguin) of one of the individual plays. These come with lots of notes explaining the text.
- If you want a novel that uses a story from a Shakespeare play, try Neil's own ***MacB***. (UBG 150)
- Or why not try Jan Mark's very funny ***Stratford Boys*** which imagines how Shakespeare's first play may have come to be written written? (UBG 230)

TALES OF A FOURTH GRADE NOTHING Judy Blume

Next?
• More books about Peter and Fudge! Try ***Superfudge***, ***Otherwise Known as Sheila the Great***, ***Fudge-a-Mania*** and ***Double Fudge***.
• Another series about a boy who isn't always good – though he always tries – is **Jimmy Zest** by Sam McBratney. (UBG 128)
• Or what about a girl who also often gets it wrong? Try Beverly Cleary's delightful ***Ramona the Pest***.

➨ Peter Warren Hatcher is nine years old and in the fourth grade. His biggest problem in the whole world is his little brother, Farley Drexel Hatcher, otherwise known as Fudge. Fudge is just two-and-a-half, and is always messing everything up for Peter. If you have a pesky little brother or sister you'll understand – Fudge can be a real pain.

He's messy, moody, noisy, and sometimes just plain weird, and you'll see why Peter finds him really annoying (especially when Fudge eats his turtle ...). But you – the reader, who don't have to have him as your brother – will absolutely love him. Because when Fudge is around, everything – going shopping, going to see a movie, having guests for dinner – is a riot!

Daniel Hahn

7-9

TALES OF THE EARLY WORLD

Ted Hughes

➨ As a child, I loved mythology: I still do – so gutsy and passionate and communal that no one could ever call it 'kids' stuff'.

I like 'invented' mythology for the same reasons. *Tales of the Early World* and its companion piece *How the Whale Became* are completely amazing, with mesmerising descriptions, clever twists and wonderful jokes. After forty-five years of reading stories, I tend to be able to guess where a story is going. But I challenge you to guess where Hughes is taking you in one of his stories. For a long time you can't even be sure who the main character is going to be – whether it's God or his earwax on the mantelpiece. You don't know if you are reading comedy or tragedy, only that the language is sweeping you along too fast for you to grab the bank and pull yourself ashore. Read it and get swept away.

Geraldine McCaughrean

8+

Next?
• The ***Just So Stories*** by Rudyard Kipling have some wonderful tales in them, many now classic, such as 'How the Leopard got his Spots' and 'How the Rhino got his Skin'. (UBG 132)
• Geraldine McCaughrean's ***The Orchard Book of Greek Myths*** contains some of the clearest retellings of Greek mythology. (UBG 177)

TALES OF TROY AND GREECE

Andrew Lang

Next?
• Rosemary Sutcliff wrote ***The Truce of the Games***, about how even enemies could be friends for the duration of the Olympic Games.
• ***Black Ships Before Troy*** is the first of Rosemary Sutcliff's Troy stories. (UBG 30)
• ***For more MYTHS AND LEGENDS see pp. 172-173.***

➨ The stories and heroes of ancient Greek myth are hugely enjoyable. And a better introduction than Andrew Lang's would be hard to find – he is a master storyteller. Maintaining the classic simplicity of the stories, through his anecdotal style he allows the heroes to become more accessible. They are characters a contemporary audience will readily identify with.

Lang weaves ancient myth with snippets of added historical detail. These condensed stories have freshness and vitality, yet retain the power and drama of their origins. Timeless phrases pop up to remind the reader just how ancient and weighty these stories are. Told at a good pace, with colour and detail to keep things vivid and lively, they will carry you right through to the end.

Neil Arksey

9-11

TARKA THE OTTER

Henry Williamson

➨ As a child, my favourite animal book was *Tarka the Otter*. It still is. I recently re-read (for the umpteenth time) Henry Williamson's wonderful story of what the dictionary calls 'an aquatic fish-eating carnivore of the weasel family'. The language the author uses is lyrical, and he paints an unforgettable picture of the beasts and birds of Dartmoor and Exmoor.

I like happy endings and have always wondered about the closing words of Tarka's story. Did Tarka escape the otter-hunters and their hounds by swimming out to sea, and thus to safety?

You'll just have to read the book ...

Dick King-Smith

10-12

Next?
- Try ***Ring of Bright Water*** by Gavin Maxwell, a true story of a man's friendship with an otter.
- Or try Kenneth Oppel's wonderful stories about bats, beginning with ***Silverwing***. (UBG 219)
- ***Watership Down*** is one of the all-time classic adventure stories, even if it is about rabbits. (UBG 259)
- ***There are many more suggestions in our ANIMAL STORIES selections on pp. 16-17.***

TELL ME NO LIES

Malorie Blackman

➨ Mike is the new boy at school who has a dark secret that he is desperate to hide. Gemma is the strange girl whom no one cares about – not even her own father. But when Gemma sees Mike, she recognises him, and knows that something links them together: something that gnaws at their insides and drives both to desperate actions.

This story races along and will carry you with it into a world of terrible secrets and frightening blackmail ... and out the other side.

It's the kind of book that keeps you reading into the night. It's stomach-churningly tense, disturbing and always thought-provoking. And in the end, despite all that happens, it's surprisingly uplifting.

10-12

Lucy Thunder

Next?
- Other Malorie Blackman favourites to try are ***Hacker*** (UBG 102) and ***A.N.T.I.D.O.T.E.***
- ***Kit's Wilderness*** by David Almond is another story of dark secrets. (UBG 135)
- Another edge-of-your-seat page-turner is Anthony Horowitz's ***Stormbreaker***. (UBG 228)

THERE'S A BOY IN THE GIRLS' BATHROOM

Louis Sachar

➨ 'There are some kids – you can tell just by looking at them – who are good spitters.' Bradley Chalkers, for example.

I first read this delightful story fifteen years ago but it has lost none of its relevance. And, in one chapter, none of its power to make me laugh and cry. Bradley is a bully who finds life less painful if everybody hates him. But the arrival of a new boy Jeff, and a young counsellor Carla, start to change all that. My favourite scenes are the ones Bradley plays out on his bedspread with his collection of little toy animals. Louis Sachar's wife is called Carla. When he first met her, she was a counsellor at an elementary school. That may be why so much of this story rings true.

Louis Sachar's later books – such as *Holes* – have rightly won him critical acclaim, but this one should not be missed.

Caroline Lawrence

9-11

Next?
- Louis Sachar is a wonderful writer, and his other books are all worth a read. Look out for the fabulous ***Holes*** (UBG 113)and ***The Boy Who Lost His Face*** (UBG 35).
- Jerry Spinelli is another brilliant American writer; try ***The Mighty Crashman***. (UBG 160)
- For an English boy with school troubles, try Anne Fine's ***Flour Babies***. (UBG 86)

THEY DO THINGS DIFFERENTLY THERE Jan Mark

➡ This weird and wonderful book captures the boredom of living in a 'new town', especially for someone as imaginative as Charlotte. She has always suspected, or hoped, that things aren't quite as dull as they seem. But it isn't until she gets to know Elaine that she discovers the bizarre world of Stalemate that lurks under the surface of their blandly uniform town.

From zen yoghurt to the mermaid factory and Dagobert the fishmonger-poet, the girls create a new and much more interesting world – much to the disgust of their classmates, who prefer to talk about diets and cellulite.

There's no one like Jan Mark for giving you a different angle on the world.

11+

Mary Hoffman

Next?
- Jan Mark's ***The Lady with Iron Bones*** tells of a close friendship between girls. (UBG 139) You may enjoy the same author's ***Handles***.
- For a chilling read about afriendship between two girls, try Anne Fine's ***The Tulip Touch***. (UBG 248)
- Geraldine McCaughrean's clever ***A Pack of Lies*** will also give you a new slant on fiction. (UBG 182)
- Another interesting and likeable character is Jenna in Joan Bauer's ***Rules of the Road***, which Jan Mark recommends on p. 205.

THIEF! Malorie Blackman

Next?
- You'll probably like the other books by Malorie Blackman such as the tense and exciting ***Hacker,*** (UBG 102) or ***Pig-heart Boy*** (UBG 187), which looks at what it's like to be made to feel different and excluded.
- Another writer whose books are full of action and drama is Neil Arksey. Look out for ***Playing on the Edge***, for starters. (UBG 191)

➡ Lydia Henson has started at a new school and finds herself accused of being a thief – which is bad enough – but then she's accused of pushing a fellow pupil in front of a car as well. Malorie Blackman's brilliant at describing how angry and frustrated you would feel when everyone thinks you've done something that you haven't. Lydia vows revenge and you can't help hoping she'll get it ...

But then the book takes an unexpected turn and Lydia suddenly finds herself blasted into a future where she did do something to get her own back, and it's not as pleasant as she thought.

All Malorie Blackman's books are exciting and thoughtful – and this one's no exception!

Andrew Norriss

9-11

THE THIEF LORD Cornelia Funke

➡ In the misty canals and crumbling alleyways of Venice, two orphans, Prosper and Bo, are on the run. They seek shelter in an old cinema with a gang of children whose mysterious leader, the Thief Lord, provides everything they need. But a detective is on their trail, desperate to find the missing piece of a magical roundabout that can control time itself.

From the very first page of this book I was transported to the wonderful city of Venice, and its twisting, fast-moving plot did not let me escape until I had reached the last page. The atmosphere of this book will soon have you wanting to explore the city's secret canals, yet the magical twist to the story is entirely believable. This book is unputdownable!

Katherine Roberts

9-11

Next?
- If you want to read another fantastic story with a Venetian atmosphere, try Mary Hoffman's **Stravaganza** series, which begins with ***City of Masks***. (UBG 230)
- You will probably also like the **Harry Potter** books by J.K. Rowling, if you haven't read them already! (UBG 106)
- How about another real place that's just been twisted very slightly out of shape? Try the London of ***A Handful of Magic*** by Stephen Elboz. (UBG 103)

Next?
Try the first of Clive Barker's new sequence of young adult fantasies, ***Abarat***. Grander in scale than ***The Thief of Always***, it is also gorgeously illustrated by the author.
• Philip Pullman's **His Dark Materials**, starting with ***Northern Lights***, will enrapture you with its subtly-altered world and sassy heroine. (UBG 176)
• Another adult author writing chilling fantasy for young people is Neil Gaiman – look out for ***Coraline***. (UBG 51)

THE THIEF OF ALWAYS

Clive Barker

➨ Harvey Swick is bored as only a ten-year-old can be. So when a stranger appears in his bedroom and offers him a stay at Mr Hood's Holiday House, how can he refuse? Who could turn down a place where all four seasons come every day, where there is nothing to do but eat and play? But the house has a darker face, and for every fantasy there is a price to be paid ...

This is a beautifully unsettling fable, an atmospheric and sinister journey of the imagination. Anyone who has ever daydreamed away an idle hour on a rainy day wishing for the lost magic of summer will find something to identify with here.

Chris Wooding

11+

THE THIEVES OF OSTIA

(Book 1 of The Roman Mysteries series)

Caroline Lawrence

➨ The year is 79 AD, and in the port of Ostia, close to Rome, Flavia Gemina is a young Roman girl with an uncanny knack for finding lost objects and a real thirst for mystery. When she sets out to discover who has stolen her father's signet ring, her investigation soon brings her into contact with Jonathan, a Jewish/Christian boy, Nubia, an African slave-girl, and Lupus, a wild and tongueless street urchin. As they become friends, a new and much more serious mystery appears ...

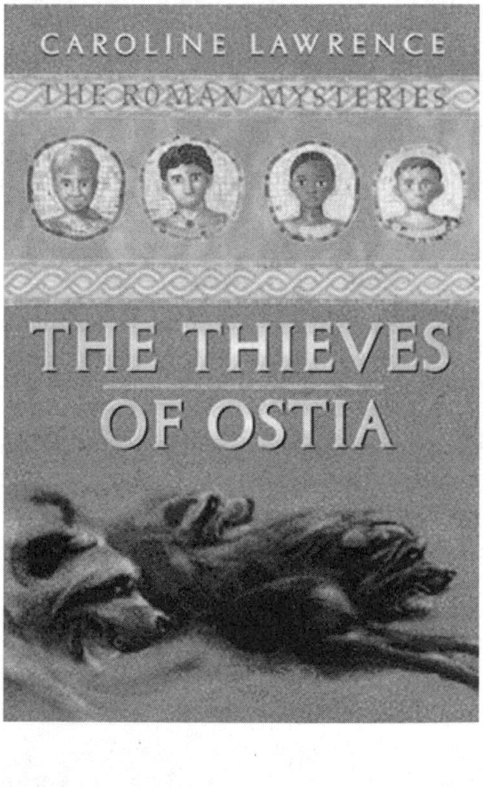

This wonderful series comprises books that can be read entirely separately, but whose plots intertwine and loop back and forth. With each volume, the mysteries become darker and more thrilling, whilst the evocation of Empire life is remarkably vivid.

Simon Puttock

8-11

Next?
• Other titles in this series include ***The Secrets of Vesuvius***, ***The Pirates of Pompeii***, ***The Assassins of Rome*** and ***The Twelve Tasks of Flavia Gemina***.
• Another series that has adventurous detection in the ancient world is Katherine Roberts's **The Seven Fabulous Wonders** books that start with ***The Great Pyramid Robbery***. (UBG 100)
• More about Imperial Rome? Try Rosemary Sutcliff's ***The Eagle of the Ninth***. (UBG 68)
• Or try the **Horrible Histories** title ***The Rotten Romans***. Read about Terry Deary's series on p. 116.

TIE-INS

'Now, read the book!'

BY LEONIE FLYNN

If you visit almost any bookshop in the country you will find, usually in the 'kids' or the 'science fiction' sections, shelves of books that are based on TV or film. These are known as 'tie-in fiction'. If something is a success on screen, most likely someone will make it into a book. You like *Buffy* or *Angel*? Great. *Star Wars* or *Star Trek*? Even better, there are hundreds of books linked to them. But how does a tie-in work?

OK, you have a good TV show. The episodes appear once a week for, say ten weeks (or twenty-two if you're American). The stories can be linked by a story arc, or they can stand alone – the story entirely told within the thirty or forty minutes of the episode. But, what happens to all the characters in the spaces not shown in those episodes? All that time not visible on screen the characters have to be doing something, don't they? Which is where the books come in. More stories, more adventures, more information about your favourite characters, and all in print so you can go back to it again and again. You like *Charmed*? Read more about the sisters and their magical problems. You like *Alias*? Read, and try and understand exactly what is happening in the show (good luck). You like Mary-Kate and Ashley? Read everything about them and their friends (and boyfriends) in the books.

And then there is *Doctor Who*. Doctor Who is just about the UK's favourite sci-fi TV show of all time. The BBC made it for years – old episodes are still shown on UK Gold and a new series is planned for next year. *Doctor Who* had some great stories – and some great tie-in novels. If you like reading science fiction, or you've seen some episodes and want to know more, try the books. There are hundreds of them. Ranging from the deeply serious to the wildly hilarious, with all the different regenerations of the Doctor starring in different books, these are tie-ins at their very best.

Most very popular shows have tie-ins for younger as well as older readers. You can usually see which ones will suit you best just by looking at the first page (the smaller

★ TIE-INS

(These aren't all things you'll find info about in the ***UBG***, but we thought you might like a few pointers about what to look out for anyway if you're interested ...)

Book of the film/TV show

- ***Billy Elliot*** by Melvin Burgess
- ***Road to El Dorado*** by Peter Levangis
- ***Arrival*** by Michael Teitelbaum (Smallville, first two episodes)
- ***The Willow Files*** (Buffy the Vampire Slayer)

Original novels

- **Jedi Apprentice** series (Star Wars)
- ***See No Evil*** (Smallville)
- ***How I Survived My Summer Vacation*** (Buffy)
- ***Ishmael*** by Barbara Hambley (Star Trek)
- ***Yu-Gi-Oh vol. 1*** by Kazuki Takahashi
- ***Charmed: Power of Three*** by Eliza Willard

the print usually means the older the reader the books are meant for).

And, of course, there are novelisations, too. These are just the story of the film or a TV episode put into print. Sometimes these will even answer nagging questions that the film/episode has raised but failed to answer. Melvin Burgess's *Billy Elliot* is a good example of this.

You'll find that some tie-in authors write in more than one invented world. Nancy Holder writes in *Smallville*, *Buffy the Vampire Slayer* and more. Diane Duane writes tie-ins as well as her own brilliant books, as does Paul Magrs. Look out for authors you like and remember their names for next time you're book hunting, because as in any genre as huge as this, some writers are bound to be better than others. Be adventurous – and ignore anyone who says these books are rubbish. Read them, then make up your own mind. And if anyone really tries to tell you they are not worth reading, you can tell them that some of the very best authors around have written for *Doctor Who*, *Buffy*, *Star Wars*, *Star Trek* ...

THE THOUSAND EYES OF NIGHT Robert Swindells

➡ Tan (short for Tristan) and his friends Simon and Diane Playfair love to play on the derelict stretch of railway line known as The Tangle, despite the ever-present threat of being bullied by Gary Deacon. But when Deacon's gang ties up the three friends in the disused railway tunnel, it's the start of a far more sinister adventure. They find the skeleton of a man, and soon discover that he was alive just four days before. What could have reduced his body to bones in such a short time? Something very scary indeed ...

As ever, Robert Swindells is great at mixing 'real' children with otherwordly adventures. Page-turning stuff, leading to a thrilling climax.

Marcus Sedgwick

10+

Next?

- Try ***The Hydra***, also by Robert Swindells.
- A really scary book is Robert Westall's ***The Stones of Muncaster Cathedral***. (UBG 227)
- If you're sure you want to be kept awake at night read Edgar Allen Poe's famous horror stories, such as ***The Raven***, and ***The Fall of the House of Usher***. But be warned – they're some of the scariest you'll ever read ...

THE THREE MUSKETEERS

Alexandre Dumas

➡ 'All for one and one for all!' is the famous motto of the Three Musketeers as they swashbuckle their way about seventeenth-century France. The three – the melancholy gentleman Athos, the brave, thick-headed giant Porthos, and the worldly priest Aramis – are each challenged to a duel by an eighteen-year-old country bumpkin named d'Artagnan from Gascony. After surviving the duels, d'Artagnan becomes firm friends with his three comrades.

The famous four uncover a plot to discredit the queen, and the adventures, skirmishes and sword fights that follow make this book one of the best classic historical romances ever written. Dumas moves us along on a high tide of excitement, devilish plots and counter-plots. We hardly notice time and pages pass.

9-11

James Riordan

Next?

- In ***Twenty Years After***, our heroes fight in France's civil wars and try to rescue England's Charles I from the clutches of Oliver Cromwell.
- Three more exciting books by Dumas are ***The Man in the Iron Mask*** (UBG 153), ***The Count of Monte Cristo***, and ***The Black Tulip***.
- Try Bernard Cornwell's **Sharpe** books, beginning with ***Sharpe's Rifles***, for more swashbuckling adventure.
- You might enjoy ***The Scarlet Pimpernel*** by Baroness Orczy. (UBG 211)

Next?
- Don't miss Jan Mark's other wonderful books. Try ***The Lady with Iron Bones***. (UBG 139)
- Another terrific tale of friendship is Katherine Paterson's ***Bridge to Terabithia***. (UBG 36)
- Two books about being unhappy at school are Nicky Singer's ***Feather Boy*** (UBG 82) and Hilary McKay's ***Indigo's Star***, the sequel to ***Saffy's Angel*** (UBG 207).
- Eoin Colfer's Benny has the added problem of moving to a new country in ***Benny and Omar***. (UBG 26)

THUNDER AND LIGHTNINGS

Jan Mark

➨ This is a wonderful book about an unlikely friendship. Andrew hasn't been happy in any of his schools, and has few expectations for his new one. But then he meets Victor – whom everyone thinks is an oddball – with a passion for aircraft that makes Andrew's own interest in racing cars seem both half-hearted and a bit too earnest at the same time. As the boys' friendship develops, Andrew makes a discovery that may change things between them, until he comes to understand Victor's way of thinking. So it's a book about change and acceptance, too. Like many of Jan Mark's books, *Thunder and Lightnings* is funny and serious at the same time. I think it's very funny indeed.

9-11

Jon Appleton

TIGHTROPE Gillian Cross

➨Ashley's life isn't easy. Her mum is ill and needs constant looking-after. The neighbourhood she lives in is run-down and the kids amuse themselves by tormenting the local shopkeeper. But Ashley has an escape route – she is a graffiti artist. At night she sneaks out, climbs walls and leaves her tag in unexpected places. Only her best friend Vikki knows her secret, or so Ashley believes.

To say any more about this dark, compulsive thriller would be a crime in itself. The ending is bound to surprise you and make you think about when you should ask for help, and when you shouldn't. The characters are strong and the background is utterly believable – *Tightrope* is truly a terrific read.

11+

Sherry Ashworth

Next?
- Gillian Cross's many other books include other nail-biting thrillers such as ***Calling a Dead Man*** (UBG 38), ***Wolf*** (UBG 270) and ***On the Edge***.
- If you like books about the darker side of life, you'll also enjoy Jacqueline's Wilson's ***The Illustrated Mum*** (UBG 122) and ***Lola Rose***.
- Older readers might also like to try Barry Hines's ***A Kestrel for a Knave***, about an underprivileged boy in Yorkshire and his pet kestrel.
- ***Scribbleboy*** by Philip Ridley is a quirkier, younger story about using graffiti to escape from reality. (UBG 211)

Next?
- You might enjoy more Diana Wynne Jones books, such as ***Hexwood***.
- Diana's books often contain elements of fantasy and science fiction but are usually rooted in domestic reality. Lesley Howarth's ***MapHead*** also uses this approach to good effect. (UBG 153)
- For an original supernatural chiller, look for ***The Bone Dog*** and ***The Ghost Drum*** (UBG 90), both by Susan Price.
- If you are intrigued by the boarding school setting then try Anthony Buckeridge's **Jennings** stories. (UBG 126)

THE TIME OF THE GHOST

Diana Wynne Jones

➨ 'There's been an accident! Something's wrong!' With these urgent words, the story begins. And something is definitely wrong for the girl who finds she is drifting along a country road, weightless and invisible, with no clear recollection of what has happened to her. All she can be sure of is that she is heading for home. When she arrives, she finds that home is a boarding school for boys. A teacher's four daughters are living in lodgings at the school. They are her family, but none of them knows she is there. Why can't she remember the accident? If she is a ghost, then whose ghost is she? And what is the evil force she can sense rising against them?

10-12

Thomas Bloor

Next?
- If you liked this, why not try some of Russell Stannard's other Uncle Albert books, such as ***Black Holes and Uncle Albert***.
- You might also want to try Philip Pullman's brilliantly, intricately constructed story, ***Clockwork***. (UBG 50)
- The **Horrible Science** series by Nick Arnold has some great titles about real science – all told in a funny way. Look out for ***The Terrible Truth About Time*** or ***Suffering Scientists***.

THE TIME AND SPACE OF UNCLE ALBERT

Russell Stannard

➡ Ever thought physics was boring? This book might just change your mind. It's the story of Gedanken, a bright enough young girl, whose uncle Albert bears a certain resemblance to another Albert – Albert Einstein. When Gedanken struggles to find an interesting topic for her science project, Uncle Albert proceeds to send her on all sorts of adventures, and she learns amazing facts about physics along the way.

Russell Stannard's great achievement in this book (and its sequels) is not only to make some of the most complex bits of quantum physics easy to understand, but to make them fun and interesting too.

9-11 **Marcus Sedgwick**

TIME STOPS FOR NO MOUSE

Michael Hoeye

➡ The mouse Hermux Tantamoq, a quiet city watch- and clock-mender, falls in love with the beautiful, daredevil aviatrix, Linka Perflinger and drops headlong into the most extraordinary adventure in which he uncovers a quest to find the formula for eternal youth. He unravels great mysteries and, much to his surprise, proves himself to be a very unusual and brave hero.

This is a book of great charm and humour as well as of daring and fearlessness – Hermux, the food- and fashion-conscious mouse is a memorable new hero, far too good to miss. With short chapters and a fast-paced story, this really is a page-turningly good read. **Wendy Cooling**

9-12

Next?
- Look out for the second Hermux Tantamoq adventure: ***The Sands of Time***.
- If you've enjoyed the fantasy, try ***Redwall*** by Brian Jacques (UBG 199), or ***The Edge Chronicles*** by Paul Stewart and Chris Riddell (UBG 70).
- If you want to laugh a lot, read Debi Gliori's ***Pure Dead Magic***. (UBG 195)
- For another mouse who has amazing adventures, try ***Mouse Attack*** by Manjula Padma. (UBG 165)

furious line, simple stories turned upside down. Me and my kids just loved his books. And there's

THE TIME-TRAVELLING CAT

Julia Jarman

➡ Topher finds a cat and takes care of her, or rather, the cat herself decides to be cared for by Topher. He calls her Ka (Egyptian for 'double') as she looks exactly like the carving of a cat that his mother, an Egyptologist, had bought for him. Topher researches ancient Egypt, and he discovers that the ancient Egyptians used to take statues of animals and servants with them when they died. Topher loves Ka and feels that she understands what he is saying. One night the most amazing thing happens: he travels back in time to ancient Egypt! But will he be able to get back home?

This book blends adventure with history, and will show you how Topher finds a way to come to terms with his mum's death. It might just make you think a little too ...

8-11

Julia Lytollis

Next?

• There are more books about Topher and Ka including ***The Time-travelling Cat and the Tudor Treasure***.

• ***Carbonel*** by Barbara Sleigh is another wonderful book about a magical cat. (UBG 41)

• ***Over Sea, Under Stone*** by Susan Cooper is a brilliant book about magic happening in the everyday world. (UBG 57)

TINTIN series Hergé

Next?

• If you like Tintin, you should try the **Asterix** cartoons by Goscinny/Uderzo. (UBG 21) Or if you think you're a bit old for those, there are many other graphic novels now available.

• What about other boy detectives? Look out for the hilarious **Diamond Brothers** books by Anthony Horowitz. (UBG 77)

• Or another classic, ***Emil and the Detectives***, by Erich Kästner. (UBG 72)

➡ Who is most famous Belgian of all time? Easy. The boy reporter with the orange quiff, his faithful dog Snowy at his side, and his loyal if slow-witted friend Captain Haddock never far away: Tintin.

These stories, originally written seventy-five years ago, are now available right around the world in many different languages. Why? Because they have a wonderful mix of adventure and danger as Tintin gets into and out of perilous predicaments with unerring regularity, and there are a few laughs thrown in for good measure.

One of the most enjoyable things about this series is the huge variety of places Tintin's adventures take him. Just like a Bond film, no Tintin story is complete without the excitement of remote and exotic locations. There's the snow of the Himalayas in *Tintin in Tibet*, the tombs of Egypt in *Cigars of the Pharaoh*, the jungles of Central America in *Tintin and the Picaros*, and even the lunar landscape in *Explorers on the Moon*.

The books feature wonderful characters, such as the bungling detective duo Thomson and Thompson (which is which?), and crazy Professor Calculus, not to mention Tintin and Captain Haddock themselves.

The stories might be old, but Tintin is as sharp and captivating now as ever he was. Be careful. If you start, you might just end up having to read them all.

8+

Marcus Sedgwick

TOM'S MIDNIGHT GARDEN

Philippa Pearce

➡ Tom has been sent away to stay with his boring aunt and uncle. There's nothing to do, no one to play with, and their small flat doesn't even have a garden. But when one night the clock strikes thirteen, Tom wanders downstairs to find the furniture in the hall has all changed. And when he opens the back door, he finds the most exciting garden he's ever seen. There are trees to climb, hidden corners to explore ... and a child from another time, Hattie, who has no one to play with either.

Tom's days continue to be boring ... but every night he sneaks outside to the garden, to live a life his aunt and uncle know nothing about. One night Hattie gives him a present: a pair of skates. When the river freezes they skate, together, the boy from now and the girl from then, miles and miles, and for me that scene is one of the most thrilling and wonderful of anything that I've read in any children's book.

Berlie Doherty

9+

Next?

- Another wonderful story by Philippa Pearce is ***Minnow on the Say***. (UBG 161)
- You might also like Penelope Lively's ***The Ghost of Thomas Kempe*** (UBG 91)and ***Moondial*** by Helen Cresswell, both tales of children who enter mysterious supernatural worlds.
- Or if you're wondering what it'd like to be the ghost yourself, then go for Alison Uttley's magical ***A Traveller in Time***. (UBG 246)

TOM'S PRIVATE WAR Robert Leeson

➡ There are some authors who never ever fail to write a genuinely good, solid story, and when I say solid, I don't mean boring. I mean a story that's beautifully crafted, completely believable, and will stand reading over and over again. Robert Leeson is one of those authors; he should be up there with all those flashy starry people, and I don't know why he isn't.

Tom's Private War is typically excellent; Tom and his gang are challenged and thrown into confusion by Scouser and the other children who have arrived as a result of wartime evacuation, and a private war develops alongside the confusion of national events. Oh, a word of warning. If you're scared of dark creepy places don't read the bit where they're down in the disused mineshafts ... oooooh!!!

Vivian French

7-9

Next?

- Anything by Robert Leeson! Tell your teachers. Convert your friends. Look for more about ***Tom in Tom's War Patrol*** and the brilliant and quite different, ***The Third Class Genie***.
- Another book that looks at what it was like to be a child in the war is ***Friend or Foe***, by Michael Morpurgo.
- A very English story of warring gangs is ***The Otterbury Incident*** by Cecil Day Lewis. (UBG 178)

TORO! TORO!

Michael Morpurgo

➡ A boy asks his grandfather the terrible question 'When you were little, what was the *very* worstest thing you ever did?' So the old man Antonito tells a story from his childhood, when he was living with his parents on their idyllic farm in Spain. Antonito witnesses the birth of Paco the bull calf and the two become inseparable. Time passes and Spain is gripped by civil war. Antonito sees his first bullfight and is horrified to learn that Paco is destined to die in the bullring. He steals the young bull and they hide out in the forest. But then the planes appear, loaded with bombs, and they are heading towards Antonito's home ...

Thomas Bloor

7-10

Next?

- You may want to read another of Michael Morpurgo's books, such as ***The Butterfly Lion*** (UBG 37) or ***War Horse*** (UBG 258).
- ***Willa and Old Miss Annie*** by Berlie Doherty is a wonderful book about the relationship between people and animals. (UBG 264)
- Michael Foreman's ***War Game*** shows a different side to war. (UBG 257)

coloured pencil make me gasp with pleasure.

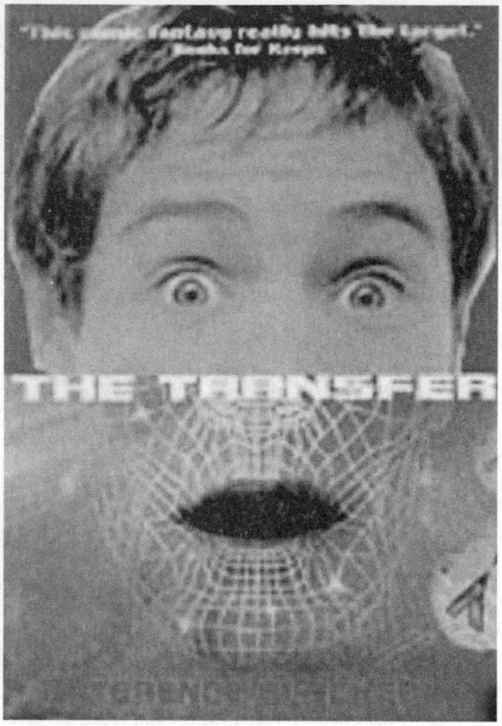

THE TRANSFER

Terence Blacker

➡ Have you ever felt that football is the most important thing in the world? Well, Stanley knows it is. Playing, watching, dreaming, thinking, he lives for football and particularly for his team, City. But City are about to be relegated, and Stanley knows he's got to do something, anything. His mum is a computer scientist, and she's working on cybertelekinesis ... and Stanley has a program he's been working on himself: 'TargetMan', with a superhero striker who has the best skills in the world – but who uncannily looks a little like an older version of Stanley. And when he puts these two things together, the strangest things start to happen ...

Football, computers and a magic boot stud take Stanley into an adventure that's more fast-paced and exciting than a cup final in extra time.

9-11

Leonie Flynn

Next?

- More football? Try ***Falling 4 Mandy*** by Chris d'Lacey or any of Neil Arksey's books: ***Brooksie***, ***Flint*** and ***MacB*** (UBG 150).
- Two other stories about computers are ***Hacker*** by Malorie Blackman (UBG 102) and Gillian Rubinstein's ***Space Demons*** (UBG 223).

A TRAVELLER IN TIME

Alison Uttley

➡ To be honest, I first read this as a grown-up but was hooked by it. It is a mixture of historical novel and time-slip fantasy. Penelope goes to stay at Thackers, an old manor house in Derbyshire. There she finds she can first hear faint voices calling, see dim figures in the flickering lamplight, and then begins to travel in time, back to a real adventure in the sixteenth century.

This is based on the author's own childhood at Wingfield. I once went to visit Wingfield and half thought I was travelling through time myself. The worlds of Penelope's real life and her experiences in the past are wonderfully woven together. The adventure she finds herself in is the Babington plot to save Mary Queen of Scots and you have a real sense of being involved in history as it unfolds. And Penelope falls in love with Francis Babington, though it is a love doomed from the start.

10-12

Helen Cresswell

Next?

- I may well have been influenced by this book when I wrote ***Moondial***, also about a girl who finds herself travelling not just to one, but two other periods of time. In my novel ***Stonestruck***, Jessica finds herself evacuated to a Welsh castle and becomes caught up in a sinister chain of children who have been turned to stone over the centuries.
- Other timeslip stories are ***The Ghost of Thomas Kempe*** (UBG 91) and ***A Stitch in Time*** (UBG 226), both by Penelope Lively. For other ideas, look at our list of timeslip stories on p. 81.
- For another book set during the reign of Elizabeth I, try Geoffrey Trease's classic adventure story, ***Cue for Treason***. (UBG 55)

THE TREASURE IN THE GARDEN

Hilary McKay

➡ Paradise House is a big, ramshackle old building which, though once a single-family house, has now been divided up into lots of flats. Among the families living there now are three children, all nine-years-old: Danny O'Brien, Nathan Amadi and Anna Lee, who are best friends, and who always have the most fun adventures.

In *The Treasure in the Garden,* Danny, trying to escape from his (noisy) new sister, starts to spend his time with the grouchy old caretaker Macdonald (who feeds him tinned steak pie and tinned spotted dick and really isn't that grouchy after all), and accidentally discovers that treasure has been buried in the garden! Will he and his friends be able to find it, or will they have to dig up the whole garden first?

Leonie Flynn

7-9

Next?
- More adventures at Paradise House? Try ***The Zoo in the Attic***, ***The Magic in the Mirror***, ***The Echo in the Chimney*** or ***The Surprise Party***, or Hilary's stories about the Robinson family, starting with ***Dog Friday***.
- Or try something by Jacqueline Wilson: ***The Cat Mummy***, say, or ***The Worry Website***.
- Henrietta Branford's spirited **Dimanche Diller** stories have a unique mix of adventure and humour. (UBG 63)

TREASURE ISLAND

R.L. Stevenson

➡ It begins quietly enough for young Jim Hawkins, son of the innkeeper of The Admiral Benbow. An old seaman comes to stay, dragging his sea-chest on a cart. But, from the first time we hear the eerie refrain – 'Fifteen men on the dead man's chest, Yo-ho-ho and a bottle of rum' – and learn of the mysterious 'black spot', we are hooked.

Once hooked, Stevenson never lets us go, us or Jim Hawkins – we're in this together. He takes us on a giddy journey of twists and turns of fate, through hope, horror and despair and back again, and all of it unexpected and thrilling. There's violence and blood and treachery (unforgettably embodied in the pirate, Long John Silver) on board ship, the *Hispaniola*, and on Treasure Island itself. And Long John Silver and his friends are no cut-out pirates, these are cut-*throat* pirates, the real thing! We live the adventure with Jim, are terrified with him and for him, all the while urging him on, willing him to win through somehow, anyhow, and bring us safely home.

Michael Morpurgo

10+

Next?
- ***Kidnapped*** by R.L. Stevenson is another brilliant adventure story. (UBG 133)
- For another pirate story, this time a little easier and much funnier, try Chris d'Lacey's ***The Salt Pirates of Skegness***. (UBG 209)
- ***Plundering Paradise*** by Geraldine McCaughrean is another piratical adventure.
- For a very modern, female pirate, read Tanith Lee's ***Piratica***. (UBG 190)

If you're looking for Terry Pratchett's *Truckers*, turn to p. 36

Next?
- You might like to read a translation of Homer's epic poem ***The Iliad***, the very first story of the fall of Troy; or a simpler retelling like Rosemary Sutcliff's ***Black Ships Before Troy***. (UBG 30)
- For historical adventure and magic, try my **Seven Fabulous Wonders** series – a mix of fantasy, myth, legend and history based on the Seven Wonders of the Ancient World. (UBG 100)
- The story of Cassandra, doomed prophetess of Troy, is imaginatively told in Marion Zimmer Bradley's ***The Firebrand***.

TROY Adèle Geras

➨ You may know the story of the Trojan War, the long war cause by Princess Helen, whose legendary beauty 'launched a thousand ships'– but Adèle Geras's *Troy* is no straight retelling of history …

This Trojan tale is told through the eyes of two sisters, Marpessa and Xanthe, who are trapped behind the walls of their city after ten years of siege by the Greek army. Bored by the siege, Aphrodite, goddess of desire, causes Marpessa and Xanthe to fall in love with the same man. A touchingly human story of love and loyalty unfolds against the backdrop of legend, lightened by comic asides from a pair of kitchen 'gossips'. But in keeping with the Greek myths, there is real tragedy here, too. Readers looking for depth and emotion should not miss this powerful book.

12+

Katherine Roberts

TUCK EVERLASTING

Natalie Babbitt

➨ Don't be put off by this book's slow descriptive beginning. You'll be gripped as soon as ten-year-old Winnie is kidnapped – as she's about to drink water from a hidden spring. Scared and angry, she's forced to go home with her kidnappers, the strange Tuck family. They tell her she can choose whether to drink from the spring or not, but if she does she'll live forever – like them. She must think about it first.

Suddenly the action speeds up with the arrival of the sinister Man in the Yellow Suit. He wants to sell the water and exhibit the Tucks as proof of its magic. Ma Tuck takes drastic action which involves Winnie. Does Winnie drink the water and live for ever? You won't know till the last page.

9-11

Julia Jarman

Next?
- If you've read and enjoyed this, you're probably ready to give anything a go, though I have to admit I haven't enjoyed other books by this author. I've never read anything quite like it and love to read and re-read it.
- Another book about eternal youth and the price you pay for it is J.M Barrie's ***Peter Pan***. (UBG 184)
- Ory try the extraordinary picture book ***How to Live Forever*** by Colin Thompson. (UBG 118)

Next?
- Anne Fine has written many wonderful novels: try ***The Book of the Banshee*** or the more hard-hitting ***Up on Cloud Nine*** (UBG 252).
- Elizabeth Laird's ***Jake's Tower*** is another dark and tense story. (UBG 125)
- And another book about good, evil and standing up for yourself is Michael Morpurgo's ***The War of Jenkins' Ear***. (UBG 258)

THE TULIP TOUCH Anne Fine

➨ This is one of the most chilling books I've ever read. Quite, quite brilliant on the nature and causes of evil.

Natalie finds Tulip exciting, and doesn't care that everyone else is so wary of her. But as Tulip's games become more and more sinister, Natalie realises that her friend will stop at nothing …

Anne Fine is a superb writer, and to my mind this is her best book. Completely un-put-downable, you are totally convinced by Natalie, the otherwise friendless narrator, describing how she is drawn into Tulip's dangerous world. The portrait of Tulip is drawn with such acute sensitivity, such understanding; the message is that no one is born evil – that we are all products of our upbringing.

10+

Malachy Doyle

Next?

- You might like to read other novels which look at what happens when opposing religious views come into contact. Try ***Between the Moon and the Rock*** by Judy Allen or Jan Mark's ***The Eclipse of the Century***, a tremendous read which, like ***Tulku***, takes you to an unfamiliar part of the world where you cannot take your certainties for granted.
- For a fantasy approach to the theme of religious conflict, read Philip Pullman's **His Dark Materials** trilogy. (UBG 176)
- Or how about something else very different by Peter Dickinson? Try ***City of Gold***. (UBG 48)

TULKU Peter Dickinson

➨ Theo is an English boy who lives in a small Chinese settlement with his missionary parents, until one day they get swept up in a war and Theo is left orphaned and alone. A chance meeting with Mrs Jones, an eccentric English plant hunter, takes Theo on a journey out of China and into Tibet and, eventually, to the Dong Pe monastery.

Tulku is a thrilling adventure story with a deeply serious theme. During his perilous journey to Tibet, Theo finds that he is also on a spiritual journey to discover if the religious certainties he grew up with can survive contact with different beliefs. After battling with the terrifying demons of Dong Pe, Theo finds his own truth at last, and learns much about tolerance and compassion.

Gill Vickery

11+

THE TURBULENT TERM OF TYKE TILER

Gene Kemp

➨ Are you one of those people who can't seem to do anything right, no matter how hard you try? If so, you'll enjoy reading about Tyke who can't get it right either. All Tyke wants to do is climb. The school tower is a terrible temptation; its bell hasn't been rung since 1945. Unfortunately, before there's a chance for Tyke to ring that bell, trouble in the shape of Danny, Tyke's best friend, gets in the way. When Danny innocently takes money from a teacher's bag, Tyke tries to help and ends up being blamed for stealing the money. That problem gets sorted out only to be replaced by another, and another.

Tyke's adventures make you laugh but they also make you think, especially at the end of the book when the author springs an amazing surprise!

Gill Vickery

8-11

Next?

- Cricklepit Combined School where Tyke is a pupil has its fair share of students who can't seem to stay out of trouble. Read ***Just Ferret*** and ***Gowie Corby Plays Chicken*** to find out what some more of them get up to.
- Another grey book by Gene Kemp is The Clock Tower Ghost. (UBG 49)
- You might enjoy reading about Jules in Lee Weatherley's ***Child X***. Jules is deeply involved in a school play whilst also juggling with family problems. (UBG 46)
- ***And don't miss our SCHOOL STORIES selections on pp 212-3.***

THE TWELVE AND THE GENII

Pauline Clarke

➡ Max finds the twelve toy soldiers wrapped in an old cloth under a loose floorboard in his family's new home. He knows the soldiers' fortunes are always watched over by 'genii', and is more than happy to take on that role for himself, and guide this boisterous troupe through their imagined battles. Before Max, however, the Twelve had some very famous genii (they used to belong to the Brontës), which makes them even more valuable in the eyes of other people. So Max has to help the Twelve solve their own crises – and save them from theft. Some of the language is quite dated, but I promise if you read this book you too will totally believe in the world of the Twelve.

9-11

Jon Appleton

Next?
- What about a story about real wars? Try ***War Horse*** by Michael Morpurgo (UBG 258) or ***The Machine Gunners*** by Robert Westall (UBG 150).
- And for real battles enacted through toy soldiers, have a look at Iain Lawrence's ***Lord of the Nutcracker Men***. (UBG 147)

TWENTY THOUSAND LEAGUES UNDER THE SEA

Jules Verne

➡ This is the story of the mysterious Captain Nemo, an Indian Prince who doesn't much like people, and the self-contained world of his super-sleek submarine *Nautilus*. When the French naturalist Professor Aronax, his faithful servant Conseil and the Canadian harpooner Ned Land begin a hazardous voyage to rid the seas of a little-known sea-monster, they have no idea that the scary creature will turn out to be *Nautilus* the submarine. Once they have made this discovery, Aronax and the others set out with Nemo to explore the underwater world together. But unbeknownst to the others Nemo's mission is one of revenge …

11+

Sara Wheeler

Next?
- If you want to read about how real submarines were used in wartime, read ***Depth Charge Danger***, by J. Eldridge, in the **Warpath** series.
- Another classic Jules Verne book is ***Around the World in Eighty Days***. (UBG 19)
- If you get the taste for classic adventure, why not try ***King Solomon's Mines*** by H. Rider Haggard. (UBG 135)
- Or for real-life exploration, read ***Kon Tiki: Across the Pacific by Raft*** by Thor Heyerdahl. (UBG 138)

THE TWITS

Roald Dahl

➡ This short novel is about a dreadful couple who play appallingly cruel tricks on one another, and are eventually outwitted by a family of acrobatic monkeys. This may not be one of Dahl's best books: the story is thin, and the only sympathetic characters are the monkeys, who don't really come into the story until the second half. But *The Twits* is still tremendous fun, especially to read aloud, and Quentin Blake's illustrations are priceless. The sheer horribleness of Mr and Mrs Twit and their nasty tricks can't help but make you giggle: Mrs Twit plops her glass eye in Mr Twit's mug of beer; Mr Twit puts a frog in her bed ('I'll bet it's that Giant Skillywiggler I saw on the floor just now,' he tells his terrified wife). Nasty, yes, but fun.

Kenneth Oppel

7-9

Next?
- You might want to read about other dreadful people and events in Roald Dahl's ***George's Marvellous Medicine***. (UBG 89)
- More nasty characters abound in Lemony Snicket's **A Series of Unfortunate Events.** (UBG 217)
- Or try Philip Ardagh's ***The Fall of Fergal*** – it's pretty gruesome too. (UBG 78)

so light, so funny and so effortless-looking. It's pure and simple genius!

TWO WEEKS WITH THE QUEEN Morris Gleitzman

➡ Colin Mudford's younger brother Luke is dying of cancer, or so his parents say. They believe the doctors who say Luke can't be cured. Colin doesn't. He's determined to save his brother.

You have to admire Colin. He knows what's important and he never gives up. When his parents send him to stay with his relations in London, to get him out of the way, he has a brilliant idea – to contact the Queen and get her doctor to fly to Australia and cure Luke. Don't let the subject matter of this story put you off. This story is a mix of sad and funny and hilarious, just like real life. You'll laugh and cry but feel strangely better for reading it.

Julia Jarman

9-11

Next?

- You might want to read ***Bumface*** and other sad funny stories by Morris Gleitzman. His characters always have interesting problems. (UBG 37)
- ***Pig-heart Boy*** by Malorie Blackman tackles illness in a more serious way. (UBG 187)
- Or try ***Up on Cloud Nine*** by Anne Fine, set in a hospital and about friendship and fantasy and strength, rather than illness. (UBG 252)

UG: BOY GENIUS OF THE STONE AGE Raymond Briggs

Next?

- You might also like other books by Raymond Briggs such as ***Fungus the Bogeyman***, which is pure gross-out! (UBG 88)
- ***A is for Aarrgh!*** by William J. Brooke is a very funny story set in the stone age.
- Another really good comic series is the **Asterix** books by Goscinny/Uderzo, all hilarious and all classic. (UBG 21)

➡ Ug and his parents live in an age when everything is made from stone: stone footballs, stone bedspreads and even stone trousers! But Ug is full of new ideas for a better world: one where food is hot, balls bounce and trousers are soft. Unfortunately not everyone shares Ug's vision of the future. Even Ug's own mother can't understand him.

To make things even worse for Ug, his inventions never seem to serve any practical purpose. His round stone that rolls down the hill is great, but what is it actually for? Perhaps with the help of his father he might actually be able to create the soft trousers he has always dreamed of …

This book is humorous, thoughtful and highly original!

Neal Layton

8-10

UNCANNY! Paul Jennings

➡ I remember loving *Unreal!*, Paul Jennings's first collection of twisted, unpredictable tales when I read it, and I've been a fan ever since. Paul writes about ordinary kids who have amazing things happen to them – surprising everyone around them. Mostly, his stories are told in the first person, which makes them very engaging – the narrators are the sorts of people you know from school and your local area. And some are real oddballs.

In *Uncanny!* we start with a corpse that's covered in tattoos from head to foot, then we meet a nude store dummy. Things get even more outrageous after that. No two stories are alike, and there's no way in the world you'll be able to guess how each one will end.

8-11

Jon Appleton

Next?

- Other great Paul Jennings titles include ***Unbearable!***, ***Unbelievable!*** and ***Tongue-tied***.
- You might also enjoy ***Seven Spiders Spinning*** by Gregory Maguire which is both spooky and silly. (UBG 217)
- ***The Day my Bum Went Psycho*** by Andy Griffiths might just be up your street if you like Paul Jennings's stories. (UBG 58) ... and Paul's collaboration with Morris Gleitzman, called ***Wicked!***, will be for sure! (UBG 264)
- And you'll probably like Susan Gates's ***Killer Mushrooms Ate my Gran*** (UBG 133) and ***A Brief History of Slime*** as well!

UNCLE J.P. Martin

➨ Uncle is an enormously rich elephant who normally wears a purple dressing gown. He has many employees and hangers-on and lives in a huge castle of many towers. When I was first asked to draw Uncle, many years ago, I wasn't quite sure how much I liked him; there was no escaping the fact that he was rather pompous. However, I revelled in the extraordinary number of characters in his world, especially the Badfort crowd – a dirty, bristly, badly-behaved collection of layabouts with names like Beaver Hateman, Hitmouse and Jellytussle. All the **Uncle** books are being reissued now, and this gallery of eccentrics and their exploits once more put on show. Watch out for that Hitmouse, though – he's a nasty little piece of work.

8-11

Quentin Blake

Next?

- Try and find one of the stories about ***Babar the Elephant*** by Jean de Brunhoff. The stories are lovely, and the illustrations are brilliant. They're very young, but who cares when they're this good?
- Or for different (but equally sophisticated) animals, try the younger ***Doctor Dolittle*** by Hugh Lofting. (UBG 64)
- For more (but very different) whimsy, try ***Mr Popper's Penguins*** by Richard and Florence Atwater. (UBG 165)

UNDER THE MOON AND OVER THE SEA: A Collection of Caribbean Poems

Edited by John Agard and Grace Nichols

➨ This is a big, bright, lively collection of verse selected by two of my favourite poets: John Agard and Grace Nichols. It is brimming with laughter and fun and delightfully inventive language. Over fifty poems capture the sights and smells, sounds and atmosphere of the Caribbean. There are poems about hurricanes and hummingbirds, crabs and coconuts, clear blue seas and pink coral beaches and much, much more. The collection is divided into five sections each illustrated by an outstanding artist, including my very favourite, Jane Ray. These musical, haunting poems will excite, challenge and inspire all those who hear them.

10-12

Gervase Phinn

Next?

- Try ***Island of the Children, an Anthology of New Poems***, compiled by Angela Huth with decorations by Jane Ray. •
- You'll probably enjoy the vivid story-telling of Joan Aiken's story collection, ***A Necklace of Raindrops***. (UBG 174)
- Or for stories about the Caribbean try Curdella Forbes's ***Flying with Icarus***. (UBG 86)

UP ON CLOUD NINE Anne Fine

➨ What if your best friend was lying in front of you, unconscious and, perhaps, dying? What if you were afraid his fall wasn't an accident?

Ian's best friend Stolly is the craziest, most entertaining and most maddening friend anyone could have. No one can make up a really convincing story like Stolly. In fact, Stolly's so happy inventing stories, living on cloud nine, that the real world sometimes gets just too boring – and then it's Ian's job to keep Stolly on safe ground.

This marvellous book turns an extraordinary story inside out and tells it with great energy and humour. It is a moving book, but a joyful one, too, with really vivid portraits of many comic characters, and a very special friendship.

10+

Sally Prue

Next?

- For another funny story of trouble-prone schoolfriends, try Gene Kemp's great ***The Turbulent Term of Tyke Tiler***. (UBG 249)
- The heroine of Gillian Cross's ***Tightrope*** has trouble fitting in; to create excitement she makes up a sort of double-life. Dealing with some of the same themes as ***Up on Cloud Nine***, this is a darker and more dramatic book. (UBG 252)
- The story of another of Anne Fine's books, ***The Tulip Touch***, is a little bit like this one; but be warned – its main character is a much nastier piece of work than Stolly. (UBG 248) If that sounds too disturbing, try her hilarious ***Flour Babies*** instead. (UBG 86)

UTTERLY ME, CLARICE BEAN

Lauren Child

➡ Clarice Bean is the third child of a family of four who, along with their mum, dad, grandad, Chirp (Grandad's canary), Cement the dog and Fuzzy the cat, live in a permanent state of pandemonium. The household itself provides many a witty situation and a multitude of clever one-liners, but when Clarice Bean steps outside its confines, the madness does not stop. We meet her utterly best friend Betty Moody, her young neighbour the persistent Robert Granger (whom Grandad calls Shouting Boy) and a further wonderful array of characters at her school, who all lend a hand to make this book one of the funniest (including some great laugh-out-loud moments) and most original I've come across in a long time. Read it – you'll be hooked.

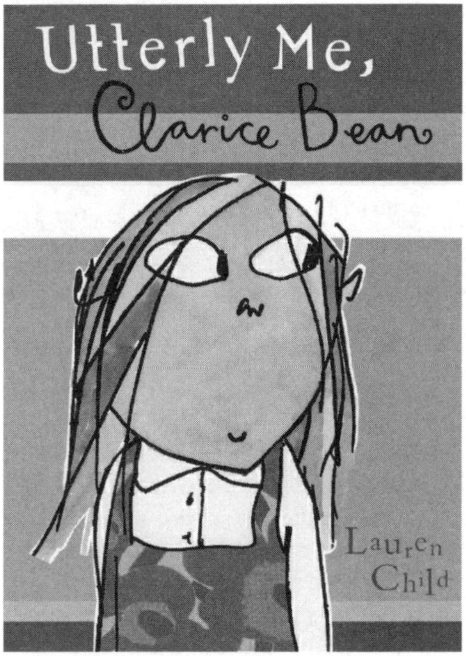

Chris d'Lacey

7-10

Next?

- Although most of the Clarice Bean stories have appeared in picture book format, don't be put off. They're really rather sophisticated and all of them are 'utterly' brilliant. Try ***Clarice Bean, That's Me.*** It's fantastic.
- And if you like wacky characters, have a look at Debi Gliori's **Pure Dead** series. (UBG 195) Great fun – and very strange! Or Philip Ardagh's equally strange stories, **Unlikely Exploits**, that start with ***The Fall of Fergal***. (UBG 78)
- ***Fairy Dust*** by Gwyneth Rees is a fun and surprising look at girls and fairies.

VARJAK PAW S.F. Said

Illustrated by Dave McKean

➡ To be a Mesopotamian Blue, Varjak Paw the kitten knows, is to be a very special cat. But his family's exclusive existence in the house on the hill is threatened by the incursion of the menacing gentleman and his two eerie feline sidekicks. Varjak goes over the wall to the Outside, where the cats don't wear collars. His mission: to find help in the shape of that rumoured monster, a dog.

But what do dogs look like? Those four-wheeled speeding objects, perhaps? And what are the Vanishings?

Aided by street-wise cats and edified by his mystical communication with Great Ancestor Jalal who teaches him The Way, Varjak learns survival and how to succeed in this gripping, fast-moving, wise novel.

8+

Chris Stephenson

Next?

- Maybe you'd like to continue exploring the world from an animal's point of view? If so, try Henry Williamson's ***Tarka the Otter*** (UBG 237), and all those creatures Rudyard Kipling wrote about in ***The Jungle Books*** (UBG 130) and ***Just So Stories*** (UBG 132).
- Look out for Adèle Geras's very funny revelations from Ozymandias the cat in ***The Fabulous Fantora Files***. (UBG 75)
- Two outstanding novels by Henrietta Branford are ***Fire, Bed and Bone***, the story of the Peasants' Revolt as witnessed by a dog (UBG 83), and ***White Wolf***, about a young wolf's quest to find and run with his own kind in the Canadian wastes.

THE VERY PERSISTENT GAPPERS OF FRIP George Saunders, illustrated by Lane Smith

➨ Gappers love goats. Each day, the bright orange, baseball-sized organisms with many eyes, crawl out of the sea to mob the poor animals. The children of Frip have to brush the gappers back into the ocean or else the gappers emit a high-pitched happy shriek of pleasure, causing the goats to stop producing milk. Such is life in the town until, one day, the gappers, led by one with a somewhat larger than average brain, gang up on young Capable's goats because they are closer to the water's edge. See how she manages the problem, through the witty text and lavish illustrations by Lane 'Stinky Cheese Man' Smith. An inspirational fable for readers of all ages – thought-provoking and very funny.

8+

Neal Layton

Next?

- Try another crazy fable, such as Andre Maurois' ***Fattypuffs and Thinifers***. (UBG 82)
- What about some Roald Dahl? ***Charlie and the Chocolate Factory*** is fast and fantastic. (UBG 44)
- What about the totally disgusting ***Fungus the Bogeyman*** by Raymond Briggs? It's wonderful – just don't show it to any adults, they'll think it's too horrible to read. (UBG 88)

A VICARAGE FAMILY

Noel Streatfeild

➨ The main character in this book is Noel Streatfeild herself (named Vicky in the story) and this is a warmly-told account of her childhood as the daughter of a poor parish vicar in the years leading up to the start of the First World War. Vicky, her two sisters and favourite cousin, John, are growing up in the loving but sometimes oppressive environment of the vicarage where Vicky struggles to be understood. Labelled as the difficult one, she suffers the consequences of a fiery nature and an inability to turn the other cheek as her father would like. This is an entertaining, funny and sad account of the years before the prophecy that 'Vicky is the one who will surprise us all ... ' came true.

10-12

Gwyneth Rees

Next?

- If you want to read more by Noel Streatfeild, I strongly recommend ***Ballet Shoes*** (UBG 23) or ***White Boots***.
- Why not try another book based on an author's childhood? Look out for ***Little House on the Prairie*** by Laura Ingalls Wilder (UBG 142) or ***Little Women*** by Louisa May Alcott (UBG 146).
- A story of a young girl growing up under very different circumstances is Jean Webster's ***Daddy-Long-Legs***. (UBG 55)

COMPETITION WINNER ★ COMPETITION WINNER

VICKY ANGEL Jacqueline Wilson

➨ I think this is the best book I've ever read. It's really sad but great at the same time. I like it because this book is like a message that tells you to be strong even when times are tough. It helped me a lot when my uncle died. This book tells you that when times are hard you don't need to cage it all up, because you have friends and family to help you.

My favourite part is when Jade is speaking to Vicky and a woman thinks she is speaking to herself. I'd recommend this book to anyone who loves reading. I think Jacqueline Wilson is a great author.

Amy Jordan, age 11, St John's Middle School

scary! 'You young dog, what fat cheeks you ha' got. Darn me if I couldn't eat 'em ...' It's a great story,

VICKY ANGEL Jacqueline Wilson

➨ Do you have a best friend – someone you spend every moment of your day with? Someone you sit next to at school (unless your teacher has already had to separate you ...), and then phone up the moment you get home? And have you ever wondered what you'd do if your friend suddenly wasn't there any more?

That's what happens to Jade, who suddenly loses her best friend, Vicky – beautiful, confident (and sometimes maybe just a bit selfish) Vicky – who's been her best best best friend since nursery school.

What will Jade do? The only person who can help her cope, who can talk to her, is Vicky, and she's gone – or is she?

Jacqueline Wilson never shies away from difficult subjects – yet however sad her stories, somehow her books always leave you feeling a little better, stronger, happier about the world. And *Vicky Angel* is one of her very best.

Daniel Hahn

9-12

Next?

- To see the story from the other point of view, try ***The Great Blue Yonder*** by Alex Shearer.
- Also read the amazing (and very sad) ***Bridge to Terabithia*** by Katherine Paterson. (UBG 36)
- More about angels? Read about the escapades of Mel and her angelic friends in Annie Dalton's **Angels Unlimited** series. (UBG 14)
- And there are lots of brilliant Jacqueline Wilsons: try ***The Story of Tracy Beaker*** (UBG 229), ***Secrets*** and ***Double Act*** (UBG 67).

THE VILLAGE BY THE SEA Anita Desai

➨ Hari and Lila live with their family in a small fishing town in India. With their mother bedridden and their father always drunk or asleep, Hari and Lila have had to grow up fast. Lila worries about food, she worries about their mother who doesn't seem to get better, and she worries about her father's next rage. Hari is especially concerned about how he will ever make money to feed the family – he knows they are all counting on him.

Desperation and confusion lead Hari to run away to Bombay, where he is forced to learn how to stay alive in a big city. Lila, as a result, is left to cope with everything at home by herself. But in this heart-warming tale neither child is really alone, for they find valuable friends who help them not only to survive, but to find hope for the future too.

Candida Gray

9+

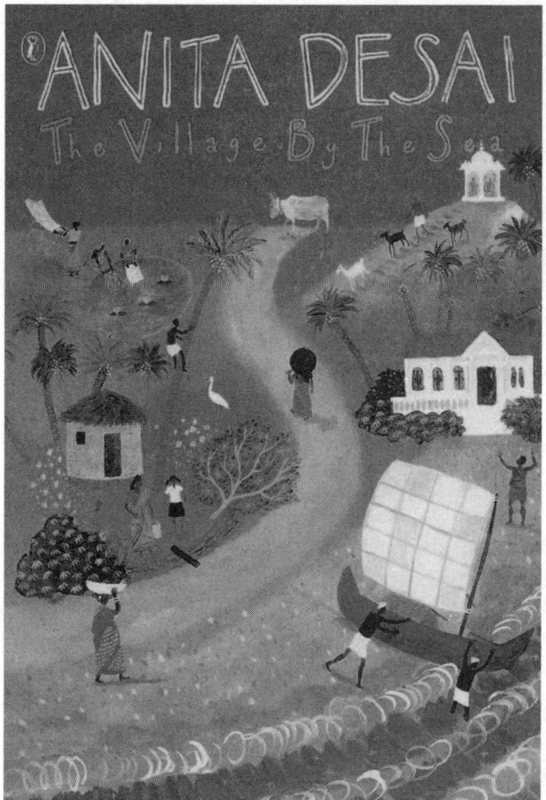

Next?

- For another story about adventure in India, try ***The Track of the Wind*** by Jamila Gavin, from the **Wheel of Surya** trilogy. (UBG 261)
- For Indian children in the UK, try Narinder Dhami's ***Bindi Babes***, the funny, irreverent but moving story of three sisters whose mother has died.
- For a very different book about children having to fend for themselves, read ***Gumble's Yard*** by John Rowe Townsend. (UBG 102)

VLAD THE DRAC Ann Jungman

➨ The hero of this funny book is a little vampire who is squeamish about blood. Like everyone else, Paul and Judy know that vampires don't exist – until, that is, they come across a baby one on holiday in Romania. The pocket-sized Vlad has slept under a stone for a hundred years and begs to be taken back to London with them.

Luckily, Vlad is a vegetarian, but he still manages to cause chaos (in the way that small aliens do when they're left home alone).

Proud, moody and funny, the tiny Vlad has a larger-than-life personality that is completely endearing without being the least bit soppy. His adventures at a football match, a fancy-dress party, school, not to mention a certain leg-biting episode, are hilarious.

Kate Petty

7-9

Next?
• Vlad has lots more adventures! For starters, look out for ***Vlad the Drac Returns***, and ***Vlad the Drac, Superstar***.
• For really funny books about aliens, read ***The Blobheads*** by Paul Stewart. (UBG 31)
• For more (slightly older) vampire stories, read ***The Last Vampire*** by Willis Hall, which is also very funny. (UBG 140)

WALK TWO MOONS

Sharon Creech

➨ The books I like best are both funny and deep like this one.

Thirteen year-old Salamanca has been told by her sorrowing father that her mother, who has disappeared after a bus ride across America, is never coming back.

She refuses to believe this, and her grandparents (a splendidly eccentric and endearing couple) take her on a journey to follow the route her mother took across the heartlands of America – through South Dakota and Wyoming and Yellowstone – to find out what really happened.

As she travels, she tells her grandparents the story of her school friend Phoebe who has a lurid imagination and whose story echoes that of the heroine.

The last chapter, where Salamanca is led to the truth in a valley in Idaho, is so exciting that one finds oneself reading faster and faster – and yet one can't bear to miss a word.

Eva Ibbotson

10-12

Next?
• You might other books by Sharon Creech: ***Absolutely Normal Chaos*** and ***Chasing Redbird*** – about family life at its oddest, and full of wisdom. Or try her ***The Wanderer***. (UBG 257)
• ***Rules of the Road*** by Joan Bauer is another American story full of life and humour. (UBG 205)

WALKABOUT James Vance Marshall

➨ A catastrophic plane crash leaves Mary and Peter alone in the Australian outback, attempting to reach safety. As their big adventure becomes frightening, an Aboriginal boy appears. He helps them find food and water and to understand this stunning, alien landscape. Peter and the boy instinctively make friends, but Mary is afraid of the blackness of his skin, of his maleness and of the thousands of years between her lifestyle and his own.

First published in 1959, *Walkabout* contains language today's reader will find shocking. But the land's vivid beauty and the Aborigines' world-view are so powerfully described, you do not doubt which is the wiser of the two cultures. A beautiful, thoughtful, very grown-up book that will take you to another world.

Helen Simmons

11+

Next?
• You might also want to get hold of the film which just as is intense and vivid.
• If you like adventure against the odds, try ***Hatchet*** by Gary Paulsen, another gripping tale of survival in a harsh, unforgiving landscape. (UBG 107)
• If you want to get more of the Australian bush, try Ivan Southall's ***Ash Road*** – an exciting novel about the terrifying power of a bushfire.

THE WANDERER Sharon Creech

➡ When thirteen-year-old Sophie signs on for a boat trip across the Atlantic, little does she know what she is letting herself in for.

Not only will this trip be a chance for Sophie to get to know her two cousins, Brian and Cody, but it will also provide an opportunity for her finally to come to terms with a tragedy earlier in her life – something so bad that she has buried all conscious memory of it. It's only when the crew of *The Wanderer* find themselves fighting for their lives in a tremendous storm that Sophie allows herself to remember the past.

I adored this book. I particularly liked the way that Sharon Creech makes you work at having to slowly piece together what has happened to Sophie, rather than telling you straight. In some ways it's a bit like a detective story and, when you've finished it, I guarantee you'll want to start it all over again.

Laura Hutchings

10-12

Next?
• Try Tim Bowler's haunting ***River Boy***. (UBG 204)
• Sharon Creech has written lots of books, and they are all worth reading – even if some might be a bit harder than this one. Look out for ***Walk Two Moons*** (UBG 256), ***Ruby Holler*** (UBG 205) and ***Absolutely Normal Chaos***.
• Or try a book by Joan Bauer. ***Squashed*** is brilliant (UBG 224), as is ***Rules of the Road*** (UBG 205).

WAR GAME Michael Foreman

➡ How rare that one person is not only a great artist, but a writer as well. Such is the case with Michael Foreman. He creates in words and pictures the story of a football match on Christmas Day 1914, the first Christmas of the Great War. Standing in the mud and rain of the trenches, faced with gunfire, rats and freezing weather, the soldiers long for home. Yet suddenly someone kicks a football into No Man's Land, and a match begins: England v. Germany. No rules. No referee. Greatcoats and caps for goalposts.

This book is all the more moving when you know that the four English soldiers are really the author's uncles who died in the war, aged between eighteen and twenty-four.

James Riordan

8-10

Next?
• You might like Michael Foreman's personal account of the last world war in the prize-winning ***War Boy***, with his own wonderfully moving illustrations.
• Ian Serraillier's ***The Silver Sword*** is about two young children's journey across war-torn Europe. It's an older, tougher read, but persevere – it is amazing. (UBG 219)
• Or try Michael Morpurgo's ***Friend or Foe*** about two boys who find two downed German airmen or another of his books, ***War Horse*** (UBG 258).

Next?
- Look out for Michael Morpurgo's ***Farm Boy*** (UBG 81) or Michael Foreman's ***War Game*** (UBG 257).
- You may like to read other books about animals. A classic is the horse story ***Black Beauty*** by Anna Sewell. (UBG 29)
- Other animals in war may be found in Martin Booth's ***War Dog***, about a poacher's dog trained to track the enemy and rescue the wounded in France during the Second World War. And don't miss Robert Westall's ***Blitzcat***. (UBG 31)

WAR HORSE Michael Morpurgo

➡ In the village hall close to Michael Morpurgo's farm hangs a small, dusty painting of a horse. The inscription says: 'JOEY. Painted by Captain James Nicholls. Autumn 1914.' *War Horse* is Joey's story, straight from 'the horse's mouth'.

Joey sees all the horrors and cruelty of the Great War (1914-18), the slaughter of men and of the horses that had to pull the guns, carts and supplies. Yet he makes it through the war, only to be sold at auction in France – and probably to be killed for meat. Will he be saved by his friend, Sergeant Albert?

You'll have to read this book to find out …

9-11

James Riordan

THE WAR OF JENKINS' EAR

Michael Morpurgo

➡ 'Take off your slipper!' demands the headmaster.

'Which one, sir?' answers new boy Christopher coolly.

It begins like a normal, old-fashioned boarding school story – Christopher is in trouble for refusing to eat his rice pudding. And yet he is anything but normal. His father is a carpenter and, as he tells his new friend, Toby Jenkins, Christopher can work miracles …

We, like Toby, are kept on tenterhooks: can Christopher really be who he says he is?

War breaks out between the 'Toffs' from school and the town boys, the 'Oiks'. Christopher's powers are put to the test as he tries to bring peace. Toby's success – with friends, rugby and Wanda, sister of the chief Oik – all depends on him.

Jane Darcy

9-11

Next?
- For more cheery tales of life in a boarding school, try the **Jennings** books by Anthony Buckeridge which are all easy to read and extremely funny. (UBG 126)
- For old-fashioned girls' school stories, try the **Chalet School** series by Elinor M. Brent-Dyer. (UBG 43)
- William Mayne's ***A Swarm in May*** is an imaginative story set in a choir school. (UBG 233)
- Of course, there are Michael Morpurgo's other books. See p. 287 for a list of those reviewed in the ***UBG***.

Next?
- Robert Westall wrote many gripping stories of the supernatural. Try ***The Stones of Muncaster Cathedral*** – terrifying! (UBG 227)
- Ann Halam writes wonderfully chilling horror novels, such as ***The Haunting of Jessica Raven*** and ***The Fear Man***.
- Celia Rees has written a scary supernatural trilogy, of which ***City of Shadows*** is the first title.
- And try John Gordon's ghost story ***The Midwinter Watch***, about a train seen travelling – though everyone knows it hasn't run for years …

THE WATCH HOUSE Robert Westall

➡ I've always loved the delicious thrill of a ghost story, but good ones are hard to find. With *The Watch House*, you're in the hands of a master of the macabre.

Anne's mother has dumped her for the summer holidays with an elderly couple living on the cliffs above Garmouth. Bored and lonely, Anne becomes obsessed with the old Watch House nearby, and its store of strange salvage from ships wrecked on the Black Middens. On its dusty shelves are the skulls of drowned sailors.

That is the beginning of an atmospheric and jumpy ghost story that will grip you all the way through, as Anne's frightened attempts to help the ghost of the 'Old Feller' conjure up a far more malevolent force. You probably won't want to read it if you're home alone …

11+

Patricia Elliott

THE WATER BABIES

Charles Kingsley

Next?

- If you enjoyed this, you might like to re-read your favourite fairy tales – especially ***The Snow Queen***. Read about Hans Christian Andersen's fairy tales on p. 76.
- You might also like ***The Secret Garden*** by Frances Hodgson Burnett, which is also about a Victorian orphan. (UBG 215)
- Also try the classic ***The Wind in the Willows*** by Kenneth Grahame (UBG 265) and *any* book written

➨ This is a rather special book. It's nearly one hundred and fifty years old and you might like it best read aloud to you.

Tom is a poor orphan who knows no other life than that of a chimney sweep, working for his cruel master, Mr Grimes. When one day he frightens a little girl, Ellie, asleep in her dazzlingly white room at Harthver House, he is forced to flee for his life. After an epic escape, he drowns – but it's not a tragedy – he turns into a water baby and now his real adventures begin.

He meets all sorts of strange creatures until, guided by Mrs Bedonebyasyoudid and Mrs Doasyouwouldbedoneby, he begins to learn the way to redeem himself and find Ellie.

Jane Darcy

9-11

WATERSHIP DOWN

Richard Adams

➨ I have always loved talking-animal books. This novel is about a 'tribe' of rabbits who have to leave their warren when Fiver, who is a bit of a prophet, foresees a terrible future if they stay. The rabbits go on a long journey, full of incidents and accidents, and finally find a new home. Yet, even as they try to settle peacefully on Watership Down, there is another threat to them, coming from a hostile tribe of rabbits who live not far away.

This is an exciting adventure story that draws you into a world of rabbits, who have their own language and religion, their own way of looking at things, their own way of solving tricky problems.

Garry Kilworth

10+

Next?

- The rabbits in this book talk, but they don't wear clothes or fight and play like humans. For books in which the animals do all those things, try **The Welkin Weasels** series by Garry Kilworth.
- A classic animal-as-animal story (without any talking) is Henry Williamson's ***Tarka the Otter***. (UBG 237)
- ***Don't miss our ANIMAL STORIES recommendations on pp. 16-17.***

WEE FREE MEN Terry Pratchett

Next?

- Eoin Colfer's ***Artemis Fowl*** is another excellent re-evaluation of the role of elves and pixies. (UBG 20)
- Philip Pullman's ***I Was a Rat!*** is another book that questions the fall-out from fairy stories. (UBG 121)
- ***Supergran*** by Forrest Wilson is the only other place where I've found such Scottish colloquialisms as 'Scunner'.
- And of course there are loads more Terry Pratchetts. See p. 287 for a list of those featured in the ***UBG***.
- You might be interested to read Terry's review of T.H. White's ***Mistress Masham's Repose*** – his own favourite 'little people' book. (UBG 162)

➨ This is the story of a girl called Tiffany who realises that she can't be the princess because she isn't blonde, so decides to be the witch instead. But when you want to become a witch on Terry Pratchett's Discworld you can't just enrol in a special boarding school. Still, when her little brother needs rescuing from the evil Queen, Tiffany knows it's up to her to save him. She sets out, helped only by a talking frog and the Wee Free Men: a tribe of tiny blue hooligans who speak an incomprehensible Scottish dialect. It's a superb story that keeps as far away from traditional fairy tale assumptions as the Wee Free Men themselves keep away from the only people they fear: lawyers.

Anthony Reuben

11+

THE WEIRDSTONE OF BRISINGAMEN

Alan Garner

Next?
• This was the first of Alan Garner's books. ***Elidor***, with its oppressive twilight world (UBG 71), and ***The Owl Service***, where the three protagonists are dragged into an ancient legend (UBG 179), are as good, if not better! Read them all and decide for yourself.
• And if you like Alan Garner's books, then you should also try Susan Cooper's **The Dark Is Rising** sequence. Dark, powerful and often deeply disturbing, the whole series is superb. (UBG 57)
• Or Catherine Fisher's **The Book of the Crow** series and try and decide if it is fantasy or science fiction. (UBG 201)

➡ This was the first book I ever read that I found totally unputdownable. I was ten at the time, and read it by torchlight under the bed-covers, desperate to discover what would happen at the end.

Colin and Susan are exploring the countryside around Alderley Edge when they are pursued by sinister creatures that are after the strange glowing 'weirdstone' which Susan wears round her wrist. In a breathtaking journey which takes them down claustrophobic mines, over treacherous wintry moorland and a floating island, and through dark, perilous forests, the two children struggle to deliver the stone to Cadellin, the wizard. If they succeed, the evil Morrigan and her deadly morthbrood will be vanquished. If not ...

I won't spoil the ending – but if you like stories with powerful magic and ancient legends, wizards, witches and forces of light and darkness, then this is the book for you.

9-12

Paul Stewart

WHAT KATY DID

Susan Coolidge

➡ This book was first published in 1872 and gives a wonderful picture of American family life at the time. I identified strongly with its heroine, the tearaway Katy Carr, especially when something similar happened to me. She goes on a new swing after being warned not to and injures her spine. At twelve I found myself lying flat in hospital for months, and naturally I re-read *What Katy Did*. The world can be a hard place, and there's nothing the matter with going to books for comfort.

Like most of the stories of its time it verges on sentimentality but I didn't mind that, or probably even notice. I just loved living with this large extended family, with crabby Aunt Izzy and the near saintly Cousin Helen (I certainly didn't identify with her!). I shared Christmas with them and even cried when someone (I won't tell you who) died ... And I much preferred Katy's brothers and sisters, five of them, to my own bossy brother and quarrelsome sister.

Helen Cresswell

9-11

Next?
• To follow, there's ***What Katy Did at School*** and ***What Katy Did Next***.
• In the same genre is ***Little Women*** by Louisa M. Alcott. (UBG 146) Also try ***Pollyanna*** by Eleanor H. Porter (UBG 192), ***Anne of Green Gables*** by L.M. Montgomery (UBG 17) and the stories about the ***Little House on the Prairie*** by Laura Ingalls Wilder (UBG 142).
• From a later period, and set in the UK, you might enjoy Eve Garnett's ***The Family from One End Street***. (UBG 78)

THE WHEEL OF SURYA

Jamila Gavin

➡ Some stories pull you into another time, another place so completely that you have to shake yourself to come back to the present. *The Wheel of Surya* is like that. From the moment I entered the first chapter, I knew I was on a journey.

It is a terrifying, extraordinary journey for Marvinder and her brother Jaspal. As India moves to Independence in 1947, civil war breaks up the country and the children's family – 'There was death in the wind.'

Separated from their mother and grandmother, the children escape across India and the ocean to find their father in strange, cold England with its different culture. This is the first novel in the **Surya** trilogy and the ending presents a new challenge for Marvinder and Jaspal.

10+

Beverley Naidoo

Next?

- You will feel drawn to read ***The Eye of the Horse*** (set in 1948 with Marvinder and Jaspal in England) and ***The Track of the Wind*** (1951, with the family reunited in India but riven with conflict). By the end you will have been involved in a truly epic voyage.
- A very good book about being a refugee is Morris Gleitzman's ***Boy Overboard***. (UBG 35)
- Anita Desai's ***The Village by the Sea*** is a story set in India, about Hari and Lila, who have to earn money to support their two younger sisters. (UBG 255)

WHEN HITLER STOLE PINK RABBIT

Judith Kerr

➡ Anna is nine years old, living comfortably with her mother, her writer father, her brother Max and housekeeper Heimpi. She is happy at school and has plenty of friends, including her best friend Elsbeth. But this is Germany in 1933. Anna and her family are Jewish. Hitler is just about to come to power and Anna's life will be changed for ever.

Judith Kerr based *When Hitler Stole Pink Rabbit* on her own experiences as a child and this gives the book a fantastic 'being-there' quality which makes it absolutely convincing and riveting to read. The title exactly expresses the utter destructiveness of Hitler's rise to power: stealing lives, childhoods, invading the everyday securities we all take for granted. Through her poignant and vivid depiction of an ordinary family suddenly overshadowed by history, Judith Kerr makes it possible for us to imagine the impossible: what would it be like if such a thing were to happen to us? The novel is a compelling story of survival and adaptation, of hope, love and loyalty. It eloquently demonstrates the triumph of the human spirit in the face of adversity, the very thing that would eventually cause the Third Reich to fail.

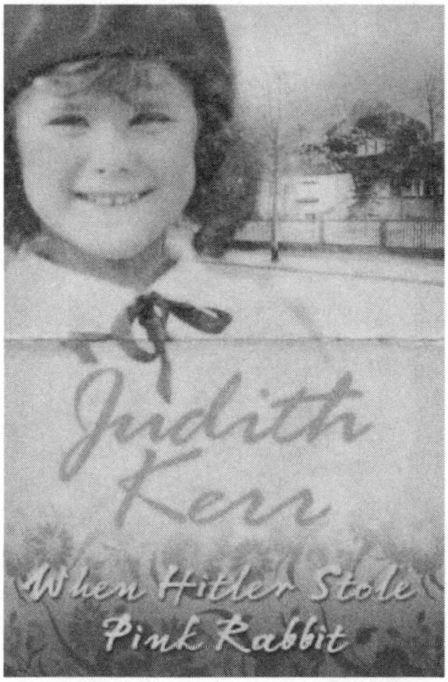

Celia Rees

10-12

Next?

- ***When Hitler Stole Pink Rabbit*** is the first part of an autobiographical trilogy. The other titles are: ***The Other Way Round*** (recently re-published as ***Bombs on Aunt Dainty***) and ***A Small Person Far Away***.
- ***Hurricane Summer*** by Robert Swindells is also set during the Second World War. (UBG 120)
- Other books about how the Second World War affected the lives of children in Europe include Lois Lowry's ***Number the Stars*** and Johanna Reiss's ***The Upstairs Room***.
- For life on the home front read ***Fireweed*** by Jill Paton Walsh.
- For a very different story about a safe and comfortable world turned upside-down, read Lee Weatherly's ***Child X***. (UBG 46)

WHEN MARNIE WAS THERE

Joan G. Robinson

➡ Anna is terrified of letting feelings into her world because she believes that everything she lets in will only be taken away again. She has already lost her family. But when Anna is sent to Norfolk to stay by the sea, she begins to dream of having a friend so secret, so unreal, that they don't really exist and therefore cannot truly be lost at all. Then Anna meets Marnie, who becomes the most real thing in Anna's world ... but is Marnie real? When Marnie disappears, Anna starts to forget her, as if she really was just a dream, and some very real children help her make the leap into the real, concrete world, and discover her own extraordinary story.

Simon Puttock

10-12

Next?
- ***Marianne Dreams*** by Catherine Storr is about a girl who, whilst ill in bed, is seemingly drawn into a world she doodles on to paper. (UBG 154)
- In ***Moondial*** by Helen Cresswell, a sundial in the grounds of an old house holds the key to time-travel.
- For a girl who has lost her identity, but discovers herself through the course of the story, read Tanith Lee's harder but brilliant ***Piratica***. (UBG 190)

WHISPERS IN THE GRAVEYARD

Theresa Breslin

➡ This award-winning story about Solomon, who is trying to come to terms with the bleak cruelties of his life – problems at school, bullying teachers, a drunken father, a runaway mother – is truly poignant. But dyslexia and a disintegrating family life are not the only demons Solomon has to deal with. When workmen dig up the rowan tree that guards the kirkyard where he likes to take refuge, an ancient and hugely malignant force is unleashed ...

A scary horror story, but so much more than just that, Solomon's battle to defeat these demons is a gripping, compulsive read. His predicament and suffering are so powerfully evoked, only those with hearts of stone could fail to be moved.

Neil Arksey

10-12

Next?
- The harder, and just as scary ***Urn Burial*** by Robert Westall, about a megalith, and the disturbing of ancient evils, is a brilliant read. Look for another Westall, ***The Watch House***, too. (UBG 258)
- Robert Swindells spins a scary story in ***The Thousand Eyes of Night***. (UBG 241)
- Theresa Breslin also writes **The Dream Master** books, about a boy who slips back in time to the ancient world.

THE WHITBY WITCHES

Robin Jarvis

➡ Ben and Jennet are sent to live with Alice Boston, a vigorous and eccentric ninety-two-year-old, in the ancient seaside town of Whitby on the Yorkshire coast. But why would an old lady that has never even met the children offer to adopt them, and how will she react to Ben, who is gifted with 'the sight'?

After encountering the mysterious Fisher Folk, Ben, Jennet and Miss Boston are drawn into a desperate struggle against the evil that stalks the dark streets of the town. Any reader who has visited Whitby, famous for being one of the most haunted towns in Britain, will recognise the various landmarks against which this chilling supernatural adventure is played out.

Thomas Bloor

10-12

Next?
- You may want to read the rest of Robin Jarvis's trilogy: ***A Warlock in Whitby*** and ***The Whitby Child***. Or try some of his many other books, such as **The Deptford Mice** trilogy. (UBG 60)
- Diana Wynne Jones's ***Witch Week***, one of the **Chrestomanci** books, also explores how the real world can exist alongside a supernatural realm. (UBG 272)
- Sally Prue's ***Cold Tom*** looks at a similar theme from an unusual angle. (UBG 50)

WHITE FANG Jack London

➡ This book is the story of White Fang, part dog, mostly wolf. It follows him from his days as a puppy in the wilds of north-west Canada, through his time in an Indian camp and his experiences as a fighting dog in a gold-rush frontier town, to the point where he finally finds a master he can trust.

Jack London's great talent lies in his ability to get inside the heads of the animals that he writes about, and he shows you the world from their point of view (I guarantee that you'll never look at the family pet in quite the same way again!). He also tells wonderful stories. The opening chapters of this book are about a hungry wolf pack hunting down two men and their team of dogs, and it's one of the most exciting openings to any book I know.

11+

Laura Hutchings

Next?

- If you enjoyed this story then try Jack London's other famous novel about wolves and dogs, ***The Call of the Wild***. (UBG 38)
- If you enjoy reading about the bond between dogs and their masters then try ***Greatheart***, by Joseph E. Chipperfield.
- And for another story of animals surviving in the wild try Sheila Burnford's ***The Incredible Journey***.

WHO IS JESSE FLOOD? Malachy Doyle

Next?

- Don't miss Malachy Doyle's excellent ***Georgie***. (UBG 90)
- ***Benny and Babe*** by Eoin Colfer, is also about small-town Ireland and is the sequel to ***Benny and Omar***. (UBG 26)
- Or what about Jerry Spinelli's ***Loser***? You can guess something of what it's about from the title, but as with all his books, you can't take anything for granted. (UBG 149)

➡ Life in small-town Ireland isn't much fun when you're fourteen and your mum's left home. Jesse Flood is good at table tennis, but when it comes to girls he hasn't got a clue. He's bored, he feels different from everyone else and, to make matters worse, he fancies the prettiest girl in Greywater.

However, if you share any of the same problems, I'm certainly not recommending that you try what Jesse does to make life more interesting – the beginning of the book finds him in a railway tunnel waiting for a train to come!

Jesse may be bored but this is a really powerful piece of storytelling. You follow him from his first encounter with a girl who wants him for more than his amazing skill with a ping-pong bat, through to what is almost a happy ending. And somewhere along the way, Jesse discovers where he fits in.

11+

Laura Hutchings

WHY WEEPS THE BROGAN?

Hugh Scott

➡ Saxon and her younger brother, Gilbert, have a daily routine – first breakfast and cigars in the *coffee shop*, then fighting off spiders, after that brushing away the remains of broken heads, and finally feeding the horrifying Brogan. They must stick to this rigid routine, because the existence of their strange world depends on it. But Saxon is troubled. She doesn't know why, but when she hears the Brogan howl she gets an eerie shiver down her spine.

Are you confused? This book is a real puzzle, one that will have you turning the pages in burning curiosity. But beware, when you reach the conclusion you are in for a real shock.

11+

Noga Applebaum

Next?

- Try Lesley Howarth's ***Ultraviolet*** – another puzzling tale, set in the future when the sun's radiation makes it impossible to go outside.
- All Hugh Scott's books have a dark and intriguing edge to them. Look out for ***Giants*** and ***The Shaman's Stone***.
- And what about checking out the two mysteries Hugh himself recommends? Look for Agatha Christie's ***The Pale Horse*** (UBG 182) and Arthur Conan Doyle's ***The Hound of the Baskervilles*** (UBG 117).

WHY THE WHALES CAME

Michael Morpurgo

➡ Everyone on the island of Bryher is afraid of the Birdman, a solitary figure who lives on the western shore. He was the last inhabitant of Samson, an island with a terrible curse on it. None of the children are allowed to speak to him but one day Gracie and Daniel find themselves on his beach and meet him face to face. They make a new friend but also begin to discover the awful truth behind the curse.

The beautiful and rugged Isles of Scilly off the coast of Cornwall are the setting for this moving tale of mystery and friendship. The story is told to us directly by Gracie, and vividly conveys her fear, bravery, joy and love at each twist of the tale.

Abigail Anderson

9-11

Next?
- ***The Wreck of the Zanzibar*** is another Michael Morpurgo story set on the Isles of Scilly. (UBG 273)
- Try ***The Snow Goose*** by Paul Gallico, also about a man living alone by the sea and the girl who befriends him. (UBG 221)
- Another book about trying to save something you love is Melvin Burgess's ***Kite***. (UBG 136)

WICKED! series

Paul Jennings and Morris Gleitzman

Next?
- Look out for these Australian authors' other series, ***Deadly!*** Paul Jennings has also written ***Uncanny!*** (UBG 251)
- Another author with a great sense of humour is Jeremy Strong. Try ***My Mum's Going to Explode!*** (UBG 170)
- ***Don't Pat the Wombat*** by Elizabeth Honey is hilarious – and Australian, too! (UBG 66)

➡ Don't you wonder how two authors ever manage to write together? It certainly seems to work, though – *Wicked!* is just as good as the title suggests. It was originally published as six separate books – *The Slobberers*, *Battering Rams*, *Croaked*, *Dead Ringer*, *The Creeper* and *Till Death Do Us Part* – and each story led on to the next one. You can tell from the titles the sort of stories they are – creepy, chilling, gruesome and very, very funny. You can also buy them in one book, called *Totally Wicked!*

Incidentally, they're *fantastic* to read out loud; get someone to read them to you at bedtime – you'll all end up under the bedclothes!!!

8-11

Vivian French

WILLA AND OLD MISS ANNIE

Berlie Doherty

➡ This is a gorgeous little book about a girl called Willa, who makes friends with Old Miss Annie. At first Willa is afraid of her, because she is very old and has twisted hands and a tiny voice, but they become close friends because they share a love of animals. There are three stories in the book, about how Willa and Annie help a goat called Joshua, a pony called Bony and a fox called Vicky.

Berlie Doherty writes with great warmth about the things that matter – sadness and happiness, people and animals, and like all the best stories, her tales stay in the mind long after you've finished them.

Malachy Doyle

7-9

Next?
- You might like the ***Tilly Mint Tales***, also by Berlie Doherty.
- Other good animal stories are ***Charlotte's Web*** by E.B. White (UBG 45) and ***Woof!*** by Allan Ahlberg (UBG 271).
- If you like gentle animal humour, try **Animal Crackers**, a series by Rose Impey. Also try ***The Golden Goose*** (or almost anything else) by Dick King-Smith. (UBG 96)

THE WIND IN THE WILLOWS

Kenneth Grahame

➨ Adventure invades the quiet riverside homes of Ratty, Mole and Badger when Mr Toad and his motor car come to visit. Conceited, excitable, swaggering, untrustworthy – yet goodhearted at the core – Mr Toad soon gets himself and all his friends into trouble. Bad trouble indeed. Toad is taken by the police to jail and while he lies in prison, the others try to recover from his mistakes. Will Toad's friends gain the courage they need? Only if they can band together to win back Toad Hall from the weasels and stoats, can they become heroes in spite of themselves.

This book was originally a series of bedtime stories told by Kenneth Grahame to his young son. When the boy went off with his governess to the seaside for a vacation, his father continued to tell him stories by letter. Mrs Grahame saved the letters and they were finally turned into the book.

Jane Yolen

➨ Read *The Wind In the Willows*, by Kenneth Grahame – the full version, not the 'retold' versions around now. Sure, it looks like a gentle tale about dressed-up animals, but it is highly strange (a toad is big enough to drive a car but can get down a water-rat hole, and is green and knobbly but can still be disguised as a washerwoman ... I mean, you don't have to be a great beauty to wash clothes, but ... really?) Anyway, that actually makes it far more fun. And don't skip the chapters 'A Piper at the Gates of Dawn' and 'Wayfarers All'. The best of all animal stories. I read it, aged ten, in the back of a car by passing streetlights and it turned me into a reader overnight.

Terry Pratchett

9-11

Next?

- Try Rudyard Kipling's ***The Jungle Book*** which is about more real animals this time, though they still talk to each other. (UBG 130)
- For another wild and exciting talking-animal story try Roald Dahl's ***James and the Giant Peach*** which has just as much adventure, but with talking insects. (UBG 126)
- Something more challenging? Try Brian Jacques's **Redwall** series, with fighting mice and a mad, dangerous one-eyed rat as the villain. (UBG 199)
- Or something gentler, easier – lovely ***Winnie-the-Pooh*** by A.A. Milne. (UBG 266)

THE WIND ON THE MOON

Eric Linklater

➨ I've always loved this story and have never read anything quite like it. Larger than life, it will fill your imagination.

There is wind on the moon, and it has blown straight into the hearts of Dinah and Dorinda, which means they will behave badly for a whole year. And indeed they find themselves in more and more trouble, until finally they run away on a daring mission to rescue their father from captivity in a distant country.

This story is such a wonderful mixture that it's hard to describe. It's a pacy adventure, a magical fantasy – gleeful and inventive, ridiculously zany, yet full of commonsense. And I've never been able to see a furniture van again without being reminded of it. You'll see what I mean ...

Patricia Elliott

8-11

Next?

- You probably know Roald Dahl's books already – darker and more anarchic than ***The Wind on the Moon***, but perhaps you haven't read his ***Danny, the Champion of the World***, about a boy and his father who live together in a caravan. (UBG 56)
- And try the anarchic *and* ridiculous Lemony Snicket's **A Series of Unfortunate Events** (UBG 217)
- Another fantasy novel with a quest element is Philip Pullman's ***The Firework-Maker's Daughter***. (UBG 84)

Next?

- You certainly shouldn't miss the sequels, ***Slaves of the Mastery*** and ***Firesong***.
- If you want to read more fantasy, why not try Katherine Roberts's **Echorium Sequence**, beginning with ***Song Quest***. Or for something a bit more challenging, move on to the classic ***The Lord of the Rings*** by J.R.R. Tolkien. (UBG 148)
- If you were interested in the colour-coded city of Aramanth and want to explore the idea of social control further, you might like to try ***The Giver***, by Lois Lowry, also about a very controlled future. (UBG 93)

THE WIND SINGER William Nicholson

➨ This warm-hearted fantasy tells the story of the Hath family, who live in the cramped Orange District of the city of Aramanth in the shadow of an ancient artefact called the 'wind singer'. When baby Pin-Pin makes a mess (literally!) of her first examination, the family is in danger of being demoted to Maroon District. But Kestrel and her brother Bowman rebel against their city's exam culture, and set out on a quest to discover the source of the evil that grips Aramanth.

So begins the first book in a fast-moving fantasy trilogy with the sort of writing that conjures up fantastic scenes in the reader's mind. The world of the wind singer is sometimes beautiful and occasionally terrifying – perhaps not surprising when you consider William Nicholson also wrote the script of the film *Gladiator*.

In this book you will meet the unpopular but brave Mumpo, who becomes Kestrel's friend when she is sent to the bottom of the class, the terrifyingly single-minded Zars, a very sad Emperor, and some unusual pirates. Kestrel, Bowman and Mumpo are endearing characters who make their world come alive without the need for massive amounts of background and detail that can sometimes make books set in such fantastic worlds a bit hard to swallow.

11+

Katherine Roberts

WINNIE-THE-POOH A.A. Milne

➨ Don't be distracted by the Walt Disney versions of these stories. The actual books with pictures by E.H. Shepard are what you should aim for.

Winnie-the-Pooh (a toy bear) and his owner, Christopher Robin, are briefly introduced in the first pages of the book, after which the reader plunges into a series of small comical adventures involving Winnie-the-Pooh, Christopher Robin and a variety of other toys. The characters do not change. Winnie-the-Pooh is always hungry for honey. Piglet is always easily alarmed. Owl is always wise (but in a blundering way) and Christopher Robin always there to rescue them from any difficulties they might get into. The stories are funny and affectionate but every now and then they can be moving too.

This book is such a classic that any more comment is probably unnecessary. The stories are wonderful fun to read aloud and the ties of affection and friendship reassure the reader and listener.

7+

Margaret Mahy

Next?

- Read other books by A.A. Milne – there's a sequel, ***The House at Pooh Corner***, and two collections of poems: ***When We Were Very Young*** and ***Now We Are Six***.
- It is worth reading the stories about Paddington Bear by Michael Bond, beginning with ***A Bear Called Paddington***. (UBG 24)
- Readers who have enjoyed this book would probably also enjoy the **Uncle** books by J.P. Martin. (UBG 252)
- The **Mary Plain** series by Gwynedd Rae is about 'an unusual first-class bear'! (UBG 156)
- Or for something a little harder, try ***The Wind in the Willows*** by Kenneth Grahame. (UBG 265)
- ***Look at our ANIMAL STORIES suggestions on pp. 16-17.***

THE WISH LIST Eoin Colfer

Next?
- For more of Eoin Colfer's comic characters, fizzing dialogue and surreal plots, try his other books, such as ***Artemis Fowl***. (UBG 20)
- You might then want to graduate to Douglas Adams's laugh-out-loud funny stories, beginning with ***The Hitchhiker's Guide to the Galaxy***. (UBG 109)
- For a very different look at death try David Almond's darker tale, ***Kit's Wilderness***. (UBG 135)

➡ The devil wants the soul of Meg Finn. But Meg, who has just been killed taking part in a bungled armed robbery, hasn't turned up in hell. Not yet. Her one good deed – pleading for the life of her pensioner victim, Laurie McCall – means she's allowed the chance to redeem herself. She must somehow help McCall achieve the four impossible-sounding ambitions on his Wish List.

The evil Belcher – half teenager, half pit-bull – dogs their every move. Their unlikely adventures are hilarious, but touching too: Meg isn't the only character to get a second shot at life, as the rejuvenated McCall discovers.

Jane Darcy

9-12

THE WISHING CHAIR series

Enid Blyton

➡ Mollie and Peter have a wishing-chair that lives in the playroom at the bottom of their garden. On their first adventure in the chair they rescue a pixie called Chinky, and from then on, the three have lots of adventures together. It's always exciting and sometimes a little bit scary as the chair flies the children and Chinky up and away to places such as the Land of Spells and the Island of Surprises. There they encounter goodies including the Windy Wizard and Mr Spells, and baddies like the Slipperies, Giant Twisty and the Snoogle.

If you ever dreamed of living in a world that really was full of magic and fairy folk if you only knew where to look, then these are the books for you!

Gwyneth Rees

7-9

Next?
- If you liked these then you're bound to like Enid Blyton's stories in the **Magic Faraway Tree** series. (UBG 151)
- Don't forget to look out for the rest of the series, such as ***The Enchanted Wood***.
- If you want to read another adventure about children who escape to a magic land, why not try J.M. Barrie's ***Peter Pan***. (UBG 184)

WITCH CHILD Celia Rees

Next?
- The sequel to this book is called ***Sorceress*** and continues the story of Mary's life in America. Celia has also written several other gripping and hard-hitting teenage books and if you like these longer, gutsier stories, you could also try one of Anne Cassidy's **Point** books.
- For another feisty, misunderstood heroine, try Tamora Pierce's ***First Test***, the first in the **Protector of the Small** series. (UBG 194)
- Or more witches? What about ***The Witch Trade*** by Michael Molloy? (UBG 269)

➡ This book is in diary form, just as if it had been written by a girl-witch in the seventeenth century. So good is the research undertaken, so effortlessly are the ways and language of the century depicted, you really do believe it's all true.

Mary is the witch child. Her grandmother has just been hanged as a witch and Mary knows that she has inherited the same dark powers. It is thought best that Mary should go to America and try to start a new life where no one knows her background (and just who is the mysterious woman who helps with the journey?). But travelling by boat is a perilous process – and the long, tiresome journey must be undertaken without arousing the suspicions of the sullen crowd that Mary must accompany.

Mary Hooper

11+

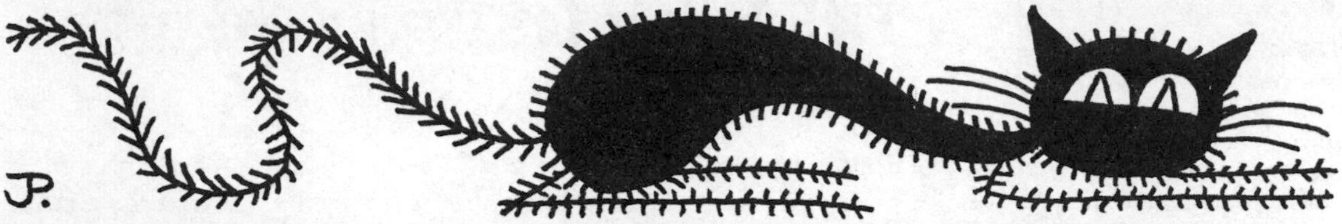

EVERYBODY'S FAVOURITE...

THE WITCHES Roald Dahl

Next?
• Other Dahl? They're all good, but start by reading ***Matilda*** (UBG 157) and the ***BFG*** (UBG 27) – if you haven't already.
• Or Neil Gaiman's ***Coraline*** which is wonderful but very scary. (UBG 51)

➨ While holidaying at a seaside hotel with his beloved grandmother, our young hero stumbles upon a witches' convention and overhears their diabolical plan: to turn all the children of England into mice. Unfortunately, before he can escape, the boy is sniffed out by the Grand High Witch, and turned into a mouse himself! Undaunted, the boy-mouse teams up with his grandmother to turn the tables on these child-hating witches.

Parents will find this a much creepier book than children: the idea of witches dressed up as sweet, normal women, preying on unsuspecting boys and girls is terrifying to any mother or father. The story starts off a bit slowly, but once the hero is racing around the hotel as a mouse, plotting to foil the witches, there is all-out excitement. The boy's cigar-smoking grandmother is a terrific character, and she and her grandson have a wonderfully tender relationship. And I loved the book's unusual ending!

Kenneth Oppel

➨ Is Roald Dahl the greatest children's writer of all time? Quite possibly. I actually missed out on most of his books when I was a kid. It was only in my teens that I started to read his work – but I soon made up for lost time! I devoured just about everything of his that I could find. He wrote so many classics; but if I had to pick a single favourite, it would have to be *The Witches*.

The Witches is a cauldron of sheer, mischievous joy. Whenever I read it I can imagine Dahl as he wrote about the ugly, evil mistresses of mayhem. He must have been laughing his socks off as he went deliciously over the top! These witches have none of the redeeming qualities of many modern-day, watered-down fictional witches. No political correctness in this book! It's all about weird, wicked, wonderful fun!

I can't give away all the secrets, but this is all typical Dahl, and sums up what makes him different and gives him an edge. He did what other writers didn't dare, and cocked a snook at the rules. In fact, he behaved pretty much the same way that stubborn, carefree children all around the world behave! That's probably why so many of us love his books – we can see our own dreaming, individual, prankish selves within them.

9-11

Darren Shan

Here are twelve more stories featuring witches and wizards:

• ***Harry Potter and the Philosopher's Stone*** by J.K. Rowling
• ***The Worst Witch*** by Jill Murphy
• ***Pongwiffy*** by Kaye Umansky
• ***Lizzie Dripping*** by Helen Cresswell
• ***Mr Majeika*** by Humphrey Carpenter
• **The Worlds of Chrestomanci** series by Diana Wynne Jones
• ***The Witches*** by Roald Dahl
• ***Witch Child*** by Celia Rees
• **The Young Wizards** series by Diane Duane
The Sword in the Stone by T.H. White
• **The Dark Is Rising** sequence by Susan Cooper
• **Jessica Haggerthwaite** books by Emma Barnes

? If you're looking for A Wizard of Earthsea by Ursula Le Guin, turn to p. 69 ?

THE WITCH OF BLACKBIRD POND Elizabeth George Speare

➨ Orphaned Katherine (Kit) Tyler makes her way from seventeenth-century Barbados to Puritan Connecticut. High spirited, free thinking and independent, everything about Kit is different, from her plantation upbringing in the care of her beloved grandfather to her colourful clothes. She immediately clashes with the strict beliefs and dour lifestyle of her aunt's household, and finds it very hard to adjust. Torn between her desire to belong to her new family and her need to stay true to herself, she finds a kindred spirit in old Hannah Tupper, a Quaker and social outcast whom the local people fear as a witch. Despite intimations of danger, Kit completely underestimates the fear and prejudice growing around her ...

This book is a gem. Elizabeth George Speare brings the whole period to life through her highly likeable heroine. Kit's story is utterly compelling, with a suitably satisfying ending – what more could a reader want?

10-12

Celia Rees

Next?
• If you're interested in witch persecution in New England, you might like to read ***The Crucible***, a play by Arthur Miller.
• Or try ***Witch Child*** by Celia Rees (UBG 267) or Chris Priestley's Salem book, ***Witch Hunt***.
• ***Burning Issy*** by Melvin Burgess is about a girl and her flight from the witch-finders.
• If you are interested in reading about wicca and witchcraft, Kate West's ***The Real Witches Handbook*** is a well-informed source of information.
• There are lots of tie-ins to the TV series ***Buffy the Vampire Slayer***, for one about their resident witch, read ***The Willow Files I*** and ***II*** by Yvonne Navarro.

THE WITCH TRADE Michael Molloy

➨ There are three types of witches – Light Witches, who are good, Night Witches, who are evil, and Sea Witches, who trade in the Ice Dust that gives the Light Witches their powers. But the Night Witches have discovered a way to make Black Dust out of Ice Dust, and with this and a host of other evil inventions, they want to destroy the Light Witches. Enter the children, Abby and Spike, who must help the Light Witches and their friends to find a supply of Ice Dust, rescue the Night Witches' child-slaves and save Abby's parents. This exciting fantasy will take you to the bottom of the ocean, to the murky shores of the River Thames and even to Antarctica.

Sherry Ashworth

9-11

Next?
• There's a sequel called ***The Time Witches***. It's just as action-packed, and takes you back to the year 1894.
• Fans of Michael Molloy's fantasy will also enjoy the **Harry Potter** books. (UBG 106)
• Or what about ***Which Witch*** by Eva Ibbotson or C.S. Lewis's **Narnia**, another wonderful series about good and evil (UBG 141)?

THE WIZARD OF OZ L. Frank Baum

➨ You have probably seen the classic Judy Garland film version of this book, in which Dorothy flies 'over the rainbow' to the Land of Oz, and finally returns home after triumphing over the Wicked Witches of both East and West. Now don't get me wrong, I do think the film is one of the best ever made. But the book is different. For a start it's longer, and takes us on after the second witchy demise, and we see what becomes of the Scarecrow, the Tin Woodman and the Lion. But the best reason you should read it is for its darkness. There's a menacing vein running through the book that's just not evident in the film. The passage with the flying monkeys is truly chilling, and despite its sometimes quaint language, this is one classic not to overlook.

Marcus Sedgwick

9-11

Next?
• L. Frank Baum wrote hundreds of sequels to it. Well, a dozen or so, at least. Look out for ***The Emerald City of Oz*** and ***Glinda of Oz***.
• Or you could try some other classic fantasy stories, such as ***Peter Pan*** by J.M Barrie (UBG 184), or ***The Box of Delights*** by John Masefield (UBG 34).
• The best English equivalent of the Oz stories is ***Alice's Adventures in Wonderland***. (UBG 12)

> **Next?**
> • For another story where myth is woven into reality, try Diana Wynne Jones's ***Fire and Hemlock***.
> • You may enjoy Adèle Geras's **Egerton Hall** series, also based on fairy tales. Start with ***The Tower Room***.
> • ***The Call of the Wild*** by Jack London is a powerful animal tale. (UBG 38)
> • Or how about ***Beauty***, which is really ***Beauty and the Beast***, the uncut version. (UBG 25)
> • Gillian Cross has written many other books – check out ***Tightrope***, in which a mysterious stalker is terrifying a teenage girl. (UBG 242)

WOLF Gillian Cross

➨ Cassy has been living with her Nan ever since she can remember. Every now and again there's a mysterious tap on the door in the middle of night, after which Cassy is always sent off to stay with her dysfunctional mother for a few weeks. This time she joins her mother and her performing friends in a squat where they prepare their new show about wolves. This is a subject that Cassy finds unsettling, as these fierce animals haunt her nightmares, and she doesn't know why. Her life is wrapped up in secrets, and no one, not even her mother, is telling the truth. Cassy decides she had enough. This time she wants some answers. But can she face the horrible consequences? If elements of this excellent thriller remind you of Little Red Riding Hood, it's no coincidence …

10-12

Noga Applebaum

THE WOLVES OF WILLOUGHBY CHASE

Joan Aiken

➨ Bonnie Green and her loving parents live happily at Willoughby Chase, even though it is a long, cold winter and the wolves are howling all around. When cousin Sylvia comes to stay, Bonnie feels things could not get any better. But Mama is very ill and must go to a warmer climate and so Miss Slighcarp is brought in to look after the two girls.

Once Bonnie's parents are out of the way, Miss Slighcarp and her nasty allies Mr Grimshaw and Mrs Brisket take over the house and send Bonnie and Sylvia to a school where they have their heads shaved, eat next to nothing and work like slaves. However, Bonnie finds she still has friends – Simon the gooseboy, and two faithful servants who help sort the whole wicked mess out.

This is an exciting tale set in the nineteenth century, full of wonderful characters – great villains, enchanting heroines and faithful friends.

9-11

Ann Jungman

> **Next?**
> • You will certainly enjoy the other rollicking adventures by Joan Aiken set in the imaginary reign of James III; these feature another daring heroine, Dido Twite, including ***Black Hearts in Battersea***, ***Nightbirds on Nantucket***, ***Dido and Pa*** and ***Cold Shoulder Road***.
> • Try ***Journey to the River Sea*** by Eva Ibbotson, in which our heroine finds herself up the Amazon with as bad a bunch of nasties as you could ever hope to meet. (UBG 129)
> • ***The Secret Garden*** is a nineteenth-century classic by Frances Hodgson Burnett, in which the sour orphan Mary is gradually turned into a happy child again (UBG 215).
> • ***Read about Joan Aiken's own favourite ADVENTURE STORIES on pp. 10-11.***

THE WONDERFUL STORY OF HENRY SUGAR AND SIX MORE

Roald Dahl

➨ All the short stories in this collection are great. Roald Dahl brings to them his usual mix of humour and originality. But the best of the lot is 'Henry Sugar' itself.

Imagine if you could learn to look through the back of a playing card and see what was on the other side. Imagine how useful that would be if you went to a casino … Henry Sugar, a rich, lazy, arrogant man, teaches himself how to do just this. Suddenly he has more earning power than anyone else in the world. But is it going to make him happy?

This is a supremely entertaining, imaginative, satisfying, pleasing story. You'll probably want to read it lots of times over. I certainly did.

10+

Susan Reuben

Next?
- There are lots of Roald Dahls to choose from. Why not try ***Boy***, the true story of his own childhood (UBG 34), and its sequel, ***Going Solo*** (UBG 96)? ***Charlie and the Chocolate Factory*** is a classic Dahl story. (UBG 44)
- If you like short stories, try Janni Howker's ***Badger on the Barge***. (UBG 22) Or maybe ***Counting Stars*** by David Almond. (UBG 52)

WOOF! Allan Ahlberg

➨ *Woof!* is the story of a boy who one evening, lying in bed, turns into a Norfolk terrier. This causes more problems than you might imagine. Like what to do when his parents throw him out of the house, how to get something to eat, and how to find some clothes to put on when he changes back …

This is one of my favourite books. Eric Banks is an ordinary boy in a very un-ordinary situation, and the way he and his friend Roy work out the best way to deal with the problem and find out what is causing it to happen make for a story you can't help but enjoy.

8-10

Andrew Norriss

Next?
- You might like to try ***Please Mrs Butler***, a collection of poems (many of them hilarious) also by Allan Ahlberg. Or his hilarious novel, ***The Giant Baby***. (UBG 92)
- And if you enjoyed the story because you liked reading about animals, there are several other writers who follow the same theme. Dick King-Smith is one of the best. He wrote ***The Sheep-Pig*** (UBG 218), which was made into the film 'Babe' and ***Harry's Mad*** about a very intelligent parrot. Rose Impey's **Animal Crackers** stories are also hugely popular.

THE WOOL-PACK Cynthia Harnett

➨ It is 1493 and Nicholas Fetterlock is the son of a wealthy wool merchant. His life seems just fine: out in the fields most of the time, a bit of schooling, and a best friend in Hal the shepherd's boy. But Nicholas is growing up, and is soon to be betrothed to Cecily, an eleven-year-old girl he has never met! On top of that, he discovers that his father's business is being ruined by Italian loan-sharks, and his uncle wants to beat Columbus to the Indies …

What begins as a pleasing journey through the Cotswolds of lush fifteenth-century England soon grows in pace to become a tense mystery, where dastardly deeds are afoot. Nicholas, Hal, and Cecily must find a way to unmask the villains and bring them to justice. This wonderful story shows that children have always been ingenious, even if parents have always been slow to believe it.

10+

Simon Puttock

Next?
- ***A Little Lower Than the Angels*** by Geraldine McCaughrean is another story about mediaeval England, this time about performing in Mystery Plays. (UBG 143)
- Or set a little later, but a great story of villains and heroes and justice prevailing, read Geoffrey Trease's ***Cue for Treason***. (UBG 55)
- Kate Thomson's ***The Alchemist's Apprentice*** is another mediaeval story about a boy on the run.

Next?
• Read anything else by Diana Wynne Jones. You never know what she'll think of next, from a young girl who discovers that being turned into an old woman can be liberating (***Howl's Moving Castle***) to a world where people from our world go on fantasy quest tours, complete with magic (***Dark Lord of Derkholm***), to the trials of a boy who accidentally frees a Norse god (***Eight Days of Luke***). (UBG 71) Wynne Jones's numerous titles will give even the most determined reader many weeks of enjoyment.
• Or try Terry Pratchett's ***The Amazing Maurice and his Educated Rodents***, which takes the story of the Pied Piper, turns it on its head, bounces it several times and throws it into orbit. (UBG 12)

THE WORLDS OF CHRESTOMANCI

CHARMED LIFE • THE MAGICIANS OF CAPRONA • WITCH WEEK • THE LIVES OF CHRISTOPHER CHANT

Diana Wynne Jones

➡ They're set in different places and different times, but these books have one thread in common: sooner or later, the current holder of the title of Chrestomanci will show up, particularly if you speak his name!

The Chrestomanci is a kind of Minister of Magic. He crosses between worlds to sort out magical problems. Magic in worlds overseen by Chrestomanci takes countless forms, from the sort that drags schoolgirls on broomstick rides to the kind that takes you to worlds where mermaids sing and a magical girl priestess wants nothing more than to attend an English boarding school. With cats, witches, music, spell-crafting families who fight like the families of Romeo and Juliet, witch hunts and people being dragged from one world into the next, you never know what interesting new twist Diana Wynne Jones will put into a story. You just have to keep reading her to see what's new!

Tamora Pierce

9-11

THE WORST WITCH Jill Murphy

➡ Everything goes wrong for Mildred Hubble in her first term at Miss Cackle's Academy for Witches. Even her black cat turns out to be a tabby kitten. Miss Cackle herself is absent-minded but their form mistress, tall, thin Miss Hardbroom, is scary, especially as she can make herself invisible and is likely to reappear at just the most embarrassing time.

Follow the adventures of Mildred, her best friend Maud and her sworn enemy Ethel Hallow as they learn all about magic spells and chanting and flying on broomsticks.

Kate Petty

7-9

Next?
• You will want to move on to ***The Worst Witch Strikes Again*** straight away, followed by ***A Bad Spell for the Worst Witch*** and ***The Worst Witch All at Sea***, all by Jill Murphy.
• **Harry Potter** by J.K. Rowling, really. It is just so good. (UBG 106)
• For another story of magic, with a cat as well, try ***Carbonel*** and its sequels by Barbara Sleigh. (UBG 41)
• And try ***Jessica Haggerthwaite: Witch Dispatcher*** by Emma Barnes. (UBG 127)

Illustration by Xara Bennet Jones, age 10, Headington Junior School

WORZEL GUMMIDGE

Barbara Euphan Todd

Next?
• I love the kind of fantasy that weaves into ordinary everyday life, and ***Worzel Gummidge*** is just that. So is Mary Norton's ***The Borrowers*** (UBG 33) and Clive King's ***Stig of the Dump*** (UBG 226); and so, if I may say so, are most of my own fantasies – ***The Night-Watchmen***, ***The Bongleweed*** and ***A Gift from Winklesea.***
• You could also try books by E. Nesbit. In ***The Phoenix and the Carpet*** and ***Five Children and It*** (UBG 85), a group of children make friends with some extraordinary, magical creatures.

➨ *Worzel Gummidge* was the book chosen for reprinting in a facsimile edition to celebrate forty years of Puffin Books. I'm not surprised. This is a book for every child. Who wouldn't want Gummidge the scarecrow for a friend? 'He was such a nice sort of betwixt and between person, not quite grown up though he seemed as old as the fields, and yet not quite a child either, though in some ways he seemed as young as they were.' He is funny, unpredictable, and given to fits of the sulks. 'Ooh aye,' he says, 'ooh aye'. He has a comical turn of phrase, and says of his Aunt Sally, 'Ooh aye, I hates her as much as a worm hates ducklings. If I could find a hatchet I'd chop her up.' Then there's his little brown-faced girlfriend Earthy Mangold and all the other scarecrow relations, including a baby. Oh, and he has a robin nesting in his jacket pocket. I read the book from cover to cover yesterday and loved every word of it. So will you. Ooh aye. Trust me.

8-11

Helen Cresswell

THE WRECK OF THE ZANZIBAR

Michael Morpurgo

Next?
• Michael Morpurgo has written many other books, and they are all worth reading. In particular, try ***Twist of Gold*** about an Irish family fleeing the famine at home to find a new life in America. Or try his ***My Friend Walter***, about a girl encountering the very mischievous ghost of Sir Walter Raleigh.
• If you find yourself interested in the sailing part of this book, try ***Swallows and Amazons***, by Arthur Ransome, and its sequels, most of which involve water and boats in some way. (UBG 232)

➨ This book has the sound of the sea in it. Taking the form of a diary, it covers a few months in the life of a young girl on the Isles of Scilly at the beginning of the twentieth century. Michael Morpurgo's wonderful, lyrical prose depicts the hardship, the joy, and the undaunted spirit of those who live by the ocean; and in particular of Laura, whose story this is.

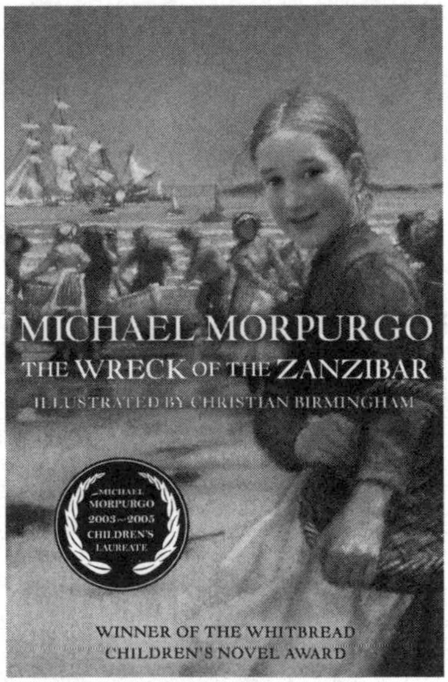

We accompany her through a season of terrifying storms and misfortunes, and see the island and the islanders through her eyes. She writes of her anxiety on finding a dying turtle, her sadness at being separated from her beloved brother, and her excitement at seeing the wrecked sailing ship which may bring salvation to her people. The book is made even more poignant by being linked to the storyteller in the present day. We feel privileged to read Laura's diary along with him, and discover the legacy she leaves for the children of Bryher Island.

The text is interspersed with, and enhanced by, Christian Birmingham's atmospheric illustrations.

A story to be read aloud, read alone, and shared with others.

8-11

Theresa Breslin

A WRINKLE IN TIME

Madeleine L'Engle

➡ This wonderfully inventive book is set partly in America and partly in the furthest reaches of the imagination. Meg's father is a top scientist, working for the Government. When he disappears, Meg and Charles, her little brother, together with their friend Calvin, set off to find him, with the help of three strange old women who are not what they seem ...

In fact, nothing is ever quite what it seems in this fantasy world. The book keeps the reader guessing all the way through, as the children and their three weird companions battle dark forces to rescue Dad from the clutches of a loathsome entity known as IT.

IT controls an entire planet – and is even casting its evil shadow over Earth. The only way to reach it is through a wrinkle in time. But once the children get there, will they ever be able to get back?

Message to all fans of fantasy, sci-fi and nail-biting excitement: read this book!

9-12

Jean Ure

Next?
- Try Philip Reeve's wonderful ***Mortal Engines***. (UBG 164)
- Or the playful ***Handful of Magic*** by Stephen Elboz, in which London is almost the same as we know it, but not quite ... (UBG 106)
- Or try ***Swiftly Tilting Planet***, also by Madeleine L'Engle.
- And do look out for Penelope Lively's wonderful ***A Stitch in Time***. (UBG 226)

YOU'RE THINKING ABOUT DOUGHNUTS

Michael Rosen

➡ If the title of this book is meant to intrigue the prospective reader and give no clue as to its subject matter, it certainly succeeds. Many children will have experienced the prospect of trying to amuse themselves for a couple of hours in a mother's workplace. In this case the setting is a museum and Frank is accosted by a skeleton who in the course of the story introduces him to characters of history and legend through sequences of fantasy-day-dreams. Through these, the reader – and Frank – embarks on a journey in which fact has to be sorted out from fiction.

8-10

Anthony Buckeridge

Next?
- Don't miss reading Michael Rosen's poetry – his poems deal with all sorts of subjects and keen readers should enjoy them immensely. There are various collections of his work.
- ***Puck of Pook's Hill*** (UBG 195) and ***Rewards and Fairies*** by Rudyard Kipling are other stories about being introduced to history in a strange and magical way. They're both quite a bit harder reads, but well worth the effort.

THE YOUNG VISITERS

Daisy Ashford

➡ This is not a children's book written by an adult but an adult story written by a child! It was published in 1919, nearly thirty years after it was written by nine-year-old Daisy Ashford. It tells the story of Mr Salteena who 'was an elderly man of forty-two and was fond of asking people to stay with him'. He falls in love with Ethel, who in turn falls in love with Bernard, who has 'tough sunburned arms' and 'very nice legs'. Poor Mr Salteena doesn't stand a chance. Daisy has obviously read a lot of adult romances (as I did myself as a child) and this is a very funny imitation of a popular Victorian romance. There is no punctuation and there are hilarious spelling mistakes. Nearly every sentence is a gem.

Helen Cresswell

9-11

Next?
- There really is nothing like this that I know of, but if you enjoy humour there is plenty to choose from. Best of all are the **Just William** stories by Richmal Crompton. (UBG 131)
- E. Nesbit's ***Five Children and It*** and ***The Phoenix and the Carpet*** are funny and fantastic adventures set and written at around the same time as ***The Young Visiters***. (UBG 85)
- Or try ***Sarah, Plain and Tall*** by Patricia MacLachlan, another book about adults as seen through the eyes of children. (UBG 210)

YOUNG WIZARDS series

SO YOU WANT TO BE A WIZARD • DEEP WIZARDRY • HIGH WIZARDRY • WIZARD ABROAD • WIZARD'S DILEMMA • WIZARD ALONE

Diane Duane

➨ Kit and Nita each find a handbook for wizards, then meet as they try to work its spells. Despite their age they are powerful; due to their age, they make mistakes – big mistakes, which they have to fix. They encounter wonderful things: wizard cats and parrots, a heroic Jaguar automobile, magic as it's practised in outer space or through computers. The boy Kit converses with subway trains, the girl Nita with trees. Duane makes our everyday world magical and heroic at the same time.

But in addition to their magical work they also have to deal with everyday family and school problems, and it's this realism that makes these books work, particularly as the series moves on and Kit and Nita grow up.

9-11

Tamora Pierce

Next?

- Diana Wynne Jones's fantasies, particularly ***Archer's Goon, Witch Week*** (one of the **Chrestomanci** books – see p. 272) and ***Howl's Moving Castle***, also present a look at magic as if we could practise it in our world.
- Laurel Winter's ***Growing Wings*** is somewhat darker, and deals with the realities faced by a young girl who grows wings. It shows her in exile from the real world, finding others like herself, and trying to learn how to fly.
- Or what about the famous **Harry Potter** series? J.K. Rowling treats us to a wonderful story about learning wizardry. (UBG 106)
- William Nicholson's ***The Wind Singer*** is about a boy and girl who discover they have special powers and must learn how to use them. (UBG 266)
- ***The Doomspell*** by Cliff McNish is a tale of good evil set in a set in a faraway frozen world. (UBG 66)

THE YOUNGEST GIRL IN THE FIFTH Angela Brazil

➨ Until I read Angela Brazil, I though a 'wizard wheeze' was Harry Potter with asthma and that a brick was for building walls.

Gwen Gascoyne is poor, plain and awkward, but bright and determined. When she gets moved up to the Fifth Form from the Upper Fourth, she's cut by her classmates, and that unspeakable rotter, Netta Goodwin, is the only person in the Fifth who'll talk to her. Netta lands Gwen into the most frightful hole, leaving Gwen to defend her honour without sneaking, and to win her place in the Fifth.

You don't have to have been in a frightful scrape, or muffed a test, or done an abominable thing, to enjoy these stories. You can still find Angela Brazil's books in libraries and second-hand bookshops. She wrote over forty school stories, between 1906 and 1947, and her novels are still as much fun as ever.

Antonia Honeywell

10+

Next?

- If you decide you like old-fashioned school stories, try the **St. Clare's** (UBG 209) or **Malory Towers** (UBG 153) series by Enid Blyton. Or the **Chalet School** stories by Elinor M. Brent-Dyer. (UBG 43)
- If you liked the ending of this novel, try ***The Story of the Treasure-Seekers*** by E. Nesbit.
- **Harry Potter** for a (slightly) more modern, (slightly) more unusual boarding-school tale. (UBG 106)

About the contributors

Don't forget to check the index on pages 284-288 to see which of the contributors' books are recommended in the *UBG*.

JOAN AIKEN has been writing for over forty years, producing classic books such as ***The Wolves of Willoughby Chase, Go Saddle the Sea*** and ***Midnight is a Place***.

DAVID ALMOND is a highly-acclaimed fiction writer. His first novel ***Skellig*** won the Whitbread Children's Book of the Year and the Carnegie Medal. He lives in the north-east of England – the area he grew up in and loves to write about.

ABIGAIL ANDERSON undertakes a variety of work as a theatre director, including shows for younger audiences which have toured to schools and theatres nationally.

NOGA APPLEBAUM used to hide between the furthest aisles in the library, reading books that the librarian thought unsuitable for her. Today, she confesses unashamedly to an addiction to teen fiction, even though some may say that her teen years are long gone.

JON APPLETON has been a reviewer of children's books, and now works as an editor of children's fiction.

PHILIP ARDAGH is a very large man with a very large beard, who has written over fifty children's books, including the hilarious **Eddie Dickens Trilogy** and ***The Fall of Fergal***.

NEIL ARKSEY scripts TV shows as well as writing books for children, including ***MacB***, ***Playing on the Edge*** and ***As Good as Dead in Downtown***.

EILEEN ARMSTRONG is a High School Librarian in Northumberland, a reviewer and feature writer for a variety of professional journals, and a self-confessed book addict since birth!

SHERRY ASHWORTH writes books for young adults, usually on sensitive issues, such as ***Fat, What's Your Problem?*** and ***Was he Worth it?***

LYNNE REID BANKS is one of the most respected of authors. She has written many books, but is probably best-known for ***The L-Shaped Room*** for grown-ups and ***The Indian in the Cupboard*** for children. She has the distinction of being the first-ever woman TV news reporter!

NINA BAWDEN has written many award-winning children's books, the most famous of which is ***Carrie's War***. ***The Guardian*** said: 'Nina Bawden's readers should be numbered like the sands of the sea.'

IAN BECK is one of the UK's best-loved illustrators. His work includes ***The Orchard Book of Fairy Tales, Five Little Ducks*** and ***Little Brown Bear***, as well as a version of ***Peter Pan***.

JULIE BERTAGNA's first paid job was serving in her uncle's ice cream van, aged seven. She subsequently decided to work as a writer instead, producing many popular novels such as ***Exodus, The Spark Gap*** and ***Dolphin Boy***.

MALORIE BLACKMAN has won many awards for her work and now lives in London with her collection of over a thousand books, her husband and her daughter.

QUENTIN BLAKE first had his drawings published when he was just sixteen. In the years since then, he has grown to become one of this country's best-loved illustrators and authors in his own right (with classic picture books like ***Clown*** and ***Mr Magnolia***). In 1999, he was appointed the first Children's Laureate.

DAVID BLANCH was a primary school deputy headteacher until he took early retirement in 1996 to work full time on ***Carousel*** magazine. He was a founder-member of the Birmingham Children's Book Group in 1969.

JENNY BLANCH is a former primary school deputy head teacher and an Honorary President of the Federation of Children's Book Groups. In 1995, with her husband, launched ***Carousel***.

THOMAS BLOOR has played guitar and sung with a band, made films and exhibited paintings. Now he is best-known as the Fidler-award winning author of ***The Memory Prisoner*** and its prequel, ***The House of Eyes***, which won the Stockton Children's Book Award.

MICHAEL BOND is best known as the author of the hugely popular Paddington Bear books, which began with ***A Bear Called Paddington*** way back in 1958. His many other books for young readers include the **Olga da Polga** series.

TIM BOWLER is the author of six books to date, including ***River Boy***, which won the 1998 Carnegie Medal.

GERALDINE BRENNAN books editor of ***The Times Educational Supplement***.

THERESA BRESLIN is one of Scotland's leading writers. Her books include ***Whispers in the Graveyard*** (which won the 1994 Carnegie Medal) and ***Kezzie***.

ANTHONY BUCKERIDGE lives in Sussex with his wife, Eileen. After a career as a schoolmaster he became a writer, creating in his Jennings books some of the best-loved characters in fiction. Besides loving Anthony's books, the editors of the ***UBG*** are particularly fond of the Buckeridges themselves, who recently invited them for tea.

MELVIN BURGESS has received both considerable acclaim and much criticism for his hard-hitting teenage fiction. He has also written less controversial books for pre-teens, including ***An Angel for May*** and ***The Earth Giant***.

MEG CABOT has worked as an illustrator and a writer of historical romances. She is author of the hugely successful **Princess Diaries** books. She has also worked as an illustrator and a writer of historical fiction.

BABETTE COLE published her first picture book in 1976, and has since written and illustrated another seventy, including classics like ***Mummy Laid an Egg!, Drop Dead*** and ***Princess Smartypants***.

WENDY COOLING is a children's book expert who has also edited many collections, including ***Centuries of Stories*** and the ***Quids for Kids*** series.

SUSAN COOPER is one of the best-loved authors for children, ever. Her **The Dark Is Rising** sequence is a modern classic – and it is also one of the very few titles in the world that the editors of this book all love equally. She was born in England but now lives in America.

MICHAEL COX is an author and illustrator. After winning the Scholastic/***Independent*** Story of the Year award, he gave up teaching to write full-time and has now written over twenty-five books.

HELEN CRESSWELL has been writing since the age of six. Her wonderful television scripts and books have earned her huge acclaim (including various award nominations) and affection among her readers.

CHRIS CROSS is the webmaster behind the book review website for and by ten-fifteen-year-olds that he and his brother Tim launched in January 2001 (www.cool-reads.co.uk).

GILLIAN CROSS is probably best known as the author of **The Demon Headmaster** series, but has written numerous other wonderful books (winning her the Carnegie Medal, the Smarties Prize and the Whitbread Award).

TIM CROSS is in charge of the reviews that appear on www.cool-reads.co.uk. He himself reads at least ten books a week, a habit which he found useful when he was a judge for the 2003 Booktrust Teenage Book Prize.

CHRIS D'LACEY is a Malteser (he was born in Malta!) but lives in England. He is author of over sixteen books, some for the very young, some for teenagers.

ANNIE DALTON tried all sorts of jobs, from being a waitress to working in a factory, before she became a writer. She is best-known for her hugely popular **Angels Unlimited** series as well as other books, all of which have a magical slant.

JANE DARCY has been an English teacher for over twenty-five years. She loves books, but can never hope to read as much, or with such pleasure, as she did in childhood.

TED DEWAN is an author, illustrator, journalist, comedian, musician and cartoonist. He had his first commission when he was sixteen. He now works in Philip Pullman's old shed, which was passed on to him much in the way of an Olympic torch.

BERLIE DOHERTY is a compulsive writer of novels, poems and plays. She has won the Carnegie Medal twice, with ***Granny was a Buffer Girl*** and ***Dear Nobody***. She lives in the Peak District and sometimes writes perched on a stone by the river.

MALACHY DOYLE's work as a special needs teacher inspired his extraordinary first novel, ***Georgie***, which was followed by ***Who is Jesse Flood?***

DIANE DUANE is an American who now lives in Ireland. She has written hundreds of books, mainly science fiction and fantasy. Her work includes tie-ins to many television shows, as well as her own creations, such as the **Young Wizards** series.

CAROL ANN DUFFY has written several collections of poetry and edited anthologies for both adults and children. She has won many awards for her work.

PATRICIA ELLIOTT has worked in publishing and most recently taught a children's literature course at an adult education college. She lives in London but has a house in Aldeburgh, the setting for her first novel, ***The Ice Boy***.

ANNE FINE has written for all ages, from young children to adults, and her amazing books have won her the Carnegie Medal (twice) the Whitbread Award (twice), the ***Guardian*** Award and the Smarties Prize. She was elected the second Children's Laureate, serving from 2001-2003.

PATRICIA FINNEY had her first novel published while she was still a teenager, and since then has gone on to write many historical novels for adults. In her spare time she takes dictation from her Labrador dog, Jack, so that the world can share his adventures and exploits.

CATHERINE FISHER lives in Wales with her two cats. She has won awards for both her fiction and her poetry, and her most famous titles include **The Book of the Crow**, ***The Snow-walker's Son*** and the slightly older read, ***Corbenic***.

LEONIE FLYNN, see p 7.

LINDSEY FRASER worked as a children's bookseller, and was Executive Director of Scottish Book Trust for eleven years. She is now a partner in Fraser Ross Associates, a literary consultancy based in Edinburgh.

VIVIAN FRENCH worked in children's theatre for ten years as both an actor and writer. She has been telling stories for more than twenty years in schools, community centres, theatres and has written over a hundred children's books.

SUSAN GATES writes very funny books, often with the maddest titles around, like ***Killer Mushrooms Ate My Gran***. She has three children and lives in County Durham.

JAMILA GAVIN was born in India, but has lived in England since childhood. Her books (which have won her the Whitbread Prize and garnered her several other nominations) include ***Coram Boy***, **The Wheel of Surya Trilogy** and ***The Blood Stone***.

ADÈLE GERAS has worked as a singer, a French teacher and an actress. Her seventy-something books to date include ***Troy***, which was shortlisted for both the Whitbread Award and the Carnegie Medal.

ALAN GIBBONS was born in Cheshire and is both a teacher and an author. . He mostly writes for older children, and his brilliant ***Shadow of the Minotaur*** won the Blue Peter Award for the 'Book I couldn't Put Down' category.

CANDIDA GRAY has degrees in theatre, art history and history, but she has always wanted to have one in literature too! Candida works in education and loves teaching eight- to twelve-year-olds.

ELENA GREGORIOU is a teacher in London. One of her favourite things is to read to her class – and to listen to them reading to her – which she considers one of the most valuable learning experiences, for both class and teacher.

DANIEL HAHN, see p 7.

MARY HOFFMAN's many successful children's books include the hugely popular ***Amazing Grace*** and ***Stravaganza: City of Masks***. She has had her appendix removed by Enid Blyton's husband. Her daughter, Rhiannon Lassiter, is also a children's writer.

ELIZABETH HONEY writes some of the best-loved stories in Australia which have won her loads of awards as both author and illustrator. She often visits schools, though as yet none in the UK.

ANTONIA HONEYWELL is Head of English at a large inner London comprehensive. She contributes regular articles and reviews to various teaching journals, and has recently completed her first novel.

MARY HOOPER started off writing stories for magazines, but now writes novels for teenagers and younger readers. Her books include ***The Great Twin Trick*** and ***Spook Summer***.

ANTHONY HOROWITZ is a writer for TV and cinema, but you'll probably know him best as author of the Alex Riderr stories (***Stormbreaker***, etc.), ***Groosham Grange*** and ***Horowitz Horror***.

LAURA HUTCHINGS is Head of English at an inner city boys' school. She does all her reading on the bus – which is the only reason she is thankful for a long journey to school each day.

EVA IBBOTSON normally writes books about magic and ghosts, but she has also written the prize-winning ***Journey to the River Sea***, an adventure story about a British girl who travels to the Amazon.

ROSE IMPEY is author of over forty books, including the wonderful **Animal Crackers** series, and direct and beautiful retellings of classic fairy stories, many of which are included in ***The Orchard Book of Fairy Tales***.

STEVE JACKSON, with his collaborator Ian Livingstone, kick-started the gaming phenomenon **Fighting Fantasy**. There are now more than seventy books in the series and they have been sold in over twenty-two countries.

JULIA JARMAN has written many books for younger children, including the ***Jessame*** stories, and the **Time-travelling Cat** stories. She lives with her husband and cat – and most of the animals in her books are based on ones she has known.

SHERRYL JORDAN lives in New Zealand and is a writer of books mainly for young adults and teens. In 2001 she was awarded the Margaret Mahy Medal for her contribution to children's literature.

ANN JUNGMAN is best known as the creator of ***Vlad the Drac***. She was born in London where she still lives (when not in Australia), and where she founded and runs the publishing company, Barn Owl Books.

JACKIE KAY is a poet who has also written widely for stage and screen. She has published various collections of poetry for children, including ***Two's Company***, and a novel, ***Strawgirl***, for older readers.

GARRY KILWORTH is author of the much-loved ***Welkin Weasels*** series. He writes for all ages, sometimes as Garry Douglas. His latest series, ***The Knights of Liofwende***, is for older readers.

DICK KING-SMITH grew up surrounded by pet animals and was a farmer for twenty years. He is one of the best-loved children's writers of today. His many books about animals include ***The Sheep-pig*** and ***The Hodgeheg***.

ELIZABETH LAIRD has always had a passion for travel, and having lived all over the world and experienced life in many different places, she is amply qualified to write her bestselling, award-winning books, such as ***Kiss the Dust***.

CAROLINE LAWRENCE is the author of the popular **Roman Mysteries**, one of the best websites on the internet – www.romanmysteries.com; she even ran a competition to be a character in her next book!

MICHAEL LAWRENCE writes, paints and takes photographs. He wants to be an archaeologist and an astronomer when he grows up. He passes the time by writing books for kids, both young and old.

NEAL LAYTON wanted to be an astronaut, then changed his mind and became an artist. He illustrates books, sometimes his own, such as ***Oscar and Arabella***, and sometimes other writers', such as ***Rover***, by Michael Rosen.

TANITH LEE has written hundreds of books for both children and adults. Her books are hugely popular both in the UK and the USA. She also has scripted shows for TV.

FRANCESCA LEWIS is a press officer and features writer for the Department for Culture, Media and Sport.

NAOMI LEWIS won the Eleanor Farjeon Award for services to children's literature in 1975. She has been the translator for various collections of Hans Andersen's fairytales and has written introductions to many children's classics.

PENELOPE LIVELY is one of Britain's best-loved writers, for both children and adults. She won the Carnegie Medal for ***The Ghost of Thomas Kempe*** and the Whitbread Award for ***A Stitch in Time***.

JULIA LYTOLLIS is a teacher currently working in Chicago. She particularly enjoys fantasy and science fiction.

GERALDINE McCAUGHREAN has written over a hundred books and plays, which have won her pretty much every children's books award going.

KAREN McCOMBIE lives, just like her heroine Ally, very close to Alexandra Palace in London. Her ***Ally's World*** series has won her a fanatical following. Apart from writing, she enjoys reading, eating crisps and belly-dancing.

HILARY McKAY's ***Saffy's Angel*** won the 2003 Whitbread Children's Book Award. Her many titles include picture books and stories for younger readers.

JOHN McLAY is a children's books literary scout, anthologist and book reviewer. He has previously worked for Puffin Books, been a children's bookseller and sold translation rights internationally.

CLIFF McNISH, as a child, loved daydreaming and superhero comics. But it wasn't until he was thirty-six that he started writing down the stories that came from the daydreams, and even then it was only because his daughter wanted stories about really scary witches.

MARGARET MAHY has been writing children's books for over thirty years. She has won the Carnegie Medal twice for ***The Haunting*** and ***The Changeover***. Margaret recently got a tattoo as part of the research for her novel ***24 Hours***.

JAN MARK, who lives in Oxford with four cats and a houseful of books, has written many novels for all ages. She gave up teaching to become a full-time writer and, since the publication of her first novel, ***Thunder and Lightnings,*** has twice won the Carnegie Medal.

PHILIPPA MILNES-SMITH is a literary agent and children's specialist at the agency LAW (Lucas Alexander Whitley). She has worked for many years in children's publishing and was previously Managing Director of Puffin Books.

MICHAEL MORPURGO's books have won or been nominated for most major children's books prizes, and earned him great affection among his very many fans. In 2003 he was appointed the third Children's Laureate.

BEVERLEY NAIDOO grew up in South Africa, under Apartheid. Her first book, ***Journey to Jo'burg***, was banned there, and this spurred her on to write more books about the country. She won the Carnegie Medal for ***The Other Side of Truth***.

LINDA NEWBERY always wanted to be a writer, and is now author of over twenty books for children. She has published novels for all ages, but is perhaps best known for her powerful books for young adults, such as ***The Shell House***.

JENNY NIMMO is the author of over forty books for children, including ***The Snow Spider*** and ***The Owl Tree***, both of which won the Smarties Prize.

ANDREW NORRISS first became a teacher and then a writer. He now works as a scriptwriter for TV and is an author of children's books, including ***Aquila***, which was made into a TV series.

KENNETH OPPEL, a Canadian, is probably best known for his ***Silverwing*** saga. When he was fourteen, he sent his first novel to Roald Dahl who encouraged him to submit it for publication!

BRIAN PATTEN is one of the best and most loved poets writing today. Along with Roger McGough and Adrian Henri he was one of the Liverpool Poets of the 1960s and he has been writing and performing ever since.

KATE PETTY is a children's author and editor. She has written the teenage fiction series ***Girls Like You***, and the very successful educational pop-up book, ***The Terrific Times Table Book***. She is the children's publisher for the Eden Project.

GERVASE PHINN is an author, poet and broadcaster, and an expert on children and reading. His collections for kids, such as ***The Day Our Teacher Went Batty***, are hugely popular. His autobiography is called ***The Other Side of the Dale***.

JAN PIENKOWSKI has been drawing since he was fourteen. He is probably best-known for the ***Meg and Mog*** series by Helen Nicholl and for his pop-up books. He has twice won the Kate Greenaway Medal for illustration.

TAMORA PIERCE comes from Pennsylvania, America, and says she was a hillbilly. As a child she loved reading and TV and spent many hours writing fan fiction based on her favourite shows. Now she lives in New York with her husband and four cats, and writes full-time in her own wonderful universes.

TERRY PRATCHETT published his first story when he was thirteen and first got paid for a story four years later. He has written books for younger readers and is most famous for his ***Discworld*** series, which has sold over twenty-one million copies and been translated into twenty-seven languages.

SUSAN PRICE hated school and for her reading and writing were an escape. Her first novel was published when she was sixteen, and since then she has gone on to win the Carnegie Medal for ***Ghost Drum*** and The ***Guardian*** Award for ***The Sterkarm Handshake***.

SALLY PRUE lives in Hertfordshire with her husband, daughters and two elderly guinea pigs. Her first novel ***Cold Tom*** won the Branford Boase Award and the Smarties Silver Award.

SIMON PUTTOCK used to sell children's books for a living, and now he writes them. His best-known titles include ***Coral Goes Swimming*** and ***Pig's Digger***.

SHOO RAYNER has written over seventy books, even though he was dyslexic and hated writing at school! His work is much loved, particularly ***The Ginger Ninja*** and ***The Rex Files*** series.

CELIA REES worked as a teacher before dedicating herself to writing full time. Her books, which cover a wide range of genres, include the acclaimed **Witch Child** series.

GWYNETH REES is half-English, half-Welsh, now living in London (with cats). Her books include ***The Mum Hunt***, ***Fairy Dust*** and the ***Mermaids*** series.

PHILIP REEVE worked in a bookshop before becoming known as illustrator of the famous **Horrible Histories** books. He is now writing books and in his first novel, ***Mortal Engines***, created one of the most intriguing worlds in fantasy fiction.

ANTHONY REUBEN is a BBC business journalist and television producer. He only got to contribute to this book because he is married to one of the editors.

SUSAN REUBEN, see p 7.

JAMES RIORDAN was born in Portsmouth. An expert on Russia, he has written over twenty academic titles, several collections of folk-tales and a number of picture books. His stories for children and young adults have won many awards and often deal with difficult subject matter.

KATHERINE ROBERTS was born in Torquay, and her career has been varied, from working with computers to racehorses. Her first book, ***Song Quest*** won the Branford Boase Award, and she is now a full-time writer.

MICHAEL ROSEN is one of Britain's best-loved children's poets. He is also a radio broadcaster and performer. Sometimes he lies in bed thinking of all the things he would write if he got up. His many titles include the poetry collections, ***Quick, Let's Get Out of Here*** and ***You Wait Till I'm Older Than You!***

KATHRYN ROSS is a former English teacher, independent bookseller and Deputy Director of Scottish Book Trust. She is now a partner in the literary consultancy, Fraser Ross Associates.

JOHN ROWE TOWNSEND is a children's author and academic. He has written a history of children's literature, ***Written for Children***, and over twenty children's books, including ***Gumble's Yard*** and ***The Intruder***.

HUGH SCOTT is best known for his supernatural and horror novels for young adults. He won the Whitbread Prize in 1989 for ***Why Weeps the Brogan***? He now lectures in creative writing and visits schools regularly.

MARCUS SEDGWICK won the Branford Boase Award for a first novel, for ***Floodland*** and his book ***The Dark Horse*** was shortlisted for the Carnegie Medal. Marcus also works for Walker Books.

DARREN SHAN always wanted to be a writer and is now a publishing phenomenon! His amazing ***The Saga of Darren Shan*** has sold in huge numbers, and each new volume is eagerly awaited across the globe.

NICK SHARRATT illustrated the cover of this book! He is also well known as the illustrator of loads of Jacqueline Wilson's novels and many books for younger kids, such as ***Eat Your Peas*** and ***Pants***.

HELEN SIMMONS was manager of Young Waterstone's in Bath, then became the Readiscovery BookBus Driver for Book Trust Scotland, taking books and authors to schools in the remotest parts of the country.

FRANCESCA SIMON is an American, who now lives in London with her husband and son. She used to be a journalist, but is now a full time writer, best known for her wonderful **Horrid Henry** books.

NICKY SINGER began her writing career at the age of fifteen. She has worked in publishing and TV and written for adults, but it is only recently, with ***Feather Boy***, that she started writing her award-winning children's books.

JERRY SPINELLI writes some of the funniest and most touching books around. He has won the Newbery Medal for ***Maniac Magee,*** and ***Wringer*** was named a Newbery Honor book.

CHRIS STEPHENSON was a bookseller for eighteen years, with a particular interest in children's books. He now works as a freelance writer, frequently contributing to ***Carousel***.

PAUL STEWART – with his long-time collaborator, the illustrator Chris Riddell – is author of **The Edge Chronicles**. Paul works every day (apart from Christmas and holidays).

ALAN TEMPERLEY lives in Scotland and can often be found on speaking tours of Scottish schools. He has written many books, including the hilarious ***Harry and the Wrinklies***, which was made into a TV series.

COLIN THOMPSON lives in Australia. He is famous as author and illustrator of some of the most brilliant picture books, including ***How To Live Forever***.

LUCY THUNDER commissions children's non-fiction for Heinemann Library. She worked previously as a bookseller and an English language teacher.

KAYE UMANSKY is best known as the creater of ***Pongwiffy***, though she has written many other books too. She has worked as a singer, dancer and actress and now lives in north London.

JEAN URE had her first novel published while she was still at school. Since then she has written and translated hundreds of books, and is one of the best loved of writers for children of all ages.

GILL VICKERY studied fine art and painting at college, and since then has worked as a children's librarian and English teacher. Her first novel, ***The Ivy Crown***, won the 2000 Fidler Award

KAREN WALLACE was born in Canada an moved to England when she was eleven. She has written over seventy books and is probably most famous for ***Raspberries on the Yangtze***.

SYLVIA WAUGH was born in the north of England and now lives in Gateshead. She began writing after following a career as a school teacher. Her first book ***The Mennyms*** won the 1994 ***Guardian*** Children's Fiction Prize.

VICTORIA WEBB has worked in publishing for four years. She lives in Richmond with her husband.

SARA WHEELER is a writer, traveller and broadcaster. She has written about her journeys, particularly to Greece, Chile and Antarctica, and is now known as an expert on Antarctic exploration.

JACQUELINE WILSON is one of the most popular writers in the country – her publishers recently gave a party to celebrate selling their ten-millionth Jacqueline Wilson book!

CHRIS WOODING is younger than all the editors of the UBG, a fact that they all find extremely distressing. In his twenty-seven years he has managed to write ***The Haunting of Alaizabel Cray*** and ***Poison*** as well as the **Broken Sky** series.

BARBARA WRIGHT is a Londoner living in Hertfordshire where she works in Pharmaceutical Research.

JANE YOLEN has written over two hundred books. An American, she has won many awards including the Caldecott Medal (for ***Owl Moon***) and the World Fantasy Award.

BENJAMIN ZEPHANIAH is a poet, performer and broadcaster. His books include the poetry collections ***Talking Turkeys*** and ***Funky Chickens***, and the novels ***Refugee Boy*** and ***Face***.

Acknowledgements

A book like this is bound to depend on the work of more than just a handful of people, and we have found ourselves enormously lucky at the generosity and goodwill shown by so many great people who have put their expertise (and enthusiasm) at our disposal.

Jane Rogers, Ruth Langley and Suzie Dent were all extremely supportive way back when this book was no more than quite a good idea. Adèle Geras and Noga Applebaum offered advice and help early on too, and have continued to do so in countless ways right through to date.

Geraldine Brennan, Candida Gray, Brenda Marshall of Port Regis School, Jenny Morris, Jane Nissen and Lisa Sainsbury all read our original, and very flawed, provisional list of 'Titles For Possible Inclusion'; their honest and well-informed comments and suggestions were crucial in refining what our book would eventually come to cover.

Thanks to all those many friends who read things for us, suggested titles for inclusion and for exclusion ('Surely you're not going to include X if you're not including Y?'); most helpful/enthusiastic/vehement of these were Abigail Anderson, Jane Darcy, Sarah Eley and Jenni Hicks.

The process of putting together such a great team of contributors depended largely on the generosity of those willing to open up their address-books for our scrutiny. Among those many people who helped us with contacts, and suggested suitable names, we should thank Ann Jungman, Sarah Wilkie and Rosemary Stones. In many cases our contact with our contributors was facilitated by agents, publicists, etc. – thanks to all those who helped. In particular Jo Williamson and Nicola Blacoe at HarperCollins and Alyx Price at Macmillan worked on this far above-and-beyond. We should also offer warm thanks to Eileen Buckeridge and Robina Masters; sadly Robina's husband Anthony passed away a few months ago – a great loss to the children's book world.

We must express our huge thanks and admiration for our contributors themselves (listed on pages 276-280) for a fantastic set of entries and essays; if you knew how much we paid them for their work you'd see quite how generous they have all been in agreeing to write for us … And many of them donated their fees to our designated charity, Hope and Homes for Children. Helen Harper made this process as easy as possible, so thanks are due to her too. We were delighted to be able to raise in the region of £2,500 towards the charity's continuing vital work.

A big thank you to all the schools that took part in the competitions and polls – we had a fantastic response, with thousands of great entries; choosing our favourite few to include in the book and on the website from the thousands submitted was not an easy task. Miranda Duffy bravely spent a weekend with us wading through boxes and boxes of children's reviews and illustrations, cutting them down to a manageable shortlist.

Of the participating schools, Arnold House, St Aloysius and North Westminster Collegiate also allowed themselves to be used as guinea-pigs in various other ways – our gratitude to the heads, staff and pupils at all these three, in particular Antonia Honeywell at NWC, Arnold House headmaster Nicholas Allen and pupils William Faulks and Andrew Mason. Max Toomey at Arnold House also gave us a layout suggestion which we used and we think looks great … Mary Cruickshank of the *TES* and Helen Child of Heathfield Junior School, Twickenham, were also extremely helpful getting this competition up and running.

All sorts of people helped us get access to exciting celebrities for 'favourite book' quotes; of these we'd particularly like to thank Natasha Lemos, Nicholas Pritchard and Emma Freud.

At various stages we had extremely useful advice on all sorts of subjects from Liz Cross, Elizabeth Hammill, Pam Dix and the Kilburn Bookshop. The all-knowing Julia Eccleshare gave us invaluable advice on many matters, as did Jonathan Douglas, whose enthusiasm for this project seemed very often to exceed our own.

Very many thanks to the wonderful Nick Sharratt for the brilliant cover, and the other great illustrators who've produced designs for the book – and all those who've kindly allowed us to reproduce their material on these pages. Thanks also to the book's designer, Bet Ayer.

The phenomenal Anne Fine was one of the first people to come on board and express support for the *UBG*, and in those early days carelessly offered to write an introduction – and was then most gracious when many months later we held her to her promise. We are very grateful for her advice back when the idea of this book was still just coming together. It was Anne who introduced us to Eileen Armstrong, who has been absolutely tireless in offering her knowledge and enthusiasm ever since we started discussing this almost two years ago – we are enormously grateful for all the many ways in which she too has helped us over all this time.

Special thanks must also go to Laura Hutchings for working her way pretty much without complaint through hundreds of books on our behalf; and to Anthony Reuben, for support, encouragement, and the mention of Supergran at regular intervals.

Araminta Whitley at LAW introduced us to Philippa Milnes-Smith, who bravely agreed to represent this project as our agent. Long after finding us our publisher, Philippa has continued to godmother the project, giving us access to all the things she knows and all the people she knows and her absolutely unwavering enthusiasm for good children's books. She and her assistant Helen Mulligan have always been delighted to help more and yet more, and indeed gave so much of their time and energy that we have now become convinced that we must surely have been the only people they represented ...

The publisher that Philippa found us was A & C Black, and the editor there Jon Appleton – for whom no praise or thanks could be high enough. Jon has contributed more ideas and time and energy to this project than we would have dared to ask for. Now that the struggle is over, we hope he's as proud of it as we are.

THE EDITORS

Versions of the book recommendations by Francesca Simon (p. 103) and Quentin Blake (pp. 149 and 152) have been published previously, the former in *The Guardian*, 28 February 2001, the latter two in *The Laureate's Party* (Red Fox, 2000).

For permission to reproduce copyright material in *The Ultimate Book Guide*, the Publisher thanks:

Artists Partners for permission to reproduce the illustration that appears on p. 147 by David Roberts from *Long Lost* by Jan Mark, published by Macmillan Children's Books.

Peter Bailey for permission to reproduce the illustration on p. 121 from *I Was a Rat!*, written by Philip Pullman and published by The Random House Group.

B.J. Kearley Ltd for permission to reproduce the illustration that appears on p. 95 by Charles Keeping from *The God Beneath the Sea*, written by Leon Garfield and Edward Blishen and illustrated by Charles Keeping, published by Victor Gollancz Ltd.

The Chicken House for permission to reproduce the cover from *Billy Elliott* by Melvin Burgess, which appears on p. 240.

Chrysalis Children's Books for the illustration that appears on p. 257 from *War Game* by Michael Foreman. Text/illustration © Michael Foreman (1997). Reprinted by permission of Chrysalis Children's Books, an imprint of Chrysalis Books Group Plc

Curtis Brown London Ltd for permission to reproduce the illustration on p. 266 by E.H. Shepherd from *Winnie-the-Pooh* by A.A. Milne. Line illustration copyright © E.H. Shepherd under the Berne Convention, reproduced by permission of Curtis Brown Ltd., London.

Egmont Books for permission to reproduce the following book covers: *The Wool-pack* by Cynthia Hartnett, which appears on p. 111; *A Series of Unfortunate Events: The Bad Beginning* by Lemony Snicket, which appears on p. 217; *The Hundred and One Dalmatians* by Dodie Smith, which appears on p. 16; *The Wreck of the Zanzibar* by Michael Morpurgo, which appears on p. 273; *Kensuke's Kingdom* by Michael Morpurgo, which appears on p. 10; *I Am David* by Anne Holm, which appears on p. 111; *The Snow Spider Trilogy* by Jenny Nimmo, which appears on p. 222; *Flat Stanley* by Jeff Brown, which appears on p. 85; *The Wheel of Surya* by Jamila Gavin, which appears on p. 181. Also for permission to reproduce the illustration by Anthony Maitland from *The Ghost of Thomas Kempe* by Penelope Lively, which appears on p. 91 and the illustration by Philippe Dupasquier from *Bill's New Frock*, written by Anne Fine, which appears on p. 28. All titles published by Egmont Books.

Faber and Faber Limited for permission to reproduce the cover from *The Iron Man*, written by Ted Hughes, which appears on p. 124; and also for permission to reprint the the illustration by Carolyn Dinan from *The Turbulent Term of Tyke Tiler* by Gene Kemp, which appears on p. 249; the illustration by Lilian Hoban from *The Mouse and his Child* by Russell Hoban, which appears on p. 164 and the illustration by John Levers from *The Time and Space of Uncle Albert* by Russell Stannard, which appears on p. 243. All titles published by Faber and Faber Limited.

HarperCollins Publishers Ltd for permission to reproduce the following covers: *Winging It* © Annie Dalton, 2001, which appears on p. 15; *A Bear Called Paddington* © Michael Bond, 1986, which appears on p. 24; *Dimanche Diller* © Henrietta Branford, 1994, which appears on p. 63; *The Great Pyramid Robbery* © Katherine Roberts, 2001, which appears on p. 100; *When Hitler Stole Pink Rabbit* © Judith Kerr, 1989, which appears on p. 261 and *The Rescuers* © Mary Norton, 1983, which appears on p. 202. All titles published by Collins Children's Book.

Hilary Hinckley for permission to reproduce the illustration that appears on p. 270 by Pat Marriott from *The Wolves of Willoughby Chase* by Joan Aiken, published by The Random House Group.

Hodder and Stoughton Limited for permission to reproduce the following covers: *The Crystal Prison* by Robin Jarvis which appears on p. 60; *A Swarm in May* by William Mayne, which appears on p. 233; *Jeremy Thatcher, Dragon Catcher* by Bruce Colville, which appears on p. 152; *Stratford Boys* by Jan Mark, which appears on p. 230; *East of Midnight* by Tanith Lee, which appears on p. 69; *Piratica* by Tanith Lee, which appears on p. 190; *The Memory Prisoner* by Thomas Bloor, which appears on p. 158; *Step into the Dark* by Bridget Crowley, which appears on p. 212; *The Treasure in the Garden* by Hilary McKay, which appears on p. 247. All titles published by Hodder Children's Books.

J.E. Huddleston on behalf of the Estate of C.T. Tunnicliffe for permission to reproduce the illustration that appears on p. 53 by C.F. Tunnicliffe from *A Country Child* by Alison Uttley. Illustration © Estate of C.F. Tunnicliffe.

Icon Books Ltd. for permission to reproduce the illustration on p. 83 from *House of Hell* in the **Fighting Fantasy** series by Steve Jackson.

Jane Nissen Books for permission to reproduce the illustration on p. 162 by Fritz Eichenburg from *Mistress Masham's Repose* by T.H. White, published by Jane Nissen Books.

The Laura Cecil Literary Agency on behalf of the Estate of Edward Ardizzone for the illustration from *Stig of the Dump* by Clive King which appears on p. 226. Illustration © 1963 Edward Ardizzone.

Macmillan Children's Books, London, for permission to reproduce the following covers: *Blitzcat* by Robert Westall, published in 1989, which appears on p. 31 (cover illustration by Jane Burton/Bruce Coleman Collection); *Penguin in the Fridge* by Peter Dixon, published in 2001, which appears on p. 183 (cover illustration by Martin Chatterton); *Strawgirl* by Jackie Kay, published in 2001, which appears on p. 231; *The Princess Diaries* by Meg Cabot, published in 2001, which appears on p. 193 (cover illustration by Nicola Slater); *The Transfer* by Terence Blacker, published in 1998, which appears on p. 246 (cover illustration by Anthony Robinson); and also for the illustration by Tim Archbold from *Jimmy Zest* by Sam McBratney, which appears on p. 128. All titles published by Macmillan Children's Books.

Orion Children's Books for permission to reproduce the following: cover illustration by Albert Uderzo from *Asterix and the Great Divide* by Goscinny/Uderzo, which appears on p. 21 and the cover from *The Thieves of Ostia* by Caroline Lawrence, which appears on p. 239. Cover design: Richard Carr. Cover illustration: Peter Sutton and Fred van Deelen. Both titles published by Orion Children's Books.

Oxford University Press for permission to reproduce the following covers: *The Demon Headmaster* by Gillian Cross, which appears on p. 59; *The Eagle of the Ninth* by Rosemary Sutcliff, which appears on p. 68; *A Little Lower than the Angels* by Geraldine McCaughrean, which appears on p. 143; *The Breadwinner* by Deborah Ellis which appears on p. 180; *Minnow on the Say* which appears on p. 161.

Penguin Children's Books for permission to reproduce the following: the illustration that appears on p. 9 from *Aesop's Funky Fables*, retold by Vivian French and illustrated by Korky Paul (Hamish Hamilton, 1997). Copyright © Vivian French 1997. Illustrations copyright © Korky Paul 1997; the illustration that appears on p. 92 from *The Giant Baby* by Allan Ahlberg, illustrated by Fritz Wegner (Viking, 1994) Copyright © Allan Ahlberg 1994. Illustrations copyright © Fritz Wegner 1994; the illustration that appears on p. 130 from *The Jungle Book* by Rudyard Kipiling, illustrated by Alan Langford (Puffin, 1994) Illustrations copyright © Alan Langford 1994 and the illustration that appears on p. 215 from *The Secret Garden* by Frances Hodgson Burnett, illustrated by Robin Lawrie (Puffin, 1994). Illustrations copyright © Robin Lawrie, 1994. Additional thanks for permission to reproduce the following covers: *Aquila* by Andrew Norriss, which appears on p. 18 (Puffin, 1997); *Ballet Shoes* by Noel Streatfeild, which appears on p. 23 (Puffin, 1919); *Bumface* by Morris Gleitzman, which appears on p. 37 (Puffin, 1998); *The Dark Is Rising* by Susan Cooper, which appears on p. 57 (Puffin, 1976); *The Endless Steppe* by Esther Hautzig, which appears on p. 73 (Puffin, 1971); *Tales from Shakespeare* which appears on p. 235; *Fungus the Bogeyman* by Raymond Briggs, which appears on p. 88 (Hamish Hamilton Children's Books, 1977); *The Golden Goose* by Dick King-Smith, which appears on p. 96 (Puffin, 1991); *The Knight and the Squire* by Terry Jones, illustrated by Michael Foreman, which appears on p. 137 (Puffin, 1999, first published in Great Britain by Chrysalis Children's Books, 1997); *Krazy Kow Saves the World – Well, Almost* by Jeremy Strong, which appears on p. 138 (Puffin, 2002); *Piggies* by Nick Gifford, which appears on p. 188; *Triss* by Brian Jacques, which appears on p. 199 (Puffin, 2002); *The Village By the Sea* by Anita Desai, which appears on p. 255 (Puffin, 1984); *Totally Wicked!* by Paul Jennings and Morris Gleitzman, which appears on p. 264 (Puffin, 2000); *The Borrowers* by Mary Norton, which appears on p. 33 and *King of Shadows* by Susan Cooper which appears on p. 111 (Puffin, 2000).

The Random House Group Ltd for permission to reproduce the following covers: *The Story of Doctor Dolittle* by Hugh Lofting, which appears on p. 64; *Clockwork* by Philip Pullman, which appears on p. 50; *A Necklace of Raindrops* by Joan Aiken, which appears on p. 174; *Go Saddle the Sea* by Joan Aiken, which appears on p. 10; *How to Live Forever* by Colin Thompson, which appears on p. 118; *The Present Takers* by Aidan Chambers, which appears on p. 213; *The Runaways* by Ruth Thomas, which appears on p. 206; *Ethel and Ernest* by Raymond Briggs, which appears on p. 186; and also for the illustration by Chris Riddell from *Beyond the Deepwoods* by Paul Stewart and Chris Riddell, published by Doubleday, which appears on p. 70, used by permission of The Random House Group Limited; the illustration by Ian Craig from *Boy* by Roald Dahl published by Jonathan Cape, which appears on p. 34, used by permission of The Random House Group Limited and for the illustration from *Emil and the Detectives* by Erich Kastner published by Jonathan Cape, which appears on p. 72, used by permission of The Random House Group Limited. All titles published by the Random House Group Ltd.

Thomas C. Lothian Pty. Ltd for permission to reproduce the illustration that appears on p. 196 by Shaun Tan from *The Rabbits*, written by John Marsden and illustrated by Shaun Tan, published by Lothian Books.

Tony Ross for permission to reproduce his illustration which features on p. 143 from *Little Wolf's Book of Badness*, written by Ian Whybrow, published by Collins Children's Books. © Tony Ross.

Scholastic Limited for permission to reproduce the following covers: *The Adventures of Captain Underpants* by Dav Pilkey, which appears on p. 40; *Harry and the Wrinklies* by Alan Temperley, which appears on p. 105; also for the illustration from *Horrible Histories: The Slimy Stuarts* by Terry Deary, which appears on p. 116. Illustration copyright © Martin Brown 1996. All rights reserved. First published by Scholastic Children's Books and reproduced by permission of Scholastic Ltd. All titles published by Scholastic Limited.

Walker Books Ltd for permission to reproduce the following: on p. 62, the front cover from *Stormbreaker*, written by Anthony Horowitz, front cover illustration by Phil Schramm, cover illustration © 2000 Walker Books Ltd. Reproduced by permission of Walker Books Ltd., London, SE11 5HJ; on p. 181, the illustration from *The Owl Tree*, written by Jenny Nimmo, illustrated by Anthony Lewis. Illustrations © 1997 Anthony Lewis. Reproduced by permission of Walker Books Ltd., London, SE11 5HJ; on p. 98, the illustration from *Gorilla*, written and illustrated by Anthony Browne. © 1983 Anthony Browne. Reproduced by permission of Walker Books Ltd., London, SE11 5HJ; on p. 166, the illustration from *Mr William Shakespeare's Plays*, retold and illustrated by Marcia Williams. © 1998 Marcia Williams. Reproduced by permission of Walker Books Ltd., London, SE11 5HJ. All titles published by Walker Books Ltd. All titles published by Walker Books Ltd.

The Watts Publishing Group for permission to reproduce covers from *Utterly Me, Clarice Bean*, written and illustrated by Lauren Child, featured on p. 253; *The Salt Pirates of Skegness* by Chris d'Lacey, featured on p. 209; *The Killer Underpants*, written by Michael Lawrence, featured on p. 127 and *The Orchard Book of Greek Myths*, retold by Geraldine McCaughrean and illustrated by Emma Chicester Clark, featured on p. 172. All titles published by The Watts Publishing Group.

All efforts have been made to seek permissions for copyright material, but in the event of any omissions, the Publisher would be pleased to hear from copyright holders and to amend these acknowledgements in subsequent editions of *The Ultimate Book Guide*.

The Ultimate Author Index

Here's a list of all the authors featured in the ***UBG*** (and the pages on which you'll find their books recommended).